The London Experience of Secondary Education

THE LONDON EXPERIENCE
OF SECONDARY EDUCATION

Margaret E. Bryant

formerly Reader in Education,
University of London Institute of Education,
and sometime Exhibitioner of Girton College, Cambridge

THE ATHLONE PRESS
London, and Atlantic Highlands, NJ

First published in Great Britain in 1986
by The Athlone Press
44 Bedford Row, London WC1N 4LY
and 171 First Avenue, Atlantic Highlands, NJ 07716

British Library Cataloguing in Publication Data
Bryant, Margaret E.
  The London experience of secondary education.
    1. Education, Secondary——England——London——History
    I. Title
    373.421   LA639.L8
  ISBN 0–485–11302–3

Library of Congress Cataloging in Publication Data
Bryant, Margaret E.
  The London experience of secondary education.
  Bibliography: p.
  Includes index.
    1. Education, Secondary——England——London——History.
    I. Title.
    LA639.L8B78   1986   373.421   85–22987
  ISBN 0–485–11302–3

Typesetting by The Word Factory, Rossendale, Lancashire
Printed in Great Britain at the University Press, Cambridge

Contents

Illustrations

Plates *facing page*

Maps
(drawn by Andras Berezny)

Foreword

The title of this study needs explanation, even apology. There is no term which can usefully describe the schooling of Becket and Bentham, of Chaucer and Coleridge, of Pepys and Asquith, of John and Charles Wesley and Frances Mary Buss. Schooling and education moreover must be distinguished. Nor is it possible to confine or define the limits of London over many centuries. A shifting and changing concept therefore is here related to an expanding and transforming entity. But there is a recognizable continuity in such demands for knowledge and skills, and London, however much it changed in extent and character, has still an identity. To give this book a title at all, and to select its contents within necessary limits, a number of Gordian knots have had to be cut. The subject matter is those stages and types of schooling, and those functions of education, which from the later nineteenth century have usually been called secondary and which have increasingly been concentrated within schools. The problem of defining London has also been dealt with by leaving the question, like the city, open. The unique openness of London has in fact had educational implications of national significance. Even the old walls which London so rapidly outgrew proved irrelevant to the forces which created and sustained educational traditions, experiments and expedients over almost a thousand years of history. When the new and expanded London was eventually provided with an administrative structure, given boundaries, and when secondary education became a function of that structure, its history has been to some extent described by Stuart Maclure in his *One Hundred Years of London Education, 1870–1970* and this study therefore concludes in 1902 or thereabouts.

Longitudinal studies of this kind are now out of favour in the history of education, which has become increasingly specialized. But understanding of process and change is central to the contribution which history can make to educational understanding, and this is especially true of what we today call secondary education. This complex and controversial subject is a comparatively neglected field in specialist history. Work has tended to concentrate on certain well-trodden areas, especially the endowed schools. Histories of individual schools are also numerous and to them this work acknowledges a great debt. But even the more successful and scholarly of these usually lack context and therefore especially in the later centuries of their history fail adequately to interpret particular with reference to wider developments. More recently research into the history of secondary education has concentrated on aspects related to contemporary polemic – the responsibility of the State, the distribution of such education and access to it in relation to social structure. Valuable work has been done, but tends to lack historical perspective and acknowledgement of both the essentially personal and voluntary nature of the consumption of such education, and past achievements of private and voluntary enterprise by agencies now often out of favour. A critical attempt at synthesis seemed desirable and timely if analytical work is to make its maximum impact.

Research for the Victoria County History of Middlesex disclosed the rich and varied traditions of schooling and education at this level in London and its environs. Without an understanding of these the history of secondary education cannot be properly reconstructed, or its concept given adequate content. The local dimension should enable sharpness of focus to give a clearer view of diversity, of demand and response, to study failures as well as successes, to discover expedients which did not outlast their utility as well as institutions which adapted or lingered on into new ages. London presents particular problems to the local historian, not only of scale and pace of change but also of demarcation – for the line between local and national history is more than usually difficult to draw or maintain. The aim here has been to concentrate on the provision for London boys and girls, or perhaps for the children of London's fascinating diversity of smaller and interconnected communities, in the belief that this will help towards understanding of developments at national and provincial level. This approach may complement work on the national picture, such as the study by Professor John Roach of the history of secondary education from 1800 to 1870.

More especially it may help to concentrate attention on the fundamental problem of the definition of secondary education. The author's preoccupation with this enigma is historical, but it is also professional and educational. Over many years at the University of London Institute of Education this question was posed to generations of students, who while preparing for a career in secondary education found it usually impossible to say what it is, or was. This failure of intelligent graduate historians to define, except perhaps in tautological terms, something they had recently experienced, and to which they were committing their professional lives, would be disquieting if it were not excused by equal confusion among politicians, publicists, administrators, educationalists. Many of these seem unsure about what it is that they are determined to provide 'for all'. Studying the London experience of nearly a thousand years of preparing boys, and then also girls, to make choices within the public world may enable us to see more clearly what we are trying to do.

The author is deeply grateful to the Worshipful Company of Goldsmiths for a generous grant towards the publication of this work. For its long research and preparation no financial help has been forthcoming. 'I hope it is no very cynical asperity not to confess obligation where no benefit has been received. . .'. This kind of history does not attract institutional or public grants or support, but while it owes nothing to patronage, it owes everything to friendship. I owe thanks to my colleagues at the Institute of Education, especially Richard Aldrich and Dennis Dean for unfailing encouragement and stimulus, and members of the History of Education Society and the Historical Association. Professor Roach has most generously read the entire typescript and made valuable suggestions. My debt to Joan Henderson, who helped with the redrafting of the original and monstrous manuscript, and to Cynthia Yates, who read and corrected the final version with meticulous care, is beyond description. Fuz Bagum and Averil Aldrich have coped with the typing with unfailing patience, kindness and professional skill. Denis Baylis has used his specialist expertise in the preparation of the index. To all of them I give my sincere and heartfelt thanks. To friendship, which even more than history makes sense out of life, I dedicate this book.

MARGARET BRYANT

The London Experience
of Secondary Education

I

The early grammar schools
from the Middle Ages
to the seventeenth century

The nature of medieval education

To developed countries in the twentieth century, secondary education is
an appetite and a necessity, it has both intrinsic and extrinsic worth. It is
an end in itself, and part of a process. It brings primary experience forth
into the public world which it helps to create and develops elementary
skills far enough to enable the individual to make social, economic and
political choices. We usually expect such education to be related to the
stage of human development which we now call adolescence, and to be
in some degree both systematic and comprehensive. To look for the
origins or early developments of such education in medieval London
might imply that their concept of it was somehow defective because it
did not yet correspond to ours. Rather it is necessary to discern how
such appetites and needs were satisfied in contemporary terms, to
discover how elements or aspects of such education were already
functioning in a society, an economy, a state, so different from our own.
The object here is to examine how education at this level operated and
changed through the centuries, to see it as a series of complex events,
part of an historical process, and so to see our own concept of secondary
education with more objectivity. London's particularly rich and complex
experience provides a study in its own right and illuminates wider
developments.

Education not only reflects the needs of society, it is a powerful force
in creating and transforming those needs. London, like other cities of
Europe, was helping to bring into being in the eleventh century a new
economic order. By 1100 it was already spilling out beyond its walls and
becoming a uniquely open city and it was rapidly being transformed
from a 'prickly commune' into a 'self-confident capital'. Although until
the end of the twelfth century England must be considered 'a
scholastically undeveloped country' London was important in giving
England 'a voice in the community of the European spirit'.[1] Of its
40,000 or so inhabitants a large proportion were highly specialized
craftsmen, while about 2000 or so heads of households were freemen of
the City, belonged to the big fraternities, paid taxes, and may be described as a merchant aristocracy. Down the river at Westminster, still
separated from the City proper, dwelt and worked an important new

1

class, the 'officiales' who represented what has been described as a managerial revolution in Church and State. As London was gradually established as the royal capital there was also an influential visiting population of members of an increasingly sophisticated aristocracy.[2] The provision and development of London education already depended on interaction and coincidence between the needs and aspirations of these sections of London's population, and upon the mutual recognition and understanding of a community of interest between them.

The immensely powerful and enterprising men who made up the merchant fraternity present something of an historical mystery for within a relatively static and hierarchical society they represented 'a shrewd and rationalist activity in which fortune, instead of being measured by social status, depended only on intelligence and energy'.[3] Were they self-made men, or had they 'risen from the ranks of the aristocracy'?[4] It is also difficult to identify the distinctive mark of their culture, that shrewd and rational calculation which could merge so unexpectedly into irrational adherence to custom, or justify generalizations which to us seem almost bizarre.[5] The thought system of the age relied greatly upon images, giving 'concrete shape to every conception',[6] and in these images it could solidify and become rigid. Practical men of all secular ranks thought essentially in concrete and symbolic terms – their very sins were numbered and personified, their salvation was carved and carried in procession before them, they walked behind in order and rank made manifest in livery, vestment and ornament. Their worldly wisdom was embodied in proverbs, in forms of law and business and in rituals of social and civic intercourse, their theology and morality in texts and parables, their experience in narratives of the past made present. Yet living as they did in a world of shared metaphor, the practical activities and shrewd speculations of these men were transforming the European economy, and in a world where the theory of the individual's place in the universe, indeed the very idea of the individual, were only beginning to take shape, they were among the few who had made choices of occupation and of style and rules of life. Moreover it was a sphere of operation which robbed them of 'certainty about their role within an evolving society and their confidence in their standing in an objective system of theology'. The Church provided no rationale or justification for their activities, indeed it expressed disapproval of them – which had important consequences.[7]

That education helped these men to see themselves as somehow outside an established hierarchy must be conceded, but it is difficult to find evidence of its precise nature. For the most part they were un-schooled, for their initiation was essentially familial and liturgical, through relationship and performance rather than critical abstraction. The household, whether domestic or occupational, was the unit and scene of instruction; the school was ancillary or incidental, often un-necessary. The same generalizations can be made about the much larger number of lesser citizens, members of the craft guilds whose skills were attained by apprenticeship of a more or less formalized nature.

What part did the ability to read and write, whether in English, in French or in Latin, play in this liberation of London's citizens? Literacy in that age cannot be considered to consist of primary or elementary skills, it must be claimed for a higher stage of education for it made reflection and reference possible, and pushed back boundaries of time and place both as mental constructs and as spheres of practical activity. Moreover the concept of literacy must be employed critically to avoid anachronism. In the earlier middle ages *literate* meant learned or scholarly, by the fourteenth century *litteratus* began to mean someone with a minimum ability to read Latin, to do more than 'spell and put together' and thus claim 'benefit of clergy'. By the mid fifteenth century London tradesmen 'are being described as *litterati*'.[8] The rise of a class of lettered laymen was a notable characteristic of the fourteenth and fifteenth centuries, especially in England.[9] Reading was increasingly needed not only for saving your neck but for civic and guild administration, for business and craft, and for devotional purposes – 'pragmatic literacy' as it has been called. The position was complicated by the three languages in which literacy had to operate. From the twelfth century an increasingly lucid Latin facilitated the expression of abstract ideas and from the fourteenth the vernacular began to reflect these possibilities. From the fourteenth century English schoolboys no longer 'did their Latins' in French, and this new interchange between Latin and English developed the vernacular still further. In the fifteenth century Lollardry encouraged reading in the vernacular, and London became the focus of the Lollard book production. In 1422 the Brewers' Company gave up the keeping of its records in Latin, which none of its members could read, and decided to use English, which some members could both read and write. Later in the century some Companies were insisting that apprentices should be able to read and write – the Goldsmiths made such a regulation in 1478. Literacy is beginning to be seen as part of an educational process. By 1489 so many persons could read that the rules of benefit of clergy had to be changed and a distinction drawn between laymen who could read and those in Holy Orders.[10]

When we turn to the question of how such literacy was attained the picture is obscure and confused. There must have been a large amount of 'sporadic and unorganised' teaching, in the City of London provided by chantry priests, song schools preparing boys to sing the church services, clerks with too little to do, parish clerks, private masters and even schoolmistresses. The Scriveners played an important part in giving what might even be called commercial education – in the year of Agincourt Master William Kyngesmill was teaching boys to read and write, cast accounts and speak French, in high-pressure short courses so that they might be made ready for London apprenticeships. The

Scriveners' Company of course had a special need for apprentices with more than basic literacy. In 1497/8 they complained that some lacked grammar, 'wherethrough oftentimes they err, and their acts and feats been incongruous . . .'. In future each apprentice when presented to the wardens was to be examined 'to see if he had his congruity'. If not he was to go to grammar school. The fifteenth century was beginning to provide at least some formal education for youths who did not aspire to the priesthood but needed to be 'rendered more capable for the mechanic arts and other worldly affairs'. Demand for literacy began thus to pass over into demand for schooling and more ambitious systematic instruction in grammar, which was the monopoly of the Church.[11]

Until the growth of cities and the twelfth-century renaissance of learning, the part played by the Church can be seen rather as holding the line than one of control or monopoly. But in later centuries the Church showed some complacency concerning the teaching of the grammar schools and outside the cities the cathedral chancellors to whom episcopal licensing had been delegated rarely exercised their powers. The evidence for the very existence or continuity of some of the schools attached to the collegiate churches is today considered inadequate.[12] But in London there is ample evidence for the continuous history of St Paul's School, the 'school of the city', at least from 1111 when Hugh the Schoolmaster appears in the records. A deed of about 1140 confirms the almost complete monopoly of the schoolmaster, who has now become chancellor, to teach grammar in the City. It is probable that Becket was a pupil and that the school had a separate building between the bell-tower and the 'forum' where St Paul's Cross later stood. By the thirteenth century the chancellor appointed a Master of Arts as schoolmaster and vice-chancellor. His duties included writing out the table of lessons and reading on the great Festivals, and holding disputations of dialectics and philosophy by St Bartholomew's Church on St Bartholomew's Day.[13] These are the disputations described by Fitzstephen in his life of Becket: 'Boys of different schools strive against one another in verse, or contend concerning the principles of the art of grammar . . .'. At carnival times, they brought 'fighting cocks to their master, and the whole forenoon is given up to boyish sport'.[14] The other contenders in the disputations may have included boys from the school attached to the monastery of St Peter's at Westminster, but were more likely to be from the other City schools allowed to teach grammar, poetry, rhetoric and logic, 'those of a school of the Arches and a school of the Basilica of St Martins the Great who claim they are privileged in these and other matters'. St Mary le Bow where he held his Court of the Arches was a peculiar of the Archbiship of Canterbury; St Martin le Grand a collegiate church and a royal free chapel with extraordinary sanctuary rights even in the Confessor's time. Fitzstephen says that other schools were allowed 'by good will and suffrance' and the St Paul's statutes imply that the chancellor kept a careful eye upon them. There is a tradition of a school maintained in the Priory of Holy Trinity, Aldgate, whose prior was always an elder-man, sat in the Mayor's Court and rode with him in aldermanic livery, for the ancient Cnihtengild had granted the soke of Portsoken to the Priory, which had been founded in 1107 or 1108 by Queen Maud.[15]

In the fifteenth century another important school was added by official patronage. The Hospital of St Anthony of the Brothers of Vienne in Threadneedle Street subsisted from about 1254 partly on the proceeds of the City's stray pigs. In 1434 further funds were provided by the Bishop of London for the maintenance of 'a master or fit informer of grammar . . . to keep grammar school in the precinct . . . or some fit house close by, to teach, instruct and inform gratis all boys and others whatsoever wishing to learn and become scholars' – making London one of the first towns to possess a 'free school'. In 1442 Henry VI added endowments to enable scholars to be sent to Oriel College Oxford, where the Hospital's former master, John Carpenter, a keen educationalist, was now Provost. The school's statutes were probably modelled on those of Eton, and St Anthony's might have become another great royal foundation with close university conections, were it not for the vicissitudes of the Wars of the Roses. But it was a considerable school, counting among its pupils (St Anthony's Pigs to other London schoolboys) More and perhaps Colet. It also had a song school providing one of the few really free places of elementary instruction known to exist in medieval London.[16]

Other schools also made their appearance. One was established in St Dunstan's in the East, a peculiar of the Archbishop of Canterbury.[17] A chantry in St Bartholomew's Smithfield had in 1444 an endowment for teaching boys grammar and song.[18] There was a grammar school in St Peter's Cornhill by the early fifteenth century.[19] In 1392 Richard Exton taught at a grammar school near the Crutched Friars.[20] St Thomas Acon was also a school;[21] St Andrew's Holborn was said to have had a school;[22] William Shipton kept a school in Vintry Ward near the Tower in 1465.[23]

Undoubtedly lay demand for grammar schooling led to this increased provision. Pressure came from the skilled craftsmen as well as from merchant ranks. There is evidence from wills that 'parents were anxious for their sons to be initiated into that world of Latin learning over which the church presided'. A baker ordered his son to be brought up in 'all learning', an alderman desired his to be educated 'to connying lerning and erudition', in 1322 another wished his sons to stay long enough at school to compose reasonably good verses. More significantly such schooling is now seen to give individual choice, the very idea of a lay or clerkly career as dependent on scholastic education is taking shape in civic life. By the late fourteenth century another father suggested that his elder son should take up common law, the younger go to university or trade. Such wills were administered by the City's Court Orphanage and this protection made it unnecessary to hurry children into marriage or occupation as a precaution against the early death of the father, lengthening the time available for education, whether scholastic or functional.[24] Two famous examples of such careers were Geoffrey Chaucer and John Colet.

Chaucer was born probably in the very heart of London, son of a wealthy vintner who also owned a couple of taverns, and clearly his education was well attended to – he possessed knowledge of the classics, divinity, astronomy, the science of his age and its scholastic learning, but the only evidence (if such it can be called) that he went to school is that the list of books left by the schoolmaster of St Paul's for his scholars in 1358 'parallels to an extraordinary degree the hypothetical list of those which Chaucer, from internal evidence, seems to have read in his youth'. We first meet him as a page in the household of Lionel Duke of Clarence, embarking on his literary, court and administrative career.[25] The case of John Colet is better documented. He was the eldest, and only survivor, of the twenty-two children of a prosperous London merchant from Buckinghamshire, a powerful member of the Mercers' Company, and Lord Mayor in 1486 and 1495. It might be supposed that the younger Colet was needed for the business, but after attending either St Anthony's or St Thomas Acon School, he was sent to Oxford and allowed to choose the priesthood and the life of scholarship, when family influence could have helped him to position in Court or City.[26]

Colet's name reminds us that education was also being transformed from within, by those subtle changes which we associate with the early Renaissance. One London schoolmaster of the early years of the fifteenth century might even be called a humanist. John Seward (c. 1364–1435), 'an excellent poet and rhetorician', was master of St Peter's School in Cornhill, and the centre of a group of scholars who met for discussion in St Paul's and at the Cardinal's Hat in Lombard Street, where one of their number, William Relyk, also kept a school. They had probably been pupils of John Leland, the noted grammarian of Oxford, and although they knew no Greek and had no new resources of Latin texts, they were 'pursuing poetry in not quite the old way', they were beginning to see the classical inheritance in perspective. Before advances in the critical understanding of Roman, and then of Greek, literature could be made, the medieval mind had to be disentangled and distanced from a classical world made intimately present and confused with contemporary culture. Seward's poetic allegory on the properties of the antelope retained the emblematic vision of the Middle Ages, but he and his friends were contributing to a new European outlook which was to put immense pressures on education.[27]

These modest and haphazard increases in the provision of schools were not achieved without opposition from the diocese. As the alternatives emerged more overtly, monopoly hardened and tried to assert itself, and by the fifteenth century fear of Lollardry added another reason for strengthening control. In 1393 several masters were accused of conducting 'escoles generales de gramer' without being properly qualified and were summoned before the ecclesiastical court. Thereupon they played on rivalry of civic and ecclesiastical authorities by seeking an inhibition of the summons in the Mayor's Court. This produced a petition to Richard II from 'The King's devout chaplains and orators', the Archbishop of Canterbury, the Bishop of London, 'the Dean of your frank chapel of St Martins le Grand', and the Chancellor of St Paul's – that is, from those in charge of what might be called the four official schools. They declared that 'the order, management, and examination of certain schools of the faculty of grammar in London and the suburbs . . . ought to belong to them . . . yet lately certain strangers feigning themselves Masters of grammar . . . wilfully usurped their jurisdiction and kept general grammar schools in the City in deceit and fraud of the children . . .'. The outcome of this petition is not known.

It is clear that resistance to the Church's monopoly was growing, fed by the demand for schooling and the frustrations and political irritations of a city which had always been ready to defend its privileges. The restrictive policies of the diocese were seen not as an attempt to preserve standards but as a desire to monopolize fees. Peculiars or enclaves of rival authority such as St Dunstan's and St Martin's were disliked. St Martin's in the early fifteenth century was the subject of a colourful row about the abuse of sanctuary rights – 'forgers took up their abode and carried on their nefarious work there' as complaint to Parliament said in 1402. By 1430 the quarrel had waxed warm, the sheriffs tried to remove a culprit from sanctuary, and by 1457 the Dean was compelled to keep a kind of rogues' register and attempt to control the more notorious. This cannot have been a satisfactory setting for the grammar school, which was probably being conducted in the nave.[28]

In this tetchy atmosphere the ecclesiastical authorities once more took the offensive, petitioning the Crown in 1445 that 'many and divers persons insufficiently learned in grammar were presuming to hold common grammar schools'. The five schools (St Anthony's now added to St Paul's, St Martin's, St Mary le Bow's and St Dunstan's) were quite enough for the needs of London. Henry VI issued an ordinance to the citizens not to 'trouble nor hinder the masters of the said schools . . .'.[29]

But the matter did not rest there. In the following year, 1446, parsons from London parishes – William Lichfield, a former Fellow of Peterhouse and rector of All Hallows the Great, Gilbert Worthington, rector of St Andrew's Holborn, John Neal, Master of the Hospital of St Thomas Acon built upon Becket's birthplace in Cheapside and within the parish of St Mary Colechurch, and John Cote, rector of St Peter's Cornhill – petitioned the King in Parliament that the shortage of schools in London caused great hurt not only to the Church; London is the 'common concourse of this land, not only for Londoners born', but for others who come up to the City 'some for lack of schoolmasters in their own country, and some for the great alms of Lords, Merchants and others' so that many would never have gained virtue and cunning without the schooling it provided. There should be 'a sufficient number of schools and good Informers of Grammar and not for the singular avail of two or three persons, grievously to hurt the multitude of young people of all this London. . .'. This resulted in an ignorant clergy (a shrewd point to make to King Henry VI), and denied education to the laity who 'needed to be competently learned for various callings'. They desired that schools should be set up in each of their parishes, and that they themselves should have power to nominate the masters. The King gave his assent, conceding to the monopolists that the Bishop of London and the Archbishop of Canterbury must be consulted.

Subsequent events are obscure. There is evidence of schools in the parishes of these powerful parsons though in some cases it is shadowy. No more is heard of shortage of schools, but this negative evidence comes from troubled times.[30]

It has been claimed that this episode was the 'turning point in the long struggle to break down restrictive monopolies', and marked the emergence of a genuinely lay education.[31] But the part played by the laity is difficult to decide. The struggle to break down restrictions of grammar education was mainly fought out in London and certainly it was based on the laity's need for schooling. The very word *laicus* was changing in meaning for it had meant *unlearned*, and so to talk of lay education in earlier centuries would have been nonsense. The cities of Europe could now be said to possess 'an exclusively lay culture' but it is still necessary to be cautious in drawing a distinction between clerical and lay enterprise. The intellectual life of the City 'fed primarily on religious interests', the 'lay spirit' was allied to a profound and ardent faith. It is true that this could be combined with criticism of the clergy. Already by the twelfth century 'the typical city father . . . was fervently anti-clerical and a princely benefactor of the church'.[32] As a parishioner the fourteenth- and fifteenth-century London merchant with his private chaplain, perhaps a small chamber for personal devotions, a library of improving books to be read aloud at meals, and even then his private pew in church, might be formidable enough, and parish priests were often men of humble origins, attainment and income. But the four petitioners of 1446 were men of very different calibre, they drew on city experience, and wielded influence over men of eminence and responsibility. Lichfield, buried in 1448 beneath the altar of his church of All Hallows the Great under a 'fair plated stone', was among the most famous preachers of his time, leaving behind notes in English in his own hand for 3083 sermons, the greatest medium of the age for propaganda and communication. Worthington, between 1439 and 1447, had beneath his notably eloquent pulpit in Holborn the lawyers of nearby Inns of Court, including probably Chief Justice Fortescue whose concerns were with courtly education as well as the law. Neal at St Thomas Acon ministered to the powerful Mercers' Company. Among the parishioners of Cote at St Peter's was John Carpenter (1370?–1441?), Town Clerk of London, compiler of its *Liber Albus*, friend and executor of Richard Whittington, Member of Parliament for the City. He must certainly have known his fellow-parishioner, John Seward. His will shows that he was a collector of books, including some of the works of Aristotle in Latin, and was a lay brother of the convent of the Charterhouse and of the 'fraternity of the 60 priests of London'. He left lands in the City 'for finding and bringing up of foure poor men's children with meat, drink, apparell, learning at the schooles in the universities, etc., until they be professed. . .'. To draw any opposition of interest of or enterprise between such a layman and his parish priest would be unprofitable and probably misleading.[33] The struggle over the schools seems much more like a struggle of London parochial clergy and laity in alliance against restrictive control imposed from outside the City or unresponsive to City needs and aspirations.

It was during this waning of the Middle Ages that the citizens of London began increasingly to demonstrate their commitment to education as the key to advancement, civic efficiency and a coherent and acceptable understanding of life. The endowed school originated in the fourteenth century and by the fifteenth century was becoming a more usual form of charity, and London citizens here made a decisive contribution, for in their hands were the necessary economic resources. From earlier centuries wealth in this sector had been generated faster than it could be soundly invested, and spurred on by theological instruction and theological insecurity (those 3083 sermons played a vital part), it became 'the custom of London' that a third of a testator's wealth should go to charity. 'Secure in this world he found it important to make preparation for the life to come.'[34] Here the particular circumstances of London families proved important. Life in London at this level may not have been nasty and brutish, it was certainly short. The merchant and craft communities were barely able to reproduce their own number, they drew constantly on new blood from the provinces. Few families survived for more than two or three generations in the direct line, and their restless ambition was sending their few surviving offspring out into the professions, the world of learning, the landed gentry.[35] Some of their earlier bequests therefore went to their places of origin. In 1507 a Londoner endowed a chantry priest at Enfield to teach children 'to know and read Latin and English and understand grammar, and to write their Latins according to the use and trade of grammar schools'. This bequest was characteristic of the transition between devotional and educational endowments. William Sevenoaks, a grocer, endowed the school at his native town in 1432, John Abbott, a mercer, one at Farthinghoe in Northamptonshire in 1443, Edmund Shaw, a goldsmith, at Stockport in 1487.[36] These bequests may be another indication that the attempt to increase the number of London schools had been successful. There was one abortive merchant endowment within the City. An immensely wealthy draper, Simon Eyre, in 1459 left a large sum to endow a grammar school in the chapel he had built in Leadenhall Market, but this was never carried out – a reminder that effective endowment had to be worked out in practice over time.[37] The view, however, that London merchants of this period in their bequests showed 'no great zeal for education' needs to be modified.[38]

The London clergy also played their part. In 1439 the rector of St John Zachary, William Bingham, a friend of Worthington and Cote, petitioned Henry VI that the decline of faculties for the learning of grammar would hinder the recruitment of clergy. He was particularly concerned with the lack of training for schoolmasters, for the degrees of Oxford and Cambridge were in higher studies of law, theology, medicine. He was given permission to found Godshouse at Cambridge for the reception of grammar students, leading to a degree in grammar.[39]

The London experience suggests that the struggle to provide for lay education was not overwhelmingly secular or laical, but was an essentially civic struggle, a manifestation of civic humanism. The all-important partnership of London clergy and laity is a theme which recurs over the centuries, and may at this time be typified by the friendship of Thomas More and John Colet. These two choicest spirits of their age were both London-born and were educated at London's grammar schools before going to Oxford – and in More's case, as he was destined for civil life, he had a spell as a page in a household of the Archbishop over the river at Lambeth.[40]

Colet's refounding of St Paul's School may be considered either as the culmination of this age, or as the opening move in the next stage of London educational development. Colet became Dean of St Paul's in 1504 or 1505, and seems to have set about the task quickly, for in 1509 he began the process of endowing the school which had existed for so many centuries as a function of the cathedral itself. A year later he petitioned the king to confer lands on the school 'wherein he purposeth that children as well to be borne w'yn youre saide citie as elsewhere . . . shall not only in continyance be substantially taughte and lernyd in Latin tung, but also instructe and informed in vertuouse condicions'. When he delivered the school statutes in 1518 he provided that his father's Company, the Mercers, 'shall have all the Cure and charge rule and governaunce of the schole . . .' which was to be for 153 free scholars. When it was assessed in 1524 it represented the huge capital sum of £2441. This lay administration was significant, it again represents that partnership between clergy and laity at a crucial period. Colet drew on the institutional and professional experience of the Church, the learning of the Renaissance, the funds and administrative expertise of the secular city. It was a truly civic enterprise, emphasizing the aim of a liberal education, the need to train children for civic responsibility and for active virtue.[41]

The heroic age of endowments

The argument so far emphasizes continuity between earlier centuries and the Tudor period. Nevertheless the sixteenth century must be considered in some respects a new age in education and, as in other aspects of history, the 1530s seem with hindsight to be the turning-point. By the reign of Elizabeth men could look back to that time with something akin to nostalgia. When John Stow was a boy the old disputations 'of their Schollers Logically . . .' in St Bartholomew the Great's churchyard, with the boys standing beneath a great tree boarded about, were still continued as a public spectacle. Colet forbade his boys to take part in this 'Foolishe babling and loss of time' but his wishes were evidently ignored for Stow remembered them there with the boys of St Peter's of Westminster (still a monastic school), St Thomas Acon, and St Anthony's, 'whereof the last named commonly presented the best schollers and had the prize in those days'. He also remembered the boys falling 'from wordes, to blowes, with their Satchels full of Bookes, many times in great heaps that troubled the streets, and passengers'.[42]

Stow was remembering the old medieval City in which he grew up and whose transformation into the frighteningly expanded giant of 1598 he lived to record. The creation of a network of schools in and around the metropolis, and indeed throughout the provinces, must be seen partly as an aspect of this growth, which contemporaries could hardly understand. A population of perhaps 60,000 in the 1530s had increased to about 90,000 when Elizabeth came to the throne in 1558 and a staggering 225,000 at her death in 1603. This is not natural increase, for the crowded pestilential city was barely able to maintain its own numbers – immigrants from all over the country and also from Europe were drawn to London by its prosperity, diversity and vitality. The civic authorities, who complained that the 'swarms of vagrants'[43] were foreigners and not their responsibility, had in many cases come from the provinces themselves or were sons or grandsons of provincial men. The commercial revolution gave London 'prodigal prosperity' and turned it into a 'boom town'.

Although London had spilt out beyond its walls by 1100, its whole population at that time could have lived within these walls. Now in the later sixteenth century there was a dramatic and frightening change. The city literally burst its bounds. Before the time of the Armada the open areas taken over from monasteries, religious houses and the inns or town houses of heads of provincial abbeys were, if not turned into secular palaces, built over, often filled in with tenement warrens. The city spread, for the most part by creeping or leaping along the existing roads and lanes, beyond the walls and even the bars around Smithfield and Holborn and Clerkenwell – out towards Westminster for the well-to-do, eastwards for artisans, and to Ratcliffe and Poplar for seafaring and shipbuilding persons – suburbs stretching in a long line west to east,

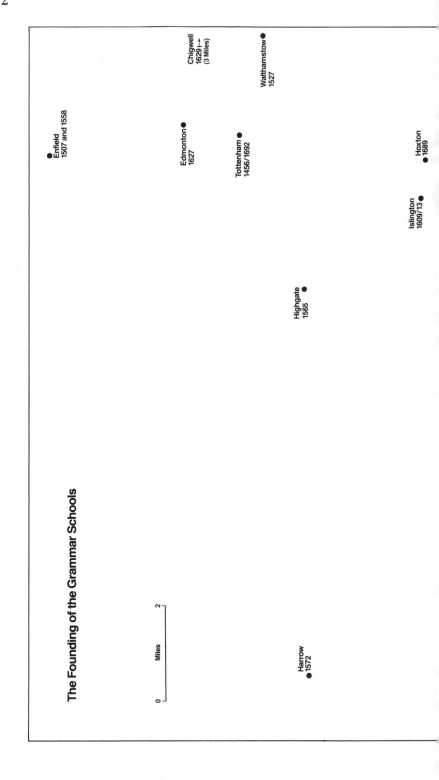

The Founding of the Grammar Schools

Miles
0   2

Harrow
● 1572

Highgate
● 1565

Islington
1609/13 ●

Hoxton
● 1689

Enfield
● 1507 and 1558

Edmonton ●
1627

Tottenham ●
1456/1692

Chigwell
1629 ⊢→
(3 Miles)

Walthamstow ●
1527

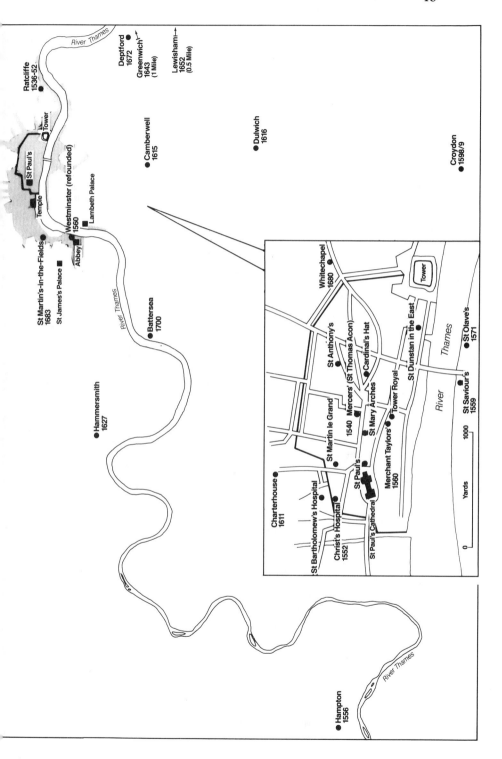

Ratcliffe
1536-52

Deptford
1672

Greenwich
1643
(1 Mile)

Lewisham
1652
(0.5 Mile)

Tower

St Paul's

Camberwell
1615

Dulwich
1616

Croydon
1598/9

Temple

Westminster (refounded)
1560

Lambeth Palace

St Martin's-in-the-Fields
1683

St James's Palace

Abbey

Battersea
1700

Hammersmith
1627

Hampton
1556

River Thames

Whitechapel
1680

Tower

St Anthony's

Mercers' (St Thomas Acon)

Cardinal's Hat

St Dunstan in the East

St Olave's
1571

St Mary Arches

Tower Royal

St Martin le Grand

1540

Merchant Taylors'
1560

St Saviour's
1559

River Thames

Charterhouse
1611

St Bartholomew's Hospital

Christ's Hospital
1552

St Paul's

St Paul's Cathedral

Yards

0   1000

and across the river, swallowing Southwark. Attempts to prohibit new buildings, or rather building on new foundations, in fact only succeeded, especially in the eastward suburbs, in heaping people together, piling up the tenements, filling in the courts and corners, digging out cellars, patching up decrepit buildings. As the decades of the Tudor century passed it must have seemed that London was beyond control.[44] It is more to the credit of its rulers and leading citizens that their civic pride and civic conscience continued to grapple with its problems and to regard them as admitting of solution, that they showed such grave and moral determination to 'create a good and civilized community' to modernize the 'institutions of their society'. Their dedication to the cause of education was particularly generous, and especially in the sixty years following the Reformation it 'may with reasonable accuracy be described as fanatical'. The old settled ecclesiastical order had dissolved, and with it the framework of administration of schooling, and the accumulation of professional expertise which had developed over many centuries. The Tudor layman needed both resolution and capital to create the institutions needed to educate the new age, and had to do this at this time of frightening urban growth. The achievements of this great enterprise must be considered in relation to the city within its region, its arc of suburbs and their still rural hinterland, where nevertheless the stimulus was felt in higher land values and more diversified employment and stirring ambitions.[45]

Foundations in the early decades of the century are few. In 1527, less than ten years after Colet delivered the statutes of St Paul's School, Sir George Monoux built his free school at Walthamstow, then a small town in the circle of hunting forest and farming country, well out round the north of the suburbs, between the Lee and the Roding, river routes for the City's food supplies.[46] The next endowment was the school in Ratcliffe, in the already crowded shipbuilding eastern suburbs, built and endowed between 1536 and 1552 and becoming the Coopers' Company School.[47] In 1540 the Mercers' Company School was added to City provision,[48] and almost from its foundation in 1552 Christ's Hospital paid a 'Gramer Schoole Mayster' and a 'Gramer Usher'.[49] Next in time are two schools well out in the rural region – Hampton, founded in 1556, probably not as a grammar but as a song school,[50] and Enfield, a small town in open country, refounded in 1558.[51] The year 1560 was an important one with both Merchant Taylors' School and the newly constituted Westminster School,[52] and between 1559 and 1571 two schools were opened in Southwark, St Saviour's and St Olave's.[53] Highgate School was founded in 1565 in a hamlet of Hornsey parish, on the rural fringe of the Hundred of Finsbury which was being quite thickly settled nearer to the northern suburbs.[54] Harrow, founded in 1572, was still in the almost wholly rural Hundred of Gore, where, however, citizens were beginning to buy land as an investment.[55] In 1598–9 Archbishop Whitgift endowed his school at Croydon, a market town grown up at the gates of his palace and perhaps only marginally within the metropolitan orbit.[56] Owen's School was founded between 1609 and 1613 in Islington, a fashionable country suburb.[57] In 1611 the most munificent endowment of all, the Charterhouse, was made.[58] In 1615 and 1616 two schools were founded in the pleasant country village of Camberwell in Surrey, Wilson's Grammar School and Dulwich College.[59] In 1627 the bequest of Edward Latymer established schools (hardly yet of grammar status) at Edmonton and Hammersmith,[60] and in 1629 Archbishop Harsnett founded schools at Chigwell, well out in the forest region of Essex.[61] Two schools in that part of Kent already affected by London's maritime development end the list – the Roan charity at Greenwich in 1643 was at first only for elementary education,[62] but in Lewisham the Reverend Abraham Colfe founded both English and grammar schools in 1652.[63] The achievements of this greatest period of grammar school endowment and building have been studied by Professor W. K. Jordan who concluded that they had transformed London from a city seriously short of school places to one where 'It seems very probable that no deserving boy with requisite ability could have failed to find a place. . .'. It is calculated that by the year 1600 there were places for 1500 youths – about 5 to 7 per cent of the male population of school age – counting only the schools in the City and in Middlesex, admittedly the most suburban county; but parts of Essex, Surrey and Kent must also, at least by the end of the period, be counted as serving London. This would probably not materially alter the percentage of places. This may be an over-estimate if consideration is given to the effectiveness of endowments,[64] and the take-up of places, for which there is often little evidence. Other factors must be borne in mind – the high death rate, especially amongst the young; the continuing practice, partly for this reason, of sending children out of town for nurture; the fact that its population was constantly renewed by immigration so that provincial grammar schools, many of them founded by Londoners, were supplying educated manpower for the capital; the existence of other kinds of education in and around the city; most important, that the very idea of schooling as we know it today had yet to be developed. The statistical evidence must be treated with great caution.[65]

Can any useful generalization about responsibility and credit for this astonishing provision of schools be made? Earlier researches concentrated on the question of the so-called decay of schools at the time of the Reformation. More lately debate has centred on the part played by the Crown. Recently the claim of the laity has been stressed. Examination of foundations in London and its region shows how complex the picture is – from what varied sources concern, capital and income for schools came in this period of instability and reformation.

First, there was what might be called corporate, public action, by the Crown or organs of local enterprise. One London monastic school of great importance was saved at the Dissolution, partly by royal action. Westminster had always been an especially royal church. Its grammar school was retained as an integral part of the collegiate church of St Peter by Henry VIII in 1540, and when twenty years later Elizabeth exempted this church from episcopal jurisdiction, she also refounded the school – its 40 foundationers are still 'Queen's Scholars'. Fee-paying town boys quickly added to its numbers, prosperity and fame. For Westminster School the Dissolution was 'a blessing in disguise'.[66]

The main crisis of Crown policy with regard to education came, not over the monasteries, but over the chantries, dissolved in 1548. The schools founded, or refounded, at this time, after what had been virtually a nation-wide survey of school provision, have been said to be 'conceived of as units in an education system serving a protestant nation'.[67] This describes too deliberate an intention – a bankrupt government facing an indignant section of the clergy was indeed obliged to concede some schools. That there are so few 'we owe to the rapacity of the boy King's ministers of state, that there are any at all to the tenacity of his ministers of religion'. One of these ministers of religion was Nicholas Ridley, newly appointed Bishop of London; another was 'that commonwealth named Latimer', thundering at Paul's Cross and before the young King himself.[68]

One school which survived was St Anthony's, though for how long is obscure. Stow describes the processions of its children in 1562, 200 of them going nut-gathering. In 1569 the boys of St Anthony's with St Paul's, Merchant Taylors', St Saviour's and Westminster, received 'Gownes geven to certeyn poor schollers of the scholls about London' by the bequest of Robert Nowell. St Anthony's seems to have existed until the Great Fire, after which it was not rebuilt.[69] Schools in the outlying London region which survived were the chantry at Enfield and Sir George Monoux's obit and free school in Walthamstow churchyard where, since 1541, an 'almespriest' prayed daily for the souls of the founder and his wife, Dame Ann, and also served the choir of the church and taught 20 or 30 children of the parish 'and nott above butt att his pleasure'. The Chantry Commissioners described him as 'Sir John Hogeson, clerke, of the age of forty years and of good usage and conversacion, litterate. . .'.[70]

The Livery Companies' schools were able to continue when lands for the endowments of chantry priests were not confiscated by the Commissioners but converted into rent charges payable to the Crown. In 1550 'the King having occasion to levy a great mass of money did require the Companies to purchase their rents, which they were loathe to do but being urged by their duty of love and service to the King' they clubbed together and bought up the lands at the cost of £18,000.[71]

In a London becoming more and more strongly Protestant, new impetus was given to endowing education in accordance with reformed teaching. The Reformer Henry Brinkelow, who had been an inmate of a monastery, took up his residence among the merchants of London and became a freeman of the Mercers' Company. He campaigned against 'superstitious' bequests and urged instead the founding of almshouses or grammar schools.[72] The Mercers were already active – when the Hospital of St Thomas Acon, in which there was probably still a school, was dissolved in 1538, their Company, which had long worshipped in its chapel, bought its property from the Crown, and covenanted 'to find and keep a grammar school within the City of London perpetually with a sufficient Master to teach 25 children freely in the same continually for ever'. They raised a loan and borrowed also from the school chest of St Paul's. The school was opened at Michaelmas 1542, at first in the church and later in a schoolhouse 'erected by the Company in the chapel under the Hall', and in 1574 the number of scholars was increased to 40. This school was supported directly from the Company's charitable funds, but also attracted later endowments for scholarships and the like.[73]

The complexities of the greatest foundation of Edward VI's reign illustrate the difficulty of disentangling credit and enterprise at what might be called official levels. In Christ's Hospital London gave the lead to other cities in coping with the problem of destitute and orphan children. Such poverty moved the City to obtain from the Crown the hospitals attached to the London monasteries. The efforts of successive Lord Mayors, reinforced by the powerful voice of Bishop Ridley, who has indeed been called the 'prime mover', succeeded in transferring them into the hands of the City, including Christ's Hospital or the Grey Friars intended for children. Under an agreement with Edward VI, who granted a charter conferring the right to hold property in mortmain, a committee was set up of citizens nominated by the City, including six aldermen, and set about raising funds so that no 'child in his infansie shall wante the vertuous education and bringing up'. Committee members set an example by subscribing a substantial £10 or £20 each, and a vigorous fund-raising campaign was launched, including as usual a sermon at St Paul's and something like a Christian stewardship campaign in the parishes, each householder being obliged to fill in a form to state the amount of his regular subscription. It was claimed, however, that 'men gave franckly, the work was so generally well lyked'.

Christ's Hospital began as an orphanage, a refuge and an infirmary, but from the outset it belongs also to the history of grammar education in the City and was soon sending boys to the universities. It added considerably to the places available, not only for orphans but also for sons of citizens who had fallen on hard times, especially as the governors early had to restrict admission to the children of citizens and freemen, so great had been the number of 'foreign' children seeking admission. Its function as an asylum was gradually overtaken by its function as a school. It attracted many bequests and endowments from London citizens from its early years, many of them assigned to its educational work, some for children from other towns or districts. Christ's Hospital has often been claimed as a royal benefaction, but it was 'not so much the King's work as the City's'. Its governance was in the hands of the City – the Lord Mayor, the Court of Aldermen and twelve members of the Common Council were governors *ex officio*, and others were elected annually.[74]

The passionate commitment of the London community to education grew with its increasing confidence and experience, and with assurance of the establishment of Protestant faith. Elizabeth's church settlement, at least for the time being, brought hope for the new doctrines and practices. The return of exiles from Europe, many of whom, in Switzerland, the Rhineland and Germany, had seen Protestantism expressed in civic academies, brought new impetus to the movement for founding and reforming schools. In 1559 a party of learned returned exiles inspected St Paul's and found the High Master 'very weak and slender'. He was removed and replaced by one who could teach Greek.[75]

Richard Hilles, who as a 'seriously-minded boy of 18' had twice fallen foul of Henry VIII's religious views, had to take refuge on the continent. He returned from Strasbourg in 1549 to find his companions on the court of the Merchant Taylors' Company divided between Reformers and Romanists. Through the troubles of Mary's reign he kept up a correspondence with his exile friends such as Alexander Nowell, and when in 1558 they began to return, he and his party were able to prevail and to found in 1560 the Merchant Taylors' School. The manor of the Rose in St Lawrence Poultney, once the house of the famous merchant and Lord Mayor of Edward III's reign, Sir John Pultney, was bought for £566 13s 5d, the statutes were modelled on those of St Paul's, and Richard Mulcaster was appointed the first 'High Master'. This school, like that of the Mercers, was supported from Company funds, but soon began to attract endowments, especially for scholarships at St John's College Oxford, for as confidence in the triumph of the Reformation at the universities grew, so did bequests for exhibitions and fellowships linking the new schools with higher education. From its beginning this school, an exceptionally large one for its time and soon with an outstanding academic reputation, educated not only sons of the Company but those of other citizens. The first boys included the sons of a minister, a plumber, a leatherseller, a carpenter, an upholsterer, a clothworker, a salter, a vintner, a grocer, a dyer, a draper, a waxchandler. In ten years' time it had begun to attract boarders, even from the north and the west country, and in 1567 was obliged to declare that its first duty was to educate burgher youths.[76]

The position and power of the City Companies place their educational work on what might almost be called an official plane. The last example of schools provided by official enterprise was at parochial level. A century earlier the lay element in demand for schools can only be conjectured. Now, not only was the parish being transformed into the basic unit of civil government, but the laity were ready to take the lead in educational provision.

Southwark on the accession of Elizabeth was struggling with many problems. The religious houses and ecclesiastical palaces which had given it dignity were pulled down or built over, some transformed into secular palaces or country houses. Its population was rapidly expanding, it suffered as an overspill area for the City, especially of the disreputable, the poor and the disaffected. At the end of the great bridge and the road from Europe, it attracted foreigners, who brought new trades such as brewing, linen- and silk-weaving, and, later, pottery-making, and also more incoherence, more diversity, more dissidence. Theatres, bull- and bear-baiting rings, stews, driven from the City by its powerful and stringent rulers, brought raffish elements. The sober residents – butchers, brewers, saddlers, tanners, etc. – must have looked with envy at the substantial provision of schools over the river. Already the parishioners of St Margaret's had shown much enterprise in troubled times and had taken over the church of the dissolved priory of St Mary Overie, whose name they changed to St Saviour's, using that of another abbey in Bermondsey. In 1559 as soon as Queen Mary was dead they sold some of the church plate and renewed the St Saviour's lease, which contained a promise that they would provide a school and that they would 'adorn' it with a schoolmaster within two years. In the meantime they let off the Lady Chapel of their old church, St Margaret's, to a baker in order to pay for the use of its church house as a temporary school, making up the funds by a further sale, this time of vestments and brass vessels. The leading spirit in this brisk enterprise was Thomas Cure, churchwarden of St Saviour's, Master Saddler to Queen Mary and then to Queen Elizabeth. 'The good benevolens of the parysshe' towards the erection of a schoolhouse had next to be put to the test, and well within the stipulated two years the purchase of the town house or inn of Lady Cobham, then called the Green Dragon, had been negotiated and the master and pupils installed. The charter states that the twelve governors 'and other inhabitants of the parish of St Saviour's, in the borough of Southwark, had erected a school at their own costs and charges in the said parish for the instruction of youth, as well poor as rich, inhabiting the said parish, in grammatical learning'. This was therefore at first supported by the parishioners by subscription and 'very probably from local rates'. Again, it attracted later endowments, by 1660 amounting to £530 including scholarships to the universities.[77]

The neighbouring, and poorer, parish of St Olave's somewhat re-luctantly founded a school at much the same time, when a wealthy brewer, Henry Leke, who held property in both parishes, left money for a free school in St Saviour's only if St Olave's should fail to build 'one Free Schole within the space of two yere from the date hereof', by March 1560. This school, which was not for the first ten years of its life a grammar school, was opened probably at Michaelmas 1561. Quarrels over Leke's benefaction continued and in 1571 Letters Patent established the school as a grammar school.[78]

Southwark in fact may, without undue anachronism, be described as being a self-constituted Elizabethan Education Authority.

This corporate, even public, provision of 'common schools' was supplemented by private, individual benefactions. Some of these were attached to existing schools as additional endowments for scholarships at school or university, etc. Others founded their own schools, though they sometimes placed their administration in the hands of corporate bodies. The London suburbs and villages and small towns, still in the surrounding open countryside, for the most part owed their schools to private enterprise of this kind. Sites in the City were pretty well used up by the reign of Elizabeth and City boys were well provided for.

These private donors represent a whole range of social, professional, intellectual concerns. First there were the merchants, especially the great merchants, whose charitable pre-eminence 'played such an important role in framing and founding those institutions and those attitudes upon which the modern society may be said to depend'. During the years 1480–1660, of the immense total sum which this comparatively small group gave to charity, 27.55 per cent was for educational uses. A relatively small amount of this, 2.55 per cent, went to higher education directly, a much larger proportion went to providing scholarships and fellowships, usually in conjunction with a school foundation, but by far the largest share, nearly 20 per cent, went to the endowing of schools, many of them in the provinces, some in the City itself through corporate giving, and others in the London suburbs.[79] Nicholas Gibson, a warden of the Grocers' Company, established a school in his native village of Ratcliffe, part of Stepney parish, in 1536, maintaining it from his own purse and then bequeathing property to his wife on trust for its endowment. She entrusted the management of the school to the Coopers' Company. The school was for 60 boys, with a master and an usher to teach the younger ones reading and spelling and the older ones 'grammatical science'.[80] Enfield Grammar School also owed its refoundation in 1558 partly to merchant wealth – a number of donors contributing, and a native of the town, William Garrett, a merchant tailor, making a gift of £50 in 1586 to build a new schoolhouse. The parish also took an active part in re-establishing this school.[81]

Wealth from a number of sources was made available for a school and almshouses founded between 1609 and 1613. As a girl, Dame Alice Owen had a dramatic escape from death when she was playing in the pleasant meadows of Islington, owned by her wealthy father, Thomas Wilkes. An arrow, inexpertly discharged, probably by one of the apprentices who were encouraged to practise this manly and useful sport in the safe fields outside the city walls, 'pierced quite thorow' Alice's tall-crowned hat, and she vowed on recovering her composure that 'if she lived to be a lady, she would erect something on that spot of ground in commemoration of the great mercy shown by the Almighty in that astonishing deliverance'. Many years and three husbands later she kept her vow, building first almshouses and then a school, surmounted by a gable with three iron arrows, for 30 poor boys, 24 from Islington and 6 from Clerkenwell. She entrusted the governance of her charity to the Brewers' Company, of which her first husband had been a member. Her second husband had been an alderman of the City of London, and her third a justice of the Common Pleas. She had 'advanced and enriched all her children' (six sons and six daughters), 'kept greate hospitalitie' and also 'in her lifetime so furthered the publique weale of this State, as her charitable deeds to the Cittie of London, both Universities . . ., especiallie this town of Islington, can testifie', said her tombstone in St Mary's Islington. This endowment was of a considerable sum, £1776, and represents the varied sources from which such capital could be accumulated – the inflated value of land near the City, trading and industrial interests, professional and official profits. Her last husband was a merchant's son and had, on his death in 1598, left considerable bequests, some to his native Shropshire, but Dame Alice was clearly a woman of considerable business powers and independence of mind – an 'intelligent, clear minded woman' as the student of her benefactions concluded. London had a long tradition of such women and of giving them freedom of operation.[82]

Dame Alice's School belongs to the most generous period of school foundations – the decades from 1611 to 1630 when the 'incredible total of £249,331 11s was provided principally by London generosity'.[83] Much of this was for provincial schools, but a large proportion of it was the result of a single munificent benefaction which gave inner London another great school – the Charterhouse. Thomas Sutton expended £13,000 on the site, and his endowment of the almshouses and school seems to have amounted to £116,000. Sutton can hardly be described as a 'great merchant' (he was never a freeman of London) although Jordan included this sum with theirs. Perhaps the overworked word entrepreneur can justifiably be applied to him. His career, and the amassing of his fortune, demonstrates the variety of ways in which disposable wealth could be drawn into the hands of men who had, at least in the last resort, the will to invest it in the human resources of the nation. The story of Sutton's fortune is not always edifying, but fitfully illuminates opportunities for profit in a changing economy, in which conduct of public service and rules of business ethics had still to be established. It also illuminates the psychology of men groping in such a situation, desirous, even greedy, of profit, but not without a sense of human obligation, and certainly with a strong conviction of divine judgment. Sutton (1532–1611) was the son of a Lincolnshire land- and office-holder. He studied at the Inns of Court, travelled in Europe, and took up a military career. Both ability and powerful patronage brought him a life appointment as Master Surveyor of the Ordnance in the northern parts of the realm. What other profits of office he may have gained are unknown, but they were trivial compared with his realization of the value to be got from the local coalfields. Between 1569 and 1580 he leased coal-bearing manors from the Bishop of Durham, and shrewdly exploited the growing demand for coal, especially in the capital. He permitted Newcastle merchants and the principal suppliers of London to operate the mining rights as a single enterprise, thus raising the price of coal from 4s to 6s a cauldron. When he moved from Berwick on Tweed to the village of Hackney in about 1580, he was already known as the richest commoner in England. He increased his wealth still further by adding to his Lincolnshire lands purchases in Essex, Cambridgeshire and Wiltshire. He almost certainly adventured his capital in overseas enterprises, and lent moneys, even to the Queen. In 1582 he married Elizabeth, the wealthy widow of John Dudley of Stoke Newington, and until her death in 1602 he resided at that pleasant manor. By 1594 he was beginning to project the foundation of almshouses and schools in Essex, until in 1611 the Earl of Suffolk, heavily committed to the building of Audley End, decided to sell the Charterhouse, and Sutton quickly negotiated its purchase, using Suffolk's official position to get Letters Patent from King James with remarkable despatch. Having drawn his will, Sutton died in December of that year. His huge benefactions became the subject of litigation, but the will was successfully upheld.[84]

The wealth of such men was a matter for contemporary social and ethical comment. In a rather earlier generation Mulcaster discussed the contribution of the merchant community to education and considered it inadequate in relation to the amount that these men had taken from the poor. 'These people by their general trades will make thousands poor. . . . They will give a scholar some petty poor exhibition to seem to be religious, and under a slender veil of counterfeit liberality, hide the spoil of ransacked poverty.'[85] Perhaps this reflects Mulcaster's unhappy relations with the men of the livery companies who ran Merchant Taylors' and St Paul's. The calculation of other people's obligations is always difficult, and the contemporary notion of the 'commonwealth' emphasized the distorting effect of gathering wealth into a few hands rather than the importance of creating wealth for a higher gross national product.

Compared with the greater and lesser merchants, landowners of varying rank contributed much less to education. Not only was the absolute level of their giving lower, but as a group they concentrated their benefactions on other causes, especially the relief of vagrancy and poverty, more traditionally the recognized responsibility of rural society.[86] The London picture is complicated by the investment in land by City men, especially in Middlesex and other surburban counties; and it is difficult to distinguish between a merchant living on his country estates and a country gentleman. In Middlesex, the most surburban county, and in Surrey, where City men also formed a high proportion of landowners, their infiltration lessened the absolute numbers of possible gentry donors. Land not only conferred a higher status, it was still the only long-term outlet for the investment of capital.[87] Once locked up in land, capital was of course no longer so readily available for charitable bequests, especially on the scale needed for education.

Two of our benefactors however may be assigned to the landed interest at yeoman level. Robert Hammond, who founded a modest little school in Hampton churchyard under his will in 1556, and by another bequest revitalized Kingston Grammar School, not yet to be counted within the London ambit, came of yeoman stock from West Molesey, a pleasant riverside village where traffic on the Thames and the proximity of the great palace at Hampton Court were stimulating enterprise and opportunity. Robert was probably only about fourteen in 1501 when he inherited his father's 'free landys and tenementes with all the Kopyeholde with in the parish of West Molsey', together with his share of £40, to be divided with his three brothers and sisters, and half-share in a Thames barge with his brother. His path from this modest start to prosperity as a London brewer twenty years later is unknown. This business was in the parish of St Andrew by the Wardrobe. In 1523 he was supplying beer under Wolsey's orders for shipment to the King's army and navy on the continent. He later figures in the Hampton Court building accounts as a carrier of goods such as chalk. Land was in fact only the basis of his fortune, which was made largely by industry and trade.[88]

Harrow School was also founded by a yeoman, John Lyon, a prosperous land-holder in the hamlet of Preston in that parish. He obtained a licence to refound the school in 1571 when he was already paying moneys for the instruction of 30 poor children. In 1590 he drafted the statutes for the school and when he died a year later, endowed it with suburban properties worth about £100 a year, to be shared with other charities. The full implementation of his scheme had to wait till his widow died in 1608. After the Restoration land values in this secluded part of Middlesex began to be pushed up by urban development, but already we may ascribe Lyon's prosperity, and perhaps his particular interest in education, to the nearness of London.[89] The yeomanry of London and Middlesex showed a great interest in education, donating 35.85 per cent of their charitable funds to it. The contribution of landed donors to schools must be measured against the increasing use of the schools and universities by yeoman, gentry and even aristocratic families.[90]

Another important group of donors was made up of professional men. These formed 6.63 per cent of all the donors of London (including Middlesex) and provided 6.59 per cent of benefactions. Over half their bequests went to education, concentrated on the universities, with only a modest proportion to schools and scholarships.[91] Three of the most

Harrow School

interesting foundations in the London region were however due to men from the lay professions. Sir Roger Cholmeley, Chief Justice of the Queen's Bench, founded Highgate School in 1565, endowing it generously for its size and location, and was given the right to frame its statutes. The Bishop of London granted to the school the chapel and former hermitage of Highgate and lands and rights on his manor of Hornsey and, as Sir Roger did not live to draw up the statutes, the Bishop also advised the governors in framing them in 1571; 40 scholars were to be drawn from Highgate and the schoolmaster was also to serve the chapel, thus providing for a hamlet far from the parish centre.[92]

The new body of 'augmentations men' and their like, who grew prosperous on the supervision of monastic and chantry property, and the growing number of officials who served departments of the Tudor state, are represented among our founders by Edward Latymer (c. 1557–1627). His father, from a family of Suffolk gentry, became Dean of Peterborough and Treasurer of Westminster Abbey, and so Edward, who held the very profitable office of Clerk of the Court of Wards and Liveries, was a second-generation professional man – a most up-to-date phenomenon for his time. Living in Ram Alley off Fleet Street, he became one of the wealthiest members of his parish of St Dunstan in the West much favoured by lawyers. He bought himself a country retreat at Edmonton and invested in lands, first in Suffolk and then in riverside Hammersmith, highly profitable for fattening beasts driven on the hoof to the London markets. He died in 1627 and left his Hammersmith lands for providing schooling for poor boys in Edmonton and Fulham in existing petty schools 'to learn to read English, to be instructed in some part of God's true religion and thereby kept from idle and vagrant courses'. His will showed no interest in the level of education especially needed for men of his own sort, the proliferating professions. Latymer's work must have brought him much into contact with the education of boys of the rank dealt with by the Court of Wards, but his membership of a City parish evidently made him sensitive to the needs of the urban poor.[93] The pattern of his giving does not conform to that of the London professional group as a whole which was strongly committed to *higher* education – 42.62 per cent of their giving went to the universities, with another 2.89 per cent for scholarships and fellowships.[94]

A colourful metropolitan professional benefactor was the actor Edward Alleyn (1566–1626), a 'theatrical entrepreneur'. The accumulation of capital on such a scale from such a precarious source as city entertainment is intriguing. Alleyn became 'almost fanatically interested in the plight of the poor in the metropolitan region' and had already shown an active interest in education. His name appears in the Minute Book of St Saviour's Southwark as one of the twelve 'discreet and worthy inhabitants' who met to appoint a new governor for the grammar school. By that time, as well as his Bankside Theatre and his new venture of the Fortune Theatre in Cripplegate, he had been appointed 'chief master, ruler and overseer of all and singular his majestie's games, of bears, and bulls, and mastive dogs, and mastive bitches', though King James had rather reduced his profits by withdrawing permission for Sunday performances. By 1606 he had begun to buy lands in Dulwich, amassing 1300 acres in five years, and began to play the part of country squire. He was interested in Sutton's plans at the Charterhouse and spent a shilling in 1617 to take boat on the Thames to visit them. After consulting the Warden of Winchester Hospital in 1613 he began building his College of God's Gift in Dulwich. He planned to have Master, Warden, Fellows and Organist, and to install poor brethren and sisters and poor scholars from the parish of his birthplace, St Botolph Bishopsgate, from St Giles Cripplegate where his theatre stood, from St Saviour's Southwark where he lived, worked and was churchwarden, and from Camberwell itself. From 1616 the College was in being, but its legal establishment was a longer matter. The Lord Chancellor made great difficulties in Alleyn's securing Letters Patent, but Alleyn succeeded in 1619, and the College was formally opened with prayer and feasting. Before his death in 1626 Alleyn had secured lands, statutes and ordinances on his College and both during his life and under his will provided funds to the value of

£9372, well nigh exhausting his estate. Legal troubles and internal wrangles weakened his foundation in its early years, which were made more difficult by the constitutional and religious struggles which soon followed.

The statutes laid down that a master and an usher were to be appointed for the school, and that the 'two masters of musique of the said College' were to teach the 12 poor scholars, three from each parish, 'good and sound learning, wryting, reading, grammar, musique and good manners'. Children of the inhabitants of Dulwich were also to be freely instructed in writing and grammar; these, however, had to pay admittance charges of 2*s* 6*d* a quarter for brooms and rods, and a pound of candles at Michaelmas. 'Forreyners' children were to pay 'such allowance as the master and warden shall appoint', but the whole number in the school was not to exceed 80. The carefully laid plans of this unusual professional benefactor were, however, very long in being realized.[95]

Last, but important among suburban professional founders, were the clergy; their contribution over our whole region must cast doubt on any classification of this massive provision of schools as a predominantly lay movement. The patterns of giving among the clergy over the whole period studied by Jordan show that the upper clergy left comparatively modest sums for religious purposes and were on the whole not much concerned with bequests to the poor, but bestowed more than two-thirds of their gifts on education, over half of this to higher education. The lower clergy were as fully committed to education, in proportions of 16.24 per cent for grammar schools, 20.70 per cent for universities, 12.12 per cent for scholarships and fellowships, and 3.78 per cent for libraries.[96] These figures, being for the City and Middlesex only, include Colet's massive contribution but not four important schools in the London region taken at its widest. Two of these, very much then on the periphery, were founded by Archbishop Whitgift at Croydon and Archbishop Harsnett of York at Chigwell; the latter gave two large schools under one roof as 'his mite of thankfulness to God, who from a poor vicar of this parish hath called me to my so high a dignity in his church'. In the English school all boys from Chigwell, and two each from Loughton, Woodford and Lambourne, were to be taught reading, writing, arithmetic and accidence, and in the Latin school the course was also to include Greek.[97]

The contribution of the lower clergy to the provision of schools for the laity must be seen in relation to the struggle of the Reformers to raise the level of education of the parish clergy themselves. Until the network of grammar schools replaced the old monastic almonry schools which had certainly, if they did little else for education, sent boys forward for the priesthood, it was indeed difficult for bishops to find candidates for ordination at all. Here, as in other educational matters, London led the way. The standard of education among the London clergy was higher than elsewhere, and this spread out to the suburbs and the surrounding villages. This in turn raised the standards of *lay* education.[98]

The Reverent Edward Wilson was presented to the large parish of Camberwell in 1578 where he remained for forty years. He was succeeded by a nephew whose education he had sponsored until he graduated at Cambridge and it is clear that Wilson, who was himself childless, realized the value of education. After the death of his wife in 1611, he spent his last years in planning and instituting a grammar school in his own parish. He negotiated with the lord of the manor an exchange of the advowson for seven acres of freehold land next to the church, built a schoolhouse and other houses which were to provide rents, and obtained Letters Patent to establish a school 'for the better education, institution and instruction of the children and youths of the poor' in the parish. The founder and after him the governors, local men of standing, were to have power to appoint and remove the Master and to make 'fit and wholesome statutes . . .'.

Compared with the complex and lavishly endowed foundation of the College of God's Gift being launched by his colourful parishioner Alleyn at much the same time, Wilson's school, modestly maintained from local rents, designed to serve entirely local needs and managed by local men, was much less ambitious. The two men were often in each other's company; Alleyn's diary records on 26 November 1618 that on his way back to Dulwich from a visit to his theatre at 'Black Friars', he called for his wife at 'Vikar Wilsone's' at Camberwell. The next day the old parson made his will bequeathing his books and lands, including those already settled on it by charter, to the governors of the school. By his pastoral labours and good management, quite slender resources had been deployed to give a small community a school which he had reasonable grounds for believing should prove adequate for its needs.[99]

The neighbouring Kentish village of Lewisham was also provided with its schools by the labour and dedication of its parson. Abraham Colfe was that comparative newcomer, the son of a parson, and in 1604 settled at Lewisham, first as curate and later as vicar. He held the rectory of St Leonard Eastcheap in plurality where he paid a curate. In his country living he was an active priest, much concerned with the welfare of the poor and in saving the common lands of the village, in what is now Forest Hill and Sydenham, from enclosure by one of James I's royal tenants, a 'Yeoman of ye Royal boiling house'. It is quite in character that he should also have spent time, patience, determination in providing his parish with educational facilities.

Money for a grammar school had in 1568 been bequeathed by an earlier vicar, but had not been properly invested, and although in 1574 a royal charter had been obtained for the 'Free Grammar School of Queen Elizabeth at Lewesham',[100] this seems to have existed in name alone. Further bequests were also ineffectual as there was no school to receive them. Another attempt to restart the school in 1612–13 seems to have been equally unsuccessful, and from about 1626 Colfe set himself to plan the re-establishment of the school on a proper footing. His marriage was childless, his family well provided for. It became his main task to get together, by enterprise and husbanding of resources, an adequate endowment. He also secured the interest of the Leathersellers' Company, which already administered lands in trust in Sydenham. On 13 July 1635 the minutes of the Court of the Company record that Mr Colfe's will had been 'receeved and locked . . . upp in safe custody in the Court House promising . . . to performe the trust according to his request . . . Wherewith hee was very well-satisfied, giving them many thanks for the same.'

Just how Colfe husbanded his resources during the next twenty years cannot be known. As early as 1624 he began to buy land, first as an investment at Edmonton, and then small plots of ground near his own church and meadows in Sydenham. His labours attracted small bene-factions from parishioners, but he complained that 'the hardness of the times and other things . . . obstructed the settling of his pious work . . .' He got his reading school built near the parish church and negotiated with the 'Jury of the Court Leet and Baron of Lewisham' to give him leave to build his grammar school 'upon a parcel of the Common Ground, lying on the side of the hill going up to the Common of Blackheath, there being no place in all my parish so fit as that to build the School upon for the more general parishes of the Hundred' – Blackheath, Greenwich, Deptford, Charlton, Woolwich, Lee and Eltham, as well as Lewisham. In 1652 the Leathersellers noted that 'Mr Colfe had opened his Free School at Lewisham, wherein he had built a Library', and resolved to follow the example of other benefactors and allow books 'as a guift of our Society so as they exceed not above six pounds'. The foundationers in this school were to be chosen from the various parishes of the Hundred, and seven scholarships of £10 a year were to be awarded to boys proceeding to Oxford and Cambridge.

Colfe secured this provision by his will, which disclosed how by 'rigid economy' practised over about forty years he had gathered together enough to satisfy himself that he could endow both the schools, and library and almshouses as well. On his death in 1657, the handling of the schools over to a City Company proved to be Colfe's most far-sighted move, for his careful endowment became insufficient, and the Leathersellers already in 1672–3 faced the fact that the estate was 'unanswerable to fulfil a discharge' on the 'uses thereof', and appear to have contributed thereafter every year to the expenses of the school.[101]

Who controlled the schools?

This achievement has been described as the 'evolution of a system of schools administered locally by lay governing bodies under the general supervision of the state. This was the major change initiated at the

Reformation.'[102] How far was there control by the state? Who did control the schools?

If some degree of uniformity and interconnection comprises a system, the schools provided by local enterprise of various kinds may be said to have such characteristics. The City drew like a magnet and exercised a powerful influence as a mart of ideas as well as commerce. Communications were comparatively good, population comparatively thick on the ground. It is highly likely that the foundation of a local school was discussed and debated outside its own immediate neighbourhood, and, in the case of a school of the standing of St Paul's, there is evidence that it formed a model widely copied – in fact, not only in the City and Southwark, but as far away as Manchester.[103] But even within a large parish such as Camberwell, with its two secluded hamlets of Peckham and Dulwich, there was room for variation and divergence, and any exchange of ideas or mutual planning by two founders known to one another both personally and professionally can only be conjectured. System in such circumstances came more as a by-product of the wide acceptance, by the sections of society who found money for education, of the Tudor order and the Elizabethan settlement, and their common adherence to cultural values and traditions. Coherence was political, moral and cultural rather than institutional. Schools were in no way linked together laterally – even their siting was usually haphazard and due to personal pieties or the availability of property. The links eventually came vertically, as a web of scholarships to Oxford and Cambridge was woven, and as masters from the universities began to flow back into the schools.

Supervision of some kind by the state may be conceded, in the negative sense at least. No Tudor sovereign, certainly not Elizabeth, would have tolerated schools overtly 'out of control' – unlikely in any case as they had been provided by ardent supporters of the social, political and religious order. The central government played only a parsimonious and reluctant part in saving or providing schools, and probably this reluctance to finance and control education was due not only to economy and lack of administrative machinery, but also to a misplaced confidence in indirect control. The crucial period here was the early part of Elizabeth's reign, when reliance continued to be placed on the licensing of schoolmasters by the Ordinary[104] and on the supervision and intrigues of the Privy Council. Elizabeth was surrounded by a group of men – including Cecil, Nicholas Bacon, Mildmay, Walsingham – who were keenly interested in education, both for its intrinsic value and as an instrument for securing the church settlement, which they interpreted on more advanced Reforming lines than Elizabeth herself was prepared to countenance. Their 'machiavel governance', as Matthew Parker, Archbishop of Canterbury, called it, encouraged the so-called puritan element and ultimately weakened control of the schools by the lay central power.[105]

How, for example, did this supervision operate when the two Southwark schools were being established by local enterprise? Their historian claims:

> There is little doubt that from top to bottom of the educational world a vast amount of scheming was afoot. Its details are little known, but here and there a dim ray of light reveals what was happening behind the scenes – in a struggle to get safe men into the right position.

The Charter of St Saviour's had to receive the royal seal, and this in turn empowered the governors to make statutes, with the consent of the Bishop – in this case, of Winchester. In some respects they were influenced by those of Winchester College, but for the most part were modelled on those of St Paul's, revised and brought up to date in a manner suggesting the hand of the new Dean of St Paul's, Alexander Nowell. He however fits ill into any picture of Renaissance plotting behind the arras. He was a sincere upholder of the Protestant settlement, but tolerant and mild, a keen angler who had been credited with the inadvertent invention of bottled beer, and was wholly thrown off-balance when Queen Elizabeth interrupted one of his sermons. Nowell had been headmaster of Westminster School from 1543 to 1553, had then gone into exile at Frankfurt, and from his return, strongly imbued with Calvinist ideas, wielded considerable influence at a certain level in the world of government and learning. In 1562 at the instigation of Cecil, he produced his *Larger Catechism*, not merely for the use of the young, but to silence those who asserted that 'the Protestants had no principles'. In 1570 his Latin *Middle Catechism* was soon translated into English and Greek but its official use in schools was delayed by criticisms from the Queen. Nowell was also on the Court of High Commission, which from 1562 had been given the power to revise the rules of schools and colleges 'as may best tend to the honour of Almighty God, the increase of virtue and unity in the same places, and the public weal and tranquility of our realm'. Nowell frequently advised on the drawing up of school statutes, and became a kind of unofficial consultant to the Livery Companies for this purpose. The tradesmen-parishioners of St Saviour's may have consulted him also.[106]

A strange experiment in intrigue and in testing the limits of the church settlement, on the part of men in high places, was the appointment of Robert Browne, founder of the Independents, as headmaster of St Olave's in 1586. Browne had already been in trouble with the authorities and written, amongst other polemics, his *Reformation without Tarrying for Any*, but he was a relation by marriage of William Cecil who took an active interest in his career, and who also had connections with Bermondsey. The entry of Browne's appointment in St Olave's governors' minute book – 'upon his good behaviour and observings these articles here underwritten' – betrays some justifiable disquiet: he did not keep the articles, he did not take Communion in St Olave's, he was responsible for 'sottish separation', he preached in private houses and disturbed the peace of congregations, and when his opinions were exposed in 1588 in *The Raising of the Foundations of Brownism*, the governors had had enough. It was not the central government but the respectable tradesman and householders of Southwark who defended the establishment. The exact date and manner of Browne's departure is not known.[107]

The first high master of the other Southwark school of St Saviour's was Christopher Ocland, whose achievements and misfortunes provide another example of the problems, even the mystery, of central control of the grammar schools of this period. After an ineffectual period at St Saviour's he later became head of Cheltenham Grammar School and while there wrote the *Anglorum Praelia*, a celebration in bad Latin verses of the martial glories of England from the time of Edward III to that of the late Queen Mary. So much impressed was the Privy Council with the educational potential of this work, especially the latest edition with 'a shorte treatise or appendix concerning the peaceable government of the Quenes Majestie', that they ordered it to be used in all common schools instead of 'divers heathen poetes . . . ordinarily read and taught from which the youths of the Realme receyve rather infectyon in manners and educatyon than advauncement in vertue . . .' This can be construed as direct intervention by the government in the curriculum, but there is little or no evidence that the instruction was ever carried out. Certainly the author of the work received little benefit – he died in great poverty and distress soon after sending a desperate petition to Lord Burghley: 'I never had anything of her Grace's hands for all my books heretofore made of her Highness . . .'[108] It is a reminder that we must 'test the Elizabethan system in action' if we are to form a true picture of the extent to which the royal power was effectively exercised.[109]

The most immediate instrument of central control was episcopal licensing of schoolmasters – the state taking over and adapting medieval ecclesiastical sanctions. In 1559 an Injunction of Elizabeth commanded that schoolmasters be examined and approved by the Ordinary, and after the formulation of the Thirty-Nine Articles in 1563 a statutory oath to them was required of all teachers, public and private. Every schoolmaster had to present himself before the Vicar General of the Bishop of London (or of Winchester south of the Thames) with a certificate of his appointment and testimonials of his fitness. His examination and subscription to the oath and his affirmation of the Articles were entered in the Subscription Book and later copied into the Consistory Court Book.[110] There is 'no doubt whatever that in the diocese of London as elsewhere teachers of grammar were closely watched', but the record does not preserve a complete, or even entirely reliable, register. For example, where from 1627–83/4, one record, a Subscription Book, can be checked against another, the Consistory Court

Books, they do not always agree, and as numbers vary considerably from year to year, it seems likely that a pending visitation from the archdeacon, or the course of national events, stimulated activity. There was a spurt in 1637 which has been explained by Laud's policies and the Ship Money crisis. After 1660 and after the Test Act of 1672 there were other bursts of subscriptions. The machinery of the diocese operated fitfully, and was also subject to the variations of a system which depended on fees (and perhaps favours). Probably it could so operate largely because schoolmasters did support the settlement of the Church and State, and the incentive for the administration of complex and time-consuming machinery was in part personal insurance and in part a question of getting the right payments. Always allowing for the real menace of state power, not much more urgency can have gone into the matter than into the fulfilment of many present-day bureaucratic procedures.

The variation of form in which the licence was granted makes exact location difficult. Sometimes the parish is specified, sometimes the licence covered the whole diocese; occasionally a school is named – St Paul's, or Colet's School, the public school of Merchant Taylors', the school in the Mercers' Hall. In most cases licence to teach in a grammar school in a particular parish does not mean that it was more than a private school or that the master did not move to other parts of the diocese. In some cases reference to a 'free school', for example that in St Andrew's Holborn, implies endowment, or perhaps a school in the church in the tradition of the chantries. The several licences granted to teach grammar in St Peter's Cornhill may indicate some continuity with the medieval school in that parish. Evidence overall is of the general level of provision of grammar teaching in the City and its suburbs, and of the preparatory teaching for 'petties', 'abecedario', reading, writing, 'such English books as are allowed', and so forth. Over all these teachers the Tudor and Stuart monarchy cast an intermittently watchful eye through clerical machinery inherited from pre-Reformation times.[111]

At local level control operated within a framework of law, finally codified in 1601 under the Statute of Charitable Uses,[112] primarily designed to protect public benefactions, which saved the Crown using its own resources, from private claims. This was backed by powers to appoint commissions of enquiry into malpractice and inefficiency by the governing bodies constituted by founders. This machinery operated only sporadically and not very effectively. In unsettled times the stability so provided probably outweighed the disadvantages of applying the doctrine of founder's intent which deprived the governors of power to adapt schools to changing needs.

Founders were careful to appoint as governors men of community standing and institutional prestige and resources. Such bodies were either incorporated (Christ's Hospital, Mercers', Merchant Taylors', St Anthony's, the Coopers' School at Ratcliffe, St Paul's, Westminster) or unincorporated feoffees.[113] Comparison between the efficiency or honesty of these two types is difficult, but London probably had an advantage in that the City Companies provided a unique source of administrative experience, communal concern and economic stability and they were on the spot. Colet placed St Paul's in the care of the Mercers because, as he said, 'though there was nothing certain in human affairs, yet he found the least corruption' in these 'married citizens of established reputation'. They were to appoint eleven 'honest and substancial menne callid the Surveyors of the scole which in the name of the hoole feloship shall take all charge and besynes aboute the scole for that one yere'. He also made exceptionally shrewd provisions for an annual turnover of surveyors to reduce collusions, and the granting of only short leases of property. This did, however, reduce the possibilities of fiscal planning.[114]

What the 'charge and besynes' about a school involved is illustrated by the records of Companies administering London schools. In the case of a City school maintained directly from Company funds, this was burdensome enough. But when administering an endowment, perhaps somewhat inadequate, in a suburban village, the duties must have been a severe interruption to business. The Leathersellers administering Colfe's schools, for example, entered into their accounts the charges for 'goeing and comeing by water from Lewsham' when they 'went thither to view the breach in the howse blowne downe with the tempest' in September 1658; in June 1660 they entered the purchase of 'paper bookes for the Schollars of the English Schole', of a 'Quart of Inke and a bottle', twelve primers and 'a hundred of Quills'.[115] The Brewers in 1678 had to cope with the problem of providing a testimonial for the headmaster of Owen's after he had got mixed up, more by folly than by design, with the Popish Plot, and had of necessity been dismissed after his licence to teach had been withdrawn by the Bishop: they 'humbly certify that he was an industrious and careful person in his place; and is a very loyal subject to his Sacred Majesty and government, for anything we know to the contrary'.[116]

The appointment of the staff was one of the most responsible tasks, often carried out with indifferent success. For their school in Ratcliffe, the Coopers in 1561 secured a scholar, Richard Reynolds, who wrote on rhetoric and Roman history, but he only stayed a year. His successor had to be dismissed after nine years for his 'evil demeanour and lack of diligence'. The next one, John Turk, stayed for an alarming period: 1594–1613. He was said to be 'lazy, insubordinate, and lacking in grammar, good letters, and manners'; it is a relief to learn that he was ultimately dismissed, even if with a pension and an almshouse. The next one proved to be unlicensed by he Bishop and found it difficult to displace the unsatisfactory Turk, who seems to have got the Bishop on his side. A new appointment again failed to satisfy the

Bishop, and when the Company did get a properly licensed master in 1616, he only stayed two years.[117]

In the matter of choice of master, the governing body was in fact well advised to seek ecclesiastical help, and this was often stipulated in statutes. Colfe provided for an impressive interviewing and appointing body to choose an 'exact grammarian . . . able to teach Greek and Latin both in prose and verse, and also Hebrew'. In 1677 the Leathersellers 'paid and spent uppon the choice of the new Grammar Schoolmaster at Lewisham at which time were present according to Mr Colfe's will many ministers from London, the Deane and Assistants of Sion College, besides the Ministers of the Hundred there abouts, a very great meeting and spent at that time £xii. viis'.[118]

Another important duty was that of Visitation – the annual examination of school, which sometimes assumed the air of combined general inspection and speech day. 'Apposition Day' at St Paul's took place at Candlemas, and a tradition of presenting a Greek or Latin play grew up.[119] Even the most powerful companies generally sought clerical help in this matter. The Merchant Taylors had their school, both scholars and masters, reviewed from its early days by the Bishop of London.[120] Others relied on parish clergy. In 1667 the Leathersellers made their visitation of Colfe's and 'mett there with severall ministers as well of London as of the parishes thereabouts who spent much time in the examination of the said schollars which was performed with strictness'. These Lewisham examinations also fulfilled the specific purpose of choosing holders of scholarships to the universities.[121] The Brewers at Islington seem to have used their annual visitation as a kind of payment by results system – giving the Master a little extra 'for his diligence' or sometimes dismissing him from his post.[122]

In the administration, even of endowed schools, the Companies sometimes had to expend their own funds – for example, the Leathersellers were doing so by 1672/3, and the Brewers declared in the early eighteenth century that 'the rents and increases of the said premises are not near sufficient to discharge their expenses'.[123] But gratitude was not always forthcoming nor perhaps deserved. Relations between the local communities and the Livery Companies were sometimes not happy. The 'feloship' was all on the side of the Company rather than of the local community, and it all too often took the outward and visible sign of alarmingly expensive meals. Even by 1640 the Visitation dinner in Islington for which Dame Alice Owen had allowed a modest 30s had reached the total of £13 19s 4d – the yearly salary of the master was £20. In Lewisham complaints arose as early as 1674, and in Islington matters began to reach a crisis in 1708 when the surveyor of the parish lodged a formal complaint, soon supported by a strong-minded vicar and several other gentlemen of the vestry. This culminated in a long Chancery case.[124]

Whether a community fared better without such extraneous help depended on the quality of its local leaders, the support they received and the adequacy of the resources at the disposal of a governing body, not only for establishing the school, but for keeping at least abreast of inflation and rapidly changing social, economic, cultural, topographical conditions. The parishioners of St Olave's, for example, had to cope with a district with proliferating industries and increasing urban over-spill, as well as plague, dissent and mounting numbers of vagrant, or at least 'unsettled', poor. The governors consisted of the minister and churchwardens, other members being mainly local tradesmen, and they were required not only to sacrifice business time (meetings were held early in the morning), but to pay subscriptions. Here also there were 'many jarrings, discontent, and inconveniences ... between ye gov-ernors and Churchwardens in relation to their distinct managing and disposing of ye Lande, Tenements and premises belonging to their parish of Olave'. The school was considered to take up too large a share of the parish resources in face of the mounting burden of poverty, and the legal position in relation to the highly profitable endowment of Horsleydown, made over to the school, was far from clear. Some kind of working compromise was reached in 1656 when part of the district was granted by the governors to the wardens for a rent of a red rose (if demanded), but this did not mollify the parishioners. The obtaining of a second Royal Charter in 1674 enabled the governors to maintain two scholars at the university and enlarge the school, but it also diverted some of their funds from education – they built a workhouse on part of the Horsleydown site, and made the school fire-engines available for the whole parish. The concern of the parish was for using its own resources in accordance with urgent contemporary priorities amongst what today we might call social services.[125]

To turn to an example of unincorporated bodies, that of Wilson's School at Camberwell was carefully constituted under the founder's statutes. It included the churchwardens of the 'Liberties' of Peckham and Dulwich, and drew on the local clergy and the services of the numerous resident gentry of a village still in pleasant open country but conveniently near to London and Westminster. Their duties were intensive and specific – to go from time to time into the school without warning and to correct anything amiss, to hold a quarterly visitation, to consult with 'men of learning' on the best methods of teaching and school organization, to manage the lands which endowed the school and look to the lopping of the trees which were to provide poor scholars with funds for pens, ink, paper, and to regulate the number of scholars admitted from outside the parish and fix their fees. Records show how troublesome these duties could be. The management of property at such a local level produced disagreeable personal squabbles with the tenants, and the governors seem gradually to have allowed too much of the resources to get into the hands of successive schoolmasters. Throughout the seventeenth century for the most part, however, the governing body remained active, even if meetings came at longer intervals, but by the early eighteenth century its numbers had reduced, no new members were co-opted, only *ex officio* members seem to have attended, and the master was gradually left to run the school much on his own lines and for his own profit. The machinery for maintaining the school as a public, community, one was not operated with enough energy, and perhaps expertise, to prevent its becoming virtually a private institution. This failure of energy and concern over the generations was one of the factors which reduced the effectiveness of the schools.[126]

Examination of schools in the London region during this crucial period in the history of the secular grammar schools does not in fact fully substantiate the claim that a 'system of schools' evolved, administered locally by lay governing bodies under the general supervision of the state.[127] Central control failed or relied too much on indirect means. The important contribution of the City through the work of its Livery Companies was weakened by the increasing divergence of these wealthy corporations and the families and communities the schools were founded to serve. Local governance, however conscientious, had to contend with changes and community stresses which were often too much for available machinery or human or economic resources. Nevertheless the 'educational revolution' was due 'in no small part to the successful efforts and labours of these unheralded and little-studied amateurs'.[128]

What was taught?

Colet founded his school to increase both 'connyng' and 'vertuous lyving', and neither the Renaissance nor the Reformation would have seen these as separable or in any way as alternatives.[129] Our grammar schools were above all to be religious foundations, increasingly emphasizing the literate basis of faith as well as culture. Moreover, by the reign of Elizabeth individual conviction for the first time mattered on any large scale. England had become a pluralist nation and this had immense significance for schooling.[130] St Saviour's was 'for the good education and bringynge up of youthe in the love, feare and knolydge of God and his most holy word, in good nourture towards the world and theyre parents, and fynally in letters and understandinge of the tongues in which is hidden and layde up the treasures of all divine and human knolydge'. In this, as in almost every school, the boys with the master were to attend church on Sundays, holy and festival days, and those of St Olave's were to be examined to see how much they brought away.[131] School days began with prayers and reading from the scriptures, and ended similarly – Colfe's School, for example, requiring a psalm to be sung at the opening of school and before going home. At Wilson's School parents were required to provide a testament and a psalm book.[132] The religious syllabus was usually carefully prescribed. The boys of St Saviour's were to study Castalion upon the Scripture, Aesop, Calvin's Catechism in Latin and Greek, and the New Testament in Greek. By 1572 St Olave's was able to specify Dean Nowell's Catechism, recently 'by the canons appointed to be taught in Grammar Scholes'.[133] Rules of conduct likewise were laid down, sometimes revealing odd preferences or prejudices – at St Paul's (1518) 'no mete nor drink nor botellis' were to be brought into the school, 'no brekefastys nor drinking is in the tyme of lernyng'; at Colfe's (1652) neither masters nor boys were to wear 'long curl'd, frizzled, powdered or ruffin-like hair'.[134] In general, however, such rules underlined the moral dimension in which all education was seen, and included behaviour in the streets, on Sundays, at all times – this was no 'hidden curriculum' but an explicit statement of shared and unquestioned values and codes. A constant battle against disorder was characteristic of the period and individual conviction must lead to acceptable conformity.

However much they may in practice have resembled bear-gardens, these schools were seen as, above all, religious and moral communities. Within this framework their chief function was the teaching of 'letters', of 'tongues', of the Latin and Greek languages and literatures. The most significant and important question here is how the Latin curriculum changed during this period, and what purposes it served. Colet set the pattern by prescribing the books to be studied (a somewhat conservative list), and commissioning textbooks at a time when the work of the comparitively new printing press was only just enabling 'bookish' education to supersede oral recitation and memorization. St Saviour's is an example of a school which followed Colet's pattern, prescribing amongst other authors Cicero, Terence, Caesar, Valerius Maximus, Justinius, Erasmi Apothegmata, Vergil, Horace, Juvenal, Persius and Ovid.[135] Morality indeed was 'based on Cicero as well as on, the Scriptures'.[136] Probably only a small proportion of the nation's schools also taught Greek, but evidence suggests that the position was better in London. After St Paul's, Westminster set the pace. Its headmaster Edward Grant produced the first Greek grammar in English. This was adapted by his successor, William Camden, and became the standard book for pupils.[137] In 1652 Colfe specified Lilly's Latin Grammar (produced for St Paul's) and Camden's Greek Grammar and 'all the best orders and exercises in use in the Free schools at Westminster, Paul's and Merchant Taylors' School and in the Public Free School at Eaton', and a good Greek dictionary was to be chained to a desk in the schoolroom.[138] The master of Wilson's School was to be able to make Greek and Latin verses, and Harsnett at Chigwell specified 'a man skilful in the Greek

BREVISSIMA

INSTITVTIO

SEV RATIO GRAM-
matices cognoscendæ, ad
omnium puerorum vtilitatem
perscripta, quam solam Re-
gia Maiestas in omnibus
Scholis profitendam
præcipit.

EXCVSVM LON-
dini, per assignatio-
nem Francisci
Floræ.

M.D.LXXIIII.

Title-page of Lilly's Latin Grammar, 1574

and Latin tongues'. Harrow statutes provided for the reading of the Greek Testament as did St Saviour's.[139] Probably only a small proportion of pupils in a small number of schools, even in the metropolis, proceeded further than this.

Apart however from the almost inevitable lead to be expected from a capital city and its region, there was probably nothing distinctive about these religious, moral and classical elements of the curriculum. More

INSTITVTIO

GRAECAE

GRAMMA-
TICES
COMPENDIARIA,
In vſum Regiæ Scholæ Weſt-
monaſterienſis.

Scientiarum ianitrix Grammatica,

LONDINI,
Excudebat Edm. Bollifant pro
Simone Waterſon.

1595

Title-page of Camden's Greek Grammar

significant was the stimulus given in London to a new and wider interpretation of the content of education. Nearness to the Court may explain the curriculum at Westminster under Camden – according to Ben Jonson 'writing' appears to have been part of the normal course, supplemented by some arithmetic, cosmography, history, music, and even modern languages. Christmas plays were used for teaching clear and correct speaking, and boys were sent to the choir school of the abbey, at a charge of 6*d*, 'for a clear and distinct elocution'.[140] Within the City itself Mulcaster, at Merchant Taylors' and then St Paul's, was an exponent of education in the vernacular – not only the teaching of English, but teaching the classical language through English. 'I honour Latin, but I worship the English', he wrote. 'Master Mulcaster's children' appeared in masques and interludes before the Queen.[141] Alexander Gill of St Paul's, Milton's high master, wrote the first comprehensive English grammar, the *Logonomia Anglica* (1619).[142] London had become the arbiter of correct English, and boys were sent to her grammar schools, such as Christ's Hospital, to acquire 'perfection in the English tongue and the right pronunciation of it'.[143] This was at that time no mere matter, as it might have been later, of genteel accent, but of consciousness of national cohesion. Nor was it only clear and acceptable speech which was acquired, but an enlarged formulation of ideas, even new possibilities of experience. While the classical languages, especially Latin, remained the key to higher education, the professions and the European, even Christian, inheritance, the importance of learning to think and write in the vernacular made these great civic or courtly schools potential makers of intellectual revolutions. From its beginning Christ's Hospital had its writing master, and the Writing School appears to have started in 1577, endowed during her life and by her will in 1596 by Dame Ramsey, whose husband had been 'Maior of thys most famous cittie'. It had its own Master and Usher and became a model of its kind.[144]

At a much more modest level, in our 'meaner and ruder schools' as John Brinsley called them, London endowed schools supplied a broader curriculum which served practical purposes for the great and growing city and its wide-ranging concerns. The Letters Patent reestablishing St Olave's as a grammar school (1571) show that it taught more than classics; it was to be 'One Grammar School, for the bringing up, Institution and Instruction of the Children and Younglings of the Parishioners and Inhabitants . . . as well in Grammar and in Accidence and other low Books, and in writing . . .' and its statutes provided the same salary for the usher as for the master, for there were more scholars 'at writinge than at grammar Seeing that we have here a great number of pore people . . . who are not able to kepe their children at grammar. But being desirus to have them taught the Principells of Christen Religion, and to wright, reade and cast accomptes, and so put them forth to prentice.'[145] At Enfield the master was to teach Latin and English 'according to the trade and use of grammar schools'. At Highgate the master was to instruct boys 'in the ABC and other English books', in writing, and in grammar 'as they shall grow ripe thereto'. Dame Alice Owen provided for boys between about seven and fourteen to be taught 'the Grammar, fair Writing, Cyphering and Casting of accompts'.[146] Harsnett founded an English school alongside his Latin school, and Colfe a reading school where boys could learn to read and write and 'be entered in English and the

Latin Accidence' before perhaps going up to his grammar school. But there also English and writing were stressed – the usher of the reading school acting as writing master. Some boys were to be prepared for the university, but others enabled to write well and 'cast up merchants' books perfectly'. Wilson considered writing of great importance and his boys used half-holidays for its practice, and every week transcribed a passage of St John's Gospel, signing it with both the Secretary and Roman hands.[147]

Some of these London endowments may have amounted to no more than the provision for the teaching of 'petties' within the foundation – Highgate is an example, and the Coopers' School instructed the master to teach the little boys 'spelling and the like'.[148] Usually boys were expected to have received this kind of instruction before they were accepted at the grammar school. At St Paul's (1578) the high master was to admit children who knew their catechism and could read and write competently.[149] The cost of such 'elementary' instruction, rarely provided free, was a serious barrier to the use of the 'free schools' by the children of the poor. At St Saviour's the boy must read English and Latin perfectly and write his name. At Wilson's the boy must read English well, write a legible hand and 'have begun or be ready to begin the study of Latin Grammar'. The difficulty of finding local boys who could do this led the governors to lower these qualifications in 1647 – 'although the sayd poore schollars to be admitted are not able to write a legible hand at their first entrance ... yet if they be able to read a chapter in the Newe Testament (bringing theire Accidence with them) they shal be admitted ...'.[150]

Other adaptations or recognition of the realities of local situations were more radical. When St Olave's got its second charter in 1674 the governors used their somewhat increased powers to diversify the curriculum by enlarging the 'writing school house' for the 'entertaining and better accommodation of the scholars'. The Great Fire of Southwark of 1676 overtook these plans, and although 'as if by Divine intervention' St Olave's was spared, the governors not only ordered better fire-fighting appliances – 'Six Pickaxes a Dozen of Shovells Six Scoopes and Two Great Hookes with Chaines to them and Roapes' – but pressed ahead with a new writing school built over the Latin school, with forms and seats as in the 'writing Schoole belonging to Christ's Hospitall', accommodating both a writing master and assistant. In 1691 a reading usher was appointed, and although he seems at first to have been fixed up on the vestry stairs, a 'new built Reading School' was ready by the beginning of the eighteenth century. St Saviour's, which was destroyed in the fire of 1676, provided an English school when it was rebuilt.[151]

Not only was the original curriculum in a number of London foundations wider than is often supposed, they were also more adaptable to changing needs. The pattern of endowments also changed

significantly – in the seventeenth century the trend was towards
providing for English as well as classical education, and more entirely
non-classical schools were also founded in the metropolitan area. As
early as 1556 the Hampton school was of this kind, though, as a
foundation from the reign of Mary, perhaps at first it looked back to
the song and chantry schools rather than to the new secular schools of
the new age. Latymer's benefactions were of the newer kind, which
merge into the later movement to found charity schools by subscription
rather than endowment.[152] Examples which retained the earlier
element of endowment were the Davenant Foundation School in
Whitechapel endowed in 1680 by the rector and his wife;[153] the
benefactions of Robert Aske of 1689 in Hoxton, administered by the
Haberdashers' Company;[154] the foundation by Sir Walter St John
under his will in 1700 of two schools in Battersea, one to teach
grammar and the other reading, writing and arithmetic;[155] and Dr
Breton's lost endowment of 1672 in Deptford to teach twelve poor
children grammar and writing.[156] Palmer's School at Grays Thurrock
in Essex, founded in 1706 by a London merchant with waterside
property there, was to teach '10 poor children . . . to read, write and
cast accounts and to instruct them in the Latin tongue'.[157] A
significant example was the school founded next to St Martin in the
Fields by its vicar, Thomas Tenison, in 1683. He had been appointed
to this, the 'great cure', in 1680 and became 'a parochial minister of
extraordinary power and originality of approach', one of the most
zealous of a group of London clergy who not only recognized the key
importance of education at a time of political upheaval and social
change, but also the need to enlist and organize the piety and
responsibility of the laity in tackling such problems with energy and
devotion. Tenison's school in its early days was to teach the elements
of literacy and the casting of accounts, and the charity then paid for
apprenticeships.[158]

Recent research has emphasized this changing pattern. A London
sample identified eleven schools founded for grammar only and two for
English and grammar in the sixteenth century, and in the seventeenth
century one grammar and eight English and grammar foundations.
Comparison with the country as a whole emphasized 'the strong lead in
this new direction given by the metropolis'.[159] Such changes are
evidence of advance towards a more diversified curriculum, more
adapted to emerging needs, rather than a decline in the schools.
Seventeenth-century episcopal licences to schoolmasters disclose a
steady decline in the number of private grammar schools. In the City
and Westminster this was accentuated by the Plague and the Fire. In
1694 twenty-eight City parishes, where previously a schoolmaster who
taught Latin had been licensed, had no grammar masters.[160]

The impulse for the founding of grammar schools however was still
active almost to the end of the century. Tottenham Grammar School

had an obscure history from perhaps as early as 1456, but its endowment as a grammar school dates from 1692 when the will of its benefactress, the Duchess of Somerset, became operative. The rules provided for the teaching of English, grammar rules, writing, arithmetic and the Catechism to children between seven and fourteen.[161] Hampton School received additional bequests which transformed it into a grammar school – the deeds of 1696 and 1697 provided for instruction in 'the English and Latin Tongue And to understand the Cathecisme now allowed by the Church of England'.[162]

The pupils

These endowed schools, provided by the varied members of the London community for the children of the community, were an aspect of that system of patronage which bound the old, pre-industrial society together vertically. The range of this chain of patronage varied – the great City schools catered for the children of the wealthiest members of the livery, as well as for poorer 'burgher youths'; the smallest, least ambitious schools may by the seventeenth century be seen as schools catering for children of a lower social rank than that achieved by their founder. But in between were the schools which expected to educate all boys from the locality and 'foreigners' who desired 'gentle learning' – the poor scholar 'on the foundation' side by side with the boys whose parents could or would pay fees. The main questions to ask relate to the cost of such education and the exclusions which this implied, the definition of 'poor scholar', and the range of social ranks which benefited from, and in turn changed, the schools. We are here concerned largely with levels and range of aspiration, and the interaction of these with the facilities provided, and their cost. Dealing with two centuries of rapid social change, and with the evidence available, it is difficult to give valid answers to such questions. The situation is further obscured by the dust raised during the nineteenth-century controversy over the diversion of endowments from 'the poor' for whom they were intended to the 'middle classes' who by then largely benefited from them. This debate, however, largely applied nineteenth-century concepts of class structure to a pre-industrial society, and so analysed the problem in terms which were irrelevant or misleading.

Endowed schools of this period were often called 'free schools', and the founders in almost all cases carefully specified the number of scholars 'on the foundation' – that is, those whose tuition was provided for in the salary of the master and perhaps usher. Sometimes it was laid down that the free scholars must come from a particular parish or locality, as at Owen's, Chigwell, Colfe's. In the great City schools this was not usually appropriate. Colet provided for the very large number of 153 scholars and St Paul's was from the beginning to be a metropolitan school – it was 'for the children of all nacions and countres indifferently'. This recalls the words of the petition of 1446 – boys came up to the City, not only because it provided facilities they did not have at home, but for its patronage, 'the great alms of Lords, Merchants and others'. At St Paul's, however, the only poor scholar mentioned was the one who 'swepith the schole and kepith the scole clene' and who received the admission money of the rest.[163] St Saviour's and St Olave's likewise do not specify poor scholars. At Merchant Taylors' there were to be 100 free scholars, 50 who could pay 2s a quarter and another 100 at 5s a quarter – this was later interpreted as implying 150 'poore men's children'. From the beginning this large school educated not only the sons of the mercantile governors but those of the craftsmen and lesser tradesmen of the City who were eager for schooling which would prepare them for their callings or open new opportunities – in the law, medicine, the public service, the church.[164] In the next century the Charterhouse was founded for the education of poor children, but from the beginning the sons of esquires and gentlemen appear as 'gownboys', and they were not children of the indigent poor.[165]

In a traditional society, class terminology is inappropriate. Most statutes made no attempt to define poverty. At Tottenham in 1710 the free scholars were to be 'the children of all such people inhabiting in ye said parish . . . as shall not have estates of their own in fee or copyhold of ye value of £20 per ann'.[166] In Camberwell, Wilson's foundation (which in its deed failed to specify exact numbers) laid down that the scholars were to be either native or resident, and the sons of poor men not assessable to taxation and the son of the senior churchwarden were to be educated free.[167] Colfe's free scholars were from the parishes of Blackheath Hundred, the sons of poor persons 'so the children be of good wit and capacity, and apt to learn', and the election was made by the parishes. In 1653 the inhabitants of East Greenwich sent forward the names of ten poor children, with their resolution that 'those who are in the parish should be preferred before others therefore wee have not chosen Hugh Goulding at this time who was not borne in the parish'. Eltham could find only two boys 'capable', and Woolwich likewise 'can find no more Redy'.[168] The test was probably not the ability to pay for such schooling, but whether it was desired and the boy's earnings could be foregone.

If it is difficult to define poverty in this context, the notion of free education must also be modified. Even for the foundation scholars admission and other fees might be demanded. At St Paul's, entrance was a modest 4d, but the scholars had also to provide their arrows, bowstring, a shooting glove and a bracer, books and wax candles 'at the cost of theyre Frendes' – no inconsiderable expense.[169] At St Saviour's, where 100 sons of parishioners were free scholars, after a steep bout of inflation the entrance fee was 2s 6d with 2d a quarter for brooms and rods.[170] Even in a modest school such as Wilson's the admission fee was 2*s* 6*d*, and in the 'weeke after Michaelmas one pound of good candles' was exacted.[171] Colet's wording, however, reminds us that patronage operated at many levels in traditional society. A boy's 'friends' might meet such charges. The King himself was maintaining two scholars at St Paul's in 1522, and a later Pauline, Samuel Pepys, son of an unsuccessful tailor, was probably maintained both at school and at university by his kinsman, Sir Edward Montagu (later Lord Sandwich).[172] This kind of informal operation of clientship, 'friendship', is impossible to quantify, even difficult to identify, but it was in fact essential to the operation of the system, and London provided exceptional opportunities. Such personal patronage was less likely to extend to the paying of fees for a place not on the foundation. Nearly all schools provided for the teaching of fee-payers alongside the scholars, both to encourage the master and augment his stipend, and to extend the usefulness of the school. The number of pupils at St Paul's was carefully calculated to fill the number of 'forms' or benches provided. Yet by 1525 the statutory number was exceeded and the high master was taking boarders.[173] At St Saviour's the headmaster was allowed to take 40 scholars from outside the parish who paid fees to him personally, 'provided that he appointed an usher at his own expense to teach them'. At St Olave's the master was allowed to take 6 private pupils 'towardes the augmentinge of his livinge' (that is £13 16*s* 8*d* a year).[174] At Wilson's School the governors were to fix the fees of parishioners' children not on the foundation.[175] Colfe allowed the master to receive other pupils, and his house would hold 26 boarders; the sons of 'ordinary people' and yeomen were to pay not more than 8*s* a quarter, and gentlemen's sons 10*s*.[176] Boarders in schools within the London suburbs or out-country were probably at this period often city children, sent for greater safety into a better air. At Harrow fee-paying foreigners 'were allowed, providing the master did not neglect the free scholars, the children of the parish'.[177] At Tottenham in 1710 the Order Book recorded 'That for the better encouragement of the master it be permitted him besides . . . to take into his school and there instruct in such learning as their parents shall desire so many other children as may be no hinderance to the well teaching of the poor children of the foundation.'[178] At Enfield, when Dr Robert Uvedale the botanist was master from 1664 to 1676, the parishioners complained that he neglected the free school for his private pupils.[179]

Probably the majority of boys who attended these grammar schools, whether those in the City or in the suburbs, were still using them as preliminary to apprenticeship. Dame Alice Owen realistically stated this in her statutes, and pupils at her school were generally between the age of about seven and fourteen. St Olave's recognized in 1572 that the boys' curriculum should serve those parents who wished to

'put them forth to prentice'. By the end of this period, although St
Olave's had been founded for all the children of the parish, 'as well
Poore as Rich', it is probable that the more prosperous families
preferred to send their boys across the river to St Paul's or Merchant
Taylors'.[180]

The hard test of the status of a school was whether it could produce
enough scholars to proceed to the universities. Nothing could more
point the contrast between the traditional, pre-industrial society which
created this network of grammar schools, and the post-industrial
society of the nineteenth century which anxiously strove to adapt them
to an entirely different social order, than the piety and devotion with
which Tudor and Stuart benefactors endowed them with scholarships
to colleges at Oxford and Cambridge, and the protracted and consci-
ence- stricken efforts of the Victorians to convert these into a system of
open competition. Here we have in classic form the sponsored and
contest mobility of modern sociology.

For the period (1460–1660) studied by Jordan, overall London
donors provided scholarships and fellowships at Oxford and
Cambridge to the value of £92,464 8s, constituting 4.89 per cent of the
charitable gifts of the city. This was a very high proportion indeed of
the nation's overall investment in education at this level, 'the most
effective of all the mechanisms for accomplishing social mobility'. A
large portion of this money, £26,235 8s, was for scholarships from
school to university – 181 scholars at a time, from over the whole
country, being maintained by London benefactions.[181] Southwark and
Lewisham were examples of contrasting districts showing some common features of the way the system operated, and the degrees of its
effectiveness. St Saviour's was endowed with scholarships by three
governors in the first half of the seventeenth century. John Bingham
donated local house property in 1617 to maintain two scholars at the
university with £6 a year each. In 1623 the provisions of the will of
Randall Carter were to maintain one poor scholar at Magdalen College
Oxford with £6 a year. Gregory Franklin endowed another exhibition
of £4 a year in 1647 at Corpus Christi Cambridge. From the beginning
the governors had difficulty in finding suitable candidates. In 1626
there was disquiet when the son of the headmaster was chosen for a
Bingham exhibition, but there was 'lack of a poor scholar'. In 1628 the
governors could be easier when Henry Caroll, a poor scholar, the son
of a widow, was sent to Magdalen with a Carter gift. Boys, however,
went forward steadily to Oxford and Cambridge throughout the
century, and their careers illustrate the contribution which these
grammar schools were making to the consolidation of national institutions. Under its second charter of 1674 St Olave's also gained the
right to maintain two scholars at the university until they had taken the
bachelor's degree, providing they had been 'first brought up in the
school' and were inhabitants of the parish. This power was little used

as boys from this poorer parish rarely aspired to university learning, while the power of apprenticing poor scholars of the school to a trade was widely used.[182]

At Lewisham the Leathersellers as governors had the duty of choosing the holders of the seven scholarships of £10 a year each at Oxford or Cambridge, given under Colfe's will, the preference to be given to a Lewisham boy whose parents were worth not more than £500. In 1657 they were able to elect 'Thomas Cordell a very poore scholler brought up in learning at the same school and now att Kings Colledge in Cambridge.' Thereafter a steady number was sent forward, though probably there were never ten up at the universities at any one time. Money for books was regularly entered in the accounts – in 1667 'Paid unto Mr Colfes scholler Samuel Alderson who upon the said Visitation was elected out of the said schoole and sent unto the university, for Bookes according to Mr Colfes will, xxiiijs.' These exhibitions were however in reality paid for by the Company, the Trust not being large enough to bear the cost. Not all the exhibitioners were the sons of poor parents: in 1675 the son of a woodmonger of Lewisham was elected; in 1670 the nephew of the headmaster; in 1674 and 1676 the sons of surgeons in Greenwich; in 1682 the son of a gentleman of Lee. Poverty must be defined in relation to aspiration, though it seems clear that the governors preferred to grant awards to the more needy. Before the end of the century this modest village grammar school, already attracting boarders and drawing on the naval and mercantile interests of its riverside situation, was producing boys who entered the church, the professions, public life.[183]

But the supply of suitable scholars began to falter – when in 1704 Henry Archer, one of the free scholars, was approved for a university exhibition, he was the first after thirteen years. This in part was due to the varying success of the successive masters of the school, but largely to the fact that the opportunity of university, or even of grammar school, learning was not demanded by the locality. In Lewisham by 1679 it even became difficult to get nominations of free scholars to the grammar school from the various parishes of the Hundred. In the Visitation that year the governers found the boys well instructed, 'only the parishioners of the severall Hambletts that are enabled to send their children to be taught gratis . . . are very remiss therein, there not being above twelve of all the parishes and Hambletts'. Lewisham parents alone had the choice of sending boys to the Reading School.[184] Whether poverty was the main reason for this failure to use the benefaction to the full, or whether social and economic changes were already within the old 'hierarchical class-less society' limiting the range of ambition, is an open question.

Grammar schools could of course be used for acquiring limited skills – enough Latin for ordinary business and all legal intercourse, reading English, writing the Secretary and Roman hands, casting accounts, perhaps – but this was not their essential purpose.

Social change was bringing new demands. Almost alone among our founders, Colet, with his Renaissance understanding of process, recognized that he was founding an *historic* institution. He left it to his 'surveyors' of the Mercery 'hooly to theyr dyscrecion' to add and diminish to his statutes as became necessary.[185] Most founders thought of their schools as providing for ever, in perpetuity, a learning which would always be valued. But from their very moment of foundation, more especially in London with its quickening life, history was overtaking these schools.

II

The Court and the City:
Tudor and Stuart alternatives
to the grammar schools

During this heroic age of the provision of educational institutions, the schools were already in some respects becoming inadequate or obsolete, and London played a key part in devising and providing both formal and informal supplements and alternatives. Here in a capital city which was now the seat of an increasingly centralized government, and which was in process of becoming the economic centre of Europe, were concentrated the social, economic and political needs and the intellectual and moral appetites which put pressures on such demands. London was a magnet for talent, skills, ambition. Its population was highly literate, speculative, practical. By the fifteenth century its scriveners were kept busy producing for an avid market, and from the arrival of Caxton onwards London became the centre of the book trade. Here was a rapidly expanding market for books of a religious nature, histories for which Londoners had a special appetite, and also works of what today we would call science, mathematics, technology, business methods. Caxton's press was in the shadow of Westminster Abbey, near the Court with its demand for fine and expensive volumes, but City merchants were among his early customers and patrons, and his successors moved his press to Fleet Street, perhaps realizing that their largest market lay in the merchant and craft communities. Gradually such printing firms congregated in St Paul's Churchyard under devices such as Our Lady of Pity, or the Three Kings, grouped conveniently both for bookseller and purchaser, who perhaps wished to browse for a book in English on the spheres and such like. In 1557 the Stationers' Company was incorporated, with its Hall nearby.[1]

The printing press was by far the most important instrument of education in the sixteenth century.[2] During this same period London was also providing more formal institutions for the training which the new state, the new economy, the new society demanded. At professional level from the fourteenth century onwards the Inns of Court were developed for the training in common law which Oxford and Cambridge failed to provide. Training in surgery, less academically prestigious than medical studies, was being given by the Company of Barber-Surgeons, incorporated with its monopoly of practice and teaching in 1540.[3] In a similar way, the constructive tension between Westminster and St

49

Paul's, between Court and City, was creating and developing new concepts of education and training at a lower level.

Courtly education

The City played an important part but princely education set the pace. At least as early as the fourteenth century, children of the royal household had received a special training and by the fifteenth century a fully developed system was in operation. Sir John Fortescue discussed the need for princes to be learned in the laws, and advised that their household education should not only include military exercises but also music and dancing. The Court to Fortescue was 'the supreme academy of the realm', and Renaissance influence made the Tudor Court in some respects a way by which the new learning irrigated a wider educational field. Young 'henchmen' were taught grammar, deportment, feats of arms, and Henry VIII was reputed to have an interest in mathematics.[4] In about 1545 William Thomas translated *The Sphere of Sacrobosco* (the Holyrood) and dedicated it to the young Duke of Suffolk, who shared his lessons with the future Edward VI. Thomas claimed that 'the discourse of the Sphere, which conteigneth as well the order of the starres and plannettes, as of the inferior elementes, is the foundation of natural knowledge'. Such matter had not before been written in English, and Thomas had to 'frame a new voice', coin new terms which he embodied in a glossary. Prince Edward also had lessons on the quadrant and the celestial globe.[5] William Buckley (1519–71) made a ring dial for the Princess Elizabeth and was for a time tutor to the Royal Henchmen.[6] From 1544 John Cheke was fellow tutor with Ascham to the royal children. An enthusiastic exponent of mathematics, especially of Euclid and the Greeks, he helped to foster their study at the university, as well as at Court.[7] The Court was also a centre of French studies. Richard Croke, who taught these as well as Greek, was engaged to teach the young Duke of Richmond, Henry's natural son, and 'such of his young gentlemen attendants' as might by their example 'more fairly induce him to profit by his learning'.[8]

It would be unrealistic to see direct connection between London education and the tutoring of these few and special children. The influence came more indirectly through new ideas and schemes for the education of the gentry and the aristocracy. Renaissance rulers were increasingly dependent on lay rather than clerical administrators, and the nobility as part of their reconstruction in the new state needed both chivalric education, schooling for civil advance and service, and new kinds of military and nautical studies.[9] Erasmus and Sir Thomas Elyot interpreted the new need as an aspect of Italian humanism with its emphasis on the civic purpose of education. But as a European phenomenon the idea of courtly education was also an aspect of growing monarchical power – or effective wielding of it. Thomas Starkey in 1535 argued the duty of scholars to serve the state and of statesmen to become scholars. A new kind of institution for the education of the nobility was needed, the massive redistribution of monastic property such as Westminster and St Albans should be utilized, 'so they nobles being brought up together should learn there the discipline of the common weal . . .'.[10] Starkey disapproved of the usual method of 'the ill and idle bringing up of youth' in the great households, but some of these must be seen as an important part of the continuing tradition of London's contribution to education: one remembers Thomas More at Lambeth Palace with Archbishop Wareham. Wolsey's household was considered a model, as well as an avenue to preferment. Thomas Cromwell employed Thomas Elyot as tutor to his son Gregory, and places in his household were also much sought after. Later in the century Lord Burghley had high standards in the household education of his wards.[11] The Tower of London itself was the scene of the education of Algernon Percy, heir to the ninth Earl of Northumberland, the 'Wizard Earl', who was imprisoned there for his supposed implication in the Gunpowder Plot. Algernon was installed near his father with numerous attendants in comfortable quarters as soon as he left his mother and nurses at six years old, and remained until he went to Cambridge at thirteen. His father aimed to train him for the public service, for the administration of his great estates, and to create in him a well-fashioned mind, 'free from perturbations and unseemly affections'. His studies were wide, including as well as exercises, dancing and music, English, Latin, some Greek, 'Arithmetic, Geometry, Logic, Grammar Universal, Metaphysics, the Doctrine of Motion of the Optics, Astronomy', and other physical and moral sciences as well as 'Politics, Economics, the Art Nautical and Military'.[12] This indicates the aims and content of a new kind of education much discussed over the previous half-century. The country squire who would rather his son learnt hawking and to blow the horn was behind the times. As Justices of the Peace such men, with 'stacks of statutes upon their shoulders', were responsible for the implementation of royal policy in the shires, and education was recognized as a necessity and sound investment. The commitment of these ranks to education from the mid sixteenth century onwards was 'unprecedented'. Many attended grammar schools, some went on to the universities, and increasingly the Inns of Court were used for the final stage of their education. Here at considerable expense young men not only studied the law, but also music, dancing, fencing. The Inns situated between Westminster and the City gave experience of public affairs and community life.[13]

The idea put forward by Starkey was kept alive by other schemes, bringing together the idea of the royal court as 'the supreme academy' and the needs of families with landed and civil responsibilities. The Court of Wards had been erected in 1540 after the Dissolution of the Monasteries, and the education of children who became royal wards because their lands were held in knight's service became something of a problem, and a scandal. 'Why is there not a school for the wards as well as there is a Court for their lands?' asked critics such as Latimer. In 1561 Sir Nicholas Bacon proposed to take such children at the age of nine from the guardians who had purchased their wardships and place then in a special academy. Bacon, with Thomas Denton and Robert Cary, had already fostered the idea of a 'school for the education of statesmen' in the time of Henry VIII. It was to be in London and its course was to be based on the study of French and Latin and the law. Now as brother-in-law of Cecil, Master of the Court of Wards, Bacon sent him a detailed set of Articles which he claimed had long been forming in his mind and which he had urged in Queen Mary's reign with no effect. His plan included studies in 'temporall or cyvill lawe' and military disciplines, classical and modern languages, fair writing, music, riding, vaulting, and the handling of weapons, and a chaplain was to be appointed as well as ushers and household attendants. These proposals came to nothing, but probably influenced a second scheme, put forward ten years later (1564) by Sir Humphrey Gilbert, for 'Queene Elizabethes Achademy', to be erected in London for 'her Maiestes Wardes and others the youth of nobility and gentlemen'. His half-brother, Sir Walter Raleigh, with his speculative and radical approach to learning and its practical applications, was associated with Gilbert in designing a course to teach 'matters of action meet for present practice'. Teaching was to be in English and the staff were to be qualified in grammar, Latin, Greek and Hebrew, in logic, rhetoric, moral philosophy (only the 'politique parte thereof' divided between 'civill' and 'Martiall pollicy'). Natural philosophy and mathematics were well provided. One mathematician was to teach 'Imbattelinges, fortifications, and matters of warre, with the practiz of Artillery and the use of all manner of In-strumentes belonging to the same'. 'Canonrie' and underminings were to be practised, and military drawing taught. There was also a riding master and a soldier, and the boys were to learn military horsemanship and to 'handle the Harquebuz', and were to practise skirmishing, 'sondery kindes of marchinges' and so on. A second mathematician was to teach cosmography and astronomy, and the practice of navigation, 'making use of Instrumentes apertaining to the same', and a fully rigged model ship and galley were to be used for exercises. Another master was to teach map- and chart-making and the rules of proportion and perspective. Medical studies were designed for practical use upon campaign, but the pupils were always to be given the 'reason philosopicall' for any ingredients or operations. A physic garden was to be used for demonstrating and surgery was to have particular attention.

Other studies included civil law and divinity, French, Italian, Spanish and High Dutch (German). A dancing and vaulting school was to be provided, and music with the 'lute, the Bandora and Cytherne, etc.' There was to be 'one perfect Harowlde of armes' to teach blazoning and heraldry. This interest in history reflected Raleigh's grasp of its importance. All the staff were to engage in research and publication. Detailed calculations of salaries and expenses were given, and Gilbert looked for a return for such outlay in a great increase of gallant gentlemen, equipped with 'chivallric pollicy and philosophie' for the Queen's service.[14] Queen Elizabeth however was not prepared to spend money, and no merchant capital was forthcoming for such enterprises.

In the reign of her successor the household of Prince Henry did to some extent realize these ideals. It was 'intended for a courtly college, or collegiate court'. Henry's tutors included Lord Lumley, an early member of the Society of Antiquaries and owner of a notable library, Edward Wright, perhaps the leading scientist of his day, and William Barlow (1544–1625) who had experimented with the lodestone and constructed for his royal pupil an 'Inclinatory Instrument' combined with an Equinoctial Dial.[15] This household could well be described by a contemporary as 'the true pantheon of Great Britain'. The Prince was said to have intended to found an academy for sons of the nobility and gentry and the King's wards which would have given special attention to mathematics and languages. Buckingham put forward such a plan in Parliament in 1621 and attributed it to Henry who had died nearly ten years before. At about the same time Edmund Boulton also devised a scheme for an academy to give fit breedings for the King's wards to avoid their being sent abroad at 'great expense of purse and soul', for not only was foreign travel becoming the necessary crown of a gallant education, but French academies were famous for teaching courtly and martial arts. Boulton's plan was sent to a committee of enquiry of the House of Lords into the state of the public schools and universities and their methods of teaching.[16] In about 1634 Sir Francis Kynaston, 'an Esquire of the Body', offered his house in Inigo Jones's Covent Garden for the academy, the Musaeum Minervae, of which he was appointed Regent. It was created by royal patent, and Charles I, who had high notions of courtly observance and learning, granted it £100 from the Treasury and himself provided books and other materials for the library and museum of philosophical apparatus which were attached to the college – mathematical instruments, paintings, statues, antiques. Pupils were all to 'prove themselves gentlemen by birth'.

The Musaeum Minervae was never securely established, though we know that it existed in 1636 when Kynaston petitioned the King for the use of King James's College in Chelsea as a refuge from the plague. Probably the King's financial troubles were to blame for its precarious existence. In May 1640 the Earl of Arundel, that notable collector and virtuoso, petitioned the House of Lords for its revival.[17]

The curriculum he proposed for supplementing the arts of action with the arts of leisure was exciting the reforming spirits of the age, shown by the interest of Samuel Hartlib, the disciple of Comenius. He had kept an academy at Chichester for the sons of the gentry 'to advance piety, learning, morality, and other exercises of industry' and planned to move it to London. Amongst his papers is one which may refer to Arundel's academy. Its course seems more exacting, the 'studies' including Hebrew, Greek, Latin, French, Italian, Spanish, to which Hartlib added High and Low Dutch; history, divine and human; oratory; poetry; experimental philosophy; mathematics, pure and 'mixt'. Exercises included riding of the great horse, arms, fencing, dancing, vaulting, limning and music, and Hartlib added four more – calligraphy, 'Double-writing', stenography and 'the history of the most principall things obvious to the senses which are the subjects of humane learning'.[18]

In the débâcle of the Civil War it was not likely that such schemes would reach fruition, but they had enough vitality to reappear in the Interregnum. Sir Balthazar Gerbier was an enterprising projector and go-between of courts and picture collections, an 'artizan architect' who had devised machines both for courtly masques and to blow up the dyke at La Rochelle. Perhaps only a man of such diverse and mediocre parts could have hoped that a courtly academy would succeed without a court, even if it were called a 'Mounte of Pietee'. It is even more surprising that Hartlib should have taken an interest and helped him, looking for a suitable situation in London and distributing his advertisements. Gerbier fixed on Bethnal Green perhaps for the convenience of the new governors of the Commonwealth, opened his academy in 1649, and advertised a wide course of astronomy, navigation, architecture, perspective drawing, limning, engineering, fortification, military discipline, the art of well speaking and civil conversation, historical constitutions, maxims of state and particular dispositions of nations, riding the great horse, scenes, exercises and magnificent shows. He appears to have undertaken to teach or display all this himself, and also gave lectures 'on navigation, succinct orations in Hebrew on the creation of the world, with an academical entertainment of music, so there be time for the same'. He also opened an academy in Whitefriars for the study of modern languages. His pretensions however were not acceptable to the citizens of the Commonwealth. Pepys sums up London's opinion of Gerbier after reading his *Counsell to Builders* – 'Not worth a turd . . . I am ashamed that I bought it.'[19]

With the Restoration the idea of courtly academies revived and received support from the Crown. In 1679 as a result of the closing of the Protestant academies in France, Solomon Foubert, who had an academy in the Faubourg St Germain, came to England with his family, helped by a royal grant and arrangements for shipping his goods including books, tapestries and large folios relating to the academy and to horsemanship. He settled in St James's, where there was apparently still some open ground for his 'Manage'. In 1679 he was in negotiation with the Royal Society which Evelyn says considered 'being Trustees and Visitors or Supervisors of the Academy . . . for the Education of Youth, and to lessen the vast expense the nation is yearly at, by sending their Children into France to be taught these military exercises. . . '. The Society does not appear to have assisted Foubert but he was given grants by Charles II, James II and William III, and his academy was used by courtiers both for practice in military exercises and for the education of their children. Evelyn went to see 'the Young Gallants do their Exercise', and observed that others not so young were rather out of practice – the Duke of Norfolk (b. 1655) had 'not been at this exercise this 12 years before'. This academy entered into family plans for the education of young noblemen such as James, son of the Earl of Ossory, heir to the Duke of Ormond, who was removed from Oxford where he was 'going backwards in his manners' and placed with Foubert to 'rid him of his fat and plegmatic humours', to 'follow both his studies and his exercises'. Young Lord Hastings, heir to the Earl of Huntingdon, entered Foubert's academy in 1695, when he left Oxford at eighteen. He went into lodgings two doors from the academy, and does not seem to have learnt much there except evil courses and 'very filthy language', as he was later described as 'so miserable a horseman, besides being very weak on horse-back, that it is impossible for him to undergo the least difficulty'. Foubert was also used by the King for the education of wards. In 1681 Lord Kinsale was removed from Oxford and sent to this academy by Order in Council.[20]

But by this time the needs of military education were changing and Foubert could offer little but practice on those formidable great horses whose restless eyes regard us from the canvases of Velázquez, Rubens or Van Dyck. From the great educative households and the earliest schemes for institutionalizing their tradition and combining it with the newer content of learning, political and practical as well as cultural, through Elizabethan and Stuart projects and experiments, the concept of courtly education had never taken root in England. The reasons for this lay deep in the social and economic structure and political experience of the nation. From the reign of Elizabeth the nobility declined in both numbers and wealth in relative terms and throughout the seventeenth century they barely held their own in comparison with the gentry. Moreover even in more prosperous times after 1660, they saw themselves less as courtiers and more as country magnates; their power was increasingly identified with their country estates rather than with the favour of the king and his service, where in fact more and more non-nobles were being employed throughout this whole period.[21]

The contribution of these largely abortive experiments in courtly education was the way they drew a new map of learning and ranged over the practical purposes of knowledge. The grammar schools with their comparatively popular base were on the whole conservative while the education of the gentry and aristocracy can be called the progressive element in this period. Only Westminster School with its royal connections and proximity to the court had anything like this width of studies. Courtly education was more utilitarian, more adapted to new needs, than the schools being founded so generously by the merchant community. But in so far as the ideal had found practical expression and had yielded positive results it had centred on London, and had depended on some cultural identity or cohesion between Court and City. Economic interests underpinned and strengthened this cohesion. The great City trading and colonizing enterprises which transformed England's world position in the sixteenth and seventeenth centuries were eagerly financed by the gentry and aristocracy.[22]

City schools

Some historians have seen something of a paradox in the 'uncritical faith in the grammar schools' and the 'infinite respect' for university learning shown by the merchant community at this period.[23] Others have seen its momentous cultural changes, amounting to a 'scientific revolution', as the work of merchants and craftsmen rather than of the established educational order.[24] The answer to this problm must be both complex and pragmatic, but must above all see London as holding in vigorous synthesis the culture of Court and City. This was perhaps expressed most vividly in the Elizabethan theatre, where for a brief period 'the colour and richness of the European Renaissance interacted with the vigour and realism of the popular tradition to create wholly new national forms'. At the Bankside, the Fortune, the Globe, the Rose, groundlings and lordlings enjoyed comedies, tragedies, histories, side by side with those of the solid citizenry who did not reject the stage and its works altogether. The triumph of London English as a national language and speech is another manifestation of this dominant and unified culture. 'Ye shall therefore take the usuall speach of the Court, and that of London and the shires lying about London . . .' wrote Palsgrave in 1530. This 'standard English' was wrought upon not only by the courtly and the learned but by the plain citizen, man of business and traveller, and gradually turned into a 'plain easy and familiar style' which by the turn of the century was an instrument 'whose precision and poetry were the hallmark' of a national civilization, 'England's cultural glory'. When boys attended London grammar schools to acquire good English, this was the currency which they sought.[25]

The vigorous life of London in this age enjoyed and supported a whole range of arts, skills and speculations, and it was pushing back the frontiers of curiosity and knowledge. It was not to Oxford and Cambridge but to London that Francis Bacon looked for 'the discovery of new arts, endowments and commodities for the bettering of man's life . . .' and the kindling of 'a light which should in its very rising touch and illuminate all the border regions that confine upon the circles of our present knowledge'.[26] Bacon's London included the court and official and legal circles, and the claim that the intellectual revolution being

wrought in the capital was 'virtually ignored by the official in-
telligentzia'[27] identifies intellectual leadership too exclusively with
Oxford and Cambridge. Court and government provided centres of
patronage, curiosity and technical stimulus and the mercantile and craft
communities played a vital part. The 'Worthy Merchant' of Nicholas
Breton (1616) was not only the 'maintainer of trade', but also the
'Sailers Master, and the Souldiers friend'. He took 'observation of time',
his 'study is number, his care his accounts'. His 'travailes' and 'eye-
observations' formed his discourse and drew into his concern 'forraine
fruits' and 'Moddels of Architectures', and he 'knows at home what is
good abroad'. 'In summe he is the Pillar of a City, the enricher of a
Country, the furnisher of a Court, and the worthy servant of a King.'[28]
This is an idealized portrait of the historically well-documented founders of many London grammar schools, but although his recognition of
the value and utility of classical learning was thus demonstrated, the
needs and perspectives of such a man could not be satisfied without
other forms of education. Measurement and observation were the instruments of the new way of looking at an expanding world. An 'Age of
Observation' was dawning. It required tools of analysis, of anatomizing
things before taken for granted. 'Intellectual dissections' lie behind the
fashion for such works as *The Anatomy of Abuses, The Anatomy of Wit*,
even *The Anatomy of Melancholy*.[29] Eventually a new view of the mind
and heart of man himself had to be accommodated. Although William
Harvey did not use the metaphor himself, he helped to transform the
idea of the heart from an organ which gave a body the spirit of life into a
mechanism which pumped blood round a machine, and the way was
opened to the radical ideas of Descartes. The tyranny of Aristotelian
philosophy was broken. Reliance upon experiment and experience
rather than theory required transformation of basic conceptual
frameworks – a huge task for education.[30]

Some of the pressures on education from the City man's 'travails' and
travels, calculations and observations could best be met by expedients.
'Writing schools', the secretarial colleges of their day, existed in London
from at least the fifteenth century[31] and certainly increased in number
during the reign of Elizabeth. A famous example was kept by Peter Bales
(1547–1610?) near the Old Bailey. He was author of *The Writing
Schoolemaster*, taught 'all manner of hands', and in 1595 won a golden
pen in public competition with a rival calligrapher. Bales was a
Londoner born and bred, his father a draper and citizen of London.[32]
The purpose of such tuition was largely vocational – forms of business,
letter writing, keeping of books, engrossing documents, all required not
only skills of composition and expression and knowledge of due forms to
be observed, but particular 'hands'. In 1611 a young man who had
secured a clerkship in the Exchange described how he 'could not write
the court and chancery hands, so my father left me for half a year with
Mr John Davies in Fleet Street [the most famous writer of his time] to

THE
WRITING SCHOOLEMASTER:
Conteining three Bookes in one; The firſt, tea-
ching Swift writing ; *The ſecond*, Truе writing; *The third*, Faire writing.

The firſt Booke, Entituled;

THE ARTE OF BRACHYGRAPHIE: that is, to
write as faſt as a man ſpeaketh treatablу, writing but one
*letter for a word : Veriе commodious for the generall encreaſe
and furtherance of learning in all Eſtates and degrees : the
knowledge whereof may eaſilie be attained by one mo-*
neths ſtudie, and the performance bу one moneths
praẽiſe . The proofe alreadiе made by
diuers Schollers there-
in.

The ſecond Boooke : Named,

THE ORDER OF ORTHOGRAPHIE: ſhewing
the perfeẽt Method to write true Orthographie in our
Engliſh tongue, as it is now generally printed, vſed,
and allowed, of the beſt & moſt learned Writers :
To be attained by the right vſe of this Booke
without a Schoolemaſter, in ſhort
time, and with ſmall paines,
by your owne priuate
ſtudies.

The Third Booke; is,

THE KEY OF CALYGRAPHIE: opening the rea-
die waie to write faire in verie ſhort time, by the ob-
ſeruations of neceſſariе Rules here ſet downe, and
by the imitation of the beſt examples that may
be procured.
Inuented by *Peter Bales.* 1. Ianu. 1590.

Omne bonum, Dei donum.

Imprinted at London by *Thomas Orwin :* and are to be
ſolde at the Authors houſe in the vpper ende of the
Old Baylу, where he teacheth the ſaid artes.

Title-page of Bales's *The Writing Schoolemaster*

learn those hands'. Bales and Davies were tutors also at Court, to Prince
Henry.[33] It was from the centres of patronage round Leicester, Raleigh
and Sidney that the invention of shorthand emerged. Timothy Bright
(1575–1616) had taken refuge with Sir Philip Sidney in the English
Embassy at Paris during the massacre of St Bartholomew. He published
his treatise on shorthand in 1588, and also wrote a 'popular treatise on
melancholy in which he compared the human body to a clock or a
windmill'.[34]

Modern languages also were acquired by private tuition or in special
schools, and again there were, especially earlier in the century, strong
courtly connections. John Palsgrave was tutor for thirty years at court and

his *L'Esclaircissement de la Langue Francoyse* (1530) was designed for a wider use.[35] From the time of the French Wars of Religion, Huguenot refugees added to the resources of study in London. The father of Claude Holyband (de Saintiens) came to England in 1564 and opened a school in St Paul's Churchyard. Claude's lively *French Schoolemaister* and *French Littleton* became very popular books for school use, and for 'all those which noo studie privately at their own study or houses'.[36] At the end of the century another writer and city teacher, Giles de la Mothe, indicated ways in which a good accent could be acquired by attendance at the French church and students were invited to repair to the author 'in Fleet Street beneath the Conduit at the Sign of St John the Evangelist where his book is sold or else in Paul's Churchyard at the Figure of the Helmet and there you shall find him willing to show you any favour and courtesy he may'.[37] Other modern languages were taught to a lesser extent but by the same means – private tuition, special, even 'crash', courses, the dissemination of manuals for self-help, and so forth.

Mathematics were in many respects the key to the new 'Age of Observation', and were also of direct practical application for a merchant whose study was number and whose care his accounts. The London contribution was undeniable and the chief point of debate is how far it must be ascribed to the importance of 'practical affairs of life',[38] and to what extent wider interests or official encouragement, also an aspect of the capital city's life, played their part. Claims for the importance of London may be made from somewhat too narrow a base. London craft skills and experience provided a foundation. The parish of St Clement's, just outside the City boundary, became famous for a succession of notable instrument-makers, whose skills stemmed from other crafts demanding precision in metal-working, engraving, clock- and watch-making. But exact mathematical knowledge was also needed, especially of the 'doctrine of triangles', and some mathematicians made their own instruments, employing craftsmen for the necessary manual work.[39] The publication of numerous works of both popular and more specialist nature contributed to the progress and dissemination of mathematical and scientific knowledge.[40] Robert Recorde (1510–58), after studying at both Oxford and Cambridge and graduating in physic, taught in London from 1547 and published his famous *Ground of Artes* (1540), a course of arithmetic and mathematics, which introduced algebra to England. His more advanced text, *Whetstone of Witte* (1557), was dedicated to the Muscovy Company. His works at first had to be printed by a foreign compositor, for Recorde had utilized, or invented, unknown symbolism for processes of calculation – plus, minus and equals signs. Recorde dealt with 'arithmetic with the pen' as well as arithmetic with counters.[41] 'Accounting' was increasingly according to the Italian system of double entry by *debito* and *credito*, and used Arabic numerals, that is 'cyphering'. There were numerous teachers of mathematics in the City who professed to teach 'accounts and reckoning' and 'cunning and feat of arithmetic, with pen and counter'; for example, Humphrey Baker, author of the *Wellspring of Sciences* (1546), advertised his school on the 'North side of the Royall Exchange next adjoining to the signe of the shippe' and taught merchants or their children or servants and took boarders.[42] Teaching of mathematics and arithmetic was well provided in London, where their study was largely practical, utilitarian and related to the needs of business life, navigation, cartography, military studies, the casting of horoscopes, surveying and so forth.[43] But leadership, even guidance, was provided from a combination of civic, courtly and learned circles, and contact with the universities, if indirect, was considerable.

In 1570 Henry Billingsley, Sheriff and Alderman of London and Customer for the Port, who had studied at both Oxford and Cambridge, published the first translation into English of Euclid, the aim of which was to assist 'common artificers'. John Dee provided a preface and its impact upon the sons of merchants and craftsmen was 'very great, setting out as it did the ways in which geometry could advance technique and foster inventions'.[44] Dee since his introduction to court by Cheke had become part of Burleigh's influential circle, and for thirty years provided advice and instruction for maritime enterprises. His great library of scientific works and his collection of mathematical instruments at Putney was an important resource and inspiration for the capital, and he was a staunch supporter of Ramus against the Aristotelians.[45] But official patronage and encouragement stopped short of funds, and the development of mathematical skills was very uneven. Stephen Borough, who had been master of Richard Chancellor's ship in 1553 and, as chief pilot of the Muscovy Company, had received instruction in navigation methods from Dee, attempted to get proper nautical training for pilots on Spanish lines, but failed to move the Queen and her ministers. William Bourne of Gravesend, a practical gunner and teacher of mathematics, tried unsuccessfully to get Burleigh interested in the training of gunners.[46]

It was the threat of the Armada which brought not official but mercantile capital into the service of civic mathematics. The London militia was under officers with no military experience, 'they have not encamped in open feelde, nor besieged townes, nor raised sconses, nor battered walles . . .'. Urged by the Privy Council, a group of London merchants and city authorities led by Sir Thomas Smith and Lord Lumley raised funds for the endowing of a mathematical lectureship. Thomas Hood, former pupil of Merchant Taylors' School, Fellow of Trinity College Cambridge, and Doctor of Physic, was appointed and gave his lectures at first in Sir Thomas Smith's house in Gracechurch Street, and then in the Staplers' Chapel in Leadenhall. He was found 'sufficientlie answerable, of very honest and courteous behaviour, affable to resolve beginners in their doubts', and he also sold his textbooks to students. After four years the lectures were discontinued, probably because they were too academic for their audience, and because, the invasion scare over, they were 'basely suffered to sink and vanish', although Hood had changed his emphasis to navigation. He continued to teach privately.[47] That trainband captains, doubtless of riper years, could be described as doubtful beginners, illustrates the difficulty of classifying *levels* of education at this period. With the foundation of Gresham College we are more clearly in the realm of higher education. Its seven professors in divinity, law, rhetoric, music, physics, geometry and astronomy were to lecture in both Latin and English to enable City audiences to profit from them. The distinguished holders of these chairs, men such as Henry Briggs (1561–1630) the geometrician who introduced knowledge of logarithms to London practitioners,[48] Edward Wright (1558–1615), a marine cartographer who revolutionized the art of navigation and lectured to the East India Company,[49] Aaron Rathborne (1572–1618), who applied the use of logarithms to surveying and developed the use of decimals,[50] were men who advanced the frontiers of knowledge and practice. Recent interpretation has emphasized the contribution which Gresham College made to the preparation for the foundation of the Royal Society. But many Gresham professors also taught privately and probably for practical and specific purposes. The College was a centre of fertile interplay between teaching and learning at different levels, between theoretical advance and practical applications.[51] The naval dockyards at Deptford formed another centre where John Wells, Keeper of Naval Stores, worked with Henry Gellibrand (1597–1636), who established the secular variation of the compass needle, and Edmund Gunter (1581–1626), who amongst other things devised a surveying chain and made the first step towards the invention of the slide-rule. Gunter had been interested in mathematics ever since his schooldays as a Queen's Scholar at Westminster. He had taught mathematics in London and lectured at Gresham College.[52]

Another mathematician with strong navigational interests was John Tapp (*fl*. 1596–1631), a former member of the Drapers' Company who taught near the Bulwark Gate on Tower Hill and published manuals, including one on trigonometry, and nautical almanacks.[53] John Goodwin, who lived in Bucklersbury, was at the end of Elizabeth's reign a *'Practitioner in the Mathematics* and teacher of Arithmetic and Geometry in the City of London'. A brass sector probably of his making is in the National Maritime Museum.[54] George Gilden (*fl*. 1614–31), an almanack publisher and mathematical practitioner, was justified in claiming for London that by the early seventeenth century 'Never were there nearer or better helps to attain mathematical knowledge than at that day and in that City'.[55] This was the transforming knowledge which was active within the intellectual and practical life of the city at the turn of the sixteenth and seventeenth centuries. Mathematical studies at this period were taken to include arithmetic, geometry, music, astronomy, astrology, dialling, measuring, navigation, architecture, and were gradually embracing the empirical sciences. Arithmetic and cyphering schools even 'annexed drawing as a subject of their curriculum'. Recorde taught pupils how 'to draw or reduce any map or card in true proportion from a great quantity to a small, or to bring a smaller to a greater'.[56] Mathematics therefore simulated both arts and sciences and served the new attitudes to knowledge which transformed the world view of men living between the age of Ramus and the age of Descartes and which in this country we associate especially with Francis Bacon.

London felt conscious pride in this multiplying and diversifying knowledge, this spirit of enquiry and observation, this desire and courage to question old theories and systems and to verify new ones. In 1615 there was annexed to Stow's *Annales* a claim that London was 'The Third Universitie of England'. Sir George Buck described how all the colleges, 'Auncient Schooles of Priviledge', 'Houses Of Learning, And Liberal Arts, Within And About the Most Famous Cittie of London' offered instruction in almost anything: law, medicine, theology, mathematics, sciences, modern and ancient languages, courtly exercises, useful arts and skills – stenography for example, very serviceable for noting 'a Sermon, Oration, Play, or any long speech'. Even the 'Art of Memorie' was taught 'within this Universitie of London'. Gresham College, the Inns of Court, Surgeons' Hall, the endowed grammar schools, Christ's Hospital and Sion College, provided an institutional structure, 'good Monuments, for the benefit and ornament' of the City provided by 'rare Cittizens, vertuous and honorable minded Merchants'. But much of the teaching and learning took place outside this structure in response to specific needs. When Lancelot Andrewes at Pembroke College Cambridge, for example, became interested in the oriental tongues it was to London he came, to 'an obscure and simple man for worldly affairs but expert in all the lefthand tongues, as Hebrew, Chaldean, Syrian, Arabian'.[57] A sound attainment of and respect for learning were thought characteristic of civic life. By the middle of the seventeenth century it could be asserted that many merchant adventurers had mastered 'the very encyclopaedia and summary of all good and necessary arts and learning', and seven years later Christopher Wren in his inaugural lecture at Gresham College congratulated 'this City, that I find in it so general a relish of mathematics and *libera philosophia . . .*'.[58]

Between the end of Elizabeth's reign and those complacent pronouncements, England's mood had changed as her course of history moved tragically into civil conflict. Although it can be argued that in this period of Jacobean melancholy, of 'economic recession, of national humiliation in politics, of doubt and self-searching in literature' the will and nerve of the City kept its buoyant confidence and optimism,[59] the cultural unity of English society was falling apart. What has been called the 'Two Cultures' of 'Court and Country under Charles I' was demonstrated in the drama.[60] City audiences attended the theatres where Edward Alleyn, who has already appeared as a founder of a grammar school, was making his fortune, and where the plays of Shakespeare, Middleton, Massinger, Jonson, etc., often contained shrewd anti-court thrusts or latent symbolism of the same tone. Cavaliers were provided with increasingly elaborate court masques, the symbolism of which was more and more strongly absolutist. The startling new Palladian architecture of one of the chief designers and contrivers of these, Inigo Jones, embodied for citizens who disapproved of 'popery, painting, and play acting' their increasing estrangement from the King and his government. In the hugger-mugger confusion of Whitehall, where city and palace were difficult to distinguish or disentangle, arose the first and only constructed part of a vast new English Louvre, the enclosed and ordered beauty of the Banqueting House, used for these masques until King Charles feared that the candles needed for their lighting effects would spoil or endanger its ceiling. This had been painted at his order by the genius who was also ambassador for the absolutist and Catholic ruler of the Netherlands – Peter Paul Rubens. The subject chosen for this masterpiece of the European Baroque was the apotheosis of James I and showed Charles, as a robust Flemish baby, being perfected by Wisdom and presented to his father. The citizens of London had limited opportunities of penetrating this enclave of Divine Right and the Baroque: they were more able to view, and disapprove of, other works of Inigo Jones – the Romish Chapel which he built for Queen Henrietta Maria, and the monstrous Palladian portico which he clapped on to the west front of the decaying but beloved Gothic St Paul's, paid for by fines from the hated prerogative courts. Inigo Jones also planned for courtiers, aristocrats and lawyers their own fashionable quarter around Drury and Chancery Lanes, outside the City jurisdiction and excluded from its franchises.[61]

London's part in nurturing the 'Puritan Revolution' belongs to a wider study than can be covered here. The War and the Interregnum were a time of lively and radical but narrowly based educational debate. Influenced by Comenius, Hartlib, Drury and the young William Petty put forward ideas for a new national education system in which science would play a part, though the curriculum would be graded for different levels of society. Some radicals advanced millennial schemes for universal schooling for a 'World Turned Upside Down'.[62] Probably these would have remained visions even if the Republic had survived: the Restoration does not seem to have been an educational event. Perhaps more important for the new curriculum was the largely contingent period of national prosperity, the dying away of inflation, the expansion of trade, the development of new financial institutions. London had become an 'unmatched commercial centre' – 'the richest and most populous city on earth'.[63] It was in the learned coteries and lively coffee-houses of this capital that wits and virtuosi, gentlemen of leisure and professionals, gradually established natural philosophy as a branch of polite learning.[64] In this sociable civic setting a new cultural synthesis emerged, reflecting the political alliance, which was to triumph in 1688, between landed magnates and mercantile and financial oligarchs. Whether true learning was advanced is a matter of debate, and discussion about the achievements of the Royal Society and its somewhat amateur membership belongs to the analysis of higher learning and education rather than here.[65] Progress in scientific understanding, however, was beginning to depend on educational process, on some sound and appropriate preparatory stage of learning which provided both specific skills and possibilities of the conceptual understanding necessary for accommodating new kinds of knowledge.[66] The commercial, industrial and financial demands of the capital continued to proliferate educational expedients and experiments which to some extent served these purposes.

Edward Cocker's *Guide to Penmanship*, 1664

Restoration London abounded not only with coffee-houses but also with writing masters and pen-men. These often waited on their pupils at their homes. Pepys, when he wished to master the multiplication table, employed such a pen-man, Edward Cocker, writing master, engraver of calligraphy and arithmetician, 'dwelling in Paul's Church Yard, betwixt the Signes of the Sugar Loaf and the Naked Boy'. Later he founded a school in Southwark and his voluminous output of copy-books gave rise to the phrase 'all according to Cocker'. Pepys's lists of pen-men, compiled when he was busy about the setting up of the Mathematical School at Christ's Hospital, are an important source of information about these

Edward Alleyn, the actor, founder
of Dulwich College, as Barabbas in
The Jew of Malta, from the
Marlowe Memorial in Canterbury

John Carpenter's statue from the City
of London School, founded in the
nineteenth century from his medieval
endowments

1 The grammar school tradition. Victorian images of two early benefactors – a
fifteenth-century city merchant and a new professional of the seventeenth century

2 City needs and the expanding curriculum. Frontispiece of Sir Jonas Moore's *A New System of Mathematicks* (1681) written for the boys of Christ's Hospital Mathematical School

teachers. Three volumes of papers and examples of their works are preserved in the Pepysian Library at Magdalene College, Cambridge, and the list of 'Surviving Maister-Pen-Men of England and more particularly in and about the Citys of London and Westminster in the year 1699' contains 64 names of 'Maisters' and their 'Abodes'.[67]

A new factor which increased their influence was the high perfection which the art of engraving had reached, enabling copy-books to be reproduced. One of the finest of these specialist engravers was John Sturt (1658–1730) who also kept a writing school near Cheapside, and then with Bernard Lens opened a drawing school in St Paul's Churchyard.[68] Such teachers clustered thickly there but after the Fire many of them were driven beyond the old walls, and they also followed their customers or pupils further into the newer suburbs. William Mason had a writing school in 'Loathbury', then one between Gracechurch Street and Cornhill, and finally in 1699 moved to the Hand and Pen, Scalding Alley, 'over against the Stocks Market', and was famous for his shorthand teaching, set forth in *A Pen pluck'd from an Eagles Wing*, and for his skill in miniature writing.[69] Thomas Ollyffe had a school in Fetter Lane, and specialized in law hands – 'Engrossing hands and the Court and the Chancery'.[70] John Ayres was 'the most eminent writing-master of his day'. He began his working life as a footman in the household of Sir William Ashurst of Hornsey, who became Lord Mayor (1693–4), and gave Ayres his early education at a writing school in Fetter Lane. He opened his own school in St Paul's Churchyard and published his first copy-book, *The A la Mode Secretarie*, in 1680. *The Accomplish't Clerk* followed, and in about 1698 *The Tutor to Penmanship*. His school offered a wide course – 'Writing, Arithmetick, Merchants Accompt's . . . Navigation, Surveying, Dialling, Gauging, Perspective, Gunnery, Algebra, Geometry, and other useful Parts of the Mathematics'.[71] This breadth of course was not unusual. Robert More junior (1671–*c*. 1727), who had been educated at his father's writing school in King Street, Westminster, set up his own in Leicester Fields, teaching 'Writing in all the Hands of England, Arithmetick, Vulgar and Decimal, Merchants Acco^ts and Shorthand . . . Also Youth Boarded or Taught Abroad.'[72] The famous City writing school of William Watts in Little Tower Street, which moved to Soho in about 1739, exemplifies the breadth and utility of the courses provided:

> Young men . . . intended for military employment are instructed in fortification, gunnery, surveying etc, and every part of knowledge for that profession, as modern languages, riding, fencing, drawing etc. Those who incline to the marine are taught every branch of navigation etc. Those who would be formed for the counting house, learn to write strong and free – to compute with ease, expedition and demonstration – to enter mercantile transactions by double entry – to know the use of all the books kept by merchants with all their

A writing-school trade card

different methods – to draw all forms of business – the nature of foreign exchange and the proper style of correspondence. The intention of this undertaking being to perfect the instructed in any branch of knowledge in as little time as capacity and application will admit, therefore they may apply as many hours of the day as best fits their conveniency, may board in the Academy or may only dine there.[73]

Here the course was wide but was used selectively for limited and specific purposes. Other writing masters themselves specialized – the ultimate was perhaps William Leekey (1710?–46) who moved his school from Cripplegate to Wapping and then back to the City, and advocated a different method of writing for 'men of bulky size and ladies laced in their stays'.[74]

Private schools for boys

London was thus the stage on which the ingredients for a new content of education were assembled. This knowledge had not at first been processed and packaged for scholastic delivery and consumption, but to this also the multifarious and urgent appetites of London were being turned. The result was to establish the private school as an obstinate element in the English educational system.[75] It is not easy to distinguish early schools giving a general education from writing masters, mathematical practitioners and the like, but from the sixteenth century a number of such schools had emerged. Sometimes they can be seen as products of, or developments from, writing schools; sometimes they reflect ideas of courtly education; sometimes they replaced the grammar schools. In the late 1570s Elias Newcomen had a school of 20 to 30 boarders, 'the children of worshipful persons', and sent some on to the universities, indicating a classical education.[76] Thomas Farnaby had a school in Goldsmith's Rents 'in a garden house . . . a fine airie place' in Cripplegate, and seems to have included geography and ancient and modern languages in his curriculum. His school rivalled Westminster until it moved to Kent (Sevenoaks) in 1636. Sometimes he employed three ushers and he was called 'the chief grammarian, rhetorician, poet, Latinist, and Grecian of his time'.[77] William Bullokar, a keen spelling reformer and one of the Elizabethan pioneers of English teaching, ran a private school.[78] 'Orthography' was an important element in the triumph of 'standard' or London English, and especially useful in commercial intercourse. Some mathematics teachers not only interpreted their subject and its practical applications widely, but also included other studies. John Speidell (*fl.* 1600–34), for example, took in boarders and instructed 'in the best and briefest ways, and (if need be) in French, Latin or Dutch'. He taught at the Musaeum Minervae.[79] French schools often taught arithmetic and mathematics, and even became established institutions of general education. Claud Holyband moved his school from St Paul's Churchyard in 1572 to the pleasant village of Lewisham and by the next year it was so flourishing that Queen Elizabeth stopped on her way to Greenwich to hear a Latin oration from the head boy. This probably became the 'Free Grammar School of Queen Elizabeth in Lewisham' which was a forerunner of Colfe's school.[80] This Huguenot influence was important in the development of the English private school.[81]

By the mid seventeenth century London was something of a centre for such schools, and the civil and constitutional disturbances of the War and the Interregnum probably strengthened them in numbers and in their function as alternatives to the grammar school. Some were kept by ejected schoolmasters, both before and after 1660. Thomas Singleton, who had been an usher at Eton, and was noted as a teacher of classics, had a school in Newcastle House, Clerkenwell, where he was said to have had 300 scholars under his care.[82] Another such school was kept in Hammersmith by Dr Edward Wolley who had been Chaplain to Charles I and then to Charles II in exile, which made it necessary for him to petition Cromwell for permission to continue to instruct youth in Latin, Greek and other exercises.[83] Thomas Swadlin, who had been minister of St Botolph Aldgate, 'much frequented by the orthodox party', was persecuted as 'one of Dr Laud's creatures' and later 'taught school in several places meerly to gain bread and drink, as in London and afterwards at Paddington'.[84] Samuel Clark, the orientalist and one of the editors of the Polyglot Bible (1657), had a boarding-school in Islington in 1650.[85] Ezekiel Tongue (1621–88), after his ejection from the new college at Durham, also taught in Islington, classical languages 'after an easy method' and writing a good hand in twenty days' time.[86] During the Interregnum William Fuller, DD (1608–75) kept a school at Twickenham where he tried to instil loyalty and churchmanship. Samuel Pepys escorted 'Mr Edward', Sandwich's son, there by coach in January 1660, leaving 'the child 40s to give to the two ushers', which suggests a school of some size. Fuller had assisted and then succeeded William Wyatt.[87]

Other schools may have flourished because the grammar schools were under attack, or simply because their curriculum was too narrow. Noah Bridges, author of *Vulgar Arithmetic* (1653), had a school at Putney 'Where is taught the Greek and Latin Tongues; also Arts and Sciences Mathematical, viz. Arithmetique, fair Writing, Merchants' Accounts, Geometry, Trigonometrie, Algebra, etc.'[88] Sir John Reresby was placed in 1649 by his widowed mother in a school at Enfield Chace, 'The Blew House, a then famous school for gentlemen's sons'. He was then fifteen and came in two years to a 'passable proficiency' in Latin, Greek and rhetoric and had learnt also French, writing and dancing.[89] These more rural schools tended to cater for the gentry and to provide a complete general and classical course. Another school of the same social type was the 'gymnasium' of Mark Lewis at Tottenham High Cross, 'where any person, whether young or old, as their Quality is, may be perfected in the Tongues by constant conversation'. This school was flourishing around 1676, and the Lord Privy Seal, the Earl of Anglesey, was so much pleased by it that he sent his sons there and enabled Lewis to secure Letters Patent for his method of teaching French, Italian and Spanish.[90]

Choice of a school of this kind for either the sons of gentry or merchant families depended on reputation and success in the particular skills and subjects needed, for boys often attended for very specific purposes. When Sir Ralph Verney was seeking a school for his second son, whom he intended for the law, he sent him first, at the age of thirteen, to the Reverend Dr James Fleetwood in Surrey, where he showed himself 'very ingenious and quick in understanding Arithmetic, wherein he hath made very good progress'. Jack himself wished to become a merchant, and after two years a school nearer London was sought. Choice lay between one in Hammersmith where the master, perhaps Wolley, had 'leave to teach', and Mr Turberville of Kensington, 'Master of French, Italian, Greek, and Latin, and of Music'. Jack spent three years, 1656–9, at Turberville's, 'preserving' his French, mastering Latin, 'amending' his writing, and learning the viol and other music. At eighteen he was dissatisfied with his education which was not of practical use and did not include merchants' accounts. In the end he prevailed over his father and was apprenticed to a Levant merchant.[91] Private schools of this kind may have been working out and formulating a new content of general education, but they were still used instrumentally and erratically, and were hardly yet related to ideas about 'education as a formative process, to be planned in relation to maturing physical and mental powers'.[92] This vital development was, however, emerging, partly because effectiveness and speed of teaching were needed to attract pupils, partly because in a wider curriculum classical languages had to compete for time and attention, and partly because the ferment of ideas and institutions of the mid seventeenth century fostered reform. In and around London experiments and expedients were thick enough on the ground for these factors to interact. At Isleworth, for example, Thomas Willis (1582–1660?) kept a school for fifty years, where he was able to practise his ideas on English teaching and the reform of Latin teaching. He published two Latin school-books, *Vestibulum Lingua Latinae* (1651) and *Phraseologia Anglo-Latina* (1655), sometimes called *Anglicisms Latinized*.[93] Nearby at Twickenham William Wyatt (1616–85) was much sought after as a teacher. He had helped Jeremy Taylor with his school and his *New and Easie Institution* of Grammar, 'In which the labour of many yeares usually spent in learning the Latin tongue is shortned and made easie.'[94] Much of Ezekiel Tongue's success and reputation was due to his following 'precisely the Jesuits' method, and the boys under him did by that course profit exceedingly'. He also devised a way of teaching writing by preparing copies printed from copper plates in red ink which the children wrote over in black.[95]

The most distinguished if not the most successful private schoolmaster in London at this time was undoubtedly John Milton in Aldersgate from 1639–40, but in spite of his contacts with reforming circles, and his tract *Of Education: to Master Samuel Hartlib*, his methods and aims seem to have been conservative.[96] In Hezekiah Woodward (1590–1675) the understanding of the need to reform Latin teaching and of new methods of teaching new subjects and new theories was united with a real understanding of the needs of childhood. He opened a school in the City in 1619, was given ecclesiastical preferment by Cromwell, and after his ejection in 1662 again kept a school, at Uxbridge. He described his own miserable grammar-school education in *A Child's Patrimony* (1640) and *Portion* (1649), and he put forward his reforming ideas in 1641 in two pamphlets whose titles reveal his discipleship of Comenius: '*A Light to Grammar and all other Arts and Sciences or the Rule of Practice*, proceeding to the clue of nature and conduct or right reason so opening the doore thereunto', and '*A Gate to Sciences* opened by a naturale key or a Practicall lecture upon the great book of nature whereby the childe is enabled to read the creatures there.' He argued that the teacher must consider the mind of the child and teach grammar so that it may be simple, beginning with the mother tongue, 'the foundation of all'; 'Hee that can stoope lowest and soonest fit his precognition to the child, he is the best teacher.' He advocated a conversational method of language teaching and the use of plenty of explanation and illustration. He urged the teaching of the sciences, they 'are lighted unto the understanding through the door of the senses and this is true enough for certaine it is that a child, yea a man also, doth taste and relish no knowledge but what he finds drencht in flesh and blood'. His justification of drawing as part of the curriculum is especially revealing of his attention to the child: 'Observe him with his little stick puddering in the ashes, drawing lines there. . . . Let us follow nature here.' Mathematics he considered should be the basis of all knowledge, but feared that it would be 'tedious and useless to tread such a maze with a child'.[97]

Woodward was certainly involved in the plans of Hartlib and Drury, their correspondence with Comenius and their plans to bring the great reformer to England,[98] but the evidence does not allow us to say how far he put any of his ideas into practice even in his own school. Nor is it easy to estimate the extent of his influence. After the Restoration he was remembered more for his 'eager' and 'fanatic' doctrines, and it seems all too probable that these discredited his enlightened educational ideas with the mainstream of practice. Probably the practical and conformist Charles Hoole was more widely influential with his *New Discovery of the Old Art of Teaching School* (1660), based on many years of experience at a northern grammar school and then during the Commonwealth in his City private school. He advocated a wide curriculum and kindlier methods, and satisfied utilitarian demands by sending his boys, perhaps for extra charge, to a nearby writing school in Lothbury, kept by James Hodder, 'where such as are desirous to learn the art of Writing, as also fractions, with Merchants' Accompts and Shorthand, may be carefully attended . . .'.[99] Although by the end of the seventeenth century boys' private schools had evolved within London and its surrounding suburbs as established institutions, the distinction between them and the writing schools was still difficult to draw. Both were a response to new conceptions of the content of knowledge and its disciplines, to the needs of society at many levels, to professional enterprise and concern. In many diverse ways practice was pushing forward the concept of education as a process related to human development.

Private schools for girls

London's contribution to the development during the seventeenth century of private schools for girls was crucial, for these were the only provision made for their education outside the home over the next three centuries. Social, economic and cultural changes had made it necessary to develop a range of schools for boys as a lay process and alternative to the old concept of familial or household education. The same changes and pressures were felt in the education of their sisters, though more slowly and to a different degree, for girls must above all be kept guarded and enclosed. The idea of personal privacy had perhaps hardly yet penetrated society, but any hint of public schooling for daughters was unacceptable and inconceivable. There was also fear that bringing a number of girls together under a 'common mistress' was dangerous. In 'such a mixture of dispositions and humours as must needs be met within a multitude, there will be much of that which is bad . . .'. 'Ill tincture' was also dangerous for boys, but it could be 'recoverable' in them, but 'hardly or never' in girls. This was the judgement passed on the school in Stepney where Sir John Eliot placed his daughter Bess in 1630 so that she could visit him in the Tower.[100] In Catholic countries new needs and old beliefs could be accommodated in the development of covent schools. In England it is surprising to find that this conventual ideal remained strong, and not only in Catholic families, and that London, in spite of its nearness to the central authority, but perhaps partly because of its nearness to the Stuart court, had early associations with the establishment of schools for the daughters of Catholic families in the penal era. The metropolitan area was also convenient for receiving such girls and arranging for their voyage to the Low Countries. Mary Ward (1585–1645), the most important organizer of the revival of such schools, was herself taken in 1606 to St Omer, and her eventual plan for an order of unenclosed religious modelled on the Society of Jesus was formed for the education of girls and the reconversion of her country. She visited London and collected pupils, and her 'English Institute' even established missions and schools in, for example, Spitalfields and Knightsbridge and, when Queen Henrietta Maria could afford some protection, in St Martin's Lane. When it was necessary to move to Yorkshire in 1642 a goodly party of children filled three coaches. After her death in 1645 it seems probable that some settlement in London was kept all through the time of the Commonwealth. When in 1669 a boarding-school for girls was openly established at Hammersmith with the 'help and countenance' of Catherine of Braganza, the tradition remained that it had been moved from St Martin's Lane. The head of the school was Frances Beddingfield who, after being with Mary Ward in Yorkshire, had gone with the rest of the community to the house of refuge provided at Paris by the Marquess of Worcester. At Hammersmith she was joined by three English sisters from Augsburg. Some protection was still necessary for the continuation of the school, and the sisters had to style themselves 'governesses and teachers having voluntarily obliged themselves to the observation of monastic rules'. In 1680 the house was visited by Titus Oates with a Middlesex Justice, the head constable and other officers. The search revealed 'divers children of several persons of quality', some popish 'books and trinkets', an 'ancient gentlewoman' who had been left as governess, and an 'outlandish person' said to be a Walloon in the service of the Spanish ambassador. Mrs Beddingfield had gone overseas, but the search party declared 'This house went under the name of a Boarding School . . . under that pretence there is a private nunnery maintained to educate the children of several of the Popish nobility.' Later Mrs Beddingfield, 'much admired for her extraordinary learning', was examined 'before His Majesty in Council' and was immediately acquitted of harbouring obnoxious persons. The protection of James II and Mary of Modena enabled a settlement to be established in London itself where a spacious house in Whitefriars was provided and '300 children quickly presented themselves'. At the Revolution the sisters from this school eventually took refuge at Hammersmith. Another attempt to revive the settlement in St Martin's Lane also failed. During this period the canonical position of 'The English Institute' was probably one of 'tacit authorization'. It was not until 1703 that final confirmation of the Rule was given, under the name of the 'Institute of Mary'. Its school at Hammersmith flourished for many years. During the eighteenth century most of the fashionable females among the Roman Catholics were educated there.[101]

Protestant London's attitude to this scarcely concealed activity was ambivalent. Hostility must be presumed, mixed perhaps with some nostalgia. The development of girls' schools within the capital was a practical response to a growing need, and it was accompanied by a debate about their purpose and nature which reveals dissatisfaction with the lack of a conventual tradition and contribution, or its Protestant equivalent. London had to provide schools for its citizens' daughters, and also to satisfy the metropolitan courtly tradition for the education of the children of the landed classes. Topographical evidence suggests that it was the first need which set the pattern, perhaps because it was first felt and combined readily with an older tradition of sending children out of town to nurse, though some schools were in the City itself. Simon D'Ewes's sisters were sent in the 1620s to a school in Walbrook kept by a pious merchant's wife.[102] Later schools tended to move out into the surrounding villages. Hackney, a pleasant village north of the City and much favoured as a country retreat, became famous by the mid century as a centre for girls' boarding-schools, 'the Ladies University of Female Arts'. When in 1667 Pepys visited Hackney Church, he confessed 'That which I went chiefest to see was the young ladies of the schools, whereof there is great store, very pretty.'[103] Before 1637 Mrs Winch's school was patronized by the City Corporation for the education of its wards. In that year Sara Cox, 'having a good portion secured to the Chamber of London', was abducted as she walked on Newington Common by the brother of one of her schoolfellows, and carried away screaming to a forced marriage in the private chapel at Winchester House – a sharp reminder of one very potent reason for the close-guarding of young women.[104] In 1643 Mrs Perwich and her husband moved their famous girls' academy from Aldermanbury to the large timber-frame house near

Hackney Church called Bohemia Palace. In this school, containing 100 and 'sometimes more of gentlewomen', from then until 1660 some 800 girls were educated. The establishment was pious, but fashionable, and showed an increasing emphasis on accomplishments. Its most celebrated pupil and later teacher was Susannah, a daughter of the proprietors. Tributes to her at her early death in 1661 describe the music at the school. Sixteen masters visited to teach the harpsichord, stringed instruments, and singing, and the pupils led by Susannah on the viol formed an orchestra and gave concerts. Dancing was taught by Mr Hazard, 'one of the rarest masters of that art in England'. Teaching was equally good in writing, accounting, cyphering, housewifery, cookery, and 'all other parts of excellent breeding', including 'curious works' with the needle, straws, wax, gums or otherwise '. . . which females are wont to be conversant in'.[105]

Nearby was Mrs Salmon's school which was well established by 1639 when Katherine Fowler, daughter of a merchant of Bucklersbury and later renowned as Katherine Philips, 'Matchless Orinda', was sent there at the age of eight. By eleven she had made progress in note-taking, could recite many passages of scripture, had perhaps learnt some French and read a little history. In 1647 on the death of his wife Sir John Bramston placed two of his daughters at Mrs Salmon's, which he called 'Hackney School'. It seems to have been acceptable to both moderate parliamentary and royalist opinion, though Aubrey states that Mrs Salmon was a Presbyterian. Katherine Fowler's merchant father had Presbyterian leanings and his daughter's skill in note-taking was acquired in recording sermons.[106]

Another schoolmistress who emphasized the more serious aspects of study was Mrs Hannah Woolley, who with her schoolmaster husband moved their boarding-school to Hackney in 1655. She published several recipe books, including *The Queen-like Closet* (1675), and in *The Gentlewoman's Companion* (1675) claimed that the female intelligence could be educated without rivalling 'the touring conceit of our insulting lords and masters'. The casual nature of girls' education outraged her excellent sense and roused her bitterness. She recommended a thoroughly practical education, but included Latin and modern languages.[107]

Mrs Woolley's misgivings were justified by many of the smaller or less famous neighbouring schools. Aubrey, for example, condemned Hackney schools as places where young maids learnt pride and wantonness and made the shrewd observation that the nunneries taught not only piety and humility, but needlework, the art of confectionery, surgery, physic, writing and drawing. Private schools might claim to teach these more useful arts, but were not in fact well equipped for doing so effectively. By the Restoration the pretentious frivolity of much of the education given here to citizens' daughters had become something of a court joke, and reference by Wycherley to 'Hackney School' was readily interpreted by his audience with contemptuous ridicule.[108]

This was social rather than educational commentary. But there was also serious contemporary debate about the nature and purpose of girls' education. Amongst the Hartlib papers was preserved a letter from 'D. D.' which may be the work of Dorothy Drury, wife of the reformer. She dissents 'from the ordinary way of educating youth' as her experience as well as her reason has taught her that the teaching of 'dauncing and curious works . . . serve only to fill the fancy with unnecessary, unprofitable and proud imaginations' quite in opposition to the 'simplicitie of the Gospell'. The 'practise common in schooles' to teach 'dressing, curling and such like' also brings 'no good to the soule or body of mankind'. 'D. D.' does not indicate what she would include in the school course, but her letter is an indictment of much current practice. Another paper in the Hartlib collection, a plan by Adolphus Speed for the 'Education of Young Gentlemen and Gentlewomen', is more positive, placing the debate about girls' schooling in its proper relation to the newer ideas about the education of boys of this rank with a wide, pious and practical curriculum. Their sisters are to learn 'all manner of needleworks, Imbroidering, etc, together with drawing on cloth for their works, the portraitures and similitudes of Birds, Beasts, Fishes, Flowers etc', fashionable styles of needlework reflecting the Age of Observation. Religious instruction, teaching by 'industruous and most judicious Penmen' to 'write, cypher, and cast accompts', and 'short-writing', French, music, dancing formed the main curriculum. Speed then added a long description of the practical course in the skills expected of a Carolean housewife: physic and surgery, the making of lotions, 'the plenary discovery of all the effects of simples', 'all rare and new devices and experiments of Cookery', with 'all physicall observations, naturall effects, operations, and cooperations of meats etc', and 'the gathering of all sorts of Hearbs, Roots, Fruits etc' (a reminder of the application of Baconian ideas to practical affairs); brewing, wine-making, distilling; the making of soap, sweet-waters, 'sanative perfumes', wax-candles, sealing wax, etc., etc., 'and all the varieties, and rare inventions and secrets that have been devised . . . with the newest and most excellent experiments thereof discovered . . .'. Most of these skills were acquired by the older methods of household education. What is new is their being taught in a school and related to the newer kinds of scientific understanding. Speed had plans for opening a school in London, but as with so many of the plans of this reforming circle, this remained on paper.[109] More likely to have been translated into practice were the ideas of another member of the circle, Mrs Bathsua Makin.

One of the most learned women of her day, sister of John Pell, the mathematician, she was governess to the daughters of Charles I, teaching them Greek, Latin, Hebrew, Italian and mathematics. During the Commonwealth she may have kept the school for young gentlewomen which Evelyn visited at Putney, which had followed Hackney in becoming something of a centre for such schools. In 1673 she opened or took over a school at Tottenham High Cross, perhaps the one where in 1628 Mrs Suzan Gardener had charge of Mary Brookes, a ward of the Court of Aldermen. Mrs Makin published her ideas on girls' education in a prospectus: *Essay to revive the Antient Education of Gentlewomen in Religion, Manners, Arts and Tongues* (1673). She developed her argument in a discussion with an 'Objector' who has 'no prejudice against the Sex'. Although a learned woman is thought to be a 'Comet that bodes mischief whenever it appears', God cannot have given women their talents that they 'may Eat, Drink, Sleep, and rise up to Play', and at the Last Day poor women will make but a vain excuse when pleading lack of education. She strongly condemned the frivolous education which trained girls merely 'to Frisk and Dance, to paint their Faces, to curl their Hair, to put on a Whisk and wear gay Clothes', and the time spent on silly tasks, 'making Flowers of Coloured Straw and building Houses of stained paper'. At her school only half the time was spent on subjects usually taught, 'works of all sorts, Dancing, Music, Singing, Writing, and Keeping Accompts'. The other half was given to the subjects essential to women, practical, intellectual and moral. Limning, preserving, pastry-making and cookery were included, but she says:

> I cannot tell where to begin to admit Women, nor from what part of Learning to exclude them, in regard of their Capacities . . . I would not deny them the knowledge of Grammar and Rhetorick, because they dispose to speak handsomely. Logick must be allowed because it is the Key to all Sciences . . . the Tongues ought to be studied, especially the Greek and Hebrew, these will enable to the better understanding of the Scriptures. The Mathematics more especially Geography will be useful; *this puts life into History*. Music, Painting, Poetry are a great ornament and pleasure. Some things that are more practical are not so material because Public Employments in the Field and Courts are usually denied to Women.

The course was arranged so that little girls entering at eight or nine, already able to read and write, could be instructed 'according to their Parts' in Latin and French, in a year to two; and further languages, music, practical subjects, astronomy, geography, history and arithmetic could be added. If only one language was thought necessary, they 'may forbear the languages and learn only experimental philosophy'. The basic course cost £20 a year, but if a competent improvement was made in the other subjects 'Parents shall judge what shall be deserved of the Undertaker.'

Mrs Makin's methods show the influence, not only of seventeenth-century scientific progress, but of the ideas of Comenius, whom she may have met through her brother. She abandoned the traditional method of language teaching, 'greater care ought to be had to know things than to get words'. Lilly's *Grammar* was useless, and her textbooks were the *Orbis Pictus* and the *Janua Linguarum* of Comenius, making use of illustrations and the child's experience. Museum exhibits were to be used, 'Repositories also for Visibles shall be prepared, by which, from beholding the things, gentlewomen may learn the Names, Natures, Values, and Use of Herbs, Shrubs, Trees, Mineral Juices, Metals and Stones.' Mrs Makin was in advance of her time and it is difficult to know how far her theories were put into practice even at Tottenham.[110]

Mrs Makin was associated with the puritan but ecumenical circle round Hartlib and Drury. Noncomformists such as Elizabeth, widow of John Tutchin, who supported herself by keeping a school in Newington Green and then in Highgate, also advocated a more 'sober' education in all kinds of suitable learning.[111] By the time Mrs Tutchin was keeping her school, Nonconformity was begin established as a recognized element in national life. Several writers of this period show that the destruction of the nunnery schools was lamented by pious Anglicans, who feared private schools as either frivolous or schismatic. Most notable was Mrs Mary Astell (1668–1731) of Chelsea. She was a woman of great learning, who in her *Essay in Defence of the Female Sex* shrewdly criticized the dilettante approach to the new learning which made science a mere satisfaction for curiosity, rather than a true advancement of knowledge, or of practical use. She also realized that if the education of girls was to improve, better teachers were needed. In her *Serious Proposal for Ladies* (1694 and 1697) she described a 'retreat from the world for those who desire that advantage, but likewise an institution and previous discipline to do the greatest good in it'. The religious nature of this college was to be 'rather *academical* than *monastic*', it was to be a 'seminary to stock the Kingdom with pious and prudent ladies'. Even, however, in pious non-juring circles this was condemned as savouring of popery, giving a greater amount of learning to women than men were prepared to countenance or encounter. Dean Atterbury, Mrs Astell's friend and neighbour, went in some awe of her sense. 'I dread to engage her,' he wrote. Mrs Astell did in fact articulate rather dangerous ideas about the position of women. She pressed the ideas of Locke too far. 'If absolute authority be not necessary in a state, how comes it to be so in a family? . . . If all men are born free, how is it that all women are born slaves?'[112]

In spite of such ideas as these, the girls' boarding-school by the end of the seventeenth century was usually more characterized by its attention to accomplishments than to sound learning or useful skills, and the teaching of these skills in a school, even if it were conceived as an extended household, was clearly much less likely to be effective than in a girls' own home. Mrs Playford's school opposite the church at Islington, then a fashionable suburban village and spa, may be taken as typical. It was advertised in one of her husband's music publications in 1679 as a place 'where young gentlewomen may be instructed in all manner of curious works, as also reading, writing, music, dancing and the French language'.[113] It was this kind of school, especially when it was in the western suburbs, which was by this period being patronized by the gentry families, for London, with its cultural pre-eminence and connections, was establishing its nation-wide reputation for girls' education. This is one significant indication of the 'cultural homogeneity' of wealthier citizens and the landed gentry which, in a style appropriate to the age of the Whig Revolution, healed that divergence between Court and City which had opened during much of the seventeenth century.[114]

Gorges House in Chelsea provides the classic example. It was the largest house in the village, famous as a school from 1676 almost until it was demolished in about 1726. In 1676 the masque *Beauties Triumph* was presented by 'the scholars of Mr Jeffrey Banister and Mr James Hart at their new Boarding School for Young Ladies and Gentlewomen, kept in that house which was formerly Sir Arthur Gorges at Chelsea'. Under Mr Portman it maintained its reputation, and in 1680 Mr Josias Priest, dancing master, removed his boarding-school for gentlewomen in Leicester Fields to this establishment, there to 'continue the same masters and others to the improvement of the said school'. In 1705 Priest was still in charge, and seems to have retired in about 1715 when Dr Richard Mead appears in the rate books. Here in 1680 the opera *Dido and Aeneas* composed by Purcell was first performed. Elizabeth Palmer of Little Chelsea, who married John Verney in 1680, learnt her skill 'on the espinette and organs and guitar' and in dancing at Gorges House, and in 1679 Edmund Verney sent his daughter Molly there, intending later to place her in 'the household of some lady of quality, paying her board and wages' – a reminder of the strength and survival of an earlier pattern of education. He took the child from Buckinghamshire to the school himself, visiting the sights of London on the way, and lingering until she was 'a little wonted' to her strange surroundings. Molly was said to improve wonderfully, distinguished herself at the school ball, and wrote home to ask whether she might learn to japan boxes. Her father approved, 'and so I shall of anything that is good and virtuous, therefore learn in God's name all good things . . . though they come from Japan and from never so far . . .'. Japanning was an 'extra', costing 21*s* entrance fee and 40*s* for materials.[115]

During the summer of 1690 Tom D'Urfey lived at this school and when in 1691 he wrote *Love for Money, or the Boarding School*, he was accused of ungratefully reflecting upon its 'housekeeping' and holding it up to ridicule – but the badness of the play was perhaps the best protection for Mr Priest's reputation, for it gives a picture unlikely to increase the confidence of parents. Two city heiresses, 'tawdry, hoyden overgrown romps', are finally carried off and married by adventurers disguised as the dancing and singing masters, while the governess seems unable to prevent her charges from climbing out of the 'jordain' window or the cellar – 'Was there ever such a contrivance? We shall have all our girls stole out of the school by baskets full, if this trade hold.' The more elegant heroine is using the school as a finishing establishment.[116]

It would be unwise to rely on a second-rate Restoration dramatist for an estimate of London's provision for the education of girls, but almost certainly most boarding-schools of this type were judged not by their intellectual achievements but by the so-called accomplishments of their pupils. The social changes which began to replace the arranged with the romantic marriage, the freer choice of partner by the young people themselves, laid increasing stress on the need for attractive social skills, whilst the rising standards of domestic comfort, the transfer of many productive processes from the home to industry, the delegation of household tasks to servants, were all placing greater emphasis on leisure or decorative arts for girls. These changes began first in the middle ranks of society, and were distinctively urban. Moreover the value of even a city heiress would be enhanced by social graces which would help her to marry into the ranks of the gentry. This helps to explain why boarding-schools for girls were a city phenomenon and used earliest by merchant and business families.[117]

It has been argued that the seventeenth century, in comparison with the sixteenth, was a time of lowered educational aspirations for women, and that the new courtly ideal, and the Protestant, especially Puritan, ideal of the woman as the docile housewife, the diligent upholder of holy matrimony in a subservient role to the husband, spelt the end of the 'learned lady'.[118] If this theory is upheld, the development of the private school must be seen as institutionalizing false or lowered standards. The very few learned ladies of the previous century were however altogether exceptional, even in their own day. Women had always been upholders of matrimony, and the London experience suggests rather a genuine attempt to meet new needs and changing ideas, to fulfil family responsibilities more effectively and with fuller resources, visiting masters being necessary for French, music and other more serious subjects as well as dancing and making straw houses. The private school must be seen as an extension and reinforcement of the home, giving to daughters some of the wider opportunities of social intercourse, and new knowledge and skills, which their brothers had.[119] That in practice it came down to japanning boxes or excelling at the school ball should not altogether invalidate the achievements of the century. Perhaps an age which depends on the television screen, the supermarket and postal offers in the Sunday magazines, should not despise those who learnt to make music in the home, to manufacture with the needle a considerable proportion of the hangings and upholstery of the more comfortable houses of their age, and to distil or manufacture agreeable articles of necessity or semi-luxury for domestic consumption.

London in the sixteenth and seventeenth centuries had not only created a network of grammar schools, but had devised and invented a range of alternative or supplementary educational institutions and expedients which reflected new economic and intellectual needs and ideas. In a capital city, expanding and quickening under the impact of a

'Commercial Revolution', private schools for boys and girls, writing or mathematical schools and masters for pupils of all ages, may be seen as an achievement to be compared with joint stock investment, fire insurance, marine underwriting.[120] It was in London also that a range of institutions for higher learning and professional training to reinforce or replace university learning had been developed. These educational provisions and institutions, moreover, manifested a reuniting of the national culture in which ideas and experiences flowed easily between citizen and gentry families.

Invitation card of the Mercers Company, showing St Pauls Schools as rebuilt after the Fire of London. from the Pepys Collection.

St Paul's in the early eighteenth century

III

From observation to Enlightenment:
London education in the Age of Reason

For the historian of education labels for periods of history serve to indicate the way in which an age defines and extends knowledge and the style in which it is verified and published. The eighteenth century was not only the Age of Reason, the Enlightenment, it was for much of its course the Augustan Age.

It was also for a great mercantile business centre a period of credit expansion which brought the 'last stage of the mobilization of commercial capital' and many of London's civic leaders were making the transition from predominantly trading to financial transactions.[1] This had important implications for the power structure of London, for the newer institutions, such as the Bank of England and the East India Company, had no place in City government, yet the great Companies, now economically relatively less important, were an integral part of the Corporation. Many bankers, stockbrokers, commission agents, preferred not to take up the obligations and ceremonials of the Freedom of the City. The Corporation therefore tended to represent the resident shopkeepers rather than the City's innovators. It was in the suburbs or out-parishes that the characteristic developments of eighteenth-century London took place and this must be remembered when tracing educational changes.[2]

At the same time London was becoming less rather than more industrial. At all economic levels it was moving from primary production to the provision of services. It was also the viewing point from which the powerful, the wealthy, the articulate, the mobile, the reflective, regarded a country which, while still a 'patchwork of distinct and separate local communities', was also a self-conscious nation developing the centralizing bureaucracy necessary for an increasingly complex and interdependent society and economy. The contrast has been well drawn between the outcry which greeted the proposal from Westminster for a national census in 1753 (not only was it unscriptural, it was also French and would destroy the liberties of free-born Englishmen), and the quiet passage of a similar proposal in 1800.[3]

These changes put pressures upon those stages of education which prepare for the public world, in its practical, political, cultural and academic dimensions. Transition towards service and administrative occupations was an 'incentive to education, an important element in the growth of the middle class and in the opportunities of rising in the world'. There were called into existence 'whole armies of contractors and clerks, public bodies and charitable institutions were employing an increased number of paid officials, and private adventure schools mulitplied. The result must have been a greater relative increase in the number of people employed in distribution (wholesale and retail), in administration and education rather than in manual labour.' Private schools may thus be seen as an aspect of an increasingly consumer society.[4] In London the extent and the variety of educational response to these needs at what we now call the secondary level was remarkable and this diversity was perhaps an aspect of Johnson's 'full tide of human existence' to be felt at Charing Cross. The literary and cultural setting of schooling is always essential to its interpretation, and the community of letters of the capital played and important part in these educational developments.[5]

London's growth and topography also had important educational implications. Unlike Paris, London kept its pre-eminence in national expansion. Around 1750 about one in six of all English men and women were either living in London or had once lived there, 'and thus been directly exposed to the social, political and cultural influences of the capital'. Immigrants were mostly young, household servants, apprentices, younger sons and so on, and settled in the suburbs.[6] For much of the century the capital's population though rising did not replenish its own numbers, but after about 1760 the annual number of burials each year decreased and in the absence of a census it was therefore widely believed that Londoners were declining in number. London's share of national population *growth* did decrease at this time, yet between 1700 and 1820 its population almost doubled, though it was not until the census of 1801 and that of 1811 that this was evident.[7]

Physical expansion was there for all to see. 'The increase of building in London has for several years been the subject of general observation,' said a writer of 1779,[8] but perhaps the curious lag in the full recognition of expanding population was partly due to the diffusion of numbers and the greater separation of social ranks which this made possible. Whereas the overwhelming impact of growth had been felt in the sixteenth and seventeenth centuries, in this age the sense of expansion was more manageable, more optimistic in tone. Elegance, like cheerfulness, kept breaking in. And it was an elegance which itself put pressures upon powers of understanding and systematization, for urban classical architecture was a language to be learned, and imposed order upon daily life. The City itself became relatively less crowded, and less important; and beyond the overcrowded and makeshift ring of old suburbs immediately outside its walls, the newer parts of the town, the comparatively pleasant airy squares and streets of Bloomsbury, the development towards the royal parks of Mayfair and the Grosvenor estates, the final linking up with Westminster, created an open city unlike anything else in Europe. It was ringed round with expanding and diversified villages, some near enough to be inhabited by commuters, or used as pleasure resorts, others far enough to remain country retreats. London education has to be seen in this wider topographical setting, as old communities were encroached upon or engulfed, better communications and safer travel linked centre with periphery, and the Londoner's sturdy determination to keep his links with his rural past and his own countryside remained obstinate. Schools once founded to serve small communities could be used in expanding villages or for boarding city children in healthier surroundings, or adapt themselves to new local needs; prestigious city foundations were challenged by changing political and academic demands; and in every part of the metropolitan area expedients and experiments of varying value abounded. The linking of the City and Westminster and the widening and quickening activity of London's countryside were symbolic as well as topographical and represented in some respects the consolidation of a governing order, its power based upon inherited or newly acquired land, but much of its wealth generated by commerce and financial and urban enterprise.

The grammar schools

Dr Johnson declared in 1776 that he 'would never consent to disgrace the walls of Westminster Abbey with an English Inscription'. Oliver Goldsmith's epitaph should be in 'ancient and permanent language'.[9] This energetic claim to 'classical stability' was the foundation and strength of the eighteenth-century tradition of liberal education. The *philosophes* themselves appealed to a 'beloved antiquity' and depicted Newton wrapped in a toga.[10] It is not possible to discuss the impact of the Enlightenment upon education without first examining its classical basis in the grammar schools. During this century Latin ceased to be a spoken language, to be used in the law courts or generally in the written discourse of the sciences and arts.[11] But if its immediate uses dwindled, it would be absurd to say that Latin became useless in an age which was committed to finding the truth of order, universality, law, within the flux and irregularity of everyday experience, by an appeal to authoritative and unchanging models. The classical tradition, especially in its self-conscious reaffirmation in the so-called Neo-Classical reaction against the frivolity of the Rococo, sought the imitation of nature which the Ancients had achieved, 'the general and permanent principles of visible objects, not disfigured by accident . . . modified by fashion or local habits'. This concept was allied to contemporary ideas of natural law and natural religion. 'The study of Antiquities was thus regarded as a means of penetrating to the eternally valid truths which were thought to underlie the superficial diversities of the visible world.'[12] A classical education was therefore initiation into stability, standards, an education for intellectual responsibility. Above all it was a political education in the fullest sense of that term, for it placed the *polis* in its temporal, spatial and cultural context and provided the skills of discourse which made public action possible. It was a source of shared metaphor.[13] During the century classical studies therefore became less narrowly utilitarian, more literary. Latin prose was neglected in favour of poetry in both Latin and Greek. The Augustan was merging into the Neo-Classical Age. Verse-composition became the hallmark of classical culture, and the much-quoted rebuke of an Eton master in the 1840s retains its ultimate justification in eighteenth-century terms: 'If you do not take more pains, how can you ever expect to write good longs and shorts? If you do not write good longs and shorts, how can you ever be a man of taste? If you are not a man of taste, how can you ever be of use in the world?'[14] Young Fitzjames Stephen probably remembered this reprimand because he thought it to be ridiculous. By his time the idea of taste was already acquiring that weak sense which a century of eclecticism, relativism and subjectivism had given it. But eighteenth-century classical education held in constructive synthesis concepts of taste and permanence, of antiquity and contemporary political responsibility, of progress and order, and it had to work through institutions which were already traditional but in some respects still precarious. It is too often stated that the grammar schools decayed in the eighteenth century, but the London experience of their varying fortunes rather demonstrates overall their achievements in continuing, establishing and developing the traditions of classical learning. This bequeathed to the nineteenth century the problem of devising educational change in the context of a securely entrenched classical curriculum, but also the men of distinction who were able to some extent to meet the challenge. Scholarship in the late eighteenth century and early nineteenth century was adding dimensions to classical learning. Porson and his like were bringing to Greek texts the exact critical purification which Bentley had brought to Roman authors, and the historical criticism of literary sources was spreading slowly from Germany, eventually being applied to the Biblical as well as classical documents. Until historical was added to textual criticism the ideas of the Enlightenment could not be fully applied to the documentary foundations of Western civilization. But it took some time for such new ideas and emphases to spread down through educational institutions, and this late eighteenth-century period was therefore crucial for the classical curriculum at all levels.[15]

The contribution of schools in London and its environs to this overall achievement was varied, and within the period of the later seventeenth and through the eighteenth and early nineteenth centuries many had reversals of fortune. The disturbances of the Interregnum and Restoration on the whole did more to stimulate alternative kinds of schooling than to weaken the grammar schools. Some masters were ejected. Robert Brooke, schoolmaster at Charterhouse, was ejected in 1643 – but then he was said to have flogged some of the boys for supporting the Parliamentary cause.[16] John Boncle, headmaster from 1651, was a supporter of the Parliamentary cause, moved to Eton in 1654, and was ejected from his Fellowship there in 1660, but his friends secured him the mastership of the Mercers' School, where he stayed for fifteen years.[17] At Highgate Thomas Carter was dismissed in 1644, it was alleged for drunkenness, but he had already served a term of imprisonment for using the Book of Common Prayer and speaking against Parliament – and Ireton was one of the governors. Carter was reinstated in 1660.[18] William Dugard of Merchant Taylors' was in trouble during the Commonwealth and perhaps spent some time in Newgate, where Milton was said to have reasoned with him. But his political position appears to have been ambiguous, for he also fell foul of authority in 1660 and was dismissed. He was however allowed to open a private school in Coleman Street.[19] Singleton of Eton was a somewhat similar case, in that he was ejected from Eton, kept a private school in Clerkenwell, and then after being made master of Reading School at the Restoration, again had to leave, partly because of his Presbyterianism, and opened a private school in St Mary Axe, which was popular with dissenters.[20] Christ's Hospital and Chigwell also suffered ejections.[21] On the whole, however, the London schools support those historians who minimize the impact of political interference on the grammar schools in these troubled times. The most notable cases of continuity were St Paul's and Westminster. At St Paul's the puritan John Langley, 'A great antiquary, a most judicious divine', was High Master from 1640 to 1657, and on his deathbed recommended his successor, Samuel Cromleholme (Pepys's Mr Crumlum) who kept the office till 1672.[22] At Westminster, the scholarly and redoubtable Dr Busby remained from 1638 until his death (in an unhealthy spring) in 1695. He courageously kept his Royalist sympathies, praying openly for Charles I on the morning of his execution, and allowing a convenient sickness to prevent his having to take the Covenant. This appearance of conformity enabled Parliamentarians to support and use the school, and in 1647 John Locke's father, a captain in their Army, got his son a place.[23]

The Restoration did not on the whole bring much benefit to the schools. Charles II made some unsuccessful attempts to exert his authority, bringing pressure to bear upon Eton, and trying to foist an unwelcome Warden on the Fellows of Alleyn's Foundation, who by pure chance were enabled to preserve a façade of both compliance and resistance. In 1686 James II tried to force a Roman Catholic Master on the Merchant Taylors but they shrewdly 'adopted a Fabian Policy' and the King withdrew his nominee. He also tried to nominate a Roman Catholic pensioner to Charterhouse, but the governors stood firm. There was a lively episode during the Popish Plot which deprived both Merchant Taylors' and Owen's Schools of their Masters. Titus Oates had been expelled from Merchant Taylors' when the Reverend John Goad was High Master and William Smith the Usher. Oates took his revenge by accusing them both of Popery. Goad, who was a successful master and had taken the school through the disasters of the Plague and the Fire and kept it in being at Kentish Town until the rebuilding, was dismissed by the Company but 'he took a house in Piccadily in Westminster to which place many of the genteeler of his scholars repairing to be by him further instructed, he set up a private school . . .'.

Goad kept this till his death in spite of the fact that he did indeed become a Roman Catholic. The Brewers likewise had to dismiss Smith, who had become Master of Owen's School, but gave him a testimonial of good conduct. Merchant Taylors' suffered another loss when Ambrose Bonwicke, a most able scholar, declared himself a non-juror, but was allowed to teach privately.[24]

English education however owes many of its unique features to the determination of the real rulers of eighteenth-century England to reduce central state powers to the minimum. In contrast to contemporary Europe with its so-called 'Enlightened Despots', in England there was no authority to attempt or desire a coherent provision or policy for education at any level. Probably more important for the grammar schools therefore than direct central interference was the ultimate curbing of the power of the ecclesiastical courts and of the Crown. Episcopal licensing, long intermittent, lapsed. The Clarendon Code operated fitfully and unevenly. Parliament and the civil courts were unprepared to exercise control; 'Far from being crippled by too restrictive an authority, the Grammar Schools suffered from a lack of authority.' Schools were controlled more effectively by local factors, by the strength of the general belief that they were designed to serve the communities in which they were placed.[25]

The progress or decline of each school must therefore be related to its locality within the broad setting of London's expansion. The type of foundation, the means of its government, brought further variety, and an all-important factor was the efficiency and success of the master, which could make or break a small local school, and had immense effect on the civic or 'great' schools which drew boys from a wider area. The prestige of the teacher was what counted with parents. All these variables must be set against a declining interest in university learning, numbers at Oxford and Cambridge falling in spite of increasing population, and an economic background of rising prices and relative decline in the value of endowments, especially when these were in country lands. This was sometimes aggravated by mismanagement or neglect, and by competition for interest and funds coming from other kinds of education, especially the charity schools.[26] Chigwell is an example of these economic pressures. In the early eighteenth century the school was in financial difficulties from the depreciation of its Norfolk lands. The governors were obliged to lower the staff salaries, that of the master of the Latin School from £20 to £8 17s, and the usher of the English School from £25 to £10 3s. They were therefore allowed to supplement their incomes by taking fee-paying pupils and in 1712 the trust was changed to reduce the number of free places in both schools. The salaries were not restored until imminent enclosure raised the value of the property, but by that time the practice of taking private pupils and boarders was established and in its golden age from 1768 under Peter Burford the school was predominantly fee-paying. This pleasant forest area was attractive to parents.[27]

In some ways this case was typical of what has been called 'Classics or

Colfe's Grammar School, Lewisham, 1831

Charity, the dilemma of the 18th-century grammar school'.[28] In these more rural communities, and with poorer or smaller foundations, if the master offered free classical teaching there was little or no demand from the pupils entitled to it from the charity. If he took paying pupils who wanted the classical teaching provided for by the foundation, he was failing in its charitable intention. Under this stress some, such as Highgate, became little more than elementary schools, others such as Lewisham and Camberwell became boarding- or day schools for boys from rather more wealthy or aspiring families. The problem had appeared by the middle of the seventeenth century,[29] but is often used to characterize the decline and failure of the eighteenth-century schools. It is true that some endowments, such as that at Lambeth,[30] did disappear during this period of political and legal disturbance, or dwindled into sinecures – this happened at Croydon and to some extent at Dulwich. It might be suggested however that the schools which continued to function were doing some service to their local communities and to London as a whole by adapting themselves. In the London region a number of schools also did in a modest way keep to the founder's intentions. Enfield had a successful period under the Reverend John Allen (1732–61) and the Reverend Samuel Hardy (1762–91).[31] Tottenham, which had only become a grammar school in 1692, seems to have kept its status.[32] Hampton, also transformed into a grammar school at the end of the seventeenth century, quietly continued to teach at least some classics.[33] Some foundations, which had been designed for a less ambitious kind of education, were more readily able to continue to meet changing needs: Owen's at Islington, for example, a village which was greatly stimulted by urban expansion and also served one of the skilled industrial areas of the City. For much of the century Latin was after all still of modest utility and other subjects were also provided. This school had the benefit of government by the Brewers' Company, and though the local Vestry challenged its management, a prolonged lawsuit decided in favour of the Company in 1718. The school's fortunes were however not really established until David Davies (1750–91) succeeded an unsatisfactory run of masters. Continuity and reasonably conscientious management were of no avail without a good teacher.[34]

The Southwark schools substantiate these points. St Olave's parish was one of those divided by the Act of Queen Anne's reign to provide for new churches in populous areas, and in 1733 St John's Horsleydown was created. Careful arrangements were made to entitle inhabitants of the new parish to use the schools, and the attention given to their right to provide a proportion of governors shows the importance given to such positions of local control, here not only of the Latin but also the Writing and the Reading Schools. Steady pressure of expanding population gave importance to the governors' powers of patronage. On the whole the management appears to have been assiduous and reasonably efficient, though there is an inevitable whiff of Georgian scandal and jobbery and at one point something of a pamphlet war – a Hogarth print on a postage stamp. The grammar school of St Olave's had always been modest in standing, but it appears to have maintained enough pupils to justify the continued employment of a Latin usher as well as the Master, and from the year when numbers are recorded, 1776, kept between 50 and 60 boys. Very few, however, went on to the university. Numbers in the writing and the reading schools were always far larger, reaching nearly 200 by the end of the century, and apprenticeships were eagerly sought.

St Saviour's Grammar School had to be entirely rebuilt after the disastrous Southwark fire of 1676. In 1690 the Reverend William Symes, 'a distinguished scholar of Balliol', became Master and immediately the number of boys enrolled rose. Soon the school had its full complement of 100 scholars and it remained full until his death in 1734, at first with parish boys or those nearby – Lambeth, Newington, and so on – but after his first ten years, from further afield – Croydon, Tooting, Reigate, Dartford, Cuckfield and Steyning in Sussex – and in his fourth decade even from as far as Somerset. Symes sent 13 scholars to the university and entered after his list of them an adaptation from Horace and Juvenal: 'These names show that even in a land of dolts and under a heavy sky learned men can be born', Southwark becoming Boeotia in his classical perspective.

After Symes's death the school did go through a period of decline under bad or indifferent masters, until 1794 when the Reverend W. L.

Fancourt began a revival. Even during this period the school could contribute to the education of scholars of distinction. William van Mildert (1765–1836), the future Bishop of Durham and founder of its University, was at St Saviour's from the age of eight until fourteen, when he was transferred to Merchant Taylors'.[35] But the historian of these useful schools prefaces his account of this period with the inevitable section on the 'Decline of the Grammar Schools, 1660–1819'.[36]

Merchant Taylors'

In writing of the greater civic schools the 'decay theory' is accommodated somewhat differently. The historian of Merchant Taylors' paints the usual picture, but adds 'Amid the general stagnation the London schools kept up their efficiency and their numbers.'[37] This particular school grew steadily, from 275 boys in 1658, to 342 in 1698 – the governors then had to reduce numbers because of overcrowding. From 1731 numbers declined for a time when the Master was suspected of Jacobite sympathies, but from 1760 to 1778 James Townley, a friend of Garrick, restored its reputation and it soon had its full 250 boys. Its high reputation brought boys from all over the country to be prepared for its valuable scholarships to St John's Oxford, and in 1750 the Company ordered that no boy could be a candidate who had entered above the fourth form. Even before that date late entry had been a disadvantage. John Byron came in 1707 from Chester School and found 29 boys in 'the Sixth – 6 at Table, 10 in the Bench, and 13 in the First Rank' – these being the labels recently acquired by the Captain, monitors and 'promptors'. Only 4 of these got St John's places, but 21 went to university, Byron to Trinity College, Cambridge.[38] Recent analysis of the school register shows that during this century the occupations of the boys' parents showed a gradual shift from merchant, manufacturer, artisan to professional, clerical, book-keeping, scrivener, not necessarily a take-over by higher ranks of society, but reflecting closely the changing occupational structure of London, where manufacturing industry was becoming comparatively less important, and more specialized financial and professional occupations were replacing more general mercantile enterprises. The Christ's Hospital admissions show a somewhat similar trend but were less likely to mirror London's social and economic developments, for this was a national institution, and the number of boys from outside the capital grew sharply in the second half of the century.[39] The history of St Paul's supports the same general conclusion that the City schools continued to fulfil their civic purposes. From 1672, when the school had recently been reopened after its destruction in the Great Fire, until 1713, Thomas Gale and then John Postlethwaite maintained it as 'one of the great educational centres of the country'.[40] These High Masters were scholars of national reputation, and noblemen and landed gentry from all over the country sent their sons to them. Then came a period of decline under incompetent or less distinguished men, and when in 1748 George Thicknesse was made High Master there were only 35 pupils in the whole school. Thicknesse had been a master of Clare's Academy in Soho Square, and then kept his own private school in Charterhouse Square. Soon a revival began: the school was filled even to its eighth form, largely now with boys from City families. Of the 950 boys admitted in his time only 65 were not Londoners. 'Grocer, Coffeeman, Watchmaker, Perruque-Maker, Wig-Maker, Hosier, Hot-Presser, Farrier, Wine-Couper, Carman, Coach-Maker, Apothecary, Hoop-Bender, Waterman, Scrivener, Victualler, Hat-Maker and Tobacconist' were among recorded parental occupations. Many (about 10 per cent) went on to the universities. The next high master, Richard Roberts (1769–1814), nominated by his predecessor, was also successful and during his long reign St Paul's once more became less metropolitan, and nearly double the proportion of non-Londoners passed through the school. This may be why in 1773 the Mercers resolved that no scholar could petition for an exhibition to the university 'until he shall have been a full Four Years in the school upon the Foundation . . .'.[41]

London's contribution to national education by taking provincial boys into its schools was long established and in turn London, largely replenished in population by immigrants, drew on the educational resources of the regions. A general conclusion that London citizens were on the whole reasonably well-served by their ancient schools must be interpreted in relation to their aspirations for their sons. University learning was the aim of the school curriculum but most wished for something more modest – enough Latin to hold up their heads in an Augustan age and for practical purposes, other subjects for more vocational needs.

Most parents of any substance were prepared to pay something towards their sons' schooling until fourteen or sixteen but were ready enough to accept patronage. The evidence does not allow any precision of calculation of the number or the status of free scholars in relation to those who made payments of some sort. Christ's Hospital is an exception but even here six masters might take six private pupils apiece.[42] Merchant Taylors' had its sliding scale of fees, the 153 scholars of St Paul's had never been exempt from some costs. Throughout the century when there was demand boys not on the foundation were admitted and were 'passed on to the foundation' after a year or two as vacancies occurred.[43] In the smaller schools of Southwark and surrounding villages, free classical instruction can rarely be disentangled from payments for boarding, subjects such as mathematics or French which were not 'on the foundation', or 'extras' such as fencing or dancing.

The 'Great Schools'

Grammar schools in London and its region were thus far from moribund during this century. In this same period certain London schools played a key part in developments in the education of the sons of the political ranks of society, those who were taking a national perspective in a country still in the earlier part of the century largely bounded by local horizons. Noble and gentry families based their power upon their estates and had in the seventeenth century often identified their political activities as much with their communities as with national politics. For them local or regional grammar schools had largely replaced the idea of chivalric or household education. Those who took a larger perspective often retained the old household tradition or looked perhaps naturally to a royal foundation such as Eton, or felt a brief attraction for the experiments with courtly academies, for national political activity still largely centred on the monarch and the Court. By the eighteenth century social and constitutional changes required a reinterpretation of political and public education. Some endowed schools, partly because their free places were not tied to locality, partly because of prestige or wealth of foundation or reputation for learning, were well placed for serving these families. St Paul's as we have seen was so used in the later seventeenth century, but during the Hanoverian period reasserted its civic purpose. London however was still the political arena and centre of national consciousness and possessed one school of supreme importance, Westminster; another, the Charterhouse, solidly established; and out in its countryside another, Harrow, which during the century moved into this category. Eton cannot be considered in the London orbit, though near enough for its influence to be felt more keenly than in the country as a whole.

London therefore made an important contribution to this development of the 'Great Schools', which had such profound and lasting effects on English secondary education. The metropolis of both the City and Westminster had been the natural setting for experiments with courtly academies, but the court gallant of the seventeenth century became the young man-about-town of the eighteenth century. While both species were probably equally objectionable to sober citizens and precarious resources of civil order, this mutation symbolized a fundmental change in political structure. And just at the time of the Whig triumph over the Crown a topographical accident emphasized the divergence of Court and City. Whitehall Palace was burnt down, the regular presence of the court was withdrawn from the capital and William III and his Georgian successors preferred to reside at Kensington or Hampton Court. Not till George III bought Buckingham House in 1762 did the sovereign reside again within the Westminster orbit, and this was to be a private, not a public, residence. This contingency coincided with a profound shift in the idea of a political education. The Victorian historian of Westminster School developed the point: '. . . before the Civil War the School drew but few boys from the class of hereditary politicians. Such statesmen as she trained rose . . . from the ranks of the squires. The King's wards and the sons of the great houses had their education in a French academy or with a domestic tutor.' Had courtly academies succeeded, 'the sons of the nobility and wealthier gentry would at School have been separated from the sons of the clergyman, the lawyer and the merchant . . . The man of action and the man of learning must in time come to the parting of the ways, but it is well that they should start together.'[44]

Westminster played a key part in the change that took place, for not only were the governors of the Interregnum unlikely to be interested in courtly academies, but Presbyterian and Puritan respect for learning, Dr Busby's great reputation, and the very nearness of the school to the scene of constitutional struggle and controversies, and its survival through them, gave significance to the fact that Parliamentary leaders preserved it and even sent their sons to it. With the Restoration it became even more usual for such schools to be used by the governing ranks. 'By the end of Busby's time Westminster was become a nursery of statesmen.' The change took time – in the reign of Queen Anne the complaint was still made that in England 'a boy must be bred either in

Westminster School

pedantry or in foppery'. But in the heyday of the Grand Whiggery the Great Schools were commonly though by no means universally used by these families.[45]

It is true that many arguments for 'domestic education' were advanced, and for some parents the ideas of Locke were influential. There was certainly no convention that a boy must go to 'the right school' – such a notion would have been entirely alien to the aristocratic temper of the age. Researches have however confirmed the impressions of the older style of school historians, who placed such heavy emphasis on lists of 'distinguished old boys'. Taking as a sample the ministers of state of the last quarter of the eighteenth century, it has been calculated that *at least* 72 per cent had been at either Eton or Westminster, and of the thirteen politicians who had not been at either of these, one was at Charterhouse and one at Harrow.[46]

Significant for the development of secondary schooling, the future men of action and of learning did share a common curriculum, that of all grammar schools which had maintained their classical status in however modest a style. In England functional differentiation between classical schools was to be by the aspirations and to some extent the social position of those who used them, and not by curriculum. The 'Great

Christ's Hospital

Schools' were by no means clearly defined. A school could move in or out of this category very quickly according usually to the efficiency and reputation of the master. But by the end of the century there was a clear distinction between these schools (whichever they happened to be at any one time) and the rest. In this way the schools of the eighteenth century, still serving an hierarchical, pre-industrial society, prepared the way for the nineteenth-century interpretation of secondary schooling in terms of social class. The later stages of this process moved out into the countryside, but its early development was centred on London, where cultural pre-eminence and wealth of endowments underwrote and re-warded those standards of classical scholarship which were by far the most important ingredients of a 'Great School', what was later to be called a 'public school'.

Although in many respects this school was a-typical, for most boys left very young, the best-loved national memories of the quality and style of this education are contained in the experiences of Charles Lamb and Samuel Coleridge at Christ's Hospital. There in the shadows of Newgate and Smithfield in the 1780s the son of a London scrivener and the orphan of an impractical west-country clergyman shared the languid and kindly neglect of the undermaster, who 'came among us now and then' but largely left them to their own mirth and uproar. Coleridge then moved into the contrasting system, across an invisible line in the great schoolroom, of the upper grammar master, the Reverend James Boyer. 'Woe to the school, when he made his morning appearance in his *passy*, or *passionate* wig.' As a 'Grecian', one of the small minority of boys working for a scholarship to Cambridge, Coleridge was not only given by him a sound classical knowledge but learnt that 'Poetry, even that of the loftiest and, seemingly, that of the wildest odes, had a logic of its own, as severe as that of science . . .'. In spite of physical hardship and miseries of homesickness Coleridge enjoyed his linguistic, literary, philosophic and geometric studies. Christ's Hospital was an exceptional school, and Coleridge an exceptional pupil. But in teaching and curriculum its classical grammar school conformed to the usual pattern, and London is entitled to its credit for contributing to the education of the two 'seminal minds' which helped to shape the nineteenth century – here Coleridge, and at Westminster, Bentham.[47]

Harrow as a case study demonstrates more typical developments and characteristics of these 'Great Schools'. Its very rise to eminence had political implications when after the Hanoverian succession in 1714 it was favoured by the Whig aristocracy, Tory Eton being tainted with Jacobitism. In 1713 the future Duke of Chandos who had 'outstanding business capacity' became a governor and put its finances in order. A wider-than-local reputation had been built up under Thomas Brian, Master from 1691 to 1730; but numbers then fluctuated under unsatis-factory Masters until 1746 when Dr Thackeray became Master. He fostered his connections with Whig families by giving aristocratic pupils special privileges and allowing assistant masters or private tutors to charge fees for non-classical subjects. His successor, Robert Sumner (1760–71), had to restore discipline after a bold challenge to influential parents and the proprietors of the boarding-houses which they patro-nized, but he retained the private tutors and under him numbers rose to 230 and then nearly 360. Fees were high and most of the boys were 'independent of the foundation'. Some local disquiet was felt about this. In 1785 when a new headmaster was to be chosen some of the governors consulted the Visitor, the Archbishop of Canterbury, about the restor-ation of 'the original intention of the donor'. Though 'the parish of Harrow is nearly 30 miles in circumference and contains near 3000 inhabitants, it gives us much concern that not one boy belonging to the said parish is now on the foundation'. 'Foreigners' had always been allowed, but they had 'entirely engrossed the school to themselves. . . . Young gentlemen from other parts of the Kingdom have driven the parishoners from the school'. Others of the governors argued that the trust was not being perverted, for the 'literary improvement' which it specified was not desired by the inhabitants, who were deterred by the expense of the universities from wanting 'a learned education for their children . . . a little classical knowledge can be of no service to a farmer or a mechanic'. The Archbishop returned no very decisive answer to this 'Classics or Charity' dilemma but on the whole supported those governors who wished to receive 'foreigners' according to the provision of the founder. A Chancery case of 1806 reached much the same conclusion, and seems to have been largely due to resentment about estate management and enclosures. The school allotment of eight acres for a cricket field became the focus of discontent. Harrow by the end of the eighteenth century was firmly established as one of the Great Schools, and under Joseph Drury (1785–1805) contained for a time more pupils than Eton. Some local boys continued to attend.[48]

The particular qualities of these Great Schools at this period are illustrated in the career of one of the eighteenth century's great eccentrics, Samuel Parr (1747–1825), the 'Whig Dr Johnson'. Educated at Harrow as a town boy, when very young he became one of its masters, but was disappointed of its headship in 1771, perhaps because he had voted for Wilkes at the Middlesex election. Thereupon some of his pupils rebelled against the governors and enabled him to establish a private school nearby at Stanmore. This was run on Harrow lines, and reminiscences of its pupils enable us to reconstruct the system – the use of classics to develop other studies and interests, emphasis on Greek studies, the 'studious cultivation, out of school hours and on holidays, of our own copious and beautiful language', the writing of themes on ethics, history, even theology. Discipline in school was strict, but in leisure time the boys ranged over the neighbourhood and its public houses and maintained their jockey club. Parr's school was not however successful and Johnson considered its opening the crisis of Parr's life; he was glad after five years to accept the mastership of the endowed school at Colchester.[49]

It is difficult to summarize the essence of the Great Schools of this period and no one school would display all their characteristics. The high standards and expectation of linguistic and literary studies, what the age called scholarship, came first, with the emphasis increasingly on Greek studies. Secondly, the republican nature of the community of boys was important; in scholastic matters the master was an acknowledged autocrat but interference with boys' leisure time or with social relationships and the hierarchy within their number was not expected, nor usually tolerated. Two further rebellions at Harrow were caused by attempts to regulate the abuses inevitable in such a situation – one led by Byron even contemplated blowing up the headmaster, but decided this might spoil the panelling on which former boys had carved their names.[50] Within this republic, while there was little equality between boys of different ages or prowess, there was usually little distinction on the grounds of rank. 'Foundationers' or 'Collegers' or 'Scholars' or 'Gownboys' were often segregated in living quarters from 'Oppidans' or 'Townboys', but while their conditions were often Spartan, even brutal, compared with those in dames' houses and so forth, this division cut across any of social standing or even of wealth. Parr's experience as a boy at Harrow was of this kind and this egalitarian element was remarked on at the time. 'In a free intercourse with equals', the stately prose of the Westminster-educated Gibbon claimed, 'the habits of truth, fortitude and prudence will insensibly be matured: birth and riches are measured by the standard of personal merit: and the mimic scene of rebellion has displayed in their true colours the ministers and patriots of the rising generation.' English travellers noted and criticized the special privileges given to rank in continental schools: 'The public schools in England disdain this mean partiality.'[51] However much in practice it may have been modified, this ideal draws attention to the importance which the training of character was given in these schools, something different from moral or religious education, and a curiously distinctive quality in English schools ever since. In the eighteenth century the character admired was robust, rational, sociable, prudent, hard-riding, hard-hitting – and would perhaps be best displayed in parliament or on the hunting field. But it also included gentler virtues, and when Parr claimed that his success with boys was due to his treating them as young gentlemen, he was referring not to their social position, but their moral autonomy.

Whatever the achievements of the endowed schools of this period, however, they had grave defects. The first was the restricted curriculum. In 1807 Lord Eldon's judgment in the Leeds Grammar School case inhibited attempts to widen the classical curriculum in endowed schools. London endowments often provided for more than the classical languages, and writing masters were sometimes employed for boys who were prepared to pay for their services – for example at St Paul's. The Mercers' School seems to have included English in the curriculum and so did Christ's Hospital.[52] It is most difficult to decide, or discover, what English in general meant in terms of content and skills. Coleridge described how Boyer 'made us read Shakespeare and Milton as lessons' while studying Greek tragedy ' . . . and they were the lessons, too, which required most time and trouble to *bring up*, so as to escape his censure'. Busby at Westminster encouraged English and mathematics.[53] Merchant Taylors', confined not by Statutes or Charter but by the views of the Court of the Company, however, had to wait for the introduction of mathematics until the challenge of University and King's College Schools had strengthened the case the headmaster, Bellamy, made to the Court as late as 1829. 'I conclude that we ought as far as possible to be upon a level with other places of education.' He advocated that the whole school should be taught arithmetic and the two top forms study geometry, algebra and mechanics. Extra 'quarter-age' would be needed and mathematics tutors were duly appointed, and from 1830 classical teaching was confined to the morning, and each afternoon given to mathematics.[54] While, therefore, it would be a mistake to judge the curriculum of endowed and classical schools on other than their own grounds, this delay illustrates one of their chief defects.

The other may also be illustrated from Merchant Taylors'. The Com-

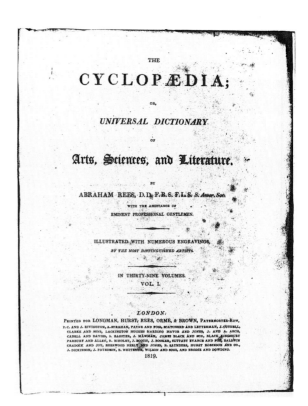

THE

CYCLOPÆDIA;

OR,

UNIVERSAL DICTIONARY

OF

Arts, Sciences, and Literature.

BY

ABRAHAM REES, D.D. F.R.S. F.L.S. S. Amer. Soc.

WITH THE ASSISTANCE OF
EMINENT PROFESSIONAL GENTLEMEN.

ILLUSTRATED WITH NUMEROUS ENGRAVINGS,
BY THE MOST DISTINGUISHED ARTISTS.

IN THIRTY-NINE VOLUMES.
VOL. I.

LONDON:
PRINTED FOR LONGMAN, HURST, REES, ORME, & BROWN, PATERNOSTER-ROW,
F.C. AND J. RIVINGTON, A. STRAHAN, PAYNE AND FOSS, SCATCHERD AND LETTERMAN, J. CUTHELL,
CLARKE AND SONS, LACKINGTON HUGHES HARDING MAVOR AND JONES, J. AND A. ARCH,
CADELL AND DAVIES, S. BAGSTER, J. MAWMAN, JAMES BLACK AND SON, BLACK KINGSBURY
PARBURY AND ALLEN, R. SCHOLEY, J. BOOTH, J. BOOKER, SUTTABY EVANCE AND FOX, BALDWIN
CRADOCK AND JOY, SHERWOOD NEELY AND JONES, R. SAUNDERS, HURST ROBINSON AND CO.,
J. DICKINSON, J. PATERSON, E. WHITMORE, WILSON AND SONS, AND BRODIE AND DOWDING.
1819.

3 The knowledge of the Enlightenment organized and digested in *The Cyclopaedia, or Universal Dictionary* (1819) by Abraham Rees, tutor at London dissenting academies

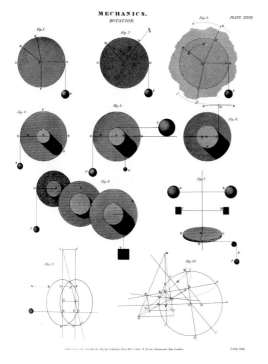

This new map of learning contributed to the birth of modern education

Salvadore Academy, Tooting, 1787

The playground at University College School, *c.* 1830

4 Private and new public schools reflect the ideas of the Age of Reason – a new understanding of children and a utilitarian and secular education.

pany and endowed schools were an integral part of that network of patronage which bound the old society together, and kept it in the service both of the State and of the Established Church. To matriculate at Oxford, or graduate at Cambridge, compliance with Anglican doctrines was necessary. Many dissenting boys attended the endowed schools, but if they hoped to gain the richest prizes, they must conform. Edmund Calamy, the historian of dissent, himself a grateful pupil of Merchant Taylors', records one instance of this, when under the headship of John Hartcliffe (1681-6) the Bishop of Winchester, the President of St John's Oxford, and other divines were examining the upper boys for Oxford scholarships and discovered that one Joseph Kentish was the son of a dissenting minister.

> They asked Mr Kentish whether he was free to receive the Sacrament in the Established Church? Telling him that, without that . . . he had better not think of the University. . . . He modestly made answer, that he had not, as yet, received the Sacrament anywhere; not being satisfied as to his being fit or qualified for so solemn an ordinance: and, he added, that as for conformity in all things to the Church of England, it was a thing of weight, and that he could not but think it would be a great weakness in him to pretend to determine or promise it, without mature and close consideration. One of the members of the Company of Merchant Taylors, a warm man, then present, cried out that he should not wonder to hear, that one that canted at that rate at eighteen, should be ready to rebel by the time he was thirty.

The boy was passed over for a less able candidate.[55] There must have been many such schoolboy Hampdens whose courage and brief tragedy lie unrecorded in the history of the endowed schools.

Nonconformist academies

The dissenting communities had to provide for the higher education of their sons and for the training of their ministries, and in doing so they made an important and distinctive contribution to the theory and practice of what today we recognize as the secondary and tertiary stages of education and their interpenetration. If London's endowed schools contributed significantly to the achievements of the Augustan Age, its Nonconformist academies were an important aspect of the European Enlightenment.

Unravelling the topographical history of these remarkable academies is far from easy, but is not irrelevant to their educational importance. They continued the work of those City parishes which had been the powerhouses of the Puritan Revolution and where academies for the training of zealous ministers had begun – Rotherhithe and Hackney for example.[56] They became a feature of metropolitan education almost immediately after the Restoration in spite of the operations of the so-called Clarendon Code and the 'nervous and violent' public opinion which it reflected.[57] Some earliest examples were in the outer fringe of villages: Richard Swift (1616–1701) who was ejected from Edgware in 1660 kept an academy in Hendon (Mill Hill) for which he paid tax for six hearths in 1662,[58] Thomas Goodwin, son of the President of Magdalen College Oxford, had an academy at Pinner from about 1690–1716[59] Other academies however were well within the Five Mile Act's range and had therefore to move frequently to avoid persecution or to preserve a decent semblance of observance.[60] At this stage they were in some respects transitory for it was not generally realized that Nonconformity would become a recognized element in church and society. Some areas quickly became centres of dissenting education and the academies became in some measure institutionalized. The support and even the protection of the mercantile community of the City played a part, and the suburbs and villages closest to the City and most favoured as residences and resorts contained the most important examples. Hoxton in Shoreditch was celebrated for its conventicles, which 'met behind locked doors, often fitted with peep-holes, and guarded by look-outs'.[61] Hoxton Square, begun in 1674 in the best and most fashionable district of Shoreditch, contained at one time and another three important academies. Islington, with Clerkenwell and Stoke Newington, was another favourite district. James Burgess, ejected from Ashprington, Devon, kept a boarding-house at Islington for the sons of citizens who went to Singleton's academy at Clerkenwell. The Reverend Robert Ferguson, formerly vicar of Godmanston in Kent, 'taught university learning in Islington'. Mr Jonathan Grew of Pembroke Hall Cambridge was 'engaged for some time in a school' at Newington Green. A Presbyterian congregation was established in this parish soon after 1660, and although there was no regular minister until 1688, such men as these were supported in their labours by this 'devoted flock' and supplemented their 'pulpit labours' by teaching in this 'succession of academies'. The Reverend Ralph Button had an academy here from 1672 to his death in 1680, almost certainly of university level.[62] At Newington Green the Reverend Charles Morton's academy lasted from before 1675 to about 1706 and was an 'open academy', that is taking some pupils who were neither Nonconformist nor intended for the ministry, and providing an advanced education for boys who usually had a good knowledge of classics before they entered. It gave in fact a university equivalent course lasting about five years, and students included dissenters such as Daniel Defoe, and those like Samuel Wesley who had failed to enter Oxford; Wesley wrote of his fellow students that many were 'persons of quality, not a few knights' and baronets' sons and one Lord's son, who were sent hither to avoid the debaucheries of the universities though some of 'em made themselves sufficiently remarkable while they were with us'. The academies were considered morally superior to the universities. Morton's 'most considerable' academy with about 50 students in residence was in a large well-appointed mansion, with accommodation for a library, 'having annexe a fine garden, Bowling Green, Fish Pond, and within, a laboratory and some not inconsiderable rareties, with an air pump, thermometer, and all sorts of mathematical instruments'. The students lived with tutors who took suitable houses nearby and some kind of student self-government was attempted, perhaps not altogether successfully, though allowance must be made for Samuel Wesley's dislike of a 'sort of democratical government'.

The history of this academy is somewhat obscure but when in 1685 Morton went to New England he was said to have kept it for twenty years. In America he became pastor of the church and then vice president of the college at Harvard, and drew up systems and textbooks on logic and physics like those he had used in England. At Islington he was succeeded as tutor by Stephen Lobb, William Wickens, and Francis Glascock, who died in 1706. The academy dissolved at his death, or a little earlier.

This ranked as the chief academy of the Independents in London. Morton himself was called by a contemporary 'the very soul of philosophy', 'whose memory was as vast as his knowledge', 'a pious learned and ingenious man, of a sweet natural temper and a generous public spirit; beloved and valued by all that knew him'. In philosophy he sought a middle way between the Calvinist and Platonist positions and he was remarkable for his tolerance and breadth of vision, advising the candidates whom he prepared for the ministry to read widely, to realize that the Church may be served by persons of very diverse temperaments and to concentrate 'humbly and wisely' on the use of notes for 'Gospel Preaching', avoiding moral and philosophical lectures. He was renowned for his mathematics, and had scientific interests – his proposal for the use of sea-sand to improve the poor soil of Cornwall was published in the Transactions of the Royal Society. His successor Wickens was an authority on oriental and Jewish studies. The curriculum was wide. Defoe who went when he was fourteen claimed that he became master of five languages and had studied mathematics, natural philosophy, logic and 'politics as a science', from a textbook by Morton, the *Eutaxia*, 'exhibiting the principles of politics exactly correspondent to the English Constitution, asserting at once the rights and honour of the crown, and the liberty of the subject'. Defoe's only criticism of academies in general was the 'want of conversation' compared with the universities and the neglect of the mother tongue. But Morton gave all his lectures in English, somewhat unusual at that time, and 'though the scholars from that place are not destitute in the languages, yet it is observed of them, they were by this made masters of the English tongue and more of them excelled in that particular, than of any school at that time'. In all, Defoe was well content with his education and in his reply to Tutchin, who had accused him of being no scholar, confidently challenged him to a contest, 'to show before the world how much Daniel Defoe, hosier, is inferior to Mr Tutchin, gentleman'.

Morton himself said that he sought to 'enable and incline the mind of man' by studies which would encourage intellectual and moral habits, to alter his 'genius and spirit' according to the information met with, especially in younger days. Logic and metaphysic would give sharpness of judgement; mathematics, solidness and sagacity; physics, 'good conjecture at the reasons of things'; moral philosophy and history, prudence; rhetoric, firmness and confidence of address; poetry, quickness of fancy and imagination. This wide course was approached in a spirit of toleration and with the emphasis on free enquiry by the students. Subscription as a condition of study was to Morton 'securing the key of knowledge and tying it fast to some men's girdles, or making it too hot or heavy for others to touch on any terms', which might 'well enough comport with popish designs to keep people in the dark, that they may lead them more quietly by the nose'. He was 'willing to have knowledge increased and not only confined to the clergy, or learned professions, but extended or diffused as much as might be to the people in general'. This is particularly significant in the light of Morton's opinions on the place of dissenting academies in the national life, a temporary need of certain sections of society.

> We are not altogether without hope that the Private Readings (in the academies) will be subordinate to the Publick (in the universities). At present it may perhaps stir a noble emulation. A poor Hackney may put a Race-Horse upon his brisker career . . . [Hereafter] our Superiors being . . . convinced of the peaceableness, and it may be, of the probable usefulness of the Non-conformists, may at last incline to be favourable . . . will not these stones that are now but hewing and preparing in the Mountains be all brought to the Universities to be there laid orderly in the Fabrick? Will not these Private Students come all to supplicate their Publick Graces, when they can receive them without incumberance?[63]

Also in Islington from 1672 until about 1707 was the seminary which ranked as the chief Presbyterian academy in London, under Thomas Dolittle. Persecution and the plague had impelled him to move his academy to several places around London, to Islington, Woodford Bridge, Wimbledon, Battersea, Clapham, Clerkenwell and back to Islington or Clerkenwell (1687). This also was an 'open' academy replacing the universities or the higher sort of education at endowed schools, for conformists as well as Nonconformists, and training only some pupils for the ministry. When Samuel Wesley knew the academy it contained between 20 and 30 students. They included Calamy; John

Ker, Thomas Ridgeley and Thomas Rowe who became tutors at other academies; and probably Samuel Jones, who later was tutor at Tewkesbury to Samuel Butler. It may therefore be argued that something of his penetrating insight into the incompleteness and paradoxical nature of scientific reasoning may be traced to Dolittle at Islington. Estimates of Dolittle's quality as a tutor vary – Emlyn called him 'worthy and diligent' rather than 'eminent for knowledge or depth of thought'.[64]

His pupil Thomas Rowe moved as tutor to a nearby academy at Newington Green, which was kept by Theophilus Gale, 'a man of great reading, well conversant with the writings of the Fathers and old philosophers, a learned and industrious person, an exact philologist and philosopher, and a great metaphysician and School Divine'. He was another tutor whose life and thought linked these academies with the old universities and with the school of Cambridge Platonists. He also had experience of French Protestantism, another influence at this period. He spent some time at Caen as tutor to the sons of Lord Wharton. His methods of teaching were perhaps more important than its content, for Gale was a pioneer of the comparative, eclectic approach, strongly opposed to tying up 'students to the confined dogmas of any one sect', encouraging the students' thoughts to 'chuse the channels where they run'. Like Morton, he looked to a time when the students in the academies would be allowed to qualify for degrees at Oxford and Cambridge, and wished the exhibitioners, for whom he provided in his will, to enter their names at some college to be ready to go into residence when the oaths were no longer required. His bequest of his library to Harvard completes his connection with the network of the academies, the ancient universities, Dutch, French and New England Protestantism.

Gale opened his academy at Newington Green in about 1665–6, and persecution caused several migrations including moves to Little Britain and Clapham. In 1678 it was taken over by Thomas Rowe, who kept it as sole tutor from the age of twenty-one until his sudden death in 1705, when this academy, one of the most potent forces in shaping eighteenth-century Nonconformist thought, came to an end. Rowe's pupils included Isaac Watts, who came when he was sixteen and stayed for four years. He was probably referring to his tutor when he said there were few 'who are sufficiently furnished with such *universal learning* as to sustain all the Parts and Provinces of Instruction'. Rowe was the first teacher in England of Cartesianism, and one of the first disciples of Locke. In natural philosophy he followed the rising influence of Newton. The notebooks Watts kept when he was Rowe's student showed according to Johnson 'a degree of knowledge, both philosophical and theological, such as few attain by a much longer course of study'. They were kept in Latin and much of Rowe's instruction appears to have been in that language.[65]

Stepney, Wapping and Bethnal Green were other parishes which contained Nonconformist academies of this early period. One was established by the Reverend Thomas Brand in Bishop's Hall near Bethnal Green where John Ker, who had also been connected with academies at Highgate and Clerkenwell, was tutor. After Brand's death in 1691 Ker carried on the academy with an interval of medical studies at Leyden. He appears not to have been in the regular ministry.[66] Samuel Palmer was one of Ker's students, and from his *Defence of the Academies* in his controversy with Samuel Wesley a detailed picture emerges. The course was planned over three to four years, the first spent mainly on logic, rhetoric, divinity, classics; in the second, logic and some rhetoric were replaced by metaphysics; ethics and natural philosophy were added in the third and fourth. Ker used a large proportion of Dutch authors, and followed the comparative method, using both Aristotle and Descartes, Heereboord and Le Clerc. He was an 'encourager of free and large thoughts'. A number of English texts were used, but daily prayers were in Latin and Ker's pupils had exercise in the formation of 'uncommon elegance, purity of stile, and manly and judicious composures' in the classical languages. Hebrew was not taught. There were probably about 17 students and the academy was 'open' although many were prepared for the ministry.[67]

At Wapping the academy of Edward Veal was established from about 1675 and continued probably till his death. It seems to have had more of a theological character: Samuel Wesley read logic and ethics here before going on to Morton at Newington Green.[68]

One of the most notable of these early 'open' examples was in Hoxton Square from 1699 to about 1729. Its tutors were Joshua Oldfield, William Tonge, John Spademan, William Lorimer, Jacques (or Jean) Cappel. It had moved from Coventry in 1696, first to Southwark and then to Hoxton Square. 'There was no house in England among Dissenters which had so many advantages.' Oldfield was educated at Lincoln College Oxford and Christ's College Cambridge, but belonged to the rather later generation of tutors who did not graduate because he refused subscription. His Doctorate in Divinity was conferred by Edinburgh. He was of the school of Cambridge Platonists and had come under the influence of Locke. Tonge was a particularly fine preacher and interested in dissenting and national history and the 'British Constitution'. Lorimer was educated at Aberdeen and had been episcopally ordained before joining the rank of 'orthodox dissent'. Spademan had graduated at Magdalene Cambridge and spent a period of exile in Holland as pastor of the English Church at Amsterdam. He 'was well skilled in philosophy and history; thoroughly versed in controversial theology; and for an accurate knowledge of the learned languages, especially the origins of the sacred scriptures, he had few equals'. He knew French, Dutch, Italian and some Spanish. Cappel was a refugee from the Protestant Academy of Saumur, noted as a centre of liberal Protestant thought, where his grandfather had also held the Chair of Hebrew, and was known as 'le père de la critique sacrée'. At Hoxton

Cappel taught the oriental languages and their critical application in the study of the scriptures. Many of the ablest ministers of the next generation, churchmen as well as dissenters, studied under him. Perhaps the most learned of them was Nathaniel Lardner.

The curriculum of this academy must be inferred from the reputations of its tutors and their works. In Oldfield's *Essay towards the Improvement of Reason* (1707) a complete scheme of education is outlined: logic, modern geography, history, chronology, laws 'including international and commercial law', current affairs, some astronomy and navigation, and mathematics, a thorough study of English, the principles of religion. Vocational preparation is considered, civil law should be studied 'to prepare the way for our own', Hebrew and New Testament Greek and ethics for divinity students, 'Mathematical Natural Philosophy with Experiments' for future doctors. It seems likely that there was a wide variety of students at Hoxton Square preparing for different callings. Oldfield's methods are also reflected in his *Essay*. He considered learning as a means of improving reason, as well as the material on which reason has to work. He aimed 'to produce the ... Habit of using our Reason in a better, and to better purpose', and he was noted for his liberal, tolerant approach and encouragement of free inquiry. Spademan also exhibited an 'exemplary moderation to other denominations of Christians', and Tonge was an 'utter enemy of all real persecution'.[69]

By this time the character of the academies was somewhat changed. The earliest schools were mainly domestic, established by ejected ministers trained at Oxford or Cambridge, and dependent on the life of a single scholar. Many of them were migratory, and they served several purposes, of which training for the dissenting ministry was only one. Later academies drew on somewhat different influences and pursued rather different purposes. Scottish, Dutch, American and sometimes French universities replaced Oxford and Cambridge in the training of tutors, and the establishment of various Nonconformist funds for the training of ministers gave more stability and a greater theological emphasis to the teaching. The Presbyterian Fund was established in 1689, the Congregational Fund Board in 1695, the Lady Hewley Fund in 1707, the King's Head Society in 1730, the Coward Trust in 1738. Their bursaries were largely to ministerial candidates, and the mid-eighteenth-century academies were therefore more concerned with vocational training than with general education, they were institutional rather than domestic and had their own trustees and subscribers. The two periods in the history of the dissenting academies overlap and fuse. Several of Ker's students received grants from the London Fund – in 1690, 9 had exhibitions, from 1690–2 the names of 21 of his students were recorded in its minutes. At Hoxton Square 15 students received bursaries between 1700–11 from the Presbyterian Fund. The Congregational Fund Board also supported students in the London area at Newington Green and at Moorfields.[70]

If earlier academies increasingly emphasized their responsibilities to the dissenting bodies, those of this 'middle period' still retained a strong element of semi-private, secular, secondary instruction. In Hoxton Square for example there were two academies which well illustrate the diversity of this mid-eighteenth-century period. Samuel Pike received from about 1750 onwards at his own home 'a select number of students for the ministry' who were supported by annual subscription and an occasional public collection.[71] Nearby in the square was a larger academy which moved to Hoxton in 1762 after several migrations. Its first tutor was Isaac Chauncey (1633–1713?) whose father was President of Harvard College. Isaac graduated there in both medicine and theology but returned to England during the Interregnum. Ejected from his Wiltshire living in 1662 he lived perhaps by medicine and his pastorate until he 'preached away most of his people'. He became sole tutor of the Congregational Fund's London Academy at Moorfields which may formerly have been Goodwin's Pinner Academy. At Chauncey's death Thomas Ridgeley, who had been with Dolittle at Islington, was appointed divinity tutor with John Eames as his colleague in languages, mathematics, moral and natural philosophy. Eames after 1734 was in charge of the academy, the only layman ever so placed. His eminence as a scholar in both classics and mathematics attracted pupils from other academies. Thomas Secker, afterwards Archbishop of Canterbury, came from Gloucester to be under this 'eminent scientist'. Eames's pupil, James Densham, became his assistant but on the death of Eames he also retired and the Congregational Fund Board had to find an entirely new staff. Dr David Jennings who had been educated at Moorfields under Chauncey was chosen as divinity tutor and made it a condition of his taking the post that Samuel Morton Savage, who had been a pupil of Eames, should become his assistant when he had finished his course. Jennings was minister of the Old Gravel Lane Independent Meeting House in Stepney and lectures were given at his house in Wellclose Square, the students being no longer in residence with their tutor. Jennings believed in the value of a 'mixed academy', receiving pupils who were not candidates for the ministry, but the Congregational Fund Board, and later the Coward Trust, were directly concerned with the management of the academy, as well as providing bursaries for theological students. At the end of their course, students had to pass trials in the presence of the committee and deliver a thesis and sermon in Bury Street Chapel. Jennings's course followed lectures on the usual branches of a ministerial education, but he added architecture, heraldry and numismatics, and 'a course for juniors' for whom 'Providence has marked out their track of life through scenes of worldly business' on the lines of his own *Introduction to the Use of the Globes and the Orrery*. Jennings as a pupil of Eames encouraged interest in physical science. The trustees had already equipped the academy with a library; Eames bequeathed to the academy all his apparatus for making experiments in natural philosophy and now the trustees had them housed, cleaned, repaired and added 'an Orrery and an instrument to show the spheroidical figure of the earth' for £33 10s. Later was added an important collection of instruments from John Horsley of Newcastle coming by way of Kendal and Warrington Academies. Another progressive feature of Jennings's course was his use of English for texts and lectures. His attitude towards freedom of enquiry seems to have changed as time went on – at first he was noted for his tolerance and opposition to 'imposing an article of faith on any man', but towards the end of his life he expelled two students for heterodox views, and Joshua Toulmin, whose views also had become inconsistent with strict Calvinism, only escaped expulsion by accident.

Jennings died in 1762 and the trustees moved the academy, now under Savage, to the handsome house in Hoxton Square where Dr Daniel Williams (founder of Dr Williams's Library) had lived. The liberal atmosphere of the academy was restored. Savage was 'a friend of truth' who 'encouraged free inquiry and threw no difficulties in the way of those who honestly pursued their enquiries, though they embraced very different views from his own'. His constant advice was 'judge for yourselves'. He excelled in mathematical science and urged the value to a minister of a wide secular learning. He emphasized the importance of style – 'The word doctrine . . . does not merely signify the matter taught, but also the manner of teaching . . . or, more properly, the act of teaching.'

One of the 8 students who transferred from Stepney to Hoxton in 1762 was Abraham Rees. Before the completion of his course, his ability, industry and attainments led to his appointment as assistant tutor at Hoxton and soon after he was elected resident tutor. He lectured on chemistry and advanced mathematics, basing his main natural philosophy course on the manuscript lectures of Eames. Then he passed on to mechanics, statics, hydrostatics, optics, spherical geometry, the use of applied mathematics in navigation, geography and astronomy. In moral philosophy he was also dependent on Eames. He allowed the methods of the freest enquiry, his students read 'all the authors of greatest repute, for and against the Trinity, original sin and the most disputed doctrines'. For twenty years his colleague under Savage was Dr Andrew Kippis, former pupil of Doddridge, who lectured in classics and *belles-lettres* and who also gave courses on oratory, the history of eloquence, the theory of language and universal grammar, and chronology. Both Rees and Kippis were becoming too unorthodox for the Congregational Fund and when in 1785 Savage died the academy was closed. Its least orthodox students with Kippis and Rees removed to Hackney College.[72]

Another group of London dissenting academies, which eventually merged to form New College (in Hampstead) in 1850, was perhaps more narrowly tied to training for the ministry, yet even here the element of general and liberal education persisted, for preliminary courses of 'grammatical learning' were found necessary.

The first of this group was the academy which eventually (in 1826) became Highbury College. It began in 1776 as a plan for evangelical

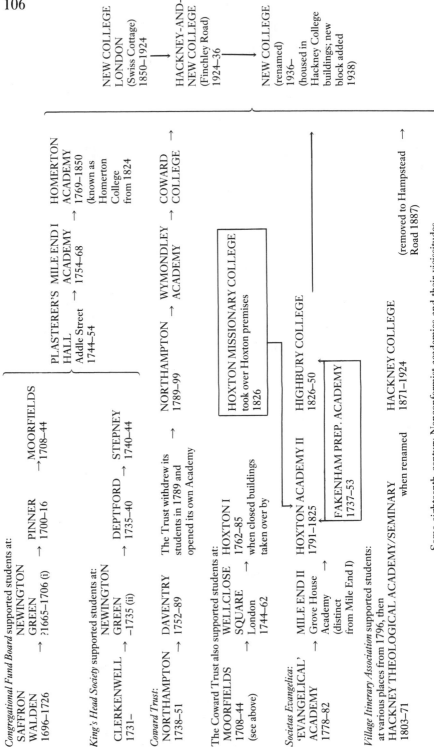

Congregational Fund Board supported students at:
SAFFRON WALDEN 1696–1726 → NEWINGTON GREEN ?1665–1706 (i) → PINNER 1700–16 → MOORFIELDS 1708–44

King's Head Society supported students at:
CLERKENWELL 1731– → NEWINGTON GREEN –1735 (ii) → DEPTFORD 1735–40 → STEPNEY 1740–44

Comard Trust:
NORTHAMPTON 1738–51 → DAVENTRY 1752–89 → The Trust withdrew its students in 1789 and opened its own Academy

The Coward Trust also supported students at:
MOORFIELDS 1708–44 (see above) → WELLCLOSE SQUARE London 1744–62 → HOXTON I 1762–85 when closed buildings taken over by

Societas Evangelica:
'EVANGELICAL' ACADEMY 1778–82 → MILE END II Grove House Academy (distinct from Mile End I) → HOXTON ACADEMY II 1791–1825 → FAKENHAM PREP. ACADEMY 1737–53

HIGHBURY COLLEGE 1826–50

HOXTON MISSIONARY COLLEGE took over Hoxton premises 1826

Village Itinerary Association supported students at various places from 1796, then
HACKNEY THEOLOGICAL ACADEMY/SEMINARY 1803–71 → when renamed → HACKNEY COLLEGE 1871–1924 (removed to Hampstead Road 1887) →

PLASTERER'S HALL, Addle Street 1744–54 → MILE END I ACADEMY 1754–68 → HOMERTON ACADEMY 1769–1850 (known as Homerton College from 1824 →

NORTHAMPTON 1789–99 → WYMONDLEY ACADEMY → COWARD COLLEGE ↑

NEW COLLEGE LONDON (Swiss Cottage) 1850–1924

HACKNEY-AND-NEW COLLEGE (Finchley Road) 1924–36 →

NEW COLLEGE (renamed) 1936– (housed in Hackney College buildings; new block added 1938)

Some eighteenth-century Nonconformist academies and their vicissitudes training for young men living in London and following their own occupations. The *Societas Evangelica* founded lectures, given in Gracechurch Street and from 1778 in Hoxton. The plan did not succeed and the academy was reorganized in 1782 on a full-time basis in a house taken for the purpose, Grove End House, Mile End, under the Reverend Stephen Addington, a former pupil of Doddridge and with experience as a schoolmaster. In 1791 the academy took the last step in its development into a normal orthodox one, when Addington retired through ill health, and it moved into the house previously occupied by the earlier academy of the Coward Trust, using its library and apparatus. Here the Reverend Robert Simpson, a Hebrew expert, was first tutor. The curriculum reflected the evangelical purpose of the college and science and classics received comparatively slight attention. The premises in Hoxton Square were enlarged, but soon found to be too 'close and confined' and in 1825 Highbury Place was bought and new buildings raised by subscription. The old buildings were offered to the Wesleyan Methodists for their first theological college. This was from start to finish in fact a semi-public institution, giving mainly theological training. In 1842 at Highbury the students had to be over eighteen 'with such preparatory instruction in Latin as will enable them to read Virgil and with some knowledge of fractional arithmetic, and the elements of geography'.[73]

The second element to merge into New College was itself more composite – the King's Head Society's academy at Homerton. This society at first was associated with the Congregational Fund Board's academy, later represented by the Hoxton Square school under Savage, but had grown dissatisfied with its management, especially with the rule which limited entry to students who had already received a classical training. The King's Head Society decided therefore in 1730 to establish an academy in Clerkenwell (later in Newington Green) where young men could receive a preliminary classical education for one or two years before proceeding to the usual theological course. The students resided with the classical tutor, the Reverend Samuel Parsons, in Clerkenwell till 1735, then for a short period with Dr Taylor, the theological tutor, in Deptford. In 1740 they were back in Stepney and from 1744 for ten years the academy was in the Plasterers' Hall in Addle Street. Then it moved to Mile End where the students were boarded by Dr John Conder, the divinity tutor, with John Walker and Thomas Gibbons as his colleagues. By this time differences between the King's Head Society and the Congregational Fund Board had been resolved. In 1768 an ancient mansion at Homerton, formerly used as a school, with two or three small houses adjoining, was taken over for the academy and in 1769 it was established there. It was renowned for its orthodoxy; the Congregational Fund Board exercised strict supervision over its students, in 1780 expelling six for bad behaviour 'in point of insolence and ingratitude'. It gave a fairly wide ministerial training, tutors such as

Gibbons and Henry Mayo ('Johnson's Literary Anvil') had a national reputation, its library of over 3000 volumes and its philosophical apparatus reflect a breadth of study. Its period of greatest distinction was under John Pye Smith, described by one student as 'Professor of things in general', 'almost a walking encyclopaedia'. Lectures were given on natural philosophy, logic, ontology, 'the Philosophy of the Human Mind', composition, rhetoric, the 'study and Use of History', and there was a full course of mathematics, the students giving 'a small portion of time to it every day'. This was in addition to the more usual parts of ministerial learning – theological, classical, pastoral. The number of students grew steadily, in 1811 the buildings were enlarged, in 1822 a new building was put up, and the institute became Homerton College. Later it merged with Highbury and Coward Colleges to form New College.[74]

Coward College, Doddridge's famous academy from Northampton, the third element in this final merging, moved to Daventry after his death, and finally after further wanderings in 1833 to Byng Place in Bloomsbury to enable the students to attend the arts lectures at University College. Its magnificent library, accumulated over these migrations, then contained 3500 books.[75]

With the foundation of New College in 1850 the connection of its various constituent colleges with general and non-professional education must be considered to be at an end. 'An instructed ministry' for the Congregational Church became the sole aim of New College, for even the proposed lay students of university level mainly found University College more central and convenient.

By the later eighteenth century the academies were emphasizing professional training. One, sometimes called Hackney College, grew out of an evangelical society for providing missions for 'the perishing multitudes of our own country as well as in the South Seas'.[76] Another, Hackney Unitarian Academy, was established in Durham House from 1812 to 1818. This did take lay students and gave a wide course of divinity, classics and mathematics.[77]

This steadily increasing emphasis on theological and professional training deprived liberal Nonconformists of institutions for the higher education for their sons, at a time when they were still excluded from the endowed schools and universities. Private schools did not satisfy the demand for control and prestige which supervision and a form of endowment by the various dissenting funds gave. In 1786 a number of wealthy liberal London Nonconformists including some Unitarians and Socinians discussed the formation of a 'New Academical Institution among Protestant Dissenters for the Education of their Ministers and youth'. A large capital fund was raised and a considerable list of annual subscribers secured, 'men of affluence, liberality and independence'. The education to be given was 'comprehensive and liberal and adapted to youth in general, whether they be intended for civil and commercial

Hackney New College

life, or for any one of the learned professions'. The institution was planned on a generous scale and on being established in Bond Hopkins House (Homerton Hall) was called Hackney College, 'not for the sake of imitating the Establishment, but because the word Academy (applied of late to every common school) does not convey a proper idea of our plan of education'. The titles Hackney New College or New College alone were also employed. The house had eighteen acres of ground and was extended, with wings giving a collegiate appearance, to accommodate 70 students 'each having separate appartments', and a good house was built for the senior tutor. Younger pupils probably were expected to board with their tutors. A prospectus published in April 1787 recommended the situation for its health and convenience, and gave assurances of attention to the moral conduct and literary improvement of young gentlemen entrusted to the care of the 'New Academy', which was to be open to persons of all denominations 'who will be encouraged in forming their religious sentiments without restriction or imposition'. The course was comprehensive – Latin, Greek, Hebrew, Greek and Roman antiquities, ancient and modern geography, universal grammar, rhetoric and composition, chronology, civil and ecclesiastical history, the principles of law and government, the several branches of mathematics, astronomy, natural and experimental philosophy and chemistry, logic, metaphysics, ethics, the evidences of religion, natural and revealed theology, Jewish antiquities and critical lectures on the scriptures. French and other modern languages and drawing were extras. Divinity students were not admitted before the age of fifteen or after eighteen and their course lasted for five years. The terms were £63 a year, with £4 4s for the use of the library; for 'young persons intended for the ministry' a 'considerable abatement' of terms was made. The staff was impressive, but unfortunately transitory and occasionally either disappointing or positively harmful. Dr Richard Price, formerly pupil of Eames, was to read lectures on 'morality and the higher species of mathematics' but he resigned in the second year. He had only three pupils capable of understanding his lectures and indeed he gave very few at all, 'both tutor and pupils being better pleased to fill up the lecture hour with agreeable conversation on philosophy and politics'. His retirement through 'infirmities and advancing age' when sixty-four was not soon enough for the college's political reputation. The classical department languished somewhat until Gilbert Wakefield, 'a most excellent classical tutor', took it over, but he only stayed a year as his colleagues found his views on public worship uncongenial and inconvenient. He proved to his own satisfaction that it was 'neither expedient nor proper' and several students thereupon developed conscientious scruples about chapel attendance and had to be removed. One delivered a warm defence of the position 'at the public examination before the assembled tutors, committee and supporters of the institution . . .'. Several parents withdrew their sons. The tutor who brought both glory and final disaster on the college was Dr Joseph Priestley who gave his services as lecturer on history, 'General Policy', and natural philosophy, especially chemistry. He was optimistic about the new college and hoped that it would eventually rival Oxford and Cambridge, and recent assessment has agreed that 'As things went in England in 1793, Hackney College was a better *Studium Generale* than either Oxford or Cambridge at the same date.' Priestley's breadth of view on the curriculum was remarkable and he urged the need for liberalizing the education of those not entering the learned professions by introducing 'some new articles of academical instruction, such as have a nearer and more evident connection with the business of active life, and which may therefore bid fairer to engage the attention and rouse the thinking powers of young gentlemen of an active genius'. He advocated history, especially the study of the English constitution, French and science, especially chemistry, classics sufficient for the reading of authors, and music. The method was to be by free enquiry.

Priestley's lectures at Hackney were however a contributary cause to the downfall of the college, just when some thought it promised 'to extend the rays of science, over the darkest regions of ignorance'. Many of its wealthiest supporters withdrew their subscriptions and also left their pews at the Gravel Pit Meeting House when Priestley became its pastor. The position was already precarious as the very freedom from internal supervision, which marked Hackney College off from private schools kept by Nonconformists and brought it into line with public schools of the period, made discipline a constant matter of concern. While an endowed and established school could weather a rebellion or two with the help perhaps of the militia and a flogging headmaster, an institution depending on subscriptions and already under suspicion for revolutionary tendencies could not afford such outbreaks. Until Thomas Belsham arrived as theology tutor in 1789 Hackney College was 'a veritable Liberty Hall', and even in his time it seems to have been impossible to control the students when carried away by the bliss of being alive in that particular dawn. Nor was it only the students. A sermon by Dr Price to the Friends of the Revolution Society provoked Burke's *Reflections*. Burke referred to Hackney as 'the new arsenal in which subversive doctrines and arguments were forged'. One French visitor to Hackney described the College to the National Assembly in June 1792 as a 'numerous band of youths' listening to 'the animated and pathetic eloquence' of Price. One of Price's sermons almost got him into trouble with the authorities, and an ex-student and a member of the college committee were both arrested and tried when Habeas Corpus was suspended in 1794–6. In 1792 a Republican Supper was held at the College with Tom Paine as guest, and the distribution of a pamphlet written by a student at the college touched off the riots in Birmingham in which ironically Priestley suffered. Nor was it possible to confine the students within the walls; in spite of all rules to the contrary they flocked to the trial of Warren Hastings and to the House of Commons to hear Charles James Fox speak on the Repeal of the Test and Corporation Acts; they caused a disturbance in a theatre by calling for 'Ça ira' instead of 'God save the King'.

These difficulties might have been surmounted had other factors favoured the survival of Hackney College. But it drew its strength and support from those very sections of liberal dissent which were discredited by the developments of the French Revolution: it had exhausted funds, confidence and goodwill in more influential quarters: its numbers had never been satisfactory – 70 students could be accommodated but 49 seems to have been the largest number in residence at any one time. Of these, 40 were fee-paying, and 9 held bursaries, 30 were 'designed for civil life' and 19 for the ministry. The hopes of the founders that not only dissenters but 'the liberal and wealthy of all other denominations will feel an interest in it, and assist in the support of the institution', were hardly realized, and not only its political but also its religious views were regarded with suspicion by orthodox dissenters. The 'annual harangues' in its support, and the behaviour of the students, had convinced the 'faithful parent, or guardian, who regards our constitution' that it would produce 'instead of peaceable and orderly citizens', instead of loyal subjects, young men 'disposed to become the violators of the law, the enemies of the Constitution which they should be prepared to defend with the risk of their lives'; and that it was the 'boasted seminary of natural religion, *the slaughterhouse of Christianity*'. Moreover the discipline was so lax that pupils did not make progress and the tutors' advanced views on flogging prevented the accepted incentive being applied. More fundamental was the fact that 'None of the rich families bring up their sons for Presbyterian parsons: they have too much sense or too much worldly wisdom.' Their sons were sent to private schools 'where they learn nothing, being sometimes better fed than taught' and then taken into the counting house at fourteen or fifteen. Keen interest in education was dying down among wealthy and orthodox dissenters, and poor youths intended for the ministry needed the support of one of the Funds not likely to patronize Hackney College.

It is surprising the College was able to struggle on for ten years, especially in that bitter decade. In 1793 it was in financial difficulties but 'a person had been found who was willing to give them 8000 pounds'. By 1796 there was 'not one advocate left for its continuance'. Price had died in 1791, Thomas Rogers, Chairman of the Committee, in 1793, Kippis in 1795. The College was closed, a forced sale held, and the buildings realized less than one-third of their cost. Contemporaries regarded the extravagance of the promoters as one of the chief causes of its downfall, the result of pride, 'setting out in too superb a style, inconsistent with the *plainness* and *simplicity* of the Dissenters'. One gloried that 'Babylon is fallen, is fallen!' The talents of the tutors when united were not enough to counterbalance the fear of Priestley's revolutionary opinions, 'the grand incendiary, now under sentence of self-transportation'. Something was saved from the wreck, and Dr Belsham continued to carry on a private seminary at Grove Place, Hackney. Later a 'new academic institution on more economic principles' was to be established at Birmingham.[78]

It is interesting to compare the causes of this catastropic failure with the factors which led to the survival and eventual success of a rather later school for dissenters. Only ten years separate the downfall of Hackney College and the foundation of Mill Hill in 1806.[79]

Disentangling the topographical and chronological complexities of dissenting academies in the metropolis over a century and a half of development may tend to distort the picture during any one decade. The extent of provision even in Hoxton, Homerton, Highbury and Hackney may become exaggerated. Nevertheless the overall impression of strength and vitality is justified by the achievements and significance of these London academies both for their own times and for the future.

The support of the trading and business community recurs as a theme in their story. This valuable interaction of academic and mercantile society was characteristic of for example Glasgow and Manchester as well as the capital, in contrast to the English centres of university learning at Oxford and Cambridge. As well as essential links with their own terrain, the London academies were linked through them with the expanding curiosity and practices of provincial England and of North Britain. The Nonconformist academies were a national phenomenon and in many ways those in the North of England were the trend-setters and models for those of the metropolis.[80] But between them and the London academies was a constant flow of influence and personalities: Priestley for example, born in Yorkshire, educated at Daventry, the inheritor of Doddridge's Northampton academy, tutor at Warrington, ministering in Cheshire, Leeds, Birmingham, and then closely associated with the last period of the London academies. He linked them not only with other centres of Nonconformist learning, but with expanding centres of industry, technology and scientific enquiry, expressed for example in the Lunar Society, founded at Birmingham by Matthew Boulton in 1766, and called the 'Scientific general staff of the industrial revolution', and the Manchester Literary and Philosophical Society.[81] This constant interpenetration of capital and provinces at a time when the national economic superstructure and its productive base were becoming more strongly differentiated, even polarized, was of great importance for future cultural and social cohesion.

The academies bridged temporarily a wider gulf – that between England and Scotland. The Scottish tradition of the 'Democratic Intellect'[82] was embodied in a distinctive education system, and based on a religious, social and legal inheritance which tied Scotland more closely to Europe than to England. Scotland looked to Roman and continental law and cherished an educational system which combined 'the democracy of the Kirk-elders with the intellectualism of the advocates' and made 'expertise in metaphysics the condition of the open door of social advancement'.[83] Principle rather than precedent was the key to Scotland's particular structure and style. Institutionally this was expressed in university courses which took their students at fifteen or even earlier, from parish schools which grounded them in Latin, and then gave them a four years' general education which included both classics and exact sciences and culminated in philosophy. At about nineteen or twenty the more dedicated or able students passed on to professional or specialist studies. There is a striking similarity between this course structure and that of the English Nonconformist academies, due not only to the strong institutional links between them but to deeply shared assumptions about the nature of knowledge, the authority of reason, the challenge to precedent and privilege, and to their secular and liberal climate and wide social intake. If the tradition and practices of the dissenting academies had triumphed in England, the circle of learning of European and Scottish classicism might have been preserved, the system of a protracted and highly specialized secondary schooling, leading to a short, specialized degree course, might not have become the peculiarity of the English as opposed to the continental or New World traditions. It was in London that the influences, needs and beliefs which had sustained the eighteenth-century academies persisted long enough to found the University of London, an idea floated in 1820, published in 1825 and achieved in 1828, open to all beliefs or none, combining classics and the exact sciences in a broad course, taking students from about fifteen to sixteen years. The Anglican King's College followed the same Scottish and Nonconformist academy pattern.[84] But by this time the cohesive forces in the more prosperous levels of English society were bringing about reforms which opened government employment and the ancient universities to dissenters of all kinds and to wider social classes and the Scottish pattern was not in the end successful. The founding of excellent schools connected with University and King's Colleges tended to defer the age of entry to university courses and the prestige of the public schools and the ancient universities was strong. The academies arose to meet the needs of a divided society, but their achievements had contributed to national cultural unity. The new society which emerged from the Industrial Revolution may have classified itself along lines which reflected religious or sectarian differences,[85] but the forces of cohesion and the triumph of toleration eventually ensured a new cultural synthesis, an 'alternative Establishment'. Here the later age of entry to university became general even as new subjects were introduced in degree courses. This transferred to the top of the secondary course problems of specialization which did not arise so soon or so acutely in Scotland and in countries such as Australia which were strongly influenced by that tradition.

The contribution of the Nonconformist academies to the *process* of education and its organization was therefore not permanent, and their only direct *institutional* legacy was the theological college, for the Anglican and Wesleyan churches as well as their own communions. Their most important and lasting influence was on the content and methods of education. It was in these academies that the critical, rational and empirical knowledge of the European Enlightenment was embodied and organized into a new curriculum.

Within this native achievement it is important to emphasize continental influences, for this new curriculum, while confining the conventional study of classical languages to a balanced place within a circle of knowledge, might overall be described as classical in the French usage of the word – it had a dignity of plan, a conception of a whole, a subordination of parts to this whole. Calvinism's strong connections with this conception of classicism underlay the dissenting contribution to a new idea of the content of education. 'The common cause which the English dissenters felt with the Huguenots gave some of them a . . . direct access to the culture which produced *Athalie*.' Dissent in the eighteenth century was not in the least insular, and 'Calvinist classicism' offers one definition of the new approach to knowledge.[86]

In this classical learning kept its place, but made room for modern languages and literatures including English, in the later part of the century branching into the elegance of '*belles-lettres*' as the Augustan softened into the Neo-Classical Age. Historical aspects of the curriculum derived from continental influences working upon a peculiarly English concern – the dissenters' passionate attachment to the Settlement of 1688 which tolerated and safeguarded their place in the body politic; this 'accommodation' may be seen as the 'characteristic endeavour and achievement of Dissent in the generation of Defoe and Watts and Doddridge'.[87] It was articulated in political, constitutional, legal studies which were a prelude to the development of modern as distinct from classical or sacred history. French influence combined with this devotion to the constitution to develop an important historical element in the curriculum, for it was from the Huguenot academies that the historical criticism of the Scriptures emanated.[88] Cappel at Hoxton for example introduced such ideas from Saumur,[89] and a century later German Biblical criticism was introduced to England at Homerton by Dr Pye Smith whose library contained a fine collection of German works.[90]

Throughout the eighteenth century therefore historical studies were developed and established as an integral part of a liberal education. At Hackney Dr Kippis included a history of literature in his *belles-lettres* course, and he lectured on chronology, 'an outline of Universal History intended to acquaint the student with the rise and fall of civilizations and the general sequence of history . . . the historical element in scripture from the Creation on was highly esteemed by Dissenters of this period'. Dr Priestley had prepared a *Chart of Chronology* and put forward a detailed rationale and content of his history course. It was to amuse the imagination and interest the passions, to improve the understanding and to strengthen the sentiments of virtue. Its emphasis was to be on cause and effect and there was to be constant reference to current topics and the citizen's duty to understand public affairs. He embraced instruction in the general uses of history, its sources, including monuments, coins, heraldry and etymology as well as written documents, its methodology, and he made use of charts, tables, models, and guidance in reading and study. His course culminated in a 'General View of Universal History'.[91] The tendency of the age was anti-historical in many respects but in the dissenting academies devotion to the Constitution combined with continental influences to secure history's development and ultimate place in the curriculum of a liberal education.

The mathematical and scientific aspects of the curriculum in the academies are perhaps more widely acknowledged and are fully demonstrated from the various London courses. John Conder (1714–81), tutor in Divinity at the King's Head Academy, put it thus: 'What is counted a polite education now is very different from what was esteemed a Century ago. Then if a man was versed in the learned and dead languages and in Aristotle's logic and metaphysics and Master of the Distinctions of the School of Divinity, he passed for a considerable scholar and a divine whereas now 'tis the mathematical learning carries the Bell.'[92] It was not only their enthusiastic study which was important but the fact that these rational and empirical elements were recognized as an integral part of the circle of learning. Eames, for example, said by his pupil Watts to be 'the most learned man I ever knew', excelled 'particularly in classical literature and in a profound knowledge of mathematics and of natural philosophy'.[93] At Ker's Academy natural philosophy was studied in the fourth year as the *culmination* of a systematic course.[94] Priestley saw science for the Hackney students not

L E C T U R E S

O N

H I S T O R Y,

A N D

G E N E R A L   P O L I C Y;

TO WHICH IS PREFIXED,

AN ESSAY ON A COURSE OF LIBERAL EDUCATION
FOR CIVIL AND ACTIVE LIFE.

By JOSEPH PRIESTLEY, LL. D. F. R. S.

AC. IMP. PETROP. R. PARIS. HOLM. TAURIN. AUREL. MED.
PARIS. HARLEM. CANTAB. AMERIC. ET PHILAD. SOCIUS.

———————— JUVAT EXHAUSTOS ITERARE LABORES,
ET SULCATA MEIS PERCURRERE LITORA REMIS.

BUCHANANI FRANCISCANUS.

IN TWO VOLUMES.

VOL. II.

LONDON:

PRINTED FOR J. JOHNSON, ST. PAUL'S CHURCH YARD.

Title-page of Joseph Priestley's *Lectures on History*, 1788

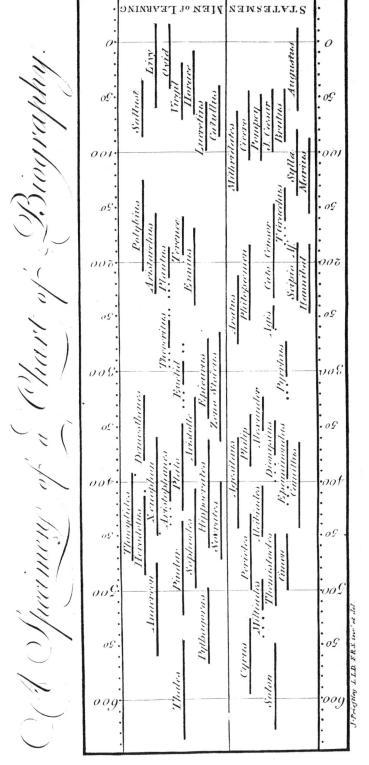

Specimen of a Chart for Biography

only as necessary in itself but as both conducing to virtue and as a practical study. 'It is by increasing our knowledge of *nature*, and by this alone, that we acquire the great art of commanding it, of availing ourselves of its powers, and applying them to our own purposes; true *science* being the only foundation of all those *arts* of life, whether relating to peace or war, which distinguish civilized nations...'.[95] The Nonconformists carried this understanding of the liberal nature of scientific and mathematical learning over into the training of their ministers, for empirical and mathematical knowledge was seen to be essential to full rationality, and therefore to natural religion. When Pye Smith gave his inaugural lecture at Homerton in 1801 for example, he outlined a plan of studies which included natural philosophy, astronomy, chemistry, natural history for the first two years, followed by ontology, the philosophy of the human mind, composition and rhetoric, history, and a full course of mathematics. The academies thus consolidated practice and theory into a new encyclopaedic curriculum, a true manifestation of the European Age of Reason. Like his better-known French counterparts Diderot and d'Alembert, Rees in 1778 re-edited Chambers's *Cyclopaedia*, and in 1802 began one of his own, which by 1819 appeared in thirty-nine volumes as the *Cyclopaedia, or a Universal Dictionary of Arts, Sciences, and Literature.*[96]

It was in these academies that a new map of learning was drawn, and new methods of exploring it were attempted. Claims here are always difficult to substantiate, for what a tutor thinks he is doing, and what his students remember his doing, do not always agree. Lecturing in English rather than Latin was increasingly practised in the academies and so was the writing of themes and attention to the native language in general. But lecturing at dictation speed was probably quite usual ('a more ingenious method for rendering instruction irksome and disgusting, cannot, I imagine, be readily devised' as an old student of Homerton College said). Lectures, once composed by a tutor of distinction, Doddridge or Eames for example, were often handed on to successors and used verbatim over several generations of students or in several successive colleges. Certainly tutors often used courses of lectures over and over again. Gibbons after 'writing his lectures for the four years following his appointment', blessed God that he had now 'acquired a Sett of Lectures for my whole future life'. Priestley was considered advanced in his methods because he read his lectures and then handed the manuscript to his students to be 'copied at leisure', while one series he gave at Hackney was printed 'in order to save the students the trouble of transcribing them'.[97]

But such practices must at least be seen in a context of greater freedom of reading and of discussion. From the end of the seventeenth century onwards several tutors were noted for the freedom of enquiry which they allowed their students, and collections of 'philosophical apparatus' at least imply some demonstration, discovery and verification.

Questioning of authority could be considered as the deliberate aim of such methods. 'The English hierarchy (if there be anything unsound in its constitution) has . . . reason to tremble even at an air pump or an electrical machine', wrote Priestley.[98] His colleague at Hackney, Price, expressed this attitude in a sermon of 1787. 'The best education is that which . . . impresses the heart most with love of virtue, and communicates the most expanded and ardent benevolence; which gives the deepest consciousness of the fallibility of the human understanding, and preserves from that vile dogmatism so prevalent in the world; which makes men diffident and modest, attentive to evidence, capable of proportioning their assent to the degree of it, quick in discerning it, and determined to follow it, which in short, instead of producing acute casuists, conceited pedants, or furious polemics, produces fair enquirers.'[99]

It was this atmosphere and attitude which held promise for the future because it enabled new knowledge, new ways of knowing, to work in the mind and open the way to more enquiry. When freedom from authority in religion was allowed, as it was at Hoxton, 'there was noticeable progress in extension of the curriculum and in methods of study'[100] and throughout the complex development of these London academies the tension between freedom and orthodoxy can be traced. The English Enlightenment in contrast to the French, retained religious commitment, but it was often at the price of orthodoxy, and 'Old Dissent' was split between Trinitarian and Unitarian beliefs.

This was one of the powerful reasons for the downfall of the last of the 'open' academies, Hackney College, for to make matters worse 'Rational Dissent' became identified with democratical or Jacobin infection. Within the classical tradition the new emphasis on Greek studies had occasionally proved politically hazardous, (Dr Parr had supported two of his ex-pupils through trial for sedition),[101] and in the dissenting tradition the connection between the ideas of the *philosophes* and the outbreak of Revolution strengthened the rebellious mood in even strictly orthodox academies such as Homerton. There 'politics pervaded every circle, almost to the exclusion of every other subject . . . attention to the advancement of knowledge and Christian piety . . . was in a great degree forgotten, and exchanged for senseless janglings . . .'. This was the College which the youthful Pye Smith took over.[102] His friendship with James Montgomery of Sheffield, prepared to face imprisonment in the cause of the freedom of the press, is a reminder that the defence of liberty was not a mere matter of rhetoric, nor of student discontent. Nevertheless the dissenting academies of the early nineteenth century had to reassert control of theological training, and it was of supreme educational importance that in this narrower context they still preserved and even consolidated the new curriculum and a tradition of open enquiry.

Mathematical practitioners

To claim that 'modern education' was formulated in these academies implies that their traditions and achievements were not only consolidated within their narrowed tradition but were also widely diffused. When social as well as ideological changes caused dissenting education to retreat into a professional enclave, it is important to question how this diffusion came about. It was largely through the channel of private and informal provision, and in this London, with its richness of enterprise and strong social and economic demands, played an important part. Private education continued to reflect the demands of both the Augustan and the Enlightened aspects of the age, as well as responding to the metropolitan needs of a nation with rapidly expanding trade and naval power and ever-increasing sophistication and enterprise in entrepreneurial techniques, and which was also developing bureaucratic structures made necessary by these other changes.

Mathematics was perhaps the key to the supplying of many of these needs and London was already a centre of operations for those practitioners who since the sixteenth century had studied the 'application of geometry to everyday affairs and skills – to time keeping and the calendar, to mensuration and surveying, to gunnery and fortification, to architecture and navigation'.[103] A study of the Hanoverian practitioners between 1714 and 1840 identified 2282 examples, and of these a high proportion were connected with London, the 'Mecca of the provincial mathematical practitioner, if he were ambitious'.[104] In 1755 James Watt himself, educated in mathematics partly by his uncles, came from Glasgow, that centre of the study of the exact sciences, to place himself for a year in the London workshop of John Morgan of Finch Lane, Cornhill, whose instruments were 'excelled by none' for accuracy.[105] Official encouragement increased the importance of London. From 1714 when the Board of Longitude was established and offered a substantial reward for a solution to the problem of keeping exact time at sea, mathematicians converged upon the capital to present their theories and instruments. Naval surveying provided a constant stimulus and when expeditions for observing the Transit of Venus in 1761 were dispatched to various parts of the world, including the South Seas under Captain Cook, there was another flurry of encouragement. During the Hanoverian period professional specialization – of astronomer, navigator, civil and military engineer, cartographer, surveyor – increased and differentiated, but they all kept closely in touch with the instrument-makers. London was the focal point of national expertise, drew on provincial abilities and in turn became a centre of mathematical education. The great Jesse Ramsden (1735–1800) for example, 'perhaps the greatest practitioner of all time', was born near Halifax, educated at a Yorkshire dissenting academy, and apprenticed to a London clothier. But he entered the business of an instrument-maker in the Strand, married the sister of another, Peter Dolland, and built up an outstanding reputation.[106] Such London instrument-makers were widely renowned and by the reign of George III rose to the height of their fame, every European observatory priding itself on the possession of their instruments. In this country, and perhaps especially in London, ease of social and professional intercourse between craftsman, professional and gentleman, scientist and technician, compared favourably with the more stratified societies of Europe. The intimacy between 'philosopher' and 'mechanic' was typical of English society, though encouragement often stopped short of financial support and European observers remarked critically that many highly skilled men had to support themselves by teaching. This was an educational advantage, since a high proportion of London mathematicians were engaged in diffusing knowledge and skills.[107]

The universities remained in the background of activity, but the influence of Newton inspired and articulated a whole world of theory and practice and it must not be forgotten that 'at the core of nearly everything that was thought, said and done at Cambridge' lay his discoveries.[108] The Cambridge contribution therefore was far from unimportant, but it was in London that on the whole the action lay. It was a London instrument-maker, John Senex, of the Globe in Salisbury Court, who printed the Dutch s'Gravesande's lucid and influential summary and exposition of Newton's *Principia*.[109] This in turn was translated into English by J. T. Desaguliers (1683–1744), who worked in Westminster and Covent Garden, giving public and private lectures on experimental philosophy. It was at these lectures that s'Gravesande, then secretary to the Dutch Ambassador, met Newton in 1715. Another member of the circle was William Whiston (1667–1757) who had been expelled from his professorship at Cambridge for unorthodox Arian views, and came to London to live by teaching, writing and a sort of mathematical consultancy. His lecture in Button's Coffee-House on Newton's system of astronomy gave Pope the experience of a Hanoverian Black Hole, 'looking forward into the vast abyss of eternity'.[110] Desaguliers also provided a link with the classical schools, for not only did he take private boarders but Westminster boys boarded with him. One of these, Stephen Demainbray (1710–82), later lectured at Edinburgh and in 1754 became tutor to the royal princes. When one of these pupils became George III Demainbray was made physician and astronomer to the King and established the Royal Observatory at Kew, with its fine collection of instruments, and George III's children studied experimental philosophy.[111] Another Westminster schoolboy, Nevil Maskelyne, (1732–1811), became so much fascinated by astronomy while still at school that he took it up as a career, eventually becoming Astronomer Royal in 1765, closely associated with many of the official mathematical projects for the rest of the century.[112] Another and more substantial link with what might be called the educational establishment was through the Mathematical School of Christ's Hospital. James Hodgson (1672–1755) wrote his *System of Mathematics* after his appointment there, 'as the Methods at that time in use did not appear to me so rational and instructive as I could wish for . . .'.[113] He was succeeded by John Robertson (1712–76) whose *Elements of Navigation* was 'justly termed the seaman's library'. When he became master of Portsmouth Naval Academy,[114] James Dodson (1710–56) succeeded him and also added to the number of mathematical textbooks.[115]

Christ's Hospital Mathematical School was expressly founded to teach navigation, and shipping and naval interests were in general a powerful influence on London education. Many mathematical teachers had been at sea, either as navigators or as teachers. In the Navy the schoolmaster only rated as a petty officer, but some went as private tutors to midshipmen. Henry Wilson (1673–1741), a teacher of applied mathematics who knew James Hodgson, was recommended in 1717 to Sir George Byng (later Lord Torrington) as tutor to his son on board the *Barfleur*, by a well-known firm of chartsellers.[116] This firm flourished as Mount Page, Nautical Stationers, from 1675 to 1800 in Postern Row, employed teachers of mathematics to keep charts up to date, and also published nautical textbooks.[117] Other nautical schoolmasters themselves kept schools ashore. Thomas Haselden (*fl.* 1702–40) served at sea for twenty years and then kept a school near Wapping Old Stairs, where 'Persons are boarded and taught Merchants Accompts and the Mathematics, viz. Arithmetic, Geometry, Algebra, Trigonometry, Plain and Spherical: the Projection of the Sphere: the Use of the Globes; Astronomy, Dialling, Mensuration of Timber and Plank, Bale Goods etc.; Surveying: Gauging Gunnery, Fortification: also Navigation after the shortest and best method: having used the sea myself about 20 years.' He also wrote textbooks, one of which went with Cook on his second voyage, and he became a Fellow of the Royal Society.[118] Nearby from the 1720s at Wapping New Stairs Joshua Kelly provided a similar course, and his stress on the 'expedition' of his methods emphasizes that such schools were doubtless used by boys and men of a wide age range, and for both broader or more limited educational purposes.[119] Haselden and Kelly must stand as examplars for innumerable schools of the same kind, clustering thickly in the City and its eastern riverside villages, and also found in western suburbs. Francis Walkingham (*fl.* 1751–85) was 'writing master and accomptant and master of the boarding school in Kensington'. He was author of *The Tutor's Assistant*, an arithmetic book which was still in use in 1868.[120] Samuel Dunn (1723–94), a native of Devon and author of *Epitome of Practical Navigation* (1774), opened a school in Ormonde House Chelsea in about 1758 where 'young men may board . . . and be expeditiously qualified in the Sciences or for business'. He worked assiduously in London scientific circles and became mathematical examiner for the East India Company's service. The official Naval Academy was established at Portsmouth in 1729 but

Ormonde House and Chelsea got something approaching official backing when in 1777 a foundation trust was formed for a Maritime School, with a board of governors and subscribers including gentlemen from the Navy and the East India Company. Its head was John Bettesworth, a former naval schoolmaster who had had his own academy in Smithfield. The private side of the academy soon superseded the official. Bettesworth took boarders for private tuition for 'all branches' of knowledge useful for a 'Sea officer, Compting House, public offices and trade'. The school became a feature of the neighbourhood with a ship, the *Cumberland*, built in the grounds, moving around on swivels, 'completely rigged with sails bent and of a capacity sufficient to admit twenty-four of the young gentlemen going aloft at one time'. The course described in *Observations on Education in General, but particularly on Naval Education* . . . which Bettesworth published with Fox, the French master, in 1782, was fairly wide, including classical and modern languages, history, politics, drawing and dancing as well as maritime subjects. It was clearly intended for preparing boys for the early age of entry to the Navy, some time between eleven and nineteen.[121]

Other mathematicians with nautical experience became visiting masters at less specialized schools. William Jones (1675–1749), father of the orientalist, had worked in a counting house, taught mathematics on a man-of-war and established himself as a teacher of mathematics in the suburbs. He was a friend of Newton, an FRS, and author of a *New Compendium of the Whole Art of Navigation*.[122] Other mathematicians kept general private schools of their own, for example John Canton (1718–72) who came to London from Gloucestershire to pursue his enquiries in the experimental philosophy of electricity. In 1738 he 'articled himself for the term of five years, as a clerk to Mr Samuel Watkins, master of the academy in Spital Square'. Here his 'ingenuity, diligence and good conduct' earned him a partnership and eventually he succeeded Watkins and kept the academy until his death, which was said to be hastened by his 'unremitting attention to the duties of his profession, and to the prosecution of his philosophic enquiries and experiments'. He had a belvedere for astronomical observations to be taken by his pupils. He was made an FRS in 1749, was chosen a member of its Council in 1751, and was a friend of Price, Priestley, and other dissenting tutors.[123]

It is thus exceedingly difficult to distinguish in such schools between specialist and general education, between the continuing tradition of the writing masters and writing schools, the private boarding-school for younger boys, and the coaching establishment for boys and men of all ages; in fact their interpenetration was forming the new curriculum of the Age of Reason. A good example was Watts's Academy in Little Tower Street, already described as perhaps the ultimate development of the seventeenth-century writing school. Under Thomas Watts (*fl.* 1715–27) as 'The Accomptant's Office' it had provided highly specialized practical courses. Its joint principal was Benjamin Worster, author of *A Compendious and Mathematical Account of Natural Philosophy* (1722). In the year that William Watts succeeded as principal Newton secured a post on the staff for the brilliant mathematician James Stirling (1692–1770), who had been expelled from Balliol for Jacobite sympathies, had travelled abroad and formed a friendship with Bernoulli, an astronomer of European renown. At Watts's Academy from 1727 Stirling gave courses in natural philosophy. Instruments for the academy were supplied by Richard Bridger of Upper Hind Court, Fleet Street. This academy later moved to Poland Street near Soho Square and must later be considered as one of an important group of London schools providing a variety of general and specialized courses.[124]

The appetites of London, its mercantile, finance and business houses, its port, its government offices, were shaping the new curriculum, and the vitality and stimulus of its cultural context were provided by the eager curiosity and sociability in which Hanoverian Londoners exchanged, advanced and consolidated knowledge. It was a clubbable age and natural philosophy excited its hopes and civilities. In this fluid situation where special and vocational needs were being met by a variety of expedients and improvisations, the vitality and stimulus of this cultural context of instruction and education were of great importance. Joseph Middleton, who had been a teacher of mathematics in the Navy, founded in 1717 a Society of Ingenious Mathematicians whose 64 members met once a week, at first in the Monmouth Head, Spitalfields; in 1782–4 it was meeting in the Black Swan.[125] John Whitehurst, a watchmaker and maker of fine instruments, came to London from Derby, where he had been a member of the Lunar Society and knew Josiah Wedgwood. He became a neighbour of Doctor Johnson in Bolt Court and 'the common resort of the scientific and ingenious of all ranks and nations'. From 1771–82 he was one of an informal group calling themselves 'the civil engineers' which included John Smeaton (1724–92), and in London he renewed his friendship with Priestley.[126] These informal interchanges and groupings expressed and strengthened the intellectual energies of the age. The classical schools and Augustan scholarship were sustained by London's literary discourse, the Nonconformist academies by the solid piety and learning of the mercantile community, and the scientific and mathematical curriculum also drew on these more informal interchanges. Moreover the lively life of the capital drew all these strands together – Dr Johnson, staunch Anglican and Augustan that he was, scorched his wig by performing chemical experiments, advised his dear Mrs Thrale that 'Nothing amuses more harmlessly than computation',[127] enjoyed the company of dissenting scholars, and justified a lengthy prose passage by saying 'Let it be considered that it comprises an account of six-and-thirty years, and those the years of Dr Watts.'[128]

During the century the organization of learning and practice became increasingly complex and formal, providing London with a number of intellectual, technical and professional focal points and powerhouses. The Royal Society, whatever its shortcomings, had two great Presidents in Newton and Sir Joseph Banks and its influence on the educational potential of the capital with substantial. The Royal Society for the Encouragement of Arts, Manufacturers and Commerce was founded in 1754, the Royal Academy in 1768, the Royal Institution in 1799. Army education also became more specialized and professional. The formation of the Royal Artillery in 1716 put much higher technical demands on its personnel, and the Royal Military Academy for artillery and engineer officers was founded at Woolwich in 1741, an important influence on general education and interacting with scientific and mathematical studies in the London area. In turn it drew on the resources of London Schools. John Bonnycastle (1750–1821), for example, kept a private academy in Hackney and later became Professor of Mathematics at Woolwich.[129] More general military preparation was not well served by the various military academies in the London suburbs. When Arthur Wellesley wished to take up a military career his parents had to send him to a French academy and it was not until 1812 that the Royal Military College at Sandhurst was founded.[130] Cartography had also become officially organized in military hands in the Ordnance Survey. Early in the next century specialist professional associations increased. The Institute of Civil Engineers emerged in 1817 from that Smeatonian group which had been meeting forty years before. It received its Charter in 1828.[131] The process is parallel to that which transformed the open Nonconformist academies into theological colleges for professionals. The days of the 'Mathematical practitioners' were over. By the reign of Victoria 'the scientist had disappeared into the laboratory, the private teacher had become a schoolmaster or a professor . . .' 'All had parted company . . .'.[132]

This increased specialization and professionalism not only made the private teacher more of a professional, it handed to private schools the responsibility of preparing specialists and professionals. The Enlightenment had created a new curriculum but its established institutions remained predominantly Augustan. The development of secondary schooling must therefore be traced next through the history of the private schools.

The Growth of London 1600–1900

Harrow

Highgate

Hampstead

R. Brent

Ealing

Chelsea

Battersea

Putney

Richmond

Clapham

R. Thames

Kingston

R. Wandle

0   Miles   5

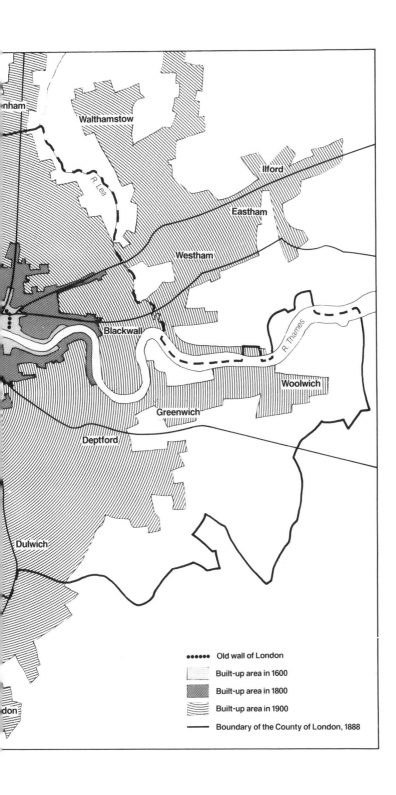

nham

Walthamstow

Ilford

Eastham

Westham

R. Lea

Blackwall

R. Thames

Woolwich

Greenwich

Deptford

Dulwich

don

●●●●●● Old wall of London

Built-up area in 1600

Built-up area in 1800

Built-up area in 1900

Boundary of the County of London, 1888

IV

The contribution of private adventure schools in the eighteenth and nineteenth centuries

Perhaps nothing has done more to distort the understanding of the history of education than the neglect and undervaluing of the contribution of the private schools. While this may be due partly to difficulties of documentation, for such schools and teachers rarely left records let alone archival collections, it is also ideological, for to give value to private enterprise in education is often unacceptable. The development of the concept of secondary education in London and its environs cannot however be understood without some systematic study of this crucial contribution, which serviced society and economy through several discernible periods. These may be described as first the development of specialized teaching by visiting masters or in 'writing schools', from the sixteenth century or even earlier until well into the eighteenth century; second, during this same period the private school of a more general character developed, and in the eighteenth century was consolidated as a substantial sector of school provision, sometimes expressing particular aspects of Enlightenment philosophy and practice. Such schools were sometimes classical, though usually not exclusively so, and religious conflicts had played a part in their establishment and continuation. In a third period, with the economic and social transformations associated with the Industrial Revolution, private schools, essential to the newly emerging and established middle classes, enjoyed a time of their greatest importance. By the second half of the nineteenth century a fourth period in which something like a systematization of private schooling begins to emerge can be discerned.

Private schooling and the Enlightenment

In the discussion of the first of these periods it has already been suggested that the private school, for both boys or girls, may be regarded as a legitimate and useful application of skill and enterprise in a city with ever more complex and specialized social, economic and cultural needs. Eighteenth-century London inherited a number of already well-established private schools from this first period. One of the best known was 'Hackney School', or 'Newcome's Academy', founded in 1685 by Benjamin Morland, who like the Newcome family had puritan

128

sympathies and scientific interests, though at the Restoration both families had conformed. When in 1703 Peter Newcome became vicar of Hackney, Morland's school was already flourishing and Henry, the vicar's son, was prepared there for entry to Cambridge. He returned to the school as assistant, married Morland's daughter Lydia and in 1721 took over the school when its founder became High Master of St Paul's. Morland's usher, who went to St Paul's with him, was James Greenwood, author or *An Essay towards a practical English Grammar* (1711) and *The London Vocabulary* (1713), an adaptation of the *Orbis Pictus* of Comenius. Hackney School had a reputation for enlightened teaching methods and became a 'seminary of much celebration, patronized by representatives of the noble houses of Grafton, Devonshire, Essex and many other families of consequence and distinction'. Henry Cavendish was probably the most distinguished of these pupils, sent to Dr Newcome in 1742 when he was eleven and going directly from there to Cambridge. Philip Yorke, first Earl of Hardwick, sent his sons to Dr Newcome. Other pupils came from City families. The Hackney curriculum was wide; it included Latin, Greek, French, Geography, mathematics and natural philosophy, and some navigation and military subjects were also taught. The boys had a degree of freedom to pursue their own interests. Botanizing excursions were something of a feature of the school, and so were dramatic performances. Every third year a play was given by the pupils, sometimes 'upwards of a hundred gentlemen's coaches' arriving for the occasion.

Teachers at the school included William Jones, the mathematician, and from 1785 to 1794 George Coleridge, the older brother of Samuel Taylor Coleridge, was assistant master. The Newcome family itself seems to have had considerable talent for teaching at least in the early part of the century. Henry Newcome died in 1756 leaving a substantial fortune and the family kept the school until 1820 when the old house and fields were sold to the London Orphan Society; since 1685 it had been a substantial source of profit to the same family.[1] The family nature of such schools corresponded closely to the scale and organization of the contemporary domestic stage of industry and business organization. The Manor House School in Marylebone was established in 1703 by Mr Denis de la Place in a large mansion with two wings standing on the site of Devonshire Mews. In 1711 its curriculum was advertised as 'Latin, mathematics, etc.'. When he died, the school was carried on by his widow and then her son-in-law, Dr Fountaine, who became its sole owner. The school benefited from court patronage, and the natural sons of many noble families were placed there – the best way to get into the school was said to be through the good offices of the midwife of the Princess of Wales. Other aristocratic pupils entered through the front door and at one time it had more than a hundred boys who made a gay procession with their flowing hair and coloured coats as they walked to Marylebone Church.[2] Another school with a long but much more obscure history was variously called Hornsey Academy or Crouch End Academy. In the next century it was advertised as 'founded in 1710' but elsewhere it was said to be as old as 1686. When John Bewick, the engraver, brother of the more famous Thomas, went there to teach drawing it was kept by Nathaniel Norton and contained 'near a hundred fine boys'.[3] These northern villages were considered particularly healthy for schools. Enfield had a famous establishment, founded as an offshoot of the Grammar School when in about 1660 Robert Uvedale obtained the lease of Enfield Palace in order to take boarders; this developed into a separate 'Palace School'. Uvedale's reputation as scholar and botanist and the healthy situation attracted pupils, and during the Plague year he claimed that the entire household escaped infection by inhaling the vapours of vinegar poured over a red-hot brick. This school does not seem to have had an altogether continuous history throughout the eighteenth century but it was well established early in the next century.[4]

The sustaining of reputation and tradition in the hands of one family was important to the development of schools of this kind, but most private schools had comparatively short lives and their reputation rested on the abilities of one or two successive owners. An example was the school kept at Isleworth from about 1698 to 1711 by James Ellis (b.1660), a non-juror. In about 1707 the guardians of Thomas Coke, first Earl of Leicester, sent him to Mr Ellis who received 'young gentlemen of quality' and gave them 'home comforts'. The fees were £50 a year with gratuities for the ten ushers – some of these must have been visiting masters for there were many 'extras' including French, dancing and drawing. Young Coke took a private tutor and four servants with him, and kept horses and a groom, but he worked hard and received a good education. From about 1711 until 1743, the Reverend Samuel Hemming took over the school and one of his assistants, the Reverend William Campbell of Eton and King's, became rector of Greenford in 1733.[5] Such erratic glimpses of a school are typical, and difficult to evaluate in detail. The sheer volume of provision is what gives it significance and private education must therefore be judged overall for the purposes it served and by its general characteristics and qualities. Individual masters or families, however much dedicated to teaching, could not have made a livelihood unless these schools had served some useful function in contemporary society.

One function was sectarian, for as well as the academies which received some degree of official support from the Nonconformist communities, there were many ordinary private schools kept by dissenters of various persuasions. A 'numerous and respectable school' was kept at Uxbridge Common by the Presbyterian Dr Rutherford from 1769 until nearly the end of the century. In 1791 the 'Annual Examination and Exhibition of this great and flourishing Seminary' lasted several days and attracted a 'very numerous and accomplished assembly of spectators' for its display of 'the elements of the useful and liberal sciences, as well as in French, Italian, Greek, and Latin'. The boys not only did well in declamation but 'showed that they understood what they read and recited'. They also, in this year of mounting revolution in France, gave a lively debate on the expulsion of the Tarquins, which demonstrated 'alertness of thought on the application of History, both ancient and modern, to the great principles of morality and political economy'. Dr Rutherford was author of a *View of Ancient History* and his effective teaching is witnessed also in his retirement to his own border country. He took a pupil with him whose parents were in India and his lessons were shared by a local boy, William Jerdan, who later ascribed 'every advantage beyond a mere school education' which he had 'to the superior course of cultivation by which mind and thought were evoked, instead of parrot rote and cuckoo repetition'. At Uxbridge Rutherford's school flourished until at least 1818 when there was still a 'considerable and respecatable seminary' attached to the Presbyterian church.[6]

Another dissenting school was that of the Reverend John Ryland, a Baptist minister, at Enfield. Ryland, active in the contemporary dissenting debate upon Calvinism and the freedom of the will, was minister and kept an academy at Northampton where he was assisted by John Clarke, a young lawyer's clerk who changed his occupation when his kindly nature revolted against attending a hanging as substitute for the sheriff. He married Ryland's stepdaughter and moved with him when he took a large house 'eminently fitted for a school', roomy, commodious, with large gardens, pasturage and paddock at Enfield, 'that charming village among the very loveliest in England'. Ryland became a beloved local character known as the 'Devil Dodger', 'stout, rubicund, facetious in manner, and oddly forcible when preaching'. The school flourished and was taken over altogether by Clarke, 'a man of nobly liberal opinions, of refined taste in literature, as gentle-hearted as he was wise, and as wise as he was gentle-hearted'. His methods were advanced, no cane was used, but 'account books' were kept for performance and behaviour. Pupils included most notably John Keats, who came when he was barely out of frocks and left when he was fourteen. Here he showed 'no extraordinary indications of intellectual character', but 'a determined and steady spirit combined with an avid curiosity' which he satisfied by reading voyages, travels, histories – Burnet's *History of his own Times* at meals, Miss Edgeworth's novels, Lemprière's *Classical Dictionary*, 'which he appeared to learn'. He voluntarily undertook the translation of *The Aeneid*, which he criticized for 'a feebleness in the structure of the work'. Clarke kept the school until he sold it in 1810, and the house remained in use as a school until 1849.[7]

Another famous Enfield dissenting school was kept at Forty Hill by the Reverend Andrew Kinross, a Presbyterian. His 'flourishing academy' was attended by Scots boys including the grandson of the Earl of Hopetoun, and James, later Duke of Roxburghe, and others of their

kind, for after the Act of Union London was providing not only for
dissenters, but for the Scottish establishment.[8] Dr James Burgh, a native
of Perthshire, was assistant to Kinross, and later had an academy at
Stoke Newington from 1747 to 1771, 'with reputation to himself and
benefit to his scholars', who included Samuel Rogers. Later he moved
to Newington Green and the school seems to have been carried on from
1770–1800 by the Reverend James Pickburn who was author of a well-
known *Dissertation on the English Verb*. Rogers and his friend William
Maltby, who later succeeded Porson as librarian of the London Institution, once ventured from the school to the very door of Dr Johnson,
when their courage failed them.[9] Another Scot, the Reverend Anthony
Crole, had an academy for the last quarter of the eighteenth century at
Queen's Head Lane in Islington. He entered the ministry through the
interest of the Countess of Huntingdon, but in 1776 became an Independent.[10] New emerging ecclesiastical preference also needed
educational provision. William Bicknell, educated at Wesley's Kingswood, established an academy at Ponders End in Enfield in 1789, which
he later moved to Tooting. The future Lord Chancellor Truro was
probably a pupil.[11] As the dissenting academies gradually gave up their
connection with general education, Nonconformist divines and scholars
put their energies and talents more into private schools – Thomas
Belsham was one example and his friend Eliezer Cogan (1762–1855)
was another. Cogan was tutor at Daventry, and after various calls
became minister at Enfield and at Cheshunt (1800) and then at
Walthamstow. Here he concentrated his labours, transferred his school
to Higham Hill and reached great fame for his teaching. His pupils
included Dr Hampden, the future Bishop of Hereford, Russell Gurney,
later Recorder of London, and Benjamin Disraeli. Cogan did not like
Disraeli; 'I never could get him to understand the subjunctive,' said the
scholar who was praised by Porson and Parr.[12]

Cogan's pupils illustrate one aspect of these dissenting schools – their
pupils represented a wide range of religious affiliations. One of their
functions was certainly to use scholarly talents and enterprise and to
provide education for boys excluded from the endowed schools, but
many of their pupils would not have attended these schools even if they
had been open to them, and many more would not go to them though
they could. Private schools probably attracted pupils largely by their
quality of teaching and curriculum, for their most important function
was the consolidation of the new and broader curriculum, based on the
classics, but including mathematics and some branches of science,
modern languages with perhaps some historical and geographical
elements, and often combined with vocational subjects. Even when a
school was still called a 'French School', as was that kept at Turnham
Green, Chiswick, by Mons. Margarot in about 1780, this probably
referred not so much to the nationality of the owner as to the fact that
French and some other modern subjects were not charged as 'extras'.

Here for £42 a year and £10 10s entrance 'young noblemen and gentlemen' were boarded and taught French, Latin, Greek and geography. Writing, arithmetic, book-keeping, Portuguese, dancing, drawing and fencing were the 'extras'.[13] In 1769 Robert Dower's Academy in Cross Street, Islington, 'a pleasant and retired part of the town next the fields', treated young gentlemen who were 'genteelly boarded' with 'the greatest tenderness', and taught them 'writing in all hands, the Latin, Greek and French languages, arithmetic, the Italian Method of book-keeping, the Use of the Globes, and all branches of the mathematics'. They were fitted 'in the most expeditious manner for the compting-house, army, navy or university'.[14] In the King's Road, Chelsea, in 1766 the Reverend William Williams BD, and Jacob Des Moulins, 'Writing Master', kept 'The English Grammar School', where they undertook the boarding and instruction of boys in 'English grammatically, according to Dr Lowth's Plan, and by his Grammar', writing, arithmetic, merchants' accounts, French, Latin, Greek and 'other branches of literature and polite accomplishments'. An indication of the use to which this kind of curriculum was put was their frank acknowledgement that particular attention would be given to boys 'whose parents designing them for trade, do not choose they should learn Latin, while those intended for 'Westminster, Eaton, Winchester, etc.', will be properly 'initiated in Prosodia and making Latin verses'.[15] The tradition and function of the earlier writing schools continued and while such schools were providing a broad curriculum, many parents were still treating the menu as *à la carte* rather than *table d'hôte*.

This is illustrated by another school in that agreeable and popular village, Islington. At the end of Colebrook Row the Reverend John Rule, who died in about 1775, long kept an academy where he aimed to 'form the gentleman, scholar and man of business'. He published *The English and French Letter Writer* in 1766, which formed a complete introduction to trade and business, and he invented a new method of teaching pupils to write in a few weeks. His school was famous for dramatic performances; in 1766 *The Agreeable Surprise*, translated from the French of Marivaux, in 1769 the tragedy of *Cato*, 'with suitable entertainments, prologues, etc.'. In 1766 a collection of poems by his pupils was published as *Poetical Blossoms, or the Sports of Genius*. It is in this unlikely setting that an advertisement for Rule's course reveals its varied, practical, even utilitarian, nature. Youths were:

Boarded, tenderly treated and expeditiously instructed in the languages, writing, arithmetic, merchants' accounts and mathematics, with dancing, drawing, music, fencing and every other accomplishment requisite to form the gentleman, scholar, and the man of business upon the most reasonable terms which may be known . . . grown up gentlemen intended for the Army, Sea Service, Trade or Merchant's Counting House, may attend as boarders.

Gentlemen designed for a military life may acquire every
accomplishment necessary for their important station by a short
attendance at this Academy. The mariner may attain in a precise and
practical manner every part of knowledge requisite for his
employment in four or five weeks with a summary compendium of
ships' accounts. Gentlemen intended for trade and the Merchant's
Counting House may be taught to write well and cast up by a short
and practical method in a few weeks. They are also taught merchants'
accounts by double entry in a very short time, with two sets of books,
one calculated for wholesale and the other for retail business, and
exactly agreeable to the practice of the most eminent merchants and
traders of London, with every other accomplishment for gentlemen
intended for trade and commerce. Finally, artificers of every sort may
be properly and expeditiously instructed in every part of science
requisite for their several professions.

The drawing master also attended pupils at home, did 'all sorts of
business in the picture way' and made designs for 'silk, tapestry,
Axminster and other carpets, etc.'.[16]

These examples are a reminder that in this period private schools
retained a strong element of their origins in the visiting-master, writing-
school stage of their development. Their very domestic and expedient
nature enabled them to fulfil a number of purposes, which was both
their strength and their weakness.

Private schools were used both as an alternative to the endowed
schools and as preparatory for them. When Charles James Fox at the age
of seven detected his mother in a blunder in Roman history he announced his decision that he should go to school rather than be taught at
home before going to Eton. He accordingly went to Monsieur
Pampellonne who kept a school at Wandsworth, 'then much in vogue
among the aristocracy'. Here he probably 'acquired his excellent French
accent' but the course must have been predominantly classical, for
eighteen months later the child decided that he was ready for Eton.[17]
Henry, later tenth Earl of Pembroke, was sent, by the decision of his
parents, to the same school from Wilton in 1743 when he was nine. His
letters home concentrate on important matters such as the supply of
venison and 'hairs' to be sent to him and the health of the little horse he
had left behind, but one is written in quite competent French for a little
boy. By 1746 he was at Eton.[18] The Manor Farm House at Chiswick
was kept as a prosperous boarding-school of about 80 boys by the
Reverend Mr Crawford and from about 1786 by the Reverend Thomas
Horne. There young Shaftesbury was sent in 1808 when he was seven
before going to Harrow. But John Copley, later Lord Lyndhurst, 'here
laid the foundations of his classical knowledge', and went direct to
Cambridge as did at least seven other pupils.[19] 'Dr Fountaine's' at
Marylebone was described as essentially preparatory, and he was said

not to have troubled his pupils with 'overmuch learning'. Matthew Lewis, author of *The Monk*, and George Coleman the dramatist, went on to Westminster and Charles, later second Earl Grey, was here three years before going to Eton, but others remained till going to the university.[20] Another school which served these dual purposes was in the Manor House of Coldhall at Ealing. It was already a school when the unfortunate Dr Dodd (later hanged for forgery) became its proprietor in 1776, then it was taken over and carried on for twenty-six years by Samuel Goodenough, later Bishop of Carlisle, an excellent classical scholar and botanist. He had charge of the sons of 'many noblemen and gentlemen of position', including Lord Bute and the Dukes of Rutland, Beaufort and Portland, and he almost certainly owed his promotion partly to their patronage.[21] Dr Weedon Butler, who had been amanuensis to Dr Dodd in his *Commentary on the Holy Bible*, set up school in Cheyne Walk, Chelsea, in about 1770 and for forty years kept it with great reputation for scholarship, 'where many persons of considerable rank and family distinction have been so thoroughly grounded in morality and gentle learning as bright ornaments to their country'. Both his sons, Weedon and George, were educated by their father until they went up to Cambridge. Weedon became his father's classical assistant and then carried on the school until 1831. George became headmaster of Harrow, and the family became part of the important 'intellectual aristocracy' of the nineteenth century.[22]

For a private school to prepare successfully for the endowed or 'great' schools, and even more to rival them for pupils, a sound reputation for classical scholarship was essential. This was the case with the Scottish Dr William Rose, translator of Sallust, who had a prosperous school at Chiswick from 1758 to his death in 1786. He was a graduate of Aberdeen and had taught at Doddridge's academy at Northampton but his school cannot be considered as sectarian. Dr Johnson praised him for his scholarship but blamed him for his leniency: 'What the boys gain at one end they lose at the other.'[23] Rose's pupil and later assistant, Dr Charles Burney (1757–1817), son of Johnson's old friend the musician, married Rose's daughter and opened a school at Hammersmith in 1786, which he later moved to Greenwich. Its prosperity was undoubtedly due to Burney's high reputation as a Greek scholar – he was said to be the equal of Porson and Parr.[24]

Dr Johnson was less complimentary about another Scottish schoolmaster, the Episcopalian James Elphinston (1721–1809), who came to London in 1752 and established his school first at Brompton and then in Kensington in a large elegant house opposite the King's Gardens. 'I would not put a boy to him whom I intended for a man of learning; but for the sons of citizens, who are to learn a little, get good morals, and then go to trade, he may do very well.' Johnson did send one pupil, young Ottway, to him in 1773. There were doubts not only about Elphinston's Latin – his translation of Martial was said to be a 'whole quarto of nonsense and gibberish' – but also of his politics – his school was even called a 'Jacobite seminary' by one disgruntled pupil. But calmer estimates show that it provided the broad curriculum, good moral and social training, and kindly conscientious teaching which attracted the kind of parents whom Johnson described. Elphinston was a good French scholar, and also taught geography, chronology, accounts, writing and arithmetic as well as providing for accomplishments such as drawing, dancing, fencing. He laid stress on the learning of English. Later he developed eccentric ideas about reformed spelling. He must however have made a financial success of his school, and his friendship with Johnson and Benjamin Franklin and his place in literary society suggest that he was a man of some sense and achievement.[25]

Elphinston's school was one which led to the claim that some eighteenth-century academies were forerunners of today's comprehensive schools. London did contain important schools which provided a broad curriculum and a choice of courses and specialisms. One was Watts's Writing School, already described. A neighbouring academy, in Soho Square, also had a history dating from the seventeenth century – Mr Meure sent a student from here to Cambridge in 1691, and in 1704 it was 'esteemed the best in England'. This may have been the same as that kept in Soho Square by Martin Clare in about 1717, its 'Old Boys' Association' dated from 1719, and in 1720 *Youth's Introduction to Trade and Business for the use of schools* was published by 'M Clare, schoolmaster in Soho Square with whom youth may board and be fitted for business'. Commercial subjects were stressed, but Clare considered that a businessman needed a liberal education, and classics were included. In 1774 he was joined as co-director by the Reverend Cuthbert Barwis, of Queen's College Oxford, and together they published *Rules and Orders for the Government of the Academy in Soho Square, London*. The main course, with board, cost £30 and included writing, arithmetic, grammar (Latin, Greek and English), geography, French, public weekly lectures on morality, religion and useful literature such as natural and experimental philosophy, 'for the explication of which a large apparatus of machines and instruments is provided'. Maps, globes, pens, ink, fire, candles, pews at English and French churches, the use of the barber and a certain amount of darning were also included. Mathematics, which included mensuration, gauging, surveying, navigation, were extra, and so were merchants' accounts and the accomplishments. There was a library for the use of pupils and dramatics were in vogue. There were special French, dancing, drawing and fencing schools, the last under the famous Angelo, who seems to have had something like a boarding-house with a 'customary entrance fee' of £5 5s or an equivalent in linen and plate.

Clare died in 1757 and Barwis's partner Barrow was perhaps the father of Dr William Barrow (1754–1836) who was head of the academy by the late 1780s. At Oxford he had won a prize for an essay on *Academic*

Education which he later enlarged and published in 1802 in two volumes as *An Essay on Education in which are particularly considered the merits and defects of the discipline and instruction in our Academies*. By then the Reverend William Whitelock had succeeded him, and in 1801 David Morrice dedicated his *Art of Teaching* to this headmaster of 'the senior academy'.

This academy served a number of functions. Its drawing school set Thomas Rowlandson and Joseph Turner on their careers by way of the Royal Academy schools. Some went straight on to the university, while John Horne Tooke and James Boswell the younger went on to Westminster. Edmund Burke entrusted his beloved son Richard 'to the charge of Dr Barrow', demonstrating 'the respectability of the school and its soundness as an educational institution'.[26]

Other academies were more specialized – nautical, mathematical, military, etc. By including these and some Nonconformist academies, together with schools such as Rule's which set out to provide for a wide variety of needs and Elphinston's which gave a broad general course with certain 'extras', it has been possible to postulate a group of academies having literary, mathematical and scientific, vocational and technical 'streams', with accomplishments and dramatic performances as another branch of the curriculum.[27] The theory that these were the multilateral or comprehensive schools of their day presupposes an anachronistic concept of secondary schooling as part of a continuous process, related to theories of human abilities and development. These academies and schools offering such varied courses were often still attended for short periods, for limited purposes and by boys of widely different ages, and even young men who needed the services of the barber, and they often readily transferred from one institution to another. It is however clear that some conscious and coherent contribution to educational practice and theory was formulating in these academies. The difficulty is to define this usefully in contemporary terms.

The claim that private schooling had a long tradition of progressive influence stretching back to the days of Priestley and Doddridge[28] has been advanced as polemic in defence of private schooling as a sector, but is perhaps more relevant as an historical hypothesis about what has been the case. The very flexibility, expediency and domestic nature of private schooling in this eighteenth-century period made it responsive to new needs and movements of ideas, or of feeling, even of sentiment – and sentiment became of increasing significance as the century drew to a close. To say that private schools put into systematic practice the ideas of Locke or of Rousseau would be making an over-strong claim, but they did both express and exploit the climate of opinions, notions, preferences and the broad experiences of living and learning through which the sense of Locke and the sensibility of Rousseau flowed into educational provision and practice. These influences, however indirectly and diffusely, helped to shape private schooling and provide the particular 'merits and defects of the discipline and instruction of our Academies', in Dr Barrow's phrase.

Locke's rejection of innate ideas, his theory of knowledge, his empiricism, his belief in reason, had direct and documented influence on the dissenting academies, and their practices and principles in turn influenced him and also flowed into private schooling, itself a demonstration of the influence of Locke's ideas about domestic education. His dislike of schools was based on his experiences at Westminster and on a general knowledge of the endowed schools of his day, but his urgent advice to parents to educate their sons at home, to 'spare no care nor cost' in getting and paying a good tutor, was difficult to apply even for the magnates for whom he was writing. For the less wealthy parent, especially the city-dweller or one not disposed to be a martyr to the education of his boys, a private school offered an attractive alternative. 'Domestic education' could be interpreted as an extension of the home, and the small size and hap-hazard organization of many schools was in fact of this nature. The same broad influence shaped the content of such education. Locke expressed the view that Latin, while necessary for a gentleman, must be kept in its place, while Greek was not necessary and French should be begun before Latin. Arithmetic, geography, chronology, history and geometry should also be taught and general and natural philosophy. This was the usual pattern of studies in many of the London schools and academies and Locke's emphasis on the importance of practical and technical subjects was reflected in their vocational courses. Watts at the Tower Hill Academy acknowledged the influence of Locke's advice that commercial should be part of general education; 'Merchants Accounts, though not likely to help a gentleman to get an Estate, yet possibly there is not anything of more use and Efficiency to make him preserve the Estate he has.' Moreover 'Business and full employment is the only Barrier to keep out the Enemy and secure the Man.' One London teacher, James Barclay, who had schools at Tottenham High Cross and Goodman's Fields and became curate of Edmonton, in his *Treatise on Education* of 1743 systematically expounds the ideas of Locke as applied to private schooling. A truly domestic education was impracticable; tutors could serve several families in this way; the curriculum should include geography, arithmetic and merchants' accounts as Latin and Greek were of little use 'to one half the world'. Children had a variety of gifts and temperaments and the 'general way of recommending the same task ... and application and progress' from them all was ridiculous. In most cases private schools did not reflect so consciously the arguments of Locke but rather the experience of a society which needed to differentiate and balance certain branches of knowledge and to refine and master certain skills and techniques. In the eighteenth century, sense was elevated to a guiding principle, for it implied the application of reason rather than mere tradition to the tasks of learning, of living, and of earning a living.

Locke lived before a concept of childhood had fully emerged, but his cool, rational and affectionate observation of children reflects a period of preparation for such a conscious idea, and he and his like inspired practices which helped it into being. Locke recommended reasoning with children within their capacity. 'They understand it as early as they do language; and, if I misobserve not they love to be treated as rational creatures sooner than is imagined.' This growing understanding of children, the development of what today would be called a psychology of learning, and changes in attitudes to authority can be discerned from the very beginning of the century.[29]

Robert Ainsworth (1660–1743), a non-juror who later inclined to Calvinist views and then attended Methodist prayer meetings, 'like old Simeon . . . waiting to see the Lord's salvation', had from 1698 onwards schools in several London parishes including 'a considerable boarding school in Bethnal Green', and then in Hackney. His *Thesaurus* gained him a reputation in classical schools, but his *Most Natural and Easy Way of Institution containing Proposals for making a Domestic Education less Chargeable to Parents and More Easy and Beneficial to Children* (1698) describes a theory of education which reflects the ideas of the early Enlightenment; indeed he acknowledges the influence of 'the ingenious Mr Locke'. Pupils may make considerable 'progress in languages' and also in arts and sciences in two years, with 'ease and pleasure both to master and scholar'. He saw the absurdity of first teaching abstract rules. Lilly's *Grammar* was slow and unnecessary, and 'any master with half a sheet of paper' could extract from it 'what is sufficient for any lad to know before he reads an author'. He proposed a conversational method, a master who could speak Latin fluently spending the entire day with the boys, it was to be a 'living language in the family'. Nothing was to be imposed as a task, there was to be no punishment of any kind, but *praemiums* which would mount up to a sufficient sum 'to buy this or that pleasant Book, neat and delicately bound'. The master was to take care that 'two or three of the last have their monies made up at the same time lest any should be discouraged'. English was to be studied, and history and geography taught with maps and pictures to form the material for language teaching, which 'being in itself, as consisting of hard and uncouth words, unpleasant, or at best insipid . . . ought to be well cook'd and made pleasant, before it is served up to children'; here there are also echoes of Comenius. Parental co-operation was to be fostered and Ainsworth illustrates the interpretation of this kind of education as an extension of the home. The placing of the school in a good air but near enough to London was to enable parents frequently to 'enquire into their son's proficiency, they may do it in summer when they have a mind to divert themselves with a walk, and in winter by coach, at a small expense'. The children were not to return home during the course, but parents paid for a monthly Latin letter from their boys. Ainsworth preferred to take only about a dozen children at a time, from six to eleven years of age, but as he made a considerable fortune by his schools it seems likely that his proposals may have been only partially put into practice with a larger number of pupils.[30]

This tradition of English empiricism reinforced more or less explicitly by the ideas of the Continental *philosophes* was considered attractive to London parents throughout the century. In 1788 Mr Harris advertised his academy in Sloane Street in the *Morning Post*. His aims were not only 'to convey the knowledge of languages, Art and Sciences into the minds of Youth', but to 'inform the heart to Virtue; to fix its principles so deep in their young breasts as to render it difficult, if not morally impossible, ever to extirpate them'. The native tongue was to come first, to pave the way for Latin and Greek or modern languages, as this removes 'Aversion and Terror'. Then the rules of Latin syntax were taught in English, which saves half the time, and when the pupil could read enough to distinguish between the different constructions and periods, these were taught formally; 'they learn thoroughly what they do learn'. Occasionally conversation was in Latin. Ancient and modern history was begun as a relaxation and a means of the education of morals and taste. 'It is likewise the best remedy against the pernicious effects of the dangerous novels that overwhelm the present age.' Kindness and politeness in the treatment of children and 'placing them in the ranks of friends and companions' always produces 'the happiest effects'. The disposition of the children must be attended to, example and reason used 'to quell any gust of passion and eradicate every peevish humour'. There was daily exercise in fencing and 'manly diversions', and youth 'intended for Trade, Navigation' etc. were 'expeditiously qualified for their different employments'. Here in this bid for custom, echoes of the ideas of Locke can be clearly heard. They have become the currency of common sense in the educational market.[31]

The children painted by Hogarth or Zoffany, dressed as miniature adults in full-skirted coats, breeches, silk stockings and lace ruffles, profited from these reforms which stemmed from Locke and the early *philosophes*. But by the turn of the century the little boys in short nankeen jackets and loose trousers painted by Hoppner, Lawrence or Raeburn belong to a different era. Through the second half of the eighteenth century new influences are at work. Native empiricism was strongly reinforced by continental influences; the impact of Rousseau's *Emile*, translated into English in 1762, the very year of its publication in France, was immense. From this period, it has been claimed, dates 'a decisive break with the prevailing ideas of education', 'the true beginning of modern progressive education'.[32] In Rousseau's work, it is true, there emerges a fully developed theory of childhood and adolescence, which unlike Locke, sees the child, and the adult he is to become, as an organism. The London schools however give ample evidence that this influence was powerful because earlier theories had prepared for it and contributed to its formation. Rousseau was expressing, and pushing to their conclusions, ideas which had been current and which had sometimes already been put into action.

There was something of Rousseau-mania in England, and its constructive results continued to find expression in private practice. One of the best-documented examples was David Williams's Laurence Street Academy opened in Chelsea in 1774. He was a 'product of the British radical and Dissenting tradition which was itself inspired by the ideals of the European Enlightenment'. Educated at a dissenting academy for the ministry, he became pastor of a Highgate congregation but his advanced and unorthodox views led him to give up his ministry and to put into practice 'a plan of education I had long considered'. His school only lasted two years and contained at most twenty pupils but was given significance by Williams's polemic writings and subsequent career as radical deist, preacher of a universal religion, friend of French Revolutionary leaders and of scientists and men of affairs such as Franklin, Wedgwood and Priestley. In his *Lectures on Education* (1774) Williams supported the main thesis put forward by Rousseau but advocated less passion and 'vague theories and visionary systems', and more common sense. Because existing educational practices were misguided did not mean that children should run about 'idly and at haphazard'. Understanding of children's development would enable the teacher to find 'a mode of instruction, suitable to the restless activity and curiosity of infancy'. The 'moment when reason unfolds as the sun rises' should be seized, and the first twelve years of life were a time when knowledge was most desired and best assimilated. The teacher should observe also the individual capacities of children and contrive incidents and provide means by which curiosity should be aroused and satisfied. Authority should not be imposed, but used to guide experience. Punishment was not used at Chelsea but a school court, headed by a magistrate who changed weekly, was in charge of rules of conduct; there was a kind of social contract which operated through 'equal laws, enacted by general consent'. Morality was to be formed by an understanding of the consequences of action. This prudential emphasis underlines the way in which the empiricism so long applied to the study of the natural world was now turning to human affairs. Williams declared that 'great attention should be given to the human mind. . . . Till this is done men in general . . . will have no rules to go on in education.' What such observation found was not always strictly rational. 'The story of human nature is a fair romance' wrote Rousseau himself. Romanticism and Utilitarianism were both products of the Age of Reason.[33]

The difficulty in estimating the influence of the *philosophes* on London schools is one of evidence, for well-developed and detailed arguments put forward on the basis of two years' experience by an advanced thinker and practitioner cannot be regarded as exactly useful for this purpose. Other schoolmasters of the London region of this period, with less claim to radical fame and more substantial educational experience, also wrote justificatory treatises which put forward sincerely held ideas, with an evident confidence in their acceptance by a certain section of the reading public and educational market. From these it is possible to deduce something of the climate of educational opinion and perhaps some further indication of practice in the last part of this century of change and enlightenment.

In 1818 William Johnstone, master of an academy in Stanmore, published the *Result of Experience in the Practice of Instruction or Hints for the improvement of the Art of Tuition as regards the Middling and Higher Classes of Society*. He claimed to have been 'accessory on different occasions to the instruction of at least one thousand five hundred boys', there was 'no department of tuition whether public or private' in which he had not been engaged. He had read 'much of what has been written on education', and tested the validity of theory by experiment and had also visited other schools to 'ascertain by trial and enquiry the chief merits of the few variations . . . between the plans of . . . numerous teachers . . .'. As a result of this research, experiment and experience he defined the aim of 'stipendiary instruction', that is teaching for which parents were prepared to pay, as a liberal education, interpreted in the light of 'the local and temporary state of the arts, the sciences, literary refinement, professional qualifications, and commerce'. To be truly liberal, education must include science and prepare the pupil to 'pursue at the close . . . whatever path in life he may then determine to be most eligible'. Specialization however must not take place too early, or the 'die of profession' be cast irretrievably before the judgement is 'capable of forming any serious election'. He then proceeds to recommend what he rightly describes as an 'Encyclopaedic Course of Liberal Education', and it is a relief to know that Johnstone was opposed to rote learning or cramming. The teacher must 'guard against misconception', and ensure that 'whatever is learned, is properly understood'. Geography, for example, was to start with local studies and the construction of maps. Each subject must be accommodated to the capacity of the pupil, divested 'as far as possible of obtuseness', and 'brought within the reach of his comprehension'. Explanation and illustration must therefore play an important part, and 'the advantages . . . from the use of experimental illustrations of scientific Instruments and Philosophic Apparatus need scarcely be mentioned'. Textbooks must be carefully chosen and a good school library was essential. Educational visits, 'little tours and instructive excursions', might be made in the holidays, to 'enlarge the scholar's sphere of contemplation, improve his general ideas, excite his curiosity, and give him satisfactory notions of space and distance'.

Discipline in the school was to be maintained by this right approach to teaching, for punishment was usually needed because wrong methods were used. Nor was Johnstone willing to replace fear by competition, which caused envy, irritation of mind and personal enmity, but interest and understanding would induce the 'habitual fulfilment of duty without the expectation of immediate praise or reward'.[34]

Unfortunately little is known of Johnstone's practical application of his elaborate theories. In this respect more is known of Moses Miall, who died in 1829 having kept for a number of years a school at Islington, which he called the Mansion House Academy. In 1822 he published *Practical Remarks on Education*, in which he made 'no pretensions to discovery nor to any new or original system', but tried to collect together what he conceived to be useful and practical from the many so-called improvements in education of 'modern times'. His views on the curriculum were perhaps less expansive but more practical than Johnstone's. He devoted two sensible chapters to the teaching of classics, but considered that they could occupy too much time, and that English should have first place. 'Modern' subjects should include geography and science, freed from its 'cumberous dress'. French should be taught orally, with plenty of practice in the use of words in different but related contexts. Too much time was often taken up in writing it, and grammatical niceties might have to be sacrificed to speaking and correct pronunciation. A school library could be used to combine instruction with amusement, through history, voyages, poetry and philosophy. Miall was greatly ahead of his time in his emphasis on physical education and its link with the enjoyable learning of more intellectual subjects, and the kindly relationship between the teacher and the taught. The teacher must give 'personal attention to each scholar'. Discipline should be maintained by kindness. 'A school is a miniature picture of society ... where the rules are founded on good sense, and suggested by humanity and benevolence for the common good, there will be little difficulty in enforcing obedience.' 'Reason and kindness appear the legitimate weapons with which we should govern the young. . . . The operation of terror is but temporary and leaves the mind with a sentiment of hatred.' Learning should be interesting and enjoyable, the child's 'labours must if possible be produced from the voluntary act of his own mind . . .'. Variety was necessary to maintain interest and relieve fatigue. Miall realized that children's abilities differed widely, and that though kindly methods would not make stupid children clever, they would enable them to make the most of their talents. In the 'public schools' such pupils must 'learn Latin and Greek or remain dunces for the remainder of their lives', but in private academies 'where there is a want of physical power of memory, attention may be paid to the cultivation of the mind by superior instruction in the native language, or by communicating a knowledge of history, or geography, and the mathematics, and endeavouring to excite attempts at excellence in drawing, writing, music'. Neither do children all develop at the same rate, 'the development of capacities is various, and in some instances so late, that it is often found, if the period of education be protracted for a year or two . . . , that perseverance is attended with the desired success, and powers of the mind are discovered which in the early period of youth the pupil was not suspected to possess'.[35] Here in these modest local educationalists we have glimpses of an important shift in emphasis. Eighteenth-century understanding of human nature had been a quest for generalization rather than individuality, for amongst the many meanings which were attached to the word 'Nature' the most usual was 'universality', 'uniformity'. Children however are apt to break out of such frameworks when once attention is concentrated on them and their development.

The kind and sensible ideas of Miall do not appear to have been profitable to him as a schoolmaster, for towards the end of his life he was in financial difficulties. Another Islington schoolmaster, the Reverend John Evans, with similar theories, was more materially successful. Born in 1767, he was educated at Bristol Baptist Academy and then at the universities of Aberdeen and Edinburgh. He is another example of the flowing together of Dissenting and Enlightenment streams of influence. In 1792 he became pastor of a City congregation and in 1795 opened a seminary first at Hoxton and then in Pullins Row, Islington. He was a prolific writer, and his *Essay on the Education of Youth* (1799?) described the teacher in Rousseauesque terms as a 'skilful husbandman' who consulted the individual differences of his pupils, and caught 'every favourable opportunity of infusing knowledge', omitting 'no means by which the intellectual and moral powers are stimulated'. The course must be varied according to the age, 'capacity and destination of the pupil'. 'Harsh treatment' which 'sours the temper of both teacher and pupil' must be avoided. Evans wrote sensibly about the curriculum; 'in the eighteenth century a more than usually extended sphere of information is expected', and advertisements for his school corroborate his claim that science was given an important place. In 1821 for example there was 'a course of lectures illustrated by valuable and complete apparatus . . . on astronomy, optics, mechanics, pneumatics, galvanism and electricity, familiarly explaining the phenomena of the universe'. He also paid attention to physical education, in 1810 enlarging his playgrounds at considerable expense, 'with other improvements conducive to the health and recreation of the pupils'.[36]

There is little evidence which can bridge the gap between such ideas and solid proof that they were put into practice but it is a reasonable inference that they reflect theories and practices which were fashionable because they appealed to both sense and sensiblity. The broad curriculum combined with vocational preferences, the enlightened methods which reflected a growing psychological understanding often expressed in language which reflects 'naturalism', the idea of the teacher as a gardener, the increasing attention to the needs of children, to their development, even to their variations of ability and temperament, the changing attitude to authority, reflect, however imperfectly, the ideas of the European Enlightenment grafted on to the English empirical tradition. Some London schools of this period helped to add this new dimension to education.

Schools for girls

Unfortunately the same claim cannot be made for girls' schools of this period. Two important shifts in the history of the family and the household combined during this very 'Age of Reason' to increase pressures, already working in the previous century,[37] towards all the more meretricious and frivolous aspects of the education of girls. The romantic rather than the arranged or business marriage gave a premium to social graces and showy accomplishments, and the transfer of processes of production from the household, and the segregation within it between 'family' and servants, began to deprive women of the wealthier ranks of their economic function, and to bring about that disastrous transformation which made them symbols of conspicuous consumption rather than partners in domestic industry and producers of the necessities of home life, bakers of bread, brewers of beer, boilers of soap, distillers of cordials, compounders of remedies, ointments and so forth. These changes probably began earlier and developed more quickly in London than elsewhere, and the capital had established its pre-eminent position as a centre for fashionable girls' schools even by the end of the seventeenth century. In the eighteenth century this was an expanding industry, and suburbs which were considered both healthy and genteel abounded in ladies' seminaries. Hackney declined somewhat in desirability and was succeeded by Islington and Newington Green in catering for the City community, with many substantial schools including Mrs Clarke's in Cross Street; the old mansion of the Fowler family, Canonbury House; the house of General Fleetwood kept as a school by Mrs Crisp in 1797; and the ladies' boarding-school which 'stood on a beautiful eminence called Mount Pleasant' in 1820.[38] St Pancras was considered an airy and pleasant neighbourhood. Highgate in 1815 had among others a long-established school of great respectability in the Grove. Edmonton was especially known for its great number of boarding-schools, for the City had a long tradition of using these northern villages for sending children to nurse.[39] Schools nearer to the fashionable and official quarters were probably more patronized by those higher up the social scale. The *Spectator* complained that 'foreign fopperies' were desired by parents and they acquired a Parisian finish for their daughters by placing them in a French boarding-school in Bloomsbury or St Giles.[40] Mary Granville, later Mrs Delany, was prepared for her expected post at court in a select academy of 20 pupils kept by Mlle Puelle, a French refugee.[41] Marylebone House, kept by Mons. de la Mare, and then by his daughter Mrs Bellpine, was a 'French boarding-school' and so was Oxford House in the same parish. Here Perdita Robinson (Mary Darby) finished her education and entered the ballet at Covent Garden, whose master had taught dancing at the school.[42] Paddington was still rural and underdeveloped but had by the end of the century at least one long-established school kept in Maida

Vale from 1799 to 1828 or later. Further west, Hammersmith was favoured for schools, and in Fulham York House, Munster House, Claysbrooke House were all schools. Chiswick was given literary fame for one particular fictitious ladies' seminary, and Twickenham had particularly select establishments.[43]

Chelsea and Kensington were however the most fashionable suburban villages for girls' schools of this period. Gorges House, Chelsea, was already famous by the beginning of the century. In 1705 Henry VIII's manor house and Chelsea Place were also let as ladies' schools. Walpole placed his two daughters nearby with Madame Nezeraum, paying high fees of £60 a year.[44] Blacklands was a French school where in 1776 Susannah, eldest child of Josiah Wedgwood, gave satisfaction for her improvement 'as well in her general carriage and behaviour, as in her music, drawing, etc.'.[45] Gough House also became a school for girls kept by the widow of an East India servant. Monmouth House was in part at least occupied by a school and Whitelands House in the King's Road began its long association with education at least as early as 1772, when it was a ladies' school where the Reverend John Jenkins lectured on *Female Education and Christian Fortitude under Affliction.*[46]

Girls' school trade card

The royal connections of Kensington began to give it some advantages over riverside Chelsea. As early as 1683 Mr William Dyer moved his school from Chelsea to Kensington, taking over that of the dancing master Hazard who had been on the staff of Mrs Perwich at Hackney. Large houses which became schools included Campden House, 'one of the most eminent establishments . . . in the neighbourhood of the metropolis', attended by 'the greatest in the land'. Notting

Hill House, Scarsdale House, Clarence House, Stormont House, Manor Hill and at least two houses in Kensington Square were also schools.[47] Some houses were even occupied as schools from the time they were built. Such was No. 22 Hans Place. It was established by émigrés, Mons. St Quentin and his wife, formerly of the Abbey School, Reading, with money provided by the anonymous publication of a novel by a former pupil, Mary Butt, later Mrs Sherwood. The St Quentins were assisted by Miss Rowden, a pupil who had been governess to Lady Caroline Lamb, and pupils included Mary Russell Mitford from 1797 to 1802.[48]

The quality of education provided in these numerous schools was of national importance, but reliable evidence is difficult to find. Advertisements have obvious disadvantages, but at least reflect marketable aspirations. In the middle of the century Mrs Philips's boarding-school in Lawrence Street, Chelsea, claimed that its rapid growth in reputation, its 'careful and polite treatment', had required 'removal to a larger house in the same street'. In 1750 and 1752 she advertised reading, writing, drawing, dancing, music, arithmetic, French, and 'all manner of curious needlework', with 'strict care for sound morals, virtuous principles, and a graceful behaviour, at moderate rates'. The young ladies received lectures on 'religious subjects and the social virtues in French and English alternately' and attended Divine Service in both English and French every Sunday. The 'prevailing custom' of sending girls abroad to be educated exposed them to 'Romish teachers' and enriched an enemy. Two 'young persons' of thirteen or fourteen were offered positions as 'half boarders, whereby they will be qualified in housewifery and notableness as well as the ... parts of education'.[49] This indicates one of the ways in which such schools were staffed and serviced, and one of the weaknesses of this kind of education was undoubtedly the lack of any guarantee of knowledge or competence in its teachers and managers. Schools tended to be judged by their products in terms of the social graces or ornamental accomplishments which were most prized. Biographical evidence is not therefore always valuable, and literary glimpses may be uncritical or unduly dramatic. In 1768 Mary Darby was placed by her unreliable father in a small school in Kensington whose mistress was 'extremely accomplished', having been 'superiorly cultivated' at her father's school for boys. She was however handicapped as mistress of a girls' school by a passion for drink and a father with the appearance of a necromancer who terrified the children with his Anabaptist views. Her perfect command of Latin, French and Italian, her ability as an arithmetician and astronomer, and her 'art of painting on silk with exquisite perfection', gradually sank under bouts of intoxication and 'pecuniary derangements'. Perhaps fortunately she had few pupils, but Mary, her favourite, shared her bedroom and remained at the school for nearly a year.[50]

Such glimpses are disquieting, yet parents set high value on the tone of a school and on its ability to give elegance of mind and manners and to make children comfortable and happy. Mrs Montague, with unpleasant memories of the dirt of her own school in Kensington, visited her favourite niece at her Chelsea school in 1772, and had nothing to criticize except the girls' stays – 'She was healthy and well behaved and perfectly clean and neat, though I called on the Saturday which is only the eve of cleanliness.'[51] A pupil at No. 22 Hans Place was visited by an equally acute observer. Jane Austen noticed especially the elegance of her hair, which would 'do credit to any education', and but for the cupids on the drawing-room mantelpiece, 'a fine study for girls, one would never have smelt instruction'.[52] Such comments underline that the girls' boarding-school was considered to be essentially domestic rather than scholastic and was rather a survival of the older system of sending girls to other families for nurture than a forerunner of the public and high schools for girls of the next century. More serious comments confirm this impression. Hans Place was considered an excellent school for Mary Mitford, for the children were 'healthy, happy, well-fed and kindly treated'. When the domestic atmosphere hardened into constraint parents were quick to criticize. Arthur Young considered Campden House a 'region of constraint and death', attributing to its 'measured formal walks', crowded bedrooms and rigid discipline, the death of his daughter. The casual acquisition of learning was not only the price paid for the social setting of the education considered desirable for girls, it was the intellectual aspect of it. At Hans Place those who chose to learn had full opportunity to do so, and 'the intelligent manner in which the instruction was given, had the effect of producing in the majority of pupils, a love of reading and a taste for literature'. Mary Mitford learnt everything because she wanted to learn. She persuaded her parents to let her learn Latin. Mons. St Quentin taught French, history, geography and 'as much science as he was master of, or as he thought it requisite for a young lady to know'. Miss Rowden with the help of finishing masters for Italian, music, dancing and drawing superintended the general course. One of Miss Mitford's biographers however saw the school differently, resenting the unsystematic and indiscriminate nature of her education by 'a pair of French emigrants, assisted by an English lady who conceived herself a poetess, and took her pupils to the theatre', allowing them to read all manner of books 'trashy and solid', dance ballets, and 'act meek plays'. It may be significant that it was at Campden House that a rare experiment in systematic teaching of girls was made. During Mrs Terry's headship (1767–91) James Rice was English master and in his *Plan for Female Education* (1791) he described his method which should 'form the mind and cultivate the understanding'. He aimed at literary appreciation and morality, and in a two years' course the girls read Mason's *Tract on Self-Knowledge*, Young's *Night Thoughts*, and *Paradise Lost*, examined sentence by sentence to test their understanding. All new words were looked up in a dictionary and listed. Two afternoons a week were given to writing 'themes' on subjects 'relating to the proprieties of conduct in social and civil life, and their respective duties towards God and man'. The growing number of girls' schools which presented medals during the period suggests that more value was being given to study and attainment. A Gough House medal of 1793 bears a figure of Minerva and the legend 'Discretion Surpasseth Eloquence'. The stirrings of demand for something better appeared at the end of the century in the circles of radical dissent. Mary Wollstonecraft was a friend of Dr Price and married William Godwin. She opened a school in Newington Green.[53]

Whatever the merits or the defects of such schools, London was satisfying contemporary aspirations and making something of a speciality in provision during this period. As well as the needs of the City and of the permanent residents of the West End and the official regions of Whitehall and Westminster, there was a growing tendency to send girls into the metropolitan area for the final stages of their education. This reflected the place of London and its suburbs in contemporary society and culture, and it was also due to the concentration of skill necessary for a system which jealously preserved a domestic and deliberately unprofessional style of schooling for girls and relied on visiting 'professors' for specialist teaching. In 1828 *The Boarding School and London Masters' Directory* described how from Easter to midsummer families crowded into the metropolis not only for the season and parliamentary session, but 'on account of the grand work of education'. Parents of 'almost every class of society' brought their children, especially their daughters, for the benefit of the 'best London masters', or to be prepared and entered for 'some eligible school, where eminent professors may be had upon easier terms than in a private lesson'.[54]

Private schooling for a class society

There are difficulties in dividing the history of private schooling into periods for they are blurred and overlap considerably. It is however possible to distinguish between schools characteristic of the Age of the Augustans and the *philosophes*, and those of this next period, say between the end of the eighteenth century and the mid nineteenth century, the central decades of the age which produced 'The Origins of Modern English Society'. The old society had generated wealth on a scale which could be contained within its own structure, and eighteenth-century private schooling was not yet serving a class society. But as this 'open aristocracy based on property and patronage' generated the first Industrial Revolution the wealth of the middle ranks could no longer be 'absorbed and assimilated fast enough to prevent the formation of a *bourgeoisie* hostile to the landowners'. The development of London private schools illustrates this period when the middle classes were beginning to identify their distinct interests, to formulate an ethos which rejected the ideals, norms, models, codes of conduct, of the old society and the institutions which had preserved and transmitted them.[55] These 'Fathers of the Victorians'[56] were driven by ambitions and acting under social, economic and moral pressures which made particular demands upon education. These were the decades in which private adventure schooling bloomed and flourished, as a distinct alternative process of education. The growth of London and its suburbs provided both stage and ideal seedbed.

The London of this age was already Cobbett's 'Great Wen' and by its end it had grown into both scene and subject of the novels of Dickens.[57] In 1801 London's population was 865,845, by 1861 it was 2,803,989.[58] Much of this was due to migration but quite early in the century the capital's population began to grow by natural increase. In this explosive period the population continued its move outwards and the City became relatively less densely populated than the newer residential areas and the suburbs. In 1801 one in twelve persons in Britain was a Londoner, by 1851 London's proportion of the whole population was slightly smaller but the impact and pace of growth was much greater.[59] London's dominance within its thirty-mile radius was increasing. Agricultural land was under hay for London's horses and stall-fed cows, used as market gardens, or overwhelmed by advancing bricks and mortar.[60] The ring of villages beyond 'the Bills of Mortality', Hammersmith, Paddington, Marylebone, St Pancras and Chelsea, had been recognized as part of the metropolis as long ago as 1769[61] and now a further ring of villages was being engulfed. Improvements in water supply already allowed expansion on the London clay. The Napoleonic Wars held up development, but the decade after Waterloo saw a building boom. The construction of the four 'Waterloo Churches', St John's near Waterloo Bridge, St Mark's Kennington, St Matthew's Brixton and St Luke's Norwood, indicates the pattern of expansion south of the Thames.[62]

The key to both intensity and lines of growth was communications. By the late eighteenth century the Home Counties were the 'most turnpiked area in England' and from 1750 to about 1836/8 improvement to existing roads was superseded by the construction of new ones. The old Roman street pattern remained the basis of new developments and eighteenth-century estate building added further well-planned road systems. The next stage drove new links between inner London and the Great North Road. After 1756 the New Road joined Paddington and Islington and continued eastwards via the City Road to Moorgate – the earliest town by-pass in history (1761). Four radial roads, the New North Road (1812), the Caledonian Road (1826), Archway Road (1813), and the Finchley Road (1826–35) relieved pressure on the Great North Road and lessened the problem of Highgate Hill. In 1826 turnpike trusts north of the Thames were consolidated by Act of

Parliament, which enabled the construction of a more satisfactory road to Tottenham (1834). Eastward the road system was improved by the dock companies. South of the river, the building of bridges (Westminster 1750, Blackfriars 1769, Vauxhall 1816, Waterloo 1817, Southwark 1819) made possible and necessary a new system of radial roads through St George's Fields, linked with their new Circus and with Vauxhall. These new roads had a rapid effect on London's development.[63] In 1829 George Shillibeer ran its first public-carriage service along the New Road from Paddington Green to the Bank of England. Within four years 600 'omnibuses' were operating, competition was fierce, London traffic was jammed, 'the solitude of Kentish Town, Paddington and Kilburn was disappearing'.[64] The horse omnibus was used only by the more prosperous of these pioneer commuters, for fares in the 1820s were about 1s 6d or 2s single from the City to the West End or Paddington, Peckham, Clapham. Places were usually booked on a regular basis, on as many as 21 coaches from Clapham which in 1825 ran daily 57 return journeys, or Paddington with 54 coaches and 158 journeys, Hammersmith with 12 coaches and 30 journeys. Once these coaches reached 'the stones' they could not take up passengers as the Hackney coach monopoly had to be preserved. Private coaches also continued to operate this kind of service. In 1860 a coach was collecting residents from Clapham Common who had booked their seats on a yearly basis. It was thus the horse omnibus or coach service which stimulated the characteristic growth of, for example, Clapham and Hammersmith, even Islington and Holloway. In these expanding villages only a small proportion of the inhabitants commuted, but this was a larger number, both absolute and relative, than any other city and it gave London and its suburbs a unique character. To the wealthier daily travellers must be added a considerable number who walked to work in the City or West End – clerks, porters and so forth trudging from Camberwell, Peckham, the northern villages. The growth of suburban villages stimulated local employment and to some extent industry also migrated outwards.[65] This commuter-village pattern was already established when the early railway lines reinforced it. The first was opened in 1836 and the 'village with a station' enabled more prosperous middle-class citizens to colonize more fully the rural districts round London. The northern lines were committed to long-distance and freight traffic, the southern lines were more interested in suburban passengers. This had a marked influence on the different developments of villages north and south of the Thames, so noticeable even today. It was not until after the 1860s that cheaper fares began to transform this pattern, especially north of the river, by enabling the 'better sort of mechanics' to travel to work.[66]

This was the new society and expanding London which this period of private schooling had to serve. In some cases well-established schools can be shown to have adapted their style to the new age, in others continuity is more apparent. In Ealing for example Samuel Goodenough's eighteenth-century school had many aristocratic pupils. In 1799 it was in the hands of the Reverend William Goodenough, still giving a classical education, but by 1840 it had become College Hall Classical and Commercial Academy, catering for middle-class needs only.[67] Nearby was Ealing Great School; this may have traced its history from 1698 when Zachary Pearce received his education at a school in Little Ealing, but its certain history began in about 1764. In 1767 a Mr Pierce (or Pearse), more renowned for botanizing than classical scholarship, was its master. Under his son-in-law, the Reverend Mr Shury, its reputation began to increase and after 1791, *his* son-in-law, Dr Nicholas, began to build up its standing until it contained about 350 pupils. It was run on Eton lines and the old building and grounds were adapted to provide fives courts, cricket pitches and so on. It was both an alternative to the public schools and preparatory to them but was used mainly by middle-class families. John Henry Newman, son of a banker, went from here to Oxford, the future Bishop Selwyn was sent on to Eton. W. S. Gilbert, who was head-boy, passed on to King's College London when he was sixteen. Other boys were prepared for the Army, and one especially interesting pupil was Thomas Huxley, son of the mathematics master, who continued with private study only before entering medical school. The school flourished throughout the nineteenth century catering for this wide range of needs.[68] The Palace School at Enfield was another which in the eighteenth century had taken pupils from the governing ranks and had solid City connections when Baron Bramwell and his brother were pupils, but later advertised as preparing for the middle-class examinations.[69]

Another school which illustrates some of the problems of adapting a family business to changing circumstances was Shield's Academy in Islington. It began in the mid eighteenth century as an 'eminent ladies' boarding-school'. Then John Shield, an Edinburgh graduate and experienced schoolmaster, married the proprietor's daughter, converted it into an academy for boys, and carried it on 'for a long series of years with the greatest reputation and success'. His pupils included John Nichols (1745–1826) of the literary anecdotes, who left at the age of thirteen after a good classical education to be apprenticed to a printer. In 1786 Shields gave it up and eventually it passed by marriage into the hands of the writing master, Mr Flower, who carried it on for forty years. His successor announced in 1835 that in this 'well-known establishment the system of education has been adjusted to the improved taste of the present day'. Greek and Latin classes were 'conducted on the plan pursued at the London University, the French language is taught by a resident native, dancing and music are comprised within the course of instruction and are subject to no extra charge'. The Islington Literary and Scientific Society delivered lectures weekly in its schoolroom, and the pupils had the 'valuable privilege of attending'.[70]

Another school which was adapted to the changes of this period was in the Mansion House, Hammersmith. From about 1770 a Scottish graduate kept this academy, considered to be one of the best in London, with a broad course which included navigation. Stamford Raffles was here for two years. It was taken over by Dr B. Duncan, formerly of Highgate Commercial Academy, who prepared boys for 'foreign and domestic trade and the public offices', and it still existed in 1839.[71]

The general direction of such changes is apparent, but very uneven, and private schools in this period of transition still served a variety of functions and families. They continued to be used by some pupils as preparatory for the 'Great Schools'. Thackeray went in 1818 to a school on Chiswick Mall, kept by Dr John Turner, his mother's cousin, who was annoyed when he was removed after three years to go to Charterhouse. In retrospect Thackeray considered that he was ill-prepared in classical studies; he also remembered being caught drawing a caricature of the master, and running away from the school. When he reached the turnpike road the roar of traffic frightened him so much that he crept back, undetected.[72] Shelley was sent to Sion Park Academy at Isleworth in 1802 when he was ten, to prepare for Eton. He was miserably unhappy, largely because he found most of the other boys highly objectionable, for they came from the small tradesman class and were using the school, kept by Dr Greenlaw, a hard-headed Scotsman of some learning, for quite different purposes. They knew well how to goad Shelley into paroxysms of rage, and he remembered them, not his severe schoolmaster, as echoes 'from a world of woes – The harsh and grating strife of tyrants and of foes'. Shelley did well in his studies but displayed revolutionary, even incendiary, tendencies and earned a reputation for near-insanity. The divergence of educational and social purposes was here heightened by poetical sensibilities,[73] and most schools of this period fulfilled their dual purposes with less drama. Durham House School at Chelsea for example which opened in 1805, had 'nearly a hundred boys training for Eton, Harrow and the Universities of Oxford and Cambridge, mostly the sons of the aristocracy and the leading families'. A local historian remembered as a boy supplying its younger pupils with white mice and fishing bait and acting as their guide when they were allowed to disport themselves in the riverside meadows of Chelsea and Battersea under the somewhat sketchy supervision of the ushers.[74]

The significant changes of this period are not seen however so much in the history of individual schools as in the overall picture which emerges from the advertisements, prospectuses and educational polemic of the period. This kind of evidence is unreliable with respect to particular practice, for not even the existence of a school is proved by an advertisement, but there is no better indication of what schoolkeepers considered saleable, what parents were prepared to buy in the educational market. Here the rhetoric *is* the evidence for several requirements which contributed significant features to the idea of education at this level.

First, there was what might be called the packaging of the curriculum. It was during this period that in schools for boys the older tradition of the writing schools, of extra subjects taught by visiting masters, of short bouts of specialized instruction for specific purposes, was further superseded by the idea of a general course, often described as 'the usual branches of a solid English education'. Elements of the old tradition lingered on, especially in the endowed schools which could rarely teach more than the classics free to foundation scholars, but in the open market fathers of the new middle classes were not prepared to pay extra for the very subjects which they most wished their boys to learn, though they were more ready to pay for genuine 'extras'. Courses therefore tended to consolidate into a general foundation, perhaps branching later into more specialized and vocational studies. If the language in which such a curriculum is described often retains its eighteenth-century flavour, the purposes being served are recognizably of the new age. In 1828 Dr David Lewis of Twickenham School offered for £52 10*s* a year 'Board and Instruction in the Greek and Latin Classics, Arithmetic, Geography and Mathematics', with preparation for the 'public Schools . . . according to their respective grammars, the regular Exercises of Composition and Versification', and finally for either of the universities, while those 'destined for commercial pursuits, are carefully instructed in every branch of knowledge necessary to their qualification'.[75] In 1821 Mr Faulkner of the Cherwell House Academy, Upper Mall, Hammersmith, prepared 'Young Gentlemen for the Universities, public offices and Foreign and Domestic Commercial business' with a course which 'is of a general character in its earlier stages, but is subsequently varied with a view to the particular destination of the pupils'. The grammar course was not needed for every pupil, but a 'subordinate regard is however paid to classical and mathematical studies where youth are designed for the counting house . . . to prepare them for this department, besides a general acquaintance with polite literature, and the formation of a good English style, they are accurately taught the French language and the principles of trade and commerce, writing with expedition and elegance, and a correct knowledge of arithmetic, and book-keeping' together with the usual accomplishments.[76]

An elaborate exposition of this theory of the curriculum is contained in the prospectus, advertisements and textbooks of Dr Daniel Dowling of the Mansion House Academy at Highgate, and later of the Mall, Hammersmith. In 1818 he prepared boys for careers in the 'civil or military departments of government, the land or sea services of his country, the Honourable East India Company's service, or the useful walks of private life'. He described himself as 'professor of the mathematics, lecturer in Natural Philosophy, and Author'. His works included *An Improved System of Arithmetic for the Use of Schools and the Counting House* (1818), *A New and Improved System of Calculation* (1829) and a *Key to Hutton's Course of Mathematics* (1818). His academy provided a common course in 'the English language, elegance in composition, Plain and Ornamental Writing, and Arithmetic . . . taught indiscriminately to all the pupils and on a plan which ensures incredible success, in a comparatively short time'. Then came the 'essential elements of a liberal education', the Latin and Greek languages, which 'are likewise indefatigably pursued unless the age and views of the students determine otherwise', and mathematics, studied 'not so much for the exquisite pleasure wherewith it fills the mind . . . as for its communication of an invaluable habit of patient research, a love of truth, and a system of accurate reasoning'. Vocational courses followed according to choice of career, 'by the proper books and a well-directed attention, and the use of the best instruments'. The French language was taught 'in its purity', 'a considerable part of the family being French, that language is spoken . . . in the House'. Spanish and other mercantile tongues could also be learnt, and 'Book-keeping, with all the routine of the counting-house and the forms of actual business', better than by the 'generality of articled clerks'. There was a well-developed scientific side, lectures illustrated 'by the most complete set of apparatus possible, and one of the largest telescopes in England'. The pupils were assisted to make experiments and observations, 'Or, if the study of Chemistry be deemed expedient, there is a laboratory fitted up with all the necessary utensils, tests, and re-agents'. The accomplishments, dancing, drawing, music, fencing, were taught by visiting masters, and were charged as extras. Dr Dowling's fees were high, from £52 10s to £73 10s, according to age, and £105 for parlour boarders, compared with from £27 6s to £29 8s charged at the neighbouring Commercial Academy of Mr Duncan, but evidently covered all the essential subjects, and also 'a constant supply of milk, fruit, and every useful vegetable in season' from the fourteen acres of good garden. This school flourished at least from 1817 to 1828 and when it was transferred to Hammersmith the terms were much the same.[77]

Languages, especially French, were often emphasized as a useful skill. In 1821 the proprietor of Prospect House Academy, Pentonville, had 'united his interest with an Establishment in France where his pupils to whom French is the first object, may go and return as convenience may require without any additional expense but their passage'.[78] At College House Boarding School in the Hackney Road the French language was 'constantly spoken',[79] and at Belle Vue House Academy in Stoke Newington an 'Education Francaises' [*sic*] was offered. 'The majority of the family, professors and domestics are French, the French language is constantly spoken, and a perfect knowledge of it is acquired without the necessity of a residence in France.'[80]

Vocational pressures were important in shaping this curriculum but the legacy of the Encyclopaedists is also apparent and numerous schools of this period advertise the place given to science, not only for vocational purposes but as part of general culture. Dr Jamieson, of Wyke House Academy at Brentford, was a prolific writer of school books on scientific and mathematical subjects between 1814 and 1846. He advertised his school as preparing youths for the professions of civil engineer, architect and surveyor, the Army and the Navy, by a 'regular and systematic course of mixed Mathematical Instruction', but this was in addition to the 'Greek and Roman Classics', English Literature, with all the 'necessary parts of a liberal intellectual and systematic education', with visiting masters for languages and accomplishments.[81] In 1835 the Reverend J. A. Emerton of Hanwell College, a school which specialized in boys entering the Army, advertised for a 'lecturer on Chemystry, Experimental Philosophy, Geology, etc.'.[82] The Reverend Robert Simpson, master of the Colebrook House Academy, Islington, and one of the founders of the British Education Society, delivered a lecture in 1835 on 'the proper objects and methods of Education, and on the relative utility of scientific instruction'. The Society should promote not only the science of education, but also education in science. At his own school lectures were regularly 'given in the Mathematical, Natural Philosophy and Chemistry department'.[83] In 1835 one schoolkeeper, the Reverend Dr Vale of the Cam House School of Arts and Sciences in Belgrave Square, evidently decided that prudence was an attractive addition to opportunity. Chemistry was included, 'and the young gentlemen are instructed and allowed to make such experiments as are not attended by danger'.[84] Much of this instruction might justify Matthew Arnold's sneer at Dr Archimedes Silverpump, PhD, of Lycurgus House Academy, Peckham, but it is clear that a marketable educational package was often expected to contain some scientific knowledge.

The eighteenth century had not only bequeathed a new content for education, but a new idea of childhood, and it was in these very middle ranks of society that this first developed and was most securely established. Many parents now looked for schools which enshrined, or at least did not violate, this image of childhood. Kindness and a domestic atmosphere were given increasing emphasis in advertisements. At Mr Freer's Tottenham Academy, 'Every attention is paid to the domestic comfort of the pupils and they are encouraged to look up to their tutors as friends.'[85] At Oxford House Academy in the King's Road, the proprietor stressed the need to make teaching enjoyable, the 'principal devotes the whole of his time to secure the improvement and happiness of his pupils ... who enjoy all the domestic advantages of a home'.[86] At the nearby College House Academy the principal's wife 'supervises the domestic arrangements, they are like one large family'.[87] In the 1830s Mr Softley kept Manor House Academy which stood 'in the midst of six acres of its own gardens and pleasure-grounds, with numerous noble gravel walks' and was situated in Upper Holloway 'entirely free from the dampness complained of in Lower Holloway' and 'being seated under the Highgate and Hampstead Hills', never felt the 'bleak winds so prevalent there'. He had expended £3000 on the rebuilding of 'his splendid mansion' and added play, pleasure and cricket grounds, fives ground, giants' stride, baths and an observatory. It was claimed to be the 'most extensive and elegant boarding school about town'. Here the pupils were 'used' as the owner's own children, the domestic arrangements were on a liberal scale and 'under the constant supervision of the principal's own wife, whose whole time is passed in contributing to the comforts and happiness of those under her care'.[88] Mr Spiller of College House Academy on Highgate Hill, near the Archway, also stressed the 'domestic arrangements, combined with excellent accommodation, and the most liberal treatment' which allowed pupils 'every comfort they could possibly enjoy even under the immediate care of their parents'. He also claimed a 'healthful situation', large grounds, gravel subsoil, and spacious views, and by 1825 was adding the convenience of 'coaches almost every hour from the British Coffee House, Charing Cross, and the Bank'. In his advertisements there also appears another motive for this stress on kindness and comfort. Parents were looking for methods which promoted rapid learning, and harsh discipline was recognized as ineffective. 'The system pursued' by Mr Spiller was 'peculiarly calculated to excite a spirit of emulation among the pupils . . . and insured the most rapid progress in every branch of education'.[89] There is evidence that a significant number of middle-class parents now objected to corporal punishment. At the Hyde Side Academy, Edmonton, where in 1840 'young gentlemen' were 'kindly treated and comfortably boarded', the principal 'aims to awaken and exercise the powers of the mind and to make memory subservient to judgement, and there is very little or no rote learning. . . . He never degrades the mind or lowers the spirit by the infliction of corporal punishment.'[90] At Mr Edney's Academy in Pleasant Row, Pentonville, the pupils were treated with parental kindness, and the 'discipline of the school is maintained without recourse to corporal punishment'[91] and at Holly House Academy, Stanmore, the 'mode of tuition' was 'without coercion'. Many schools emphasized reward rather than punishment and medals are numerous in this period. They also no doubt acted as advertisement.[92] The consumers of private schooling of this period may not have endorsed the terms of these advertisements, but they must have attracted customers for there are here authentic echoes of a new middle class consciously rejecting the para-military code of the upper ranks of the old order, and in the open market at least schooling could not afford to be slow, ineffective and painful.

Nor were these parents prepared to tolerate the abuses which the system of the public boarding-schools made inevitable. Leaving large numbers of boys of mixed ages to their own devices during their leisure time in order to preserve manly independence led to practices which by an aristocracy might be put down to experience within a broad range of tolerance, but which outraged the middle-class conscience and sensitivity to social judgement. Until the old public school system, 'a republic confronted by an autocracy',[93] was reformed or decently formulated in the 'prefect system' and organized games, middle-class parents demanded, and got, moral and social supervision from the schools. Boys at private schools also were better supervised in their studies for the 'great schools' had often gone on the principle that 'you can take a horse to water, but you can't make him drink'. In his *Remarks on the Theory and Practice of Education and an Outline of the Course of Studies pursued at . . . Elm House, Edmonton*, Dr Ireland divided his comprehensive discussion under four heads, intellectual, moral, religious, physical, and made it abundantly plain that nothing must be left to chance.

> The greatest care is taken that everything which is learnt is learnt thoroughly, regard being always had to developing and strengthening the powers of the mind. Strict care is taken to cultivate the moral and religious principles. The Establishment is conducted upon the plan of a well-regulated and united family, so that a right spirit may actuate each of its members, who are watched over by the affectionate solicitude of the principal and his wife.[94]

The impact of such solicitude upon its unfortunate subjects is palpable in the printed address distributed to his pupils by Mr Robson of Hyde Side Academy, Enfield, in 1842. After an exhausting survey of the curriculum, Mr Robson turns to the boys' hours of leisure:

> You have read in the fable, of the bow which required to be occasionally unstrung to keep it in order. So it is necessary that your studies should be relieved by amusement. You have here, beside the national and delightful occupation of gardening, ample space for all the sports of your age. . . . We have many places in which you can enjoy the best and most manly of games, cricket; there is a fine piece of water . . . in which you can, under my care, learn to swim . . . and on our half holiday there is not a nook in this beautiful country that we will not explore. I say *we*, for I will accompany you, to point out the charms of nature, examine with you the subjects of natural history that we may meet with, and blend instruction and amusement with exercise.[95]

Private schools of this period were characterized by the demands of the new urban middle classes for a broad and strongly utilitarian curriculum, by their accommodation of a new concept of childhood, by their emphasis on competition rather than coercion, but above all by their constant supervision of their pupils. It was this characteristic which was felt by contemporaries to distinguish private schools and by the time of the Taunton Inquiry set up in 1864 to investigate the education of the middle classes it was of some national concern, even seen as a threat to social cohesion; 'Middle-Class Education' had become a 'Question'.[96] The Commissioners, nearly all university and public school men, displayed some of the qualities of explorers in an unknown territory surrounded by hostile tribes and in need of interpreters. They took pains when examining witnesses from private schools, such as Clarendon House at Denmark Hill, to establish the degree of constant supervision of the pupils.[97] The Reverend J. M. Brackenbury of Wimbledon School, which prepared 100 boys, mostly for the military colleges, the Civil Service and the Indian Civil Service, tried to help the Commissioners to an exact analysis. Asked about the degree of freedom in his school compared with that in the public schools he replied:

> I think the public school system is the best for the genius of the English character. We assimilate our system, and I think all private schools should assimilate their systems, as much as possible to the public school. We give our scholars great liberty. We allow them to go to the village for three quarters of an hour a day, and they roam the country checked by roll-calls every two hours. We encourage, and very successfully, cricket, football, and other athletic sports.

He admitted that his school differed in that the boys' work was more fully supervised, all study was done in school, 'You may call us, perhaps, somewhat of a hot-bed of instruction.' But he would wish that private schools could adapt their internal organization to that of the public schools, where 'the self-government and responsibility of the boys tend to make them self-reliant, manly, generous'. Private schools could do much to extend this benefit of a 'certain freedom of action, a feeling that he is trusted' which 'is necessary as the air he breathes, to the development of an English school-boy'.[98]

While it would hardly be conceivable that Mr Dombey should have little Domey's name down for Eton, by the 1860s such assimilation was becoming acceptable, not because the middle classes had capitulated to aristocratic values, but because their own values were penetrating and transforming the upper reaches of society. During this vital period however private schooling had developed characteristics which became integral to the idea and practice of secondary education and the development of a system of private secondary schools even seemed possible.

A system of private schools?

London's needs and resources had stimulated the development of schooling by supply and demand for the new middle classes, 'private adventure schooling' as its critics often called it. In the mid century metropolitan pressures and opportunities interacted with growing state concern to produce some of the machinery for a system of such schooling.

That unsatisfactory category of evidence, the scholastic directory, discloses the change that was taking place. A *Scholastic Directory* of 1861[99] still listed schools 'for Ladies and Gentlemen' alphabetically under the name of the proprietor, as a *Boarding School and London Masters' Directory* had done in 1828, and as the trade directories continued to do. But directories of 1872, 1879 and 1884 listed 'our Endowed and all the leading schools of Great Britain' and our 'Endowed Schools and our Higher and Middle Class Private Schools and Colleges' as institutions arranged topographically and classified according to management and ownership, giving the qualifications of staff, numbers of pupils, the curriculum followed, the examinations entered, charges, and connections with other branches of education.[100] Here is a new conception of such schools, still private property, but publicly accountable and part of a national network.

London played a significant part in this change. The Brougham enquiries,[101] the earliest attempt to investigate popular education, revealed the sheer quantitiy of metropolitan private schools and alarmed their keepers into forming the London School Society to oppose a 'general system of National Education'. Professional concern was hardening into the defensive self-interest of a pressure group. Its *Scholastic Journal* fought bitter battles against dawning state interest, the pretensions of elementary school teachers, meddling bodies which aspired to examine private schools, and perhaps above all against the 'feeble, foolish and misdirected attempts' of the College of Preceptors.[102]

This was founded at Brighton in 1846 and moved to London in 1848, eventually in 1887 to its own building in Bloomsbury Square. In 1849 it was incorporated by Royal Charter and women were admitted.[103] Its origin lay in the need for 'some bond of union between the members of the profession' and for 'some body which can represent their views and wishes'. The first need was for some public reassurance, for the pressure of demand convinced private schoolkeepers that they 'must exert themselves to bring about . . . improvement' in their own ranks. The publication of *Nicholas Nickleby* (1838) still rankled, the pretentious pomposity of Dr Blimber (1848) was almost more damaging. The beginning of the examinations for teachers in elementary schools was seen to threaten teaching as a business. In private schools 'the chief, if not the exclusive object, is to make an income', and 'many of these persons are utterly unfit, both morally and intellectually, to be intrusted with the care of the young . . . some proof of qualification, both as to the amount of knowledge and the art of conveying it to others' should be required, at first for assistant masters only.[104] From the very beginning part of this examination was in the theory and practice of education.

The Deed of Trust for scholarships to Cambridge is presented to the Chairman of the City of London School committee, Warren Stormes Hale. The Headmaster, Dr Mortimer, is on the right.

The Beaufoy mathematics medal (1852)

5 The City of London School, one of the most significant and influential in the nineteenth century, attracted support from progressive industrialists. The Beaufoy family, vinegar manufacturers of Lambeth, gave £9,000 to encourage its reformed curriculum and spirit of emulation.

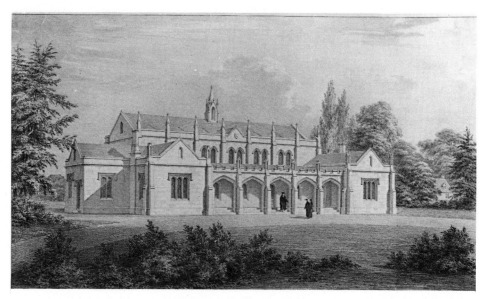

Camberwell Collegiate School

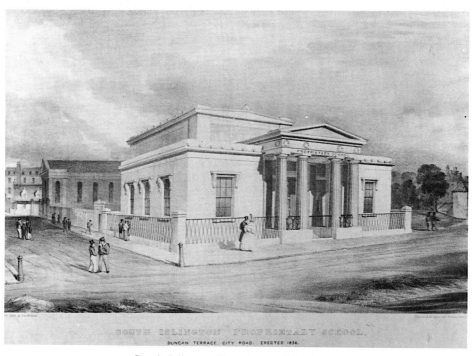

South Islington Proprietary School

6 Education by investment, in both Gothic and Classical style. By the beginning of Victoria's reign London was ringed with proprietary schools of moderate Anglican persuasion, providing liberal and broad courses.

Diplomas were instituted for Associates, Licentiates and Fellows of the College, but unfortunately *membership* (MCP) was open to established schoolkeepers with no examination at all, and this undoubtedly undermined the reputation of the college and its income. Membership declined in spite of other advantages – regular meetings, an agency for assistants, the publication of the *Educational Times*, a Benevolent Fund for 'aged, distressed and afflicted schoolmasters', and a rather ill-designed 'Preceptors' and General Life Assurance Society' which had to be hurriedly wound up. Fortunately a scheme for the examination of schools was sanctioned in 1850 and put into practice in 1854. These were the first of the so-called 'Middle Class Examinations'. For the first time schools recognized the need for public accountability, examinations taken as a warranty of a general school course, not tied to the receipt of public money, nor to university entrance or scholarships. The method of examining also, by printed papers simultaneously taken by all schools using the service, was new in this sector, based on the Queen's Scholarship technique for examining pupil-teachers. This system is now so much an integral part of secondary education that it is easy to overlook the significance of these College of Preceptors' examinations. They were held twice a year and taken at three levels for both boys and girls – the first class for pupils not usually below fourteen or above seventeen, the second class for pupils of about twelve years and the third class for those between eight and ten or eleven. Their chief aim was to give teachers an independent assessment of their own teaching, but they quickly established a modest public reputation and the higher certificates earned exemption from the preliminary examinations of the Law Society and the Pharmaceutical Society and from medical examinations, as a certificate of a good general education, for the packaging of the curriculum now enabled it to be more readily marketed. The fees from these examinations saved the College financially, enabled it eventually to build its own headquarters in Bloomsbury Square, which in turn was profitable, for it could be sublet to numerous organizations and conferences.[105]

The Taunton Inquiry and Report brought further progress for its criticisms caused the College to tighten its regulations for membership. It was then examining nearly 2000 pupils a year, it had elected women members on to its Council, and extended its attention from the examining to the training of teachers. In 1862 the Social Science Congress discussed the Newcastle Commission on Popular Education's proposal that the universities might examine certificates for 'Middle Class Schoolmasters'. Robson, secretary of the College, contributed a paper on the need for 'Academical Degrees in the Science of Education . . .' and there was a useful discussion on the importance of learning how to 'develop the mental faculties' rather than 'impart instruction'.[106] But the desire of the College of Preceptors to connect the private schools with other sectors of education, especially the universities, led only to

frustration. In 1871 it established its own lectureship in education, held
by Joseph Payne, who from the beginning had examined in pedagogy.
Two years later this was converted into a Professorship in Education,
the first in Britain, and plans were made for founding a training college
with its own practising school. This failed for lack of support and funds,
but was revived when the new headquarters seemed to offer another
opportunity. A scheme for one year's professional training for men over
eighteen, with practice in London schools and maintenance grants of
£20 a year from the College, had a brief life. Tollington Park College
was one of the schools used. The headmaster of this school for 350 boys
'in the second grade of education' gave the student 'constant daily
practice under a master', weekly criticism lessons, and time for private
study and attendance at evening lectures. The headmaster considered
himself so successful that he had taken the young man on to his staff.
But there was not sufficient support for the scheme in general, for
headmasters, especially of endowed schools, 'rather admired training
than made use of it'.[107]

From its early years the College had considered the question of a
Teachers' Register 'as a means not only of informing the general public
as to the qualifications of men and women who undertake to teach, but
also of increasing the inducement to qualify by training and examination,
and of rendering the whole body of teachers more compact and influential'. Robson in his Taunton evidence urged that legislative action
should regulate entry into the teaching as to the medical profession. He
had something of a brush with the Commission over the restrictive
nature of the proposal, Lord Stanley asking caustically, 'You would
allow parents to teach their own children without a certificate, I pre-
sume?' Robson held his ground, only conceding that it should not be a
penal offence to set up a school without certificate, but unregistered
masters should be unable to recover fees in a court of law. In this, as in
the training of secondary teachers, the College was far ahead of the
possibilities of the day. Such proposals also lost the College support
within its own clientele, for it is easy to see why the London School
Society was alarmed at such 'misdirected' attempts.[108]

But the College of Preceptors received support not only from shrewd
or enlightened private schoolkeepers, but from a number of influential
men and women who saw it as the nucleus of a new system of education
– Miss Buss of the North London Collegiate School, Dr Richard
Wilson, headmaster of St Peter's School, Eaton Square, Dr Jacob of
Christ's Hospital, A. K. Isbister, headmaster of the East Islington
Proprietary School and later of the Jews' College and the Stationers'
School, H. W. Eve, headmaster of University College School, who gave
evidence for the college to the Bryce Commission of 1895 and repres-
ented it at the Cambridge Conference on Secondary Education in 1896,
Dr Wormell of the Cowper Street Schools, later the Central Foundation
School, Dr Haig Brown, headmaster of the Charterhouse, the Reverend

J. R. Major of King's College School. Robson, secretary from 1859, was a London graduate who had taught for fourteen years at University College School. The Treasurer from 1837 to 1881 was Dr C. H. Pinches, the 'son of a well known City schoolmaster', and himself the owner of a very successful private school, Clarendon House, who had been examined by the Taunton Commissioners. He was succeeded by Isbister.[109] All these brought experience of reformed or newly founded London schools, experimenting with an emerging concept of secondary education. If the work of the College is to be assessed historically, it must be seen not only as the attempt of a vested interest to gain respectability and stability but as part of a whole complex of educational movements which were bringing modern secondary education into being.

But the College's policy of working with the endowed schools was a further reason for its failure to satisfy private schoolkeepers; for in the end it failed either to bring the private sector within a coherent system of national education, or to retain the confidence of private schoolkeepers as guardian of their interests. In 1883 the Private Schools' Association was founded to represent them in the decade leading to the Bryce Inquiry.[110] Nor did the College of Preceptors satisfy or adequately provide for the demand for the scientific study of education as the foundation and work of the Teachers' Guild showed.[111] The reasons for the College of Preceptors' failure, and its survival, were complex and difficult to disentangle, but it was attempting to build a new kind of secondary education at a time of unparalleled pressure, with no help from the state, little as yet from the universities, and on the insecure foundations of education as a business enterprise.

The economics of London private schools during this climax period of their social utility are mysterious. The provision of such schools was an important local industry, engaging the capital, skill and concern of large numbers of people and having an effect on the property market. But no useful estimate of the amount invested in education in London suburbs could be made. The evidence of advertisements in the scholastic press confirms that the London suburbs were considered the most desirable situation for such schools until well into the 1880s. But judging from sample evidence of 1882 the offers for schools and partnerships, and the sums asked for sale or transfer, varied so widely that while some factors, leasehold or freehold for example, may not yet have been raised, teaching as a business appears to have been as rudimentary as it often was as a skill. The amount offered for investment or purchase was intended to relate to the social class for which the school provided, the fees charged, the neighbourhood, and must also be interpreted in relation to the difficulties of the trade – the need for reliable partners or assistance, the pressure of success, precarious health, the necessity of retirement and so on.[112] The Bryce Commissioners gave some consideration to the business problems of private schooling. They reported that 'although the decrease in the number of private schools since 1868 has been considerable, there is still a large amount of capital invested in them'. It was the smaller day schools which had tended to go out of business, they were rarely remunerative but 'a private boarding-school, when placed in an attractive district, can generally command good support'. The evidence of these advertisements confirms that the London suburbs continued throughout this period to be such a district. Two keepers of suburban schools, in giving evidence for the Private Schools' Association to the Bryce Commissioners, estimated that average capital expenditure on private schools over the whole country was £2,817 – girls' schools £1,831 and boys' £3,603. Miss Olney had for this enquiry visited a large number of girls' schools in the suburbs. She found as well as preparatory schools, three main types of secondary school – those preparing pupils for 'work in after-life in various branches'; those preparing for university and other examinations, carried on in 'fine houses, furnished with every modern appliance'; and those with a curriculum 'more suited to a life of leisure' on which 'an immense amount of capital must have been spent'.[113] Llewellyn Smith in his survey of suburban private schools made at this time for Charles Booth, gave another side of the picture. Many such schools were 'mere mushroom growths'. A comparison of the lists of private schools mentioned in the London Directory for 1889 and 1890, respectively, shows the disappearance of 71 schools, and the establishment of 38 in the interval. When capital was successfully invested in this manner, when the school in fact became profitable, 'there is an almost irresistible temptation to raise the fees ... and so place the school out of reach of the class who need it most'.[114] In London, while urban expansion gave many openings for the investment of capital in schools, and tended to depreciate in value just those properties most suitable for them, the pace of change brought many dangers. A writer in 1865 for example described the 'Difficulties of a Middle-Class Schoolmaster' after sinking his money in setting up a school in the suburbs. He got on well enough when the school was under his sole charge, but as soon as it grew larger it decreased in efficiency as he could not afford to pay a proper assistant on the fees which the parents would pay. His own difficulties had been aggravated by his rashness in getting married at thirty when he should have waited till forty. Scarcely any proper accommodation for a school was to be had, for small houses had too small rooms and large ones were too great a burden. The population of London was shifting, children were birds-of-passage, the able ones were transferred to public schools and most left at fourteen.[115] Schools of this kind, evidently within the inner radius of the suburbs, suffered from the competition of the proprietary as well as the elementary schools, and here larger houses were older and in bad repair. From the economic point of view, private education was contributing to its own difficulties by stimulating demands which it was increasingly expensive to meet. As a market commodity it had to attract customers. Tottenham School in 1879 advertised its eight acres of ground with cricket fields, running path, swimming bath recently built, covered fives court, warm baths for winter use, specially built bedrooms and classrooms, separate studies for senior boys, workshops, laboratories, school library, new and complete sanitary arrangements, and separate infirmary.[116] The coming of gas lighting, piped water, water-closets, placed a capital burden on enterprises which had to rely on using old property when it was abandoned by the outward move of the better-to-do suburban dwellers. The development of the railways contributed to the mobility of the population, but brought dangers to investment. In 1861 Mount Pleasant House Boarding School at Sunbury advertised its beautiful and healthful situation, fourteen acres of ground, the buses leaving Piccadilly several times daily and the railway to Hampton Court. A neighbouring school added the attractions of cricketing, boating, fishing.[117] But in areas as fortunate as this, easy transport drove up the price of property, while in the northern suburbs it altered their pleasant rural character.

Success however was not independent of educational utility as the fortunes of individual schools show. John Vine Milne, an external graduate of London, for example, invested £100 in 1878 in a few inky desks and boys and two houses knocked into one in Kilburn, and provided a modest preparation for the universities, professional examinations and matriculation. In the 1890s, he moved the school to Eastbourne as a preparatory school for boys under fourteen.[118] W. Brown, an ex-elementary schoolmaster who had also been in teacher training and inspecting, bought Tollington Park College in 1879 and developed it, and its branch school at Muswell Hill, as thoroughly successful 'organized science schools' for 400 and 225 boys up to the age of 16.[119] The College House School at Edmonton, in a large rambling house next to the Bell Inn (of John Gilpin fame) continued the useful tradition of the suburban boarding-school from about mid century. Its economics were essentially domestic rather than institutional, providing not so much a livelihood as a way of living for its owner, his domestic and scholastic staff and his numerous family, the boys educated at the school, the girls 'exchanged' with other boarding-schoolkeepers. Its prosperity was destroyed not by the coming of the railway through its pleasant grounds but by the provision of workmen's fares which altered the neighbourhood, and this school also moved to Eastbourne.[120]

The most considerable expense of such education came when its development brought about a revolution in teaching technique and staffing requirements. Larger schools teaching a wider range of subjects in their ordinary course invented that particular Victorian system of mass production which still in the mid twentieth century is considered 'normal' educational practice at the secondary level: groups of children of roughly the same level of attainment (whether by age, progress, or ability) were taught on lines resembling the workshop practice of moderately sized factories. The 'standards' of the elementary school became the 'forms' or 'classes' of the 'high-school' or 'collegiate' system. Victorian teachers showed much ability and ingenuity in evolving teaching methods appropriate and efficient in such a situation. 'Teaching power' became increasingly necessary. These changes in the economics and organization of learning in the schools were reinforced by changes in philosophy and discipline as competition replaced punishment as an incentive, and classes of a certain size and teaching of a particular kind became more necessary. These changes were gradual but increasingly rapid and cumulative and by the end of the century they revolutionized the economics of private schools. In larger schools employing a number of 'form-teachers' the school staff must cover the normal curriculum, which led eventually to increasing specialization and further demand for qualification and higher pay of assistant teachers.[121]

London schools reflect all aspects and stages of this Victorian transformation for here were united every variety of need and practice with every opportunity and facility for exchange of ideas and experiments. The staffing position early in the reign is illustrated in numerous prospectuses. When in 1858 the proprietor advertised his Highbury New Park Collegiate School, he gave no qualifications, but in 1861 he was described as PhD and Member of the College of Preceptors, and in 1879 as FRAS, and was giving lectures at the British Museum on Assyrian antiquities. He secured the headmaster of King's College School as examiner, and there was an imposing list of visiting masters, including the 'Late Tutor to the Prince of Orange', and Hafiz Sudrool Islam Khan Bahadoor for the 'Hindostanee and Persian languages and other acquirements necessary for gentlemen proceeding to India'. Other visiting masters taught 'Painting, Drill, Callisthenics, Dancing and Deportment'. The school 'was designed to prepare the sons of gentlemen for entering on a Collegiate or Professional career', students attending London University could 'have a comfortable home', and classes were 'also formed for qualifying youths to enter upon Commercial and Mercantile engagements'. This schoolmaster was drawing on all sources of prestige – the standards and standing of the proprietary schools, the craze for popular culture, the appeal of snobbery and the frankly incomprehensible. Least important in the whole pretentious structure were the 'two resident masters' whom he employed and who probably did a great deal of the work.[122] In schools of this type it is still the visiting staff who have any pretence to qualifications or prestige and in an area so thickly provided with schools, it was unlikely that qualified men were willing to become 'ushers' for longer than was necessary.

This was aggravated by the kind of supervision which parents expected in private schools, for while the proprietor of a private school had a financial interest in the preservation of middle-class taboos, it placed an intolerable burden on the assistant staff, further depressing their position. At College House, Edmonton, the third member of staff was the 'English master, a shy, awkward, shambling creature' who had 'drifted down' to teaching by 'strange by-ways of misfortune, perhaps of misconduct'. He had been an actor, understudy to some tragedian, and now was the drudge of the school, 'the slave of the other masters, and the butt of the boys'. He remained during holidays as he had no home 'and there was always some boys to be looked after'. During playtime it was his duty to be with the boys, and he 'walked up and down, up and down, by the playground wall', reciting or reading scenes from Shakespeare. The author of these memories, 'very little, very quiet', walked with him.[123] Schoolmastering of this kind was the resort of failures or a temporary expedient until abilities could find a better outlet. London had some remarkable schoolmasters of this latter kind: for example Thomas Huxley at Ealing Great School and H. G. Wells at Milne's Henley House at Kilburn. Wells 'was not a great schoolmaster. He was too clever and too impatient. He had the complete attention of the class once when vivisecting [*sic*] a frog (kindly provided by a day-boy) but school life was not lived at that level, and on the lower slopes we lost him.' The most remarkable of these 'birds of passage' was Vincent van Gogh who acted for a time in 1876 as assistant at two small and precarious private schools in Isleworth and whose letters preserve something of the intense miseries of such teaching.[124]

In this way the demands upon assistant teachers and their career prospects were transformed by the economics of private schooling. Higher pay for well-qualified assistants could bankrupt a school, and as schools grew in size and capital requirements, teachers could no longer regard their time as assistants as a probationary period before they set up their own schools. In this way education as an investment of skill helped to undermine education as an investment of capital, and teaching as a profession helped to destroy teaching as a business. This was probably the underlying reason for the strange paralysis and fossilization which eventually overcame the College of Preceptors. During the last decades of the century it was putting its main energies into the struggle for Teachers' Registration and the professional training of teachers, while the average owner of a private school was unlikely wholeheartedly to support policies which inflated the value of his assistants.[125]

Though containing within itself the seeds of its own destruction, the possibility of a system of secondary schooling by private enterprise during this climax period deserves to be judged on its own terms for its ability to satisfy contemporary needs, rather than on later standards and assumptions about state responsibility for secondary education. A speaker at the Social Science Congress of 1858 expressed both the criticisms and the convictions of this particular period, when he viewed education from a European perspective, praising the education of the upper classes for producing the 'character of the educated English gentleman of which we are so justly proud', but criticizing middle-class education as faulty in comparison, and bad in itself. 'It has great pretentions and show without substance or solidity. There is no superintendance whatever . . .'. Should England therefore follow the example of Europe and have a system of education, he asked, and answered by recalling that Europe also had passports, conscription. The English lack of system had elasticity, it 'forges new links which bind class to class', and above all it paid great attention to moral training. The aim must be to achieve the best of both the continental and the English conception of secondary education.[126]

Advertisements for London schools during this period indicate what the middle classes themselves desired, and what they were prepared to pay for in the open market. There is plenty of evidence of that 'curse of England . . . the obstinate determination of the middle-classes to make their sons what they call gentlemen', which Macaulay had diagnosed as early as 1833.[127] Many schools were advertised as 'for the sons of gentlemen'. Colleges and 'collegiate schools' abounded, for the name had reassuring echoes of external standards, a systematic course, and connections with other branches of education. Often such schools advertised that they were 'in Union with the College of Preceptors', listed the public examinations for which they prepared, and hinted at 'modern improvements' – the 'plan of education combines the various modern improvements which have been introduced into the scholastic world with the solid excellencies of the more ancient system'.[128] Many private 'grammar schools' were advertised but their emphasis was often on current needs rather than tradition – for example Church House Grammar School at Ealing, established in 1815 'for a sound general and practical education . . . for the Professions or Commercial Business of life',[129] or Paddington Grammar School, 'to provide for the boys of the upper classes a sound education, similar in tone and character to that of the older foundations, but more economical and better adapted to the requirements of modern times'.[130] This distinction between traditional and contemporary conceptions of education was sometimes indicated in the name – the Eton Park School of Modern Instruction in St Pancras, for example,[131] and the South Hornsey Latin and Modern School, divided into sides preparing for the 'Universities, King's College, Eton etc.' and for commerce, the Army, the Civil Service, law, etc.[132] Schools of commerce were openly advertised, and middle-class schools proclaimed by name their social purposes.

The single factor which emerges clearly from the advertisements for these London schools is the vocational one, for the social factor was confused by the fact that no one, least of all the middle classes themselves, knew who belonged to this 'independent body of the nation'. Fearon, the Assistant Commissioner investigating London private schools for the Taunton Commission of 1864–8, also concluded that the middle classes could be characterized by their vocational approach to education. The middle-class boy left school between the ages of fourteen and nineteen. Moreover it was possible 'to divide the middle-class into its different strata'. The 'first grade' contained a small number whose sons remained at school till about eighteen and there was no sharp distinction here from the upper class, boys passed from one to another 'at the last moment, owing to change of fortune, development of ability, success at examinations'. In the second grade, 'the most genuinely "middle" of any part of the class', boys left at sixteen or seventeen. The third-grade boys left at fourteen or fifteen, and in this 'large and interesting class of children' it was often difficult to distinguish sharply from the lower classes. Their education he considered to be 'the worst in Britain'. These leaving ages were determined on social or economic grounds. A boy left when it was necessary or considered suitable that he should earn wages. 'Few parents now-a-days withhold schooling from their sons during the school time of their life.' London parents decided the length of school life by reference to the family's place in society and the boy's future employment.

On the basis of this classification Fearon reviewed the private schools of the metropolis in relation to other kinds of provision. In the first grade were a few endowed and proprietary and expensive private schools. In the second grade he placed many grammar and endowed commercial schools, some proprietary schools which had started as middle-class schools, and a large number of private schools 'such especially as are in connexion with the College of Preceptors and the better among which prepare for the local examinations of Oxford and Cambridge'. In the third grade with the badly endowed or neglected grammar schools were a very large number of private schools and these had benefited since the Revised Code had destroyed much of the attraction of the upper forms of the elementary schools for the lower middle class by withdrawing grants from any instruction above the most basic subjects and skills.[133]

To London boys leaving schools of this kind a wide commercial, financial and professional field was open, if their previous education enabled them to undertake the usual method of in-training in banking houses, trading companies and the newly emerging professions. Between 1841 and 1881 professional occupations trebled, and constituted a substantial element in the middle classes, enjoying moreover rising recognition, remuneration and status. To enter such a career however demanded a much more exacting professional training, based on a sound general education. Place in society depended upon the career chosen, for to be a gentleman it was not yet necessary to have been to a public school, but to have acquired higher education or professional standing. To some middle-class families this was an important consideration and in this way social aspiration reinforced the vocational purposes of schooling.[134] As the older system of patronage and apprenticeship died, the newer system of competition sharpened the demands upon education. The reform of the Civil Service and the Army reflected and quickened changes in business and professional life. Boys could more rarely be placed at any level by family interest or personal negotiation. The pace and scale of business organization, the demands of technology, the pressure of specialization, were mounting, and it does not seem surprising that conscientious parents looked to the schools for results. The Taunton Commissioners blamed them for giving 'inordinate value to mere show', or perhaps worst of all, considering no education worth having unless it could speedily be turned into money.[135] Yet fathers had to have something to show prospective employers, and no one else was prepared to provide money for their sons. The days were passing when Anthony Trollope, having spent long and entirely fruitless years at two suburban schools, one public and the other private, was offered a clerkship in the Post Office through family connections, and secured it in spite of an entrance 'examination' which disclosed that he could neither write legibly nor knew the multiplication tables.[136] One by one respectable and reasonably secure and satisfying careers were being professionalized or entered through competitive examinations. From the side of the employers the pressure was the same. Faced with an unparalleled growth of business and personnel, banking and commercial houses of all kinds were beginning to look for some methods of assessing possible recruits which would replace personal recommendation. Some external standards for schools and some public assessment of pupils were becoming necessary to the labour market. The purely private area of education was an unchartered sea to both parents and employers. External examinations were needed and were mulitplying in the middle years of the century. The College of Preceptors was the first, the Royal Society of Arts followed in 1856, the Oxford and Cambridge Locals in 1857. In 1859 the Department of Science and Art examinations began.[137] Such examinations were a powerful factor in linking the system together as London witnesses before the Taunton Commission emphasized. The registrar of London University concluded that the effect on private and proprietary, but not grammar schools, had been 'substantial'. 'All the subjects required by the University are specifically and regularly taught' in the ordinary school routine. He asserted that 'those who obtain the best knowledge of classics, are those who have the greatest power of grasping the other subjects', advancing the same argument, at another level, with which Macaulay, Trevelyan and the other middle-class intellectuals justified the designing of the Civil Service Examinations for those who had taken honours at a university.[138] The headmaster of the North London Collegiate School entered for the Oxford and Cambridge Locals 'about as many as any school in England'. The stimulus 'decidedly increased the tone of study and application in the school'. It leavened, in fact, 'the whole lump'. The Senior Examination was of great value for the professional and middle classes, it was a 'stamp and guarantee of acquirement and it encourages them'. He admitted however the cramping effect on the syllabus – too much was required in history and geography – and on the curriculum – science could only occur occasionally, when preparing for the Oxford examination: 'We cannot afford an afternoon for chemistry or the steam engine.'[139] Another London headmaster considered that the multiplicity of examinations caused difficulty. He submitted a list of textbooks required by twenty-two examining bodies in classics and modern languages in 1865, to illustrate their diversity and lack of co-ordination. The demands of society were overruling the needs of children and teachers.[140] The genuinely educational advantages of even a minimum external standard and a severely formal syllabus were however seen to be giving some coherence, purpose and framework, as well as raising standards.

A very large number of London schools of all grades made use of these public examinations. As examples, Eagle Hall Collegiate School in Southgate in 1872 prepared for the 'Civil Service, the Preliminary Medical, the Incorporated Law Society, the Oxford and Cambridge Middle Class, and Other Examinations'.[141] The College, Tollington Park, prepared for the University Locals, the College of Preceptors, Civil Service, Royal College of Surgeons, Apothecaries' Hall and Pharmaceutical Society examinations.[142] There is a difficult borderline between general education and cramming. Cromwell House in Highgate was a school divided into 'several courses of study', designed to 'give distinct and efficient prominence to each particular line of education' – preparation for the public schools, universites, Army, Navy, Civil Service – 'and to provide that amount of individual attention for want of which so many pupils fail to make a satisfactory progress in their studies'. Two neighbouring schools in St Pancras in 1879 illustrate the overlap between general education and coaching. 'The Collegiate School' in Camden Cottages prepared for the University Locals, the preliminary examinations of the Royal College of Surgeons and Apothecaries' Hall, entrance to 'Eton, Harrow etc.', the Civil Service, the College of Preceptors, whose first-class certificates 'are recognized by H. M. Judges, and by the General Medical Council, as guarantees of good education', exempting holders from the preliminary examinations of the Law Society and the various Medical Corporations. A special class for the study of navigation was under the headmaster, 'who holds a certificate as Captain from the Examiners of the Board of Trade'. Nearby, there was a coaching establishment where payment could be made by the month or even the hour for special classes or private lessons and there was also a correspondence course at slightly lower fees.[143]

These examinations, especially those of the Council of Military Education (1857–70) and the Directorate which succeeded it, made a profound impression on the schools. Although some provided an 'army side', the public schools did not respond adequately to the curricular demands and standards which the military reformers hoped would send boys with the 'education of a gentleman' forward to Woolwich,

Sandhurst, or Addiscombe, the East India Company's military seminary (1809–61), either as cadets, or for direct entry by purchase, for even these had an examination to pass from 1851 onwards.[144] Private enterprise swiftly filled the gap. Fearon for example reported on one 'Private School of the First-grade', which specialized in preparing for competitive examinations – Woolwich and Sandhurst entrance, direct commissions, the Indian Civil Service, the Naval College at Portsmouth, the Marine Artillery, the Home Civil Service, and open scholarships, chiefly to Cambridge. The standard of teaching was high and 'appears . . . to have a remarkable effect on the pupils'. The impact of the examinations was 'direct and severe', and the only question was whether 'owing to their highly technical character', their influence on general education is most for good or evil?[145]

Military and other 'crammers' so rapidly became a feature of the educational scene, that Canon Moseley of the Council of Military Education said before the Taunton Commissioners that already these 'special schools' intervened to 'erect a sort of screen' between the schools and the Council.[146] Their establishments were numerous in London. The Kilburn and St John's Wood Civil and Military Institute, founded in 1859, prepared for a representative series of examinations – the Indian Civil Service, the Indian Engineers, Woolwich, the Staff College, Ceylon Civil Service, Indian Telegraph, Sandhurst, Direct Commissions, Home Civil Service, and the universities.[147] Some included the Indian Forests examinations. The courses at these establishments were fairly wide. Castlebar Court at Ealing included English, mathematics, drawing, geometrical and mechanical, Latin, Greek, French, German, Italian, Spanish, Arabic, Sanskrit, 'natural and experimental Sciences and the Moral Sciences'. Rochester House at Ealing added 'Surveying and Plan Drawing'.[148]

There was still a strong element of general education in these courses, and the boys who took them were often of secondary age. Castlebar Court took boarders between sixteen and twenty-one years of age. The Practical Military College at Sunbury, established in 1855, took youths form sixteen years in its junior department.[149] The coaching establishment begun by Captain James and his colleagues at South Kensington in 1881 had older men preparing for the Staff College and promotions in the Militia, and a country branch for younger pupils, but the majority of its students was of upper secondary age as 'boys from the public schools do not gain such success in the various examinations because they do not have the opportunities which are absolutely forced upon them in Lexham Gardens'. Discipline held first place, Captain James and his colleagues laid great emphasis on the 'moral influence on boys committed to their charge'. The Oblate Fathers of St Charles College sent him their boys. He had 'an excellent tutorial system', the thirty-nine classrooms being 'constantly occupied by one of the forty-seven tutors'. 'No one', as its most distinguished pupil said, 'who was not a congenital idiot could avoid passing thence into the Army.'[150]

These coaching establishments charged heavily, and could be attended for short expensive bouts in the old writing-school tradition. A supreme example was an establishment in Powis Square, Notting Hill, whose results made high termly charges an investment – Michaelmas, thirteen weeks, £82 resident, £39 day; Lent, twelve weeks, £76 or £36; Easter, nine weeks, £57 or £27. During seven years 118 vacancies out of 237 in the Indian Civil Service were 'carried off' by its pupils, and successes in other examinations ('all of these are much more easy') were 'too numerous to mention'. Readers were referred to the Blue Book of March 1876 on the 'Selection and Training of Candidates for the Indian Civil Service' for 'Special Proof of the goodness of the education given'.[151] This was the age of payment by results. Old distinctions of professional standing, newly created intellectual and academic distinctions of competitive examinations, distinctions based on calculations of future emoluments, promotion, security, status, were all reflected in the price families were prepared to pay. Military coaches charged highly, for they drew on classes which had been accustomed to the purchase of commissions (abolished in 1870), or who regarded the Army as a social preserve, as well as on aspiring families who saw the value of making their sons officers and gentlemen. The newly competitive Civil Service likewise drew on traditions of public service as an honourable career, and new areas of prestige in the colonial services reflected older traditions.

The newly emerging technical professions rested precariously on the somewhat ramshackle structure of private education but some schools gave specialist courses. The West Metropolitan Academy in Quebec Street, Hyde Park, for example, was 'conducted on those broad and liberal principles which can alone form the good man, the correct scholar, and the virtuous and enterprising citizen'. The principal took his scholars 'for vigorous healthy exercise daily in Hyde Park', and in 1831 a twelve-year-old pupil solved one of the mathematical 'juvenile problems' in the *Academic Chronicle*. It was in fact a secondary school. In 1840 it advertised a 'Class for Mechanics, Architectural and Geometric Drawing' under a Civil Engineer, which embraced 'sectional and perspective drawing, architectural plans, elevations, etc., plans of surveys, mapping, perspective, ornamental designing, art floors' work [this last may refer to the recent revival of the skills of medieval titles] etc.'.[152] In 1840 the 'High School for Mathematics, Engineering, etc.' was opened in Charles Street near the Middlesex Hospital, 'important for those designed for the Engineering Profession'.[153] From 1872 the Crystal Palace School of Practical Engineering was taking pupils over sixteen who had a suitable general education for courses to prepare them to take articles under either civil or mechanical engineers. It provided a preliminary course also and gave considerable facilities for practical work. 'There is a Colonial section of the school, designed particularly for gentlemen who are going to the Colonies or abroad as explorers or settlers, affording them so much practical knowledge or scientific or mechanical work and expedients, as shall enable them best to utilize the means at their disposal, especially when entirely dependent on their own resources.' Subjects included surveying, levelling, drainage, boring for water, ventilation, rope-making, shifts and expedients of camp life, growth of wood and modes of clearing, felling, grubbing, etc., timber-work, carpentry, stone-work, making bricks and tiles, wheelmaking, mineralogy, geology, chemistry and general forging. The principal of this outward-bound venture in the outback of Sydenham was a Member of both the Institutes of Civil and Mechanical Engineering.[154] By 1895 a School of Electrical Engineering was advertised in Princes Street, Hanover Square.[155] In the last decades of the century another special vocational need produced both secretarial colleges or crammers and schools giving general education and commercial skills – in 1880 for example George Clark founded a college in a small house in Southgate, which was an immediate success, largely because of its results in the Civil Service examinations.[156] The examinations of the Science and Art Department were underpinning provisions of this kind. The senior division of the Islington School of Science and Art had in 1879 about 220 scholars daily.[157] The Berners College of Experimental Science was founded in 1860 to teach 'Science theoretically and practically in all its branches, and is in connexion with the Government Examining Boards'.[158]These 'science schools' were for one social level what the 'military crammers' were for another.

Through the various stages of their development private schools provided an essential and substantial element in education.[159] Whether private enterprise in education, or schooling as a market commodity, is desirable, it is difficult to see how Victorian London, or Victorian Britain, could have engaged on its extraordinary adventure without the almost heroic ingenuity of such schools as these, and they must be analysed as an essential element in the development of secondary education. Private schooling failed however to build a system of such education, or indeed to convince contemporaries that they could, or should, do so. Education was not only a market commodity or a private transaction.[160] Even when paying a generous tribute to the work of private schools, Frederick Temple, then bringing to the bishopric of London a lifetime of educational experience, showed his distaste for such a concept when he spoke in both concrete and symbolic terms of some schools 'conducted in ordinary houses, the classes being held, we have heard, in the upstairs room or the downstairs room, or perhaps in a little adjunct or shed built at the back . . . children could not be properly taught under these circumstances'.[161] In 1895 Temple may be said to be speaking for men such as himself who had been striving for two generations to bring secondary education securely back into the public sector.

V

The middle-class education question
in the reign of Victoria

The challenge

For the most part private schools serve private practice. As the nineteenth century advanced, the changing structure of society and state drew the new middle classes more overtly into the public sector. The economy generated a larger, more specialized, more diversified, professional cohort; social ethics demanded new kinds of corporate concern and action; politics were gradually penetrated by new class interests and eventually became a sphere of direct middle-class operation as well as of influence and pressure. The metropolis led the way and with the other great civic centres experimented with educational institutions which would serve these public purposes. Private schools did adapt themselves to new needs, but the evidence suggests that the middle classes began to demand something more coherent, even systematic, carrying more assurance than improvements devised by private adventurers. Moreover, it became increasingly clear that the economics of such enterprises were not able to carry the cost. Capital investment had to be secured in other ways. The temper of the age was reforming and prudential, but the concept of secondary education which had begun to emerge in Revolutionary France and which had indeed been systematized by Napoleon, and spread through much of Europe, was not only tarred with the Jacobin brush, it was alien to English empiricism. English society preferred to conceive of schooling as a function of social structure and the debate about middle-class education became increasingly prominent, explicit and articulate as the century advanced.[1] Although middle-class distrust of what was considered a corrupt, exclusive and monopolistic political system gradually diminished after the repeal of the Test and Corporation Acts and the first reform of Parliament in 1832 and of the municipalities in 1835, state action or interference in this sector of education was still for the most part inconceivable or unacceptable. Nevertheless the middle-class education question was no longer considered a matter only of private or sectional interest. During the years between the two electoral reforms, 1832 and 1867, concern over this question mounted. In 1852 the *English Journal of Education* declared it to be 'the greatest educational problem of the day'.[2] In 1861 *The Times* said: 'The political centre of gravity is confessedly somewhere in the middle classes. ... Yet ... the great educational movement of the last fifty years ... has scarcely visited [this] intermediate region.'[3]

The problem was one first of definition and then of provision and control. As early as 1832 Thomas Arnold advocated state organization of middle-class education – there was no 'regular system of secondary education', and something comparable to the public schools and the universities should be provided for these classes who were at the mercy of private adventurers.[4] Matthew Arnold carried his father's European outlook forward into the next generation, but even then he was in advance of his times. Public concern in these earlier decades usually had to operate through less official channels, more directly under the control of those who wished to use the schools, and more easily penetrated by their influence and ethos, even if leadership and authentication were provided by a sometimes patronizing aristocracy or more usually by the intellectual 'aliens' of Matthew Arnold's analysis.[5] As late as 1883 Lord Norton could write of the 'national repugnance' which had always been expressed at placing 'in the administration of the government, the intellectual and moral training of the independent body of the nation'.[6] Twenty years earlier Lord Fortescue had argued that this 'homely strength and honest independence' could best be provided for locally by county schools.[7] He was concerned particularly with the farming communities, but the experience of London and its suburbs had for well over thirty years demonstrated that local response was essential to the success of experiments of this kind. At this level it is difficult to separate private from emerging public interest. Enterprise was extremely diverse and complex. In spite of accumulating experience in the difficulty of making even good private schools pay their way, it was still taken as axiomatic that schools for the middle classes should aim to be self-supporting. Public concern might seek to eliminate, reduce, or collectivize the profit motive but the laws of supply and demand must be applied. Only by local studies can public elements in the newer kinds of middle-class education be discerned, and the beginning of what was later to become state enterprise in secondary education traced amidst the complexities of the classic age of private enterprise and urban growth.

In London middle-class education was one aspect of the new urban society, of the process of both creating it and coming to terms with it. Learning to live in cities can be seen as 'a kind of training that society had to undergo . . .'.[8] This was not the romantic London of Dickens, with its enveloping fogs, flickering lanterns or gas-lights, unbanked, encroaching, laden river, mounting and shifting piles of dust and excrement, its unreflecting, intuitive, emotional inhabitants, for whom schooling could do little, for learning was no substitute for spontaneous living, and calculation was usually equated with inhumanity. This on the contrary was the utilitarian city, driving, grasping, measuring, calculating, suppressing, restraining, training the spontaneous in favour of the logical, the formulated, explanation or action. The educational needs of boys growing up in such an environment were practical, but almost at the other end of a continuum from those fifteenth-century schoolboys and apprentices of London, who were learning to see their world, its meaning and possibilities, in concrete, symbolic terms. This new abstract city of the nineteenth century both generated and demanded a utilitarian ethos and philosophy. Novelists might embody the city and its challenges in symbols and images which both terrified and fascinated the romantic imagination, but the practical, civic mind could no longer personify and visualize its problems and hopes, nor narrate itself into understanding. It must instead theorize, calculate, and first of all, classify.[9]

The secular response

It is not surprising that among the first attempts to reflect upon a new and more systematic education for inhabitants of London, not only at working-class level, but higher up the social scale, were those of the Philosophic Radicals. James Mill discerned that there was in London 'an aggregate of persons of middle rank collected in one spot . . . the like of which exists in no other spot on the surface of the earth'.[10] And to these middle ranks society must look for secular salvation. In 1814 Mill with Place helped by Bentham, Ricardo and Wakefield laid plans and collected subscriptions for opening a 'superior day school' on monitorial lines, and even began negotiations for a site either in Bentham's Westminster garden or Leicester Square, both venues with ineradicable disadvantages. By 1822 difficulties had obliged them to abandon the scheme and return the money.[11] This seems to have hurried forward the plans of the Hill brothers for a branch of their Birmingham School (first opened in 1803) in the London suburbs; they wished to make their fortunes by establishing a network of such schools catering for large numbers at moderate cost. Their father, Thomas Wright Hill, had been a student under Stephen Addington of Mile End and the Hoxton Square Academy, and a friend of Joseph Priestley, an interesting link between eighteenth-century dissenting academies and these experiments in a new education for the middle classes of the new century.[12] He and his sons Matthew Davenport, Rowland and Arthur, and then Arthur's son George Birkbeck Hill, consistently practised and developed the application of Utilitarian ideas to education throughout the century. Early contacts with Bentham, Mill, Brougham, with the ideas of Locke, Rousseau, Pestalozzi, and with the methods of Bell and Lancaster were embodied in their *Plan . . . for the government and Liberal Instruction of boys in large numbers* (1822 and 1825), and carried out at Bruce Castle, Tottenham. The Hills aimed to establish moral principles and habits, to develop the powers of the mind and body, and only thirdly to communicate knowledge. The curriculum included science, and the English subjects and languages were deferred 'to a comparatively late period'. Methods emphasized activity and interest, and hobbies and studies of the boys' own choice were ingeniously used as incentives. Discipline was based on a school coinage which would buy the things schoolboys really want – holidays and privileges.[13] The school's constitutional government was 'a replica in miniature of the great social body, of which the pupils, as Englishmen, are hereafter to be members', and the criminal code was the work of the boys with the masters *ex officio* magistrates. By the time of the Taunton Inquiry, this system had changed somewhat to incorporate the Platonic ideas then so powerful, and some boys had been made 'guardians' whose standing depended on the behaviour and industry of ten charges – one felt his responsibilites so keenly that he contemplated suicide.

In its early days the school attracted much attention and support from its sympathizers. The *Edinburgh Review* declared that it 'seemed more than most to ensure that boys had less useless suffering and more play in the process of becoming men'. Bentham himself inspected it and was enthusiastic, and he, Grote, Hume and other radicals sent boys. They also came from the new republics of Greece and South America and a Hillska Skola was founded in Stockholm. The Society for the Diffusion of Useful Knowledge was eulogistic. But the influence of Bruce Castle was perhaps less than these high hopes promised. It remained a modest private school for about 80 pupils advertising in 1872 and 1879 that it prepared for the 'Universities, Learned Professions and Commercial Pursuits'.[14]

University College School was also founded under Utilitarian influence. Unlike Bruce Castle, which was entirely a family business, its connection with University College and its element of semi-public support enabled it to survive and establish itself as a flourishing public school. Yet revolt against these was the reason for its establishment. The great 'Winchester fagging row' led to the suggestion in 1828 that 'the middle and upper classes have founded the University of London. Why not a school in connexion with this? The new institution is a legitimate produce [sic] of the disgust universally entertained for the absurdities of the old ones.' In 1832 the school was opened in rooms provided by University College, under T. H. Key, whose Taunton evidence thirty years later described a flourishing non-sectarian day school of 340 boys between seven and about seventeen. A great advantage was that pupils could enter University College for about a year before going on to Oxford or Cambridge, avoiding the danger of its being considered as preparatory for the public schools. Its able and progressive headmasters; its central position – 'close to the Gower Street Station of the Metropolitan Railway and only a few minutes' walk from the termini of the North Western, Midland and Great Northern Railways' on which season tickets were granted at half price; its enlightened curriculum meeting 'the wants of the middle-class in London. . . and also supplying a better education to the highest class', were all factors in enabling this school to make a satisfactory profit from fees of £5 per term at its opening, rising only slightly during the century. In 1879 there were 600 boys under H. W. Eve who had been master of the modern side at Wellington before taking this post. Key's discussion of the school's discipline and curriculum illustrates its Utilitarian philosophy. Religious teaching was absolutely excluded though masters who took private boarders were free to deal with the matter as they chose. The course was not prescribed but selected by parents after discussion with the headmaster. All but 10 per cent took Latin ('as a common rule we recommend it'); Greek was only taken after the age of thirteen – by about 60 boys out of the 340. About 80 took German, and all studied French; English received much attention and in the early forms practice rather than grammatical theory was emphasized. Arithmetic and mathematics were very strong and some book-keeping was taught, but on the whole parents did not want it even if their sons were going into commerce. Physical sciences were taught, first theoretically and then practically to a class of 24; 'They have a laboratory of their own and do things as well as talk about them.' Chemistry was an innovation, and the 'ordinary sciences of observation', botany and zoology, had occasionally been taught, but not considered successful. Physical, rather than political, geography was emphasized. Eve was a vehement opponent of history, from which boys could learn little philosophy, 'only facts which had no significance'. Music was abandoned as it was taught out of school time and the boys considered it a punishment, but drawing was taught by a large staff of masters and was much valued by middle-class parents. Importance was given to the teaching of political economy or social science. 'I am not sure that I do not place it above everything except arithmetic', its precondition. 'The question of moral character connected with it I attach a very great value to.'[15]

University College School established itself as an important influence on London schooling, an unusual example of an idea, even a theory, securing a foothold in the pragmatic fabric of English education. Another London school, which embodied a rather less precise ideology, was less successful. The liberalism of the mid-nineteenth-century exhibitions found educational expression in the founding of the International College at Isleworth. In 1863 Paris Exhibition prizes were offered for essays on the advantages of educating together children of different European nations, and a society was founded to carry out the project. Its English directors included Cobden, Kay-Shuttleworth, and Professors Huxley and Tyndale. Four schools, 'entirely free from any government control', were planned in England, France, Germany and Italy. They were to follow a 'uniform programme of study' embracing 'all the subjects necessary to an education of the highest order, whether the pupils intend to follow commercial pursuits or the learned professions'. Boys could pass easily from one school to another and acquire four languages fluently. In England the site chosen was Spring Grove, Twickenham, 'one of the healthiest and most accessible spots near

London, approved on sanitary grounds by Sir James Clarke and on the loopline of the South-Western Railway'. The Prince of Wales opened the new building in the thirteenth-century Gothic style; the first headmaster, Dr Leonard Schmitz, had been his tutor, and then rector of the High School at Edinburgh. The school curriculum subordinated classics to modern languages and science, whose course was devised by Huxley.

The International College had difficulties from the beginning, instruction of the 'motley assemblage of pupils' proved very difficult and the quality of the teaching does not seem to have been high. One old boy remembered that while all men are brothers 'it is not logical to infer ... that all brothers are better for each other's society'. Discipline seems to have been precarious and in 1870 the locality was shaken by a revolt, caused by the stopping of holiday privileges. The boys barricaded themselves in with supplies of food and tobacco, with reserves 'granaried' at a public house nearby, and the police had to be called in. Finance was never satisfactory and numbers were disappointing. In 1872 the total of day boys and boarders was said to be 300 but by 1887 the average number of boarders was put at 100 with a limited number of day boys. It was popular with well-to-do merchants of the north, and this brought the school's most distinguished pupil, Frederick Delius, who gained a reputation as a violinist and composed his first song in its sanatorium after being hit over the head with a cricket stump. In practice the high-sounding project for educational free trade seems to have produced a conventional second-rate boarding-school. In 1890 it closed and the building was sold to the Borough Road Training College.[16]

The Utilitarians and their liberal successors were explicit in their educational purposes: the new secular city needed to be explained, serviced, and managed. But if Bruce Castle, University College School and the International College over several decades set out to equip the various levels among the managers of the new society, there remained the task of inducting those who could only be managed if they understood and were prepared to co-operate with the managerial ideal, and these included the holders of numerous and complex ranges of lower-middle and upper-working-class occupations. Here the appetite for education was especially keen, for on it depended possibilities of staking claims to the precarious territories between these levels of society, styles of life and aspirations. It was an educational area where problems of definition were acute even for those who strove to find an alternative rationale for society. The early movement for the provision of popular schools by the co-operative movement was stronger in the north than in the south of England, but London radicalism did provide some ground for experiment. In the Gray's Inn Road a school for both day pupils and boarders, with infant, junior and senior sections, was opened as part of the Labour Bazaar. The curriculum included music, dancing, physical education, and French and Latin for older pupils, and the

'Science of Society' was taught by free discussion. The children, to emphasize its republican tone, wore a uniform 'similar to that worn by Greek youths in former days', including the toga (an unusual item of Greek attire) and sandals. The school declined even before the collapse of the co-operative movement and the Grand National Trade Union; it was never perhaps suited to the working class, and the high fees (£2 2s a term, boarders £2 2s a month if their parents were co-operators) put it quite beyond their reach.[17] A few London schools continued to uphold this ideal, one attached to the John Street Literary and Scientific Institute gave for 6d a week a 'comprehensive and practical education' which included, as well as the usual basic subjects, grammar, the elements of geography, mathematics and vocal music, and 'an introduction to the Knowledge of the Inductive Sciences'; another, 'one of the most complete secularist institutions in the country', was the school of the Metropolitan Institution, which in 1860 had 200 pupils. These however, as with private schools on the same lines, really catered for middle-class children, they were quite out of the reach of the poor.[18] At the time of the Taunton Inquiry Joshua Fitch noticed the same problem in the north, where successful and superior British schools, Wesleyan, and even some National schools, together with schools such as that attached to the Mechanics' Institute at Leeds, had 'by their own excellence attracted children of a superior class'.[19]

London was however to make a substantial contribution to the development of this level of education through the work of William Ellis (1800–80), a highly successful underwriter whose educational work was firmly rooted in City experience and Utilitarian philosophy. His life and business career coincided with the social and economic development of the century and his meeting with James Mill and his circle formulated his ideas, especially about the importance of a particular kind of education to the happiness, well-being and cohesion of society. To this cause he quietly gave over a quarter of a million pounds, and John Stuart Mill described his zeal as 'apostolic'. In 1826 he put forward in articles in the *Westminster Review* the importance of the inculcation of 'the laws of conduct which affect human well-being', the 'science of character', the 'art of being, and of doing good', the 'Religion of Common Life', and those studies which helped children to apply these laws in industrial and civil life.[20] Ellis experimented with various titles for his course – social economy, social science and so forth – but its purpose was constant and was predominantly moral. When he recommenced his active work for education in 1835 his friendship with George Combe and W. B. Hodgson brought him allies on the national stage. He tried out his teaching at a boys' British school in Camberwell and there began training a body of teachers who could simplify 'a very abstruse subject . . . so that children can readily comprehend it'. For years he conducted a teachers' class on Saturday mornings in his City office, sometimes with as many as 50 members. He was involved with Combe

The Gospel Oak Schools, 1865

in establishing the Secular School at Edinburgh and provided its first master, William Mathieu Williams, and he was also connected with the secular movement in the north of England. When, however, he began to finance his network of London schools, he avoided the label as it had been an 'occasion for reproach'.

His first venture in 1848 was to provide substantial aid to the Chartist school of William Lovett for working-class boys in the National Hall, Holborn, himself teaching 'the science of human well-being'. In 1848 Ellis began his most characteristic enterprise – the first 'Birkbeck' school was opened in connection with the London Mechanics' Institute, Southampton Row, largely financed by Ellis, with contributions from associates, and even from the Corporation of London. This was the first of a number of highly successful schools named modestly after the founder of the mechanics' institutes. In Finsbury a disused chapel was holding a school of 280 boys in 1852; in Vincent Square, Westminster, another old chapel was taken in 1850, and at one time this had 300 pupils. In Bethnal Green a chapel was taken as freehold, and Ellis felt able to adapt the premises, opened in 1851, and by 1870 containing 400 boys and girls. A specially built school at Peckham became the model enterprise; its headmaster was W. A. Shields, one of Ellis's most successful teachers. The building for 400 boys and girls had soon to be extended to hold nearly 1000. At Kingsland in 1852 there began another highly flourishing school, ultimately for between 500 and 600 children. The last school was set up at Gospel Oak in 1862, for 500 children, and this one was named after its founder. By 1870 it had 650 pupils.

These Birkbeck schools were not at first intended for middle-class children, but even with the munificent support of Ellis they were obliged to charge fees which enabled them to cover running costs, and by the time of the Taunton Inquiry they were said to have been founded 'with the object of affording in them a type of what the education of the middle classes should be . . .'. Ellis hoped that his demonstration would persuade other school managers to adopt his methods. When in 1865 the schools were vested in trustees, the deed declared that the schools were intended for the education of children of small tradesmen and other persons of moderate means. The charge seems to have been around 6*d* a week. In 1884 the Kingsland Schools charged £4 4*s* a year. After 1870 the competition of the Board schools made it even more necessary to raise the fees and make them 'middle-class schools' supplying what was 'most urgently needed under our present defective system . . .'.

These schools were distinguished by their methods and their curriculum. There was great emphasis on explanation, teaching was 'not by tasks but by collective, conversational and catechetical lessons'. The curriculum emphasized science, chemistry, mechanics, geography, and above all physiology, taught for its civic purposes, designed to send out pupils 'intelligently prepared to co-operate in the future with the legislator who would enforce vaccination and the medical officer of health'. More important still was the moral dimension in which urban and industrial society was conceived, 'every part of knowledge was to be subordinate to the laws of conduct which affect human well-being, and by obedience to which only can the welfare of the individual and the community be attained'. Ellis saw this first as a rational basis for individual conduct, 'the science of character', and he emphasized not only the classic Benthamite appeal to enlightened self-interest but also the 'feelings of reverence and benevolence'. Unfortunately the social interpretation of these moral ideas was less unexceptionable, for Utilitarian application of the theories of the classical political economists included in the children's lessons such precepts as 'Capital can never oppress the workman', and that if thrown out of work by the beneficial results of technical progress, men should not complain but adapt themselves. It was claimed that these lessons of the 'Rules of Conduct in Harmony with the Truths of Economic Science' were transmitted by home lesson to parents, 'with unmistakable satisfaction'. It was not from the more easy-going English capital, but from the less receptive Scottish one that reports of revolt by the parents came. Edinburgh fathers staunchly refused to accept the dogma of Lesson 27, 'Competition is one of the most efficient agents for diffusing the benefits of industrial enterprise over the whole world', and gave lessons at home refuting those given at the Secular School.

In London however the Birkbeck schools filled a very real need and flourished until the competition of the Board schools and of growing technical education brought nearly all of them to an end. Only the Gospel Oak School survived, to be recreated in 1889 as a public secondary school for 200 boys, strong in applied art and science and with social economy still in the curriculum, with fees of £2 2s a term.

It is difficult to assess this contribution by Ellis to the development of the idea of secondary education. His benevolence was quiet and un-obtrusive but his influence can be traced in many educational directions; for example he and Shields taught at University College School, he lectured at Crosby Hall, one of his teachers became master of the Jewish Middle-Class School in Red Lion Square. The Prince Consort invited him to teach political economy to the Prince of Wales and the Princess Royal. His secularism was never aggressive, nor anti-Christian, and at least one active Anglican educationalist, Canon William Rogers, re-garded him as one of the most religious of men, and both accepted his help and later returned the generosity by becoming Chairman of the Trustees of the Birkbeck Schools. The problem of providing schooling for this social level could be seen either as divisive, or as bridging a social gulf between the lower-middle and upper-working-classes. Ellis and his fellow secularists at least made an honest attempt, in a confused and rapidly changing civic situation, to bring order out of educational chaos.[21]

Church of England response

Secular theorists might be well equipped to make sense of the city, but could choose to take up or ignore the cause of middle-class education. The Churches had no such choice for they were urged to provide education of all levels. Coleridge in 1829–30, when opposing Brougham's policies, argued that Church and State were partners in national education and while primary education should be entrusted to the parochial 'clergy', a semi-clerical character should be given to teachers of more advanced studies. He was interpreting much scattered and unsystematized practice and provision, and working out a coherent theory of the work of the *clerisy*, the Church in action in the secular, non-sectarian sphere. The Church as the 'third estate' was failing to counterbalance the various interests of society and therefore to secure and improve 'that civilisation without which the nation could be neither permanent nor progressive'. Coleridge's 'National Church' was not to be identified with either the Church of Christ, the Catholic Church, or with the Church of England, and his 'clerisy' was made up of clerical persons, rather than parsons.[22] But the matter looked somewhat different from the top of Highgate Hill than it did down in the front line where the clergy of all denominations were essentially, inexorably, committed to an urgent, desperate attempt not only to make city life supportable but to make civic living explicable. To the Established Church the task had to be total. No part of the city, no inhabitant of it, could be said to lie beyond its responsibility. Yet the Church was still organized for a stable, rural way of life. London's ecclesiastical fabric was in complete disarray. North of the river the Bishop of London was responsible not only for the exploding metropolis but for the whole of Essex, a huge hinterland, while south of the river the Bishop of Winchester had the swarming and spreading 'Borough' and southern suburbs as a kind of appendage attached to his rich and rural diocese. Within its widening boundaries, London surged and grew through and over its ancient parochial structure, and submerged a widening ring of suburban and rural villages, facing its clergy with topographical, demographic, sociological, pastoral problems which must have seemed impossible of solution. Transformations of attitude and understanding were as urgent as changes in organization, structure and distribution of resources. Before the Church could respond effectively to what came to be known as the 'condition of England question', a new and acceptable version of the theory of the relation between Church and State had to be worked out in practice – the Church had to have a new reformation. It was the 1830s which decided that this should come from within. The contribution of the London parson to the cause of middle-class education in the nineteenth century was part of this 'new reformation', continuing the tradition of the City clergy of the fifteenth century and of Elizabethan and Jacobean clerical benefactors. It was the challenge of the City which both focused and precipitated the necessary changes.[23]

The impact of City experience can be demonstrated in a personal but highly significant case – Charles James Blomfield[24] became rector of St Botolph without Bishopsgate in 1820 after a career very much on the old rural and academic lines. Perhaps even in country livings the clergy were recognizing that the old order was not as clearly laid down as it seemed, but in his City parish Blomfield responded quickly to the needs of shifts and growths of population, widening and diversifying opportunities, increasing possibilities and aspirations as well as bewilderments and problems. He became an ardent exponent of education, his infant schools were a model, he campaigned actively for the National Society, and he helped towards the transformation of the parish charity (ward) schools from the usual elementary kind, giving the children 'such useful learning as is suited to their condition', into schools eventually preparing for 'more advantageous occupations . . . than what are termed "charity children" generally attain'.[25] When Blomfield became Bishop of London in 1828 he had already developed that concept of the Church's duty to the City which was to be of such importance for the task of remedying the 'terrible deficiencies of his teeming diocese'. At a national level his immense abilities, driving energy and dynamic moderation played an important part in the setting up of the Ecclesiastical Commission in 1835, which 'probably saved the Church'. Here he worked with that conscientious and moderate churchman, Sir Robert Peel, and these two men may be compared in their growing understanding of the shift from rural to urban society in these vital decades between 1830 and 1850, just as the repeal of the Corn Laws symbolized or epitomized the political recognition of the shift in the balance of population.[26]

In the meantime Blomfield had on his hands a metropolis in a state of 'spiritual destitution'.[27] Already some rebuilding and 'church extension' had taken place. The Hackney Phalanx of High Churchmen, founders of the National Society, had also founded the Church Building Society in 1817 and secured substantial parliamentary grants for building churches where local initiative demonstrated the need. In zealously Evangelical Islington for example, in 1825 the erection of three substantial churches was set on foot.[28] Rival societies, the low Church Pastoral Aid Society (1830) and the high Additional Curates Society (1837), were founded to increase the supply of assistant clergy and, however much Charlotte Brontë may have considered that too many of them descended upon the Yorkshire moors, in London's thickly populated parishes curates could always be put to good use.[29]

These early achievements did not even keep pace with the increase of population. By the time Blomfield began to tackle the problem at diocesan level, it was clear that government funds were no longer politically feasible and that the general indictment of neglect of the towns by the Church must be answered by redistribution of church funds as well as by local effort.[30] In 1836 Blomfield produced *Proposals for the Erection of a Fund to be applied to the Building and Endowment of Additional Churches in the Metropolis* and 'expatiated over the whole metropolis by building fifty churches at once'. He had to see the problem of London as a whole, he had a concept of the total civic community. He appealed to the City Companies and to merchants and bankers of London, and received £106,000 for his fund by the end of its first year.[31] Christ Church, St Pancras, was the first church built with this money. Prosperous parts of the capital began to realize their responsibilities for more destitute areas. A fund collected at St George's Chapel, Albemarle Street, enabled St Jude's Whitechapel to be completed.[32] South of the Thames, London's parochial problems were in the hands of that 'last of our old prince bishops', Charles Richard Sumner, whose early fashionable career and promotion by favour of George IV hardly presaged his evangelical devotion and admirable administration as Bishop of Winchester from 1827 until his retirement in 1868. Although he opposed the setting up of the Ecclesiastical Commission, he loyally carried out its designs. He formed a Church Building Society for his diocese and a special Southwark Fund for schools and churches, and spent a considerable part of his munificent revenues on trying to bring the Church into the service of the people of south London.[33]

The motives for this 'Church Extension' movement both north and south of the Thames were broadly pastoral. Blomfield 'considered that to build a new church in a district where the means of public worship were wanting was a sure way of increasing the number of clergymen in that district and that it would be a centre from which would radiate all around' not only the truths of Christianity but also 'the various benevolent institutions of schools, visiting societies, dispensaries, etc. . . .'.[34] By the 1830s 'few churchmen can still have doubted . . . that a parish was not complete without an educational apparatus',[35] and to Blomfield with his London experience this 'apparatus' must serve varying social levels. Schools were needed for children of the middle classes, to whom the Church of England made the least appeal, and who now had increasing political power. Several of the areas whose parish structure was revitalized and renewed during this period provide significant examples of experiments in education at these levels.

Weldon Champneys's ministry to a population of 33,000 in Whitechapel was a case in point. The titles of his voluminous evangelical works, such as *The Path of a Sunbeam* (1845), do not indicate the tough practicality of his work in actively promoting the parish institutions which might help to make working-class life in the East End less incomprehensible and unmanageable as well as a little less unpleasant – a local association for promoting the health and comfort of the industrial classes, a provident society, schools for boys, girls and infants, a shoeblack brigade, a 'Ragged School', the first Church of England Young Men's Society for mutual improvement, and an office for the payment of the London coalwhippers to avoid their having to collect their wages in public houses. Such was the local apparatus towards which Blomfield's policy had been directed, and if Whitechapel seems an unlikely setting for an experiment in middle-class education, that is to leave out of account both the rich texture of the new urban society, and the diverse demands created and stimulated by this revitalization of local institutions. Chamneys was able to remodel local charities to bring forward a scheme for the Whitechapel Foundation Commercial School, approved by Chancery after amendment in 1858 and built in Leman Street for a cost of just over £4000. It provided instruction 'in the principles of the Christian religion, reading, writing, arithmetic, the Latin, French and German languages', and also in 'such language, arts and sciences as to the trustees shall seem expedient'. Prayers were Anglican but there was a conscience clause. The boys were to be between seven and fifteen years of age, able to read and write and of a good character and health. Preference was given to boys of the parish, but 'foreigners' were admitted for an extra 5s a quarter. In 1868 the Charity Commissioners allowed the 'native' fees to go up to £1 and £1 5s a year to enable better salaries to be paid to the masters. At the opening there were 50 scholars and by the 1860s the numbers were well over 200.[36]

By that time Champneys had returned to his native parish, St Pancras, as vicar (1860). Here he inherited a parish which had been an almost classic case of reorganization. Already by 1825 the growth of its population had been considered spectacular, and since then a whole generation had been born and had grown up amid the sights and sounds of railway construction. In 1843 the Ecclesiastical Commissioners were empowered to divide parishes into new districts.[37] The huge parish of St Pancras was arduously subdivided into twenty incumbencies, under the devoted guidance of Canon Thomas Dale, another Londoner and an Evangelical who took on St Pancras with the especial purpose of putting into practice the policy of Peel and Blomfield who had promoted him. As Professor at University College and King's College and as a private schoolmaster in Camberwell, Greenwich and Beckenham, he had already had experience of London's varied educational needs, and one of his assistants, the Reverend David Laing, who had offered to take over the Holy Trinity district and to help with the reorganization, was working with the Governesses' Benevolent Institution and Queen's College. In 1850 when St Pancras still contained 200,000 inhabitants they decided to establish a school for middle-class boys. A public meeting resolved that 'regard being had to the wants of this populous and increasing locality, it is . . . expedient that a Public School be established, in which a thoroughly sound commercial and classical education based on religious principles can be afforded on reasonable terms'. Plans were submitted for approval to Blomfield, and the North London Collegiate School for Boys was opened under the headship of W. C. Williams, one of Dale's curates. 'There is no greater proof of the progress of Camden Town than its possessing such an institution for the sons of its middle-class residents', wrote a local historian in 1874. It opened in a disused piano-manufactory which had already been used as a Nonconformist chapel and a temporary Anglican church – such being the property pressures of urban expansion.[38]

Williams remained headmaster for the rest of the school's life; it eventually became his private property, but he still considered himself as acting for the parish clergy who could come into the school at any time and examine a class. It contained 350 boys in 1861 and in 1869 the classical department had 250 pupils, the junior school 50, and the commercial department 120. The parents chose the course largely according to their own social standing and one 'with direct reference to mercantile life' was 'forced upon' Williams to meet their views. He confined the school to boys from middle-class homes, and refused sons of 'rising artizans', such as drivers and proprietors of omnibuses. The fees were £9 9s a year and Williams was able to cover the cost and get good masters from the universities for about £120 to £200 a year. The school's reputation enabled them subsequently to get good appointments.

Williams retired in 1886 and the school died with him – already in 1878 he had warned the middle-class schools that they must do more to face the competition from the Board schools which gave such a superior education that all appointments under Government would fall to their pupils. He had shown concern for all the educational needs of the parish, urging Dale to establish a school above the National School and below his own, 'for the next stratum', at about £2 2s a year, 'for that they ought to get a thoroughly good instruction in reading, writing, arithmetic, geography and French': they would not 'care about Latin'. Popular lectures could be added upon 'a variety of subjects which everybody ought to know something of'. The school should prepare for the Civil Service, clerkships and so on.[39]

Another incumbent who provided for middle-class educational needs in his parish was the Reverend T. R. White, rector of Finchley, who was able in some measure to draw on the ancient parish charities to found in 1857 the school which became Christ's College, in a Gothic building of great gloom with ingenious and somewhat experimental ventilation and lighting systems. The school had early staffing difficulties and its boarding fees of £40 and £50 a year were too low to provide a sound education. White had bought the lease and the next headmaster raised the fees and transformed the school into a thriving institution, with a good sporting and scholastic record, preparing boys for the 'Universities, Professions, Military and Naval Colleges and all competitive examinations'. In the 'Modern Department' boys were 'fitted for mercantile pursuits' and modern languages were stressed. After White's death in 1877 the school became independent of any parochial control but continued to be a Church of England school. By 1895 it was difficult to compete with the endowed schools and the emerging secondary school system. A scheme to turn it into an endowed school came to nothing, and the next purchaser opened negotiations with the Finchley Urban District Council and the Middlesex County Council. Christ's College became the first school in Middlesex in which public secondary education under the Act of 1902 was provided, but the headmaster was allowed to keep his existing staff and the chapel service.[40]

Finchley was created by the outward movement of the middle classes, Camden Town was in some respects an almost archetypal middle-class neighbourhood, while Whitechapel may seem a surprising setting for a middle-class school. Another example however confirms the danger of predating the development of the almost single-class neighbourhoods made possible by later railway policy. The Reverend William Rogers (1819–96), a breezy and unconventional young man, had somehow displeased his vicar in a Fulham parish, and in 1845 was made by Blomfield the reluctant perpetual curate of St Thomas's Charterhouse, carved out of the huge parish of St Luke's between the City and Islington. The stipend of £150 a year represented comparative liberality. Blomfield as governor of the Charterhouse got the church site on an out-of-the-way corner of its playing fields, and in 1847 induced the Ecclesiastical Commissioners to apply to it part of the revenues of St Katherine's Coleman Street (which had a bare 666 inhabitants).[41] Rogers's downtrodden and impoverished district, created by Blomfield's policy, illustrated its problems and limitations. Rogers later complained of this 'mania for erecting churches in all sorts of inconvenient places' and declared that St Thomas's 'should never have been built'.[42] The boundaries of the parish, owing to the objections of St John's Clerkenwell, cut out any house of a better description, and Rogers served a population which made such living as it could from 'ministering to the pleasures of the more wealthy districts by which they are nearly surrounded'. Costermongria he called it, and after 'visiting the district he saw that it would be utterly useless to attempt to reclaim [them] . . . and he determined to devote his energies to the establishment of schools'.[43] Beginning with a few children in a blacksmith's empty shed, Rogers transformed his disreputable district into a network of schools, each creating further and perhaps unexpected appetites for education. At one stage a thousand of his parishioners, two-thirds of them unable to write their own names, petitioned the President of the Council for more provision. Most of this schooling was of an elementary level, but not only did one kind of schooling lead to demand for higher levels, the diverse social composition of even such a bedraggled neighbourhood was disclosed by this active policy. Rogers had a boys' second 'National School of a superior kind' charging between 3*d* and 6*d* a week, a corresponding girls' school providing French, domestic economy and fancy needlework as extras. The St Thomas Charterhouse Middle Class School in the Goswell Road under a clerical headmaster was in 1859 'one of the pioneers of this kind of education'. In 1872 it trained boys at £4 4*s* a year for 'Commercial Pursuits, the competitive examinations of the Civil Service, and for the University Local Examinations', teaching French, Latin, mechanics, natural philosophy and book-keeping, besides the 'subjects of an ordinary English education'. It continued to fill a real need and was not closed until 1906.[44]

While this kind of sporadic enterprise depended on local initiative and response, for it 'was largely in the parishes that the social concept of the establishment was to be worked out',[45] it can still be seen as an aspect of diocesan policy, and a genuine attempt to comprise 'all that distinguishes the fourth from the nineteenth century, and London from Laodicea'.[46] The work of the Church for elementary education is acknowledged and often criticized but the Anglican contribution to secondary education is nearly always identified with the decaying or outmoded grammar and 'hospital' schools rather than with an energetic, diverse, inventive and temporarily highly successful series of experiments during this crisis period.[47]

The problem was largely one of funding. Parochial enterprise alone was clearly not enough to bring the Church of England's educational

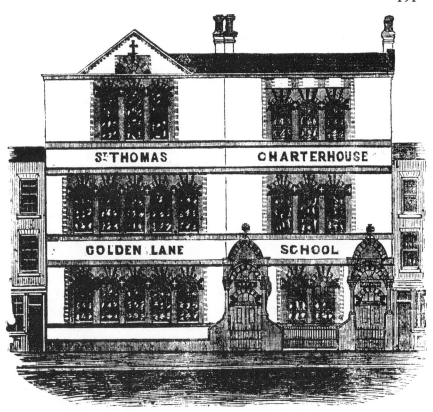

St Thomas Charterhouse

effort into line with the needs of the expanding middle classes. The *Quarterly Review* pointed out that the parish system in great towns such as London 'breaks down altogether'. 'The rector of many a large metropolitan parish presides over a small oasis . . . in the midst of a desert of dissent, indifference, and infidelity.'[48] The two bishops had already realized that some centralizing agency must be brought to bear on the problem. If government aid was not available, nor government interference acceptable to the middle classes, at least National Society resources might bring some coherence and help to their schools, and secure their loyalty to the Established Church. In April 1838 Blomfield communicated to the National Society 'the outline of a plan, which his Lordship had in contemplation, together with the Bishop of Winchester, for establishing an Institution in the Metropolis with a view to improving the education of the middle classes of Society by securing to them the benefit of sound religious education, in connexion with the other branches of instruction usually professed to be given by the best commercial schools'. By July the legality of using the National Society's funds for this purpose had been established and the idea of setting up middle schools, now combined with plans for diocesan boards of education and training establishments for masters, were embodied in a circular to be sent to all bishops.[49] The proposals of Blomfield and Sumner had coincided with the campaign of the High Church group which revivified the National Society and established its Committee of Enquiry and Correspondence. Its background was less metropolitan, its plan for diocesan boards and seminaries connected with the cathedrals, and a central training college, was national in scope and in some measure related to making the old society with its cathedral chapters and village and county hierarchies more acceptable and useful to contemporary needs. The urban concerns of the two metropolitan bishops were woven into this ambitious scheme. The schools connected with cathedral chapters would teach general subjects and drawing, surveying, and 'the sciences of agriculture and commerce', and would be seen as a source not only of choristers and parish clerks but of better-educated teachers for National schools, who would also have the incentive of 'rising up to a middle school', that is promotion to middle-class schools. The National Society in 1839 reported on the 'possibility of entering . . . into communication and connection with that higher class of Institutions which have lately been denominated Middle or Commercial Schools', and emphasized the crucial need for better teachers with better salaries for the schools for the poor, and for 'that large and respectable body who need no pecuniary assistance'. London was to have a central normal school, a 'Collegiate Hall' in connection with King's College where the master of this 'Queen's College' was to be professor of education. This part of the plan came to nothing but the metropolis did gain St Mark's, Chelsea, with its attendant practising school and Whitelands College with an interesting school for girls.[50] The ideas of the two London bishops had already been more explicitly put into action in the setting up of the 'Metropolitan Institution for the Establishment and Improvement of Commercial Schools in the Metropolis and its suburbs, in connexion with the National Church'. Its patron was the Archbishop of Canterbury, Blomfield and Sumner were its Presidents, and its committee included the Reverend T. Dale, Gladstone, T. D. Acland, and Dr Daltry, the powerful rector of Clapham who had been professor of mathematics at Haileybury. The committee's work was aimed at 'that great division of the community . . . between those who are brought up at our Universities, our old classical Schools . . . and those who will avail themselves of our National and Parochial Schools'. This cause was of 'national importance as well as of vast private benefit' and 'the capital city of the empire was obviously the place in which the improvement should commence'. The plan was to establish a 'Central School' for the training of masters and to form local schools in connection with it as well as to enter into friendly relations with the proprietors of existing schools, which would be received 'into union', a concept probably borrowed from the system of King's College. In 1838 a house had been taken near Soho

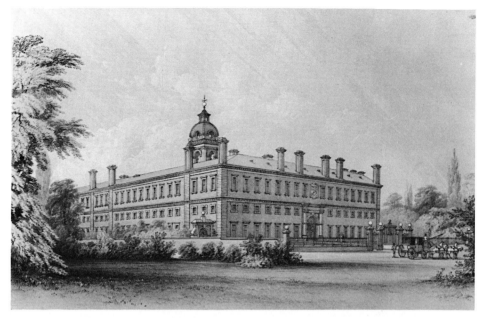

Royal Naval School, New Cross, 1844 (now Goldsmiths' College)

Mill Hill School, 1830

7 Provision for sectional needs by corporate enterprise and finance. The school for naval officers' sons was projected in 1833; the Protestant Dissenters' Grammar School of 1808 moved into these buildings in 1826.

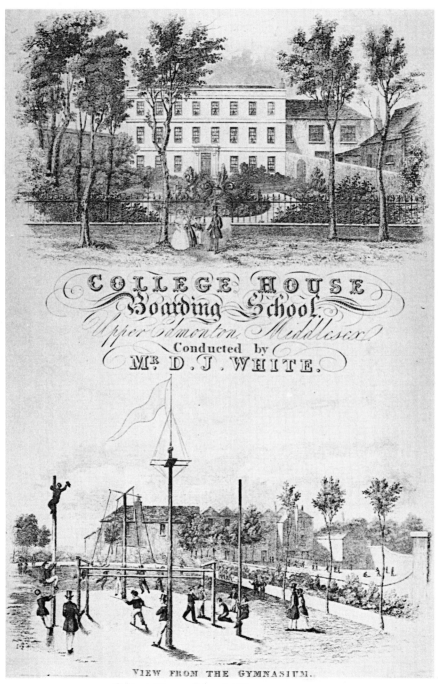

COLLEGE HOUSE
Boarding School
Upper Edmonton, Middlesex
Conducted by
Mr. D. J. WHITE.

VIEW FROM THE GYMNASIUM.

College House School, Edmonton, *c.* 1840

8 The Victorian private school serviced the new class society. The playground and gymnasium are under the watchful supervision of the ushers.

Square, which could accommodate 250 boys, a clerical Cambridge graduate had been appointed headmaster and a lay undermaster with visiting French and music teachers chosen. In 1839 there were already 28 pupils, by 1840 there were 103. The fees were £1 5s a quarter, £1 for subscribers, as the school was partly financed by this method, though it aimed to be self-supporting. The 'system of education' was carefully devised.[51] What is emerging here is not only a concern with newly discerned levels of secondary education, but a redefinition of the content and aims of such education. Thirty years before the Schools' Inquiry Commission formulated its ideas on three grades of middle-class school, the Established Church began gathering experience in this field. In the Soho School religious instruction 'in the Truths and Duties of Christianity according to the Doctrines of the Church' was by a study of the scriptures in detail, with interpretative questions, answered by looking up references and parallel passages 'which when not discovered by the pupils themselves are pointed out by the master'. The questions related not only to the meaning of the passage but 'its practical application to themselves'. The pupils seemed to enjoy this and wanted more. Languages included English, taught grammatically, Latin and French, the grammar studied as it arose from reading. In history, geography and 'the elements of Natural History and Philosophy' 'interesting and instructive' works were read and a 'strict catechetical examination' occupied the time usually given to learning by heart. Geography was much emphasized and taught by the use of large maps and the boys were taught to draw these accurately themselves. 'Arithmetic and the Elements of Mathematics, including Mensuration' were taught with 'attention to principles as well as the practice of calculation – the pupils were made to reflect and know the reason for their methods of working'. Mensuration was acquired by actual measuring and simple diagrams 'chalked on a convenient surface'. The 1841 report described the 'Unremitting attention . . . paid to Penmanship' and the frequent dictation which was 'useful towards securing orthography, attention to what is said and quickness and fidelity in committing it to paper'. Great pains were taken with English composition. Linear drawing and vocal music were 'cultivated with pleasure and profit', there were easy lectures in the sciences and mechanics. The monitorial system was partly used, but was not meant to be relied on 'beyond such as is merely mechanical. . . '. The elder boys were used in offices of trust and a small library was managed by the boys themselves. Examinations were to be public, twice a year, by the Bishop or members of the committee.[52]

As the school was to be a training centre for masters rules were drawn up for this purpose, and it was hoped that 'a race of men will be gradually bred up, who will undertake the office of school-master with superior qualifications and requirements'. Not only the 'mechanical routine and methods of instruction' should be acquired, but 'a large store of diversified information' and an 'extended culture of their own minds'. The headmaster of a school on similar lines from Cheltenham and a master from the Proprietary Grammar School at Brighton had attended for a short time and a third candidate had received a certificate. In 1840 the Institution was even planning a similar school for girls.[53]

Wider influence was hoped from the system of 'schools in union'. Anglican control was assured; an annual report was to be made to the Metropolitan Institution and the qualifications of the masters approved. Several private schools responded to this scheme during the short time it was in operation. One of them, the East Islington Commercial School, was designed to bring to the new Districts of St Paul's and St Stephen's, with a population of nearly 11,000 a 'fair field for the establishment of a school of this kind', a 'sound moral and religious education, combined with the various branches of useful knowledge, at a reasonable charge and under good security'. Latin was part of the main course, but French and drawing here were extras. This school was created by the Metropolitan Institution policy rather than aided by it; another was established in Upper Chelsea – the Metropolitan Branch School – and a third which had existed since 1832 was planned to serve Marylebone and Paddington. On the whole the committee was satisfied with progress. Proprietors of schools reported that parents were responding well. Mr Stevens of the Diocesan Commercial School, Hammersmith, had been dubious whether they would want an education 'essentially religious and loyal' but had gratifying results. 'The advantage of a unity of pursuit throughout the school I find almost incalculable.' The boys were excited to 'constant emulation' by the system of public examination, and 200 parents flocked to see the spectacle.[54]

When the London Diocesan Board of Education was established, it took over the work of the Metropolitan Institute, all the schools in union agreeing to transfer themselves to it, and it continued to supervise the Soho School.[55] In 1842 the fees had to be raised and by 1843 as it had become self-supporting it was transferred to the ownership of the headmaster, now a layman, 'a gentleman highly recommended both for his attainments and piety'. The numbers continued to rise, and in 1844 it was hoped that evening classes might be started, especially if the 'Metropolitan Drapers' Association succeeded in decreasing the hours of opening of shops'. But in the following year the Soho lease expired and the Board gave up all interest in the school.[56] The hard fact was that the whole scheme was too fragile to continue and the resources and energies of the National Society and of the Diocesan Boards were absorbed in the task of setting up training colleges.

Between 1841 and 1866/7 little was done but the movement to help middle-class parents revived during the years before another measure of electoral reform. The *Saturday Review* wrote of 'the vast tract of howling wilderness of imposture' between upper-class education (they 'have taken care of themselves') and that of the lower classes ('which have been well cared for'[57]) and the Reverend Nathaniel Woodard considered that this dangerous area was breeding 'Communists and Red Republicans. . . . Unless the Church . . . gets possession of this class we shall reap the fruits of an universal deluge.'[58] Not many were so hysterical, but the Reverend Robert Gregory (1819–1911), who as rector of Lambeth had contrived to get government grants for parish schools of a superior and more expensive kind, and who was now working closely with Woodard, urged on the National Society its responsibilities towards the lower middle classes and the 'aristocracy of the working classes'. Among such boys were the sons of clerks, small employers of labour, foremen, warehousemen, and skilled mechanics. 'In after life they will often be placed in positions where they will extend a powerful influence over the numerous class immediately below them . . .'. This was important not only because of the forthcoming extension of the franchise but in the interests of class harmony – 'a kindly and considerate spirit should influence artizans in their intercourse with their employers'.[59] As a result a new Middle Class Schools Committee of the National Society decided to aim at the standard generally understood 'by the term "Commercial Education"' and to proceed on a system of grants for buildings or any other approved purpose. A separate Special Fund for the Metropolis was instituted to facilitate securing 'the assistance of public bodies in the City'.[60] Schools should be aided towards being self-supporting, inspection was essential, and the area served by a school need not necessarily coincide with a parish.[61] This aid to existing schools would not be affected by the legislation pending as a result of the Taunton Inquiry. The greater number of schools aided were 'in and about the Metropolis' – for example the school attached to St Mark's College, Gregory's in Lambeth, a school at East Peckham (£400 at 1 per cent), the St Pancras Church School (£300 towards building a school for 400 children at a cost of £5050), St John's Kennington. The inspector, the Reverend F. L. Bagshawe, a scholar of Trinity College Cambridge, continued his work for some years, spreading sweetness and light and class harmony by means of examinations on the lines of the Oxford and Cambridge Locals (music, mechanics, perspective drawing and German were noted as additional subjects), and he was even given paid examiners as assistants.[62] But the scheme was never successful. The Endowed Schools' Act of 1869, the problems facing the voluntary schools after the Education Act of 1870, fears by the Society that funds intended for the poor might be 'diverted to children of a higher rank', all contributed to the failure of this second attempt at systematic help to secondary schools of this 'third grade'. Above all it was lack of demand from the schools. By 1876 mentions of the work have disappeared from the Society's annual reports.[63] London's little Philistines must struggle towards the light of culture and sound Anglican principles with no assistance from the National Society.

Anglican enterprise was able to make a much more substantial and systematic contribution to a higher level of London secondary schooling. Since the end of the eighteenth century methods of funding education through investment by proprietors had been attempted. Endowments of the old kind were drying up and were under much criticism for their 'dead hand', their inability to adapt to changing needs. The system of subscriptions characteristic of the 'Age of Benevolence' was for the most part identified with the spirit of the charity schools for the 'labouring poor'. What the new age needed was a method of getting the middle classes to invest money in the schooling of their own children over and above the paying of fees, the buying of education from the open market. If the 'plant' and a reasonably stable academic and educational community were to be secured, more public capital as well as income was needed. The interim answer was the 'proprietary school', a school on joint stock principles. The earliest of these schools in London was the Philological School founded in Marylebone in 1792, 'for Educating and Clothing the Sons of Clergymen, Naval and Military Officers, Professional Men, Merchants, Manufacturers, Clerks in Public Offices, and the Higher Order of Tradesmen, in Reduced Circumstances'. It sprang from 'the Philological Society' which had a library and held monthly lectures to subscribers; for a higher subscription a boy could be nominated, if able to read and not more than twelve years old. 'Any boy of a good genius and desirous of continuing his studies will be taught the languages and sciences.' Ten boys intended for the ministry were to stay until nineteen, 10 were prepared for the Navy, and 20 for mechanics. Older boys were to help in teaching the younger ones. The school had strong Evangelical connections, Lord Teignmouth was president, services at the Bentinck Chapel were attended and here its 'Charity Sermons' were preached. Collections for it were made in sympathetic churches such as Holy Trinity Clapham (Lord Teignmouth's own parish). The school had management troubles for it was working out practices between earlier forms of charitable endowment and control, and later proprietary rules. Subscriptions rather than capital endowments bring particular risks even if ensuring greater adaptability. In 1798 the Society suffered from the 'scandal of a bogus collector' and in 1834 complained that 'many persons have mistaken the spirit and intention of those rules which confer greater privileges upon the higher Subscribers, by considering that it is sufficient on their part to pay the amount of their subscriptions only as long as the boy presented by them remains in the school' – a constant difficulty of schools provided by this particular semi-charitable expedient.

The Philological School survived its earlier difficulties and in 1827 gained royal patronage. In 1834 it contained 140 scholars: sons of naval and military officers, 16; of professional men, 12; of clerks in public offices, 17; of merchants, manufacturers and the higher order of tradesmen, 35; and 60 'Contributory Scholars'. Its Visitor was the Bishop of London, its headmaster and secretary since 1827 Edwin

Abbott, who remained headmaster for forty-five years. In 1827 it moved to a site in the New Road where in 1857 new buildings in the style of the 'Domestic architecture of the fourteenth century' were put up. Fearon in 1869 classed it as one of the best specimens of the 'middle-class school of the second grade' in the district, 'managed and taught with judgement and ability'. No corporal punishment was used, but discipline was kept by a system of monitors. A general education was given to boys leaving at sixteen or seventeen, arithmetic and mathematics were the backbone of instruction with Latin, French and German. The fees were £9 a year and only drawing was an extra. An annual examination was held and a large number of prizes and scholarships given, every boy was ranked by marks for good conduct and diligence. In a district where there was great demand for such a school Fearon concluded that its popularity was due not only to the decided excellence of the teaching but to the fact that the masters were all laymen, and to the prominence given to arithmetic.[64]

Another school which was partly proprietary but financed also by charitable subscription and endowments was the Royal Naval School, projected by several naval officers in 1833, and opened in temporary premises in Camberwell, 'for enabling less affluent naval and marine officers of not lower than ward-room rank . . . to give their sons a sound general education'. Dr Bell gave almost £10,000 to be applied to the general maintenance of the school on his Madras or monitorial system. Investors had preference in entry and fees for their sons. In 1840 the school was incorporated and in 1844 removed to its handsome new building in a pleasant revival of Wren's style, on the site of a former school, the County Hill Academy in New Cross, and was opened by the Prince Consort in the presence of 'a vast concourse of naval officers'. It had a headmaster in Holy Orders and provided a wide liberal curriculum (English, French, Latin, Greek, ancient and modern history, geography, arithmatic, navigation, mathematics, natural philosophy, and German) for between 200 and 300 boarders. In 1890 when New Cross had become comparatively insalubrious, the school removed and was renamed Eltham College, admitting also non-naval pupils.[65]

The same somewhat experimental combination of donations, subscriptions and investment financed the London University (later University College) and its lower department. University College School had a significant ideological and pedagogic influence on other London secondary schools, but in the absence of any secular administrative structure it could form no part of a system. With the foundation of King's College and its school the first attempt at a coherent organization of education at secondary or higher level became possible.

This foundation was not merely a riposte to the 'godless Institution of Gower Street' but was part of a comprehensive Anglican campaign for fulfilling the Church's national educational responsibilities in the new urban society. The clerics most active in the venture had much metropolitan experience, Howley, Bishop of London until his elevation to Canterbury in 1828, Blomfield as his successor, and Dr George D'Oyley, rector of Lambeth, whose grotesque charge of 54,000 souls when he took the living in 1820 had increased to 130,000 when he died twenty-six years later – by which time he had built thirteen new churches, one of which, St Mark's Kennington, provided the first Principal of King's, William Otter. Another parish clergyman active in the cause, later to be Principal of the College and then Bishop of Lichfield, was John Lonsdale of St George's Bloomsbury, a district with a vast range of social and pastoral problems, for the St Giles area was one of the worst slums of the capital. Men such as these were well placed to diagnose educational needs and responsibilites. The open letter to Sir Robert Peel from Dr D'Oyley which launched the King's campaign emphasized that growth of population, especially of the middle classes, and of 'a strong spirit of intellectual improvement', indicated the need.[66]

King's, like London University, in its early period was more of a secondary school than a college of university standing, reminding us not only that adolescence was then still an ambiguous and imperfectly defined stage of development, but of continuing difficulties in drawing boundaries between secondary and tertiary education. Its 'general course of study' designed for youths admitted at the age of sixteen constituted it as a kind of sixth-form college for the London area,[67] used both by boys going directly into the newly emerging professions or into commerce, and by others to prepare for Oxford and Cambridge. For most of the reign of Victoria it functioned as an element in London's provision for what today would be called the secondary level of education. The history of the college however belongs properly to that of higher education while its 'Lower Department' or school was from the beginning conceived as 'totally distinct from the higher', affording 'an education, preparatory to it'. Its curriculum was to embrace Anglican religious instruction, with classics, mathematics, English literature and composition, 'and some modern languages when desired'. The inconvenient slope of the piece of land next to Somerset House acquired for the college obliged basements to be constructed, in one of which this school was installed, while even lower down medical students dissected corpses. This, together with the rise and fall of the unembanked Thames with its sinister debris lapping up to the arcading on the river front, must have lent a somewhat Gothick air to the boys' subterranean lives. Parents however seemed willing to pay £15 15s a year for boys nominated by a proprietor, or nearly £18 18s if they were not, for the school was an instant success, greatly embarrassing the Council by inflating through capitation fees the salary of the headmaster, the Reverend Dr John Richardson Major, to more than twice that of the principal of the college, even that of the second master comfortably surpassing it. In 1832 there were 150 boys; in 1833, 319; in 1834, 404;

in 1835, 461. There was an attempt to fix 350 as the maximum number but by 1843 there were nearly 500, in 1846 a peak of 518 was reached. The staff had to be considerably increased and the scales of capitation hastily trimmed while more and more of the basement was adapted for classrooms and a refectory provided under the terrace on the riverfront. From the beginning it proved impossible to prevent boys staying in the school after the age of sixteen, when they were supposed to transfer themselves to the college above. The excellent and systematic teaching of the school (at lower fees than in the college) tempted parents to leave Dr Major to prepare their boys for Oxford and Cambridge and he was understandably loath to hand over his best pupils and their fees. The school's prosperity and popularity were to contrast to the often disappointing and uneven progress of the college, sustaining it through difficult times.

Like University College School, King's, a large efficient centrally-placed school with a thoroughly modern curriculum, both liberal and utilitarian, and leading to a systematic or vocational course of further education in the college, was providing an important educational service for London, and the boarding-houses kept by masters (all in orders) continued its tradition of serving boys from further afield.[68] But the Anglican character of King's enabled much more to be achieved. The Church's territorial structure as well as its allegiances brought a network of useful suburban schools into being and helped to ensure their standards. As early as November 1829 Prebendary H. H. Norris of Hackney wrote to the founding Committee of King's, enclosing the prospectus of 'a school to be established in this parish . . . for asserting the same principle which led to the formation of King's College' and asking whether 'any regulations have yet been adopted . . . by which such establishments' as the Hackney Church of England School 'can be taken into union with King's College'. This was the beginning of an important development. 'Public attention being now directed to the expediency of establishing local or district day schools for the purpose of affording a sound and liberal education at a moderate expense to the sons of professional and mercantile men and others', the College Council hastened to impress the importance of Anglican principles upon their organizers and to offer 'union with King's College' to 'form a centre of a system of education for the middling classes of society, combining the advantages of a judicious and extended cultivation of the intellectual faculties with the careful inculcation of religious truths and moral duties.'[69]

Success depended on joint stock enterprise being active at local level, and in the metropolis the movement was already active before 'union with King's' gave it added impetus and coherence. The Western Grammar School, Brompton (sometimes called the Brompton Church of England Grammar School), had been founded in 1828 and tried the Madras system, but 'came to the conclusion that it was inefficient in its

application to the course of studies' followed.[70] In 1831 the Society for
the Diffusion of Useful Knowledge, recognizing that 'the advantages
afforded by the formation of proprietary schools having rendered the
desire for their establishment very prevalent', thought it helpful to give a
full account of the rules of the Pimlico Grammar School in the parish of
St Peter's, Eaton Square, 'in order to facilitate their introduction into
those places where a superior and economical course of instruction is
required'.[71] Other foundations followed quickly. As well as some provincial schools, Hackney and Kensington Schools were among the first
to be taken into union with King's, and by 1836 St Peter's, schools in
Stockwell, Islington, Stepney, Camberwell, Blackheath, West Ham, and
the Forest School at Snaresbrook in Essex, had been founded and the
Western Grammar and the Philological School had also joined the
scheme. In 1850 the Collegiate School at Croydon was added and a
school formerly connected with the Metropolitan Institution which now
moved up the social scale as the All Souls and Marylebone District
Grammar School. At the Taunton Inquiry the Westbourne Collegiate
School was also listed and in 1871 St John's College in Kentish Town.[72]

Such schools had to satisfy certain conditions; the London High
School in Tavistock Square, converted into a proprietary school 'in the
plan and principles of King's College', evidently did not meet these.[73]
The headmaster and his 'regular assistants' were to be members of the
Church of England, echoing the rather odd arrangement at King's
where all professors had to be Anglicans, except those for modern
languages and oriental literature, curious subjects such as these allowing
for deviancy, even unorthodoxy. Although there seems to have been no
formal inspection of schools, standards and ethos were to some extent
assured. Pupils were able to contend for the junior scholarships of the
College Departments of General Literature and Science and of Applied
Sciences and to become Associates (AKC) in a shorter time. Later the
Council also wished to be 'fully satisfied' that the school was 'required in
the particular district in which it is proposed to be established', the
headmaster must not be the proprietor, the College must be free to
inspect the arrangements for study and recreation and the books used,
and periodical external examinations must take place and be reported.
Tangible benefits to the schools were perhaps small – but the common
prize-giving in the great hall of the College was nevertheless a symbol of
what was most needed – prestige, assurance, an end of isolation.[74]
When the early success of the London proprietary schools is contrasted
with the situation in Bristol the importance of King's College is apparent
– an attempt to found a proprietary college there in 1831 failed because
of suspicions of its radical and irreligious nature, a 'Bishop's College' as
an Anglican counterblast soon became moribund, and it was not until
1860 that a third attempt by a group of businessmen was successful in
founding Clifton College on a proprietary basis and by that time the
revival of the public schools confined its benefits to a more exclusive

level of civic society.[75] The London system allowed for local variation and gave a much broader social base while giving the necessary minimum of confidence and support.

Only local investigation can uncover the individual characteristics and fortunes of these highly important schools. 'Clerical agency' continued the tradition of the 'four powerful rectors' of the fifteenth century, but the part played by the laity was active and crucial – their demand for education for their sons, their management and business acumen, their capital, were essential to success. The fortunes of these schools provide a kind of barometer of the need for middle-class education in London and its suburbs during the reign of Queen Victoria.[76]

Whether or not Evangelical Islington was spurred on by rivalry from High Church Hackney, its indefatigable inhabitants were among the first to set on foot plans for a school in January 1830. Its purpose was 'to provide an education ... under the most able Masters that can be procured at a very moderate expense' where 'the parent will have an opportunity of keeping a constant, watchful eye over the morals, manners, health, and progress of his child'. The Madras system 'as practised at the Charterhouse, is, as far as is practicable to be adopted', presumably on economic as well as educational grounds, for compared with the nearly £18 18s of King's College School, the fees were not to exceed £10 10s a year 'to comprise every expenditure except that of printed books and mathematical instruments, which are to be supplied by the Institution at cost price'. The cost of travelling by the newly developed omnibus system might be borne by parents who used King's College School but not these local schools. The school was to be established by 'a Proprietary of not less than 100 shares of £15 each', no proprietor might hold more than two. There were to be twelve directors, all Anglican, chosen from among the proprietors living within four miles of the school. The proprietors might nominate one scholar for each share, 'but no scholar is to be admitted without the consent of the Directors, unless he be the son of the nominating Proprietor' and for an admission fee of £5, extra sons might be entered by holders of two shares. If a proprietor made no nomination the directors might fill up the vacancy.

By February 1830 the school was instituted, the money was quickly subscribed, and in October the same year the 'neat building of brick, in the Elizabethan style of architecture', with spacious and handsome schoolrooms, another for the French master, several 'cloakrooms, apartments for washing and other accommodations', with a covered playground and 'ample room for exercise and recreation' was built at a cost of £1967 9s 6d. At the opening 125 shares had been subscribed and 67 pupils admitted. After three months the figures had reached 139 and 99, and after the first year, owing 'to the soundness of the mechanism, and the skills and assiduity with which that mechanism is worked' as well as 'the Divine favour and blessing' the figures were 170 and 150 and the list had to be suspended 'before the School by an overgrowth should so press upon the strength and energies of the Headmaster and exceed the range of his active superintendance, as to endanger the tone and vigour of its internal system'. The building was enlarged and more masters were appointed, including a popular drawing master 'of great respectability and approved talent'.

Rapid success and growth demonstrated the needs of the neighbourhood. The curriculum provided 'a course of education for youth, to comprise classical learning, the modern languages, mathematics, and such other branches of useful knowledge as may be advantageously introduced', together with sound Anglican instruction. This course qualified 'the rising generation of this community not only, if need be, for literary pursuits, and the more scientific professions, but for the beneficial discharge of their respective duties in the various employments and social relations of that sphere of life, in which they move'. Such a school opened the universities to their boys, or prepared them for business, commercial and professional life, and local parents accepted not only the prestige, but the utility, of the classical side of the course. 'If it may seem . . . that too large a share of time and attention is devoted to what are called the learned languages', the headmaster explained, 'through them we hope to lay the foundations of all useful knowledge, historical, geographical, political, scientific. . . . A total rejection of these is incompatible with a liberal education . . .'[77]

The school was adapted to the needs of a large middle-class suburb and the proprietors seem also to have been fortunate in their choice of this first headmaster. They had consulted Samuel Wilberforce, who did not like their particular brand of Evangelicalism, and asked Newman to suggest someone to 'creep into the midst of the beehive and poison the Islingtonians'.[78] The Reverend John Owen Parr of Brasenose College Oxford combined 'high classical attainments' with 'sound religious principles' and 'the art of imparting knowledge with suavity of manner and firmness of purpose'. He also showed a remarkable and unusual ability to appreciate and combine the theories and practices of Bell and Pestalozzi. 'Alone, the system of Bell is deficient in a purely moral influence. It wants a largeness of intellectual freedom and expansion. It uses not, if it do not, as may justly be feared, abuse the social affections of humanity. That of Pestalozzi, on the other hand, seems to want arrangement and regularity, being not sufficiently straightened and confined within precise limits, but rather luxuriating in a vagueness and eccentricity of course.' Parr therefore proposed to unite them, 'bringing the one to bear on the whole, collectively, in the practical detail of instruction, the other on the mental development of each individual in the school, as well as on the spirit of the social intercourse subsisting among the boys. Beneficial results in the management of human affairs are, for the most part, produced by a compensation of forces, a balance of antagonistic powers.'[79]

Unfortunately Parr could not long demonstrate this admirable example of the Anglican genius for the middle way, for the Islington Proprietary School was not free from those difficulties which a new type of institution must encounter. The endowed schools according to current opinion had suffered from not only the deadness of tradition but also from the freehold nature of their headmasterships. The newer schools had to work out a system of staff appointments giving both headmaster and his staff security in relation to managers and directors, who were usually amateurs in matters of education. In 1836 the dismissal of the second master by the directors led to the resignation of the headmaster as well. The new headmaster was the Reverend J. Jackson, later Bishop of Lincoln and then of London.[80]

Islington might in the 1830s be described as the archetypal middle-class neighbourhood – in fact for a time it supported two proprietary schools. The South Islington Proprietary School was also 'designed to afford a liberal education suited to the advance of society, to the sons of professional gentlemen, merchants, and respectable tradesmen', and was also for a time in union with King's College. Its building was in the Grecian style.[81]

A contrasting area, but equally needing this kind of school, was Blackheath, still a rural community well separated from the City, but with a steadily increasing population, including prosperous City men with their houses round the heath and the rather less well-to-do who could still afford the regular coach service to Fenchurch Street at a shilling a journey. There were many boarding-schools in and around Greenwich, and Colfe's School also at this period largely served boarders. 'A day school was needed which would give a complete secondary education of a more liberal type . . .'. The initiative came from leading laymen and from the Reverend Andrew Brandram and the Reverend Joseph Fenn (a noted Evangelical with nine sons) of the new church in Blackheath Park. Their whole style of operation was purposeful, speedy, even experienced, indeed the model of the Islington Proprietary School was acknowledged. They met in the Paragon and decided to establish the school, and promptly the next day (27 January 1830) drew up rules for a proprietary of 100 shares of £20 each and formed a committee. Barely a month later a more general meeting of applicants for the shares resolved that the school be established 'having for its object the providing a course of education for youths, to comprise classical learning, the modern languages, mathematics, reading, writing, arithmetic, history, geography, and such other branches of modern science and general literature as may be conveniently introduced'. Regulations were drawn up for the nomination of pupils by proprietors and trustees, officers were appointed, and very shortly the committee was seeking for a 'centrical' position for the school. Delays in opening the school were due not so much to educational doubts as to the problems of a select and developing residential district where boys in quantity were not welcome, and ownership of land was complex, there being 'considerable doubts . . . as to who were freehold tenants and what were their rights'. The Commissioners of Woods and Forests and the royal Ranger of Greenwich Park and the Trustees of Morden College were involved. The matter of noise 'or rioting', even the danger of fruit and cakes being sold to the boys, were dealt with by severe rules – any audible sign of joy on leaving school was subject to a mounting scale of penalites, culminating in dismissal, and it was felt that 'a quiet habit will be established at once and no inconvenience felt'. Problems of negotiating the use of property as a school delayed its opening until January 1831 and by then the necessary clerical headmaster, the Reverend Sanderson Tennant, and his assistant had been appointed. Twenty-five boys, one of them John Mason Neale, later the hymnologist, presented themselves, and by the end of 1833 there were 113 boys – 47 boarders were accommodated not by the regular masters but by licensed boarding-house-keepers. The new school building was opened in October 1831. These practical men let no grass grow under their feet. Shares were eagerly sought and £20 shares were changing hands for as much as £70. A dispute among the proprietors in 1834 led to a split and the founding of the New Proprietory School. For a time local demand was enough to support both schools but by the later 1840s the position had changed, the new school became a private school, and the original school went through something of a crisis, with dwindling numbers and an apathetic staff. The foundation of Greenwich Proprietary School in 1849 increased competition. It was at this period, in 1849, that the school ceased to be in union with King's. The committee took vigorous action, replaced most of the staff, including the headmaster, and appointed the Reverend Edward John Selwyn of Trinity College Cambridge in his place. He became something of a 'great Victorian headmaster' (on a small scale). He built up the school, especially by inducing more able boys to stay until they entered the university, and in the last two years of Selwyn's headship every boy in the Upper VI won an open scholarship to Oxford or Cambridge. By 1860 there were 204 boys in the school and by the time Selwyn resigned in 1864, 275. The boarding-houses (now under masters) were flourishing. Boys came from all over England and considerable numbers from Northern Ireland. But numbers continued to fluctuate. This was a time when the curriculum was being diversified, masters' salaries had to be improved to compete with the revival of the public schools and the reform of nearby endowed schools such as Dulwich. Improvements in numbers meant extending the accommodation, for example two new classrooms 'with provision for the exhibition and stowage of chemical and scientific materials and instruments'. After a high-water mark of nearly 300 boys in 1870, decline was pretty steady.[82]

In attempting to assess the contribution of these schools to London secondary education the first point to note is the breadth of their curriculum. From about 1830 there were in many of the suburbs large (for their period, often very large), efficiently organized schools offering courses containing very much the range of subjects expected at the end of the century. It is surprising that Fearon is reporting on them for the Taunton Commission should have given as one reason for their early success that they were founded before the 'general desire for modern instruction had made itself felt'.[83] True, the classics predominated; in some schools it received traditional emphasis – the Westbourne Collegiate School in 1863/4 described its classical course as including composition in verse and prose, and the 'principles of rhetoric' were included in the English course – but this school was in a suburb likely to support such literary aspiration and was under the patronage of Archdeacon Browne, late Classical Professor at King's.[84] In general parents supporting these schools not only acquiesced in, but valued, the place given to classics as it kept their boys' options open as well as giving prestige and a commonly accepted liberal culture. But the 'learned languages' had to take their place in all cases with mathematics, modern languages, English grammar and literature, sometimes history and geography and a certain amount of science, though the degree to which this was systematized was in some cases minimal, at least in the early years. In 1850 the All Souls and St Marylebone Grammar School announced its course as including Greek, Latin, English, French, German, mathematics, the 'Elements of Physical Science', mechanics, hydrostatics and pneumatics, drawing, arithmetic and writing, with ancient and modern history and religious and moral instruction. There was a separate course for pupils designed for the Army or Navy, or for 'Commercial pursuits'.[85] At Blackheath, advantageously placed for both naval and military reinforcements, by 1832 astronomical lectures were being given and in 1833 Professor Ritchie, lecturer at the Royal Institution, lectured on natural philosophy and mechanics, and a tutor from Woolwich on pneumatics and hydrostatics. Such lectures might be described as endemic – geology appeared in 1850 and two masters from the Lower Naval School, Greenwich, had also given courses on the steam engine and on chemistry. This seems desultory, but makes a respectable enough showing in comparison with other schools of the time. A Blackheath pupil in the 1880s recalled that all boys had the opportunity of learning some science 'even if one was not on the modern side'.[86]

As the century went on vocational pressures brought more system into these 'modern sides'. In 1850 King's College School itself, when its numbers had declined somewhat from its peak number of over 500, took the step of dividing into two 'sides', but although the modern side kept up better than the classical, it did not really flourish until the somewhat forcible retirement in 1866 of the first headmaster, Dr Major, less efficient and vigorous with the passage of years. With the promotion of the Reverend G. F. Maclean as Headmaster, and the Reverend J. Twentyman (from Cheltenham College) as Vice-master and head of the

modern side, a vigorous period of expansion and reorganization began –
by 1873 the previous record of numbers had been passed, due it was
said not only to better masters and discipline but to the 'better
classification' of the pupils and the organization of matriculation and
other special classes. In 1880 the high-water mark, 631, was reached –
quite a lot of boys to fit into a basement. In 1872 the school was
advertised as in three divisions: the Division of Classics, Mathematics
and General Literature, designed to prepare pupils 'for the Universities,
for the Theology, General Literature and Medical Departments of the
College, and for the Learned Professions'; the Division of Modern
Instruction, to prepare 'for general and Mercantile pursuits, for the
Department of Applied Science at King's College, and for the Military
Academies at Woolwich and Sandhurst'; and a Lower School 'to give a
thorough education up to such a point as will prepare pupils to enter
either of the two Senior Divisions'.[87] Blackheath created a Special
Department in 1852, to be 'devoted to the instruction of candidates for
direct appointment in Her Majesty's or the East India Company's
service and for cadetships in the Military Colleges at Woolwich,
Sandhurst or Addiscombe; and to elementary theoretical training of
those pupils who are intended for the profession of civil engineering'.[88]
The Kensington Proprietary School seems to have had connections with
the East India Company from the beginning, being 'founded by the
servants of The Honourable John Company', and with thirty cadetships
at Addiscombe. In 1848 its curriculum included Hindustani and civil
and military drawing and in 1869 its modern department included
oriental languages, civil drawing, civil and military surveying and military
hill drawing, fortification, civil engineering, as well as the more usual
subjects.[89] Another proprietary school preparing especially for the Indian service was St John's College, Kentish Town, founded in 1859,
whose headmaster in 1871 had been Principal of the Government
Training College, Madras, and where Bengali and Hindustani were
taught.[90]

The Islington School was also divided into classical and modern
sides, but in this district the special connections were clerical – it
provided many of the holders of the Church Missionary Society
scholarships at King's – and with the City. Mathematics were encouraged and systematically taught, and the French teaching was
good.[91] This school, with Kensington and Blackheath, 'contend on
equal terms, and not infrequently with success, against the great public
schools, for the highest prizes which Oxford and Cambridge offer to
freshmen'.[92]

No claims for the curriculum of these schools can be made independent of a standard of teaching which enabled them to reach their
objectives. There is sound evidence for claiming that some of the
teaching was excellent, much of it good, reflecting a critical approach to
pedagogic problems and practice, for these schools could only flourish

by distinguishing themselves in some useful way from the private and later the endowed schools. They sought to combine the reassurance of an Oxford and Cambridge or Trinity man in Holy Orders, with innovatory ideas and a sensitive response to the educational market – were they not joint stock enterprises? Occasionally there are glimpses of consumer reaction. The Dean of Westminster, G. G. Bradley, in 1884 wrote a portrait of his schooldays, when between 1830 and 1840 he passed through 'zones of educational influences of very marked and characteristic types'. From a Brighton preparatory school dedicated to the acquisition of information by rote he went to a 'much respected master' on Clapham Common where the Latin Grammar was committed to memory, and thence to the Stockwell Proprietary School. Here be was taught by a young man fresh from mathematical honours at Cambridge, 'full of fire, enthusiasm and original ability'. The man was an educational radical, who in Latin gave a very few rules on the blackboard, roused interest with some comparative philology, 'the science of language', taught the boys to group facts together, and provided explanatory geographical and literary background. At least one lesson a week was given to natural science, and mathematics was 'coloured with the warm glow and activity of the teacher's mind'. The teaching Bradley experienced here influenced his educational ideas for the rest of his life.[93] This remarkable teacher was certainly Charles Pritchard who had himself been for an unprofitable time at Merchant Taylors', and then at a private school in Poplar, where he had learnt the use of scientific instruments, and first saw 'a retort, an air pump and an electrical machine'. At Stockwell from 1833–4 he developed his own ideas of teaching science.[94] These schools arose from a need for innovation and experiment though they probably conceived of themselves as conservative – mediating to a new society a liberal culture which they were little disposed to criticize in any sharply conscious way. But the middle classes were in the forefront of the forces of social transformation and however unusual it is to think of the Anglican, often Evangelical, clergy and laity of the early and mid nineteenth century as radicals, each age needs and breeds its own innovators. These schools were part of the process by which a new social structure and moral code were established and serviced. They belong essentially to the period when the new middle classes had attained a self-consciousness which drew a sharp distinction between themselves and the old prescriptive, corrupt, aristocratic order with which the endowed and public schools were identified. Many proprietary schools, especially those founded in country districts – Cheltenham and Marlborough for example – developed into public schools of the newer kind and the London schools pioneered some of their characteristics and aspirations. Blackheath was one of the schools represented at the first Headmasters' Conference at Uppingham in 1869 – Selwyn its headmaster had been runner-up to Thring when he was appointed there, and his son became Thring's successor in 1887.[95]

There was in fact a good deal of interchange of staff between the proprietary and the public schools.[96] The example of the London schools almost certainly reinforced the demand for the broadening of the curriculum of the endowed and public schools and they pioneered new attitudes to school social life and leisure time. Urban schools could not leave such activities entirely to boys' own supervision and middle-class parents were in any case not in favour of such an anarchic practice. Kensington for example seems to have developed an early emphasis on organized sports. In 1838 when 'athletics were quite in their infancy' the first of a well attended and organized series of sports days was held (in 1869, 2000 were present before the first race was held) and by the end of the century the school seems to have prided itself that 'our so called intellects counted for something, our bodies counted for more'; 'for the most part our ordained future was to be doing on the fringes of civilisation' – that is, India by way of the military colleges.[97]

Interchange of ideas, practices, teachers, and interchange of pupils also linked the proprietary with the public schools. Parents were sometimes prepared to risk an older boy amidst the moral dangers of a boarding-school, or perhaps managed to afford the higher fees for able sons who had proved their abilities and ambitions. For whatever reason the London schools were often used as preparatory for the public schools – an interesting case, because of his future influence on middle-class education, was Joseph Lloyd Brereton (1822–1901) who was at Islington under Jackson before going to Rugby under Arnold.[98] M. G. Glazebrooke who became headmaster of Clifton in 1891 went from Blackheath to Dulwich before going on to Oxford.[99] The danger of this practice to the prosperity of the proprietary schools was only combated temporarily by successful headmasters such as Selwyn.

Kennedy of Shrewsbury gloomily declared to the Clarendon Commissioners in 1861, 'I do not see how any of the old foundation schools, except the few which have fashionable and great connections in their favour, can hold their ground against the tide of joint stock education,'[100] but in the long run he was mistaken as far as the London schools went. The early success of the schools was in some ways deceptive for it concealed the disadvantages of this method of financing and managing schools which essentially served a public purpose rather than private profit. Education has never been a profitable field for investment, the shareholders usually went to the wall, and even if they had risked their money in the interests of their sons' education, were not necessarily competent or knowledgeable in governing a school. Islington had early troubles when the directors in 1836 dismissed the second master, and a 'minority of the directors, reinforced by a number of respectable inhabitants', considered that the whole affair would harm the school and the parish.[101] Another damaging dispute deprived Stockwell Proprietary School of its brilliant master, Pritchard. He built up the school by recruiting 140 pupils, and proposed a systematic

THE

STOCKWELL GRAMMAR SCHOOL,

Close to the Clapham and Brixton High Roads.

THE PARTICULARS AND CONDITIONS OF SALE

OF THE EXCELLENT

LEASEHOLD PREMISES,

FOR MANY YEARS KNOWN AS THE

Stockwell Proprietary Grammar School

WITH GROUNDS OF NEARLY HALF AN ACRE,

PROMINENTLY SITUATE IN THE

STOCKWELL PARK ROAD,

Only a few minutes' walk from the Brixton and Clapham Stations on the London Chatham and Dover Railway, suitable either for continuance as a School, or for the purposes of a Public Institution, or available, on extension of the Lease, for

THE ERECTION OF NUMEROUS PRIVATE HOUSES,

Held for an unexpired term of 39 years at a

GROUND-RENT OF £40 PER ANNUM.

Possession will be given on completion of the Purchase.

Which will be Sold by Auction by Messrs.

EDWIN FOX and BOUSFIELD

AT THE MART, TOKENHOUSE YARD, BANK OF ENGLAND,

On WEDNESDAY, the 26th of NOVEMBER, 1873,

AT TWO O'CLOCK PRECISELY.

May be viewed, and Particulars obtained at the Mart, Tokenhouse Yard ; of

Messrs. **MILLER & SMITH**, Solicitors, 3, Salters' Hall Court, Cannon Street, E.C.; and of
Messrs. **EDWIN FOX** and **BOUSFIELD**, 24, Gresham Street, Bank, E.C.

Poster advertising the sale of Stockwell Proprietary School, 1873

science course. 'I think it preposterous to regard any man as . . .
educated unless he has some intelligent acquaintance with the physical
nature of the food he eats, the air he breathes and of the general
structure of the heart which beats within him.' But he was constantly
hampered by the parsimony and interference of the proprietors, 'no
doubt amiable and honourable enough in their own individual spheres,
nevertheless as governors of a place of education . . . wholly out of the
beat . . .'. It was therefore as master of Clapham Grammar School,
created as a proprietary school especially for him in 1834 by his
sympathizers, that he did his best teaching. It was generously equipped
with an observatory, packed with scientific apparatus, and in 1842 its
Committee of Management handed over the entire running of the
school to Pritchard. Before he retired in 1862 he had taught St George
Mivart, C. P. Scott of the *Manchester Guardian*, Charles Grove,
Alexander Herschel, Sir George and Sir Francis Darwin and J. P.
Gassiot, the future City benefactor of scientific education. The
Stockwell School continued without its best teacher, and by the 1860s
was in decline.[102]

The most dramatic case of harmful interference by proprietors was
that of St Peter's College, Eaton Square, where in 1879 the Reverend
B. W. Gibsone had been for 'many years Headmaster of the oldest and
most promising Proprietary School in that quarter of London containing
the Royal Palaces and the Government Offices'. He applied for a Royal
Charter but a few shareholders, presumably regarding this as the end of
all hopes of private profit, 'desiring to realize their capital by breaking up
the newly incorporated Association', and having no hope of carrying
with them a majority of the 200 members, resorted to the 'cruel expedient of pretending that the Headmaster was a scamp, and had
reduced the College to insolvency'. Long investigation in the Courts of
Exchequer and Chancery decided that both these charges were false,
pupils were increasing, and a 'dividend of £12 odd on each share i.e.
more than its value for thirty years' had recently been paid. An impressive testimonial signed by two archbishops, five bishops (including
London and Winchester), numerous other leaders of church and state,
the heads of each of the seven great public schools and so forth, was
presented to Mr Gibsone, but the damage was done and St Peter's
expired.[103]

For most of the schools decline was slow and often concealed. Fearon
discerned their weakness in the 1860s. Stepney largely for local reasons
had since 1863 become a private school and Hackney struggled to keep
up the curriculum of a classical school 'without having scholars suited to
that grade of education'. Islington was doing well, but was having
difficulty in competing with endowed schools. Kensington was in a
better position as it had a few exhibitions to Oxford and Cambridge.[104]
In 1866 this school was apparently so prosperous that it planned to move
to new and much larger premises where 300 boys could be accommo-

dated, but this proved illusory. Three years later it was necessary to reorganize its finances and it emerged as a 'Foundation Grammar School' still in Kensington Square, its property vested in trustees; 'by this change of system, the School, which has now for sometime been in danger of dissolution, is placed beyond the reach of those accidents that are inseparable from a Proprietary constitution. It is a permanently Endowed School . . .'. Life governorships now conferred the privilege of nominating pupils without giving any proprietary right.[105] Blackheath, even when it appeared more prosperous than ever before, at the end of Selwyn's tenure, was in reality only just paying its way. There were no reserves of capital, for example, to keep the school building adapted and enlarged for new needs, and directors, 'estimable . . . in many ways . . . consisted chiefly of retired colonels and stockbrokers of strong evangelical views, but entirely ignorant of method in education'. Competition from reformed boarding-schools, and newly organized neighbouring schools such as Dulwich, was serious. It is likely that Selwyn resigned because he could not secure a sensible policy of adaptation to new conditions from the poorly attended committee. Over the next twenty years of apparent success it became clear that it was impossible to maintain a school 'on the fees paid by parents, unless the school is large and the fees are high. There must be assistance either from endowments or from the taxes and rates'. In the 1880s the committee even contemplated transferring the school to the Church Schools' Company, but this was turned down by the proprietors.[106]

The fluctuating fortunes of King's College School underline these challenges and difficulties. Already by the 1860s it was under pressure from the challenge to the classical tradition and the growing 'cult of the boarding-school and the passion for playing fields' which drew 'many possible pupils away from urban day schools which taught in cellars, exercised in sunless back yards, and promenaded in sinful streets'. The revival under Dr Maclean was probably due not only to his reorganization of the school and modernization of its curriculum but also to his introduction of newer public school features, but though very substantial, the success was comparatively temporary. In 1880 when he retired there were 612 boys but two years later this total had sunk to 538, and throughout the 1880s the decline was catastrophic; by 1897 there were only 166 pupils – this in spite of the levelling of the playground, the acquisition of playing fields at Wormwood Scrubs, the introduction of new matriculation and commercial classes, better science teaching, the lowering of the fees, even bringing some of the classes up from the basement into the light of day. It became clear that the school must move, and in 1897 it migrated to a site on Wimbledon Common.[107]

There was no such reprieve for the other Anglican proprietary schools. Some dwindled into preparatory schools – Kensington was scheduled as such by the London School Board in 1891. By 1900 it had come to an end, and was later occupied by the Kensington School of

Science and Art.[108] The All Souls and St Marylebone School had made a virtue of necessity and adopted a 'Scheme of Work [which] corresponds with that of the Lower Division of King's College School, and is intended to prepare boys for the Upper School'. By 1891/2 this school and the Forest School, the Western Grammar and the Philological School were the only ones 'in Union' with King's College.[109] The Blackheath School (which had long given up the connection) staggered on a little longer. By 1906 it was on its last legs, in spite of an effort to revive the boarding-house system, the setting up of a cadet corps during the Boer War, and good work at football. 'It seemed as though it was no longer wanted by those upon whose support we had to rely for existence.' The closure in 1908 seemed sudden, but was in reality the end of a long decline.[110]

The history of this group of Anglican London schools reflects topographical change – the outward spread to the suburbs which deprived Hackney and Islington of suitable pupils; the sharper classification of population which made areas such as Stepney almost wholly working-class; the contrary process which made urban villages such as Blackheath less select. Educational change played its part, for secondary schooling was rising in cost with greater specialization, wider curricula, higher standards, but social change was predominant. The newly conscious middle classes of the early decades of the century were more united in their rejection of certain aspects of the old society and its values than in any real identity of interests and needs. For a comparatively short period it seemed that a truly urban class would identify its educational needs through such schools as these, but as the century went on the great diversity of wealth, aspirations, style of life, even of allegiance, within these highly complex groups of people widened and schools which depended entirely on their fees and their investment no longer had a solid base on which to operate. By the end of the century the more wealthy and aspiring had once more identified themselves with the upper classes and wanted schools of the new public school type – either day schools such as Dulwich, and the older London schools now in rural settings – or they were prepared to go the whole way and use boarding-schools.[111] It is significant that the only two of all these schools to survive to the next century were the Forest School, which was essentially a rural boarding-school, and the Philological School, which continued its excellent tradition of systematic 'second grade' education, not usually attempting to prepare boys for the universities or higher professions. The less affluent and ambitious continued to need schools of this kind. Perhaps the Western Grammar School survived for a little longer as one of the last of these schools 'in union' because it adapted itself to provide a 'systematic course of Practical Instruction' aiming at the 'various Public Professional and Commercial Examinations'. The course included book-keeping, and reference to the nearness of the South Kensington Museums suggests a scientific or technical emphasis.[112]

It would be a mistake however to classify the nineteenth-century metropolitan proprietary schools as failures. True, they dwindled and vanished, but they are best seen as brilliant improvizations, drawing on academic, social, financial resources to solve a particular educational problem, and bequeathing to future generations the expertise of many soundly, if somewhat narrowly, educated men, but few institutions which had outlived their day.

Nonconformist schools

The great years of Nonconformist contribution in London to the development of the concept and process of secondary education were in the eighteenth century. During the nineteenth century, while they were making a major contribution to the wealth and growth of London, its Protestant dissenting citizens created some notable schools, but these were more imitative than innovatory. Dissenters wished to provide for their boys along lines available to those for other sections of the community rather than experiment boldly with new systems and new content. The Nonconformists were perhaps becoming part of the establishment – an educational establishment being transformed by their previous contributions and reformed by their experience.

This is illustrated by the first of these London foundations – in 1808 Mill Hill School, which was significantly called for its first sixty years not an academy but a Protestant Dissenters' Grammar School. The gap left in their educational facilities by the dramatic collapse of Hackney College was serious.[113] A number of London merchants under the chairmanship of Samuel Favell, Master of the Clothworkers' Company, met at a tavern in Cheapside in 1806 to discuss the idea of establishing a school 'for affording the best means of a sound, learned and pious education'. At first they considered a day school 'in a healthy part of the Metropolis', but houses in the City were found to be too expensive, and it was moreover considered that 'there would be dangers, both physical and moral, awaiting youth while passing through the streets of a large, crowded, and corrupt city . . .'. Even the inner suburbs, the setting for so many of the academies of the eighteenth century, were no longer thought suitable, and the Committee determined to find a site 'at least ten miles from London' for a boarding-school. An exploratory party, including Favell and the Reverend John Pye Smith of Homerton College, eventually chose Ridgeway House in a rural part of Hendon, which since the seventeenth century had associations with Nonconformist education, where they hoped that 'the rising generation would imbibe the elements of sound literature and the principles of the Evangelical religion, and thus become a credit to the institution, the joy of their parents and blessings in every relation of social life'. Money was already being collected by subscription, but the sermon preached at Mr Gaffie's Meeting House in Broad Street in January 1808 by the Reverend John Bogue seemed to be primarily a public-relations rather than a fund-raising exercise.[114]

Later somewhat shrill assertions that the middle classes not only *should* pay the market price for education, but wanted to do so, were being formulated, and these Nonconformist London citizens of the middling rank found it necessary to defend their subsidization of a liberal education for boys whose parents could afford quite high fees, on the grounds not only that their community must be secured by a learned and pious ministry and membership, but that general and intelligent benevolence depended on a 'cultivated mind with religious principles'. The cry of the widow and orphan would be the better heard.[115]

The school opened with 18 boys, all introduced through a member of the Committee. The fees were £45 a year with a considerable reduction for ministers' sons, and some boys, paying even lower fees or none, were 'taken under the society's patronage'. The classical course had been carefully laid down and from the outset the school was 'to secure a first rate classical and mathematical education'. French and drawing were provided as extras, and aspects of a broader curriculum, including some science, were planned; globes, an orrery and other instruments were provided. The school's syllabus and methods of religious instruction were prescribed in some detail and used the Westminster catechism, with modifications in the case of boys from some Baptist congregations. From the beginning Anglican boys were accepted, continuing the eighteenth-century tradition of meeting the wants of parents who distrusted the moral climate of established public schools.[116]

Mill Hill forms a bridge between eighteenth-century Nonconformist academies, provision for middle-class education in the nineteenth century, and the public schools of its closing years. In the varying fortunes and changing character of the school the evolving idea of such education can be traced. Fluctuations of success depended on problems which the school shared with comparable experiments in other sectors. A system of control had to be worked out if the school were to be publicly accountable. The independent churches had accumulated some experience in this respect, but by their very nature lacked any central organization which could provide machinery. The informal community of dissenters, academic, ministerial and commercial, of the City and its suburbs produced a committee of able and earnest supporters, but early disasters were at least partly due to its constant interference and attempt to retain and increase its own influence by dividing authority between chaplain and headmaster – Wesley's organization of Kingswood School may have been an influence. The Mill Hill Committee was so busy in every detail that it soon found it necessary to divide itself into five parts, and the headmaster was supervised and harassed frequently and thoroughly. He could not appoint his own assistants, and even the list of classical texts to be studied was altered without his being consulted. In 1826 the school, apparently well-established in numbers and reputation, moved into a handsome new building in the Grecian mode. But on Public Day in 1828 these dissensions reached their culmination in a truly memorable scholastic scene – the older boys throwing all the school benches into the pond, and the younger ones turning on the taps of thirty urns of boiling tea awaiting the visitors.[117]

Fluctuations in the quality of the staff were also serious, and in its first twenty-seven years the school had seven headmasters. Fortunately in 1834 Thomas Priestley, who had been on the staff for seventeen years, was appointed headmaster and for eighteen more years gave the school stability and good teaching. He met and admired Thomas Arnold, and to some extent tried to adopt some of his ideas. But although Priestley's long tenure gave him a stronger position, the Committee was still liable to meddle. The venerable Dr Pye Smith brooded over academic standards – he examined the school regularly until his death in 1851 – and its morals and orthodoxy – he once hurled away into a far pew a volume of Voltaire which he found himself about to present as a prize. The rest of the Committee had less educational experience and made less positive contributions. Priestley did good work within the limits imposed on him, but even before his death in 1853 numbers were declining and a disastrous period of wavering policies and contradictory interferences through the rapid tenures of four more headmasters brought the school to closure in 1868. Debts prevented the managers from selling it to the last headmaster. The Protestant Dissenters' Grammar School was experiencing financial crises similar to other schools trying to satisfy this level of educational need without adequate capital. What saved it in the long run was the genuine denominational need which it satisfied, and in the short run the energetic work of an old boy, Thomas Scrutton. In 1866 he became treasurer at a time of keen interest in this level of education, and succeeded in winding up the old committee, enlisting important new support such as that of the benevolent Samuel Morley, organizing the contributions of Congregational, Independent, Baptist and Presbyterian ministers and congregations, and applying to the Charity Commissioners for a new trust; 1869, the year of the Endowed Schools' Act, saw the second foundation of the school, now called Mill Hill School, and the appointment of a really effective headmaster, Dr R. F. Wearmouth, ensured a period of success. Two new railway lines, the Midland and the Great Northern, contributed by opening stations in the village.[118]

Dr Wearmouth was not only a good scholar, teacher and manager of boys, he had a coherent educational policy which brought the school into line with wider developments. He made systematic use of the University Local examinations and made the London Matriculation the chief goal of the senior boys, with remarkable success. Perhaps he should have raised their sights further and put them in for Oxford and Cambridge scholarships after the abolition of the tests in 1871, and this, together with increased competition from reformed endowed schools, now provided with conscience clauses, lay headmasters and even dissenting governors, may have accounted for a decline in numbers in the last years of his rule. On Wearmouth's resignation in 1886 there followed a second struggle to save the school from extinction; Scrutton 'headed the rescue party once again'. They appointed in 1891 J. D. McClure, who brought the school triumphantly into the twentieth century, with a wider and more liberal curriculum, a school chapel, laboratories, music facilities, and a higher standard of scholarship.[119] By this period a boarding-school of this kind had to attract parents who wanted more than a reformed local grammar school could offer, and Mill Hill, with its magnificent buildings and situation, could draw on the loyalty and help of a particularly active Old Boys' Club (1878), as well as denominational allegiance. While other London examples do not altogether do so, the final success of Mill Hill does support Fitch's statement, based on his survey of Yorkshire proprietary schools, that they only succeeded when they were denominational in character.[120] During the century its periods of crisis almost exactly corresponded with those of emerging secondary education in general, and its ultimate prosperity and success also reflected polarization within middle-class education.

The demand for the education of clergy sons on the provision of middle-class education was important both quantitatively and qualitatively, for in the nineteenth century there was a keen demand for schooling for sons of the manse and the parsonage, difficult to meet in times of rising costs. Mill Hill took ministers' sons, and in 1811 another school for the sons of Congregational ministers was founded in Lewisham – a pleasant village much favoured for scholastic enterprises. After seventy years it moved to Caterham.[121] Another foundation supported by the interdenominational evangelical London Missionary Society and the Baptist and Congregational Missions (as well as the Church Missionary Society in its early days) was the school and home for missionaries' sons at Blackheath from 1842. A similar school for girls had been opened at Walthamstow in 1838, a rare case of provision made for sisters before their brothers. The Blackheath School moved into Eltham College when it was vacated by the naval school in 1912.[122] The expansion and proliferation of the professions during this period created a number of similar schools and both reflected the importance of education as a means of social confirmation in a more specialized society, and influenced its standards and nature and, inevitably, also its cost. Such schooling was needed to enable sons to maintain or improve on the professional standing of their fathers and, as professional standards steadily rose, even maintaining this put increasing pressure on education. It became necessary not only to have the right vocational preparation, but also 'the education of a gentleman'.[123]

The case of middle-class schooling for Wesleyan boys emphasizes the importance of clergy sons. The Wesleyan Connexion had made excellent provision for the sons of its itinerant ministers in Kingswood and Woodhouse Grove and therefore clerical pressure and leadership were lacking in a campaign for secondary schools: as one minister said in

1869, 'The preachers have excellent schools of their own, and perhaps this is one reason why the want of our more respectable people has not been attended to.'[124] Moreover, it was not until 1878 that laity were elected to a representative session of Conference, hitherto entirely a clerical body. During the early decades of the century the Connexion suffered many inner tensions and the Wesleyan body may be said to have lost its hope of successful mission to the urban poor. It made heavy demands on its middle-class laity and its members grew steadily in prosperity and educational aspiration.[125] Proprietary schools, with active Connexional interest, were founded in Sheffield (1838) and Taunton (1843), but although in 1847 a meeting was held in Spitalfields to consider the establishment of a school for the sons of Methodist laymen, this did not materialize for nearly thirty years, and then it was founded in Cambridge.[126] The proportion of Methodists to other Nonconformists was lower in London and its suburbs than almost anywhere else in urban England,[127] yet the Wesleyan position emphasizes the paradox that, while they were important both in contribution and composition in the creation of demand for middle-class education, Nonconformists played a relatively small part in providing for it. Perhaps the most significant evidence the Wesleyans give for the history of metropolitan secondary schooling at this period is negative. A numerous, varied and in-tellectually demanding body of middle-class parents was apparently able to find suitable or adequate schools in a situation increasingly described as one of crisis and shortage. Where did Wesleyan boys from moderately prosperous homes go to school in London? Many of them no doubt to private schools, and there were some very good ones.[128] But it seems probable that as in the earlier decades of the century many Wesleyans did not regard themselves as altogether or finally separated from the Established Church, and as the Evangelical movement provided much common ground, these parents were prepared to use Anglican schools. When the Tractarian and Oxford movements drew denominational lines more sharply, and Woodard and his like began to see middle-class schools as a means of winning back dissenters to the established fold, and as Wesleyans identified themselves more completely with dissent, the situation changed. Alarm that Wesleyan boys would leave their parents' church led to a conscious movement for denominational sec-ondary education.[129]

The extraordinary effort of the Wesleyan community in providing 743 elementary schools between the setting up of their Education Com-mittee in 1837 and 1870[130] had important results for the idea of secondary education nationally, and it perhaps supplied the most ex-panding need of metropolitan Wesleyans of the middle classes – for the 'third-grade schools' of the Taunton analysis, catering for children leaving between about twelve and fourteen. Matthew Arnold mingled praise and blame of these Wesleyan schools – praise for their quality, blame for their comparatively high cost (often 3*d* to 4*d* a week), which restricted their benefits largely to the children of skilled artisans and lower-middle-class parents. He commented on the high proportion of qualified teachers, the surprisingly good attendance, many of the pupils being 'recruited from a class of society in which parents exercise ... supervision over their children's proceedings', and it was common practice for children to buy their own books. It was from such a school, in Highbury, that Arnold took Thomas Healing, whom he asked the Department to appoint as his assistant. He had criticisms also of the London schools, those of 'middling or average merit' did not reach as high a standard as those of other districts he had inspected, and he wondered whether the excitement and intensity of London life was perhaps too powerful a distraction rather than a stimulus. But these schools more and more convinced him that the middle classes should be able to benefit from grants and from inspection.[131] On the other hand, the Wesleyans intended their schools for the poor. Westminster Training College, with its large practising schools, had purposely been built in a district 'proverbially destitute' and arrangements were made here as elsewhere to pay the fees of poor children. The parents, as the principal said to the Newcastle Commission, did not feel pauperized because such help produced kindly feeling, they saw that their 'neighbours have cared'.[132] This emphasizes an aspect of Wesleyan social structure which was able to make an important contribution to the idea of educational process. Even the best National schools were rarely able to bridge the gap between the upper working- and lower middle classes. But while in the Wesleyan Connexion social distinctions might be strong, the detested element of patronage was absent, and Methodists refused to define elementary education altogether in social terms – in this respect they resembled the Jewish community. Though it must be remembered that this 'alternative establishment' did not include the really poor, here at least were the beginnings of an understanding of elementary and secondary education as part of a continuous process, and as part of a shared culture, deeply imbued with religious values and a strong sense of community and communion. One prominent Wesleyan educationalist proposed at the time of the Taunton Inquiry that a whole ladder of educational opportunity should be set up by the Connexional schools, allowing promising elementary boys to reach the universities, which should have colleges assigned to Methodist students.[133] The same ambition was evident at the college in Westminster. Like the Church training colleges, but perhaps with more real success, it attempted 'higher subjects' to improve the 'general capabilities' of the students and tried to attract young people from the middle classes. By the time of the Newcastle Commission some ministers were even sending their daughters.[134] Under its second principal it was something of an educational powerhouse, and here Dr Rigg was able to consult and exchange views with Dr Temple, when Bishop of London, with Cardinal Manning and with Canon Gregory, and to discuss problems and to lend books to Dean Stanley and Lady Augusta. It is a pleasing ecumenical picture, and not without significance for the development of secondary education. This liberal attitude prevented the Wesleyan contribution from being of an entirely sectarian nature.[135]

The Society of Friends also had a regional and central organization, though not so strong as that of the Wesleyans, and an intellectual and social ethos which made very clear demands upon education and, like the independent churches, Quakers already had experience of providing schools at secondary level.[136] Quickened by the Evangelical Revival, they were active in many movements for social reform including popular schooling. They had no ministry or ministers' sons or daughters for whom schooling must be provided, but they had a deep conviction of the importance of the individual and the dignity of all occupations, which led them to an understanding of the need to provide serious and practical schooling for all children of their Society. Their empirical, vocational, even utilitarian views led them to conclude that the greatest need for 'guarded education' in the early part of the new century was for their less affluent children, both boys and girls. Ackworth School near York had been founded in 1779, and gradually coeducational 'Meeting Schools' on this pattern were extended to cover the country. For the London area, including (in parallel with Anglican territorial divisions) the eastern counties, the old school of industry in their workhouse in Clerkenwell was gradually transformed, the children were separated from the old people and moved to Islington in 1786, where more time was given to schooling and less to labouring. By 1811 the age of leaving was fourteen, which could be extended if needed, but the school did not yet give as high an education as Ackworth.[137] In 1811 the London Friends decided to 'extend over a wider area the benefits of their school in Islington Road', and in that year the London Yearly Meeting debated its support until 'many friends said they were heartily tired' of the question. In 1825 the school moved to Croydon and in 1879 to Saffron Walden, developing much in line with the slow changes in secondary schooling in general.[138] Quaker parents had always been encouraged to keep their children at school until fourteen, a leaving age which identified these schools with Taunton's 'third grade' rather than elementary schools, but throughout the century standards rose; in 1879 a Quaker Education Conference advised parents 'to leave their children at school at least till sixteen'. By the end of the century the 'Ackworth schools' were following a curriculum which included languages, mathematics, sciences, and were therefore considerably more expensive than they had been. These 'Meeting Schools' were, as an Inspector's Report of 1905 said, passing on 'to work of a more ambitious character'.[139]

From the early part of the century schools on the Ackworth model did not satisfy all the educational needs of London Quakers, many of whom were both wealthy and influential, and the Meeting for Sufferings in

London in 1828 took the responsibility of helping to provide and supervise a school for boys whose parents could afford high fees. Foremost in taking action was William Allen, who as well as campaigning against the slave trade, acting as treasurer to Lancaster's society, financing (and interfering with) Owen at New Lanark, working with Humphry Davy and lecturing at the Royal Institution, putting the Duke of Kent's financial affairs in order, taking the Czar Nicholas to a Quaker meeting, managed to find time to become a leading trustee of the Grove House School at Tottenham.[140] This had been bought and established by means of a loan subscribed by Friends, and trustees bore famous Quaker names – Gurney, Hodgkin, Lister, Barclay – and represented local families already associated with education in that pleasant village.[141]

Tottenham had long connections with Quaker schools. Richard Claridge had in 1707 opened such a boarding-school near the High Cross which passed into the hands of the Foster family and gave a wide education including as well as classics, modern languages, merchants' accompts, useful branches of mathematics and 'just sentiments of religion and virtue'. Thence it went by family connection to the Coars – Thomas Coar had published an English grammar for Ackworth School. The Tottenham School became a notable preparatory school for little boys.[142]

In 1828 the Foster family provided five trustees for Grove House, two of them still resident in Tottenham, but although London and local connections were important, the school was also providing for a national need. One of the first subscribers was Richard Darby of Coalbrookdale – Abraham Darby had been a pupil at the Coar school – and his son was sent to Grove House. From the beginning Grove House had more than personal connections with the new technological society to which the Quakers were contributing so notably. The curriculum was wide and included Latin and Greek ('taste for the elegance and style of these languages' was to be imparted), literature, 'the principles of religious liberty and the British Constitution', geography and history, 'particularly as illustrative of the Bible', and the history of the Society of Friends, mathematics, pure and as 'applied to mechanics, navigation and astronomy', and natural philosophy, not only as mental training but to give 'a clearer and enlarged vision of the wisdom of the Supreme Being in the wonderful regularity of the Laws of Nature'. Modern languages were not mentioned in the original course but appear to have been soon included. The course fostered science and technological curiosity from the beginning – Joseph Lister could not have regarded his education there as irrelevant to his career or even to his fame.[143]

For fifty years this was a highly successful school, closely supervised by the trustees at the London Meeting for Sufferings. In the early days interest was regularly paid on money loaned, and by 1840 a substantial proportion had been repaid. It is clear that wealthy Quakers were content to regard this as a useful and modest investment. Fees were high from the beginning – £94 10*s* – and John Ford of Ackworth in giving evidence to the Taunton Commissioners stated that the richest members of the Society did not use his school – 'They send their sons to an institution at Tottenham, a sort of proprietary school, called "Grove House", where it is 100 guineas per annum against our 50 1.' The distinctions within middle-class education were accepted by Friends as by the rest of society.[144]

By this period the school was in fact beginning, like the other proprietary schools, to experience difficulties. In the late 1850s the accounts began to show a loss, partly due to heavy capital expenditure on raising the standards of the building, such as installing warm baths in 1854. But the committee obviously placed the decline partly at the headmaster's door, and in 1860 replaced him. The new appointment, Arthur R. Abbott, proved someting of a cuckoo in the nest. He had been headmaster of Hitchin School and was businesslike and ambitious. He negotiated a generous, even inflationary, salary with the committee, secured further and expensive improvements to the building – new classrooms, common rooms, studies – and gradually secured more independence, more financial stake in the enterprise. Undoubtedly the school increased in size and efficiency. In 1879 the fees had risen to £120 a year and the school claimed to prepare boys thoroughly for 'the Universities, for Matriculation in the University of London, or for direct entrance on Commercial life', and they could stay until they were twenty, thus providing a range of education comparable to that of the Catholic colleges at the same period. The amenities of the school included workshops, a chemistry laboratory, a library, cricket ground, running path, swimming bath, covered fives court, and a boat-house on the River Lea and 'every facility for rowing exercise'. But the interest and control of the Society of Friends had weakened. By 1871 the original trustees had all gone, except one old and infirm Foster; in 1873 the headmaster gained permission to allow boys to attend places of worship other than the Friends' Meeting House; and in 1877 Abbott declared his intention of taking Anglican orders. The trustees sold him the school premises and goodwill for £11,000 and were left with a sum of £7600 for investment. In the event they had much the better of the bargain, for Abbott's private school immediately failed. Its end seems to have been hastened by some sort of scandal, but the neighbourhood was rapidly changing. The Great Eastern Railway had taken part of the school grounds in 1865, but it was cheap fares which changed the amenities and social composition of Tottenham.[145]

Perhaps the decline and fall of Grove House can be connected with a period of transition which brought Quakers more into the mainstream of society, more ready to use other schools. By the second half of the century London Quakers could not be immediately distinguished from their fellow citizens by dress, language and so forth. Certainly by 1883 a new 'Higher Class School' was recognized as needed if Friends were to escape from what was now seen as their enclave, and three years later a paper for the Friends' Central Education Board declared 'Our need for a New Public School'. The argument was partly based on the danger of the Society's losing its future leaders when they did not receive a 'guarded education'. The resulting outburst of activity discovered that the Grove House trustees had ceased to meet, and that the £7600 was lying unused. The Meeting for Sufferings of 1886 established a new Board of Management and, amidst controversy over the desirability of segregated schooling and the need for a school for wealthy Friends, there emerged a limited liability company, the Friends' Public School Company Limited (1888). Quaker middle-class education, like that for other sections of the community, had assimilated its style and standards with those of the higher classes. The universities were now free from religious test, and there was less dislike of boys mixing with those from other families – there was increasing evidence that boys were attending schools of other denominations. The school, which was founded under the 'cognizance' of the Yearly Meeting, was to be in the south of England, but by this time London and its suburbs were no longer considered suitable for a public school of the type envisaged, and the site chosen was Leighton Park near Reading: and there the school opened in 1890.[146]

The development of middle-class education for London Quakers has some interesting points of comparison and contrast with that for other denominations. They were early in recognizing the need of the more modest section of the middle classes, liberal in interpreting the courses provided at all levels. In some ways the compact, interconnected body of Quakers was almost a paradigm of middle-class society at its best, or as it would wish to be in its times of worthier aspiration. It may be that the ideal was too high, in the early decades the insulation too complete. Over the whole nation, and in a longer perspective of time, their influence was significant, but in the surging metropolis, and in the crisis years, the Friends appear to have played a lesser part in the development of secondary education.

Roman Catholic provision

The development of Roman Catholic schools in London during this period raises some interesting questions about the emerging concept of secondary education and its social and economic determinants. It also underlines the insular nature of English education, for here lively and systematic European and transatlantic influences and ideas contrasted with the native amalgam of tradition, expedient, common sense and the operation of market forces.

There were Catholic schools in London throughout the penal era and fashionable private schools for boys became possible by the end of the seventeenth century.[147] In the next, more tolerant century such schools could be quite openly established. One was kept by John Walker, the lexicographer, at Kensington Gravel Pits (now Notting Hill Gate) in partnership with James Usher (1720–72), who put up the capital for this 'school for Catholic Youth' and kept it till his death.[148] But the old Roman Catholic community was introverted in its outlook, comparatively static or declining in numbers, and although Bishop Challoner gave serious attention to the needs of education, neither of his schools for boys above the elementary level was situated in London. His specifically mercantile school was at Sedgley Park, near Wolverhampton, a district earlier affected by industrial change.[149] Already in London the steady influx of Irish immigrants was creating a problem of Catholic popular education, and the needs of the middling ranks were beginning to be realized on the eve of the Relief Act of 1791 which brought the penal era to an end. In 1787 the Catholic Committee, appointed at a general meeting of English Catholics to promote their interests, proposed 'the setting up of a school which shall afford a system of education proper for those who are destined for civil or commercial life'. This was not successful and education of this kind continued to depend on private schools, which multiplied after 1791 and soon received an influx of skill and experience from *émigré* priests and teachers from revolutionary Europe.[150] The revival of Roman Catholic education was stimulated by these exiles and sympathy engendered in influential English circles, but the 'great' schools or colleges founded at this period provided a classical, and in some cases a seminarian, education for high fees, and settled far from London. The nearest was St Edmund's at Ware (1793) which took over a private Catholic academy, tracing its descent from a seventeenth-century school.[151] The centre of Catholic gravity was far from the capital and the Catholic community still lacked a middle class, especially in the urban concentrations of population; in London probably comparatively few Roman Catholic working men rose into the 'aristocracy of labour'.[152] An indication of the greater needs and aspirations of immigrant groups of workers for this level of education was the school for German children in Whitechapel, established by 1841 as the St Boniface's British and Foreign Catholic Preparatory and Grammar School, under 'the patronage and inspection of the Rt Hon. T. Wyse', to 'prepare talented children of the humbler classes to become useful settlers, tradesmen, artists, merchants' clerks, masters and teachers in British Colonies . . .'. The curriculum included 'all the preparatory branches of science', and Latin, French, German, Spanish, Dutch and Russian.[153]

As the century passed, Catholic families began to fill this confessional social vacuum. 'The wealthy manufacturer, the successful merchant, the keen-eyed speculator, introduce a new element of social power, which they double in their sons by securing to them the benefits of a liberal education.'[154] After the Oxford Movement, converts provided these classes with a 'formidable intellectual armoury', and those in orders who were unable to continue in the Roman Catholic priesthood were especially useful in educational causes. Thomas Allies in 1850 opened a school in Golden Square, which then moved to the Priory at St John's Wood. Archdeacon Manning (already a widower) brought to Catholic educational policy a keen sociological insight and purpose. In his Anglican days he had been especially aware of the needs which had been created by rapid growth of population, wealth, knowledge and skills which called 'into existence a whole people below the highest and above the lowest of earlier times'. Later, as Archbishop of Westminster from 1865–91 and head of the hierarchy, Cardinal Manning played a key part in the struggle for Roman Catholic education at this level. He saw this as not only supplying a legitimate and distinct need, but as binding together the disparate sectors of Catholic society, where, as he wrote, 'between the rich and the poor there were individuals, but no classes. In the Catholic Church in England there were no gradations such as exist in the social order of the English people.'[155] In discussing this complex situation, and a personality of such subtlety and ambiguity, historians do not easily agree about Manning's priorities or his effectiveness in meeting them, but there can be little doubt of his impact on the metropolitan educational scene at all levels.

This must be put into its context. Even before the restoration of the hierarchy, in July 1848 a meeting of London clergy and laymen had discussed the opening of a 'School conducted on Catholic principles at which a good education might be obtained at moderate cost ... an object much to be desired in Metropolis'. From the outset this school was conceived as an expression of the interdependence of the various elements of Catholic society – its sponsors included the 'Old Gentry' – Arundel and Shrewsbury and Wyse for example – and it was 'under the direction of the Catholic clergy' of the old mission, and Dr Wiseman consented to be its patron. An exhibition fund was set up and the parish clergy were to nominate suitable boys. Headmaster and staff were sought among graduates from Oxford and Cambridge, 'now Catholics', and the first headmaster was J. M. Glenie, 'late of Mary Hall, Oxford', and the second, James Stewart from Trinity College Cambridge. It was called first the London Catholic Classical and Commercial School, and later the Catholic Middle School, but it sought not only to cater for an emerging need, but to knit these middle-class boys into Catholic society. Its liberal education aimed to prepare them for 'mercantile pursuits and for all those situations in life for which a good general education is required', and at the same time to fit them to enter the Catholic Colleges and 'for that course of study which is required by the London University'. The general course included English, Latin, Greek, French, German, arithmetic, book-keeping, mathematics, geography and history, with 'Elements of drawing and vocal music' for a small extra charge. Religious instruction formed 'an integral part' of the course, but non-catholics were accepted and not expected to attend these lessons.

This school was in fact launched as a communal enterprise, and it was financed by an appeal to the Catholic body generally. 'Guarantees' of £100 each were sought, and enough was promised for the school to be opened in John Street at the end of 1848, but it had a short life. By the following autumn the guarantees were having to be taken up and the original fees of £6 6s a year had been raised to £8 8s. By 1851 the school had faded away. The structure had been impressive, the need perhaps too slight or not met with enough precision, a constant or recurring problem at this complex of social levels.[156]

By the time this school had modestly expired, the restoration of the hierarchy in 1850 had provided the Capital with a diocesan organization which at least identified its focal points at Westminster and Southwark, though like the Anglican bishops each was responsible for a huge extra-metropolitan area. Within their boundaries parochial structure could be improvised alongside emerging city needs, especially those created by the huge influx of Irish immigrants which coincided with the first decade of diocesan organization, and brought overwhelming problems of popular education. In tracing the development of the middle-class educational policy, this must always be borne in mind, as resources could never be diverted from this multiplying and mounting problem.[157]

When Wiseman, now Cardinal, arrived in his diocese in 1850, he was faced with a formidable array of tasks, and he relied greatly upon the work of communities of religious. The Jesuits were already settled in Farm Street, but within a few years Redemptorists, Passionists, Marists, Oratorians, were established, and at his death in 1865 there were fifteen such communities of men in his diocese as well as many for women.[158] This had great significance for the future of middle-class education. After the failure of the Catholic Middle School in 1851, apart from numerous private schools, the only schools catering for this level in London were those for about 50 boys and 50 girls established in Somers Town in 1799 by the Abbé Carron from France.[159] Certainly a number of London boys must have attended the great Catholic colleges, but they could only help the better-to-do who required a classical curriculum. It was therefore another landmark in the development of Catholic secondary education when in 1854 the Brothers of the Christian Schools, the De La Salle Brothers, sent two of their number to investigate the educational needs of England. Their vocation and their rigorous training enabled them to contribute to all levels of education,[160] and Wiseman, his right-hand adviser Manning, and Grant, Bishop of Southwark, welcomed them eagerly. The Brothers decided to begin modestly by opening a middle-class day and boarding-school in a house near to the church of the Redemptorist Fathers at Clapham, where they could also help in their primary school. A house near Clapham Common was rented for £100 per annum, and the school was duly advertised as being opened 'to meet the wishes of a great number of Catholic families', on the model of the De La Salle schools in France, Belgium,

Italy and America. The situation was extolled as healthy, and omnibuses ten times an hour linked it with the centre of London. 'The Brothers endeavour to instil into their pupils habits of order and gentlemanly manners', to make them 'good Christians, dutiful sons, and useful members of society'. Pupils were admitted between seven and twelve years of age and the curriculum was wide, including mathematics and modern languages, French and German and 'the Rudiments of Italian and Spanish' if desired, book-keeping, 'the Elements of Physics, Chemistry and Natural History', a significant addition to the John Street menu. The practical course and low fees made available a kind of education greatly needed, and the professional training of the Brothers – six companions had soon arrived from Paris to assist Brother Barthélemy – ensured standards. As funds for renting the house also came from headquarters, English Catholic middle-class education was receiving handsome resources of skill and capital from overseas, and for a level of education where it was urgently needed, for the temptation, especially for the converts from intellectual and professional circles, seemed always to interpret middle-class education in too classical and aspiring a manner. Indeed the educational ideas of this group drew the Catholic colleges further into the orbit of Oxford and Cambridge, at the very time when social change was reinforcing the need for a more utilitarian secondary education. This problem of educational definition and diversification was vividly illustrated by the fluctuating fortunes of the Clapham school, St Joseph's College, as it became. It soon outgrew its original premises and moved to a larger house with plenty of grounds, but there were difficulties in drawing on teachers from France or other countries in which the Order operated, and when a Brother from America arrived to take over the school he found a flourishing scholastic community, rather on French lines, but with alarming debts. The logical remedy of raising the fees only brought a disastrous drop in numbers; a Canadian successor pursued an equally unpopular and unsuccessful policy of strict economy and short rations, and after eight years' useful existence it looked as if the school would have to close. What saved it was the decision of the Order to wipe off the debt from their central funds, and this also ensured the continuation of a second school which had been founded in 1860 in Southwark, at the express wish of the Bishop. This prospered as St Joseph's Academy and removed to larger premises at Kennington. The London clergy urged the Order to open a third secondary school and for a time this was successful, in a building in Holborn, described by one of the brothers as a place with 'no space, no light, no air, not even an inch of ground for sixty-four persons'. Here they did manage to assemble and teach, for a space of three years, something like a hundred boys, but then it was abandoned. Boys for such a venture seemed in endless but erratic supply in Victorian London.[161]

The Clapham school's most successful period began in 1870 when

Brother Potamian, American by birth and with diverse teaching experience in Canada, arrived to take up an appointment on the staff. Potamian found that the science course at St Joseph's was already in process of reform, a laboratory had been set up helped by supplies from the continent, and the science side of the library improved. Was this influenced by the nearby Clapham Grammar School, until recently under Pritchard?[162] As director of studies Potamian concentrated on the scientific aspects of the curriculum, and on the use of the various 'middle-class examinations'. Good results brought a steady increase in numbers – 100 by 1873, the majority boarders. Potamian himself worked for matriculation and then a London degree, proving himself a distinguished academic and an excellent teacher, affable, thorough, stimulating. The school prospectus laid stress on science, 'instruction in Physics, Chemistry, Drawing, Mechanics, Land-Surveying, Natural History, is aided by complete sets of apparatus, models, diagrams, specimens, and a well furnished laboratory'. But the school retained a balanced diet – 'the young gentlemen will receive a good English and classical education'. To middle-class parents of moderate means, the utility of science and the emphasis on external examinations made a strong appeal, and for higher ambitions London Matriculation was entered as well as the University Locals.

St Joseph's College was perhaps one of the most significant middle-class schools of Victorian London, and it is sad that ignorance and insularity prevented its influence being more widespread. The contribution of the Order to the educational section of the International Health Exhibition in 1884 astonished and impressed large crowds. 'Until the present exhibition probably not above a score or two of people in England had heard of these Brothers . . .' as *The Times* put it. Yet there were then 11,000 of them actively engaged in teaching 306,000 children scattered all over the world. It was the objectivity and system of the teaching, and the emphasis on well-designed and prepared illustrative and practical materials, which attracted such interest. The English exhibits were 'not to be compared' with them (except perhaps for the strength of our school desks).[163]

During these middle decades of the century, Catholic schools for this level were steadily increasing. The Augustinian Fathers opened St Monica's Priory in Hoxton Square in 1864, the Josephites a school in Croydon in 1869. The Brothers of Mercy, a Belgian order, had been introduced into London by Cardinal Wiseman in 1855, and their large school, St Aloysius, moved to Hornsey in 1879.[164] Especially important was St Charles's College, established by Manning in 1863 in Kensington when he was still superior of the Oblates of St Charles to whom he entrusted the school, with his nephew, Father William Manning, in charge. This was designed as a middle-class school but it was several years before its curriculum was as wide as Manning wished. By 1868–9 it included Christian doctrine, English, history, Latin, Greek, geography, botany, mathematics and trigonometry, natural philosophy and drawing, and when by 1872 the senior classes were large enough astronomy, political economy, zoology and geology were added, with French and German and some fringe benefits such as mythology. The fees were higher than those at Clapham, aiming at a rather higher social level. In 1879 there were 100 boarders and 40 day boys, it was advertised as 'teaching the usual course of a Public School', and the fees had risen to as much as £63 a year for senior boarders. In 1874 a lavish new building had been opened in Notting Hill, costing £40,000. The Oxford and Cambridge Locals, London Matriculation and a variety of professional examinations were all prepared for, and throughout the last thirty years of the century the school made an important contribution to the increase in numbers of Catholics in the professional classes – Army and Navy cadetships, entrance to Woolwich, the Indian and the Home Civil Services, the law, medicine, chartered accountancy, the newer technical professions such as electrical engineering.[165]

By 1880 Manning was able to survey the progress of middle-class education in London at a meeting at Archbishop's House with some satisfaction. Eleven schools were giving a broad and suitable curriculum to 340 pupils (more if a wider sweep of suburbs was included), more attention was being given to English history, modern languages and science, and satisfactory examination results included 377 passes in the recent Science and Art papers, some indication of proper attention to technical and less expensive needs.[166]

During this same period the Cardinal Archbishop had been deeply involved in the long and complex struggle over Catholic higher education, which was enmeshed with the changing social structure of the Catholic community and was as much a social as an educational or even a religious debate in which London played a key part. 'The demand for university education had . . . to be viewed in the nature of a class struggle for power and influence.' As the higher classes hoped to see Oxford to some extent as a 'safeguard against the energy of the London-educated middle-class . . .', it was also to some extent a regional struggle.[167] 'London-educated' here must be interpreted widely to mean those who had followed school courses, whether at distant Catholic colleges or metropolitan and other day and boarding-schools, shaped by the demands of the Matriculation examination, and perhaps then taken external London degrees at 'colleges' or by private study. But the phrase also indicates the shift of social and topographical equilibrium from the old Catholic provincial gentry to the urban middle and professional classes, and their differing aspirations for their sons. Other towns, especially Liverpool, were important, but Manning's part was central, not only because of his sharp social focus on education, but because of his metropolitan experience and commitments. The Catholic hierarchy was beginning to look at England with a somewhat different perspective, from a rather different angle. 'London's compromising atmosphere' begins to be felt.[168] Historians disagree about the extent to which Manning and his fellow bishops, or his rival Newman, read the real needs of their times and of the future, and the debate has implications for the secondary level.[169]

Whether the Catholic University in Kensington is seen as the result of his determination to secure clerical control of higher education and to perpetuate the social isolation of Catholics, or on the contrary of his attempt to serve the new classes and so enable Catholics to play their part in the new society, it is certain that Manning gave a decisive lead in its rather hasty establishment in 1874 by the hierarchy, and that it added a dimension to Catholic, largely metropolitan, education rather similar to University or King's Colleges. Like them it admitted boys at about seventeen and provided a variety of courses both general and vocational. 'The growth of the middle and upper classes of our Laity, and the opening of the career of professional and public service, render it necessary to lay at least the foundations of a system of higher studies ... in Modern Languages, Constitutional Law, Physical Science in application to certain professional employments, and above all, a sound course of Mental Science and of the study of the Philosophy of Religion, with a more complete and scientific treatment of the Faith ...'.[170] Manning secured government undertaking that its candidates would not be excluded from the Civil Service by being compelled 'to study in Colleges where we are unable to send them', Kensington students should be admitted 'on a parity with other Colleges'. Their 'two years of approbation' after passing the ICS examination could therefore be passed at the Catholic University College.[171] The school attached to the College, however, unlike University College School and King's College School, was a private venture of the rector, Monsignor Capel (Monsignor Catesby of Disraeli's *Lothair*). His Catholic Public School in Warwick Road had existed before the College was founded and was to be the overt reason why the site was chosen – another was probably the fashionable nature of the neighbourhood and its attractions for higher social support. It was intended that Capel should give up the headship of the school, but he never did so. He involved himself in debt for it, launched a joint stock enterprise for its extension, and declared that to him the university was as Leah, and the school as Rachael – moreover he said this to Lord Petre, who had invested not only in the University College, but in St Charles's College as well to which this school was a serious threat. In 1879 Capel's venture was advertised as the Kensington Catholic Public School and had survived the Catholic University by a year.[172] In 1878 this had been hurriedly removed, under a cloud of financial and even moral scandal, to more modest and unsullied premises in the Cromwell Road; in 1882 what was left of it was incorporated into St Charles's College as a Department of Higher Studies, where it functioned until the death of Manning's successor in 1903, ceasing to have 'national significance' but still serving a 'purely local and diocesan clientèle'.[173] It had been 'squall and squabble to the end' and had cost the Cardinal £10,000, leaving him 'poorer than a Church mouse'.[174] The reasons for its failure belong to the discussion of higher rather than secondary education. But Rachael's fortunes were involved with those of Leah, threatening something of a gap in education for the better-to-do London middle classes, who perhaps hankered after the more aristocratic Jesuits. Capel seems to have hoped that the Jesuits would buy his public school and allow him to continue as headmaster but the Jesuits were not prepared to accept his conditions, and moreover acknowledged the opposition of Manning, as Ordinary of the Diocese. Capel, bankrupt, was obliged to sell to the diocese without conditions. Manning hoped that 'the miseries and sins of rivalry and ill feeling' were brought to an end, but it was not easy to escape from such a web of rumour and intrigue. The Jesuits suspected that Manning was going to open a college as a rival to their Beaumont founded in 1861 in Warren Hastings's old house near Windsor. Manning indignantly repudiated this. He 'intended to form a school in South Kensington for boys resident in their homes' but nothing would induce him to 'do so unbrotherly an act' as to try to rival Beaumont.[175]

While we may acknowledge Manning's sincerity in action, his feelings towards the Society of Jesus were far from brotherly and correspond more to our expectations of the Victorian Anglican archdeacon than the Catholic cardinal. He probably brought some prejudices over with him, and experience and reflection did not change his views. Above all he considered that the Jesuits would not, could not, supply the levels of education which he recognized as among the great needs of London. Classical studies must not be allowed to distort the middle-class curriculum, which should emphasize scientific and commercial sides.[176]

This whole confused and perhaps unworthy episode had in fact strong connections with the social and academic definition of secondary education. The equally complex episode which followed hard on its heels had little practical outcome of provision of secondary education, but also in its very confusions revealed problems of defining and providing it. Manning unsuccessfully tried to keep a middle-class school in being on Capel's site, and considered asking the Christian Brothers to open another school for the 'middle and East of London'.[177] This project got entwined with an ambitious plan launched by two laymen, W. R. Conolly and W. A. Dalton, for a 'Great Central Middle Class' school for Catholic boys, on the lines of King's College and University College Schools, the City of London, Charterhouse and Westminster, combining classical and modern sides, preparing 'for the Press, for the desk, for the foundry, for Government appointments'. 'There is a Classical education, an English or a Literary education, and a Commercial education, which do you want?' as Manning shrewdly asked. The Christian Brothers shared these doubts, feared that the supply of suitable teachers would be overstretched, and agreed with the Cardinal that there were not enough Catholic boys who could afford the proposed fees as well as the railway fare to Charing Cross or the Embankment. Manning caused a survey of such boys to be made, disclosing a number using such schools as the North London Collegiate, University and King's College Schools, Cowper Street, the City of London, St Mark's, but it was highly doubtful that they would attend the proposed central school. Its financial basis was also insecure and Anglican experience of proprietary schemes was apparently ignored. Add to all this Manning's fear that this was another bid by the Jesuits 'to make capital out of our middle-class movement' and it is clear that the scheme had little chance of success.[178]

In the end a somewhat ridiculous mouse emerged from the mountain. The Brothers at Clapham agreed to take boys for a fee inclusive of railway fare to Victoria or Ludgate Hill where they would be met. A similar arrangement was made at St Charles's. The Victorians were much addicted to Bradshaw as a solution to intractable problems, but it is hardly necessary to say that this one did not last for long. One new school however did come from all this intrigue and contention. The Brothers of the Oratory opened a middle school in Brompton, under a lay headmaster, charging only 13*s* a term, and teaching English, history, geography, writing, mathematics, French, drawing and scientific subjects, with Latin if required.[179]

After this a period of comparative calm ensued, and as the dust settled it became more than ever clear that the work of the religious orders was essential to Catholic secondary education, perhaps especially amidst the pitfalls of the London property market and with increasing competition from reformed endowed schools. New foundations included the Franciscan St Bonaventure School at Stratford in 1877, moved to Forest Gate in 1884, the Marists' St John's at Islington, the Salesians' at Battersea in 1887 where inexpensive and practical preparation for business and commercial life was stressed, and in 1897 the Xaverians opened Clapham College.[180] By then Manning was dead and his successor, Cardinal Vaughan, invited the Jesuits to open St Ignatius College, Stamford Hill, in 1894. There, in a large dilapidated Victorian house, they provided, not the high classical education which Manning had feared, but a pretty down-to-earth diet. In the Southwark diocese they opened Wimbledon College in 1893. St Charles's College continued to provide for the upper middle classes of West London until it closed in 1905. By then this function had been taken over by the Ealing Priory School of the Downside Benedictines, opened in 1902.[181]

That even the devotion of the religious orders was not able to bring security to under-capitalized education on the open market principle was demonstrated by the later fortunes of Brother Potamian's school. In the 1880s St Joseph's College was growing steadily in numbers and reputation, but Clapham was changing as a neighbourhood and the premises were too cramped for further expansion. In 1886 negotiations began for a property in Tooting and in 1887 Tooting College was opened in magnificent new buildings, with room for 200 boarders and as many day boys. The fees were now about £52 10s for boarders and £15 15s for day boys, and it was planned to add higher classes for degree work. But this venture had stretched the Order (and perhaps the neigbourhood) too far, and Potamian's business acumen proved less than his educational and academic abilities. Attempts to clear the debts might have succeeded if Potamian had not been moved in 1891 to the Institute's training college in Ireland. Disaster followed; his teaching and educational direction were necessary for the school's survival at a critical period, and in 1895 the building was sold. It says much for the reputation which the Christian Brothers had built up in South London that the school was able to survive in a small nearby villa, and later move to Denmark Hill and thence to Beulah Hill in 1904 and gradually build up its numbers again. St Joseph's Academy also prospered; it moved to Blackheath in 1919.[182] This belongs to the history of twentieth-century education, when the anti-clerical and secularist movement in Europe strengthened the Catholic orders in England, just as the demands of the 1902 Act became pressing.

Jewish education

The education of the Jewish community of London during this period provides illuminating comparisons and contrasts with that of their Christian fellow citizens – like the Anglicans they had to solve organizational problems in an expanding city and diversifying economy and, as with the Roman Catholics, deep historical social divisions within their ranks complicated both the purposes and provision of schooling and their relationship with the wider civic and national community. Moreover the lines of their suburban dispersal were particularly sharp and disclose the topographical determinants of secondary schooling even more clearly than with other communities.

Almost from the time of their re-entry or re-settlement in the seventeenth century London Jewry was divided into two communities, the Sephardim and the Ashkenazim. The communal history of Jewry in London is the story of the attempt to impose cohesion and self-discipline upon its members and in the nineteenth century these London citizens approached their problems in a characteristically 'Victorian' and English way.[183]

By the beginning of the nineteenth century there may have been between 20,000 and 26,000 Jews in England, of whom 15 to 20,000 were in London, a population which had doubled or trebled between 1750 and 1800.[184] The Ashkenazi community was itself divided into several groups, and the desperate influx of destitute immigrants pouring into London throughout the second half of the eighteenth century was still putting immense pressure upon them.[185] The Sephardim may usefully be compared with the old Catholic gentry families, and like them they desired not divisive and special provision, but such assimilation with their non-Jewish neighbours as was compatible with the maintenance of their faith and the limits of their civil status. Many prosperous members of the Ashkenazi community had also become Anglicized and shared this attitude.[186] The first half of the nineteenth century was a comparatively stable period numerically for London Jewry, there was only a trickle of immigration and natural increase accounted for the growth of numbers to about 30,000 by 1850.[187] The most important demographic development was the growth of the Jewish middle class. Jewish society was still a pyramid with a broad base but the lowest rung of occupations had now been taken by the Irish. At mid-century probably about 5 per cent were upper middle and 30 per cent middle class. Thirty years later these estimates are 14.6 per cent and 42.2 per cent and Jewish occupations on the eve of another great wave of mass immigration were showing increasing diversity.[188] Occupational was accompanied by topographical change, and by 1850 about one-third of the London Jewish population lived outside the traditional area of the City and its east end.[189] The building of synagogues plots their spread to Finsbury, the West End, Bayswater, Kensington, Maida Vale and north and east to Highbury, Islington, Dalston, Hackney. In the later part of the century Jews from Eastern Europe once again filled the East End, but 'if 1880–1914 is the period *par excellence* of the immigrant quarter, it is equally the period of the rise of Jewish suburbia'.[190]

Demographic, social and topographical change put pressure on religious institutions. The problems of the beginning of the century forced the Ashkenazim, like the Anglicans, to co-operate and evolve institutions capable of cutting across mere congregational or parochial groupings. In 1802 Solomon Herschel became Rabbi of the Great Synagogue and then Presiding Rabbi of the three City synagogues, the Great (1722), the Hambro (1724/5) and the New (1761, Bricklayers Hall in Leadenhall Street) and in 1808 he concluded a treaty between these and the Western Synagogue. For the first time the London Ashkenazim could speak with a united voice.[191] In 1835 the Conjoint Synagogues had been brought into being and in 1870 the United Synagogue. In 1842 Herschel was succeeded by Dr Nathan Adler and under him the Jews of the metropolis further developed a centralized ecclesiastical organization which had a close parallel with non-Jewish institutions. The Jewish church had not only to keep its 'parochial provision' up to date, it had to develop 'diocesan' organization and perspective. An episcopal flavour began to creep into the Chief Rabbinate.[192]

All these challenges and changes had strong implications for education. As with other denominations the first to be recognized was the need for schooling for the Jewish masses. Not only was this necessary if movements of assimilation and toleration were to be encouraged, the Jews shared in the general belief in schooling as a social discipline as well as mental, moral and religious training. This was the background to the founding of the Jews' Free School in Spitalfields in 1817 which at first united somewhat uneasily the Talmud Torah of the Great Synagogue, giving advanced Jewish instruction to nominated pupils, with a school on the Lancastrian system for Hebrew and English elementary instruction. This became one of the most efficient elementary schools not only in London but in the whole country, and Jewish social structure and culture gave it more continuity and coincidence with the secondary stage than was the case with contemporary Gentile schools, except perhaps those of the Wesleyans. From the beginning the school had remarkable features. Its first headmaster, H. N. Solomon, had a liberal conception of elementary education, but it was under his successor, Moses Angel, that the school achieved its greatest distinction. He was one of the most remarkable teachers and headmasters of Victorian England. By 1879 his school was 'the largest educational establishment in the British dominions' with 1600 boys and over 1000 girls; by 1894 there were some 3600 pupils. It had been recognized in 1853 as a training institution for Jewish teachers and had early developed many of the characteristics of a 'higher grade school' with a broader curiculum and far more effective methods of teaching than most such schools. 'Of the 48 teachers on the staff, no less than one-third were pursuing advanced University courses of study.' In 1898 a technical wing was added at a cost of £19,298. It has been claimed that this school was a prototype of the large London secondary school of today, or the day department of a large polytechnic. The Jewish community was true to history when it reconstituted this school as a secondary school after the Second World War, and later developed it on comprehensive lines.[193]

In 1820 the Westminster Jews' Free School was reorganized from the Talmud Torah of the Western Synagogue. In 1846 a school for girls was added and in 1853 the two were amalgamated in Greek Street.[194] Another mid-century venture which provided for social and cultural regeneration within the Jewish community and also had strong overlap with the emerging needs of secondary education was the Jews' General and Literary Scientific Institution, opened in 1845 in the Bricklayers Hall, and supported by Dr Adler, Hananel de Castro and many of the leaders of the London Jewish community – Goldsmiths, Montefiores, Rothschilds. It provided excellent social and educational facilities, a library, and eventually preparation for the Royal Society of Arts examinations and it was even suggested that it might provide schooling on the 'Birkbeck system', particularly for clerical and technical training. But its influential supporters fell away, and were in any case fearful of creating a ghetto, while its more humble members desired more specifically Jewish studies. The building was then occupied by a comparable Anglican venture which had been started in Crosby Hall and it is interesting to compare the decline of the Jewish experiment with the success of this Anglican enterprise to provide educational facilities for City youths, mostly clerks, which kept going long enough to merge into later aided systems for further and technical education. It became the City of London College. The very success of the struggle for Jewish emancipation may have contributed to the closing of the Jews' Literary Scientific Institution.[195]

Middle-class Jewish children like young Christian Londoners attended private schools of various grades,[196] but some schools for them received community support. A school attached to the West London Synagogue in Lincoln's Inn Fields opened in 1845, at first for choristers and the children of the poor, but it was soon giving a superior kind of education for which parents paid. The headmaster was trained by William Ellis and as Christian children were admitted it could receive government grants – this synagogue had always been suspected of unorthodox, even heretical tendencies. After several moves the schools settled in Red Lion Square where 300 boys, 150 girls and an infants' school were taught on what was variously described as 'the Birkbeck system' or 'Pestalozzian lines'. Monitors were used, but rather as prefects, and they were given a special room which was also fitted up as a museum, and the school had a laboratory. Inspectors' reports, including those of Matthew Arnold, were enthusiastic but in 1872 the school decided to withdraw from government inspection and was developing along middle-class lines. The Jewish community recognized the duty to 'foster amongst Jewish Englishmen that spirit of independence and self-reliance which is one of the noblest characteristics of our Anglo-Saxon brethren'. In 1878 it became the West Metropolitan Jewish School for Middle Class Pupils and eventually the Jewish Middle Class School. But the boys' school was already in decline as competition from the reformed endowed schools made it unnecessary; middle-class Jews preferred their sons to be educated with those of their non-Jewish neighbours. The girls' school was handsomely rebuilt near Bedford Square by the generosity of Miss Goldsmid, who was concerned with the training of Jewish teachers, and renamed the Jewish High Class School for Girls; it prepared for the Cambridge Higher Locals until competition from the suburban girls' schools brought its closure in 1896.[197]

In the mid nineteenth century, a time of emancipation and acceptance, and of strong religious leadership from the 'Grand Dukes' of Anglo-Jewry and from the Chief Rabbi, Dr Nathan Adler, some systematization of provision was attempted. He came from a learned German rabbinical family, and brought a European perspective to the confused and compromising scene of Jewish education. Within a month of becoming Chief Rabbi he had circulated his policy to all congregations throughout the British Empire, including plans for educational establishments 'from those which are calculated for infants ... up to such as are to extend their salutory influence to the future, by training proper and efficient teachers'. His task might be compared with that of the Anglican founders of King's College, or the leaders of the National Society in their attempts to extend its work more widely through the social hierarchy, or with the problems of Cardinal Manning. Adler, looking round the ragged metropolitan scene, had to devise his system from anything he could lay his hands on.[198] He planned a college which would train students for the Jewish ministry or as readers and future wardens of congregations and produce 'a new class of spiritual leader, one learned not only in the details of biblical and Jewish law and in Talmudic literature, but who also shared in the intellectual interests and activities of the larger world into which Jewry was entering'. It was also necessary to train preachers, for the pulpit was being established in the synagogue, and nineteenth-century Jews, like nineteenth-century Christians, were much addicted to sermons, until recently considered both heretical and dangerous.[199] The practical plan which Adler proposed had elements both of the Nonconformist academies of the eighteenth century and the more recent University and King's Colleges and their Schools. As well as a college there was an urgent need for a 'public Day School for the sons of our middle ranks' on the lines of the City of London School. The institution should provide sound general and liberal education for boys, with religious instruction, and clerical education for the higher students, who would then go to University College for secular studies.

In spite of some opposition from influential laymen who objected to the segregation which such a school would encourage, the scheme was at last got off the ground in 1855 and the college and school opened in a house in Finsbury Square, then still the centre of Jewish social and intellectual life, with 33 pupils. Dr Louis Loewe, who had been proprietor of a private boarding-school at Brighton, was headmaster. The venture was financed from community funds and by subscriptions, donations, and fees of £10 a year, and support was expected not only from the nation but from the empire. From the beginning the Sephardim also supported the venture and provided the first holder of the first scholarship endowed at the College in 1856 to commemorate the first election of a Jewish Lord Mayor of London.

The Jews' College, like University and King's College, demonstrated the same problem of definition of secondary and higher education. At first the school was better attended and more prosperous than the college. In 1863 there were 71 boys and only 3 students, but under the principalship of Michael Friedländer, which lasted from 1865 to 1907, the real needs of the Jewish community in the metropolis, the nation and the empire shaped and changed the college and it emerged as a professional institution, corresponding to the theological colleges of both Anglican and Nonconformist churches. In 1881 the Jews' College moved from Finsbury to Tavistock Square, in order to be near University College where its predominantly theological students attended for secular studies. Two years earlier, in 1879, the school department had closed. The centre of gravity of well-to-do Jewry had shifted westward, and there was 'a growing indisposition on the part of the community to send their sons to a Jewish day school, however excellently taught'. The same attitude shaped the higher part of the college, which had originally been intended for the education of students who did not want to enter the ministry as well as for more vocational studies. Like the Roman Catholic gentry, however, more wealthy Jewish families preferred their sons to have the opportunity of mixing with other young men for their university education. The college did maintain some connection with the secondary level of education for it became necessary to reconstitute an 'Elementary class' for boys between thirteen and sixteen to prepare them for London matriculation, but its pupils were all intending ministers.[200]

Jewish middle-class education in the nineteenth century was overwhelmingly influenced by the desire of Anglo-Jewry to avoid segregation. Less well-to-do middle-class Jews were attempting to use the endowed Christian schools. This was challenged in the 'Bedford Case' of 1839 when the Lord Chancellor ruled that they were not eligible. 'This case', he said, 'is one more instance of the normal aversion of Jews under conditions of tolerance to the segregation of their children.'[201] It was therefore all the more important that schools were being founded at this time with no sectarian tests. University College School had Jews amongst its most generous supporters – Isaac Lyon Goldsmid and two others found the £30,000 to buy the Gower Street site of the school. Many Jewish boys were among its pupils. The City of London School had no religious tests – it was used by Roman Catholic boys, and Jewish boys distinguished themselves there. In 1851, of its 600 pupils 17 were Jews, including the school captain.[202]

It was not long however before schools barred to them by the Bedford Case began to admit Jewish boys. In remodelling their constitutions the schools reported on by the Clarendon Commissioners made it possible for Jews to attend. Some even opened Jewish houses – Dr Chotzer's at Harrow, for example; and the headmaster of Dulwich College 'exerted himself with zeal, generosity of feeling and good sense' to secure admission of Jews in 1870. But on the whole schools of this kind did not attract Jewish parents; they disliked boarding-education and were revolted by the fagging system even in its reformed style. It was all the more important therefore that the Taunton Inquiry schools should be opened to them. A deputation of the Board of Deputies of British Jews waited upon Forster, who was able to reassure them.

Although the Endowed Schools' Act of 1869 and its aftermath were of great significance for Jewish secondary education, many Jewish boys had already been attending such schools, and had been received with toleration and kindness under the watchful eye of such headmasters as

Dr Major of King's College School.[203] Some London schools, such as the Cowper Street Schools, in areas with large Jewish communities employed Jewish teachers, not always for specialist Hebrew teaching alone.[204] But it was the Taunton reforms which regularized the situation and led to the collapse of the school attached to the Jews' College and the boys' school in Red Lion Square.

During this period, it has been said, the Ashkenazi Jewish community was struggling 'painfully towards a system of education which was new and was eventually to produce the Anglo-Jew, that unique species so puzzling to Jews abroad; the Anglo-Jew who could live a happy and complete life in this tolerant environment of England . . .'.[205] This was helped by the fact that Londoners as a whole were still seeking a system of secondary education. When a stage of education was systematized, and even more when it was secularized, the Jewish community was pushed towards what might be called sectarian provision. When prosperous and Anglicized middle-class Jews moved out into the suburbs, they contributed to the growing demand for the state to provide for secondary education, but as this system developed in the twentieth century there grew with it some demand for special Jewish schools – this 'Jewish Secondary School Movement' belongs to the present century.[206]

The Middle-Class Schools' Corporation: a case study

One London school almost epitomizes the evolution of secondary education from middle-class schooling in the nineteenth century. In origin this might be classed as an Anglican enterprise, for it sprang from the initiative of the Reverend William Rogers, that 'Liberal Churchman of the strenuous sort'[207] already encountered devising ingenious educational institutions, including a middle-class school, in one of Blomfield's reorganized districts.[208] His labours had received some public recognition; he had been appointed to the Newcastle Commission, to a stall in St Paul's (but 'without any provender in it') and in 1863 to the Rectory of St Botolph's without Bishopsgate[209] which may be said to have contributed significantly throughout the century to the formulation of ideas of metropolitan education. When Rogers took over the parish its schools were already providing for a higher level of education than some ward or National schools, but he thought poorly of them. The catechism monopolized 'far more than its fair share of attention' and innovation was resisted. Soon Rogers got the charity garb worn by the children abolished, the school placed under government inspection, and all children from the ward admitted 'whether they could produce their baptismal certificates or not'. Less than three years later the boys' school had five masters, a curriculum teaching not only the 'three Rs' but English grammar and composition, letter-writing, book-keeping, history, geography, drawing, music; it had a circulating library, cricket and football clubs (playing in the Victoria Park), a boys' drill club every

Thursday evening, and all this for only 2d a week. Evening classes in subjects such as higher mathematics and mensuration provided opportunities for young men 'fitting themselves for the walk of life they may pursue by acquiring a sound, practical, and commercial education', and others for boys in subjects 'essential to a sound commercial education' were 4d–6d a week. Plans for more ambitious schools were endangered by the Great Eastern Railway, which swallowed up the school site. Complex and indomitable financial and territorial negotiations produced new schools in 1870–1, not only on the old level, useful enough for City boys, but also for 'a better class of boy' at 9d a week, under the Reverend J. H. Smith, who came from St Thomas Charterhouse Middle Class School to be Rogers's curate especially to help with the project. A middle-class school for girls completed this educational complex, which in 1874 comprised:

	Pupils
Upper Boys' School	70
Lower Boys' School	313
Upper Girls' School	160
Lower Girls' School	129
Infants'	168
Evening classes	85

Their development was very much under the supervision of Rogers, and of Smith until he left in 1875 to become headmaster of Alleyn's School at Dulwich, by which time the schools had amalgamated as the Upper and Lower Schools of the Ward of Bishopsgate. When the Board schools began to cater for elementary education this school concentrated on the higher level for all its pupils. In 1884 the government grant was given up, as it cramped the curriculum. The headmaster in 1885 was a science graduate, the school was inspected by Fellows of Balliol. Two years later the railway was again advancing upon it and the school had to close, but by that time Rogers's enterprise beyond his parish and wider educational developments enabled it to find a haven in the Central Foundation Schools, which must next be described.[210]

Rogers's robust figure (kept in trim by an occasional outing with the Puckridge Hounds) and practical mind (perhaps equally well exercised in discussion with his friend Jowett at Balliol or with Dean Stanley at Westminster)[211] had soon become well known in the City. His educational achievements in his present and former parishes and as chairman of the governors of Dulwich College[212] made it natural for men to look to him for leadership in this sphere. As he moved about his parish and the City, he found that he had much 'to do with the class of people such as clerks and what may be called the lower middle class', and parents frequently asked him when he was going to do something to establish middle-class schools. 'The more I enquired into the matter, the more I found that there was a great demand for that sort of school' among 'clerks and tradesmen with moderate resources'. He was moreover convinced that the City would be ready with support and was over-optimistic about getting help from idle City Charities.[213] Rogers prepared a circular which he 'scattered . . . far and wide in civic circles' inviting 'earnest attention' to a scheme 'for extending the means of education to the people employed in the City of London. . . . There is a large middle class composed of tradesmen and people employed in the City for whom no public education is provided for they are naturally enough unwilling to send their children to the Ward or National Schools, and are debarred by various circumstances from availing themselves of the advantages offered in St Paul's, Merchant Taylors', and the City of London Schools.' His experience in St Thomas Charterhouse was cited to show that a school of that kind could be self-supporting if the cost of site and buildings was met, and he was confident that the City Companies, the great commercial firms and so on, 'will no doubt cheerfully take part in the establishment' of such a school. Finsbury was proposed as a good area, 'not only on account of its open and airy situation, and being at the same time accessible to the Metropolitan railway termini', but also because a site might be had from the Ecclesiastical Commissioners.[214] The result was a meeting 'of Bankers, Merchants, Clergymen, Magistrates, Members of the Corporation of London, and other Gentlemen held at the Mansion House of the Lord Mayor', who took the Chair on 7 November 1865 to give practical effect to this 'Scheme propounded' by Rogers. It was resolved to establish a school 'which shall prepare the Scholars for the practical Work of Life', and a committee was set up. Its activity and expedition reflected not only City leaders' recognition of the needs of the class they wished to help, but also their own need for boys who could usefully enter their employ and take advantage of the usual methods of informal in-service training in the 'great City Corporations, Banking Houses and Mercantile Establishments in London, all of whom are deeply interested in the cause of Education'.[215] The committee and its subcommittees set about fundraising and ensuring civic support, co-opting the Sheriffs, the Masters of the twelve great Livery Companies, the Governor of the Bank of England, the Bishop of London, the Dean of St Paul's, the City Members of Parliament and so forth, and by 20 November had prepared a comprehensive scheme not only for the first school, for 800 to 1000 day boys, but also for other schools to be 'in communication' with this first or central school. It was agreed that Finsbury would be the best situation as at that point the 'Railways, North and South, converge and give facilities for children living in the Suburbs as well as Children of Parents resident in the City'. The curriculum was to be a preparation for 'the Industrial and Commercial work of life', and 'such as will not have the effect of excluding any of the Classes for whose benefit the Schools are founded' – a careful piece of social observation which had practical long-term consequences.[216] A deputation despatched to the Charity Commissioners, although well received, produced no practical effect.[217] Fund-raising occupied much of the committee's time, for however cheerfully the City might subscribe, it did not do it readily. By July 1866 £54,103 had been promised, £46,221 actually paid. Memorials to the Bank of England eventually secured its £1000; an application to Common Council eventually extracted £1000 'in aid of the Fund for establishing a system of Middle-Class Education'.[218] The City Companies received reminders and memorials and gradually produced their contributions. The list of business companies subscribing was impressive, and even more so was that of individuals – Rogers himself with £1000, William Ellis the same sum.[219] A full report on the City Charities was commissioned.

Where personal influence could be brought to bear there was limited success – the Datchelor's Charity of St Andrew's Undershaft gave £3000, Sir Sydney Waterlow, himself a generous subscriber, undertook to get information about the charities of St Edmund King and Martyr, and in 1871 the trustees of the Barnes Charity of St Margaret's Lothbury used their obsolete funds. But it was on the whole a disappointing business, which was considered to have destroyed any hope of establishing a *system* of schools.[220]

In the meantime the Charter had been secured, and the enterprise was incorporated under the title of the Middle Class Schools' Corporation, with power 'to erect one or more school or schools in the Metropolis and the suburbs thereof, and to carry on therein a system of education of a practical character, based on sound religious principles, and such as shall be calculated to fit the scholars for the industrial and commercial work of life . . .'. The headmaster was to be a member of one of the universities of the United Kingdom, the Bishop of London to be Visitor, and subscribers of £100 were life governors with power to elect a council of twenty-one members, plus the Bishop and the Lord Mayor.[221]

Getting a site was more difficult than getting a Charter and ambitions gradually dwindled. At first it was thought that the governors of the Charterhouse, which was said to be moving into the country, might sell the whole or part of their building, but Merchant Taylors' School got in first. Clements Inn was investigated. The Proprietors of the London Institution in Finsbury Square 'declined to avail themselves of the proposition to amalgamate'. In the end after some hesitation the former French Protestant Hospital in Bath Street, City Road, was accepted in May 1866 'for temporary purposes' for three years, with an option on permanent possession. Negotiations with the Ecclesiastical Commissioners for a permanent site eventually fixed on Cowper Street where land and leases of neighbouring property, including a Nonconformist tabernacle and a public house called the Barking Dogs, cost the Corporation around £29,000. The lowest tender for an almost agressively plain building was accepted – £15,787.[222] Later in the same year the committee expended another £3500 for York House and its grounds in Southwark for a second school, for 'the necessity exists equally in other portions of the Metropolis'. It was clear that funds were already running out, and for the 'erection of the second school, and the development of the system throughout London, further funds will be necessary'. Rogers was hoping to establish schools 'all around London. . . . We shall include places like Hoxton and Islington.'[223]

At this early stage not only financial but religious difficulties inevitably raised their heads. Rogers was convinced that sectarian education was unnecessary. 'I believe the class who would come to these schools are those who fill the chapels and churches, and therefore I do not think we shall be bound to look after the religious instruction as we are in a National School, one founded for missionary purposes . . .'.[224] His impatience with those who raised the sectarian issue gained him his nickname, for, called upon to speak at the inaugural ceremony of the school on the Bath Street site, he somewhat incautiously said, 'Hang economy, hang theology, let us begin.' As the notable and evangelical City philanthropist, George Moore, said, cancelling his subscription for £1000, 'Mr Rogers may be an atheist but at any rate he is a gentleman.'[225] This £1000 caused some trouble to retrieve: eventually Moore relented and subsequently also endowed scripture prizes in the school, making provision that if it should become 'entirely secular' the money was to be transferred to other middle-class schools.[226]

It was not only the more crotchety City subscribers who had misgivings. Canon Woodard inevitably thought the worst. Writing to J. P. Gassiot, of Clapham, wine merchant and scientist, one of the most generous and tireless supporters of the school, he made his position clear – unsectarian education was unreligious education, although elsewhere he angrily declared that he did not object 'to Jews, Parsees (as Mr Rogers told us), Socinian and other sectaries uniting to obtain a secular education for their children'. Woodard was pressed to start an opposition school in London but evidently thought success unlikely.[227]

At least from the point of view of practical success, Hang-Theology Rogers was justified. The denominational issue was apparently either solved or unimportant in what became the Cowper Street Schools. From the beginning the Bishop of London, the broad-minded and educationally experienced Tait, was involved. He consented to become Visitor, and acquiesced in an early resolution proposed by the Nonconformist Samuel Morley and seconded by Woodard's correspondent, Gassiot, that 'It is the intention of the originators of these Middle Class Schools that in all the arrangements the rights of conscience and the liberty of opinion should be carefully maintained and preserved.' The newly appointed headmaster, the Reverend William Jowitt from St Thomas Charterhouse Middle Class School, had been ordained deacon and priest by Tait who testified to his devotion to education and added that 'he is well acquainted with the feelings of parents and children of the Middle Class, and has the power of attracting their sympathies'. Jowitt with one of the governors waited on the Bishop to arrange 'a friendly and private conference' with the governing body in July 1867, presumably to discuss the school's plan for religious education. When the school was in session Tait visited it and 'all its class rooms . . . and had expressed himself satisfied with the arrangements'.[228] When Tait was elevated to the see of Canterbury, the Council at once approached the new Bishop, Jackson, from Lincoln, who had been headmaster of the Islington Proprietary School and had extensive parish experience in that part of London early in his career. 'Emboldened by their knowledge of your Lordship's deep interest in the Education of the young, and of your previous experience of the wants and circumstances of the Metropolis, the Council feel certain that your Lordship will appreciate their exertions in securing for the thronging populace of this vast City and its Suburbs a provision for that Middle Class Education which has hitherto been so lamentably deficient.' Jackson acknowledged his 'warm and deep interest in the cause of education and especially that of the great middle class, which was the very backbone of our body corporate'. He attributed their neglect partly to such events as the Eldon judgment, perpetuating classical schools 'where they could not possibly be needed'. The new examinations system had 'as yet reached a very little way below the surface. . . . The result was that the middle classes had been receiving an education not fitted to bring out their mental faculties or to discharge their duties in life.' These schools could remedy this by teaching 'based on principles which, combined with good sense and tact, enabled a master to secure soundness and depth of religious teaching, without interfering with the religious scruples or objections of parents'.[229]

This tactful policy paid off. Rogers declared: 'The religious question has never assumed any more portentous proportions than the withdrawal from prayers of a few Roman Catholics and of one little fellow whose father called himself a "freethinker".' The school was attended by a large number of Jewish boys and Jewish masters were appointed.[230]

The early history of the school was one of unbroken success in achieving its carefully defined objectives. In its temporary premises 500 boys seemed to be the maximum possible and by the end of the first term this figure had almost been reached. In the following March 650 had been squeezed in and 200 applicants were besieging the door. 'The great success which has attended the present experiment shows the correctness of the view entertained, that there was a very large demand for middle-class education in London.' 'Wherever I go into such places as banking houses and the like', said Rogers, 'the clerks all thank me of their own accord. They say how much obliged they are, it is the very thing they have all been longing for.'[231] The laying of the foundation stone of the new building in December 1868 was something of a civic occasion, the Mayor and Sheriffs in official robes, driving to the place in their official carriages, the City of London Militia providing a guard of honour; the boys acted as choristers, the headmaster read prayers, the City MP (Tite) thanked everybody. He described how he had in his capacity as employer 'examined lads who had learnt little that was of value in business. They could rarely read well, and never write well. Lately a youth was sent to a friend to see what could be made of him. He had learnt a little Latin and Greek and taken two or three prizes; but he had not been taught the multiplication table . . .'. The school should aim at 'a good commercial education, coupled with as much religion as could be introduced in the limited time available for it . . .'. The Lord Mayor emphasized that the school unlike many large foundations was not to be allowed to glide imperceptibly away from the class it was intended to benefit, 'the middle class and especially the lower middle class'; they must therefore keep the cost down, or increase the number of branches of instruction or lengthen the school life of the pupil – give value for money in fact.[232]

Some of these civic statements may have appeared somewhat blunt, even at the time, but there is no doubt that the curriculum of the school was the basis of its continuing success. Here boys received for £1 1s a quarter (by 1879 £5 5s a year) an education 'not much inferior to that of the sons of gentleman for which £100 or £150 is usually paid'. After the move into Cowper Street numbers stood steadily at 1000 'except during one term when we had 1250 and were compelled to fit up the cellars as classrooms'. 'There is no better passport to a City bank or counting house than an education at the Middle Class Schools, and every week brings applications for promising boys.'[233]

Its distinctive feature was the absence of classics as part of the general course, and thorough and effective teaching especially of subjects considered vocationally useful. An early university examiner described how in the absence of Latin he was 'prepared to expect greater completeness in the teaching of other subjects; but . . . did not anticipate finding that degree of thoroughness which pervades the teaching. In my opinion the absence of the classics is more than compensated for by the sciences and the proficiency evinced in English and French.' The interest of the boys was shown 'by the bright, intelligent manner in which they answered' the examiner's questions. He recommended tentatively that trigonometry should replace book-keeping. The headmaster had to resist some pressure to teach Latin, and looked forward to the day when the universities would dispense with it – he considered it 'hard that the London University did not do so now'.[234] In 1870 when Joshua Fitch inspected the school, Latin was still not included and he considered the headmaster was right – the 'slender knowledge' of it 'attainable by boys who were leaving the school for business at fifteen' often proved a very 'sterile possession'.[235]

From the beginning the mathematical teaching was outstandingly good, and was in the hands of the man who in 1874 became the second headmaster, and a significant figure in the development of ideas of secondary education at this period – Richard Wormell. He had been trained at Borough Road, was for seven years headmaster of public elementary schools, qualified himself with London degrees, eventually obtaining his Doctorate of Science.[236] He was appointed as one of the first staff at a salary of £180[237] and was loudly cheered by the boys when his teaching was praised at the Cowper Street foundation ceremony. His 'unremitting exertions' had been crowned with great success and inspired the Lord Mayor to hope that when it was seen that this system of education 'supplied the wants of the people, thoughtful men all over the country would imitate the example set in London', especially as national pride was damaged by the fact that 'for years past our middle class education had been inferior to that of France and Germany . . .'.[238]

Wormell contributed to another important aspect of the curriculum, its science teaching, important from the beginning, and with the new building it was possible to make proper provision to give 'greater efficiency' to its teaching. The Gilchrist Educational Trust gave grants for science apparatus and the governors frequently allowed expenditure for this purpose. When the new hall was added to the building in 1875 'mechanical rooms' beneath it were 'supplied with science apparatus from the valuable collections of Mr Gassiot' and the council began to contemplate a fully developed technical department.[239] Dr Lyon Playfair had already given an excellent report on the science teaching and had indicated that 'if the undertaking was properly supported by the citizens of London, the school could become one of the glories of the metropolis'. His suggestion that the 'process of instruction' might be more developed was evidently followed up, for three years later the University of London examiner remarked upon 'the habits of accurate observation and manipulative skills evinced by the pupils', which convinced the council of the 'propriety of giving larger space and better appliances for Practical Scientific Instruction'.[240]

So important did this side of its curriculum become that the next stage in the history of the Cowper Street School belongs properly to the development of technical education in London, but it was important that this experiment above all helped to redefine *general* education for the middle classes and provide a context in which more specialized or vocational aspects could usefully develop – the curriculum included music, gymnastics, and sports such as fives, as well as utilitarian and liberal subjects seen to be of relevance to boys leaving school at fifteen or sixteen.[241] Fitch's report in 1870 emphasized that 'the general character of the School was remarkably life-like and intelligent and its effects on the mental activity of the pupils was very marked. He had rarely seen a school so thoroughly pervaded with the spirit of work, or affording such strong evidence of the sympathy and interest with which the scholars followed the explanations of their teachers.' The linguistic training considered essential to a liberal education was here supplied by the systematic study of English and French. In the sixth form boys were able to give careful analysis of 'a difficult English sentence', showed a critical and detailed knowledge of certain works of Shakespeare and Spenser, and in general demonstrated 'that their studies had taught them to use their own language with precision and judgement'. The discipline of the school was excellent and 'was largely owing to the perfect influence of the Headmaster and to the loyalty with which he had inspired the boys'. At the beginning of each day 'each class headed by its own master ... went through various quasi-military movements and evolutions' to the music of the school brass band, so acquiring 'not only healthful physical exercise, but a manliness of bearing and a pride and interest in their school'. This gives a glimpse of the growing identification of the middle classes, even of the lower middle classes, with the state, with overt political power, for the growing impact of the Army competitive examinations on schools had to be matched by changes in sentiment and conviction. It would have been unthinkable to imagine boys from this class in the ranks of the Army say at Waterloo – even at Inkerman – somewhere between the Wellingtons and the Raglans and the men whom they commanded. While this school did not yet directly respond to Army examinations, in schools of this kind a social and political transformation was now being both reinforced and demonstrated.[242]

Cowper Street kept its distinctive curriculum, though in due course Latin was introduced for those boys who wanted it. Some boys were entered for the Oxford and Cambridge Locals and 'some of the boys, whom it was impossible to restrain, have carved out for themselves distinguished careers at the Universities', as Rogers put it.[243] But this was the exception; the age of leaving continued for some time to be lower than in the 'schools of the first grade'. In 1879 of 1150 pupils there were fewer than fifteen in the sixth form.[244] By 1885 Dr Wormell reported that the 'altered state of the educational arrangements of the Metropolis' was bringing about a different balance in the school. There was an upward tendency in the age of admission, nearly 50 per cent of the boys entering that January had passed the VI and VII standards in an elementary school, and while in 1878 there had been 455 boys below the third form and 687 above, in 1885 the figures were 148 and 759. All the boys still came from the middle classes, from those who could afford to keep them at elementary schools long enough to gain a scholarship to Cowper Street, but he considered it an 'ominous sign for the future' that 'a Clerk's desk was the summit of their ambition'.[245] What had been the chief purpose of the school was becoming a danger to its future as educational standards and aspirations were rising. Rogers himself considered that the 'prospects with which it set out have been to a considerable extent thwarted – and nobody is more gratified that such has been the case than I am – by Mr Forster's Act of 1870, and the consequent gradual levelling up of the educational condition of the metropolis. The cost of education has increased with the raising of the standard . . .'.[246]

Financial support proved insufficient to fulfil the hopes of the founders. The 'school in fact never became self-supporting after all, and the £75,000 which . . . has been expended on it has been none too little to maintain it in efficiency'.[247] The plan to build other schools was early abandoned. The Southwark site was sold and hopes of founding a girls' school were frustrated and delayed.[248] Continued pleas to the City Charities had little success at this stage, and the occasional generosity of a City Company, usually for specific purposes, such as the £105 from the Merchant Taylors for the 'Mechanical School Room' in 1874, or the contributions of the Drapers and Clothworkers for technical education in 1877, was inadequate.[249] What had been glowingly described at the outset of the enterprise as 'gratifying proof that munificence was not extinct in London, and that the citizens were as capable as those of old of displaying a noble generosity on behalf of their own generation and of posterity'[250] had once again proved that private enterprise of this kind could not do the whole job. It had also demonstrated that the middle classes were certainly not unwilling to accept help for the education of their sons, and this at the very time when Matthew Arnold was writing that 'The great middle classes of this country are conscious of no weaknesses, no inferiority; they do not want any one to provide anything for them.'[251] He was of course urging the middle classes to accept state aid, but before that stage could be reached the possibilities of reformed endowments had to be exhausted. The next stage of the history of the school founded by the Middle Class Schools Corporation therefore belongs not only to the development of technical and commercial education, but to the struggle with the 'Dead Hand' of charity.

VI

'It's past praying for':
The reform of London endowments

The nineteenth-century inheritance

Many experiments and expedients for devising and providing schools for the middle classes contained an element of philanthropy – confessional, sectarian, civic, personal – for the 'Contours of Early Victorian Benevolence' were ample and luxuriant, and education at this level was recognized as a need, an investment, an insurance. Here the nineteenth was building upon the experience of the eighteenth century, both of charity and self-help. Amendments and interpretations of the Statute of Charitable Uses of 1601 had established education as a public benefit irrespective of its connection with poverty as the criterion of charitable status.[1]

Some interesting schools were provided charitably for children of a particular occupation, belief or community. The Clergy Orphans' School grew from the Corporation for the Relief of Poor Widows and Children of Clergymen and the Stewards of the Feast of the Sons of the Clergy. At first only assistance with apprenticeship was given, but in 1749 a society was formed for 'Maintaining and Educating poor Orphans of Clergymen . . .' and from this grew the Clergy Orphan Schools, one to be in Yorkshire, the other, in London, which was opened in the rural village of Acton in 1804 and incorporated as 'The Society for Clothing, Maintaining and Educating poor Orphans of Clergymen of the Established Church . . . until of age to be put apprentice'. To ensure proper supervision by the committee the schools were moved in 1812 to St John's Wood, boys and girls side by side, until in 1855 the expansion of Lord's Cricket Ground and the gift of land at Canterbury brought another move. The headmaster was in orders and the education included Latin but was of a practical type. In 1810 the 'Madras system' was introduced and in 1840 the 'scheme of instruction' was revised on the basis of a higher commercial education.[2] Later in the century St John's Foundation School was established in Clapton in 1852 for the sons of poor clergy financed by subscriptions from private donors and collections in churches. Regulations safeguarded the right to presentation of foundation scholars. In 1867 it was a classical school with 63 foundation boarders and some private day boys, taught by three resident graduate masters, with visiting teachers for French, drawing and drilling. It moved to Leatherhead in 1872 and later also took the sons of laymen.[3]

The Freemasons attempted from 1798 to provide education for the sons of needy members and by 1852 had enough funds to buy Lordship House in Wood Green, Tottenham, a village attractive for schools. There 70 children were admitted in 1857 and eight years later it was rebuilt to accommodate 215. At that time it was giving a 'thorough commercial education', but by the end of the century, when £150,000 had been received in subscriptions, it moved to new premises at Bushey and was giving a 'sound public school education'.[4]

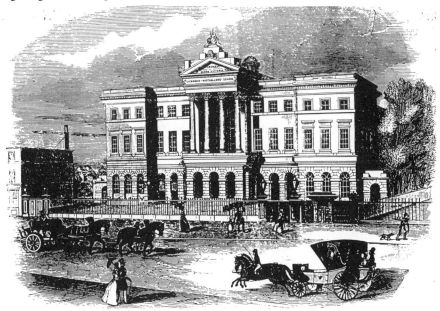

The Licensed Victuallers' School
(for ground plan, see p. 444)

An interesting school which emerged from the growth of Friendly Societies in the late eighteenth century was established by the Licensed Victuallers, whose trade involved physical danger and uncertainty of life. In 1802 their Friendly Society took the lease of Kennington House on the Cornwall Estate to establish a school for the children of deceased or impoverished fellow traders, to be 'soundly instructed' in the doctrines of the established church, reading, writing, arithmetic and geography, and the girls in plain needlework, household and laundry work. Its aim was to avoid 'over-education', and fit them for good apprenticeships or household positions. By 1836 success required better premises, and the Friendly Society secured incorporation by Letters Patent as the Society of Licensed Victuallers. The old house was demolished and Lord Melbourne, in the name of the King, laid the foundation stone of the handsome classical building, a monument to the concern of 'individual tradesmen who have to contend against peculiar disadvantages and burdens . . .' and who had thus rescued over 700 boys and girls from poverty and ignorance. By 1844 the new building contained 112 pupils.

The Warehousemen and Clerks' Schools, Croydon

This useful school of about 150 pupils remained in Kennington until 1922 when the Victuallers sold the building to the Navy, Army and Air Force Institutes and moved the school to Slough.[5]

Another school catering for a particular occupation was the Warehouseman's Clerks' and Drapers' School which had begun in the business premises of that notable philanthropist and businessman, George Moore, in Bow Churchyard. It moved in June 1866 to new buildings in Purley, opened by the Prince of Wales.[6] Moore, the 'Napoleon of Watling Street', who on retirement had 'plunged into philanthropy with the same zest he gave to business,' was also concerned with the Commercial Travellers' Schools founded at Pinner in 1845, and secured Dickens's interest. Their 'pleasing and commodius collegiate Gothic structure' was opened by the Prince Consort in 1855. Wings were later added so that the schools could house 200 boys and 100 girls for a 'superior education'. Funds came from voluntary contributions, three trustees 'hold the school as it were', the headmaster told the Taunton Commissioners, and it was managed by a board of thiry-six elected by the subscribers, half of whom were employers and half commercial travellers. The school fund was to some extent an insurance. Education and board were free to orphans or children between seven and twelve at entry whose fathers were unable to follow their occupation and who were elected by the subscribers. The religious difficulty caused no problems; parents chose between the Church and the Westminster Catechisms and all went to the parish church on Sundays. The University Local examinations were used, and the curriculum followed the 'subjects that are usually taught in middle-class schools' – a little Latin, a good grammatical knowledge of French (they leave 'pretty good French scholars'), arithmetic of all kinds, some mathematics, physical and commercial geography, grammar analysis. Science was 'not taught to any extent', and book-keeping was on the whole left to be learnt at the business houses to which most of the boys went at fifteen, 'the same class of house as the father was employed', commercial travellers being a 'very distinct class'. Such commercial houses usually remitted their premiums and the school had applications six months in advance. The girls' school followed a similar type of course, 'a good education for their class in life', with English subjects, French, but 'no other accomplishments'. There was greater difficulty in getting that kind of education for a girl, and in placing them out. Some became governesses, after further training as articled pupils, some went into warehouses where 'a great number of females' were employed in general millinery and dressmaking and trimming departments. The school was far from coeducational – the boys and girls only met at prayers and meals and, in spite of great care and trouble 'taken to keep them as distinct as possible, there is a tendency to advance towards each other' for a girl by fifteen and a half was 'frequently quite a woman'. By 1884 their leaving age had become sixteen in line with the general rise in standards of this level of education.[7]

Matthew Arnold took Olympian exception to this method of providing and designing schools. Licensed Victuallers and Commercial Travellers had a 'natural taste for bathos still strong', and 'sheer schools' composed of their offspring, bringing them up in an 'odour of licensed victualism or of bagmanism' was not wise training, but a gross example of Philistinism and of doing as one likes. Royalty should not compound the error by extolling such 'energy and self-reliance'. This is not one of the more attractive passages in Arnold's analysis.[8] Responsible provision for their children and the working out of a system of education which made a practical contribution to the idea of general and vocational schooling should be interpreted more positively, as indeed it was by the Taunton Commissioners.

The Commercial Travellers' Schools, like many institutions provided by investment or subscription, had hopes of becoming endowed.[9] Some endowments of the older kind were created in nineteenth-century London. An interesting donor was George Green, an eccentric 'old-fashioned low-churchman frightened by ritualists',[10] who in 1840 endowed two schools in Poplar, for 200 boys and 200 girls and infants, to give education somewhat above the elementary level.[11] But it was not only his anti-Puseyism which justified the description of Green as eccentric, for endowment of this kind was almost an anachronism. Throughout the century, mistrust and dislike of their abuses and obsolescence mounted, and it is in the long and uneven progress of reform of charitable trusts and not in concern for the political control of schools that the beginnings of state concern with secondary education can be discerned. Here 'charity, self-help, and state action mingled and interacted in a confusing fashion'.[12] The picture is further clouded by the passions which were aroused and in London the sheer wealth and complexity of endowments were seen against a background of urban problems and opportunities unmatched elsewhere. Fearon,[13] in investigating the metropolitan area for the Taunton Inquiry, wrote of the maldistribution of these London charities, 'sown broadcast and blindly over the land with all the partiality, all the inequality, all the profusion, all the waste which voluntaryism necessitates . . . creatures of accident and the sport of chance, yet utterly wanting in flexibility and the means of adapting themselves to the shifting requirements of the time. . . . Bones of endless and extravagant contention in the Courts of Law . . .' Sometimes such schools were closed for years when they were most wanted, or were 'not supplying the education the people want at a reasonable price, but offering them instead *gratis*, with a sort of mockery, something they do not want, and often would rather do without . . .'. The situation was the result of a lack of any directing, supervising intelligence, and of an undue love of independence, 'so peculiar to Englishmen'.[14] This was an echo of Matthew Arnold's ironic comment on the danger of 'doing as one likes', from another of those alien intellectuals, men 'conscious of their capabilities, often intolerant of their social superiors and inferiors, with a sharp cutting edge to their Liberalism, not remarkable for their sympathy towards what they regarded as unsystematic or disreputable'.[15]

Fearon's reforming zeal clouded his sense of history. These endowments had not been 'sown broadcast and blindly', but carefully and responsibly planned to serve communities since engulfed or transformed by urban growth and social change. And half a century of controversy and effort had not only led up to the Commission of 1864 which he was serving, but had considerably changed the situation he was investigating and the attitudes he was criticizing. The theory that educational institutions, especially the grammar schools, remained unreformed until the outcome of the Taunton Inquiry in the Endowed Schools' Act of 1869 is perhaps less true of London even than of other parts of the country. What Fearon represented was not the beginning of reforms, but a culminating point in one stage of a process of reform.

From the early years of the century concern with the plight of the poor and a utilitarian urge to remedy ancient and untidy abuses united with the desire to investigate and reform endowments into a national movement with strong metropolitan expression. In 1810 Anthony Highmore's *Pietas Londinensis* tabulated the immense charity resources of the capital city. At this period there was a general movement to reform the administration of charities and to correct suspected malpractices rather than to alter their direction or design. This 'current of reform' could be called 'Scottish-Whig-Utilitarian' and it brought not only elementary but even what became secondary education into the orbit of state concern. The work of Brougham directed attention to the essentially urban nature of the new economic environment and the important part which education must play in the new competitive, individualistic society which was taking shape. The 1816 Select Committee on the Education of the Poor in the Metropolis (a significantly early use of this word), with Romilly, Wilberforce, Macintosh and Babington under Brougham's chairmanship, seemed mild and limited in intent, but managed to sniff its way up the educational ladder to Christ's Hospital, St Paul's and Charterhouse, and to hint that small numbers were being boarded and clothed rather than large numbers educated. Brougham had got his foot in the door.[16] The next inquiry was to be more extensive and though he failed to broaden its scope beyond educational charities, Dr Ireland, vicar of Croydon where one of the more 'rancid' of these awaited investigation, protested that 'the principles of Adam Smith or the Scotch economists . . . threatened to supersede the established maxim of the law of the land and of the constitution'.[17]

The nation-wide investigations which followed eventually produced a 'Domesday Book' of charities. One team was formed to sit in London,[18] and the Analytical Digest of its findings, compiled in 1840, issued in 1843,[19] disclosed, not unexpectedly, that London was the most 'liberally endowed of all', with more than 47,000 acres scattered throughout the kingdom and more than £1,825,000 capital, to which most of Middlesex's £370,000 must be added, and some of Kent's £310,000. The total income for London was £250,000, out of £1,209,397 for the whole country. Not all these were educational funds, as it had proved impossible to isolate these from other benefactions.[20] Such facts made the establishment and development of central machinery imperative, but it was not until 1853 that the Charity Commissioners were set up,[21] and then with only imperfect powers, neither had the procedures and powers of Chancery been effectively reformed. It remained suicidal for a charity, especially a small one, to resort to the law.

As the facts emerged, the attack changed in direction and took on a particularly urban character. Not only abuse and malpractice were suspected or denounced, but the very obsolescence and the inflexibility of charities. The doctrine of *cy pres*, devised at the end of Elizabeth's reign to protect the public purpose of endowments against private depredations, was called into question, the donor's intention had become a 'dead hand'. The Utilitarians especially challenged the very concept of charity itself. In 1824 the young William Ellis, later a notable benefactor to London education, expounded his belief that benevolence had been demonstrably ineffective, even harmful. As its volume mounted, so distress and destitution had increased. Ellis ventured to hope that indiscriminate almsgiving was 'less general than formerly in town', but feared 'that it is far from being discontinued in the country'.[22] The pressure of new and mounting urban problems lay behind this movement to redirect and redefine charity. It was not industrialization so much as the new city which needed new kinds of education. The difficulty of restraining indiscriminate giving however was demonstrated a quarter of a century later in Sampson Low's *Charities of London* (1850) which again attempted to quantify the extraordinary 'variety and multiplicity' of the capital's benevolent agencies.[23] How much more difficult to direct and control ancient endowments, designed for another age, entrenched behind the doctrine of founder's intent, at the mercy of the Circumlocution Office and, at local level, Bumbledom and Turtledom, for the deepest mistrust was reserved for the City of London itself.

Detailed analysis is necessary to estimate how far these fears were justified. Clear causes of downright dishonesty seem to have been rare. A confused case concerned the Latymer and other bequests at Edmonton. Here the exceptionally well-paid mastership had, from 1781, got into the hands of the Adams family. John Adams junior (1802–28) had some success in increasing the numbers to 106 boys, keeping Latin in the curriculum, but providing in general a broadly useful course, aiming at 'the City's need for clerks which created a market for boys who could write and calculate', in line with local demand. Under the next Adams, Charles Henry, the rapidly expanding community became increasingly restless and, after appointing new trustees in 1844, in 1848 the Vestry meeting obtained an official investigation. For nearly twenty years suspicion and anger mounted. The school was ineffective, Latin had ceased to be taught and little else was learned, boys going largely for free clothing which they did not always receive though some of them sometimes got double outfits. The schoolmaster was secretary to the trustees. The accounts were in complete confusion, and although the newly constituted Charity Commissioners were drawn into the investigations in the 1850s nothing was cleared up and by 1861 it seemed that 'more than the equivalent of a whole year's income had been misappropriated', £952 3s 0½d being unaccounted for by the trustees. In 1863 another Charity inspector was called in, but even he failed to make clear what had happened and who was liable. In 1866 Adams was relieved of the secretaryship but remained headmaster with his son, the fourth of the dynasty, as assistant until, after Fearon's scorching inspection of his school for the Taunton Inquiry, he resigned in 1867. The most recent historian of the school does not hesitate to imply that the missing money had found its way into his hands.[24]

Without making windows into men's souls, the exact line between incompetence and dishonesty is often difficult to discern. By 1711 the chest containing the deeds of Highgate School had been lost.[25] In Deptford exhaustive examination of records and witnesses by the Commissioners in 1819 was unable to find what happened to a legacy in the South Sea stock bequeathed in 1672 to Dr Breton's School for Grammar and Writing. The school was maintained, at elementary level only, by a receipt of £6 16s 10d from the remains of the endowment, and

1*s* a quarter from parents for pens and ink. The parish maintained the schoolroom where 12 boys were educated and the master also had private pupils.[26]

Maladministration was far more evident. Within the London area the rising value of real property was an important element in the ability of endowments to serve expanding and changing communities. But management of property by bodies of local trustees had in several cases led instead to dwindling revenues. Letting property on long leases was common for it saved trouble when boards of trustees met at increasingly long intervals, and local interest or knowledge wavered. In Camberwell the master of Wilson's School had been allowed not only to manage the property, but to get much of it into his own hands, and as he had spent a great deal of capital on improving these old houses to accommodate private pupils, the governors found it difficult to sort the matter out. In 1818 the Commissioners found that the school, under William Jephson, the third of that dynasty, had 25 to 30 boarders at £42 a year, and 12 free scholars taught classical learning entirely separately in the old dilapidated schoolroom. A local solicitor, an old boy of the school, began proceedings in Chancery, and the churchwardens and trustees were also stirred into activity. They sought Counsel's opinion and in 1820 declined to grant the master renewal of the leases.[27] It was not only such bodies of local governors who had failed in this respect. The Coopers' Company, trustees of Gibson's School in Ratcliffe, had imprudently leased some of its property for a long term to the East India Company in 1770. Moreover only about a quarter of the income went on the school. The master's salary had been fixed at £73 10*s* a year in 1813, no usher had been appointed for a long time, and the school consisted of 30 foundation boys and a few private pupils, paying a small weekly sum and usually elected to the foundation when there was a vacancy. There was no classical teaching. The 1818 enquiry spurred the Company into greater interest. A committee was appointed and found that income from property in Fenchurch Street, bequeathed in 1563, had gone into the funds of the Company and not to the charity. During a decade of activity the school was to a considerable extent revived, but it was not until the late 1840s, after a long lawsuit with the East India Company, that more funds became available. The headmaster of the Mercers' School was called in as educational consultant, a new master was appointed, and in 1848 the school was reopened by J. B. Firth, the Master of the Company who had taken a great interest in the reforms. This was the highly successful school reported on by Fearon.[28]

Another disastrous practice of management was the custom of letting for fines, re-leasing at the old rent with sometimes only a token payment for increased value.[29] At Croydon Archbishop Whitgift had regularized this practice by ordering that only short leases should be granted, and relet at the same rate with substantial fines, which should be distributed amongst the schoolmaster and almspeople – a practice much to the advantage of local public houses and to dishonest masters, and one of the ways in which Dr John Rose swindled the endowments when in 1812 he presided over a school with no pupils. This unsavoury case had been disclosed before the time of Brougham's Commission, by a special Court of Inquiry set up by the Visitor, the Archbishop. By 1818 reforms in the system were already substantially, though slowly, increasing the income of the charity.[30]

Another malpractice was the use of educational endowments for the relief of the poor. As these in many cases did not want, or were not in a position, to avail themselves of such endowments, and as the mounting tide of urban poverty threatened to overwhelm small rural communities and urban parishes with once manageable problems, this was understandable, even perhaps laudable. It also had the advantages of relieving the poor rate. This was a practice sharply condemned by the Commissioners and was a special temptation in the case of 'town schools', those more or less administered by the local community. Moreover, many school endowments were not clearly separate from almshouses or other agents of poor relief.[31] St Olave's governors had since the seventeenth century taken a leading part in parish business in Southwark. The report of 1818 disclosed that 75 per cent of the income of the foundation was spent on the school and the rest went to charitable expenses.[32] At Enfield in the later eighteenth century, where the school no longer taught grammar, timber, valued at £1849, from one of the estates of the original charity, had been sold and 'the proceeds applied to the relief of the poor'.[33] An inner city example was St Clement Danes where the William Breton estate in Holborn, of £41 value, was left to the churchwardens in 1552; by 1814 the capital value was £9000 and the parishioners were challenging the obstinate use of the money for general parish purposes, although as long ago as 1701 the Commissioners of Charitable Uses had made orders to prevent this diversion of funds. In 1816 the courts directed that the whole income should be properly applied, but in 1837, when this had reached £4000, the misuse still continued. A lengthy Chancery suit produced in 1844 a scheme intended to provide some organized system of education for poor children in this crowded commercial district, as well as assistance for hospitals and almshouses built at Tooting in 1849. The Charity Schools had moved into fresh premises in 1820, new infant schools were built in 1852 and 1862 and then two middle-class schools were opened, the Holborn Estate Commercial Grammar School for Boys, with 53 pupils, and the St Clement Danes Middle Class Girls' School, with 16 at first. These provided comparatively cheap education for local children, especially useful in a legal district, and were praised as a precedent by Fearon.[34]

Much malpractice and maladministration was disclosed by this half-century of enquiry and controversy, but it would have taken an unbroken succession of Daniels in judgment to keep this motley col-

The school-room at Westminster

9 The nineteenth century had to develop new styles of teaching and grouping pupils. For a brief period some schools tried the monitorial system at secondary level.

St Olave's School, Southwark, 1855

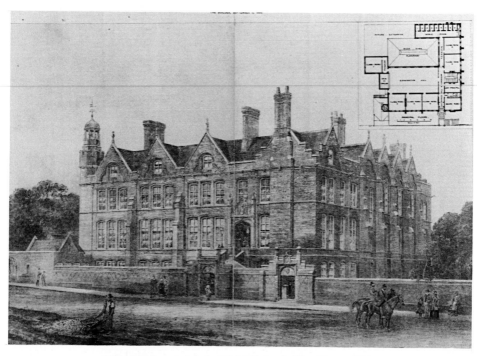

Haberdashers' Aske's Girls' School, Hatcham, 1886

10 The St Olave's building was severely criticized at the time for its ostentatious inconvenience. By 1886 the girls are beginning to share the Elizabethan dream – even the users of the Deptford road appear as retainers and sportsmen.

lection of endowments on the lines laid down by their founders. 'The thing is past praying for. The old order of things is gone by', as Fearon put it. 'Their founders would probably recognize very few of these institutions if they could now revisit them.'[35] Inertia did as much as incompetence or dishonesty, for perhaps trustees could best do their duty by allowing social demand to shape the type of education provided. At Croydon the vicar, Dr Ireland, was a powerful advocate of 'popular education' and when in 1812 he wished to found a National School as a counterblast to one just opened on Lancastrian principles, there was Whitgift's School, swept and garnished, empty after the ejection of the infamous Dr Rose. The logic of the situation was clear, and Counsel's opinion found 'no objection to allowing the Schoolhouse or part of it to be used for teaching the proposed National School if it was not required for the purpose of a grammar school'. And so the foundation building was used for many years to come. In 1832 the headmaster of the foundation told the Bougham Commissioners that he never had any free scholars as there was no demand for classics.[36]

At Highgate Cholmeley's school had long become an elementary school and although the 1818 enquiry stirred the governors to action and the erection of a new schoolhouse, it was run like a National school on the Madras system. But in 1821 the attempt of the governors to legalize their long misuse of the school funds by creating a new parish at Highgate and attaching the school funds to its needs, aroused local bitterness. As the neighbourhood changed, a reform party gained a judgment from Lord Eldon in 1824–6 that the school was for the learned languages and, though the governors had acted in good faith, the character of the grammar school must be restored. In 1832 new statutes were approved, 40 boys were to be educated on the foundation, and the master, who was to teach personally in the school in spite of his pastoral responsibilities, could take 'pay-boys'. It was not however until 1838, under a new vigorous headmaster without parochial duties, that the school began to thrive. Mathematics and modern languages were added to the classical curriculum, and boys were prepared for the universities and the professions. Boarding-houses and a cricket field were acquired. The social demands of the neighbourhood, which had earlier depressed the school to elementary level, had now changed sufficiently to support a school of this type, providing that boarders added to its resources. But its usefulness to the poor of Highgate was marginal.[37] Tottenham was another school which in 1818 had sunk to elementary level, with only 50 boys in a dilapidated building. In 1840 the trustees appealed for subscriptions and rebuilt it to accommodate 120 but at Fearon's enquiry there were only 42 boys present, and the schooling was inferior to that of the National and British schools nearby.[38] At Battersea, the Sir Walter St John boys were sent to the local National School as the endowed school had ceased to exist altogether.[39]

Local initiatives

The eighteenth-century dilemma of 'classics or charity' was in fact the fundamental problem which faced trustees endeavouring to meet both their obligations and local needs. The nineteenth century was making the problem more complex, as varying and overlapping levels of middle-class educational demand developed, and as proprietary schools provided by other agencies stimulated and competed for supplying these demands. London foundations on the whole provided a broader curriculum that is sometimes supposed, but if writing, with all that implied, and mathematics were included in the course as well as classics, they all too easily, as at Stepney, Tottenham and Enfield, encroached on and overwhelmed the more ambitious subjects. At Owen's School in Islington a fairly modest level of course for boys leaving at fourteen had been laid down by the foundress, and the Brewers' Company had on the whole found this met local demand. In 1818 they attempted to repulse the enquiries of Brougham's Commissioners, but in the end submitted to examination. There were then 30 foundationers and 25 private pupils, and Latin was available to all, though only the private pupils wanted it. On the whole the report was favourable but the Brewers were stirred to more enterprise. The income of the almshouse property had increased in much greater proportion than that of the school, while it was the expanding demand for the school which needed the money. Chancery permission to pool the resources of the charities was gained in 1826 and schemes for rebuilding were being discussed. At this point delays were caused by a parishioner, over-anxious to secure a 'better establishment' of the school, filing an information in Chancery against the Company. This held the reforms back for a mere eight years, but in 1838 it was possible to resume plans, and in 1840 a new school, 'a pleasing and picturesque structure in the Elizabethan style of architecture', was opened. This was an instant success, the 42 admissions doubling by 1841, and in 1858 120 been reached. It provided a useful commercial education for boys between seven and fourteen, nominated by the Vestry and the Brewers. The classical curriculum had completely gone.[40] The Brewers were better able to maintain this at another foundation for which they were responsible, Alderman Hickson's benefaction of 1686, the Tower Hill Grammar School. This remained a thoroughly useful little classical school which they provided with a new building in 1852. In 1864 it was 'full and flourishing' with 60 boys: 20 on the foundation (14 from All Hallows Barking, and 6 from St John's Wapping) and the rest paying 20s a quarter. The headmaster was a Cambridge graduate, paid £120 a year plus capitation fees, and there was an assistant master at £120 a year and visiting drawing and French masters. It did not close until 1889, an interesting indication of the late operation of the shift of population from the City.[41]

Other endowments, such as Colfe's and Wilson's, were only able to maintain their secondary character because the headmaster took boarders as private pupils, they had virtually become private schools. In the early nineteenth century the Wilson's governors were lamentably lax. Between 1803 and 1811 they did not meet at all, in 1813 a meeting did not produce a quorum, and again from 1814 to 1817 meetings stopped. In the 1820s they made a laudable effort to restore their school, urged on by a new and vigorous incumbent of Camberwell, J. G. Storie, who had a staunch ally in Dr D'Oyly, the rector of Lambeth, so active in educational causes. The property was first retrieved from the master's control, the school statutes were revised to provide reading and arithmetic as well as classics free to the foundationers, Counsel's opinion enabled the governors to develop the resources of the estate, and an acre of land was sold for extending the churchyard and the funds invested. For a time the school revived; by 1830 there were five forms and 12 boys on the foundation, the education was of a good standard and affiliation to King's College was considered. But this prosperity was short-lived, and when the Proprietary Camberwell Collegiate School, which was in union with King's College, opened in 1835 with the active help of Mr Storie and influential parishioners, this seems to have given Wilson's a mortal blow. Pupils dwindled, its dilapidated buildings unfortunately survived the fire which destroyed the church of St Giles in 1841, the headmaster retired in 1842,[42] and then, just as the governors were contemplating new action which the Grammar School Act of 1840[43] might have facilitated, the endowment fell into the hands of Chancery. A zealous parishioner laid information with the Attorney General alleging a breach of trust, and desiring that the case be referred to a Master in Chancery. The governors were then powerless to carry out schemes of reform as the matter was *sub judice*. Not till 1845 was the case decided: Chancery agreed to pensioning the retired master, pulling down old buildings, letting some land on building leases, and rebuilding a new school when funds reached £1500. Alas, the cost of the legal action swallowed up available capital, and although Camberwell was developing as a desirable residential suburb, the leasing of the building lots went slowly, and the helpful and zealous rector was followed by one uninterested in the cause. Neither were the governors competent, for in 1860 they were granting leases at £220 per annum for 79 years – an estimated profit to the lessee of between £600 and £700 a year. Meanwhile the school was temporarily extinguished.[44] Enfield was another foundation which was crippled by litigation, here due to a series of unfortunate disputes between the trustees and successive headmasters. Between 1819 and 1846 £2838 was thus spent, and the school had already lost funds through misapplication of endowments.[45]

These last cases demonstrate that it was not only local inertia or mismanagement, combined with social pressures, which distorted or destroyed endowments, but the expense, delays and inadequacies of the law devised to protect them. The case of St Olave's illustrates the interaction of changing and confused demands on levels of schooling with administrative misjudgement and breakdown. The 1818 enquiry showed that the classical and English schools had an income of over £1000 a year, but the so-called Classical School was not only much smaller than the English School, it was very imperfect in its standards and sent virtually no scholars forward to its universities – the last had been the schoolmaster's son some years before. Local demand for this kind of schooling was rare and the governors resisted attempts to take 'foreigners'. Some improvements were made but unfortunately the renewed interest of the governors, local businessmen with little educational knowledge, led them to consult Dr Russell, the new young headmaster of the Charterhouse, who recommended the adoption of the monitorial system then being tried at his own school. There it enabled a man of 'exceptional vigour and capacity' to cope with large numbers – in 1818, 238 boys and five masters, in 1825, 480. After 1832 the system was abandoned but at St Olave's it lasted until about 1855, undermining quite respectable efforts of both headmaster and trustees to raise the standard of the school. Some pupils were sent on to the universities, the school was twice rebuilt, when the new London and Greenwich and then the Croydon railways drove it forth. The second move inspired the Court of Governors in 1855 to draw up a new scheme of education, again consulting Dr Russell, no longer at the Charterhouse, and also Dr Mortimer of the City of London School. These educational experts accepted the main feature of the plan to unite the schools (three, including a Branch School which had been opened at Vauxhall) under one head in the new building, but one of the governors wrote to raise the problem which was fundamental to the nature of the school – 'The Inhabitants of the Parishes may be classed as Clergymen Professional Practitioners Merchants Captains and Officers of Merchant Ships Tradesmen and Shopkeepers, and on the other hand a large majority of industrious Artizans and daily labourers.' He believed that 'the first Class of Inhabitants . . . neither can nor will avail themselves of the Schools, unless they are kept entirely distinct from each other'. Victorian social attitudes made the original design of the community school unworkable.

The new headmaster, the Reverend Henry Hayman, a Londoner educated at Merchant Taylors' and St John's Oxford, was however reasonably successful in raising standards, abolishing the monitorial system, and introducing the University Local examinations. In 1859 he was succeeded by one of his assistants, the Reverend Andrew Johnson, who presided over the laborious reconstruction of St Olave's. Fearon gave a graphic description of the difficulties encountered.

Hayman had already attempted to get the governors' permission to admitting fee-paying boys from outside the parish at the Classical School, to help raise the academic standard. In 1864 the governors produced a Scheme before the Charity Commissioners for dividing the school into three departments (classical, commercial, English) under one headmaster. In the first department parishioners' sons were to pay a maximum of £6 6s year, non-parishioners a maximum of £12 12s, and were to be eligible for the school's valuable exhibitions after three years at the school. All were to be admitted by examination. In the second school the fees were to be £2 2s, and the English School 'should continue free'. A system of scholarships was to link the three schools together, and the apprenticeship fees, so long valued in this district, were to be continued. Eventually all was approved, notices were posted on the church doors, and in July 1865 the two Vestries met. St John's agreed to the scheme, but 'St Olave's in a very stormy meeting condemned it'. A public meeting then totally threw it out. Fearon sought out some of the critics who had attended this meeting but could understand no very rational reason for their opposition. One 'small tradesman' who had been very active 'objected to any imposition of fees. Thought it ought to be "a free school, and free for ever". Said there were no upper classes to patronize the classical school; and that the tradesman did not care for classics; all they cared for was plain English, French and arithmetic. They did not want Latin, pure mathematics or science. Thought it was "destroying the tradesman's birthright" to make him pay for the commercial school, or "to admit foreigners to compete with him". . . . Said that there had long been a general dissatisfaction with the school for "*peddling with classics*".' This, said Fearon, was in spite of a real effort of the present headmaster to use the Local examinations to broaden the course and to 'fix a curriculum suitable to the different classes of scholars'. Fearon's small tradesman however was convinced that fees were a fraud upon his rights, and was especially 'piqued at not having been consulted at all in the matter'.

So great was the ferment that the opposition appealed to the Charity Commission, St John's Vestry also rescinded its approval, conferences and committees were held, and Scheme Number II emerged, conceding the fees in the commercial school. Both Vestries sanctioned this scheme but this time one of the governors took up the opposition, another public meeting was called, condemning Scheme II *in toto*. Here one line of argument was that it 'deprived the poor man's son of his classical birth-right which might one day make him Lord Chancellor', the master was 'deliberately undermining the grand old Latin foundation'. However, as the two Vestries had accepted it, the governors felt able to go forward to the Charity Commission.

Fearon's duties at this point took him from the scene, but soon curiosity prompted him to enquire how things were getting on. A protagonist reported that several violent parochial demonstrations had taken place, and then the blow had fallen, the Charity Commissioners had acknowledged that 'after deluding us for nearly two years . . . they had no power to make any order'. The opposition of even a single individual was enough to reduce the Commission to impotence. This Fearon put forward as a strong argument for an 'authoritative educational board, which may save their noble foundation the ruin which has swallowed up so many endowments'.[46] Progress in reforming the law on charities had indeed been inadequate. The Act of 1853 had provided that trusts which could not be revised *cy pres* might be reorganized by schemes such as those for St Olave's, but experience had demonstrated that this was only possible where they 'offended no local interests or opinions'. The Charitable Trusts Act of 1860 attempted to strengthen their powers but was another half-hearted measure, for it only applied to small charities and was not altogether precise.[47]

It is difficult to make any overall judgement about the disclosures and results of this half-century of enquiry in London. Complexities, confusions and incompetencies were drawn into the light, together with dishonesty, laziness, negligence and sheer stupidity. Alongside these exposures, a great deal of effort at reform was made, and much was achieved. How much of this was due to the enquiries and criticisms, and how much of it to the general movement for educational reform is difficult to say, and the influence of experiments such as the proprietary schools was strong. It was a half-century in which the initiative still lay entirely with the local agencies, and their achievements have probably been underestimated because the critical intellectual voice of the Arnolds and the Fearons dominate the documents of the new bureaucracy which was taking shape.

The local agency which was most deeply distrusted and criticized by the radical reformers was the City of London itself, the corporation whose wealth, power, prescriptive rights, archaic customs and indulgences summed up the unregenerate order, 'turtledom'. Its refusal to co-operate with the Municipal Reform enquiry confirmed the Utilitarians' worst suspicions.[48] Yet during this period it created a school which from the year of Victoria's accession helped to shape ideas of secondary education in the capital.

From 1442 to 1827 the City through its Chamberlain had been responsible for the education and clothing of 'John Carpenter's children'. From the time of the Reformation their schooling was probably at one of the City grammar schools – the only evidence indicates Merchant Taylors'.[49] The five tenements which comprised the estate were by the eighteenth century largely represented by holdings in St Giles in the Fields, remaining fairly constant in value until 1713 when a steady rise began – £130 in 1742, £238 in 1781, £750 in 1826, £2500 by 1863. From the time of John Wilkes's Chamberlaincy the money was swept into the general City accounts and only the money specified in Henry V's reign was applied to the charity. When in 1821 the Chamberlain provided particulars of the City's charities for the Brougham Commissioners' tenth report, the parents or friends of the four children received payment for their schooling, and were required from time to time to bring the copybooks of their children, and other specimens of their progress, to satisfy the Chamberlain 'of the proper application of the testator's bounty'. No money was left to pay for clothing. It was clear that the level of education, and the amount applied to it, in no way corresponded to the possibilities of the endowment, and the matter was made more complicated because Carpenter's will could not then be found.[50]

The publication of the Charity Commission Report in 1823 did indeed justify the classic Benthamite belief in the importance of facts and of public scrutiny. It was clear that the greatly increased revenues were not being applied to the charity. There appeared, however, to be in the City Corporation a 'genuine and widespread desire to put matters right'. The first solution which emerged in 1826 was that four boys should receive full board and clothing and a classical and commercial education at Tonbridge School, and at the age of fifteen each to be given a premium of £100 'towards his advancement in life'. The firmness of Dr Knox, the headmaster, saved them from being tricked out in blue charity uniforms with silver medals 'denoting the objects of the said Charity', and extended their school life to sixteen, though not to eighteen or nineteen as he would have preferred.[51]

More radical Common Councillors were not satisfied with this solution and one, Richard Taylor, a printer of scientific interests and liberal views (his nephew founded the *Manchester Guardian*), recommended the setting up of a day school in London for a much larger number of boys. This was too advanced a proposal, and a considerable part of the benefaction continued to be 'carried to the credit of the City's cash'. Again in 1828 Taylor tried unavailingly to get the use of the bequest 'for the largest possible number of sons of bona-fide freeman-householders of the City and none other'. In 1832 further complaints were made and a Select Committee was formed, and in the next year an ally became chairman of the City Lands Committee, Warren Stormes Hale, a wax-chandler who had made a fortune by being the first English manufacturer to apply industrially the discoveries of French chemists in animal and vegetable fats. Through such channels and chinks did the forces of change work their way into an apparently archaic and impenetrable fabric. Until a problem could be identified by external criticism and taken up by friends of reform within the citadel, progress was unlikely.[52]

The second stage of the reform of Carpenter's endowment brought up in an acute form the question of founder's intent, or how citizens of the reign of William IV could redefine 'study at school' in the reign of Henry V in terms of the needs of boys of their own day. And what kind of boy? Not many were now born within the City as the donor had specified, poverty had not been a condition in the original terms, and only in the seventeenth century had 'Freemen's Children' become the usual formula. There was an area of real debate, and also a general feeling that charity should go to those who needed it most. This was not only a period of charity and municipal reform but also of approaching Poor Law enquiry. The Corporation, investigating the London Workhouse, secured an Act of Parliament (1829) to abolish it and use its property for a school for destitute children, Christ's Hospital no longer fulfilling this purpose. The Board of Governors of the workhouse was therefore charged with the duty of setting up a school at the same time as the more radical reformers of Carpenter's bequest were advocating the same thing. The two projects and teams became confused, and the workhouse spoke of 'a school which might emphatically be termed the High School of the City of London'. By 1832 they had produced a plan for the 'City of London Corporation School'; it was to be for the poor and on monitorial lines, but they spoke of it also in more grandiloquent terms, procured a grant of £2000 from Common Council, and began to cast eyes towards the Carpenter charity, still only used for four boys. Taylor was a member of both camps. Matters came to a head just at the time of the last Reform Bill crisis at a stormy meeting in May 1832, when argument ranged over the choice of a school for the poor, or for resident householders of the City. The outcome was a resolution that the school should be for 'the maintenance, clothing, education, and apprenticing of poor children', but that it should 'as regards the Male Children' be 'what is commonly known by the name of a Grammar School'. On this insecurely contradictory basis fund-raising for this charity school continued, a Guildhall ball was held, an unsuccessful invitation to the Princess Victoria being a small indication of the forward-looking nature of these plans.[53] The school was to be within the City, and in 1833 the site of Honey Lane Market, nearly opposite Bow Church in Cheapside, became available. The 'Corporation School' governors approached the City Lands Committee under Hale, just when it was examining the Carpenter estate, recently augmented by the sale of lands for improving the approaches to London Bridge. The Committee agreed that the school governors could have the market site, but only if their plans were altered to 'secure to the Citizens of London a School for the education of Children on a more extensive scale and on the most liberal and improved principles . . .'. It was also proposed to Common Council that the Carpenter Bequest should be consolidated with the Corporation School if these terms were accepted. The double temptation was too much for the workhouse party, 'for the sake of the Carpenter Bequest and the Honey Lane Market site they abandoned the cause of the poor and destitute'. During the subsequent negotiations within the City machinery the governors even gave up their own control of the proposed school, and a committee of the City Lands Committee was given the responsibility, Hale being its chairman. In February 1834 Common Council received the report of the negotiations, the City Remembrancer was instructed to prepare a draft Bill, introduced in the Lords by Brougham himself. It was at the Committee stage that an amendment separating the workhouse funds from those of the school was negotiated between Brougham and Shaftesbury on the one side and Hale and the Remembrancer, Tyrell, on the other. The rights of the poor had been upheld, but ironically the workhouse governors had lost on all fronts, their charity funds were now left in the hands of their rivals, while Hale and his party had the site, the endowment valued at £900 a year,[54] and the 'Act for establishment of a School on the Site of Honey Lane Market in the City of London'.[55]

The complicated circumstances which preceded the foundation of what by now was called the City of London School raise the whole question of the diversion of funds intended for the poor to the use of the middle classes. This appears in some ways to be a classic case. True, the funds recently collected for the education of the poor had been safeguarded and, after sixteen years, Hale was able to secure the opening in 1854 of the Freemen's Orphan School at Brixton. But the school which opened in Milk Lane in 1837 in a building predominantly Tudor-Gothic in inspiration, designed for 400 boys, had been planned to give for moderate fees a classical and commercial education, and the pupils, while few of them were from wealthy parents, were solidly middle-class. Carpenter scholars had free education, an allowance for books and a premium on leaving, and at first they were also boarded; but these were certainly not working-class boys. The problem was partly one of founder's intent, for the doctrine of *cy pres* was yet to be fundamentally challenged, and Carpenter almost certainly had grammar education in mind. But it was more a question of the way the educational needs of the City were defined by its more radical, reforming element. Hale and his colleagues had a conception of a school for 'the religious and virtuous education of boys, and for instructing them in the higher branches of literature and in all other useful learning', which was in line with the educational experiments so much in operation elsewhere in the capital. They were looking to King's and University Colleges and their schools, and to the other proprietary schools being founded. Hale himself had a lively interest in such education as a function of a social structure which was itself seen as a recent achievement, and, in the service of a new economy, generating wealth on an unprecedented scale. The distribution of this wealth was considered to depend more on the individual enterprise made possible by education than by any almsgiving of the kind appropriate to the old order. It is significant that just about thirty years later he presided as Lord Mayor over the Mansion House meeting which gave practical effect to Canon Rogers's scheme for the Middle-Class Schools' Corporation. In that same year, also at the Mansion House, he was able to entertain the 637 boys of the City of London School to champagne, chicken and boar's head.[56]

From 1834 to 1836 Hale and his committee, now the City of London School Committee, were planning the school within the framework of the Act. An incident quite worthy of Trollope or Dickens hints at the radical tinge of the enterprise. Hale invited Brougham to lay the foundation stone of the new building, whereupon the Lord Mayor first threatened to write personally to the Lord Chancellor forbidding him to

WINCHESTER *VERSUS* BROUGHAM, OR A RUMPUS OVER THE FIRST STONE OF THE CITY OF LONDON SCHOOL!

Cartoon of the Lord Mayor and Lord Chancellor Brougham

do so, and then declared that if he 'attempted to lay the stone he would be instantly arrested'. The committee stood firm, the Lord Mayor appears to have cooled off, and when the school was opened the then Lord Mayor took his proper part in the ceremony. It could therefore be said that a school founded in 1442 was not opened until 1837.[57]

The problems of the Carpenter bequest were not over. The £900 charity income which the Act of Parliament allowed for the running of the school soon grew inadequate for its rising costs, while the capital of the charity increased substantially. In spite of economies, especially in the size of the classes, it became necessary to raise the fees, and it was not until 'Old Citizens' began to rise to positions of influence on

Common Council that enough money began to be put into the school. It also began to attract numerous bequests for scholarships, university exhibitions and so forth, for example the important Beaufoy scholarships which did so much for the teaching of English, and those founded for modern languages in 1858 by Sir William Tite, who was later to take an interest in the Cowper Street Schools. The City of London became second only to Merchant Taylors' for the wealth of its leaving scholarships.[58]

Important claims have been made for the pioneering work of the school. Its first curriculum was broad, the general course included English, classical and modern languages, 'writing, arithmetic, and Book-keeping', 'elements of mathematics and Natural Philosophy', geography, history, choral singing, lectures on 'Chemistry and other branches of Experimental Philosophy', and religious instruction. Special courses were provided in Hebrew, drawing and some extra languages, and 'superior classes' were to be formed in 'the higher branches of literature and science', mathematics, physics, logic and ethics. The significance of this course was that it was an 'emancipation from a narrowly classical curriculum ... partly achieved through the needs of commerce'. The utility of the course was not restricting or illiberal, and in the hands of a remarkable series of headmasters 'a new and broader conception of humane learning was built up'.[59] There is truth in this, but it is unjust to the previous experience which London schools had accumulated. The headmasters of University College School, Professor T. H. Key, and of King's College School, Dr Major, had helped to construct the curriculum, and the first three headmasters had close connections with other London proprietary schools. The Reverend John Allen Gilkes, appointed in 1836, had been head of the Camberwell Collegiate School,[60] and he was succeeded in 1840 by the great Dr G. F. N. Mortimer who had been head of the Brompton Proprietary School since 1833; under him the City School soon reached nearly 500 boys.[61] The third head was the greatest of all, Dr Edwin Abbott (1865–82), who had been brought to the school as a boy in 1850 by his father, the highly successful head of the Philological School.[62] What the City of London School was able to contribute was not so much the actual pioneering of this type of curriculum as its development, consolidation and testing out in a context with resources and stability, where the prestige of the City gave it weight and influence. The Clarendon Commissioners remarked on this. The majority of the boys in 1861 left to go into business, but for the small number who stayed on the classical and mathematical education was so good 'that all who go to Universities distinguish themselves', and this prestige had influence throughout the school. 'Parents who must be supposed to have ... strong reasons for desiring a good practical education for their sons ... are content that they should follow a course of instruction in classics ...'.[63] H. H. Asquith, perhaps one of the school's most brilliant pupils, paid tribute to the teaching he received, a classical education of the highest quality.[64]

The influence of this breadth and quality of course was all the more wide as the school was from the beginning non-sectarian, it early admitted Jewish boys, it was used by Roman Catholic families. Again it has been claimed that it was the first to do this, but University College School was certainly before it, and Anglican proprietary schools, including King's College School, also followed a similar policy.[65] But the prestige of the City of London was high, and it moreover appears to have continued the ancient City tradition of catering for boys from outside London. Boys travelled in daily from around London, and others from a distance 'lodged close by the school for the purpose of attending it'. On the death of their grandfather, the Asquith brothers came to live with an uncle in London to attend the school. When he moved back to Yorkshire the boys stayed on in London lodgings. Herbert, the elder, was only twelve and yet it was the 'end of any effective home background'. There is a curiously mediaeval ring about it.[66]

The boys, spilling over from their overcrowded building in Cheapside, led lives which were almost part of the public life of the City itself, following cases at the Old Bailey, using St Paul's, the Law Courts, the National Gallery and so forth almost as an extension of their classrooms. As Asquith said, 'brought into contract . . . with the sights and the sounds and the life of a great city, [we] brought into our reading an element which could not be contributed from elsewhere – mixed our knowledge . . . with actuality and reality'.[67] It was an important reminder that the City has always played an essential part in educational stimulation. Local civic enterprise had provided a great day school which not only strengthened a newly emerging conception of secondary education, but whose very centrality gave it nation-wide influence and significance.[68]

Local action during this important half-century was also parochial, and this at a time when urban parish organization was under increasing and intolerable pressures. The parishes of Southwark were trying to deal with an unprecedented scale and pace of change, not only the general population explosion and the contrary process of outward movement to new suburbs, but also the revolution in the capital's lines of communication. New bridges built over the Thames (Lambeth, 1862, and Tower Bridge, 1894, were added to those already mentioned)[69] converged upon and carved up the Borough, making it more accessible for commerce, industry, dwellings. Then came the railways, the London Bridge and Deptford in 1836, extended to Greenwich in 1838, the London and Croydon in 1839, the London and Brighton, the South Eastern. Most of these generated suburban traffic. The last, the London and South Western, was largely for long-distance trains to Southampton. All this activity was at its height in the 1840s and 'completed the process of detaching the more affluent classes from Southwark and left the area a prey to industry and commerce'. Factories and slums filled every nook and cranny. Bermondsey and Rotherhithe still remained more attractive and open, and there was a steady movement of population from the old Borough centre towards what was in fact the less healthy, lower ground – Fearon noted that 'There is a large middle-class population in the south and east of [St Olave's and St John's], viz, in Bermondsey, Newington, Rotherhithe, etc., almost entirely unprovided with grammar school education.'[70]

The efforts of the parishioners of St Olave's and St John's to supply these wants and adapt their school to these conditions have already been described. St Saviour's was both less ambitious and more successful, at least for a time. The endowment was smaller, £387 15s 1d in 1818, and 68 boys were then receiving an entirely classical education – here the statutes allowed the master to take boys from other parishes when he had time and room for them. The governors were already conducting their own enquiry when the request for evidence was made by the Commissioners in May 1816. This stiffened their resolve, and they tightened up the rules, made sensible adjustments about salaries, hours of opening and so forth, but did not attempt anything more spectacular than securing the residence of the master. The school continued to be modestly useful until in 1843 its site was taken for the new Borough Market. New and smaller buildings were put up in Sumner Street, not so pleasant as the old situation near the church. In 1850 a Chancery Scheme secured some modernization of the curriculum and imposed fees on all boys. At the time of the Taunton visitation there were 109 boys, and open scholarships and Indian Civil Service appointments were still being won. It was not until the 1870s that the final decline of the area caused dwindling numbers. It would be too much to claim that the St Saviour's governors were remarkably energetic and effective, but they had shown a continuing sense of responsibility and adapted the school to some extent to new needs.[71]

A parish with very different problems was St Dunstan's in the East, on the other side of London Bridge, which had contained one of the oldest, if the most shadowy, of the grammar schools of medieval London. Numerous benefactions accumulated in the parish, some to the ward and charity schools and some for apprenticeships – it is not always easy to distinguish the level of education intended. By the early nineteenth century, with a resident population already beginning to dwindle, the parish Vestry was administering charity funds from about twenty-four sources, yielding an income of over £3000 a year from valuable City sites such as Great Tower Street, Thames Street, Mincing Lane, or property in suburbs just beginning to increase in value, Sydenham, Lewisham, Catford. In 1820 Brougham's Commissioners called on the parish officials for information, which was reluctantly supplied after legal advice had been taken. It would be an exaggeration to say that after this things began to move quickly. In 1833 information was filed against the rector and churchwardens in the name of the Attorney General – the Vestry clerk seems to have effected a temporary rescue. In 1845 the parish appointed a subcommittee to examine all its trust property. In 1851 the Home Secretary instructed the Attorney General to take steps about St Dunstan's charities, and process in Chancery began. In June 1865 a public meeting was called in the parish, and produced a plan for using the endowments for providing a new school; 'Education was a great feature of the day; and they might do in that direction a great deal with their surplus charities.' Only one year later a draft Scheme emerged. 'Owing to the enormous prices of London ground suitable and the very significant tendency of large London schools to move out from the centre, the school should be placed at such a convenient distance from London as to be accessible by railway and that it should therefore be built on the Charity Estate at Catford Bridge in the parish of Lewisham immediately contiguous to a station on the Mid-Kent line of the South Eastern Railway Company, whereby proper playgrounds may be secured for recreation.' The rest of the estate could then be 'improved for building purposes' and the proceeds would be 'fully adequate to the maintenance of a large and eminently useful public undertaking sufficient to engage first-class talent in masters and to supply first-class education to the pupils adapted to the circumstances of the present-day'. In 1867 this Scheme was approved by Chancery.[72]

This wealthy City parish had needed much goading from the centre, but at last a useful school seemed to be taking shape on the horizon. But this was further delayed by the Taunton Inquiry and the Endowed Schools Act of 1869, for this Scheme proved not to conform to the specifications of the Endowed Schools' Commissioners, who also objected to the site, as there were other endowed schools nearby. The trustess were in a dilemma: if they acknowledged the Commission's authority they 'must undergo a Scheme', and if they did not they could not get anything from them, 'consequently we were hung up'. The trustees tried ineffectually to argue that as there was no school to be reformed, the case did not fall within the Commissioners' scope.[73] Nearly twenty more years' litigation, even reaching a petition to the Queen in Privy Council, passed before a new Scheme, No. 390, emerged in 1883, and St Dunstan's College did not open until 1888.[74] Its development therefore belongs to the post-Taunton period, but its genesis comes from before it.

Bodies of local trustees and governors varied greatly in the energy and efficiency of their response to new conditions or to promptings from the centre. In some more gross cases the developing machinery of the Charity Commissioners felt impelled, and was able, to take action. The great Dulwich charity had long been partly ineffective and a prey to litigation on account of the obscurity of its statutes and its complexity, for not only was it a combination of school and almshouses, but it benefited both old and young in four widely separated parishes, St Botolph's Bishopsgate, where Alleyn was born, St Giles Cripplegate, the site of his Fortune Theatre, St Saviour's Southwark, where he had been vestryman and churchwarden, and Camberwell, his country retreat where his College of God's Gift was raised. In 1834 the Charity Commissioners found only 12 boys in the school and a master unconvinced that he ought to teach Latin. The rental was then £7881. A suit in Chancery followed and in 1842 produced a charming small new 'grammar school', designed by Barry on *cottage orné* lines, with two masters at salaries of £150 and £50. In 1847 there was ineffective complaint from St Saviour's about the lack of benefit to their parish, and when in 1854 the able and vigorous Charity Inspector, Thomas Hare, descended upon the school, he found 10 boys, taught on mornings only, alternately by the master and the usher. Only 5 boys learnt grammar, and even they studied French rather than Latin authors.[75] The Dulwich College Act of 1857[76] dissolved the old corporation and established a new body of governors, eight elected by the privileged parishes and eleven appointed by the Court of Chancery. The master and usher were pensioned off with £500 and £446 a year. The educational part of the charity was to be entirely remodelled. The Act provided for upper and lower schools, with boarding scholarships for the privileged parishes. In the Upper School the boys were to stay until eighteen, and the education was to be of a grammar-school type, including Greek, modern languages and science. In the cheaper Lower School Greek was not included and apprenticeship fees replaced university scholarships. There was to be a ladder of awards between the two schools.

The Dulwich College case illustrates not only the problems of reforming an endowed school, but the need for some system of schooling for the capital, for here the educational needs and resources of two City and one Southwark and two suburban parishes were interlocked, and it proved almost impossible to provide places in the right kind of school and the right locality for boys entitled to them. Rumours of the resuscitation of Dulwich College stimulated the other grammar school in Camberwell, Wilson's, to revive its plans for reform.[77] The Vestry of St Botolph's Bishopsgate took a lively and continuing interest. In 1856 they objected to the balance of representation of the interested parishes on the proposed new governing body, but optimistically welcomed the idea of two large schools 'for the exclusive benefit of the four parishes' with 'a class called Boarders' who would pay only for the cost of their maintenance, and 'all of whom are to receive a liberal and good education'. As the property should increase in value so would the benefits. At the Vestry meeting of 9 September 1857, in between an item about Burial Board fees and another on rating for the Gas and Water Companies, the churchwarden explained the provision of the Dulwich College Act. Consultations with the Charity Commissioners, joint meetings with St Luke's Finsbury (the successor of St Giles), St Saviour's and Camberwell were held. Too much money was being expended on the Upper School and on pensions to retiring governors, the Lower School was not getting its fair share of foundation scholarships for boarders, the principal benefit to St Botolph's as the distance was too great for day scholars; the constitution of the governing body was 'most objectionable'; the resources of the endowment were not increasing as quickly as had been hoped, and yet extravagant expenditure, such as a £300 architect's fee for the new building, was undertaken. At the meeting which presented an address of condolence to the Queen on the death of the Prince Consort, the Vestry expressed 'most respectfully but at the same time most earnestly and distinctly the extreme regret and disappointment they feel, four years after passing an Act of Parliament (which they had hoped would have improved the administration of the affairs of the College) to find themselves in a worse condition than they were under the old Scheme'. In this year Canon Rogers became chairman of the Dulwich governors and also rector of St Botolph's and could be said to be running with the hare and hunting with the hounds. His progressive educational ideas presumably recommended him to the somewhat militant mood of the charity reformers, but by December 1868 the parish had decided that only local schools would benefit them.[78]

While these tensions were mounting, in 1859 the two schools had been opened and by the time of the Taunton Inquiry there were 130 boys in the upper and 90 in the lower divisions. A modest but still precarious start at reform had been made.[79]

The Schools' Inquiry Commission

Far from being made necessary by the lack of educational reform, the history of London schools suggests that the Taunton Commission was needed[80] because enough reform had already been attempted to disclose local difficulties and especially the inadequacies of legal machinery and theory. Not only was 'knowledge being accumulated, the will to use it was gathering force'.[81] The very nature and status of charitable endowments was called in question.

By the 1860s, the attack on *cy pres* had become radical. Fitch, deeply experienced and concerned in the reform of endowed schools, argued in 1869 that it should be illegal to devote money by will to public objects 'except through the agency of some recognized body which was amenable to public control'. Private persons must be restrained from tampering with 'any one of those great national interests such as education . . . which demand organization and fixed principles, and . . . complete readjustment from time to time . . .'.[82] J. S. Mill considered that 'We have well nigh seen the last of the superstition which allowed men who owned a piece of land or a sum of money five hundred years ago, to make a binding disposition determining what should be done with it as long as time or the British nation should last . . .', but he was wary of Fitch's extreme position. It smacked of 'the very spirit of the overcentralising governments of the continent'. After a term of fifty or a hundred years endowments might be diverted to new purposes.[83] Arthur Hobhouse put the more extreme, and in some ways the most informed, case. The public should not be compelled to accept bequests, 'the grasp of the dead hand shall be shaken off absolutely and finally', there should 'always be a living and reasonable owner of the property to manage it in accordance with the wants of mankind'. Robert Lowe went even further and would have abolished endowments altogether.[84]

The intellectuals who were providing both the theory and practice of the new state were working upon and within a 'governing class increasingly accustomed to change and reform, increasingly persuaded of the possibility of progress . . .'.[85] Leaders of Church and State had to be enlisted. Within the ranks of the Church there was no one more influential in educational affairs than Frederick Temple. Already in 1856 in *Oxford Essays* he had raised the matter of the 'great resources for education which were then wasted in the form of endowments', and the duty of remodelling the grammar schools in order to organize the education of the middle classes. Before his appointment to the Taunton Commission Temple was studying the accumulating volumes of the Charity Commissioners. The Inquiry strengthened rather than formed these convictions which he embodied so ably in the first volume of its Report. He was already convinced that 'Secondary education in England required, above everything, to be organized'. Schools were 'isolated units, without any established relation between their situation or purposes', and their reform had been handled 'without free adjustment to the wishes of the locality, and without subordination to general plan'. Nor were the Charity Commissioners qualified to give educational guidance.[86]

Among statesmen Gladstone was a powerful ally. In 1863, on the eve of the appointment of the Commission, he criticized the exemption of Charities from taxation and provoked an alarmed deputation, including both Archbishops, Lord Shaftesbury and the Duke of Cambridge. This in turn roused Gladstone on that same evening in the Commons to attack the sacrosanct nature of the testamentary bequests. Those who wished to be benevolent should give money away while they were alive to feel the sacrifice. Existing charities were often a source of scandal, it was 'too much to suppose that [they] are managed by Angels and Archangels', and public grants to institutions would have the salutary effect of making the public a party to their management.[87] This was heavy ammunition for the advocates of state intervention.

Debates among theorists, administrators, even churchmen, were not so likely to rally public opinion as the reporting of scandalous cases, or the utterances of Gladstone. When *The Times* (Trollope's *Jupiter*, after all) supported Rogers's efforts to broach charitable funds for his City middle-class school, it was by suggesting that he was opening up 'a field of action which is perhaps wider than he contemplates'. Helping parents, who were finding 'extreme difficulty in discovering a school

Endowed and Proprietary Middle Schools
1864

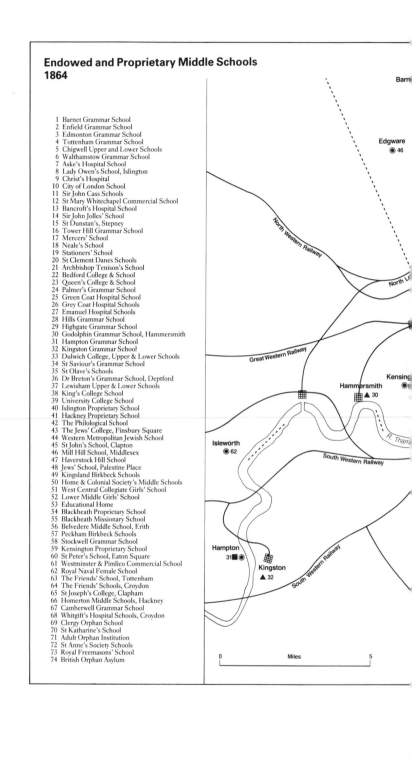

1 Barnet Grammar School
2 Enfield Grammar School
3 Edmonton Grammar School
4 Tottenham Grammar School
5 Chigwell Upper and Lower Schools
6 Walthamstow Grammar School
7 Aske's Hospital School
8 Lady Owen's School, Islington
9 Christ's Hospital
10 City of London School
11 Sir John Cass Schools
12 St Mary Whitechapel Commercial School
13 Bancroft's Hospital School
14 Sir John Jolles' School
15 St Dunstan's, Stepney
16 Tower Hill Grammar School
17 Mercers' School
18 Neale's School
19 Stationers' School
20 St Clement Danes Schools
21 Archbishop Tenison's School
22 Bedford College & School
23 Queen's College & School
24 Palmer's Grammar School
25 Green Coat Hospital School
26 Grey Coat Hospital Schools
27 Emanuel Hospital Schools
28 Hills Grammar School
29 Highgate Grammar School
30 Godolphin Grammar School, Hammersmith
31 Hampton Grammar School
32 Kingston Grammar School
33 Dulwich College, Upper & Lower Schools
34 St Saviour's Grammar School
35 St Olave's Schools
36 Dr Breton's Grammar School, Deptford
37 Lewisham Upper & Lower Schools
38 King's College School
39 University College School
40 Islington Proprietary School
41 Hackney Proprietary School
42 The Philological School
43 The Jews' College, Finsbury Square
44 Western Metropolitan Jewish School
45 St John's School, Clapton
46 Mill Hill School, Middlesex
47 Haverstock Hill School
48 Jews' School, Palestine Place
49 Kingsland Birkbeck Schools
50 Home & Colonial Society's Middle Schools
51 West Central Collegiate Girls' School
52 Lower Middle Girls' School
53 Educational Home
54 Blackheath Proprietary School
55 Blackheath Missionary School
56 Belvedere Middle School, Erith
57 Peckham Birkbeck Schools
58 Stockwell Grammar School
59 Kensington Proprietary School
60 St Peter's School, Eaton Square
61 Westminster & Pimlico Commercial School
62 Royal Naval Female School
63 The Friends' School, Tottenham
64 The Friends' Schools, Croydon
65 St Joseph's College, Clapham
66 Homerton Middle Schools, Hackney
67 Camberwell Grammar School
68 Whitgift's Hospital Schools, Croydon
69 Clergy Orphan School
70 St Katharine's School
71 Adult Orphan Institution
72 St Anne's Society Schools
73 Royal Freemasons' School
74 British Orphan Asylum

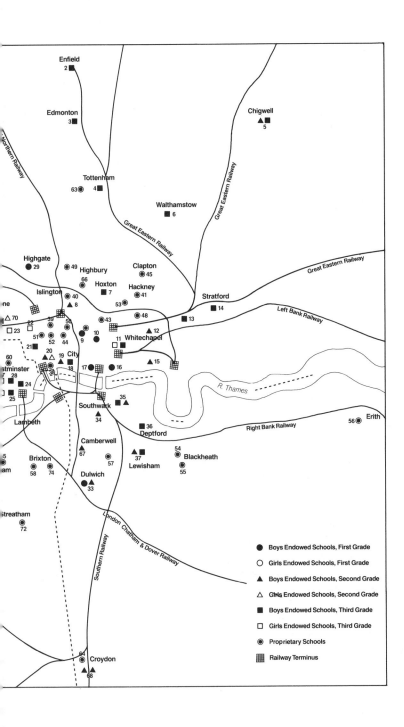

Enfield
2 ■

Edmonton
3 ■

Chigwell
▲■
5

Tottenham
63 ◉ 4 ■

Walthamstow
■ 6

Highgate
● 29

◉ 49 Highbury

Clapton
◉ 45

66
◉
Hoxton
■ 7

Islington
◉ 40

Hackney
◉ 41

Stratford
■ 14

ne
△ 70

22
□
□ 23

39
◉
50
◉

53 ◉

◉ 48
■ 13

● 12

▲ 8

◉ 43

5◉
52
◉
44
◉
10
●
9
●

11 Whitechapel
□ ■

● 16
▲ 15

21
□
60

20
▲ △
19 City
▲
18
17 ●

stminster
7
28
■ ■

38

24
■

25
□

Lambeth

Southwark
■ ▲
34

35
■ ▲

R. Thames

■ 36
Deptford

Right Bank Railway

Erith
56 ◉

Camberwell
▲ 67

5
Brixton
58 ◉ 74 ◉

◉ 57

Lewisham
▲ ■
37

54
◉
55
Blackheath

Dulwich
◉ ▲
33

streatham
◉
72

Northern Railway

Great Eastern Railway

Great Eastern Railway

Great Eastern Railway

Left Bank Railway

London Chatham & Dover Railway

Southern Railway

64
◉ Croydon
▲ ▲
68

● Boys Endowed Schools, First Grade

○ Girls Endowed Schools, First Grade

▲ Boys Endowed Schools, Second Grade

△ Girls Endowed Schools, Second Grade

■ Boys Endowed Schools, Third Grade

□ Girls Endowed Schools, Third Grade

◉ Proprietary Schools

▦ Railway Terminus

where their children can receive a decent education', was exactly the purpose for which charitable funds should be used, and Gladstone's attack was recalled. 'What he wanted to prove was that the income of all Charities ought to be taxed ... what he did prove ... was that some Charities ought to be suppressed altogether.' Already the Taunton Commissioners were poking about, 'exploring all parts of the kingdom, worrying country gentlemen about schools of which they are trustees ... teasing schoolmasters and school committees with all sorts of questions about education ... and vexing the boys themselves with unusual and unlooked for examinations'. It 'will be fortunate if the zeal for education, which is one of the best features of the present generation, provokes the reformation of our charitable foundations, which has been too long delayed'.[88]

It was in this highly polemical atmosphere that Fearon was poking about the London schools, and vexing and teasing masters, boys, governors. Representing the very body of intelligent opinion which urgently advocated administrative rationalization and the strengthening of central control, it is understandable that he should have underestimated what had already been achieved by local agencies, often in his opinion of a ramshackle kind. In many other respects he presented a brilliant analysis of London's provision of secondary education. It was during the course of this investigation that this term was established as an accepted part of educational terminology, indicating that a new dimension was being added to the concept of schooling for certain classes of society and levels of learning. Fearon's analysis of school provision in the London region was topographical, social, educational, emphasizing elements of process, systematization and interconnection which were then being built into changing ideas of secondary education. In the metropolitan area more than anywhere these could be observed and dissected by the keen minds of the new agents of the new style of government.

Fearon's assignment was the 'vast labyrinth of schools and educational institutions of all kinds and sizes within the postal limits of London,' a circle of some twelve miles from Charing Cross – a reminder that London was still a postal district rather than an entity.[89] He had to ask for more time and even then felt that he was only on the threshold of his inquiry when he presented his report. His area consisted of the Cities of London and Westminster, nearly all Middlesex, and parts of Surrey and Kent.[90] The 'Clarendon Schools' were excluded, but he had in his area the largest endowment in the country, Christ's Hospital, with an income of £42,000 plus its site and buildings, though Lyttelton wrote its report.[91] Fearon estimated that the 'aggregate net endowments for secondary education in the metropolis may be set down at 84,000 l. per annum', with primary endowments in addition. These were to serve a population of 2,803,989, and consisted of twenty-four schools, of which three (Christ's Hospital, Dulwich, St Olave's) were double foundations.

Leaving out Christ's Hospital, Fearon counted this as twenty-five schools:

> 7 classical with 1417 scholars
> 9 semi-classical with 1159 scholars
> 2 non-classical with 577 scholars
> 2 elementary with 88 scholars
> 1 in abeyance, and
> 2 others united with other primary schools.

The lower departments of the two double foundations made up the total.[92] In addition Fearon had to take private schools into account, an assignment he approached with some noticeable distaste, but without an attempt to survey these schools there would have been 'very little insight into the real relations of the grammar schools to a large and influential portion of the middle classes'. Here their real wants and tastes could be ascertained. But he found statistics of any value impossible to compile, and it was only towards private schools for girls that he was able to evince much understanding. The proprietary schools he approached with more sympathy, regarding them as a useful part of the educational apparatus of the capital, but he distrusted their strong 'element of privacy', and considered that, like the railways, that inevitable Victorian image, they 'cannot altogether escape public responsibility'.[93]

Topographically Fearon divided his area into four districts, each with its recognizable characteristics, needs and wants. District A, the north-east part, lying north of the Thames and east of the Edgware Road, was 'mainly commercial'. District B, the south-east, lay east of the road from Charing Cross to Vauxhall, was commercial, but also military and naval; it abounded with 'crammers' and villas, and private schools 'literally swarm'. The south-west (C) mainly consisted of villas and their accompanying private schools 'of the "respectable" kind'. District D, the north-west, was 'the fashionable and official division'. There mainly resided 'the upper classes; those whose sons are at Eton and Harrow and other superior schools. . . . But the sub-division is also *official*', with a 'great number of porters, messengers, door-keepers, clerks of every degree, and other persons connected with the Government offices', who are 'generally intelligent, anxious about their sons' education . . .'.[94]

Fearon also considered the capital as an organic whole, by a minute examination of the transport system and its impact on schooling. He related the eight great railway arteries, 'which together drain the metropolitan counties of Middlesex, Herts, Essex, Kent and Surrey', to his topographical pattern, collected tables of fares, with reductions for schoolboys, and calculated any extra omnibus fare, and the cost of a school dinner, sometimes provided then by the porter's wife. He concluded that for better-off middle-class Londoners, those using schools of the first, and some of the second, grade, 'the precise locality of a day school within the radius is a secondary consideration. For them we may lay down the maxim, "Every school in London is a day school for the

Londoner".' This applied only to those 'in easy circumstances'. Some of the second-grade schoolboys, and all of the third, required schools within walking distance. Not only would a rail and omnibus fare make a vital difference, but in most cases the father did not travel by rail daily either, the family dined in the middle of the day.[95]

Fearon's social analysis was an able exposition of the classic Taunton differentiation of the strata of society in educational terms. His brief was to enquire into the education of the middle class, but this had to be defined. 'There was a time when this might have been done by wealth and property, and their outward signs, dress, equipage, and the like. That time has gone for ever, and is only known to antiquaries and readers of novels. Neither can we define the middle class by its occupations. . . . But from an educational point of view the difficulty vanishes. Educationally, one *can* make a distinction between the upper, middle, and lower classes . . . and that a very exact distinction too. And what is more, one can subdivide this middle class into its different strata.' The lower classes wanted, or received, primary education only and removed their children when about twelve or thirteen; the upper classes educated their sons until well after eighteen; the sons of the middle classes left school between fourteen and nineteen. 'Few parents', he decided, 'nowadays with-hold schooling from their sons during the school time of their life.' This tautology therefore had to be resolved by how this was defined. In the middle classes a small number of first-grade schools catered for boys who wanted education until eighteen or nineteen. Here the division from upper-class families was not sharp, and such boys might at the last moment, 'owing to change of fortune, development of ability, success at examinations', which made a special impact in the metropolis, require to pass on to university or professional education. Second-grade schools catered for boys who left at sixteen or seventeen, 'in every respect the most genuinely "middle" of any part of the class'. The third grade blended with the lower classes, leaving at perhaps fourteen or fifteen, and 'contains a very large and interesting class of children, a class whose education is probably at present the worst in Britain'.[96]

It is still so often stated or implied that the Taunton Commission *prescribed* three grades of middle-class school, that it is worth emphasizing that Fearon at any rate *described* the schools, which in themselves were disclosures of social structure in London and its sub-urbs, and for which parents were prepared to pay, and at which they would keep their sons until they had to earn a living. The Report as a whole tended to be critical of these parents, 'their indifference or ignorance . . . are among the chief hindrances to education at present'. They too often 'did not care at all', or gave 'inordinate value to mere show', or thought 'no education worth having unless it could be speedily turned into money', but the Commissioners recognized that the ultimate decision must rest with them. 'What they require their children to be taught, that if it be practicable, shall be put within their reach.[97] Fearon, in his grass-roots investigations, occasionally showed rather more sympathy. In reporting on the Whitechapel Foundation Commercial School he noted 'a tendency on the part of the shopkeepers among the trustees to decry the instruction in Latin, Euclid, and other scientific branches of study; but this has been counteracted by the influence of the rector; and there is *salt* even in these utilitarian views. After all, the school is for the benefit of these shopkeepers. It is their children who are being taught there; and their influence ought to be felt in shaping the curriculum.' So also should that of the superior mechanics, makers of delicate machinery and instruments, who used the school. Fearon may have looked forward to a time when standards were raised by state funds and rational administration, but he accepted the social and educational facts of his age.[98]

In his educational analysis, Fearon's estimate of London's schools of the 'first grade' was that they were on the whole useful and effective. The City of London School he considered the most important in the district, admirable for its organization and curriculum and its practical adaptation to the needs it served. The staple of instruction was science, the science of number. 'Arithmetic, mathematics and chemistry form the bases of the intellectual nutriment.' The dead languages were deferred until the boys were older. Teaching methods were thorough, the memory well-trained, but explanation, and therefore understanding, was stressed. The cost of the schooling he calculated, including fees, fares, lunches, as £23 6s 6d p.a., making the school 'practically open to all respectable persons residing within twenty miles of St Paul's Cathedral'. The cost was low because 'the masters are underpaid, and the boys are overmassed'. Some classes were as large as 60. These were managed partly by good teaching, partly by good organization; older, backward boys were not allowed to 'fester', because what was euphemistically called a 'removal system' got rid of those who did not keep up, and promotion was by examination. Another point in the school's favour was that the masters were appointed for one year only; they had no debilitating 'freehold' in their posts. This Fearon judged to be the nearest approach to his idea of a good secondary school.[99]

Of the other first-grade schools, Christ's Hospital was the most important boarding-school, doing valuable work but in need of serious reform: 'if touched with a bold and skilful hand, it would go far towards making London and its neighbourhood the best educated locality in the world'.[100] Dulwich was 'in transition, and it was rather soon to judge 'whether that future ought to be spent in aiming at the establishment of another great classical school, or in endeavouring to provide the best pattern of middle education'. Highgate School was 'decidedly useful', though there was much that still needed to be reformed. Two central schools were also put into this category – the Tower Hill Grammar School had recently acquired a new headmaster who showed 'genuine zeal and efficiency' and the methods and discipline were good when the school was visited in May 1865. But the boys mostly left at fourteen and Fearon doubted the value of maintaining a small school, with no room for expansion, in such a central situation. It is even more curious that he should have put the Mercers' School in this class, as the Company resolutely maintained that it was their private school, refused him any information, and his visit in May 1865 convinced him that to keep a school for the free education of 70 boys, with no admission examination, all taught in one large schoolroom shut up 'on the river side', was a 'needless waste of power'.[101] These 'first-grade' schools were all in Fearon's Sub-district A with the exception of Dulwich. Only good railway facilities therefore enabled them to serve the capital and its suburbs adequately. The Commission was also prepared to agree that for this class the proprietary and better private schools should be counted, and St Paul's, Merchant Taylors', Charterhouse, Westminster and Harrow had not been included as they had been investigated by Clarendon.[102]

In Fearon's estimation London's schools of the second grade were also serving the capital well. He did not find 'any gross cases of neglect or abuse', and while there was great room for improvement, 'whether it is owing to the stimulus conveyed to them by the greater numbers, activity, and intelligence of the London population, or to the greater value of their property, or to the attraction which a metropolitan mastership offers, or to a combination of these with other causes', they 'seem to me to be in a much better condition than those which I have visited in the country'.[103] He does not suggest that the reforms of the last few decades had been at least partly responsible, yet Owen's School at Islington, the school at Whitechapel, the Coopers' Company School in Ratcliffe, St Saviour's in Southwark, were useful second-grade schools because they had been remodelled by local effort, and he carefully set out the facts of these cases.[104] Colfe's School at Lewisham, for example, had been revived by the Leathersellers' Company under a Chancery Scheme in 1857. It had therefore only been in operation again for six years when Fearon visited it. He found 59 boys present out of an enrolment of 61 (13 were boarders with the headmaster). The school was 'in all respects efficiently taught and conducted'. It was a classical school, but mathematics, French and English were 'well and carefully taught'. There was a half-yearly examination, 'through the post', by an external examiner appointed by the Company, which continued to spend more on the school than was derived from the endowment. It is difficult to see why this school was placed in the second grade, compared for example with the Tower Hill School, except that it had not yet had time to prove itself.[105]

Another recently established school was the Godolphin School, Hammersmith, formed from miscellaneous benefactions for decayed gentlemen, the apprenticing of poor children, and general education, by

Chancery Schemes of 1852 and 1859. It had been in its new buildings since 1861 and contained 30 foundation scholars and 150 fee-paying boys, mostly sons of 'professional men and persons of independent income'. The clerical headmaster aimed at a 'decidedly classical' education and a system of 'bifurcation' was attempted, which in practice created a Remove form where more French and mathematics were taught, 'a kind of refuge for boys, who from idleness, neglect of early education, or other causes of mental incapacity, do not succeed in their classical studies . . .' Fearon assessed this with some discernible dislike as 'a fair specimen of classical schools for the middle class'. It was 'taught with conscientious care' and the 'methods used for governing, reviewing, and conducting the ordinary routine are judicious and effective'. He did not think however that this was the level of education most needed in the neighbourhood. A serious general criticism of schools of this grade was that there were too few of them, and they were badly distributed – seven in his District A, three in District B, one each in Districts C and D.[106]

London's third-grade schools enabled Fearon to give full rein to his powers of criticism, and he abused them rather as Dr Johnson did the unfortunate joint of beef. He listed fourteen of these schools – St Martin-in-the-Fields (Archbishop Tenison's), the Cass School Aldgate, two Westminster endowments (Hill's and Palmer's), Enfield, Edmonton, Tottenham and Walthamstow Grammar (the Monoux charity), St Mary's Stratford (Sir John Jolles endowment), Chigwell and Lewisham lower schools, Neale's Mathematical School, St Olave's, and the Deptford school, which had more or less disappeared.[107] His first criticism was their uneven distribution; even in District A, where 'as is very natural and proper, the greater number of these schools are found, there are large spaces, great blanks . . .', for example between the Great Eastern and Great Northern Railways (Hackney, Hoxton, Dalston, De Beauvoir Town, Kingsland, Highbury, Islington) where only one *second*-grade endowment, Owen's, was situated, and the docks region, Stepney, Limehouse, Bromley (by Bow), where the Coopers' School, also of the second grade, was 'full to overflowing' and had a waiting list of 300. In these districts therefore the education of the lower middle classes was 'to a very slight degree in satisfactory hands'. The two proprietary schools which to some extent supplied the want, the Home and Colonial Institution in the Gray's Inn Road and the Congregational Normal School at Hackney, were both committed primarily to the training of teachers.[108]

Even where they existed however, there was little advantage to be gained from these third-grade schools. They were in every respect inferior to the elementary schools which these parents would not use. Fearon contrasted with relish the bright, well-warmed, lighted and appointed National school with the 'decayed structure, looking like a compound of an old-fashioned dwelling house and a hen-roost or barn' of the tottering, bare and dirty endowed school. Here, in comparison with the methodical certificated elementary teacher, an untrained master, with 'no professional study routine', his heart in 'anything rather than the work of grinding the elements into a rising generation of shop-keepers, market-gardeners, and publicans', taught ineffectively and with no proper equipment. Moreover this 'primary education bewitched' was ludicrously expensive to the community, even if free to some parents. Fearon, reminding us that he was an HMI practised in putting children through the hoops of the Revised Code, calculated the annual cost of schooling of boys at Enfield Grammar School as £3 1s 5²⁄₁₅d, double that of a National school; at Walthamstow as £8 2s 5³⁄₁₇d, four times; and at Edmonton £5 6s 5¹³⁸⁄₁₇₈ d, three times the cost. The middle class, he concluded, 'pays pretty dearly for its reverence for the past, or its timidity for the future, or its dislike of Government guidance and initiative, or whatever else it is that paralyses it, and prevents it from rearranging on a broad and economic basis the whole of its small grammar schools'.[109]

A special class of third-grade schools contained the 'Hospital Schools' where children were boarded, clothed and taught free – for example the Green and Grey Coat Schools, Emanuel, Bancroft's, Aske's. Fearon described these as part of secondary provision, as they took children of labourers, porters, messengers, policemen, those in government employment and 'very small shop-keepers' who might have been scholars at National schools etc., and gave them a rather wider and longer education, 'the first elements of a liberal education'. As they were then apprenticed or became clerks, these hospital schools took children out of the labouring class. For these schools Fearon had a special dislike. They represented to him and his like a survival into the new age of open competition and contest of the old age of patronage and sponsorship. They were filled by private favour, after no admission examination, and parents such as 'persons on duty in the Houses of Parliament and the other public offices in Westminster', assured of a free education for their offspring, often left them quite uninstructed until they got their place. Examinations during the school life of their gently docile scholars were 'nothing more than a little entertainment for the governors and their friends'. They lived an isolated monastic life which would benefit by the admission of day scholars to 'enlarge their sphere of competition and observation'.[110]

Fearon's criticisms of London's endowed schools were far-reaching, and although they were especially forceful in relation to the third grade, they ranged over the whole provision of schools. He attempted to explain what was wrong with their teaching, with what as taught in them, and with their administration. The masters of the schools were un-trained and, in the poorest schools, had neither breadth of knowledge nor method. They did not know how to classify and explain knowledge, to demonstrate principles and general laws. They used bad or archaic textbooks. Where graduates were employed they were often 'passmen', and the ordinary degree at Oxford or Cambridge was 'not a guarantee of any but the most rudimentary intellectual capacity'. But even 'class-men' had no professional preparation for secondary teaching. He noted especially the lack of 'scientific' teaching, by which he meant the systematic process of teaching by explanation. This applied to arithmetic and mathematics as well as to languages. Modern languages were often begun too late and taught by inferior teachers, even foreigners – his criticism here was of inability to communicate skills and often of poor control. Drawing was badly taught and was not helped by lack of parental discrimination – they merely wanted to see 'pretty results. . . . The mercantile classes have not much knowledge or appreciation of the principles of art.'[111]

The poorness of the teaching was related to the narrowness of its content, for it was not only the limitations of school statutes which kept the classics in their dominant place. 'The instructors', said Fearon, 'know very little of anything else. They will have the first place for their idol, grammar. They set him up. They clear a space for him, they demand half the school time for his worship.' This resulted in a curriculum suited to boys who continued their studies to twenty-one or two, but for middle-class boys, even in first-grade schools, it 'shows about as much wisdom and kindness as to prepare an elaborate dinner of six courses for a friend whose train is starting in 15 minutes'. The results were demonstrated by the pitiable attainments in classics of boys even at Christ's Hospital. The buyer of such schooling 'can only consume a certain quantity' and Fearon, who had entered upon his enquiry with a prejudice in favour of Latin and Greek, had become convinced that 'the middle class is justified in its prejudice against the attempts so commonly made to force classics upon it'. Among the mercantile classes of London, 'who now patronize private schools but would gladly use the endowed schools, I find a great desire for less instruction in classics and more thorough teaching in modern subjects', he concluded.[112]

Want of suitable external standards aggravated such poor or inappropriate teaching. Some endowed school statutes required and provided for regular examination of the boys, but this was not always carried out, nor was it often effective; Enfield School for example was never examined. If neighbouring clergy or schoolmasters were asked in, they usually prophesied 'smooth things', as 'no man of sense deliberately sits down on a thistle'. No endowed school used the College of Preceptors examinations, the offer of the Syndicate of the University of Cambridge to inspect and examine 'middle schools' was expensive, and no London grammar school had taken it up. The Oxford and Cambridge Locals had little effect either on these schools. Only Dulwich and Whitechapel prepared whole classes for the examinations, and bad schools 'refused to take the medicine'. Tutors from Oxford and Cambridge were used by some first-grade schools such as Highgate and the City of London, but for second- and third-grade schools these examiners tended to be 'Gulliver among Lilliputians'.[113]

Behind all these weaknesses and failures lay that *bête noire* of the utilitarian reformer, bad management, for which Fearon reserved his most stringent criticism. The 'mercantile classes' were themselves profoundly dissatisfied, not only with the curriculum, but the inefficient administration of these schools. There were at least eight different *sources* of authority involved in the management of thirty-three grammar schools within his area, and five distinct *kinds* of authority, with wide variations. Of City Companies Fearon was especially scathing; they were only interested in the education of the sons of their own members, and certainly not in children lower than 'the bulk of their own livery men and freemen'. Private trustees were often neglectful, uninterested. '"I hate", said one of the trustees to me, "the very name of the school . . .".' If they were local they tended to lack educational knowledge or to be too much engaged in 'local politics or parish polemics'. One school seemed in this way to have vanished in a dispute between a local chemist and the vicar. If they lived at a distance they failed to attend meetings and matters were left too much in the master's hands. In general Fearon considered them to be 'not an efficient body of men; in fact it was the utmost limit of their efficiency' to have kept themselves 'without the grasp of the law'.[114]

At the centre Fearon wanted a rationalization of confusions and conflicts. The Court of Chancery was slow, irregular, expensive, uncertain. Seven schools in his district were urgently awaiting reform, while St Clement Danes was constantly undergoing revision and Enfield was crippled by legal costs. There was little consistency in Chancery's regulations. In the matter of boarders Highgate had been allowed an unlimited number, St Saviour's and Camberwell 8. Above all, Chancery lacked educational knowledge. The Charity Commissioners were on the side of enlightenment, but had neither enough authority, nor expertise.[115]

Fearon had justification for many of his strictures, and his overall desire for reform commands sympathy. His brilliant report however is not free from over-generalization or exaggeration, special pleading and inconsistency. His argument for adaptation to local and social needs does not fit easily into his overall desire for administrative neatness. The needs of Highgate and Bankside for example were very different, and the Chancery solutions on the number of boarding-places may not have been the result of inconsistency but of flexibility. The particularity and varied possibilities of historical situations tended to be ironed out by the administrative reformer. Just as he had underestimated what had already been achieved by agencies for which he had little sympathy, so he pre-empted solutions to complexities and irregularities which did not accord with his style of thinking and his convictions. The future however was with the bureaucratic reformer, not with the jumble of civic and suburban expedients inherited from the past or recently improvised or overhauled.

Fearon's Assistant Commissioner's report was among those which exercised a noticeable influence on the general report so ably prepared by Temple himself. The advocacy of the need to see the endowed schools as a whole, as 'local contributions to the higher education of the country, which might be freely adjusted to changes as they occurred' necessitated a central agency with knowledge and power, and local boards as well. Acceptance of various levels of secondary education related to largely middle-class social demands led to recommendations for the recasting of schools into a 'neatly articulated system, almost Gallic in its symmetry'. Intense dislike of free education stemmed from determination to get rid of patronage, of charitable grinders, of choice of children for schools on irrelevant grounds. Open competition would be an instrument of educational rationality, creating opportunities for able children from any social class to receive an appropriate schooling. Prizes must come 'from something in the boy himself, and not in the circumstances of his parents'.[116]

The aftermath of Taunton

The Endowed Schools Act of 1869[117] did not embody the recommendations which Fearon would probably have considered crucial – local boards, and a permanent central supervisory agency. Nevertheless it went much further in breaking the grasp of 'the Dead Hand' than might have been feared.[118] Hobhouse himself was one of the three Endowed Schools' Commissioners appointed, and his colleague Lord Lyttelton, Gladstone's brother-in-law, was also well-known as a radical reformer in this field and the author of the critical report on large foundations, including Christ's Hospital. The third, Canon Robinson, a Broad Churchman, was a friend of Foster and had training college experience.[119] Their powers enabled them to disregard *cy pres* for certain types of endowment, to take the initiative in reforming trusts, and to consider localities as a whole. How they fared in this formidable task is amply illustrated in the story of London's schools. Their slow labours shaped the secondary schooling of generations of young Londoners.

Again, however, it is important to stress not only the radical changes which the 1869 Act made possible, but also continuity with the more unsystematic and localized reform which preceded it. Much reshaping had already taken place, much educational experience had been gained. The headmasters and staff of schools remodelled after 1869 came either from proprietary schools or rejuvenated public schools, or from endowed schools which had experimented in various ways. Slow though the progress on Schemes after 1869 was, it is difficult to see how it could have taken place successfully unless there had been men capable of steering the schools into new waters.

St Olave's illustrates both these continuities. Fearon had used its problems to draw attention to the urgent need for new machinery. As it happened, the old system enabled the parish to get a new Scheme for the school from the Court of Chancery in April 1869. It divided the school into three departments, classical, commercial and English. The upper division was open to non-parishioners at not more than £8 8s a year, parishioners paying only an entrance fee of £4 4s and having the other two schools free. This led to a vigorous development. By 1875 there were 280 in the classical school, with 190 paying fees of £6 6s, and the other two schools had 250 and 230 boys. The Oxford Local examinations were used, boys were going on to the universities, both in mathematics and classics. Science was introduced gradually, and the headmaster gave up his house to be turned into laboratories. This also enabled him to move to a more salubrious district, Blackheath. In 1887 the Local examinations had done their work and were now cramping the curriculum as St Olave's had in fact passed in ten years from a third-grade to a first-grade school. In 1876 the headmaster, Johnson, was elected a member of the Headmasters' Conference. Boys came to the school from all parts of London, particularly from Rotherhithe, and made full use of the new railway stations, though it is interesting that in spite of the occasional boy who penetrated on foot the abandoned and foggy railway tunnel of the London Hydraulic Power Company, the river remained not a physical, but a psychological, barrier and few boys crossed the Thames to the school. The system of promotion through the three grades of school worked well, and 'prizes were principally carried off by boys from elementary schools'.

All this development took place before the Endowed Schools Act was brought to bear upon St Olave's. In 1877 the Commissioners produced a draft Scheme for reforming the governing body, but local objections were raised. In 1884 another Scheme was published which proposed that the 'elementary' school should be abolished, and the foundation should consist of a grammar and a science school. Finally in the Scheme of 1890 the three schools were kept, and the old governing court or corporation, representing local families, businesses and parish interests, was replaced by a board of representative governors. The school's historian states the 'blunt and basic truth' that this foundation was now firmly within the grip of a central authority which 'was taking the first tentative steps towards the building of a national system of Secondary education'.[120]

Change of administration facilitated rather than initiated further developments. Johnson had repeatedly put forward scathing criticisms of the old building, designed for the monitorial system. In 1890, when the character and government of the school were at last settled, plans for a new building became possible. Before it was finished there was a new headmaster, W. G. Rushbrooke, an Oxford man who had been both boy and master at the City of London School. He was allowed to modify the plans in many important ways which enabled the building to serve until 1968. Rushbrooke carried the school vigorously forward in further modernizing the curriculum and methods of teaching. He emphasized physical education and tried to identify St Olave's with public-school practices and ideas at a time when these were considered to represent the progressive aspect of secondary education. In 1896 the decline of the neighbouring St Saviour's led to the suggestion that the two schools should be amalgamated, and this was carried through in 1899, under a Charity Commission Scheme which applied some of the endowment to a girls' school. St Olave's and St Saviour's represent the achievements, and limitations, of both local and central enterprise over the periods both before and after the 1869 Act.[121]

Another case, which Fitch put forward to the Endowed Schools' Enquiry of 1886 as an example of London achievements 'typical of the general views and plans' of the reformers, was Haberdashers' Aske's Foundation. This began in 1689 when Robert Aske bequeathed £20,000 and the residue of his estate to build a hospital as almshouses for twenty poor men of the Company and to educate twenty sons of its poor freemen. The Hoxton institution had to some extent been modified to keep in touch with educational needs. Dr Mortimer of the City of London School had been consulted in 1849 and had recommended French instead of Latin, in 1858 mathematics and science had been suggested, in 1866 the parishioners of Hoxton had tried to get the school opened to their children, but it was not until the Endowed Schools' Commission was able to formulate a Scheme that radical reform was possible. By this time it was difficult to find twenty decayed members of a small and prosperous Company who wished to live in almshouses in Hoxton. Instead, pensions of £50 to £60 a year were given to thirty members. The 'twenty little haberdashers' entitled to free board and education were replaced by 30 exhibitioners with £30 and £40 a year towards any school they chose. 'Having thus amply satisfied the original trusts, the entire residue was then made applicable to the establishment of large public day schools in London.' Two schools, for 300 boys and 300 girls, were in Hoxton, and by 1886 had 429 and 278 pupils, a large number from local elementary schools. The leaving age was at first sixteen but was raised to eighteen in 1883. At Hatcham New Cross the Company administered the estate of another trust, the Jones charity. Here they hit upon the happy idea that the provision of middle-class schools would 'prove a material benefit to both charities, for whilst on the one hand Aske's would have the advantage of a site much healthier than that of Hoxton and which would be most accessible by means of the various railways meeting at New Cross, on the other hand, the erection of the Hospital and schools would materially increase the probability of letting the [Jones] land for building . . .'. Here two schools were built, boys and girls at first being on the same site. The fees here were about £7–£8, but there were exhibitions and scholarships of a very liberal kind. There were therefore 1262 children being educated by this foundation in 1886.[122]

Aske's was one of the hospital schools which had so much roused

Fearon's powers of criticism, but another of these was the cause of a serious setback to the working of the Endowed Schools' Act and its 1874 amendment by Disraeli's government. The Act had run ahead of public opinion. 'Our experience in attempting to work the Act has shown that the country was hardly prepared for its reception'.[123] As Hobhouse had put it, 'I always looked upon ourselves as missionaries sent to lighten the heathen . . .'[124] and the inhabitants of Westminster proved quite ready to oblige him in his desire for martyrdom.

The Commissioners wisely did not select London as a whole as one of the areas for their 'topographical system' but tackled the Westminster charities, partly because it 'seemed to invite large and early reform', partly perhaps because it was on their doorstep, perhaps even partly because it meant engaging battle with the City of London itself. Emanuel Hospital especially was one of those antipathetic foundations giving free board and elementary education to a small number of children chosen by patronage. From this and other endowments there seemed a hope of producing a rational structure of secondary schools for an important and thickly populated part of the metropolis. Success would undoubtedly have been a great encouragement to similar plans. Conversely, failure set back the possibility of planning reforms elsewhere on a rational regional basis.[125]

The Dacre charity (Emanuel) was a sixteenth-century benefaction operating from 1603 and providing for twenty aged poor and twenty children from Westminster, Chelsea and Hayes in Middlesex. The revenues did not mature enough to open the school until the next

Emanuel Hospital, Westminster

The carved school-room at Great Campden House, Kensington, *c.* 1840

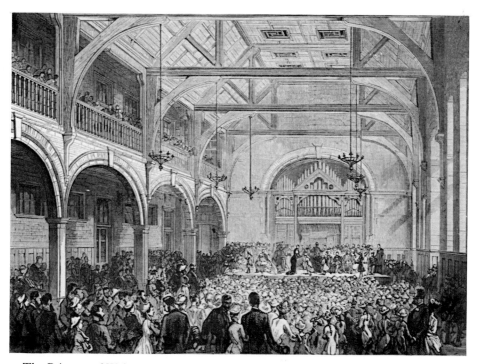

The Princess of Wales presents prizes at the North London Collegiate School, 1879

11 The transformation of girls' education, from private enclave to public occasion.

Miss Buss, founder and headmistress of the North London Collegiate School, with her successor, Dr Sophie Bryant, the new professional, first woman Doctor of Science of the University of London.

Dr Haig Brown, headmaster of Kensington Proprietary School and of the Charterhouse, former pupil and active governor of Christ's Hospital.

Wm Haig Brown

12 The essential talents.

century, but when Yorkshire estates became more profitable, the governors, the Lord Mayor and Alderman of London, put up new buildings and the so-called Brown Coat School opened in 1756. Here ten boys and ten girls were 'to be brought up in virtue and good and laudable arts'. Revenues steadily mounted and the governors with some conscientiousness strove to enlarge the benefits. Pensions were increased, more children were helped, new and extended buildings were put up. By 1847 the school consisted of 60 children. Some incidents in its history do not altogether endorse Fearon's generalization about docile and monastic communities, but there was certainly an air of Hiram's Hospital about the whole foundation. The delightful and large gardens and charming buildings were not far from the Abbey, the master's house was roomy enough for private pupils or boarders from Westminster School, his position was usually regarded as a stepping-stone to ecclesiastical preferment – it was all perhaps too much like Barchester for the zeal of a reforming Commissioner. Moreover Westminster abounded in such schools. The Grey Coat Hospital was opened by the parish of St Margaret's in 1698 and in 1851 had 67 boys and 33 girls. St Margaret's Hospital dated from 1624, and as it was given its Charter by Charles I and £50 a year by Charles II it was sometimes called King Charles's Hospital, though it was also founded by the parish. Its 25 boys wore green coats and 6 of them had yellow caps in honour of another benefactor. Palmer's, or the Blackcoat School, for 20 boys, was founded by a clergyman in 1654, and Emery Hill's School, a lay foundation, also for 20 boys, dated from 1674. All these together, with an income of about £7000 a year, educated 230 children in multi-coloured garb who must have flickered feverishly before the eyes of the reformers.[126]

The governors of Emanuel planned in 1869 to replace the almshouses by out-pensions, and to move the school into the country, admitting extra children as fee-payers. But in 1870 the Commissioners produced a radical plan, 'supposed to be a theoretically perfect scheme for the education of the Middle Classes of Westminster', as one bitter Aldermanic critic said. It was proposed to unite all the endowments and establish a boys' boarding-school near London, and two days schools in Westminster with 300 boys in each. For girls there were to be a boarding-school for 120 and the original Grey Coat Hospital for 300. These schools would no longer be free, but generous exhibitions were to be provided.[127]

An embittered dispute broke out in press and Parliament over these ambitious plans. The hope of educating over a thousand children from the charities probably overstretched available income. The City resented its threatened loss of power and patronage. The inhabitants of Westminster perhaps had more legitimate ground for opposition as admission to the schools was not to be by need, but by competitive examination. The City Solicitor sounded the alarm, the Mayor and Alderman petitioned the Committee of Privy Council, denying 'utterly that these and similar foundations were intended or ought in future to be established only for boys who possess brilliant abilities'. At a Mansion House meeting a descendant of the Dacre family was produced who rambled somewhat about Shakespeare, grammar schools and the right to gratuitous education. Letters to *The Times* wrote of the 'pauperised system of management'. In Parliament Lord Salisbury came forward strongly and with obvious relish as the champion of the poor against the principles of competition and confiscation, and pilloried the Scheme for its devotion to the middle classes (for whom he perhaps lacked sympathy). Sharing public attention with the Tichborne trial, Emanuel Hospital became a test case, 'one of the most notable precedents on the supervision of education by the state', as *The Times* said. Far from depriving the poor, the Scheme would restore benefits to local people, for 'the effects of patronage' had been 'seen in the number of City children introduced in the School'. The *Spectator* underlined the outmoded ethos of the hospital school, where a less useful education than an ordinary elementary one was given to children who were compelled to wear a ridiculous dress, live in a 'little monastic community', and trained to be grateful to their benefactors and respectful to their patrons.[128]

After three months of controversy, the City won a victory by the defeat of the Scheme in the House of Lords. 'The triumvirate of autocrats sitting in secret in Westminster' then produced a new Scheme leaving the almshouses to the control of the City Corporation, setting up for the schools (much as in the earlier Scheme) a new governing body, including representatives from the City and from the School Board for London. The Commissioners stood firm by their principle of competitive entry and the award of exhibitions and scholarships 'on merit and not by patronage'. The necessarily limited number of children must 'deserve it by self-help and self-control on the part of themselves and their parents'.[129] They also borrowed a weapon from their opponents and organized a petition signed by over 6000 citizens of Westminster supporting this Scheme, which was pushed through by Gladstone in 1873, making ominous reference to City privileges, a city 'fed with charities, gorged and almost bloated with charities'.[130] The Emanuel Hospital case had indeed many repercussions. Even the Commissioners' friends admitted that some of their published opinions and plans had 'caused alarm' and had in some cases seriously impended harmonious action, though charges that they had earned a reputation for 'wholesale and unncessary interference' were dropped.[131] The case enabled Disraeli to replace the Endowed Schools' Commissioners with more conciliatory agents, but it also sent rumblings of anger and alarm forward towards the next obstacle to the reform of endowments, the City Charities. 'This poor little business of Emanuel . . . may thus prove the occasion of a great undertaking . . . reorganizing the Metropolis of a nation.'[132]

From this conflict there eventually emerged, for boys, the United Westminster Schools. The suburban boarding-school, Emanuel School, was opened in 1883 in the former premises of the Royal Victoria Patriotic Asylum on Wandsworth Common. The fees both for boarding and tuition were to be moderate, and the school was modelled on Woodard's Ardingly in Sussex.[133] Its first headmaster had experience at the City of London School and the Godolphin School, and his successor came in 1893 from Christ's Hospital. It began with 67 boarders and 12 day boys, but a year later there were 215 altogether and by the end of the century 350, 160 of them boarders. A quarter of the boarders were holders of scholarships of varying value. In its early years this school was of a 'second-grade' standard. Most boys left at sixteen, even fifteen was common, and seventeen was the latest age they could remain without special permission. The University Locals and College of Preceptors examinations were taken and only gradually did a few aspire to London Matriculation. Science was from the first an important part of the curriculum and in 1896 good laboratories were built. As Wandsworth began to lose its rural charm the situation became less suitable for a boarding-school, and in 1910 Emanuel became wholly a day school; boarding-scholarships were provided elsewhere. The school had established itself as an important part of educational provision in south London. Its standards had risen, and it was at this time of transition that a new headmaster arrived who was determined to make it 'one of the great schools of England' where boys would learn 'to live a corporate life'.[134]

In Westminster there remained the Palmer, Hill and St Margaret Schools, which in 1899 were combined by a Consolidating Scheme as the Westminster City School. Here the education was of a less aspiring kind where, as Roby put it, an attempt was made to provide a good school 'for the lower sections of the middle-classes' with entrance exhibitions for poor boys.[135]

The Endowed Schools' Commissioners had on the whole had their own way educationally with the Westminster schools, but had destroyed themselves in the process. Hobhouse had already gone to India, his successor, Roby, and Lyttelton were both replaced, and their Charity Commission successors trod more warily. The hope of dealing systematically with endowments in a locality, and thereby trying to remedy the failure of the Act to set up local boards, had to be abandoned. On the one hand, the Emanuel case strengthened the hands of obdurate local vested interests or opponents of rational change, on the other it placed some of the initiative once more in local hands, and where enlightened local leadership prevailed, properly co-ordinated Schemes could be devised in co-operation with the Commissioners. In London the very density and variety of endowments enabled some achievements in local provision – planning would be too ambitious a word to use – and the picture is further confused by London's rapidly expanding and shifting development.

Hammersmith demonstrated both problems and achievements. By 1879 the Latymer schools were reorganized. Since 1863 the boys had been housed in a new school which at first held 200, still clothed and badged by the Charity, and the education was of an elementary kind.[136] In 1878 a Scheme divided it into Latymer Upper and Lower Schools. The Lower School eventually passed into the hands of the London County Council[137] but in 1895 new buildings for the Upper School between King Street and the river were opened by Temple, now Bishop of London. Here fees were charged, scholarships were provided from the foundation, and the education was of a secondary standard. Already in 1896 the numbers had reached 300 and the buildings had to be extended with five classrooms, science laboratories, workshops. By 1901 there were 450 boys. The first headmaster, the Reverend C. J. Smith, had been a Latymer School boy, trained as a teacher at St Mark's Chelsea, and later headmaster of the Higher Grade School at Cambridge. He took his degree in 1884, returned to the staff of his training college, and was ordained in 1886; an interesting case of experience crossing the line between elementary and secondary schooling.[138]

In the meantime, in 1884 St Paul's had moved to Hammersmith,[139] and the Godolphin School, about which Fearon had doubts, was already feeling this competition when Latymer Upper School was opened. In 1900 Godolphin closed, and its funds were united with Latymer endowments (£8000 capital and £500 a year) to form a girls' school.[140] The remodelling of charities can only be said to have catered for secondary schooling in this suburb in a somewhat wasteful and haphazard fashion. It must however be conceded that London's development was prodigal and unpredictable.

The East End is another interesting study where girls and boys must be considered together. This area remained more mixed socially than its stereotype in the national conscience often admits. There were numerous endowed elementary schools in the eastern suburbs, and as early as the 1850s, Canon Champneys had discerned the need for secondary education for boys and continued to get some of the local charity funds for his Commercial Foundation School.[141] In 1888 this useful school was further strengthened by union with the Davenant Foundation which, from 1680, under the will of the rector of St Mary Matfelon, Whitechapel, had provided school and clothing for 40 poor boys and 30 poor girls: later, under Dr Bell's system, numbers were considerably increased. Eventually, after the merger of 1888, the Commercial Foundation School in Leman Street moved altogether to the Davenant Foundation premises in the Commercial Road, which were considerably extended to provide a broader course. By this time (1896) the various grades of schooling had converged into the concept of secondary education generally associated with the Bryce Report, but for at least fifty years the appetite for such education had been present in this East End parish.[142]

At the George Green School in Poplar the curriculum developed along secondary lines, for boys the usual English subjects, modern languages, Latin, science, drawing, drill, music, and a strong emphasis on technical instruction. From 1894 the school had grants from the Technical Education Board, and in 1895, as well as other sciences, it was teaching chemistry and elementary engineering, and thinking of including building construction when funds would allow. Painting, instrumental music and Greek were extras. The Cambridge Locals, Science and Art, Civil Service, London Chamber of Commerce examinations were taken, and boys were entered for Finsbury Technical College, the Bow and Bromley Institute, and the University of London. The teaching was thorough and methodical. The girls, who originally had no Latin or science but domestic economy and the 'laws of health', had the upper storey of the building and played on the roof if it was fine. By 1895 they were learning Latin, and extras included dancing, the guitar and banjo. There were then 137 girls paying £4 4s a year, 'mainly the daughters of professional men and the better class of tradesmen'; 50 were from Poplar, 38 from within a radius of two miles. There were scholarships and one exhibition, and one pupil had 'attained considerable distinction at the North London Collegiate School and afterwards proceeded to Girton College, Cambridge'. The school's financial position was precarious, and the Blackwall Tunnel was threatening its premises.[143]

The first East End endowment tackled under the 1869 Act was the Coborn School. The widow of a Bow brewer had endowed this at the beginning of the eighteenth century for poor boys and girls. Her executors were to found a separate school or combine the funds with those of Sir John Jolles School at Stratford (the St Mary's School of Fearon's list). By 1869 numbers had risen to 250 boys and 170 girls organized as a National school. In 1873 a Scheme was prepared to reorganize it as a secondary school for 200 of each sex. The buildings of the old Stepney Proprietary School in Tredegar Square were purchased and extended. This experiment was not successful and in 1886 the girls' school closed. During this same period the Coopers' Company, whose boys' school was flourishing in Ratcliffe, had also decided to apply some of their trust funds to girls, and in 1878 opened a school for them in Mile End Road. This was highly successful and had to move to larger premises in Bow Road. In 1886 the Charity Commissioners demanded to know by what authority the girls' school had been founded and brought considerable pressure on the Company to agree to a merger with the Coborn charity. The Stepney and Bow Foundation (1891) resulted, half the governors coming from the Company and half nominated by local and educational authorities. The Cooper boys moved into Tredegar Square with the Coborn boys, the Bow Road premises were used by both the Cooper and Coborn girls.[144]

Parmiter's charity school and almshouses in Bethnal Green were reorganized under a Scheme of 1884 to provide a secondary school for

250 boys, 40 of them scholarship holders. The fees were to be between £3 and £6, and the curriculum included Latin, mechanical drawing, and 'such subjects of technical training as the Governors may fix from time to time'. A girls' school for 'not less than one hundred and fifty scholars' was to be set up when funds had accumulated. By 1890 the boys' school had 321 pupils.[145] Another East End primary charity, the Raine's Foundation in Wapping, was also promoted to secondary level – in 1897 for boys and in 1904 for girls.[146] To this provision must be added the Central Foundation Girls' School in Spital Square, and some places at the Cowper Street Boys' School provided by the reorganization of the Bishopsgate Schools.[147] It can therefore be claimed that a variety of agents, to some extent supervised and co-ordinated by the Commissioners, had provided quite amply for the secondary schooling of children of these East End parishes.[148] Here social change, which did by the later decades of the century make this part of London very much the domain of classes which had not previously demanded secondary schooling, was to some extent counteracted by educational change, as standards and aspirations rose, especially after the Board schools began to make their impact. It was not until the depopulation of the East End in the mid twentieth century that these useful schools moved out further into the suburbs.

The Endowed Schools Commissioners had aimed not only to rationalize provision in a locality, but to systematize the levels of schooling. In this respect also their successors from 1874 had to proceed more cautiously. There was general acceptance in the Taunton Report of the usefulness of the classification of schools into first, second and third grades, but there was less agreement about the strength of the demarcation between them. Lord Harrowby had been almost carried away by the beauty and clarity of the idea: 'I should like to club the grammar schools with some relation to locality, and I should like to say, you shall be a good lower middle-class school; you shall be a middle middle-class school; you shall be a higher middle-class school, that which is now called a grammar school.' Others such as Canons Moseley and Rogers wanted to keep the distinctions clear because they feared that classics would usurp the curriculum needed by the lower grades. Latin, said Rogers, who put his conviction into practice at the Cowper Street Schools, would be the thin end of the wedge, a schoolmaster would be tempted to 'go on to Greek' and then to get his boys 'off to the University', to the neglect of the majority who wanted a different kind of education. On the whole the Commission favoured a decent flexibility; schools should enable boys to go as far as possible; education was the 'social bridge which unites all classes in England above the mere day labourer', and Latin was 'the cement of this'. The first Commissioners adopted the Taunton grades as the 'basis of our action', but already by 1872 had enlarged the maximum age at 'the two lower grades to 15 and 17 respectively'. Where possible separate schools were established, but sometimes demand only justified internal subdivisions or departments. It was accepted that a school would suffer by attempting too much, the 'necessary result was a failure of some of the objects, or imperfection and superficiality in all'.[149]

As the slow and necessarily unsystematic work of the Commissioners proceeded from 1874 to 1899, the situation changed under their hands, the various levels of schooling fused into an idea of general secondary education, encouraged and made possible both by their own work and the experience upon which they drew and which they incorporated into their policies. The Taunton guidelines can be discerned in their London schemes, blurred by educational pressures, and redrawn by changing social attitudes.

The 'Battle of Dulwich' illustrated this point. At the time of the Taunton Inquiry the two schools, reformed under the Act of Parliament of 1857, were already developing under the Master, Dr Carver, and the chairman of the governing body, Canon Rogers. But the ideas of these two powerful Victorian personalities were very different. Rogers wanted both first- and second-grade schools to emphasize science and to serve the less well-to-do inhabitants, not only of Camberwell but of the other privileged parishes, which included his own. In some ways he helped to defeat his own objects, for astute business management, especially in selling parts of the estate to railway companies, hugely increased the assets, making it possible for Carver to realize *his* ambition, to create a public school. When the new buildings, almost an embodiment in brick of Ruskin's 'Stones of Venice', were opened by the Prince of Wales in 1870, Carver's policy began to triumph. His early successes bred further success, for Dulwich village, largely in the hands of the governors of the estate, was growing fast, was served by several railway lines and attracting parents who wanted to make use of the school. Local families therefore had an interest in supporting Carver. 'We have at Dulwich the only first grade school in South London. . . . It has proved successful beyond parallel. . . . It is well known that the college has made Dulwich and the neighbourhood what they are, and that hundreds of families have taken up residence there solely because of the great educational advantages', wrote a correspondent in the local press. By 1882 Rogers had lost. He resigned his chairmanship in 1895 telling A. H. Gilkes, who had succeeded to the Mastership in 1885, 'You wish to make Dulwich a public school and I have no wish to enter into a conflict with you.' By 1904 it had 699 boys, boarding-houses, a school cap, cricket and football fixtures of the right kind. It had 'finally asserted its place among Public Schools by winning the Ashburton Shield . . .'. Its fees were between £25 and £35 a year. It was 'providing the professional and mercantile classes' with 'the same kind of education and school atmosphere that the richer members of the same classes obtain by sending their sons out of town'.[150] The lower school had a more difficult struggle to establish itself. It had never occupied the same buildings but was scattered about the village. In 1875 the Reverend J. H. Smith, Rogers's curate at Bishopsgate and collaborator in his schemes for middle-class education, became headmaster, and in 1887 the 400 boys moved into new buildings for 600. In the beginning it had had a more restricted curriculum, but from this time developed rapidly. Smith, 'a master of his craft', insisted on well-equipped science laboratories, first for physics and then for chemistry. He paid great attention to music. By the end of the century London Matriculation was being taken, and by 1911, when the school was completely full, it was considered to be the goal of all boys taking a public examination.[151]

Some of the endowment, combined with a local primary charity, was also used for a girls' school, the James Allen's Girls' School, a cause which always enlisted Rogers's sympathy.[152] He also secured some of the endowment funds for his Cowper Street School. As early as 1871 the Middle-Class Schools' Corporation had approached Hobhouse, regarded by Rogers as an ally, in hopes of being 'admitted into relations with the Endowed Schools' Commission', but this had not proved legally feasible. In 1887 the Great Eastern Railway had finally sliced through the site of the Bishopsgate Schools and this, together with the Dulwich connection, enabled the Charity Commissioners to move in. Under a scheme of 1891 the Bishopsgate boys were sent to Cowper Street, while some of the Alleyn endowment was also used for scholarships paying half the fees there for boys of parents living or working in the privileged parishes. St Botolph's Vestry shrewdly proposed that the school should be called Alleyn's Central Foundation, as a recognition of present benefits, and in hopes of encouraging more. This however did not take, and henceforth it was named the Central Foundation School. Its sister school in Spital Square was also endowed.[153]

This benefit to two of the parishes for which Alleyn had originally designed his charity was described by Leach as a depredation on the rights of Dulwich College, 'the indomitable rector of Bishopsgate carrying off £50,000 as his share of the plunder'. It is curious that Leach as an historian should have been imprisoned within a concept of secondary education which had only been recently formulated, but which as an administrator he was helping to consolidate and implement. In his history of the Dulwich charity he accuses Rogers of advancing the interests of his own parish, and depriving Dr Carver's boys, and of regarding 'all social and therefore educational strata below the level of Eton and above that of the Board School' as of 'one dead level of mediocrity in intellect and culture'.[154]

Croydon is an interesting case study in the difficulties of identifying appropriate levels of education for it was a commuter town rapidly developing in numbers and prosperity. Between 1871 and 1901 its population grew from 56,000 to 134,000, and it was surrounded by its own little satellite suburbs, villages such as Addiscombe which were linked to it by its own small railway network, as Croydon was linked to the capital. This pushed up the value of property and increased the wealth of the Whitgift endowment. The complexity of the social composition of such a community put keen pressures on education. Local tradesmen and businessmen demanded commercial education and resented having to use private schools; professional parents, especially those who could not afford to send their sons daily to the City, wished for a revival of the Grammar School, while the Church party argued the constantly growing need for popular education. By the later 1870s a ratepayers' pressure group of superior artisans, shopkeepers, clerks, had been formed, and became the Whitgift Hospital and Croydon Charities Committee.

The endowment itself laboured under particular difficulties. The Church party had already secured possession and early attempts at reform in 1858 had entrenched the National School more firmly in a new building. The Archbishop being the Visitor, the Charity Commissioners were powerless to interfere, while the Archbishop's desire for reform was ineffective because he could not draw on the support of the Commission. By 1869 reforms had proceeded far enough for Tait to lay the foundation stone of a new Commercial and Middle School of the Hospital of the Holy Trinity in Croydon in the 'Perpendicular Collegiate style'. The 1869 Act and the appointment of the new Commissioners only brought confusion, for they disapproved of the new plan and found much local distrust of the level of education proposed and of the patronage of the governors, all appointed by the Archbishop. In the event the school was built and opened without the approval of the Commissioners, and the new headmaster, an Oxford man, arrived with hopes of creating a public school with inadequate facilities, a scheme of fees which encouraged parents to keep their boys in the lower school or take them away early, and sharply divided opinion in the town. In 1881 a Scheme was finally drawn up which also established a middle school. This was an immediate success and by 1894 a second such school was contemplated. Whitgift School only struggled towards success early in the next century when its scale of fees was rationalized and its course was both widened and integrated, and from this point the school's crisis of identity was resolved.[155]

Another example of an attempt to satisfy two levels of education from one endowment was Sir Walter St John's foundation in Battersea. In 1700 he had left thirty-one acres in the parish of Camberwell to endow a graduate schoolmaster, to teach rudiments to 20 poor boys, and some Latin and Greek to any other scholars 'at a salary from their friends and parents'. It was always difficult to combine the two kinds of teaching and from 1800 to 1852 the school virtually ceased to exist. From 1852 to 1873 there were numerous attempts at reform, and then in 1875 an upper school was opened in St John's Lodge on the hill above Clapham Junction, where soon 80 boys received a 'lower grade grammar' type of education for £12 a year – Latin, modern languages, a little science. A middle school was built in Battersea High Street, with fees of £2 a year, and as marshy Battersea was being developed for lower-middle-class housing, it was an immediate success. By 1879 it had 285 boys and was used as a practising school by the neighbouring training college. As the more pretentious school was in difficulties, the Commissioners advised closing it and transferring all the endowments to the middle school. Just at this juncture, 1880, the endowment was enriched by the sale of land to the London and South-Western Railway Company and a new headmaster took over the Clapham branch, raised the tone of the education, adding Greek and successful science teaching, and rapidly increased its numbers from 48 to 160 in ten years. In 1893 the Commissioners negotiated a new Scheme, the upper school became Battersea Grammar School, where the character of the education was 'recognized as that of a first-grade school of the modern type, not excluding Greek, but placing most insistence on modern subjects'. Again Leach was critical: all the funds should have gone to this school, and the other been handed over to Battersea Training College.[156]

The contrast between this attitude and the importance which the Taunton Commissioners had given to third-grade schools indicates the development which had taken place in the whole idea of secondary education during the last thirty years of the century. At the outset of the enterprise the Endowed Schools' Commissioners had to use much time in reorganizing elementary endowments, especially in the flurry of denominational activity caused by Forster's Act of 1870. But as that began to take effect, and School Boards were gradually established, the position changed. While regretting that there should be a 'broad distinction' between elementary 'schooling of the children of the labouring class' and other schools, the Commissioners' Report of 1872 maintained that their duty under the 1869 Act of 'putting a liberal education within the reach of all classes' was best attained by giving them 'advantages which they cannot expect from other sources'.[157] This justified the use of primary endowments of the charity school kind for secondary education, in the East End parishes for example, and these seemed especially appropriate for third-grade schools or for scholarship schemes.[158] In 1883 the Commissioners summarized the provision of third-grade school places in the metropolis with the number of pupils in attendance:[159]

	Boys
Battersea	300
Bow	128
Clerkenwell	285
Greenwich	365
Hackney	326
Hoxton	355
Westminster	700

	Girls
Bow	84
Camden Town	387
Greenwich	319
Hackney	248
Hoxton	246
West Ham	244
Westminster: St James	273
St Martin	160
Greycoat	326

But the slow pace of reform meant that rising standards of elementary education were overtaking the need for third-grade schools. The higher commercial school, for example, which was to be set up in the parish of St Luke's Finsbury as part of the reorganization of the Dulwich charity, was never built, partly due to a 'doubt whether there would be a sufficient demand for it even if established'.[160] The day branch of the United Westminster Schools (Westminster City School) in Palace Road had been designd as a third-grade school. It was attended by the sons of artisans as well as of other classes, and its emphasis on science and mechanics and its almost unbelievably successful performance with the Science and Art Department examinations (so unbelievable that the master was accused of malpractice), made it especially useful for boys going into technical and clerical posts. But other pupils went on to professional or higher education, and the school stressed that its emphasis was on a good general education. If it had been conceived as a third-grade school it had soon developed a curriculum which served more varied and advanced purposes.[161]

The Roan Schools at Greenwich were also intended as third-grade schools, formed originally by a scheme of 1873 from various charities for primary schooling, and in one case for training domestic servants. The boys' school was opened in 1877 and the girls' a year later. Their fees were about £6 a year, and the cost of the buildings and of numerous scholarships were met from the endowment. Boys from elementary schools in the parish could also enter for half fees, and it was considered that 'a large class of persons whose children attend public elementary schools . . . if sufficiently attracted, will pay £3 a head for secondary education'. In 1886 there were 100 such assisted boys and 80 girls at the two schools. Here also technical education was important and by 1893–4 the London County Council was making a grant of £1000 for the cost of instruction in science, drawing, manual training, domestic economy and commercial subjects. Both schools were in a 'high state of efficiency', sending boys and girls on to the universities.[162]

The Addey and Stanhope School in Deptford was formed in 1893 from a number of charities, Dr Breton's of 1672, Dean Stanhope's of 1715, and Addey's Charity which had been used in 1822 to provide a school on Dr Bell's system. This could hold 600 children, though it was rarely full. In 1893 a consolidated Scheme provided a day school for boys and girls, 'so conducted as to qualify for grants from the Science and Art Department'. Fees were between 3*d* and 9*d* a week or 3*s* to 9*s* a quarter, the curriculum had no Latin, but included modern languages, mathematics and mechanics, theoretical and practical chemistry, physics including electricity and magnetism, physiology, drawing, shorthand, the 'use of tools for working in iron, clay or wood', singing, 'the Laws of Health', and drill; with cookery, needlework and domestic economy for the girls instead of one or more of these subjects. Scholarships were provided. Sidney Webb represented the London County Council on the governing body.

The school was designed to appeal to parents in the neighbourhood, it was successfully taught as an 'organised science school' and it had distinguished examination results. But although it had 200 pupils in its first year, by 1897 these had shrunk to 39 boys and 53 girls, children largely from artisan homes and a few from 'the class of clerks and shopkeepers'. The Commissioners attributed the decline to the delay in moving to new premises, the raising of the standard of entry to comply with Technical Education Board regulations, and perhaps 'as regards boys, a certain indisposition to attend a mixed school . . .'. Probably competition from Board schools, some of the higher grade, was a more fundamental cause for the faltering start of what became a useful school when it was more clearly differentiated at secondary level.[163]

The various grades of secondary school were being consolidated, partly by this pressure from below making the third grade unnecessary, but also by a general raising of standards. Owen's School, Islington, classed as a second-grade school by Fearon, could be much improved by fees and competition instead of patronage, 'the stimulus of an independent and careful written entrance examination'. The Brewers were stirred into preparing a Scheme and by 1878 this was approved. It involved the demolishing of the almshouses, the extension of the school, proper salaries for head and assistant master, fees between £3 and £6, a graduated entrance examination, with preference for boys from the founder's favoured parishes, and scholarships. The leaving age was to be fifteen, but some exhibitions were provided for boys to go on to places of 'liberal, scientific, or professional education'. The school soon began upward progress. By the time a new headmaster, James Easterbrook, arrived in 1881 Owen's was ready for transformation. He had been Senior Mathematical Tutor at St Mark's and was above all a pedagogue, a believer in method, system, organization. He built the school rapidly into one of the most efficient and effectual schools in London. Relentless pressure, exact discipline, meticulous organization were perhaps reminiscent of contemporary business practices. Within the decade numbers had expanded to nearly 400. More classrooms, an enlarged modern languages department, laboratories, art and music rooms were built and in 1896 £10,000 had to be spent in structural development. The Brewers must have considered this as investment in an ongoing enterprise, founded by a businesswoman, situated in a district with strong City connections, sending many of its pupils there to work, run on first-class competitive lines.

External examinations at this period must be seen as a liberating influence, opening up lines of communication, tightening connections, testing response between schools, parents, public, labour market. This is how Easterbrook used such examinations. The Cambridge Locals had already been introduced and through them Owen's boys pitted their talents 'against those of other progressive schools throughout the country'. Between 1885 and 1909 Owen's position was unchallenged. London Chamber of Commerce, Science and Art, Civil Service examinations were also taken and, as the aspirations and leaving age of the school rose, the London Matriculation – by 1903 there were 46 successes. Soon university awards were added. By the end of the century Owen's days as a second-grade school were almost forgotten, and in 1906 Easterbrook was elected a member of the Headmasters' Conference. He has been called the second founder of the school, for he applied his educational genius to build up the type of school 'needed in the expanding academic and commercial world of the late nineteenth century'. The Taunton policy of reforming a second-grade school suited to a particular foundation and locality had made possible its development as a school of another kind, serving not only limited ambitions but enabling boys to 'go as high as they could'.[164]

St Dunstan's College illustrates another aspect of this rise of standards – the transformation of the curriculum by the leaven of science. By the time the school was opened[165] demands on secondary education were rising, and it is significant that the foundation stone of the elaborate Elizabethan Gothic structure was laid by the Alderman of Tower Ward, but the building declared open in 1888 by a scientist, Sir Henry Enfield Roscoe. In the meantime the governors had advertised for a headmaster for the College which 'will provide a liberal education for 400 boys from 8 to 17 years of age, of whom 60 will be boarders in a Hostel. . . . The education will aim at fitting the scholars for manufacturing, commercial and professional pursuits, special attention being paid to scientific, technical and commercial education, in connection with which excellent Laboratories, Lecture Rooms etc. will be provided.' The rest of the curriculum was the usual wide course, Greek being an extra.

The headmaster who was appointed was Charles Maddox Stuart, the son of a London India merchant, educated at Harrow and at the South Kensington Royal College of Chemistry before study and research in Germany and the Natural Sciences Tripos at Cambridge. His educational experience was equally valuable for he had worked at Clifton College (a proprietary foundation) under Canon J. M. Wilson, who had taught science at Rugby and written influentially on its educational theory. Stuart had then gone as assistant master to the High School at Newcastle under Lyme where a disciple of Temple, Kitchener, from the Rugby staff, was trying to build up a new first-grade school from a reformed endowment. This most unusual headmaster moreover found in the agreeable village of Lewisham a resident who was not only an ally in the building up of science courses at St Dunstan's, but a national pioneer of new methods of science teaching, Henry Edward Armstrong. For Professor Armstrong the arrival on his doorstep of St Dunstan's, with its exceptional headmaster and well-equipped laboratories, must have seemed an equal advantage. He was able to use the school as a laboratory for his heuristic method which liberated science teaching from the strait-jacket of 'cram' for the Science and Art Department examinations.[166]

Science had long been established within the secondary curriculum but the significance of the collaboration between the St Dunstan's governors, the Commissioners, Stuart and Armstrong is that they helped to redefine science as part of a general education, and from their philosophy of its method 'heuristic tenets' spread to other school subjects. It also was one of the factors which raised the cost of secondary education. These were the kind of standards against which all London secondary schools were being measured, for although most of them still served largely local communities, they mainly served the same labour market, and the growth of the external examination system and developing educational centralization brought pressures as well as stimulus and cross-fertilization of ideas and practices.

Wilson's School at Camberwell had been crippled by litigation and moreover was entangled in the great Dulwich endowment reorganization, which both raised false expectations and delayed the passing of a Scheme until 1880. At one time it was suggested that Alleyn's lower school should absorb and augment the Wilson endowment, but the governors were determined to restore their school at the centre of Camberwell, where there was now a population of 150,000, consisting largely of 'small professional men, clerks in City and government offices, journalists, tradesmen and labouring folk'. From 1872 plans for a school of second-grade type for 200 boys were being formed, but when the building, designed by Robson the London School Board architect, was finally erected, its financing had partly to be a matter of faith. It was opened in 1883 and estimates of Camberwell's need for such a school were justified; it grew rapidly and in 1886-7 extensions to take 350 boys were necessary. The curriculum was the usual broad course, with Greek as an extra, the headmaster was an Oxford man with middle school experience in Birmingham and Reading, the fees were £10 a year. From 1885 external examinations were entered – the College of Preceptors, gradually superseded by the University Locals, and from 1888 the annual examination offered by the

Syndics of Cambridge University. The Science and Art Department's examinations were an important source of revenue to the school, which continued to be cramped by shortage of funds, and by the short time parents kept their boys at school. The school was attempting to give a rising standard of general secondary education with inadequate means, and it was this which obliged it to receive help from the London County Council through its Technical Education Board. But this grant was dependent on the building of new laboratories, which would not bring in extra income by accommodating more boys, only improve the education of the existing number.[167] It was this kind of dilemma which strengthened the claim of the state to aid or provide the kind of schooling which it had been hoped would be funded by reformed endowments.

Each school had to meet this challenge. Squeezed into the site now occupied by the London School of Economics, St Clement Danes, which had impressed Fearon with its up-to-date interpretation of middle-class needs, was both much beset with slum clearance and enriched by rising property values. In 1875 the charity income had reached £5000 and the two secondary schools were enlarged. In 1882 the demolitions to build the Law Courts and later the clearance of the St Giles area to construct the Aldwych and Kingsway meant a decline in numbers. Numerous schemes were suggested for other uses of the funds and the buildings, but although the girls' school did eventually succumb, that was not until 1916, and the boys' hung on and survived. This was partly due to its central and accessible situation, but also to the success of W. J. Addis who became headmaster in 1899. He had been on the staff at Owen's, and then sixth form master at the Central Foundation School, and with this relevant experience and much energy and ability he revived the school, built up its numbers, got it recognized by the Board of Education (1904), appointed a permanent graduate science master, entered pupils for London Matriculation. When he handed on the school to W. P. Fuller in 1907 it was ready for further development. Fuller had been educated at Kingswood, and in London had taught at Emanuel and University College School, and he took the school even more firmly into the higher grade, eventually necessitating a removal to fairer fields.[168]

In the rapidly changing northern suburbs of the Lea Valley two of the old grammar schools which had so much roused Fearon's scorn made the grade with the help of the Commissioners, but the third did not. Enfield began negotiations in 1872, was permitted to sell estates and charge fees. In 1876 it reopened as a lower grade secondary school, Latin being among the extras; the numbers began to grown and by the end of the century a satisfactory partnership with the Middlesex County Council had developed.[169] Tottenham was reorganized in 1876 and rapidly developed as a school of a standard high enough to qualify for grants from the local authority.[170] Latymer's at Edmonton, on the other hand, had an unhappy history of mismanagement, and the industrial development of the Lea Valley, together with the impact of workmen's fares on the railways, expanded and changed the neighbourhood. The poverty of agricultural labourers was replaced by urban and industrial poverty. After the sordid troubles of the 1860s the endowment was reorganized in 1868 into two divisions, and the Reverend C. V. Dolbé was appointed headmaster of 'Latymer Upper', the middle-class school and its elementary partner. He had been curate of St Thomas's Charterhouse and second master of its middle-class school, and brought another of its staff with him as his chief assistant and master of the lower school. He seems to have been an effective and devoted teacher and strove hard to bring his school up to the standards which were expected. But though by 1877 there were 270 boys in the school, the lower division was always more popular with the townsfolk and the trustees did not give Dolbé adequate backing. The danger signal came when in 1893 two Lower School boys won Middlesex County Scholarships but were not allowed to hold them at the Upper School because it did not 'satisfy the minimum standards set by the County Authority'. In the same year Latymer Upper failed to get the grant for building a science laboratory which had been given to Enfield and Tottenham Grammar Schools by the County Council. When Dolbé retired in 1897, he handed on a school tottering towards extinction; yet it was still a wealthy foundation. The trustees, not the headmaster, had failed to enable it to reach the standards required by the newly emerging system of secondary education.

The school took several years to die. The new young and able headmaster eventually in despair took to the bottle while wrangles continued between factions among the trustees and, after 1902, the new Middlesex Education Committee, with the Board of Education dragging out negotiations 'in accordance with a minute under which all municipalizing schemes are being delayed to introduce a system of uniformity in dealing with schemes of this character' – a fine example of a desire for central administrative neatness taking precedence over local needs. By 1909 the school contained 56 boys, the 'whole secondary school population of a town of 55,000'. In 1910 it closed. When it was reopened later in the same year, it was as a municipal coeducational school, and although the foundation made a small contribution, most of its funds were frittered away on small projects to save the rates.[171]

The scholarship ladder

This gradual redefining of secondary schooling at a higher level was partly in educational terms – cultural, intellectual, professional – but it was also economic and social. Explicit in the Taunton Report was belief that redeployment of endowments was the answer to the problem of middle-class education. This was by no means unchallenged at the time, and has since led to accusation that the Commissioners took funds intended for the poor and handed them to the middle classes.[172] Leaving aside the usually irrelevant discussion which took place then and now over the definition of 'the poor' and 'free-schools' (for terms were carried to and fro across the semantic gulf of social and economic transformations), it can be stated, without either much risk or profit, that the scholarship system devised by the Commissioners was not sufficiently generous, the ladder was narrow and precarious. The problem is further confused by the rising cost of secondary, and the rising standard of elementary, schooling, for as fees rose while prices of other commodities fell, the lower middle classes were also more in need of scholarships for their children, and more willing to send them to elementary schools to qualify for them.[173] Another complication was that working-class aspiration to secondary schooling was probably sometimes more limited than the means of achieving it. From the 1870s, however, conscious demand for the redistribution of endowments was voiced by working-class leaders, R. Applegarth, for example, writing of the monopoly of the middle classes in 'enormous and misused endowments'.[174] Until a concept of such secondary education existed in a social group, it could not arouse ambitions and motivation to overcome daunting obstacles. As it is not possible to estimate how far short in number and value were the scholarships provided, nor the extent to which working-class children failed to take advantage of them, the problem is usually prejudged on ideological lines.

From the first years of the implementation of the Act of 1869 this question was under debate. It was discussed in the Commissioners' Report of 1872. In evidence to the Select Committe to enquire into the working of the Act, presided over by Forster in 1873, Lyttelton and Roby, now responsible for London, defended entry to the reformed schools by competition. This was, as Lyttelton put it, during 'what we call our Emanuel time', and questioning was often concentrated on its peculiar problems. Challenged that the proposed scheme would 'entirely deprive the class of recipients who now benefit from it', Roby maintained not only that many inmates of the Hospital had been middle-class children, but that the new arrangements would restore the school to the poor. The small shopkeepers in Tothill Street, the orphan child of a policeman or a 'porter in any of the offices' might still be benefited, but only if they deserved a place by merit. However poverty did remain one criterion of selection. At St Martin's School for Girls, two-thirds of the free places were to be for pupils from neighbouring elementary schools, and one-third for girls 'who by reason of orphanage or other adversity' should be considered by the governors to need such help. Here the problem was one of definition and newly constituted governing bodies would still be exercising a degree of unwelcome patronage. Roby throughout his evidence showed an understanding of the sociological importance of family ethos, it was not only the 'child of parents better circumstanced pecuniarily' who would succeed in competition. He was pressed to recognize the 'condition of the working classes in London and other large towns', the daily life of 'arduous struggle' which would ensure that children of upper-working- and lower-middle-class homes would 'have a very great advantage'. This he conceded, but he maintained that needy parents existed in the lower middle classes and higher up the middle classes also, where it would be the 'bitterest trial and humiliation if they could not give their children a high education'. Mixing these children with those from other classes would make a school 'vigorous and effective'.[175] What is missing from Roby's evidence is any explicit recognition of the need for a child's contribution to family income or the expense of maintaining him at a secondary school. Free clothing was connected with the old system of patronage and subservience. In 1873 the idea of helping to clothe a schoolboy was in fact more likely to emanate from those who hankered after preserving the old order than from any looking forward to the ideas of the welfare state.

The fact to Roby was that 'no endowment whatever . . . is large enough to admit everybody; and you must make a selection'. This must be by merit, and the central problem must remain its definition and identification. Did merit 'mean intellectual capacity or ability'? Roby maintained that moral conduct would inevitably be included. Industry was the *sine qua non* and family attitude would play a central part. Lyttelton reinforced this. Merit was not something with which a boy was born. This system of awarding places would enable children to acquire merit. Roby described safeguards which it was hoped would minimize unfair advantages to boys from richer homes, but denied that help from homes where more encouragement and incentives were given should or could be counteracted.

The measuring of merit remained therefore the main educational problem. Competitive examinations would play their part, and also the schoolmaster's 'estimate of the boy's performances for some time'. Salisbury in the Lords had made play with 'admission by merit' being 'part of the jargon of the day', which could only 'mean competitive examination'. Lyttelton therefore stressed the responsibility of governing bodies to devise means of giving rewards to 'something which shows work, effort, self-discipline in the child himself . . .'.[176]

The first mention of endowments and the confiscation of the rights of the poorer classes at the Trades Union Congress was made in 1881.[177] This problem was one of continual concern. In 1883 the Commissioners emphasized the need for inspection of endowed schools to ensure 'advancement of children from lower to higher grades of education', for some scholarship schemes were inoperative or imperfectly carried out, and there was no proper machinery in law. Policy must continue to aid third-grade schools, that is middle-class schools, but must pay due regard to the interests of the poor, providing 'as many Scholarships as the Endowment would permit giving free education to boys coming from

Elementary Schools as well as Exhibitions that would . . . carry them on to places of higher Education'.[178] In 1883 Lord Fortescue demanded detailed information and the returns to his questionnaires sent to all endowed schools provide an analysis of the position. Behind such statistics lay many problems, and the complexity of the situation must have put difficulties in the way of those most in need of help.[179] By the time of the 1886 enquiry, another Select Committee under Sir Lyon Playfair, the atmosphere was more critical, even acrimonious. Democratic advance, experience of municipal reform, a growing understanding of the realities of working-class life, a strengthening belief in state social policy, the rise of an abrasive and influential group of politicians, especially Joseph Chamberlain and Jesse Collings, concentrated attention on the class bias of the endowed schools' policy. There was savage criticism of school fees, of the system for the award of scholarships, of the use of elementary endowments for secondary schooling.[180] Defenders of the Commission stuck to their convictions that those who could pay should, that the schools could not be financed at their new educational level without these fees, that the only way to choose scholarship holders was by some proof of merit, that elementary endowments should be used to provide something extra, not for the relief of the rates, and that if possible the best use of them was to enable 'some pupils to move up a rung or two of the educational ladder'. Both sides had strong arguments and sincere convictions. Much of the confrontation can best be seen as the expression of a society in uncomfortable transition, working painfully at new ways of defining and approaching problems. The class society was no longer seen as an achievement but as something which required amelioration, transformation, even redemption. The 'Age of Equipoise' was over and a new stage of social and political conflict or adjustment did not make for comfort, consensus, easy solutions or even mutual comprehension.

The evidence given to the 1886 Committee does give a number of sharp glimpses of the operation of the Act in the Metropolis, and reveals the extraordinarily complicated interactions which it produced. Richmond, secretary to the Committee in 1873, considered that the third-grade schools were being 'trodden on' by the elementary schools. Their cost had been higher than had been hoped, and their fees did not cover the whole expense of education at Roan's and the United Westminster School for example, which had to be kept going by such fees.[181] Fitch, with wide experience of elementary education and liberal attitudes, had given close attention to the impact of the scholarship system on the elementary schools. While inspecting these in Lambeth he had 'observed with interest the effect of those scholarships' for Roan's, the 'great Dulwich Foundation', the Haberdashers' Schools at Hatcham, Wilson's, the Datchelor girls' school at Camberwell, and had concluded that the character of the teaching was improved, the whole tone and aim of the competition excited 'an honest ambition among the scholars'. The 25 or so open scholarship places each year in the Lambeth district, a figure which indicates the inadequate scale of provision, showed the children that there was 'something higher to be aimed at, and that there are opportunities open to those who are diligent and clever'. He was not prepared to say that any children who did not get scholarships were encouraged to go on to secondary schools because of this, nor how many of the winners belonged to the working class. At Roan's a large proportion of the pupils was from elementary schools, and these would then have a chance of exhibitions to places of higher education.

Fitch also had the opportunity to observe the attitude of some headmasters of first-grade schools to scholarship boys. Dr Abbott at the City of London had 'always taken a great deal of interest in those measures which tended to send up boys from the elementary schools'. He had received a good many such scholars, about five or six a year, and considered that in conduct and diligence they compared favourably with 'the best of our pupils'. Some unfortunately left before the fourth year, but about half gained foundation scholarships at sixteen and passed on to the university. He did not think however that the numbers should be increased. As one of the governors of St Paul's, Fitch took 'a special interest in watching the growth of the exhibition system there'. The 153 foundation scholars who had previously been chosen by the Mercers' Company were now selected by competitive examination, but the candidates could not be from elementary schools unless they had been to an intermediate school first, for attainment in Latin and mathematics was tested at twelve to thirteen years of age.[182]

An emerging system

Within the limitations of the social assumptions of their age, the Commissioners who implemented the Endowed Schools' Act conceived these scholarships as not only rewarding diligence and cleverness, dispensing at least some personal and social justice, but as helping to form separate schools, and different types of school, into something of a system, linking elementary with secondary schools, and secondary schools of varying levels together. In London it is not possible to quantify their success, nor easy to evaluate it, but there is evidence of growing interconnection and systematization by this means. This in turn prepared the ground for administrative links when they became possible through the reform of local government and the growing realization that secondary, like elementary, schooling needed state help. In fact, as at Enfield, Tottenham, Camberwell, it was through their own scholarship systems that the local authorities first formed connections with the endowed schools, and it was through its Science and Art Department examinations and grants that the central authority did so. Both these posed a threat to the balance of the curriculum; there were signs that the 'technicalization of schools, which have hitherto given that sound general education which is the basis of all proficiency, is proceeding at a rapid rate; and it is possible that it may be carried too far'.[183] Moreover the burden of the Commissioners' work was increased as the County Councils appealed for the revival of schools suitable for aid from the 'whisky money'.[184]

The new local government structure of 1888 and 1889 brought an additional problem for the Commissioners as they entered the last decade of their work. They had from the first been trying to develop the representative character of school governing bodies. In London the denominational issue did not loom so large in their composition as it did in the more sectarian Midlands and North, but the complexities of local government structure were greater. As early as 1873, for example, Roby had described how in forming a mixture of official, co-optative and representative members, they had given nominations to town councils, school boards and, if there was neither, 'we very often take the vestry', and had occasionally 'taken a direct election by the rate-payers'.[185] When the London County Council was created the Commissioners hoped for the 'interposition between the local administrators of individual Charities and our Board as the agent of central control, of a representative local authority', and endeavoured to create a working partnership.[186] They calculated in 1893–4 that at least half the local means of providing education above the elementary level lay in the scope of their jurisdiction, and it was therefore 'essential . . . that the work of the two agencies should be co-ordinated'. They had approached the London County Council to ask whether it 'would be disposed to take part in the government of a large number of secondary schools in the metropolis' and as a result the Council was to be 'connected administratively with governing bodies having charge of thirty-six secondary schools in London'. The Commissioners considered that this would give the new Council 'an experience of much value and suggestiveness' in formulating its educational policy. It might especially encourage a sound development of general education as a basis for technical instruction.[187]

By the time the educational work of the Charity Commissioners was taken over by the Board of Education after 1899, the pattern of endowed schools in and around the capital had been transformed. Over eighty years of effort to bring the great wealth of charities, many of them ancient, into the service of the new city and suburbs had passed through various phases of activity. For half a century the initiative had remained with local agencies, often spurred into action by central enquiry and criticism, and more was achieved in this way than has sometimes been supposed or admitted. The Taunton Inquiry was not so much a turning point as an important milestone. From 1869 a 'directing and supervising intelligence'[188] was brought to bear on secondary education. Although the early attempts of the Endowed Schools' Commissioners at a coherent policy of reform came to grief in 1874, their successors, in a more piecemeal and conciliatory fashion, did adhere to certain principles of action: attempting to devise appropriate levels of secondary school, sometimes relating these to one another with regard to particular needs; creating a network or ladder of scholarships which would widen the middle-class base of the schools and draw in able working-class children; and in the final years of the great enterprise, working to connect this emerging school system to the new framework of local administration. These slow labours interacted with other levels of educational development, and with other work for the provision of schooling for the middle class. By its very success it created an appetite for education which helped to raise standards already being stretched by social, economic and intellectual developments, and this in turn distorted its achievements. The various levels of what was now called secondary education were consolidated at a period of rising working-class aspirations, and this tended to widen a gulf which the scholarship system was designed to bridge.

Educational policy can rarely keep pace with social change, and in London the momentum of this was enormous, and made more complex by topographical transformations. At the beginning of this slow process of reform, London's greatest surge of growth was beginning, but it was still a City, still a place of residence as of business, surrounded by an immediate ring of old slums which had once been huddled in the ditches against the city walls, and then by pleasant, semi-rural residential suburbs to the north and east, connected to the west with the legal quarters and with Westminster, the centre of government, and with the fashionable areas of Bloomsbury and the royal village of Kensington and riverside Chelsea. The northern villages were either still remote in the old forest belt, or protected by their hills. South of the river lay the Borough and Lambeth, still residential as well as industrial and commercial, and separate villages and market towns just being invaded by the earliest 'commuters'. By the time of Fearon's inquiry this picture had become much expanded and overlaid, but it was still to some extent recognizable and even tied together by the railway system. By the last decade of the century it seems remote, archaic, though the final phase – for example, the opening up of 'Metroland' in the north-west, the engulfing even of the Surrey villages as far as Croydon – was a twentieth-century development. Because London, through most of the nineteenth century, remained essentially a commercial and administrative City surrounded by identifiable villages, the old pattern of endowed schools laid down centuries before had still some correspondence to community needs, and decades of charity reform strove to revitalize and adapt it. But by the last decades of the century when further sources of endowment had also been tapped, it was clear that state intervention was necessary if secondary education were to be soundly financed.

VII

'The most important event in the history of the country': The transformation of girls' education in the reign of Victoria

London and the genesis of change

'The emancipation of women, which is perhaps the most important event in the history of the country, can be only studied as a whole in London itself', wrote Sir Walter Besant in 1909.[1] In this the development of secondary education played a key part.

London had always had a special place in the provision of education for girls and as a business community it had a long tradition of allowing women more independence and freedom of operation than was usual in society as a whole.[2] By the nineteenth century it shared with other metropolitan centres such as Manchester, Liverpool and Edinburgh, but in greater degree even than these, a concentration of demands and a social and occupational structure which stimulated new developments. Interaction between the business, administrative, academic and fashionable nuclei of the capital and its proliferating, aspiring, responsive suburbs provided a topographical and economic seedbed for this transformation.

London was the first urban area to have a modernized police force. It is easy to overlook the importance for female emancipation of streets where unprotected women were able to pass to and fro in comparative safety.[3] This was a gradual process and even towards the end of the century in some parts of the capital was a matter of comment. 'Oh, Miss, now it's like Heaven; there's a lamp-post and a policeman at every corner', as an East End woman said to Octavia Hill.[4] As the movement for the better education of girls and women was in some respects most significant among the middle classes, where respectability was so much prized and protection could not easily be afforded by plentiful servants and private transport, little could be achieved until freedom of movement was possible.

In the early stages stimulation of communication was perhaps the capital's most characteristic and vital contribution to an adjustment within society so profound that it may be claimed as a revolution. In London not only was there a diverse and quickly responsive market for educational experiments, but women reformers could meet and exchange ideas and experience and give mutual support and en-

311

couragement. London's function as a social, cultural and political centre brought together those women, often from political, intellectual and clerical families, whose domestic education had been superior to that usually given to girls, or who came from less orthodox sections of society – for example, Emily Davies, and the Shirreff, Leigh-Smith and Garrett sisters. Metropolitan centres in the north, such as Manchester, Liverpool and Leeds, filled the same function and, in a more circumscribed way, cathedral and old county towns also.[5] In London such women also found the support of intelligent, progressive, wealthy, and influential men in the City, in government and parliamentary circles, in the new university colleges, at the Inns of Court, in the literary and journalistic community, in the multiplying professions and among clergy whose urban pastoral responsibilities brought increasing sociological and psychological awareness of new needs, pressures and tensions. Without the help of men such as these the movement could hardly have got off the ground, let alone achieved so much in such a remarkably short space of time.[6]

Moreover, the working out of new provisions, practice and philosophy must be seen as an aspect of the general movement for reform of secondary and higher education. In this respect London was an especially fertile field. The numerous experiments in middle-class schooling for boys, progress in methods of its finance and management, together with the emerging metropolitan further and higher education sector, made London a kind of forcing-house for parallel and interconnected developments for girls. The vitality and coherence of civic society, often obscured by inequalities, injustices, inertia and hysterical or stubborn resistance to change, were nevertheless demonstrated in this immense reordering and redistribution of educational provision between the sexes. Besant was making a well-founded claim for London's part in the essential prerequisite for the emancipation of women.

Systematic and public provision for girls' schooling and higher education had to be built on existing private practice, particularly profuse and diverse in London and its suburbs. Because the foundations on which improvements had to be built were so ramified and precarious,[7] policy was necessarily opportunist even while principles and convictions were both prerequisite and being formulated in action. In each succeeding episode in the story of the vital half-century between about 1840 and 1895, on the eve of the Bryce investigation, the various forces at work in London can be discerned reacting upon one another and upon the movement, locally and nation-wide.

The first episode, the founding and development of Queen's College, demonstrated the interaction between the pastoral problems of a rapidly developing middle-class suburb, the fashionable West End of Victorian 'society', and academics working through the first decade of a new concept of education for boys and young men. This first college to redefine the needs and capacities of girls grew out of the need to improve the private sector, in particular the qualifications and position of the governesses who were largely responsible for giving girl snatches of disconnected information and trivial or showy accomplishments. In 1843 the Reverend David Laing, one of the team working with Canon Dale on the reformation of the huge parish of St Pancras,[8] became secretary of the somewhat moribund Governesses' Benevolent Institution, founded earlier in the century to provide assistance in temporary difficulties and annuities for the aged, and Laing found a horrifying number of his parishioners in desperate need of such help.[9]

To provide a home between engagements and 'a good address' for applicants to posts, a house in Harley Street was taken. An attempt at registration brought a huge number of applicants and revealed distressing cases of hardship. In 1845 a system of examinations to raise the status and tone of the profession was considered, but revealed a degree of ignorance which demanded teaching, not examination. Courses were started at the Harley Street home, which attracted large numbers of women, and 260 certificates were issued in the first year. Evening classes were free. In 1847 a library was opened and made available 'for the pupils of the college and female teachers in London'. By this stage plans for the founding of Queen's College were emerging from the work of the Governesses' Benevolent Institution and the name of Laing is overshadowed by that of one of the members of its committee, the Reverend F. D. Maurice, professor at King's College, who must be considered the actual founder. 'He took compassion on the sisters of his boy pupils . . .' He considered that this first college for women would be either 'a model or a warning', and must not be narrowly vocational for it was impossible 'to provide education for the future governess except by offering it to all who may become governesses', driven into it, as the College Report of 1849 frankly says, by family misfortune (especially before the Limited Liability Act).[10] A Committee of Education of the College was formed, another house taken, and a staff of professors drawn from King's College – including Charles Kingsley, Stopford Brooke, Sir Henry Craik, Henry Morley, Dean Plumptre. A Lady Resident was to receive the pupils and take general supervision, and Lady Visitors, women of position in society, acted as chaperones. At first the supply of these was overwhelming as it was fashionable to be on the Committee of Queen's or one of its Visitors and this 'easy acceptance by London society' was an important element in success. Financial support was not so readily forthcoming and Laing wrote anxiously of 'the unexpected coldness of the public towards this its best work'. The difficulty of getting money was not owing to any objection to the scheme 'or to secondary schools; it arose from a general indifference to the whole subject of women's education'.[11]

The College was opened on 1 May 1848. A very wide course was offered from which 'compounders', who undertook and paid for the main course, selected subjects partly according to their own choice and partly from some which were considered basic studies. 'Non-compounders' attended for individual courses, and there were in addition special optional courses. The founders wished from the outset to establish that there need be no limits to the studies of girls, and by their methods the professors aimed to ensure depth of understanding.

Queen's continued to help governesses, but from the first the two functions of the College, a school or college for a very wide range of age and previous attainment, and an institution for providing training, instruction and examination of teachers, required much careful adjustment and discussion. Although they ended by 1855, and Queen's never became a training institution, it is difficult to over-estimate the importance of these courses for teachers. Miss Buss for example was among the first evening students. 'To young beginners', she wrote, 'they opened a new life.'[12]

Growing as it did out of the Governesses' Benevolent Institution, the management of the College was a matter for gradual adjustments; at first there was 'not the proper framework and machinery which a college ought to possess'. From its early days it claimed to be a public institution, incorporated and largely depending on public support, though unendowed. One of Queen Victoria's ladies-in-waiting, the Hon. Amelia Murray, who had already raised money for the Governesses' Benevolent Institution, secured the sympathy and patronage of the Queen and a Royal Charter was granted in 1853. The governing body consisted of the Visitor, the Bishop of London; a Council inherited from, and in the early days shared with, the Governesses' Benevolent Institution; and a Committee of Education 'consisting of the professors of the college, who had the arrangement and control of all matters directly relating to education'. The members of this last body held office during life, and the chairman had the title of Principal. When the Reverend Llewelyn Davies, brother of Emily Davies, was re-elected as President in 1879, four women members were added. The Lady Visitors from the beginning had their own meeting whose minutes formed reports to the Committee of Education, but the College had in effect been governed by men. From 1875 the 'Lady Resident' assisted in the deliberations of the Council. Gradually therefore Queen's College evolved a system of government suitable for a semi-public institution, and it succeeded, not only because of its social acceptance and situation in a central residential district with a plentiful supply of pupils, but also because its nearness to King's College enabled its professors to give unsparingly of their time.[13]

From the beginning the chief problem of curriculum and methods of teaching had been the varying ages and abilities of the students. 'Young Ladies' over the age of twelve were admitted, and each department included a junior as well as a senior class. In addition there were 'preparatory classes for young ladies of nine to twelve years of age'. The difficulties of teaching even the main age range as a group were aggravated by the inadequate education which most had previously received, but Queen's adhered to the ideal of a secondary education for girls which aimed at independence of study and free choice of course and the professors made few concessions to their classes. Gradually methods were found which worked. The preparatory classes for girls of nine to twelve were, from the beginning in January 1849, placed under a 'Lady Superintendent', and 'lady tutors were to help such of the less advanced pupils as may desire it'. Gradually Queen's College School emerged as a separate institution within the same premises, combining the 'preparatory class' with the 'preparatory department', or earlier part of the college, with Miss Parry as first headmistress. The age of entry was reduced to six and the teaching was on Pestalozzian lines, training in method was considered an important qualification for the staff, and pupil-teachers were taken.[14]

Throughout the early history of Queen's there are close parallels with developments in boys' education. King's College and School had also to work out a process and content for new kinds of institutions and to try to build a system of Anglican schools of its own kind. There was even some attempt to develop a system of 'Schools in Union' with Queen's College, on the lines of King's College's affiliated schools. But unlike King's, Queen's could not offer them any useful concessions in higher education courses leading to a recognized qualification, nor did it have any system of school-level examinations which would help to bring the standard of 'schools in union' in line with its own. No system was in fact evolved, but Queen's did help to create some kind of standard and lessen the isolation of girls' schools. In 1860 a speaker at the Social Science Congress could take it as a matter of course that such schools would be encouraged by correspondence with Queen's College.[15]

Queen's may also have had some influence on the founding and early development of Bedford College, though the two institutions ultimately took divergent paths. Bedford illustrates the contribution of more radical academic circles and the strong tradition of dissenting experiment within the capital, leading back to the Nonconformist academies of the Enlightenment. Mrs Elisabeth Jesser Reid (*c*.1794–1866) had been interested in the idea of forming a college for the higher education of women for some years and in 1847 'opened her house near Brunswick Square for a course of lectures for women'. Although as a Unitarian she moved in different circles, she is said to have helped in the founding of Queen's, and was certainly 'all alive to the new female College which has been instituted for the education of governesses . . .'. Its success encouraged her to launch a similar college. Some question arose at the time as to the need or wisdom of starting a second in much the same neighbourhood, but several of the most influential members of Queen's gave 'cordial encouragement and approbation'. Mrs Reid wanted an undenominational college, one in which women were actively associated in the management, and she looked to wider purposes. It would be inexact to think of her in 1849 as envisaging a university college for women, but she had in mind an institution which would develop on those lines.[16]

The college was opened in October 1849 in 47 (now 49) Bedford Square. Trustees were appointed, a constitution of a general, an executive and a ladies' committee had been worked out and adapted by July 1849 to a more workable scheme of Council and Board, each containing women members, and a body of 'Lady Visitors' modelled on those of Queen's. The early days of the Ladies' College, Bedford Square, were considerably more beset with constitutional and financial difficulties than the other college, partly due to the very presence of women in its government, for which there was no precedent, and they had little experience. The staff moreover lacked the coherence of the body of Anglican professors, nearly all drawn from King's College. The professors of Bedford came some from King's, some from University College. Many of them were men of pronounced individual, even unorthodox, views. There were many changes of staff. An ill-advised attempt to secure a 'balance of creeds' on the staff led to an absurd situation which could be parodied: 'Wanted, a Professor of Physical Geography . . . who must not be a Deist, nor a Puseyite, nor a Unitarian, nor a Roman Catholic. A liberal Churchman or a Quaker will be acceptable, if not too deep in Rationalism.' By 1852 however signs of improvement were apparent in an increase of students, a more stable staff, the establishment of some few scholarships. As with Queen's the problem of inadequate preparation had to be solved by the setting up of a 'Junior School', opened in January 1853. Girls were admitted at the age of nine and received 'instruction in the ordinary English subjects', with French, Latin and German. The parallel with Queen's is close, and Miss Frances Martin, who was appointed to the charge of the school, had been one of its early students. In 1854 there was even some discussion of a union between the colleges, but one friendly conference seems to have ended the matter. Girls' education was certainly the richer for the similar but ultimately divergent development of the two institutions.

The establishment of the school may have brought more prosperity to the College, but Mrs Reid was afraid that it would swallow its parent. 'Now that we have the nucleus and the name, let us not suffer it to die! My dread is that it merge in the school.' She died in 1867 and left under her will a trust in the hands of three women on whom she could rely to carry out her intention of making Bedford a college of higher education. In 1868 they closed the school abruptly. This cannot be regarded as the end of Bedford's contribution to secondary education as for many more years it continued to provide what would today be considered as sixth-form courses. After the removal of the College from Bedford Square to York Place, Baker Street, girls were still continuing to enter inadequately prepared for anything other than these, and for a time in 1877 a scheme for establishing a new school was considered. By this time however progress in girls' education was far enough advanced to stimulate the development of genuine higher courses.[17]

Although Queen's founded no system, and Bedford was eventually incorporated in the higher sector of education, their influence was profound and in the long run helped to make possible a new kind of systematic secondary education for girls. The next episode provided the model upon which the system was eventually based.

Frances Mary Buss was born in the parish of St Pancras in 1827, the daughter of an unsuccessful but gifted artist and a mother able and determined enough to recoup the family fortunes by setting up a small preparatory school run on Pestalozzian lines in Kentish Town, after taking a training course at the Home and Colonial Institute in the Gray's Inn Road. Her daughter joined her, taking a select number of young ladies as pupils in 'the essential points of a liberal education'. She had been teaching since she was fourteen at the little school where she received her own education. When Queen's College opened she walked from Camden Town to Harley Street four nights a week to attend lectures and gain three certificates. In 1849 the family school had grown enough to move to a larger house and in 1850 Miss Buss opened a new school in Camden Street and named it the North London Collegiate School for Ladies. The first prospectus said that the success of the North London Collegiate School for Boys had shown the need for 'a similar step being taken' for the education of girls: 'both originated at a public meeting, and both have the same moral guarantee so far as regards the clergy of the parish', but Miss Buss's school was 'completely private in regard to buildings and all money expenses'. She had the support of Laing, who gave generous help and regularly visited the school until his death in 1860, and of Canon Dale. Miss Buss and her parish clergy had the neighbourhood in sharp focus.

> Of all the various suburbs of our vast metropolis this district . . . is more thickly inhabited by Professional men than any other. Its proximity to the City and the busy part of London on the one hand, and on the other to Regent's Park and the open parts about Hampstead, and Highgate and Holloway, render it peculiarly convenient as a place of residence for that large and influential part of Society known as the middle class.

Queen's served the girls of wealthier families and had aristocratic patronage and powerful academic support. Miss Buss succeeded in creating a school which became a prototype. She had an intense belief in the need for and moral importance of the education of girls so that 'the future mothers of families . . . may be enabled to diffuse among their children the truths and duties of religion, and to impart to them a portion of that mass of information placed by modern education within the reach of all'. Such a conviction, coinciding with the wants of the families she served, enabled purpose to emerge from the early experimental stage as conscious and guiding policy. Every detail of the school Miss Buss created, its curriculum, discipline, staffing, her very social engagements, the clothes she wore, all were designed to create and sustain support for her school and adapt it to the needs of girls who would carry its policy and practice into widening circles.

From its beginning this family-venture school had a broad curriculum including Latin and some study of science. Mrs Buss helped with the younger girls; Mr Buss taught drawing, 'Botany, Zoology, Geology, and Astronomy, each illustrated with profuse diagrams' and gave a series of chemistry lectures, illustrated by experiments or at least 'smells and explosions', and also elocution; the brothers of the headmistress, who later took orders, taught arithmetic, Latin and scripture. Laing visited to teach divinity. Miss Buss aimed at a type of teaching which would 'train the youthful mind to habits of thought, instead of burdening the memory with merely a number of words'. She wished to arrest attention and excite a habit of observation by lessons 'of a conversational character'. There was a serious difficulty of finding women teachers who had a good enough general education, or any training in methods of teaching. 'Government trained' mistresses were not available, nor was their 'deficiency in the accomplishments' easily overcome. Eventually she was able to persuade some of her own old girls to take courses at the Home and Colonial Institute and return to her staff, where she could continue their training in the 'power of teaching' by requiring them 'to draw up sketches of their lessons . . . to make their lessons oral, and to reproduce the teaching from the children by rapid questions, of course combining these with a certain amount of home lessons'. Dependence on textbooks at any stage was discouraged. Miss Buss's views on educational method were remarkably sensible. In practice perhaps her system tended to be self-perpetuating and the young women who taught the middle or lower forms often lacked confidence and knowledge, but from its beginning the school flourished. In 1850 there were 60 pupils in the first term. Numbers rose rapidly and other houses had to be taken. For twenty years it grew steadily and by 1865 there were 201 pupils.[18]

During these decades, the 1840s and 1850s, progress had been impressive, guided by the more liberal and perceptive leaders of academic and ecclesiastical circles, with active and pragmatic contributions from enterprising women, in whom these early reforms released a remarkable energy and enterprise. This success was built on social, cultural and educational demands concentrating and fermenting within the expanding city. As early as 1841 the *Westminster Review* claimed that there was 'General agreement . . . that there is no good in female ignorance. On the subject of intellectual education, public opinion and practice have undergone a complete change within a very few years ... The battle of Education, which was fought for women ... is now altogether won'.[19] Concession had come largely from the need to make good wives and mothers, but the reviewer challenged the argument that one half the human race should have its reason cultivated in order to benefit the other half.

Moving within radical literary journalistic circles the writer, probably Harriet Martineau, both was over-optimistic and underestimated the dangerously ambiguous nature of the usual argument for concessions to improved educational opportunities for 'half the human race'. Twenty years after this article appeared there was need for a rallying of the forces of reform, and some more systematic attempt to capitalize both on the gains already made and on the growing demand for better education for boys. This campaign, for such it must be called, was gathering force during this early period, and became centred on the so-called Langham Place Group. Here the capital performed its vital function as an exchange and mart of ideas, policies, strategies, tactics, both inside the education campaign and linking it to other movements, such as those for improving the legal position of women and for their political enfranchisement. It drew women also into the demand for a better analysis of the new society, which led to the founding of the National Association for the Promotion of Social Science. This became a forum for ideas on female education, and with its peripatetic annual conference linked metropolitan and provincial activities. The greatest obstacle was the isolation of girls' schools, which not only prevented and inhibited change, but was also the characteristic, disguised as modesty and womanliness, most prized by opponents of more public scrutiny and accountability. To secure these was the triumph of the 1860s.

The lineage of the Langham Place Group, like that of the Social Science Association, can be traced from the campaigns of the 1830s for law reform, largely Benthamite in inspiration and philosophy. Here allies from politics, the secular radicals, and the legal profession added their particular contributions – John Stuart Mill, Matthew Davenport Hill, Lord Brougham, Mr Sergeant Manning, Monckton Milnes, George Hastings. The Society for the Amendment of the Law took up the cause of the legal position of married women, and was joined by Barbara Leigh-Smith, daughter and granddaughter of radical members of Parliament, inheritors of the Clapham Sect tradition. Unlike her cousin Florence Nightingale, she did not have to struggle to establish her own freedom of operation. With her aunt, Julia Smith, she had been one of the early students at Bedford, and she was unique among women of her era in that on her majority in 1848 her father had secured to her a personal income of £300 a year for life. She and her friend, Bessie Rayner Parkes, granddaughter of Joseph Priestley, prepared and published documents on the laws concerning women, and organized drawing-room meetings, and it was here, in about 1856, that the Women's Movement may be said to have been born. The active and articulate women who were drawn into this pressure group took a house in Langham Place, the 'Ladies' Institute', a rallying point and a recruiting ground as well as a headquarters, and there the *Englishwoman's Journal* began publication. This in turn attracted women such as Miss Jessie Boucherette who felt 'deeply the helpless and necessitous condition of the great number of women obliged to resort to non-domestic industry as a means of subsistence'. Soon a Society for the Employment of Women was established, which drew attention to the size and desperation of the problem and to the deficiencies of education which aggravated it; thus members of the group were drawn into experiments with remedial and vocational teaching.[20]

Annie Carey, in her women's classes at the School of Design in Gower Street, used art teaching 'to raise and extend the intellectual culture of the students'. Women were so imperfectly educated that books and lectures were of little use as a remedy, but the discipline and concentration of drawing could gradually develop the powers of perception and a real concern for knowledge could appear for the first time. In Charlotte Street a school was founded by Jessie Boucherette to give 'a solid English education to young girls and to teach older women to write a letter grammatically, to calculate rapidly without a slate, and to keep accounts by single and double entry', to enable lower-middle-class women to find employment as clerks, cashiers, saleswomen, service in telegraph, railway ticket and post offices. The Portman Hall School in Paddington was run largely under the guidance of Barbara, now Madame Bodichon, and supervised by the other Leigh-Smith sisters, 'to bring a thoroughly good education within the reach of the lower middle-class'. Elizabeth Whitehead, who later played a part in the formation of the Working Women's College in 1864, taught here regularly, and Octavia Hill gave lessons in French, drawing and English. This school was advanced in its ideas, coeducational, undenominational, and aiming at a mixture of social classes. A unique corps of volunteer teachers gave lessons in drawing, physiology and the laws of health, and social economy. Children from a wide district were attracted, and the success of the experiment at a charge of 6*d* a week enabled Madame Bodichon to urge the Newcastle Commission to adopt a suggestion for giving 'Government certificates' to volunteer lady teachers for specific subjects. This would have helped to solve the problem of effective teaching for middle-class schools. Octavia and Miranda Hill later, in 1860, under the advice of F. D. Maurice, opened their own school near Marylebone Church where a sound and intelligent education was given, including the study of Latin and the sciences, and the pupils had plenty of exercise in Regent's Park.[21]

Experiments of this kind could not be more than palliatives for the few, or gestures to the future. It was Emily Davies who chiefly devised the policies which made practical and overall advances possible. The daughter of the rector of Gateshead, her formidable abilities as an administrator and her determination, controlled passion and commitment as a reformer had already been active in her father's parish and in the guidance and support she had given to her friend, Elizabeth Garrett, in her efforts to qualify for the medical profession. Now she brought the experience of the industrial north to the London centre. Miss Davies had already met Barbara Leigh-Smith and been introduced by her to the Langham Place set when, on her father's death, she and her mother moved to London to be near her brother, the Reverend Llewelyn Davies, who was a disciple and colleague of Maurice at Queen's College, and rector of a Marylebone parish. His rectory in Blandford Square was opposite the Leigh-Smith house. Miss Davies assumed the leadership of the educational aspect of the woman's movement, as Barbara Bodichon's husband was a French doctor practising in Algeria. Miss Davies was conservative and conventional, wily, tough, even somewhat unscrupulous. Her principles were coherent, uncompromising, her policies conciliatory, empirical. She was proving a theorem by the methods of diplomacy: girls and women were capable of learning and studying the same subjects as boys and men, assessed by the same external examinations, even if contemporary practice was unsatisfactory and in a process of change and reform. Her remarkable qualities, which would have made her a successful 'Secretary of State or the Governor of a Colony', Miss Davies quietly and dangerously deployed in West End drawing-rooms.[22]

The first victory was to get the Cambridge Local Examinations opened to girls, and an important ally, Henry Richard Tomkinson, Secretary of the London Centre, was secured. He became both friend and adviser of Miss Davies and had more influence over her obstinate but receptive mind than most people. From him and from Dyke Acland she learnt the importance of avoiding over-large demands which would require old-established institutions to commit themselves in principle. The campaign also increased the group's experience of committee work, lobbying and publicity.

Without previous improvements in girls' education, the sudden permission to allow girls to take the Local Examinations on an experimental basis at the London Centre in 1863 would have been of no avail. Candidates were hastily assembled from Miss Buss's North London Collegiate, from some of the better private schools already influenced by her, and from the Queen's and Bedford schools. Their performance was quite satisfactory, except in arithmetic. 'The want of an external qualification could hardly have been better demonstrated,' declared Miss Davies promptly, while Miss Buss hurriedly reorganized her mathematics department. The attack on the isolation of girls' education had successfully begun, and tactics and strategies were further practised and improved in the continuing campaign to secure permanent and nation-wide permission from the Cambridge Syndicate in the following year, 1864.[23]

The significance of the Taunton Inquiry

Equally important for the future was Miss Davies's next opportunist coup to get girls' education included within the scope of the Schools' Inquiry Commission, appointed in 1864. Her situation at the administrative centre, the efficient committee, experienced in the Cambridge Locals affair, and her alertness enabled her to take instant action when it was realized that so little regard was given to this aspect of the wide and ill-defined 'middle-class schools' question' that those who drew up the terms of the Commission had forgotten to exclude it. Grudging permission was secured for assistant commissioners to survey girls' schools as far as they could find time, and for women witnesses to be examined. For the first time the state had acknowledged its interest in the education of girls not attending elementary schools. The ally who had helped in this victory was H. J. Roby, then Professor of Jurisprudence at University College London, and Secretary of the Commission. His career as a reforming tutor at Cambridge, as one of the founders of the Local Examinations, as second master at Dulwich College, and his friendship with Frederick Temple had given him the experience and breadth of vision to see that the emerging sector of secondary education must include girls as well as boys.[24]

This inquiry gives a penetrating survey of girls' education in the capital city and its suburbs at the very time when forces of reform were acting like yeast within it. Over many parts of the country men of the calibre of James Bryce and T. H. Green made discerning and damning studies of the 'want of thoroughness and foundation; want of system; slovenliness and showy superficiality, inattention to rudiments; undue time given to accomplishments, and those not taught intelligently or in any scientific manner, want of organization' of girls' schools. The survey of London by Fearon shows the Victorian administrator and intellectual at the same time at his most innovatory and bewildered. Like an illustrious contemporary of very similar background, Fearon was entering a kind of looking-glass world. The anthropological flavour of some of his observations and the unrealistic, even apocalyptic, nature of his proposals demonstrate both the depth of the gulf between male and female education, and the earnestness and determination which were beginning to bridge it.

Fearon proceeded by circulation of an enquiry among proprietors of schools, by inspection and examination, and by a form of enquiry among 'ladies and others taking a practical interest in the question', and correspondence with teachers and promoters of schools. He found a degree of interest much greater than he expected:

I remarked among several lady principals and teachers, both in public and private girls' schools, a desire to improve their own teaching and their own knowledge of the best educational methods, and to raise the standard of instruction in their schools, which demands my highest sympathy and respect. It is evident that a large number of persons who may be supposed to have the best knowledge of the condition of girls' education in England are profoundly dissatisfied with it, and that a movement has begun which is being pushed with so much vigour and discrimination, so much spirit and judgement, that it is not at all likely to be suppressed or die out for the present.[25]

The classifying of girls' schools in his district caused him some trouble. Primary or elementary education at a 'properly conducted and inspected' National school presented few difficulties, but secondary education was a less specific concept, and it was impossible to decide when this merged into 'superior education', if indeed any system of such education could be said to exist at all for women. He could only therefore surmise that secondary education ended at about eighteen or nineteen, and he was reluctantly compelled to classify girls' schools as first, second or third class by the age of leaving, as he had done with boys' schools. 'The questions whether a girl should receive any, and if so what general education, in what subjects, up to what age, under what conditions, seem all to be new and unset in this country. For girls there is no academical life, almost no professions, and until one comes to the borders of the labouring class, few trades or businesses which can stimulate or determine their education.' It was therefore almost impossible to define middle-class education for girls.[26]

Perhaps the most interesting group comprised the small number of 'second-grade' schools which he described. The St Clement Danes Middle Class Girls' School had been opened in 1862 'For the advancement of girls in useful and appropriate learning and good manners'. Daughters or wards of resident parishioners between seven and fourteen were following a curriculum which included Anglican religious instruction, grammar, writing, arithmetic, 'general history', needlework, singing, 'elementary and geometrical drawing', for 15*s* a quarter with French and German as 'extras'. The headmistress, a 'well-educated gentlewoman', had a salary of £100 and a house, and with two assistants taught 57 girls, all of whom lived within five minutes' walk of the school. Fearon regarded this as a model for the future.[27] Other schools catering for the same level had been founded by voluntary enterprise. The West Central Collegiate School for Young Ladies had been formed by an association of ladies who collected funds and managed the school, to 'meet the wants of a large number of respectable tradesmen, professional men, retail shopmen, etc. who find themselves unable to meet the expenses of higher schools and colleges'. It gave a 'good preparation for domestic or business life', and Fearon found 63 pupils between ten and fourteen generally from the immediate neighbourhood. The fees were from £7 17*s* 6*d* to £11 11*s* , with some 'extras', and the Cambridge Local examinations were taken.[28] The Great Ormond Street Proprietary School for Girls nearby had a link with the Working Men's College and provided for a slightly lower social level, 'daughters of shopkeepers and others of the lower middle class who will have to earn their own livelihood when they grow up'. Fearon considered that such schools deserved the greatest encouragement and were sadly in need of endowment.[29] Queen's and Bedford Colleges represented the only 'attempts which have been made in London to establish girls' education of the first grade upon a thoroughly public basis, in colleges offering guarantees for the soundness of the education similar in kind to those afforded by public schools for boys', though, he added, 'without sacrificing that retirement and unobtrusiveness which are considered essential for the preservation of the freshness and refinement of the female character'. He deplored that they were more expensive than was necessary, and that 'our unhappy social divisions' made them 'less widely useful than they might be'.[30]

His general observations gave substantial support to the reformers. Lack of system and social exclusiveness which put undue emphasis on showy accomplishments were the root of the trouble. The 'weight of social pressure' was heavy; 'the question of manners or style, or as it is sometimes called in school prospectuses, of "deportment", is considered so much more a vital question for girls than for boys. . . . It is impossible not to recognize that social exclusiveness . . . and accomplishments are the two great educational shibboleths whereby most parents test girls' schools.' Even for the 'first grade' of schools provision was most inadequate, cost high, buildings unsatisfactory, overcrowded both in classrooms and dormitories, there was no 'scholastic furniture' or 'essential apparatus', 'common tables and chairs of household use' were employed 'at which the pupils sit in disorderly array', there was a distressing want of playgrounds and attention to physical education. Callisthenics were often an 'extra' and most games were desultory and of little use as a 'real diversion to the players' minds'. Croquet he admitted to be a game of skill and much interest, but it led to a 'deal of lounging and stooping'. Above all he criticized the courses of instruction and the quality of the teaching, and strongly supported the need for external assessment. Even at Queen's no satisfactory system had yet been applied. 'General proficiency in one subject', he reported, 'seemed undesirable . . . I am aware of the present low condition of female education, but surely it can hardly be and at any rate is not likely to continue so low as to require such a humiliating programme as that of the third-class certificate of general proficiency?' His overall criticism was that the examinations were internal. In the beginning an outside examination would probably have had too many terrors, but now perhaps the time had come for a 'higher line'. Bedford College earned his praise for taking a step, 'almost without parallel among institutions of this kind', in appointing external examiners. Such comments demonstrated the value of masculine investigation of what was still something of an educational ghetto, an endorsement of the action of Miss Davies and her committee.[31]

Fearon's summary of the improvements 'generally desired in the district' was a large increase in means of sound education of girls, and endowments shared with boys' schools. Educational boards should be set up to reform endowments; to establish infant or preparatory day schools 'for children of professional or mercantile classes', and good lower day schools for girls, 'a kind of girls' grammar schools' in different parts of London; to provide 'good upper day schools for girls which should afford at from eight to twelve guineas an advanced instruction in language, mathematics, logic, some branch of natural science, and art; with continued physical training; intended for pupils between thirteen and eighteen years of age'; and finally establish or support 'central institutions for the superior education of young women', with scholarships, professorships, libraries, laboratories.[32] He wrote as if he were devising remedies for an imaginary community, an unknown country which he had only begun to explore. His proposals went far beyond what was practicable, or anything which most London parents consciously desired. Miss Buss from her immediate experience was able to express their wishes more realistically in her evidence to the Commissioners. 'I feel most strongly from the people I have to do with – professional men with a comparatively small income – that they can obtain help with the education of their boys, but that no assistance whatever is given in the case of their girls, and that even when able and willing to pay for a good education they cannot get it.' With tears in her eyes, and trembling with emotion, Miss Buss shrewdly indicated the way in which girls' secondary education in London was within a few years to be devised and systematized. It was this sensitive awareness of the needs of the scholastic market, allied to a firm grasp of educational principles, which characterized her evidence throughout. She had no illusions about the general standard of girls' schools. 'I think such education as they get is almost entirely showy and superficial; a little music, a little singing, a little French, a little ornamental work, and nothing else.' She faced this 'large demand for accomplishments' and persuaded parents by demonstration that what they really wanted for their daughters was a solid and broad curriculum. 'The parents we have had to deal with are always willing to take the routine as it stands,' she said firmly. Nor did she have difficulties over entering pupils for the Cambridge Locals, which had given 'a great impulse to the study of English and arithmetic. The parents themselves were quite willing to accede to them.' They were also ready to trust the school in matters of religious instruction, and her school was quite unsectarian. She was prepared to think that parents were not generally apathetic, but two intractable problems remained. In times of hardship a daughter's education would always be a casualty, and when girls left her school there was no inducement to continue their education. 'They can read in a loose desultory way, but serious study is considered unnecessary and unsociable.' The need and appetite for further education of some kind was being created by success: the Cambridge Locals had done a 'great good' already, girls had 'something to work for, some hope, something to aim at, and the teachers also'. No undue excitement or strain had been observed – indeed Miss Buss, though she did not tell the Commissioners this, would not have allowed or tolerated them. When asked for her opinion about the specially modified type of matriculation examination, introduced for women by the University of London in 1866, she was cautious. 'Something better might be thought of', but as an interim measure it seemed useful.[33] She did not mention that she agreed with her friend Miss Davies that special examinations for women were dangerous and proved nothing, and as the university was still resisting the admission of women, this was an attempt to propitiate them with a second-rate article. In practice, and as an interim measure, this examination proved, like the Cambridge Higher Local, to be a useful qualification for teaching and so helped forward the cause.[34]

Other women witnesses from the London education scene showed the same cautious, empirical, practical approach. Miss E. E. Smith, a member of the Council of Bedford College, described the defects of girls' education as chiefly 'want of thoroughness', and the reluctance of parents to accept the need for 'discipline and mental training'. In demanding accomplishments they wanted their daughters 'to have refined tastes' but forgot that these 'must be based on knowledge'. She had not been involved in the campaign for the Cambridge Locals, but was in favour of them as they were the same for girls as for boys. Higher education would be pointless unless professional openings provided a goal to work towards.[35] Miss Frances Martin, superintendent of the school attached to the college, was doubtful of the desirability of external examinations. She was afraid of 'cram' and valued the freedom of teachers to plan their own courses and methods, and she also thought that higher education for women might diverge from that of men.[36] This division over the question of examinations and the need to take the same courses as men cut right through the women's movement. On the whole the London movement, led by Miss Davies and Miss Buss, was on the side of equality and similarity of examinations and courses.[37] The Taunton Commission provides a review of ideas being formulated in practice, and of a group of remarkable women, as well as men, who were prepared to operate outside an established framework. The Commission was supremely important, not only for its practical outcome in the Endowed Schools' Act of 1869, but because it brought the whole question into the public arena, stimulated debate, and gave confidence to people who were challenging the most deeply cherished myths of their age.[38]

The London Association of Schoolmistresses

The importance of the work is illustrated in the formation of the London Association of Schoolmistresses in 1866 'out of a desire on the part of schoolmistresses in London and the neighbourhood, and especially of those who through the working of the Cambridge Local Examinations had come into mutual communication, for some means of drawing together on a common ground'. 'No plan could be carried out without mutual confidence', and it was found that schoolmistresses 'were singularly isolated, some teachers having scarcely so much as a speaking acquaintance with any professional associate'. London had not been first in the field, as at the preliminary meeting in 1866 to meet 'several gentlemen connected with the Schools' Inquiry Commission' a representative of the Manchester Schoolmistresses' Association was present. Soon a more formal constitution was adopted, apparently modelled on the Manchester one, and the business of the Association was admirably conducted throughout, Miss Davies being secreatry for most of its life. Membership was not confined to headmistresses; assistants and anyone interested in girls' education might join. At first meetings were held in the homes of leading members but soon the headquarters of the Society for promoting the Employment of Women were used and there a library was built up and looked after by Miss King, its secretary. Before long the Association was in correspondence with similar groups of teachers, at Brighton, Bristol, Leeds, Liverpool, Reading, as well as Manchester, and with the Irish Schoolmistresses Association, and these became corporate members. Some individuals, such as Miss Kyberd of the famous Chantry at Frome, became corresponding members. The London Association therefore acted both as a receiver and as a disseminator of ideas and information through the country. Its activities reveal the degree of professionalism which had already developed among schoolmistresses, largely here from private schools, and the skill of these women in using pressure-group techniques. 'The Association adhered with considerable strictness to its original idea of occupying itself chiefly in the elucidation of questions having a direct bearing on the business of school-teaching . . . and discussions have been of real use in the diffusion of what may be called technical knowledge on the subject of education.' They were on such themes as examinations and competition for girls and young women, the systematization of their schooling, the need for thoroughness, the problem of accomplishments, the need for objective standards. An intelligent attempt was made to decide what 'schemes of instruction' should be followed at different stages of school life and what standards and content should be expected at different ages. 'The relations of growth to Education' were examined. Less popular or more serious subjects such as Latin and political economy were encouraged and methods of teaching received much attention, the 'Lecture system as applied to School teaching', 'Oral teaching against teaching by books'. Moral training was emphasized – aspects such as 'School Honour', 'Emulation as a motive power in education', echoed some of Fearon's strictures on girls' schools. The problems of organization of schools as they became larger and more systematic were reflected in discussions on timetabling and the relation of headmistress and assistants. Such topics indicate the content gradually being given to the concept of secondary education over this period. Other services provided by the Association were its library, lists of school books, registry of posts for governesses (later usually called assistants) and 'professors' (soon modernized as 'Visiting Teachers'). Courses of lectures were arranged – Dr Hodgson on an introduction to economic science, Joshua Fitch on 'Methods of Teaching Arithmetic'.

The other aspect of the Association's work was more out-ward-looking, showing 'sympathy with public educational movements. The large number of candidates for the University of Cambridge Local Examinations, presented at the London Centre, may probably be attributed in a great degree to the influence of this Association. The projected College for Women at Hitchin has also been cordially supported.' A memorial on the higher education of women was sent to the Schools' Inquiry Commission. When the Scholastic Registration Association sought co-operation, the London Schoolmistresses insisted that registration of female teachers was included and women taken on to its committee. When the provision of girls' schools began to improve with the implementation of the Endowed Schools' Act, the London Association of Schoolmistresses took the Association of Headmistresses of Endowed and Proprietary Schools into corporate membership. It was this movement which eventually made the separate organization of London Schoolmistresses unnecessary, and it was wound up in 1887–8. It had pioneered a new idea of professional interchange and solidarity, antedating even the drawing together of headmasters under Thring's leadership in 1869. During its twenty years of active life it had played an important and not altogether local part in a revolution in secondary education.[39]

The new High Schools

The frustrations and delays in applying the Endowed Schools' Act, especially Miss Buss's difficulties in getting its support,[40] were the background to a letter to *The Times* in January 1872 from Mrs William Grey. She deplored the poor response to Miss Buss's appeal: 'People do not care about the education of girls and do not think it worth giving money to', but the education of women was fundamental to family well-being, and moreover the latest census had shown how far women now outnumbered men, and many 'must at some period or other of their lives be entirely dependent on their own exertions for support'. She appealed to the 'richest city in the globe' to sow a 'seed which will bring forth fruit a hundred fold'.[41]

The richest city in the globe may have been slow and reluctant in subscribing to this cause as a general proposition, but it had accumulated a fund of experience in financing the education of boys by joint stock enterprise and local initiative, and it contained a huge unsatisfied demand for better education for daughters for which parents were prepared to pay and invest modestly. The next momentous development in girls' secondary schooling drew on these factors and can only be properly understood as part of the history of secondary schooling as a whole.

Here a new group of women reformers came to the fore. Mrs Maria Grey and her sister Miss Emily Shirreff were remarkable and intelligent women who had already written penetrating studies of the deficiencies and possibilities of home education for girls. Mrs Grey's husband had been a nephew of Lord Grey and they moved not only in fashionable but also in Whig reforming and intellectual circles, which included Benjamin Jowett, Thomas Huxley, Herbert Spencer, the Grotes, F. D. Maurice. Henrietta Stanley, the wife of a Whig politician and mother of a numerous family, brought into this circle a whiff of the Regency, of earlier, less inhibited days. She had used Mrs Grey's *Thoughts on Self-Culture* in the education of her own daughters. She was drawn into the work for more public education for girls and became one of the first Lady Visitors at Queen's by the influence of Maurice whose church in London she attended, for although she spent most of the year busy with her progeny at their country home, she of course visited London for the 'Season' and the parliamentary session. Before 1869 she had to keep in the background, as 'it is not liked to see my name before the public', but when her somewhat saturnine husband died she, like that other widow, Mrs Grey, became one of the most active participants in the movement which was drawing these women into the legislative, public orbit.[42] Not only was the implementation of the Endowed Schools' Act dependent on active lobbying, but after the Education Act of 1870 women were eligible to sit and vote on school boards. Emily Davies and Elizabeth Garrett were elected to the London Board, and although Mrs Grey failed to gain the seat for Chelsea, she regarded her reluctant entry into this contest as a turning point in her life and that of her sister. It concentrated their attention even further on the educational aspect of the women's movement, especially the campaign for girls who would not attend Board schools, now the least well provided with appropriate schooling. This, Mrs Grey declared, was 'not a woman's question but a man's question, a national question'.[43]

A national movement to combine existing efforts was launched by Mrs Grey in a paper at the Royal Society of Arts in June 1871, urging the sharing of endowments and the creation of an Educational League or Union to effect an 'Educational Charter of Women', demanding provision of schools, and registration and improved training of teachers. Over the country as a whole this was an urban movement: Mrs Grey campaigned in Liverpool, speaking to the North of England Council for promoting the Higher Education of Women and enlisting the sympathy of Mrs Josephine Butler, a connection of her late husband. Here also she met Miss Beale of Cheltenham and other supporters such as Professor Sidgwick and Professor Stuart of Cambridge. The next step was taken at the Social Science Congress, held that October in Leeds. Mrs Grey contributed a paper 'On the Special Requirements for Improving the Education of Girls', and Miss Mary Gurney of Wimbledon an important analysis of Miss Buss's work, setting forth for the first time an explicit plan to use the North London Collegiate School as a model for schools moderate in price, socially inclusive, non-sectarian, with courses 'the same as in boys' schools', with teachers who could 'call out the powers' of the pupils and 'produce thoughtful women, ready for every emergency of life'.[44] A committee was formed at this Leeds Congress and the National Union for the Education of Girls of all Classes above the Elementary was in being. Lady Stanley became a Vice-president, as did other influential figures, including Lord Lyttelton, the Endowed Schools' Commissioner, his daughter Lady Frederick Cavendish, and the Bishop of Exeter, Frederick Temple. The objects of this 'Women's Education Union' gradually brought girls' education from the pioneering to the professional era, operating with not a nineteenth- but a twentieth-century concept of secondary education.[45]

The Union's most urgent practical task was to form 'a limited Liability Company, for the purpose of establishing Public Day Schools for Girls, which should give a first-class education at fees as low as was compatible with the Schools being self-supporting and paying a fair interest on the capital invested'. Forty years before, the boys' proprietary schools had been established by the same means and there are some indications that this experience was drawn on. Dr Barry of King's College was actively involved; it was in the drawing-room of the headmaster of the Blackheath Proprietary School that he and about one hundred local residents met Mrs Grey and Miss Shirreff in 1878 to discuss the possibility of a girls' high school in the neighbourhood. It would seem unlikely that decades of experience, accumulated by the comparatively small number of people working in the field of middle-class education, were ignored.[46]

The method proved more permanently successful for girls than it was for boys. Even royal patronage was secured in the person of the conscientious, active Princess Louise, Marchioness of Lorne, in spite of the Queen's violent dislike of the women's movement. In 1872 the new Girls' Public Day Schools' Company was launched at an Albert Hall meeting, with Lord Lyttelton in the chair. It had nominal capital of £12,000 in 2400 shares held by such people as the founders themselves, James Kay-Shuttleworth, Joseph Payne, Joshua Fitch, Anne Clough, Dorothea Beale, Frances Mary Buss, and Samuel Morley – the last an interesting link with City philanthropy.[47]

Chelsea was chosen for the first school and Durham House, a dilapidated property, once the home of Isaac Newton and since a private boys' school, was rented. The early difficulties of this school dispel the myth that the high school movement 'was hailed with joy at the beginning'. The first headmistress, Miss Porter, recollected that they 'had to strive for years against continual opposition'. The house was unsuitable, the district dubious, and the GPDS Council at first inexperienced and fumbling. Miss Porter soon, in 1875, moved to one of the first endowed schools for girls, Bradford Grammar School. When the Chelsea school moved to Kensington in 1879, it began to flourish under a headmistress, Miss Hitchcock, who remained in the post until 1900. More fundamental, the very fact of this kind of education for girls was extraordinary to many people. Revolution was implicit in the word 'public' in the title of the new Company. 'It is not easy to realise how great was the innovation that we should be thus all assembled together in a public school', as one of the first pupils remarked. Moreover the Company deliberately increased and risked disquiet on two points of principle. The schools were to allow no social distinctions and they were to be non-sectarian. At Chelsea the early pupils represented every class 'from an earl's daughters to a very small tradesman's in the neighbourhood'. Miss Buss had overcome this prejudice against the mixing of classes and the Company schools eventually did so. At the time of the Bryce enquiry it was remarked that Company schools solved the difficulty of providing schools in Surrey for both the 'residential and villa population' and the 'local population', that is for daughters of parents who commuted to better-paid or professional work and the tradesmen of the neighbourhood. In Wimbledon, where social distinctions were very marked though not based on wealth, the High School also overcame them.[48]

But not even Miss Buss had attempted undenominational religious teaching, though girls might withdraw from Anglican instruction, and she had many Jewish pupils. The Company Schools were therefore breaking new ground. Here the relaxed attitude of the capital helped for it notoriously lacked urgency in denominational rivalry, and the first Company Schools, at Chelsea and Notting Hill, were able to avoid any particular trouble. In the case of the third Company school, out at archiepiscopal Croydon, the problem raised its head. Dr Tait tried to get the Council to allow 'definite religious instruction for children of Church of England parents', but this was refused. At Bromley in 1882, three Anglican incumbents, a Wesleyan and an Independent minister led the local demand for the opening of one of the schools. 'We have pleasure in drawing the attention of the Council to this town as a convenient centre for establishment of one of their schools. The . . . want of a high-class school for girls is seriously felt . . .'.[49]

After the two pioneering schools, the Council decided to open a school only when local demand was demonstrated by the formation of a local committee and the taking up of a 'certain number of shares (usually four hundred) enough to cover the initial expenses of the school'. In this way schools were opened all over the country, and in London and its suburbs – at Hackney (Clapton) 1875, St John's Wood (South Hampstead) 1876, Highbury and Islington 1878, Maida Vale (Paddington) and Dulwich 1878, Blackheath and Wimbledon 1880, Bromley 1883, Sutton 1884, Brixton (later Streatham Hill) and Sydenham 1887, Putney 1893. A 'Middle School' at rather lower fees was set up at Clapham in 1875 and a High School there in 1882. They were later combined. This policy tested the demand and proved that while it might be difficult to obtain gifts, either large or small, for the education of girls generally, 'there was little difficulty in getting share contributions from parents for the establishment of schools for their own girls'.[50]

The local nature of the need had another important effect. When travelling was considered dangerous or undesirable for girls, it provided a network of schools which were capable of expanding as suburbs grew and the idea of public education for girls was accepted. At Sydenham a resident moved to this affluent open suburb from North London where his daughter had attended the Company School at Highbury. He found no school nearer than Dulwich, now considered within easy distance. A colleague of his, a nephew of Lady Stanley, 'brought the wants of Sydenham before the Council'. A local committee of 'influential people', share subscriptions, 'premises at a fair rent and plenty of girls' were all secured and the school opened in 1887 with 20 pupils. Three years later there were 237.[51]

Local strength could turn to weakness when a neighbourhood changed or when endowed schools began to supply the demand. The Hackney and Clapton school closed in 1899, Highbury and Islington in 1911; Maida Vale, later called Paddington and Maida Vale, was transferred to the London County Council in 1911, Dulwich to the Church Schools' Company in 1913.[52]

Each school soon developed an individuality and fees varied from £9 9s to £15 15s, according to the locality. Slight local variations in the courses were allowed by the Council; Highbury included book-keeping, and the Kensington area was considered suitable for Greek and became famous for its music.[53] But there was no general policy of bowing to the market. The aim of the Company was to free girls' education from the notion that something special, and usually inferior, was required for them. The course was to be considered as a balanced whole – religious, literary, scientific, linguistic, aesthetic and physical. Girls were entered for the Cambridge Local examinations in the junior and senior divisions, and in the early days for those of the College of Preceptors; later seniors were examined by the Oxford and Cambridge Joint Board.[54] Each school was eventually organized into three divisions, and the junior departments soon had kindergartens run on Froebelian lines. Emphasis was laid on the 'progressive class system', by which girls could proceed up the school in a systematic way, following in each subject a course which developed logically and was related to their stage of growth. In practice this was difficult to attain as pupils entered so badly prepared and with such disparate attainments, and still often attended for short periods or in fits and starts. Many of the classes contained a wide range of ages and some girls who were unlikely ever to make much progress. It was however a scheme of study and scholastic planning which consolidated nineteenth-century experiments and bequeathed to the next its characteristic internal system of secondary organization. In 1900 this, with some features peculiar to the high schools, was described by Miss Gadesden, headmistress of the Blackheath School:

> The pupils are divided into Forms or arranged in divisions for special subjects. School hours are approximately from 9–1 ... Practical Chemistry and Greek are sometimes taken in the afternoon, as are piano, violin, dancing and special drawing lessons. Lessons for the next day can be prepared at school or at home. Most carefully prepared tables of homework are made to suit the requirements of each girl based on her position in the School, her ability and her power of work.[55]

To maintain standards and coherence the Council did not only depend on external examinations, but in 1878 appointed a Schools' Inspector of their own, the Reverend William Jowitt, headmaster of Canon Rogers's Cowper Street Schools, who could relate the problems with which these girls' schools were faced to those which had already emerged in boys' schools – the proper autonomy of the head-teacher, the development of a fully professional assistant staff for larger schools organized on the class system, the broad curriculum leading to higher professional or business education, the appropriate use of public examinations.[56]

The girls' schools had the added problem of finding staff with any adequate academic training, and moreover recognized, as the boys' schools rarely did, the need for professional training as well. Some of the early headmistresses were truly remarkable women, but could only be described as amateurs. Miss Porter had training college experience at a private establishment near Tiverton for the preparation of governesses.[57] Miss Morant Jones of Notting Hill, outstandingly successful in building up academic standards, had teaching experience in Guernsey.[58] Miss Dorinda Neligan of Croydon however had not taught before, though she was perhaps prepared for her work as a pioneer headmistress by having served in the Red Cross and being left in sole charge of Metz during its siege in the Franco-Prussian War.[59]

Eventually it was such schools as these which broke the deadlock of lack of adequate teachers by producing students for higher education. By 1895 271 external scholarships to university colleges had been won by Company schools, 587 students had been provided for university colleges, 245 degrees and diplomas had been obtained and 141 students had gone on to training colleges.[60]

The success of these schools stimulated other enterprises. The wife of the Reverend Francis Holland, considering the needs of her husband's Marble Arch parish, was inspired by the history of St Cyr and had 'been going about to some of the great High Schools to see their system of teaching'. She admired these interdenominational schools but the Church should also provide secondary day schools for girls, where continuity of religious teaching was secured and worship could form an integral part of education. For this end Mrs Holland and her husband worked together. He encountered the need at confirmation classes, she during parish visiting. Neither was wealthy, and it was necessary to secure investors for a company, the Church of England High School for Girls Limited, which was formed in 1877 with the Bishop of London as Patron. A house in Upper Baker Street was taken, between a blindmaker's yard and the railway, and adapted at moderate cost so that it could be easily converted if the venture should fail. First pupils were secured by forays by Holland on friends with suitable daughters. Miss Gertrude Frost, an old friend who taught at the Notting Hill High School, became the first headmistress and the reluctant parents of twenty-one-year-old Miss Vyner were persuaded to allow her to embark on a professional career as assistant mistress. In this way the ingredients of a successful and necessary school were assembled. It opened with 15 pupils in October 1878, and soon there was 'no doubt that the school was needed and appreciated'.

The fees were low as the school was intended for the daughters of the clergy, or professional men, and income was from the beginning the chief anxiety. In 1880 however the company paid a small but unexpected dividend and a second school was started in Graham Street at the request of Mr Wilkinson, vicar of St Peter's Eaton Square, later Bishop of Truro. After 1882 the formation of the Church Schools' Company with schools in Kensington, Streatham, Stroud Green and Dulwich made it unnecessary for Holland to begin more schools. Probably his schools were already supplying this need within the London area, for the Church Schools' Company had little success here, while both the Baker Street and Graham Street Schools flourished. Not without problems of management: fortunately the schools were rescued by Mr Moberly Bell, husband of one of the Ladies' Committee and father of five pupils. As business manager of *The Times* he was 'charmed by Canon Holland but horrified by the state of affairs'. He revolutionized the system of accounts and placed the whole organization on a thoroughly business like footing. The systematic education of an old pupil enabled her to take over the secretaryship under his guidance. The days of the uninstructed struggles of women pioneering in administration were drawing to an end. It was now possible in a district of this kind to find amateurs with both trained minds and the leisure for voluntary work, and the efficiency and pace of social adjustment quickened accordingly.[61]

Endowed schools for girls

By 1895 witnesses for the Girls Public Day School Company could claim to the Bryce Commission that 'there would appear that there is something approaching a sufficient provision of high schools for girls in the London district', and also that their work had stimulated the reorganization of endowments.[62] Both these claims need some caution. The high schools provided for the 'first grade' of education and were comparatively expensive. And it may be that concentration on their provision to some extent diverted attention from the struggle for endowments. From its beginning the Women's Educational Union set up a special committee 'to restore to the use of girls the endowments originally intended for their benefit, and to obtain for them a fair share in the other endowments applied to education'.[63] Later an Association for Promoting the Application of Endowments to the Education of Women was formed, with Miss Davies, Miss Clough, James Bryce and Joshua Fitch on the Committee, and especially urging the need for second- and third-grade schools. It estimated that in 1871, 225,000 girls over the whole country were awaiting secondary education.[64] But later the Union seems to have lost some of its active interest in this cause, especially after the Endowed Schools' Commissioners, their redoubtable allies, had been replaced by the Charity Commissioners in 1874.[65]

The difficulties of securing endowments, and the strengths of support for the Commissioners and their staff, were demonstrated when Miss Buss tried to place her school on a 'more public footing'. Her appeal met a pitiful response and the necessary step could only be taken by the formation of a trust to which Miss Buss handed over her highly profitable private property. A new North London Collegiate School was built in the Camden Road and in the old building a second school, the Camden School, with a lower scale of fees, was provided for girls leaving at about sixteen. Eventually some endowment from private subscriptions, the Clothworkers' Company, and a local charity, the Platt Charity of St Pancras administered by the Brewers' Company, was secured. The assiduous and almost conspiratorial assistance of the Commissioners, Lyttelton, Hobhouse, Robinson, and their assistant William Latham, had been crucial.[66]

Over the country as a whole the replacement of the Endowed Schools' Commissioners in 1874 brought a much less positive and committed policy towards the needs of girls. Even in the eye of the storm, in London between 1869 and 1874, schemes for twelve endowed schools for girls were approved, while in the much longer period from 1874 until the end of the century there were eleven.[67] Some of the loss of impetus was undoubtedly due to the slowing down of any enterprise gradually fulfilling its purposes. Yet progress was painfully slow. Seventeen years after the Act, witnesses before the Select Committee on its working emphasized the prejudice against the diversion of funds to girls: 'The education of boys is more favoured by parents than that of girls.' Many schemes for girls 'are in the nature of postponed clauses'. Nationally, girls' schools of the first grade were still comparatively deficient and, while girls were badly provided for in the lower grades, this was true of boys also. The Commissioner whose district included London reported that there had been an attempt 'to give substantial effect to Section 12', but 'we only regret that our success has not been greater. . . . Even where an endowment was large, and had improved . . . greatly in value, our proposal to apply a proportion of it to female education has frequently encountered determined opposition, and seldom received active support from the locality.' Public opinion however was on the move. There 'has been a very remarkable change', which Richmond ascribed to the success of the girls' schools already established under the Commissioners' schemes, 'as evidenced by the attendance of scholars', and also 'to the great public work which has been carried out by the Girls' Public Day Schools' Company' and the greater interest taken in secondary education as a whole. Now, 'provided it may be done without seriously endangering the work' for boys, help for girls was often supported and even urged upon the Commissioners. He cited St Olave's as a case in point. Fearon considered that this was especially the case in areas 'where there is a greater interest in education and social well-being', 'where the whole life of the country is more energetic and active'.[68]

Energy and activity however had to overcome many difficulties. As early as November 1869 the subject of establishing girls' schools came up before the Committee of the Middle Class Schools Corporation, and it was 'considered advisable that a scheme should be prepared and laid before the Council'. In the following spring Mr Jowitt, headmaster of the school and later inspector for the GPDS Company, reported 'a very interesting correspondence . . . between myself and the parents of my scholars'. They had been asked to 'express an opinion whether the system of our Day School here could be beneficially extended to girls', in spite of the 'difficulties if not dangers' which it was alleged might arise. Seven hundred answers 'expressed great satisfaction with our boys' school and entire confidence in the success of this new enterprise for female education if undertaken by our Corporation', gave 'unanimous evidence' of the 'deplorable state of girls' schools' and offered 'upwards of 200 girl pupils to any day school that may be opened'. A meeting was to be called at the Mansion House to raise funds for such a school, the business of finding a site began, and negotiations with the Datchelor's Charity opened. It was hoped that funds would be forthcoming for 'securing for the City a Model Girls' School'.[69] In the meantime Canon Rogers had been taking advice about a suitable headmistress, and Florence Nightingale and Dr Jowett of Balliol had recommended Miss Anne Clough, who accepted. Unfortunately while financial difficulties were dragging on she took on other responsibilities.[70] Meanwhile Rogers's parish school, the Bishopsgate School for Girls, to some extent provided an education of the kind desired, under the headship of Mrs Stanton who had been trained at

Whitelands. It entered girls for the Science and Art Examinations, those of the College of Preceptors, and even sometimes for the Cambridge Locals. French and Latin were taught as 'specific subjects' and the tone and quality of work was high.[71] This was the school used for practice by the Maria Grey College.[72] In 1887 the Great Eastern Railway acquired the site of the schools and the girls' school was eventually rebuilt in Spital Square, a 'handsome building of red brick with terra-cotta facings'. By this time, 1891, a Charity Commission Scheme was at last secured for what now became the Central Foundation Schools. Mrs Stanton remained headmistress of the girls' school at a salary of £100 a year with capitation fees; later it was fixed at £250. The school fees were between £2 and £5 according to age. Girls could enter at seven, and the broad curriculum was of the high school type, though Latin was not included in the main course. There were 100 Alleyn scholarships and some exhibitions, which were by the end of the century being held at Maria Grey College, University College London, and Bedford. In 1897 the school had 363 girls, more than it could properly accommodate, and it was nearly always quite full. Their parents were mostly commercial travellers and clerks, resident in the north and east suburbs; 80 girls travelled more than three miles, 107 more than one mile, and 176 lived within a radius of one mile. Most of the girls left shortly after they were fifteen, only two were over seventeen. There were sixteen class teachers, three music teachers, a French mistress and an art master. Most of the mistresses had been 'trained at a training college for teachers', two held London degrees.[73]

Application of endowments to girls' education was hampered and hindered by all the problems which beset the same reforms for boys, and by some peculiar to itself, and over the country as a whole progress was erratic and fortuitous. In London the sheer luxuriance of possibilities meant that even modest achievements brought useful improvements, especially after travelling became less difficult for girls.

One of the earliest successes was an example of the redeployment of a number of small charities to form a new school. Mary Datchelor's will had secured monies for the upkeep of her tomb and to her sisters the exclusive right to a vault in the parish of St Andrew Undershaft, and in 1726 the property was augmented by the Dutch Coffee-House in Threadneedle Street. The charity supported several doles, apprenticed two poor childen and so forth. Its value rose through the nineteenth century, and in 1863 the coffee-house was sold for £30,000. By a Scheme of 1871 two-thirds were to be applied to a school for girls. No suitable site was available in the City parish and a couple of houses in Camberwell were bought. There the school was an immediate success, more charities were added to it in 1879 and 1881 and a new school was built at a cost of £12,000. By a Scheme of 1894 the Clothworkers became governors of the school and of its endowments for as long as they continued their substantial support. From 1877 Miss Rigg, daughter of Dr Rigg of Westminster College, was the highly successful headmistress; by the end of the century she had a staff of twenty assistants and there were over 400 pupils. There were 18 entrance scholarships and some exhibitions, one of £50 to Girton College.[74]

The two Haberdashers' Aske's Schools were examples of the updating of endowments for both boys and girls. The Hoxton girls' school was from 1888 under Miss Edith Millar, a scholar of Newnham who had been headmistress of the Girls' Grammar School at Dewsbury, and she had a staff of twelve, two of them graduates, and a visiting music mistress. Fees were about £4 4s a year. By 1890 there were over 200 girls, mostly over twelve or thirteen as the neighbourhood was 'an obstacle to the attendance of younger children'. The majority left at sixteen. Parents were mostly clerks, shopkeepers, commercial travellers in the northern suburbs of Highbury, Canonbury, Islington. Some girls went on to the new University colleges, Newnham, Aberystwyth, and to Maria Grey College or the new physical education college at Dartford. But by 1897 the number of girls was declining owing to changes in the neighbourhood, and the school was moved to Acton in 1898.[75]

The Hatcham school was from the beginning planned as of a higher grade than that at Hoxton, and when it moved into its new and separate building in New Cross, it rapidly fulfilled the Haberdashers' expectations. The fees were over £9 a year. The headmistress, Miss Connolly, had a salary which in 1895 came to more than £700, her ten assistants were comparatively well-qualified, one a London graduate, one with a Science Teacher's Certificate from South Kensington, two with Froebel Certificates, one with a first-class Diploma in Cookery. There were 333 girls, most of whom remained until seventeen; there were 17 girls over eighteen years of age; 28 pupils were being prepared for special groups of subjects for the Higher Local Examinations; and there were leaving scholarships to Newnham and Lady Margaret Hall. The parents were mainly professional or business people, but a considerable number were clerks and shopkeepers. The girls came from the immediate neighbourhood, which the Haberdashers were developing as middle-class housing, but also from Greenwich, Woolwich, Forest Hill, Camberwell and Lewisham. About 20 per cent travelled by train to school.[76]

In these examples girls had to some extent been helped by the lead given by City men and the interplay between City Companies and the suburbs, where they administered and profited from real estate left in their trusteeship. London's unique topographical structure helped in another important respect: the number of charity schools for girls founded in both inner parishes and in villages since absorbed into London suburbs. St Clement Danes had provided a middle-class school for girls even before the Act of 1869. Lady Eleanor Holles School was created from a charity school in 1874.[77] The provision of secondary schooling in the East End of London for both sexes had been achieved largely in this way. In 1873 another girls' high school was created in that area from Bonnell's School in West Ham, and by 1906 contained 210 girls, with a headmistress who was a mathematician from Newnham.[78] Prendergast's Foundation in Lewisham was also used for a girls' school,[79] as was James Allen's charity in Dulwich. He was Warden and then Master of Alleyn's College of God's Gift from 1712 to 1746, and established and endowed a 'reading school' to teach poor boys and girls. The mistress and her little school were accommodated in a local inn. The Kensington property which financed this modest venture enabled the James Allen's Girls' School to be founded as part of the great Dulwich modernization. The 1857 Act enabled a superior girls' elementary school to be built in the centre of Dulwich Village for 150 girls, paying between 2*d* and 4*d* a week. It was never more than half full and the lack of provision for girls parallel to that for boys in Dulwich College was criticized by Mrs Grey and her colleagues. In 1882 the Commissioners however produced a Scheme for a less prestigious school for 300 girls, paying fees of between £3 and £8 a year, and following a high school course, with Latin if the governors thought fit. Twenty scholarships and six leaving exhibitions were provided. A laboratory was later built from a grant from the Technical Education Board, and chemistry, physics, botany and mechanics were taught. The need to earn grants led the examiners in 1898 to express 'a hope that science teaching may not be allowed to usurp too large a place in the school curriculum'. By the end of the century (1897) there were 307 girls on the register, the standard aimed at in the highest form was the London Matriculation, and girls were sent on to Bedford and Holloway Colleges. It exemplified the tendency of girls' schools to move up from second- or third- to first-grade education.[80]

St Martin's Middle Class School for Girls, later renamed St Martin's-in-the-Fields High School, used charities which had accumulated in this populous and fast-developing parish over two centuries, the latest being Dr Richard's Gift of 1830 (very much in the old style) for the clothing, education and support of four girls at the parochial school. The newer style of school was set up by a Scheme of 1873, varied by another in 1894. Its object was a 'practical education', for girls between seven years of age and not over sixteen, with fees between £2 and £5 a year, and no admission charges; scholarships were to cover fees, cost of materials, and in some cases 'to reimburse the parents the expense or loss of keeping their girls at school'. Two-thirds of the scholarships were to go to girls educated at 'some public elementary school' within the parish for at least three years. Exhibitions of about £30 a year might be provided at 'any college or place of higher education of women, or at some boarding-school . . . or at any training institution for schoolmistresses or governesses . . .', and these could go to girls from an elementary school, presumably to cater for the needs of pupil-teachers. The course included English, drawing, vocal music, needlework, domestic economy and the laws of health and natural science, and 'some modern European language'. Religious instruction was subject to a conscience clause, and the governing body was not to be subject to religious tests. It included representatives of the Vestry, the School Board, the London County Council and its Technical Education Board, which enabled a well-qualified science mistress to receive a salary of £120, far higher than that of any of her colleagues. At the end of the century the school contained 155 girls, 109 of them from within a radius of a mile, mostly daughters of 'shopkeepers, lodging-house-keepers, publicans, and hotel-keepers, though there are a few of the professional class'.[81]

Schools created in this way, from what had been primary endowments, avoided undue competition with the needs of boys as did endowments for girls. In 1881 William Ward gave an endowment of £20,000 for a City of London School for Girls.[82] The Skinners set up a new school for girls in 1886–90 in Stamford Hill.[83] Sharing of an endowment which had been solely applied to boys' education was much more controversial. Dame Alice Owen's School was founded in 1878 as a sister school to Owen's, and St Olave's was another example.[84] Even St Paul's eventually released some of its wealth for a girls' school, but the Scheme of 1874 was not carried out until 1904.[85] All too often the girls had to wait. The Latymer Foundation Scheme of 1878 contained Clause 64 – 'If and when the funds admit, the governors shall apply to the Charity Commissioners . . . for a supplementary Scheme for establishing a school for the education of girls of the same general character . . .'.[86] Indirectly the competition of Latymer Upper School and St Paul's School, after it moved to Hammersmith, was responsible for the actual transfer of an endowment from boys to girls. The Godolphin and Latymer School for Girls was set up after the Godolphin School for Boys closed in 1900.[87] Sometimes the sacrifice of sharing endowments dwindled into scholarships for girls. St Dunstan's for example made a number tenable at Prendergast Girls' School.[88] This scholarship system for girls was open to the same criticism as it was for boys: Jesse Collings complained that the Prendergast scholarships 'are of such a character that I do not think it possible that the poorest classes . . . can be benefited'. For three third-grade schools in the London division, taken as samples of scholarship provision in 1887, the occupations of parents listed by two of the schools were boilermaker, painter, clockmaker, charwoman, bootmaker, goldwire drawer, carpenter, nurse, foreman, railway porter, sempstress, printer. The third school reported that 'very few are the children of parents supporting themselves directly by manual labour . . . but rather of small employers in such trades, small shopkeepers and clerks'.[89]

Denominational and private schools

During this 'long haul' in providing for girls, denominational and private schools continued to play a vital part. Some Nonconformist schools especially emphasized the element of serious purpose and thorough study which was so necessary to the raising of standards. There were some very good Methodist private schools for girls. In 1852 Miss Hannah Pipe moved her school from Manchester to Clapham Park, developed by Cubitt for substantial middle-class housing; strongly influenced by Thomas Arnold, she called her school Laleham Lodge. Nearby was another school, Queenswood, which at first had ministers' daughters and was then formed into a limited liability company. It later moved to Hatfield. The Wesleyan School founded for the daughters of ministers began in Clapton, but later moved to Southport.[90] The school for the daughters of Congregational ministers, Milton Mount, was opened out at Gravesend in 1883, and the school for the daughters of missionaries at Walthamstow moved further out of the London orbit to Sevenoaks in 1878, under the headship of Miss Unwin, daughter of the Principal of Homerton College, the redoutable Voluntarist.[91] In London and its suburbs, the Roman Catholic orders contributed substantially to both the provision and the concept of girls' schooling. They shared belief in seriousness and solidity of study and added a systematic educational philosophy and practice derived from confessional and continental sources. The Society of the Sacred Heart for example was founded in France in 1800 by Madeleine-Sophie Barat who had been educated by her seminarist brother on the same lines as his pupils at the local *collège*. She took this tradition into her Order, and when she was invited to open schools in England, she transplanted it here in 1850. Even though fashionable pupils at Roehampton were quite unable to aspire to the full rigour of the course, this remained recognizably Gallic, and preserved the idea of a systematic and intellectual education for girls throughout the century.[92] The Sisters of the Faithful Company of Jesus had several schools in London. At Isleworth, Gumley House catered for 'girls of the upper rank' in a boarding-school of about 50 to 60, where the 'education is much higher than is required for the local University Examination', and they also had a day school of about 50 to 60 girls, St Mary's High School. In Clarendon Square, St Pancras, the Order opened in 1863 a middle-class school with fees of only £4 4s a year. In Poplar they began in 1880 at Howrah House two schools, a 'Boarding School for Young Ladies' and a 'High School for Girls', kept quite separate.[93]

There was a considerable number of such schools in and around London and as pressures on Catholic resources were severe, they were obliged as the century advanced to take fee-paying non-Catholic pupils, and thus considerably increased the overall supply of secondary places, often however 'for the Daughters of Gentlemen', or 'young ladies of the higher classes'. As the movement for the improvement of girls' education developed, their role became more conservative, for many of them maintained an ideal of specifically feminine schooling which was not in sympathy with the claim to an education similar to that of English boys. Prospectus entries even at the end of the century emphasized the strengths of the old traditions of domestic education, with references to

'Parlour Boarders', 'health and deportment', 'the best professors', 'London masters'. The 'accomplishments' were often mentioned, 'callisthenics' survived. The curriculum of Howrah House was probably typical – 'English in all its branches, the French, German, and Latin Languages; Music, Singing, Drawing, Painting, Dancing, with the newest dances, and all kinds of plain and fancy needlework'. Foreign orders could offer special advantages in language teaching, and sometimes pupils could pass on to a European convent 'in Rome, Paris, Vienna, etc.'. In some schools there were qualified secular mistresses – the Catholic High School of Our Lady of Sion had a headmistress with a London BA and a Maria Grey professional qualification, assisted by a 'Staff of Certificated English and Foreign Teachers'. But the use of public examinations was now often mentioned. At the Convent of the Assumption pupils were prepared for the Cambridge Locals 'when parents desire it'; at the Convent of Jesus and Mary pupils who had passed the Oxford Senior were prepared, if desired, for the London Matriculation and Intermediate Arts Examinations.[94]

By the end of the century such convent schools were an important part of London's provision for girls but they held aloof from the emerging system of secondary education. This was partly due to their strong tradition of social exclusiveness, and partly to their experience of continental interventionist, anti-clerical policies.

Private schools of this period continued to fill a vital function for many girls who would never be allowed to commit themselves to a high-school course, or a public institution. Some private schools had been deeply influenced by the revolution which had taken place. Such was the school opened in Hampstead in 1886 by Miss S. A. Olney, who had been member of staff and headmistress of GPDS Company schools and who gave evidence to the Bryce Commission on behalf of the Private Schools' Association.[95] Another was the Hammersmith High School, established about 1878 with a committee which included Sir Charles Dilke and Miss Buss and which claimed to give systematic teaching of the new kind.[96] Some aspired to give higher education; Elgin College in Bayswater for example prepared for the Higher Locals, and Frankfort House in Stoke Newington took 'students wishing to qualify themselves for teaching' by the 'French diplomas'. The difficulty of evaluating such claims however is demonstrated by the University College for Ladies in St John's Wood. It was under a 'Committee of Education' including Dr L. Schmitz, was 'established for the higher education of ladies, and is designed to hold a position for the training of daughters of the upper classes analogous to that occupied by the public schools for the instruction of their sons'. Its course was that of the usual boarding-school, the accomplishments given academic respectability by 'the system of the Royal College of Music, and of the Continental conservatoires', and of the School of Art in South Kensington'. Extras included the harp, zither, china painting and Hebrew.[97]

The achievements of the century

By the end of the century progress in London had been substantial. The various company schools catered on the whole for the first grade of girls' education, and reformed endowments to some extent served as well second- and third-grade needs; the confessional and private schools helped at all levels. To these must be added the coeducational schools attached to polytechnics, and some charitable schools such as the Victuallers' and Commercial Travellers'. Varied fees catered for the extraordinarily complex levels of the urban middle classes. Higher grade Board schools and pupil-teacher centres added to the provision by the last decade.[98] An inadequate number of scholarships helped some elementary school pupils but the majority of these were from the lower-middle- or skilled-working-class families who used the more aspiring voluntary schools or began to use the Board schools, sometimes as a deliberate way of qualifying for assisted secondary education. Within this secondary system however, and between its grades, there was more interchange of ideas and personalities, and more unity of ethos, than might have been expected. Schools founded as 'second' or 'third' grade increased their aspirations and standards. The deliberate policy of social cohesion in the 'first-grade schools', the lack of professional alternatives to teaching for the new women graduates, the determination of the secondary headmistresses to organize a unified profession, all contributed. So did the strongly shared value-system of the age, the especial expectations, which any family aspiring to respectability, let alone gentility, had of its womenfolk, and the need for the education of women and girls to identify itself in a socially acceptable manner.

How far the achievements of this period provided enough secondary places for London girls it is impossible to say. The rapid filling up of schools as they were created strongly suggests that there was always a deficiency of provision, but desultory attendance indicated that education for girls was still not generally accepted as a continuous, cumulative and indispensable process. The Stepney and Bow Foundation Schools serve to illustrate the situation in 1895 – the boys' school with accommodation for 580 was not yet full, the girls' school contained only two short of the maximum number, 254. They were mostly the daughters of clerks and tradespeople; 118 travelled to school by railway, and there were more girls over twelve than under that age, implying 'that the school is largely used to supplement the education that is got elsewhere'. Many stayed only two or three years, and while this meant that it was 'of great service to the district', it meant 'no little difficulty' to the school itself. Girls had gone with exhibitions to Aberystwyth University, and Bedford and University Colleges, London.[99]

Such were some of London's achievements within a national transformation. Did the capital make any special contribution to the causes and impetus of this extraordinary change in the education of women and girls? Cultural, intellectual and social leadership undoubtedly may be claimed, but demographic and economic factors also had a metropolitan dimension which grew in importance as throughout the nineteenth century imbalance between male and female population was increasing. In 1841 there were 358,976 more women than men in England and Wales, in 1901 1,070,015, about one-third of them below the age of marriage.[100] This census moreover emphasized that this problem was greater in urban than in rural areas, in London and the Home Counties than in the rest of the country.[101] The 1911 census produced more detailed evidence. In three prosperous and three poor London boroughs the proportion of unmarried women to unmarried men varied considerably. In Hampstead for every 100 unmarried men between thirty-five and fifty-five there were 291 unmarried women, in Kensington 409, in Chelsea 260. For Woolwich, Shoreditch, and Bethnal Green the figures were 81, 59 and 81 respectively.[102] Even when corrected to allow for a high proportion of domestic servants in wealthier areas, these figures were startling. A social or educational system which assumed that women would marry was unrealistic, and while working-class women in London certainly suffered from extremes of under-employment and under-payment, middle-class women were increasingly seen as in need especially of education for self-support.[103] The work of the Langham Place Group in the mid century had disclosed that even in London, the most expanding and diversified labour market in the world, which since the eighteenth century had been passing from the productive to the service stage of development, the economy had not yet generated enough suitable work for middle-class women, and that there was strong male competition for any such posts. It was the gradual transformation of this situation by urbanization and what has sometimes been called the second or consumer industrial revolution, which gave added impetus to secondary education for girls in London.[104]

Fearon, summarizing his London enquiries for the Taunton Commission, described how professional men with fixed incomes and commercial men of limited means might look 'anxiously' at their little girls and reflect how to prepare them for a precarious future, or to 'reap the advantages of the hopeful future which is opening out before them' as higher education for women became a possibility.[105] Miss King, Secretary of the Society for the Promotion of Employment of Women, giving evidence before that Commission, was able to report some practical progress. Women were beginning to be employed in the electric telegraph offices. Positions of responsibility for them however were rare, usually in rural areas, and put strains on inadequate educational foundations – these few girls could write good letters and spell.[106]

Another area in which some progress was made at this period was in the various branches of design and art and craft work. Schools of art were considered to be both genteel and to have 'powerful and abiding moral influence' in training girls in accuracy, observation, steady perseverance, and punctual regularity. In 1862 only two took women students, South Kensington and the college in Queen's Square, Bloomsbury, which had formerly been the female portion of the Government School of Design in Somerset House. A large number of girls entered at fifteen and sixteen, 'just at that age when they require some object or pursuit to engage their attention'. The majority became teachers, but many other possibilities opened up – engraving, lithography, heraldic designing, and illustrating children's books, wood-carving, even the 'lighter decoration of dwelling houses'. Much of this work, often in trades and skills already overcrowded, must have been precarious and sporadic, and unlikely to provide the secure living which one private school of drawing and modelling in north London claimed for its young women students if 'a British Bank collapses, or Death makes a call on the head of the family'. Nevertheless it was a sphere in which women could hope for and did secure some employment, if not real independence, especially in the particular conditions of London's small-scale and skilled industrial organization, and this increased as the century drew on. In 1884 for example there were a considerable number of female students in the applied arts colleges who were 'learning the art of wood-engraving, and doing it very successfully'.[107] This strengthening tradition in the education of girls meant that in the last decade of the century they appear in the debate and the story of technical and commercial education not to make any abstract claims, but almost as a natural, if minor, part of the scene, as employees of commercial or industrial firms, as holders of scholarships under the Technical Education Board, as pupils in laboratories provided by its grants, as students at the polytechnics, even side by side with the boys in the secondary schools attached to them.[108] By this last decade of the century the transforming economy and central and local administrations needed their services, and were generating employment for 'lady typewriters', clerks, assistants in department stores, and so on. Lower wages and salaries played an important part in establishing their share of such service and distributive posts: 'It only means that the work is transferred from a man to a woman at a lower wage.'[109] The social base of this kind of work was widening. In earlier decades girls from good voluntary or Board schools not only had an educational advantage, but the recognition of their need to earn money was uninhibited by middle-class pretensions. The *Quarterly Review* argued in 1881 that there was plenty of employment for lower-middle-class girls and that help should concentrate on 'gentlewomen' of limited means. Professor Fawcett when Postmaster General increased employment and prospects for women in the government service. From 1875 Sir John Tilley had filled posts in the Post Office Savings Banks from their ranks by competitive examination after nomination. The number of applications was 'saddening to contemplate'. There was constant pressure from competition for scarce jobs upwards through society, the skilled workers' daughters challenging the lower-middle-class girls, and so on.[110] This provided pupils for an interesting range of schools, such as the Addey and Stanhope in Deptford.[111] By the last two decades the demand for secondary education was immensely stimulated, both by the needs of the labour market and the plight of middle-class finances and changing attitudes. The years of prosperity were over by 1870 and, in a time of steadily rising prices, families were unwilling to lower their aspirations.[112] The report on Surrey for the Bryce Commission drew attention to the very large number of girls in the suburban districts who, as soon as they left school, had to earn money in some way or another. 'They either go into shops, do clerical work, or begin teaching themselves. Some go out as day governesses or nursery governesses, some try to get situations in the Post Office, or work as type-writers. For them, cheap secondary schools would be a great help. . . .'[113] This was reflected in private schools. As early as 1884 Woburn College in Guildford Street advertised 'special preparation . . . for the Post Office (Lady Clerks') Examinations', and the Thornhill College for Ladies, established in Barnsbury since 1854, prepared for the 'Civil Service Examinations'.[114] More significantly for the future of girls' education, the high schools were also responding. The GPDS Company School in Paddington announced in 1894 that not only had it sent students to Newnham, Westfield and Somerville Colleges, but that one pupil had 'gained a clerkship in the Bank of England. These posts have lately been opened to women, and are gained by a competitive examination subsequent to nomination by a director.' By 1907 one old girl was a 'girl clerk in the office of the Prudential Assurance Company'. She reported that there were two other pupils from the school among the 400 women on the staff. In the same year another former pupil wrote of her experience working in the GPO. 'The year I passed fifty vacancies . . . were offered and no less than 488 candidates sat . . .'. Her sister had obtained by nomination a post in the new typing section in the Accountant General's Department. In 1908 the headmistress of this school reported that 'a class for typing and shorthand has been formed . . . I hope that it may grow to provide a useful technical training . . . for girls who are intending to take up secretarial or business work.[115] The Manchester High School for Girls, under the famous Miss Burstall, had already had such a department since 1901. But headmistresses were divided on this matter. At a 1914 conference Miss Rigg of Mary Datchelor favoured it, Miss Walder of the Roan School 'did not feel that secondary schools should provide special courses'. Most headmistresses who provided commercial subjects saw them not only as vocational preparation, but as aspects of character training – 'meticulous accuracy, earnestness, business-like habits, personal neatness, a certain type of manner, sympathetic yet not fussy, deferential but not servile'.[116] The girls' high schools in this way made a powerful bid for employment opportunities over pupils from elementary or higher grade schools. Girls' secondary schools, under increasing pressure from a labour market which was beginning to need skilled girls and women, nevertheless sought to preserve an ideal of general education, and directly vocational or trade schools for girls as for boys were a development from the higher grade Board schools and not from the secondary schools. London gave a lead to the country as a whole. The first was opened in the Borough Polytechnic in 1904 and others followed, some, such as the Blue Coat School at Greenwich, using old endowments.[117] This separation of the strands of secondary education was bequeathed as a problem to the twentieth century but the London experience demonstrated the importance of economic factors in creating and extending schooling for girls at all levels throughout the nineteenth century.

The contribution of girls' secondary education

These immense achievements in providing schooling for girls had far-reaching significance for the concept of secondary education being formulated in these crucial decades at the end of the nineteenth century and setting the pattern for almost three-quarters of the next. Girls' schools established the idea and practice of professionalism in secondary teaching; they defined the curriculum and its purposes in new ways, entrenching especially the literary, expressive and practical subject and non-denominational religious teaching as essential aspects of a general, liberal education; they provided a comprehensive approach to physical education; they emphasized and reinterpreted the pastoral dimension of the school's responsibilities; and they helped to formulate a process of education related to stages of human development.

Throughout the century London had played its vital part in providing a meeting place for women reformers, and as secondary schoolmistresses passed from the pioneering to the professional stage in their work, it became the arena in which formal associations came into being. The London Association of Schoolmistresses has already been described. In 1874 the first meeting of the Association of Headmistresses was held in Miss Buss's house, attended by the heads of Milton Mount College, Gravesend, the Grey Coat Hospital, Notting Hill and Chelsea High Schools, the Camden School, St Martin's Middle Class School, and Manchester High School, with Miss Beale of Cheltenham in the chair – already it represented Company, denominational and reformed endowed schools, and throughout its history it kept this openness to all kinds of secondary schools.[118] The Association of Assistant Mistresses was formed in 1884.[119] Such associations, of very remarkable women facing new and rapidly developing problems and opportunities, were the focus of much progressive thinking on all levels of education. Perceptive contemporaries recognized that they were able to make a distinctive contribution because, in Thring's words, they were 'fresh, enthusiastic and comparatively untrammelled', in contrast to the schoolmasters who were 'weighed down by tradition, cast like iron in the rigid mould of the past'.[120] The women themselves were perhaps more conscious of the *lack* of the tradition which gave their male colleagues a framework within which to operate, and above all, they were aware of their lack of formal qualifications, both academic and pedagogic. This professional insecurity, shared with many private schoolmasters, lay behind the creation of the College of Preceptors in 1848, which was spurred on by the contemporary developments in the training of elementary teachers. London schoolmistresses actively participated in the College of Preceptors,[121] and were very much aware of the work of Whiteland's College, established in 1842 by the National Society in a house in Chelsea which had been a seminary for young ladies. This tried to attract middle-class girls as students but they were usually too ill-prepared, having been given 'a little external dressing but rarely any internal culture'.[122] In any case the teaching skills which Whiteland's imparted could not be used in secondary schools, for the 'Government will not allow it'.[123]

But although much was written at the time and since, and with justification, of the miserable lack of knowledge and skill of many private governesses and schoolmistresses, girls' education had here more of a positive inheritance than has perhaps been realized. The long tradition of domestic education had its strengths, as the ideas and achievements of women such as Miss Buss herself demonstrated. The oldest training establishment for women teachers belonged to this tradition.[124]

In 1818 Mrs Sophia Williams, already experienced in charitable work, drew attention to the needs of the young persons who have 'by birth, great claims upon society', the orphan daughters of naval and military officers killed in the Napoleonic Wars, and of the clergy. She interested Queen Charlotte in her scheme for an 'Adult Orphan Asylum' (later Institution) to train them as governesses. It was to be a memorial to the Princess Charlotte, but subscriptions were disappointing and in 1819 it was decided to drop the idea and begin the institution on a reduced scale. The patronage of the Princess Augusta and the labours of a committee of gentlemen enabled two houses in Mornington Place to be taken and to admit 16 wards to be trained as teachers, 'as artists, or as useful members of society in domestic conerns'; 4 were fourteen years old, 2 fifteen, 4 sixteen, 3 seventeen, 2 eighteen, and 1 each was nineteen, twenty, and twenty-one. In these early years they also contributed funds by their 'work', some taking pupils in music, dancing or general instruction, others by their needles. A fortunate pair of lace ruffles worked for King George IV brought a subscription of £100 and royal patronage, which has continued to this day. 'Wards' were presented by donors and subscribers on a system akin to that being devised by boys' proprietary schools.[125]

Gradually the Institution worked out its policy and practice. The admission of girls at fourteen was found to be too young: the 'Institute was formed, not to educate children, but to finish the education of young women, and to forward them in their way through life . . .' but selection at a later age disclosed that some 'for want of previous instruction or mental weakness can never be fitted for that occupation in life' for which they were intended. Some spent their first year in trying to learn what they should have been taught in earliest youth, and they were therefore to be examined as soon as convenient in the 'rudiments of Education (more especially English Grammar, Reading, Writing, Arithmetic and the principles of the Christian Religion)'. In this way they could be got rid of 'before making up their wardrobe', but were still on a year's probation.[126]

In 1824 the Institution moved to a house in Regent's Park, Nash giving his 'gratuitous services as architect' and a piece of ground at a rent of £100 a year.[127] There it continued to educate and train between 30 and 40 girls and women at a time. It afforded an education 'at a period of their lives when they most stand in need of counsel and protection, during the five or six years previous to their arrival at confirmed woman-hood', and enabled them 'to procure for themselves a sufficient maintenance without descending from the rank in life in which they have been born'.[128] The curriculum, as well as a 'superior course of religious instruction' under 'clerical superintendence', emphasized 'sound and useful knowledge'. Latin and German were added after 1843 to enable the words to teach boys and accomplishments were stressed for professional purposes. They were to be qualified to teach not only in private families but in schools, and on leaving were examined by the Bishop of London.[129] The demand for their services was great, and when they had obtained posts they were still regarded as 'Senior Wards' and given asylum when necessary. The committee also regulated the salaries which they demanded. In 1832 these were increased to secure 'more just remuneration for the cultivated talents and general acquirements which they will carry with them . . . and to enable them both to maintain a respectable appearance and to make some little provision for future exigencies'. Students were much sought after by private families.[130] By the time of the Taunton Inquiry, the Adult Orphans' Institution had changed little, but it was to respond to its recommendations and to the stimulus which it gave to girls' education, as we shall see.[131]

One strength of this domestic tradition of teaching was its inheritance from the Enlightenment of ideas of childhood and its development and of the responsibility of the 'educative family', usually the teaching of young children by the mother herself, or her substitute. The Pestalozzian Institution of the Home and Colonial Society, established in the Gray's Inn Road in 1836, provided London with another source of teacher training, at first for the primary age, but by 1868 it had recently taken up 'the question of secondary education on an extensive scale'. It taught subjects which 'female teachers in secondary schools' wished to teach, instructed them in the theory of teaching, and gave them practice in a mixed secondary school on the premises. In 1894 this moved to Highbury Hill House and became the Highbury Hill High School for Girls.[132]

The part played by Queen's College from 1848 has already been described, and although its training courses for teachers did not last long, their influence was if not profound, at least dramatic.[133]

Miss Buss's evidence to the Taunton Inquiry sums up the position during that vital decade. She herself was armed with three Queen's certificates and her conviction of the need for professional training was passionate. Her difficulties in getting staff who could carry out her enlightened views of teaching method were described to the Taunton Commissioners for she insisted on exposition and explanation 'accompanied by rapid questions' in the Socratic manner. By sending her young staff to the Home and Colonial Institution she secured a 'certain amount of teaching power'.[134] The reminiscences of an intelligent pupil, Mary Thomas, who entered the North London Collegiate School in the early 1880s, demonstrated however the inadequacy of such improvised training.[135] Miss Buss hoped that the new pedagogic skills from the teachers' training colleges could be used in secondary schools and as the pressure of demand for such teachers became acute, they brought about important new enterprises in their training. The Teachers' Training and Education Society was founded by the Women's Educational Union in 1876 to meet this need. A scheme for a non-residential undenominational college, to train teachers for both secondary schools and their kindergarten and preparatory departments, and preparing for an external recognized qualification, was worked out and was incorporated under licence from the Board of Trade. Before the college opened Cambridge set on foot plans for a university diploma in education.[136] Mrs Grey approached Canon Rogers, always a friend to women's education, and asked him to allow his girls' school in Bishopsgate to be used as a training school. 'He very cordially agreed that it should be, and he also lent, rent free, a small house, or rather part of a small house, in which the students had lectures.'[137] In May 1878 the Training College for Teachers in Middle and Higher Schools for Girls opened with four students.[138] They gave demonstration lessons in Mrs Stanton's excellent school[139] and took the examinations of the Cambridge Training Syndicate as soon as they were established. From 1883 for teaching in preparatory departments the Bishopsgate College was a pioneer in Froebelian methods. It also set up a lower division to prepare students for the Cambridge Higher Local as a qualification for its own professional courses. Staffing was a problem and at first experimental. In 1880 Miss Agnes Ward, a connection of the Arnold family, who had been teaching at GPDS Schools, became principal. Mrs Stanton acted as 'Mistress of Method', visiting lecturers helped with academic and pedagogic studies – James Sully, Canon Daniel from Battersea Training College, Oscar Browning from Cambridge. The College was well supported by the London educational community – Dr Rigg of Westminster College, Dr Abbott of the City of London School, Lyulph Stanley (later Lord Sheffield), son of Lady Stanley and prominent on the London School Board, the Reverend T. W. Sharpe, who from 1890 was senior HMI for the metropolitan district.[140]

After five years the college outgrew its premises – it now had 53 students – moved to Fitzroy Square and opened its own practising school.[141] But its position was precarious. Financial support was minimal and the College faced competition from the Cambridge Training College for Women, opened in 1885, and later from the Mary Datchelor course. In spite of these difficulties an appeal for funds for a permanent building drew support from the Pfeiffer and Gilchrist funds and from the Clothworkers' Company and in 1892 a college and school were built in Brondesbury, then an area of market-gardens and open fields with grazing cattle.[142] Here the Maria Grey College, as it had been called since 1885, used its Brondesbury and Kilburn High School for intensive and carefully supervised practice teaching, students also acting as form-mistresses, watching classes, and learning pastoral and administrative duties. They came from such schools as the North London Collegiate and the GPDS Company schools, and in 1890 Mrs Stanton's school supplied a student. They were not only of much more use to the newer kinds of girls' school, but they were able to command rather better salaries, of about £80 a year.[143]

At this period there was a considerable revival of interest in Froebel's ideas and, while these directly applied to the teaching of very young children, indirectly they had great influence on women teachers at secondary level. Froebel teachers were used as form-mistresses in the lower parts of schools and high schools had their own preparatory departments. In 1874 the Froebel Society was founded, with Miss Emily Shirreff as president. In 1894 the Froebel Education Institute opened in North End Road, Fulham, for students and a few children, and it was soon enlarged to contain a model kindergarten for about 160 pupils.[144] At Maria Grey Miss Elsie Riach Murray became head of the Froebel Department at the end of the century. She was an early exponent of Dewey's philosophy and an international figure in the 'Child Study Movement'.[145] The high schools also acted as training centres for kindergarten teachers. In 1900, at the Paddington and Maida Vale High School, Agnes Ward, for example, gave a course of lectures to parents and friends of the school's preparatory department, where students were trained and prepared for the examinations of the Froebel Society by the kindergarten mistress, who had been a student at Fulham. In 1901 four girls were being prepared for the Elementary Examination of the National Froebel Union.[146]

Company schools contributed to the training movement by taking a few student teachers at secondary as well as preparatory level. The most far-ranging provision was at Clapham where, under the legendary Miss Woodhouse who became headmistress of the combined Modern and High Schools in 1898, there was established a training college with four departments – the secondary training department for post-graduates, the kindergarten Froebel department, the training department for teachers of drawing in secondary schools, and a course for teachers of domestic subjects in secondary schools.[147] Fitch was justified in claiming that the Company had forwarded 'the due training and pre-paration of highly qualified teachers'.[148] In 1902 the London schools of the GPDS Company felt experienced and confident enough to submit a complete scheme for the training of graduate women teachers, to operate in conjunction with the newly formed London Day Training College. Professor Adams, its first principal, had acted as consultant. Theory would be taught at the College, supervision of practice given in seven Company schools.[149]

Another girls' school which contributed to the training programme was Mary Datchelor's. A Secondary Teachers' Training College attached to it was opened in 1888 with 26 students. By 1905 there were 34. Miss Rigg was principal of both school and college.[150] To all these experiments must be added the training department at Bedford College. This was opened in 1892 in the charge of Mary Thomas, an old pupil of Miss Buss and student of Miss Hughes's College at Cambridge. Bedford was alarmed by the competition of this college for its own students who intended to teach, a reminder of the precarious nature of such higher and professional training. In 1895–6 the Bedford De-partment had 13 students.[151] Because of its non-sectarian character it was chosen to train nuns for the staff of the Cavendish Square College of the Society of the Holy Child Jesus founded in 1896 by Cardinal Vaughan to train women teachers for Catholic secondary schools. In 1897 it was recognized by the Cambridge Education Syndicate.[152]

This period of intense and enterprising activity brought a new di-mension into secondary education. How far girls' schools were penetrated and transformed by these ideas can be demonstrated from the history of the Adult Orphans' Institution. Soon after the Taunton Inquiry the effects of drawing girls' education, even tentatively, into the public arena can be seen. The headmaster of the nearby Philological School was brought in to teach the wards Latin and higher mathematics and the 'Analysis of the English Language', and Mr Meiklejohn gave lectures on 'The Theory and Practice of Teaching'. Princess Christian, daughter of Queen Victoria, became the active Lady President and the Institution became the Princess Helena College. It was decided to open it to paying boarders and younger day pupils, and the students in the upper division (between seventeen and twenty-one years of age) were to receive classified Diplomas on qualifying.[153] One of the first Maria Grey students, Julia Walker, became Lady Principal.[154] Soon the Regent's Park building could not accommodate such expansion. A new college and high school on a site of nine acres in the village of Ealing was planned on a system 'designed to meet the criticisms of the Schools' Inquiry Commission'.[155] Its committee included Dr Bell, the headmaster of Marlborough, Mr Eve of University College School, Joshua Fitch, Professor Huxley, the Dean of Westminster (Dr Bradley), and most significant perhaps of all, the Reverend William Jowitt, now incumbent of Stevenage, former headmaster of the Cowper Street Schools and Inspector of the GPDS Company schools: a hitherto somewhat introverted institution was to be thrown open to new influences and experience.[156]

In 1882 the Prince of Wales opened the new building, Miss Williamson from the Notting Hill High School was appointed Lady Principal, election of the wards by subscribers was abolished and the Education Committee began to look into the 'systematic outside examination of the College'.[157]

From this there grew a boarding-school, retaining for some time an element of teacher training, and a day high school. By 1886 numbers had risen to over 200, and by 1895 to 257, the day girls greatly outnumbering the boarders who usually, including the wards, remained at about the 50 mark. The College at first took the Cambridge Locals, including the Higher Women's examination, the college of Preceptors' for younger pupils, and was inspected by the University of London. By 1888 London Matriculation was taken and in 1892 the College progressed further up the academic ladder by placing itself under the Oxford and Cambridge Board of Examiners, on the same conditions as the GPDS Company. It had also become a centre for University Extension lectures.[158]

While the boarding and day schools were kept separate except for lessons, the plan retained the 'original object of the institution' by allowing wards being trained as 'governesses' to assist in the school. Education on 'the most modern lines' was given with the 'view to fitting Pupils to take their position in any society as refined, cultured, and healthy women'. In 1890 the college branched into technical education, training its future teachers in domestic science and other practical subjects, including book-keeping and shorthand, as the 'demand for Technical Teachers is very great'. The school was affiliated to the Forsyth Technical College, a voluntary enterprise in Kensington. In 1892 one of the wards obtained two teaching certificates from the London Institute for the Advancement of Plain Needlework and was appointed needlework mistress at the West Ham High School.[159]

The very success, however, of the newer kind of girls' school, and the opening of higher education to women, made it unnecessary for Princess

Helena College to remain a training centre for teachers. It served its wards, now more in the nature of scholarship holders, better by sending them on to the other institutions for this specialized work and its future was that of a girls' high and boarding-school. It followed much the same path, though at a later date, as Queen's College, its partner in the pioneer training of governesses.

These achievements must be seen in contrast with the failure of professional training for schoolmasters. The lectures of the Cambridge Training Syndicate began in 1879 and were well attended at first. By 1881 their few students were mostly women. Its examinations were also mostly taken by women. By 1899 only 28 university men had been granted certificates. A Training College for Secondary Schoolmasters was initiated in 1883 in Finsbury by a group of headmasters 'of First Grade Schools'. Its principal was Courthope Bowen from the Grocers' School and it was provided with rooms and teaching practice at the Cowper Street Schools by Canon Rogers. It was a complete failure. In 1895 the College of Preceptors tried a scheme of one year's professional training for men over eighteen, but it had no support and closed after two years. The problem was that, although some headmasters paid lip-service to training, it brought few professional advantages when a university degree was still considered an adequate qualification.[160] By the end of the century the number of women graduates who were entering the teaching profession was making its impact, and there was some anxiety lest they, also, would neglect the need for further training as indeed the vast majority of them did, if only for economic reasons. The very considerable momentum which had been built up in the pioneering and early professional days however carried the movement forward into the era of university participation in teacher training. It is hardly too strong a claim that the idea of a profession of secondary teaching was established by women. This new professionalism, building on the ideas of the pioneers, and the best traditions of girls' education, enabled these women to make important contributions to the theory and practice of secondary education.

First, the curriculum. In claiming to study the same subjects as boys, the girls' schools had not abandoned their own birthright. The course of the new girls' schools had added Latin, sometimes Greek, mathematics and often some science to the usual English subjects and modern languages and had transformed ornamental accomplishments into serious study of music and drawing, and kept plain needlework, often as an aspect of social service. The grants of the Science and Art Department and the Technical Education Boards had strengthened the scientific element in this course and the demands of the labour market emphasized commercial and related subjects.[161] In the last two decades of the century increasing pressure came from the movement known as 'Social Darwinism', a complex of ideas on national efficiency and health, social progress, and even racial purity, which emphasized the role of the wife, mother and home-maker. To some extent the new type of schoolmistress shared or was prepared to accept such ideas and the Association of Headmistresses formed a special committee in 1895 to discuss the place of domestic science in the curriculum. But when it came to sacrificing the broad liberal curriculum and intellectual development of girls to their position as 'guardians of the race', to selling 'the intellectual birthright' of girls for 'skill in making puddings', the GPDS Company was ready to make a stand, and even to sacrifice grants from the Board of Education by not complying with its regulations on systematic training in housewifery. Their philosophy of the curriculum however remained comprehensive, and it was the headmistresses who were responsible for the inclusion of practical and aesthetic subjects as an optional group in the School Certificate examination which operated from 1917.[162]

It was also in girls' schools that a fully developed and comprehensive theory of physical education was put into practice – medical inspection with proper records for each pupil, individual remedial exercises if necessary, gymnastics and musical drill for all, and organized games for recreation, character development and further supervised physical training. Some of this was an inheritance from the deportment, dancing and callisthenics of the old tradition, some from the good sense and breadth of understanding of the pioneers, some from the boys' schools. It was also necessary to counteract the hysterical fears of overstrain and overpressure on girls, often put forward as an argument against their improved education. To all this was added a new professionalism, especially the influence of Madame Österberg, an exponent of Ling's Swedish exercises, who taught the students at Whiteland's and introduced her system into London Board schools. In 1885 she set up in Hampstead the first residential college for training specialist PE teachers, with the first fully equipped gymnasium of its kind in England. Here she developed her own system, combining Swedish and German elements with vaulting and apparatus of her own design, team games, including netball and basketball imported from the USA, and also more individual sports such as tennis, squash and swimming, and dancing which included waltzing and national dances. Students studied anatomy, animal physiology, relevant sciences, hygiene and the theory of movement. Madame Österberg was relentless and autocratic, determined to 'send the drill sergeant packing', for only women could and should educate other women. She was able to select her students ruthlessly, her fees were high, and her college was essentially training middle-class girls to teach in middle-class schools. In 1895 its success made a removal to Dartford necessary. Soon colleges were set up throughout the country. In London, both Chelsea and Battersea Polytechnics had physical education colleges for women.[163]

Alice James described theory and practice in London schools at the end of the century in her *Girls' Physical Training*. Her introduction quoted Browning, Ruskin, Herbert Spencer and Froebel, emphasized the pressure of intellectual work, the nature of childhood and youth, the 'essentials for character building secured by means of the child's play', the need for 'fusing the *mental* and *physical* training' if the nation was to reap benefits from education. Her exercises with plumes, dumb-bells, rings, balls, were designed 'on natural and wholesome movements' and to give real enjoyment. She also urged that field games should be encouraged. 'In the playing field young people . . . acquire virtues which no schoolroom training can give them . . .', high standards 'of physical and moral health'.[164]

Such physical education was seen as an integral part of a general and liberal education. One of the outstanding headmistresses of the period, Miss Woodhouse of Clapham, expressed this philosophy of the curriculum in her Presidential address to the AHM in 1908. 'In these days the curriculum must be thought out and defined in relation to the child and its growing activities. The perception of the relation between the two is, of course, our great debt to Froebel and those who have developed his point of view . . .'. Professional ethos emphasized this newly emerging psychological interest and the importance of the individual girl, while the still precarious foothold of women in higher education and the labour market, as well as the need for discriminating social responsibility, demanded 'sympathetic insight into the double need – the needs of the pupil on the one hand and the waiting world on the other'.[165]

This approach to the curriculum was not only liberal and comprehensive, but also pastoral, and girls' schools of this period greatly strengthened this aspect of secondary education. Attention to the growth, health, disposition and abilities of the individual pupil combined with the inevitable need for protecting and sheltering girls, of reinterpreting the old idea of chaperonage if the new schools were to be socially acceptable.

The special ethos of the women's teaching profession also emphasized the relations between the process of education and stages of human development, although confusions were caused by social attitudes: 'Apart from class distinctions, the stages of primary, secondary and tertiary education show themselves as real – though not with great black lines of departmental separation between them,' said Dr Sophie Bryant, the second headmistress of the North London Collegiate School, in 1904.[166] From the beginning of the movement women teachers had been challenged by these problems of demarcation. What should be expected of girls of different ages at different stages of schooling? The London Association of Schoolmistresses spent a number of its sessions discussing these large questions, which were made more opaque by the low standards attained by most girls, and their erratic, desultory attendance.[167] The education of boys had also to delineate borderlines between secondary and higher education, and

University and King's Colleges for many decades occupied a middle ground. Queen's and Bedford Colleges had additional difficulties and only worked out gradually a suitable process of education, progressively organized in stages which became common practice in girls' schools. In 1884 for example the City of London College for Ladies in Finsbury Square, claiming that it had been established thirty years earlier as a branch of Queen's College, had three departments: a kindergarten for girls and boys under eight years old, 'conducted on the principles of Pestalozzi and Froebel'; a 'Transition Class' preparatory for the upper school; and this upper division in which girls were prepared for the College of Preceptors' and University Local Examinations. Senior classes 'may be attended by ladies who do not follow the whole course', and some were prepared for the 'Cambridge, Oxford and other Higher Examinations for Women, including those of London and St Andrews Universities'.[168] Divisions such as these set a pattern, and the high schools were able to build on the experience of these pioneering days. With their kindergartens and preparatory departments, they tended to fix the age of transfer to the lower division of the secondary school proper at about eleven, and the taking of the various levels of the Oxford and Cambridge Local Examinations made the ages between sixteen and eighteen or nineteen the usual period for senior studies for the special examination for women of the University of London, or the Cambridge Higher Local. These years were not yet clearly distinguished from higher education, especially while the Higher Local Examination not only replaced the Cambridge Previous for Newnham students, but was taken instead of a degree course in some cases.

London thus was catering for many girls and women who needed and wanted higher studies, but would never have been allowed to commit themselves even to a high school course, let alone an Oxford or Cambridge college. Some private schools of this period taught to a very high standard: for example Mount View School, Hampstead, was a pioneer centre for the University Extension lectures of Canon Ainger and Professor Seeley from 1878. Pupils entered for the Higher Locals, and some went on to Newnham and Somerville.[169] For a time King's College for Women provided for these same needs. It began in 1871 as a series of extension lectures for ladies in Twickenham, where the lecturer happened to live, and in 1878 the vicar of Kensington, two of the staff of King's, Dr Barry and Professor Warr, and a number of local ladies, arranged lectures in Kensington Vestry Hall. From these developed King's College for Ladies, not merely a growth from King's College, but a response to local need. Girls and women of secondary age and above flocked to the classes. In 1885 the Council of King's decided to constitute it the Ladies' Department of the College, and as such it was inaugurated in a service in St Mary Abbot's, and installed in two converted houses in Kensington Square. During this whole period it was providing studies on the borderline of secondary and higher education,[170] just as at a different social level the polytechnics were displaying the same confusion, or flexibility, in meeting the needs of girls and young women.[171]

In these ways the reform and extension of girls' schooling made important contributions, both pragmatic and philosophical, to the theory and practice of secondary education over the nation as a whole, for boys as well as girls. The women actively involved in this complex process themselves recognized the part played by the new urbanism in adding new dimensions to the emerging system of schools: 'The tendency of our times is eminently social. We live too close to each other in our crowded cities for it to be possible any longer for each man merely to live and let live. We realize, as never before, the amazing complexity and subtlety of the ties that bind together all members of a community, the far-reaching consequences to many of the "negligencies and ignorance" of one.'[172] Besant rightly observed that London played a key part in a revolution in the education of women and girls, which enabled them in turn to add new dimensions to the emerging system of schools.

VIII

'Reorganizing the metropolis of a nation': The City of London and education in the nineteenth century

The reform of London government

London is not only a 'place in space, but a drama in time'.[1] The constitution of London has always been 'unique among British municipalities'. Itself a County of ancient privilege, it has no Charter of Incorporation, but is a 'Corporation by prescriptive right', and the development of its constitution is in its own hands.[2] This was the formidable entity which constituted for nineteenth-century London education both an obstacle to progress and a source of wealth for investment in reform.

Municipal reform in 1835 did not touch London. The powers possessed by Common Council, the Commissioners declared, 'enable the Corporation, if so disposed, to apply remedies . . . without the assistance of the legislature'.[3] But until the City was reformed, the rest of the Metropolis lay in hopeless confusion. It 'was in the eye of the law no town; it had no legal being; it was but a collection of townships, and manors and parishes, and extra-parochial places, which owned no common ruler, save King and Parliament. Geography and remote history had done their worst for the Metropolis . . .'.[4] In comparison with re-formed or newly constituted cities, such as Birmingham, in London only ecclesiastical administration, both Anglican and Roman Catholic, operated within any framework, which in education placed the secularists at a continuing disadvantage.[5] Even after the creation of the London School Board in 1870 the failure of the Endowed Schools Act of 1869 to create local machinery perpetuated this for secondary education.

Before 1857 there was no readily available definition of 'London'.[6] The administrative problem was compounded by demographic as well as topographical change. Other municipalities had been reconstituted partly by extending their boundaries to include new suburbs, but as the Commission of 1853–4 declared, this was impossible in London which had become a 'province covered with houses'. The metropolitan district was 107 times the size of the old City for the population of the whole capital had doubled in the last fifty years, but that of the City had remained nearly stationary. Its importance now 'arises not from its population or even from its rateable property, but from its central

ANOTHER "BITTER CRY."

ALDERMAN. "OH, BUMBLE! JUST TO THINK OF IT!—NO MORE HALDERMEN!!"
BUMBLE. "AR SIR! IT'S WUSS THAN THAT!—NO WESTRIES! NO BEADLES! NO NOTHINK!!"
BOTH (*despairingly*). "OH, WERDANT 'ARCOURT! WERDANT 'ARCOURT!"——   [*They bust into tears.*

The persistent image, *Punch*, 19 April 1884

position, and from the magnitude of the mercantile and pecuniary transactions which are daily carried on within its limits'.[7] It was a problem not of space and of quantity, but of qualities and nature. The very *idea* of the Metropolis had to be formulated and it has even been argued that this resulted from the activities of cartographers, statisticians and social reformers. The title of Brougham's educational enquiry is an early, significant, use of the concept. The Metropolitan Police date from 1829 and it was not until 1830 that 'the word Metropolis began to appear in map titles'.[8]

London became a 'cockpit for reformers'.[9] The Utilitarians were early critics of the City's powers of patronage, the freehold and archaic nature of many of its offices, the position of the Livery Companies – 'trades-unions of the mercantile class', claiming their funds as private property when they were the 'accumulated produce of a public tax . . .'. The Corporation could not rightly claim to be 'a representative institution' and the 'judicious and economical' application of its funds was much open to doubt. This was serious because 'objects embraced by municipal institutions were much more extensive than was generally supposed', and included education, 'schools for children, colleges, and scientific institutions' – a claim relating more to Benthamite theory than to current practice except in relation to charity funds. Here the Utilitarians suspected mismanagement, it was a 'standing miracle' if the inhabitants of London received any benefit from 'such a method of government'. These educational funds were estimated as £65,426 0s 4d for the City of London, £5952 0s 2d for the City of Westminster, and £18,243 10s 1d for the County of Middlesex, divided between grammar and non-classical schools and bequests not attached to any particular school: £89,621 10s 7d in all. This was very much a blanket estimate including every possible bequest and it must be remembered that during this period the unreformed City was creating its own successful school.[10]

The Commission of 1854 led to the creation of administrative Vestries and District Boards, thereby strengthening localism, and of the Metropolitan Board of Works, relating more to London's preoccupation with sanitation than education. Its work emphasized the idea of metropolitan London as a reforming, radical concept, or slogan.[11] Criticisms, pressure groups, schemes mounted. The Metropolitan Municipalities Association favoured the 'big idea, if not a practical one, [of] giving the antiquated central authority of the City of London a sort of india-rubber expansive power of extending itself to the extreme limits of the present Metropolis'. The London Municipal Reform League, which was led among others by James Firth, radical MP for Chelsea, and Arthur Hobhouse, advocated the counter-policy of absorbing the City into a new municipal region on lines inspired by Mill's *Representative Government*.[12] Select Committees, Government and private members' bills worried away at the problem, and inevitably the reform of local government became not only a struggle between localism and centralism, but a party issue. When Salisbury formed his precarious second administration in 1886 he had to concede county councils to Chamberlain and his followers. Firth had been killed in an accident and did not see the creation of the London County Council (LCC) in the second instalment of legislation in 1889, but the Corporation of London was left for future treatment 'as a sort of strange animal pickled in spirits of wine . . . [when] the turtle was well on its back and the Government might do exactly what it liked with it'.[13] As an administrative county the new LCC included the City, as a judicial county it did not. At first of course it had no educational functions.[14] The LCC alarmed the Conservatives from the outset by falling into the control of the Progressive Party 'committed to the extinction of the City Corporation and the reform of the City Guilds'. In 1894 another Royal Commission was appointed to consider the merging of the City and the County, but before its recommendations were acted upon by the lukewarm Rosebery, first Chairman of the LCC, Salisbury returned to power and amidst local and national vituperation the London Government Act of 1899 created the Metropolitan Borough Councils as counterweights to the LCC and left the City 'unamalgamated'.[15]

In the very year that the LCC was created the Technical Instruction Act was passed[16] and in 1890 the curious episode of the whisky money placed £170,000 a year in the hands of the authority over and above any rates voted for this purpose. London was one of the counties which did particularly well out of this strange expedient.[17] But the new Council delayed action; there was a feeling that 'the City should be called upon to devote more of its vast resources to educational purposes'.[18]

The controversy over the City's wealth and especially that of the Livery Companies continued to be interwoven with disagreements over the government and administration of London. 'Turtledom' was identified especially with the twelve great Companies, their wealth and public influence balanced, it was claimed, by no public responsibility. The City Guilds' Inquiry Society, 'a small knot of agitators' under the leadership of Firth, was formed in 1876.[19] By the 1880s the TUC was taking the matter up and in 1885 the wealth of the companies was referred to in the Presidential address: 'What has become of the vast sums of money which have been left in bygone times for education, for help to the poor? . . . It would never have been bequeathed if the ancient donors could have forseen its use for costly banquets, middle-class education and other foreign purposes.'[20] Gladstone, more immediately dangerous and perhaps aware of the weakening of the City's old Liberal ties, was increasingly critical, even hostile, and one of the first acts of his administration of 1880 was to appoint a Royal Commission on the City of London Livery Companies.[21] Twelve large and sixty-two minor ones had a trust income estimated at about £200,000 per annum and from 1862, when the rents of certain educational foundations had greatly increased, this was distributed as three-eighths on almshouses and similar causes, three-eighths (£75,000) on education and one-quarter on miscellaneous charities. Educational expenditure was divided between classical education, both schools and university scholarships (£35,000), and middle-class schools for both boys and girls in the provinces as well as the capital (about £40,000). The Companies claimed that this often included expenditure from corporate income. In addition £150,000 corporate income went on benevolent objects: about £10,000 on the relief of poor members, £90,000 on other charities and about £50,000 on education. This covered exhibitions at the universities (now including London) and at Company schools, some in connection with the London School Board, some at the newly founded colleges for women at Cambridge. Almost all the Company schools were assisted from corporate funds. Technical education had received large sums. The Companies not only maintained that they had exercised their responsibilities with fairness and generosity, but that they had the right to do so without interference, and the claim was even made that surplus funds from endowments might be absorbed into general income.[22]

The attitudes of the Commissioners as embodied in their report were perhaps equally predictable. On the whole the membership under Lord Derby had been reassuring, but between for example Firth, the active municipal reformer with strong centralist views, and Alderman Cotton, an archetypal City man, Master of the Saddler's and the Haberdashers' and member of the Fan-makers' Companies, Lord Mayor in 1875, there was 'no possibility of agreement'. Firth supplied Observations and a Memorandum, arguing that the 'Livery Companies are an integral part of the Corporation', 'unproductive bodies', a 'hindrance to commerce and a loss to public revenue'. Cotton supplied a Protest and with Sir Richard Cross and Sir Nathaniel de Rothschild signed the minority report.[23] The majority report, however, recommended a moderate course, the establishment of a commission similar to that for Oxford and Cambridge, enabling the state to carry out limited reforms. In 1885 the Liberal Government fell and in twenty years of Conservative rule little was done. This was not altogether due either to failure of will, or the complexity of the situation; the 'position of the companies, legal and otherwise, was not as indefensible as the more eager reformers made it out to be'. The management of trusts by minor companies was better than most, and expenses of management were usually paid from corporate funds.[24] Some of the benefactions of larger companies were impressive, although the educational charities needed more 'systematic management' and 'unity of purpose', and 'should be treated as a whole' as Counsel's opinion put the case. The evidence of that highly experienced City Charity Commissioner, Thomas Hare, though fundamentally critical, tended to the same conclusion as regards education.[25] This position remained substantially the same in 1951 when evidence to the Nathan Commission admitted that the senior

Companies never developed long-range programmes, but many of their decisions were taken collectively, setting up a single target and then saying 'Now this is what we want to subscribe, and how can we best do it?'[26]

When the educational work of the Guilds during this period is examined closely and overall, the nineteenth-century polemic begins to seem less relevant, for as the nation as a whole had not at this time assumed responsibility for financing and directing secondary education, the City and its Companies provided both funds and some attempt at least at public policy and provision. Moreover this emerging plan for secondary education had national influence.

The independent rating system of the City, based not upon residence but on business occupation, provided a source of income for the rest of London and enabled a reservoir of capital to accumulate and flow into under-capitalized services such as education. The same could also be said of the funds of the Livery Companies. That this flow was not adequately regulated by public control or public policy was increasingly attacked during a quarter-century when democratic theory and machinery were gaining strength, and when the need for a national policy for secondary education was increasingly recognized. Nevertheless secondary education in London received significant benefits by this means, partly by pressure from without, partly by fear and philanthropy within, just at a time when new ideas were being incorporated into a changing tradition. These concerned the need for education for girls, the importance of technical and commercial education, the social and pastoral dimension which educational institutions needed in an increasingly urbanized and abstract community. Moreover while many City men like Alderman Cotton remained wholly 'unreconstructed',[27] there was also a reservoir of intelligence, and of social, intellectual, business and administrative experience, which was put at the service of education. During the course of the century, this has a recognizable development and change in style and direction. Earlier benefactors were caught up in the debates over popular education, and the clergy still predominated in leadership at secondary level. Later this stage of schooling received more attention from civic and business leaders. The generation of philanthropists such as George Moore contributed in a princely fashion to popular education but only warily supported Canon Rogers with a subscription.[28] Alderman Cotton (1822–1922) served for nine years on the London School Board and was its first chairman.[29] Samuel Morley (1809–86), who regarded the distribution of his fortune as a business requiring as much time and thought as its amassing, was converted to the need for state elementary schooling. His work for further education in partnership with Emma Cons, remembered in the name of Morley College, emphasized the importance of self-help in education and opportunities for extension courses rather than systematic provision at secondary level.[30] Although

William Spottiswoode (1825–83) died before Morley, his educational work has a much more modern flavour, perhaps because of his mathematical and scientific achievements. He was a member of the so-called X Club, the most influential scientific pressure group of his day. London played a significant part in the development of scientific institutions, not only because it was the capital, but because of the stimulus of business life and overseas trade.[31]

Sir John Lubbock (1803–65), scientist and astronomer, was another distinguished representative of this tradition. In between his work for the British Association and the Royal Society he not only found time to steer the family banking firm through the commercial panics of 1847 and 1857, but he took an active interest in the Society for the Diffusion of Useful Knowledge and was the first Vice-Chancellor (1837–42) of the new London University. His son (1834–1913), who became the first Baron Avebury, left Eton early to work in the family bank, but assiduously followed his study of natural history, helped by his friend Darwin. He became one of the leaders of the banking world, a distinguished scientist in his own right, and an influential public figure, Liberal MP for Maidstone and then for the University of London. His public work for education was considerable, and he contributed much to the discussion of the nature of secondary education. He also was a member of the X Club.[32]

Sir Frederick Bramwell (1818–1903) was educated, like his elder brother George, at the Palace School at Enfield, and their banker father apprenticed them both to the Goldsmiths' Company. George decided to study law, played an important part in the modernization of City practice in the Companies' Act and the enactment of limited liability, and became a law lord noted for his championship of freedom of contract, and through the Liberty and Property Defence League a staunch upholder of the City's independent position. Frederick turned to mechanical engineering, did notable work in hydraulics, atmospheric pressure and steam locomotion, and then combined his mechanical abilities with his powers of exposition and advocacy in a career in the legal and consultative side of his profession. His experience and connections might have been designed to enable him to contribute to the technical elements in secondary education.[33]

Roundell Palmer, first Baron Selborne (1812–95), Lord Chancellor in Gladstone's cabinets of 1872–4 and 1880–5, was a member of the Mercers' Company, like his father and grandfather, by right of descent. He had keen theological and scientific interests, and while the one, being of a High Church tendency, identified him sometimes with conservative educational policies, the other combined with his City connections to involve him in the movement for technical education.[34]

A City man whose educational work may be said to sum up the changes during this period was Sir Sydney Waterlow (1822–1906). Educated at St Saviour's, belonging like Morley to the Nonconformist community of the City's old northern suburbs, apprenticed to the Stationers' Company in 1836, he had a distinguished civic career, became Lord Mayor in 1872, and Liberal MP for the City from 1874. He took a lifelong interest in education, in the founding of the Stationers' School and as chairman from 1873–93 of the United Westminster Schools and of Emanuel School until his death. He served on the Livery Companies Commission and signed its majority report.[35] The City produced many men of this stature, and while many of them staunchly supported its independence and right to direct its own bene-factions, it would not be exact to describe the flow of capital and expertise with which they were concerned as haphazard or private. While their efforts were independent of public control and direction, private benevolence was planned and operated on business lines which corresponded sensitively to civic needs and civic lines of communi-cation, and in the later part of the century such activity became less personal, more corporate. Active involvement in the management of schools as well as the provision of funds was usual. Behind these leaders lay a business community keenly aware of the need for new or improved kinds of education.[36]

Moreover the matter was vigorously kept before their eyes. It can be forgotten that the City and its immediate fringe 'beyond the bars', even as its residential population dwindled, was full of schoolboys. As its flavour of sociability and domesticity faded, such boys must have appeared more numerous and obtrusive, more incongruous than their Tudor and Stuart predecessors who had piled their satchels in St Paul's churchyard before falling to battle with each other, or attacking the sober citizenry. The life-styles of the Victorian City, its work ethic thrown into relief by the gradual divorce of dwelling and counting-house, accorded ill with the lively life of even industrious and decorous schoolboys. Supervision of leisure-time and provision of school dinners was still largely in the future. From the City of London School in Milk Street, from St Paul's still in its cramped churchyard quarters, from Merchant Taylors' in Suffolk Street, from the Mercers' School on College Hill, from the little grammar school by the Tower of London, from the court off Fleet Street where the Stationers' boys were crowded, from Neale's Mathematical School nearby, from the austere neighbour-hood of Old Street where Rogers's enterprise had assembled over a thousand of them, boys flowed out into the City's chophouses and bun shops or lunched in the bar of Cannon Street Station on a glass of stout and an Abernethy biscuit. They crowded its omnibuses and railway carriages. They fought their battles in styles not unlike those of centuries before: as there was also a large rival boy population in the City, ritual fights between for example the boys of Merchant Taylors' and the youths from the printing works opposite further enlivened the scene. Just beyond Temple Bar the boys of King's College School multiplied in their basement, and nearby in the slums behind St

Clement Danes the boys of its middle-class school in gown and mortar-board picked their way warily amongst hostile inhabitants. At night-time and at the weekends the boy population shrank, but small ones might be found wandering at dark in their nightshirts (having been let down from a bedroom at Merchant Taylors' in a sheet), or groping their way across the debris made by the building of London Bridge in search of herrings for a fag-master's supper. Some were still turned out of Christ's Hospital for the day to amuse themselves as best possible in the deserted City, shivering as they gazed into the print-shop windows. Inhabitants who ventured into the neighbourhood of the Charterhouse, almost a 'town in itself', ran the risk of being lured on to the Green and badgered by the gown boys, a Sunday sport known as 'boxing'. Boys could be found rowing on the Thames, fishing in the Lea, swimming in the New River, drinking in the taverns, poking about in coaching inns and debtors' prisons, and enjoying the executions outside Newgate, or sporting in the somewhat disreputable Peerless Pool at Islington.[37]

Charterhouse Green

The schoolboy Asquith would have agreed with the pronouncement 'I do not like towns, but I think they are very necessary when one is young.'[38] But the Clarendon Inquiry considered the streets of London 'not the most desirable place for boys to spend their leisure time in'. Four of its nine schools were in the Metropolis, containing 690 boys, 188 of them boarders. Already parents were doubting the suitability of the centre of London for boarding-schools, and Charterhouse and Westminster had seriously declined, but the demand for day places was great.[39] The Taunton Inquiry gave a fuller and more realistic estimate of the number of schools and places already existing, and the threat which this inquiry represented released more of the wealth of the City and the Livery Companies for education. The Companies even felt some complacency over their educational efforts, and in the debate on the Endowed Schools' Bill the exemption of City schools unless the Commissioners could report mismanagement was proposed; these schools, it was claimed, were 'admirably well managed'. Forster contested this, though some, especially the City of London School, were models of this level of education. There were eight municipal schools with 1512 scholars (45 undergraduates from these were studying at the universities), and twelve Company schools with only 1090 scholars (35 undergraduates), and the average cost of these schools was much higher than in the municipal schools. They must take their chance under the act.[40]

The contribution of the Livery Companies: Schools

The contribution of the Livery Companies was in administering educational endowments, and in providing schools from their corporate funds, and it is difficult to distinguish clearly between these two methods.

The Merchant Taylors claimed before the Clarendon Commissioners that not only did they maintain their school out of their funds (to the tune of almost £2000 in 1862) but that it was 'theirs simply, and that no one could challenge their act if they were to abolish it altogether'. The Commissioners received this with caution, for the school had attracted rich endowments, especially scholarships to St John's College Oxford. On the whole however, they gave a good report. For the school's 262 boys there were ten assistant masters, four of them for mathematics, who taught for the whole afternoon each day, 'considerably above what we have found in any other school'. Hebrew and drawing were taught and English literature, ancient and modern history, geography and French received 'a fair share of attention', but there was no science. The classical teaching showed 'marks of much care in selection and diligence in application', and this and the generous closed scholarships attracted many pupils from far afield. Merchant Taylors' however was strongly characterized by its civic nature and its setting amid the tall warehouses and fogs of Suffolk Street. The Commissioners did not recommend changes in the government of the school, but wanted natural science and German to be included in the curriculum, and limited competition for admission to replace the Company's 'absolute right of nomination'. Leaving scholarships should reflect the whole curriculum of the school and not be confined to classics.[41]

As well as administering the endowments of St Paul's the Mercers' Company defrayed 'the whole of the expense' of their own school 'out of their corporate funds', though it had attracted endowments, notably the benefaction of Thomas Rich in 1672 of property in St Mary Axe and in West Ham. The school, originally in the Hospital of St Thomas Acon, moved to various places within the City; the Old Jewry after the Great Fire, Budge Row, then Watling Street. Its revival had begun when in 1778 the Company appointed the Reverend Mr Taylor to report upon it and accepted his recommendation that writing and accounts should be added to its curriculum. In 1804 the Company appointed its own management committee and began a much more active policy of keeping the school in line with new educational needs. In 1808 it moved to College Hill near Whittington's house, and there in 1829 the Company built a new school for a larger number of boys. By 1832 there were 70 receiving a general classical education with some mathematics and merchants' accounts. Fearon was critical, especially of its indiscriminate free education, and in 1876 after the criticism by its own visiting committee of the 'insufficiency of the probationary examination required to be passed by the youngest class of candidates for admission', the Company improved the entrance examination and imposed a capitation fee of £5 on all boys, now 125 in number, except the 25 free scholars of the original foundation. Greek was not to be required and 'the best possible modern and commercial, rather than a classical, education' was to be the aim. Boys already in the school who were aiming at the university were transferred to St Paul's. By 1880–1 there were 150 boys in the Mercers' School and the buildings were hardly capable of further extension. To celebrate the five-hundredth year of their Charter, the Mercers in 1892 bought Barnard's Inn in Holborn for £43,000 which they extended and adapted to take about 250 boys at a cost of between £20,000 and £30,000.[42]

The Stationers' Company was one of the earliest to respond to the climate of criticism in the mid century by founding a new school using both endowments and their own funds. The Company consisted of 'persons of all ranks of life, from the leading publishers of London, down to pressmen and compositors' and these skilled craftsmen were among the best paid of London artisans and had a tradition of valuing education. Leaders included such members as Sydney Waterlow and William Spottiswoode who not only recognized criticisms but were committed to the advantages of reform. The suggestion for the use of obsolete endowments for almshouses was replaced by the idea of a school and in February 1852 the Court of the Company accepted the plan and made over £5000 available from four charities of the late-sixteenth and seventeenth centuries which had provided for 'the support of a preacher at St Paul's Cross; gifts to the poor of the parish of St Faith; doles of money, Bibles and the like'. Five years' delay was caused by the need for Chancery approval, and then the Company bought Mr

Tyler's printing house in Bolt Court for £6000, and adjacent premises in Hole-in-the-Wall Court, and the Assistants of the Company spent generously in time and money to get the buildings ready. In spite of the cramped situation, they would accommodate 'something like two hundred or three hundred boys' and had 'the advantage of a play-ground ... though a very small one ... an unusual prize in the City'. The school was opened in 1861, and intended for the sons of members of their own Livery, especially its 'lower classes', and care was taken to advertise it widely in printing houses and so forth. But journeymen parents lived in the suburbs, and preferred to use local National or British schools, for although the fee for foundationers was only 6s a quarter, the expense of travelling together with the level of schooling provided put it out of their reach, or ambition, while tradesmen, professional men, clerks and others were eager to 'come forward'. The Company therefore took the advice of the headmaster and opened it to non-members for fees of £6 a year. It contained 65 boys when Fearon visited it, 80 by the time its headmaster gave evidence before the Taunton Commissioners, and 150 by the time the Report was published.[43]

This headmaster, A. K. Isbister, was a graduate of Edinburgh, with teaching experience at an Islington proprietary school and the Jews' College, active in the affairs of the College of Preceptors, one of its honorary secretaries and editor of its journal. His Taunton evidence put the school into a broad educational perspective and displayed contemporary pedagogic theory. Its curriculum was designed at first to include 'the principles of the Christian religion; reading; writing; arithmetic; land-surveying; book-keeping; geography; drawing and designing; general English literature and composition; sacred and profane history' and such other 'branches of education' as the Company should decide. Isbister had expanded this course intelligently to provide not only what parents needed but a system which developed 'the thought of boys' and made them 'mentally stronger than they were before'. Latin and French were 'essential subjects of study'; great attention was paid to 'physical science, arithmetic, book-keeping, and good writing, as they have a direct practical application to the business of life' and every boy learnt drawing. Isbister gave a detailed description of the science course, which was connected 'as far as possible with geography' because 'our difficulty with physical science is this, that there are a multitude of facts which it is difficult, with young boys especially, to get them to retain in their minds unless we group them around some familiar subject'. Chemistry presented difficulties because it easily 'came to be an affair of explosions' and boys paid more attention to noisy experiments 'than to the principles involved in them'. It was taught therefore more by means of diagrams, more convenient and less distracting in a large and crowded school.[44] The school was approved by one of the City's sharpest critics, William Gilbert, who in his evidence to the Livery

Companies' Commission held it up as a model of what such schooling should provide for a much wider number.[45] By 1892 the school had outgrown its premises; the Company bought a two-acre site in Hornsey and put up new buildings at a cost of £13,000.[46]

The 'Graceless Grocers', as Firth had described them,[47] were spurred into educational activity by the Endowed Schools' Act. A number of small obsolete charities were drawn upon, but the Scheme which originated at a Court of Assistants meeting in December 1870 for a middle-class school in North London also depended on the use of Company funds. The Endowed Schools' Commissioners approved a formal Scheme in 1872 (though they refused to sanction the use of prison charities), a site was purchased in Hackney Downs and the building in the domestic Gothic style, costing £27,000, was finished by 1876.

To the historian this school had a number of especially interesting features. While the Commissioners had insisted that as the school was to use endowments left for the poor of London it must be within three miles of the City, the Company had chosen a neighbourhood being rapidly transformed by the cheap railway fares of the Great Eastern line. By 1876 Hackney had ceased to be a middle-class preserve in the old style. Almost the last vestige of its rural past was the preservation of Hackney Downs by the Metropolitan Board of Works, and the school had some trouble with the Lammas rights which local inhabitants claimed over some of the school playground. The Grocers from the outset planned a school for the new Hackney, a middle-class school 'to give a practical education suitable for the children of that class who desire to educate their children up to the age of fourteen'. They consulted Canon Rogers, and appointed as headmaster Herbert Courthope Bowen, a Cambridge prizeman and second master at the Cowper Street School. The fees were £6 a year, the curriculum included the usual English subjects, history, commercial and physical geography, surveying, book-keeping as well as mathematics, writing, drawing, French, singing, the 'Elements of Science', but Latin, together with shorthand and some more ornamental studies, was taught after school hours. The building and school organization were progressive for its date, with fifteen classrooms 'fitted on the Prussian system', library, dining-room, and even a tuck shop, but as yet no separate science rooms or gymnasium. It would hold 500 and by 1878 the numbers had reached 389, each boy bearing on his serge winter cap or summer straw boater the Grocers' crest of a camel laden with spices.

Thereafter the numbers began to decline and the course of events suggests that the reason was that even in this neighbourhood the level of education was depressed in relation to the ambitions of parents. Courthope Bowen was dedicated to the central importance of English language and literature in the curriculum. 'Style of thought and expression' must be closely attended to, without this the piling together of facts was like an attempt to build a house without tools. But parents, both skilled tradesmen and those in commercial and professional occupations, wanted an education which included Latin. In 1881 Bowen, who had had other differences with the governors, resigned and a year later became first principal of the short-lived Finsbury Training College for secondary teachers.

At this very time Longley, the Charity Commissioner, in giving evidence to the Livery Companies' Commission, emphasized the need for schools of the second or third grade, 'a sort of superior elementary school', and agreed that the Haberdashers in Hoxton and also the Grocers' School were doing useful work of this kind 'amongst a large and new population'. The parents of Hackney evidently thought differently. The second headmaster came, not from Rogers's middle-class school, but from the rival tradition which had defeated his purposes at Dulwich. The Reverend Charles George Gull was an old boy of Dulwich College, and after Oxford and endowed school posts, returned there as assistant master and earned the gratitude of Dr Carver by founding the Dulwich College Rifle Corps, perhaps its final declaration of public-school standing. Gull was a man of strict discipline, and at Hackney he made Latin the 'predominating subject throughout the school'. Science was only slowly given more attention but by the end of the century Gull had persuaded the Company to build a chemistry laboratory and engage a science master. He also built up sports facilities including five courts, and acquired grounds at Edmonton costing £3000, the boys' fares being subsidized by the Company. A house system was introduced in 1892, and an old boys' club (the Clove Club) was formed in 1884.

Gull was deliberately modelling the school on lines quite different from those originally laid down by the Grocers but if it is to be judged by numbers – 495 in 1890 – this was what the neighbourhood wanted. The school opened choice of opportunities to its boys, yet Gull had a struggle to raise the level of academic aspiration; most left at fifteen after the Cambridge Junior Local examination. London Matriculation was introduced and gradually the number of academic successes increased. As late as 1896, however, the Company reminded Gull that the school's purpose was 'to prepare sons of the middle-classes for life in manufacturing industries, rather than guide them to the universities'. This school illustrates the transformation of secondary education, the convergence of its various levels, and also its mounting costs. By 1900 the Company's subsidy to the school was £3736 15s 6d, and numbers were falling as the proportion of tenement buildings in the area increased. It was decided in 1904 to offer the school to the new Education Committee of the LCC. As a maintained school it was able without any substantial change to serve the new working-class population.[48]

The Skinners' Company, long concerned as trustees of Tonbridge School, expanded the use of the endowment by providing middle-class schools for boys in Sir Andrew Judd's Commercial School in the same town (1888), and another school of the same type in Tunbridge Wells (1880). In London they used a number of small charities for the Skinners' Company Middle School for Girls, opened in 1890 at Stamford Hill which was then being converted from a district of large houses 'into streets of moderate sized houses'. By 1902 it had 350 pupils.[49]

Other companies continued to administer charities and to supplement endowments from their corporate funds – the Coopers at Ratcliffe, the Leathersellers at Colfe's School, the Brewers at Owen's in Islington, the Tower Hill Grammar School, and further out of town at Aldenham in Hertfordshire. The educational work of the Drapers' Company provides a case study, complex and ambiguous, for the degree of secrecy which they preserved makes it difficult to distinguish between charitable and corporate expenditure. The Drapers expended on the 'furtherance of General and Technical Education', a sum rising from £2659 5s 10d in 1870, to £7157 7s 3d in 1879. About £3000 a year of this was on a school opened in 1861–2 at Tottenham, the Drapers' College, for the sons and grandsons of the Livery, where boys were educated, boarded and clothed free.[50] In its early years at least the Company expended on it money from the balance of educational endowments, including that of the Sir John Jolles' School at Stratford-le-Bow. This aroused the criticism of Fearon in 1864. Although founded in 1617 as a school 'in grammar and the Latin tongue' it had become little more than an elementary school under a former pupil-teacher and Fearon found it 'unmethodical', 'badly classified' and doing 'as much harm as good in the neighbourhood'. He accused the Drapers of lack of interest in lower levels of middle-class education and of spending money on their College for boys whose families could well afford to clothe them and contribute to their education, instead of restoring secondary education in the locality which Jollies had intended to benefit. The difficulty lay not only in modernizing the Drapers, but in discerning demand for such education in the eastern suburbs.[51] The Company also administered at Mile End Bancroft's Charity of almshouses and school. By the later eighteenth century it had already become necessary to use corporate funds to improve the buildings and salaries of the masters and in 1820 it was resolved regularly to supplement the school's income in the same way. In 1879 it was decided to sell the Mile End estate and move the school to Woodford, where ten acres were bought for £9000 and buildings put up at a cost of £50,000 from corporate funds. Negotiations with the Charity Commissioners were tough, for the Drapers 'were anxious to have in return, so to speak, for the large additional money endowment, a large number of free places at their disposal by nomination', as Longley said in his evidence in 1884, 'we have reduced the number considerably . . .'. The matter continued under review and the Company provided further funds, for example for laboratories. By

1915, of the 100 boarders, 70 received their education free and of these 20 were nominated by the Company and 50 were selected by the LCC from public elementary schools. Some of the day boys also had scholarships and exhibitions.[52]

The other educational charity which the Drapers administered in the London area was the Green Coat School at Greenwich, endowed by Sir William Boreham in 1684. The school was for the sons of watermen, seamen, fishermen and inhabitants of East Greenwich 'especially of such loyal men as have served the King in his wars' and the instruction was supposed to have a seafaring flavour. In 1860 Hare found a small depressed charity school and local complaints of lack of nautical instruction. In 1882 negotiations with the Charity Commission began and a scheme was drawn up for a new school, Sir William Boreham's Nautical School, intended to have a curriculum including practical mathematics, and the application of steam and machinery to navigation, navigational and nautical astronomy, surveying on land and water, at least one foreign European language, and natural science. Instead, however, it was decided to pay the fees of 100 boys chosen from the elementary schools of the parish at the upper division of the Greenwich Hospital School. Here their lives were made a misery and they were known as Water Butts from the initials on their nautical caps. They were accepted only when they were able, being day boys, to maintain the honour of the school against the common enemy from the Roan School, boys having different ways of solving educational problems from Drapers and Charity Commissioners. The curriculum followed at the Upper Nautical School was designed for 'the training of the boys in the principles and practice of navigation, nautical astronomy and all those branches of knowledge which conduce to the producing of a skilful navigator and a competent knowledge of the scientific principles'.[53] The needs of the Navy and merchant marine had long been recognized as a special technical demand upon education in the metropolis.

Technical education

It was during this period that a working definition of technical education began to emerge. At the time of the Taunton Inquiry the 'notion' of such education 'was almost entirely new to the country'.[54] Playfair's famous letter to this Commission, drawing attention to the poor performance of the British exhibitors at the Paris Exhibition of 1867, may be thought of as an opening salvo in a campaign for something which had scarcely yet been usefully defined.[55] The Select Committee of 1867 under Samuelson, and the Royal Commission (1870–5) set up as a result (Devonshire), were significantly on 'Scientific Instruction' and at this time the usual interpretation given by leaders such as T. H. Huxley was the teaching of scientific principles, not specific skills, and certainly not workshop practice. The processes by which technical instruction came to include both scientific and more practical learning, and its connections with general elementary and secondary education, were worked out in the last three decades of the century. The second Royal Commission under Samuelson was to enquire into Technical Instruction (1884) and by the time of the Bryce Commission (1895) one definition of technical education put forward included 'everything which prepares a man or a woman for the walk of life which he or she intends to pursue'.[56] This added an important dimension to secondary education and here the City of London made significant contributions.

As a crucible for concocting new ideas of technical education, and compounding them with the recent brew by now nearly always labelled secondary education, the capital and its region had advantages and disadvantages. By 1881 its population had risen to 4.5 million, by 1911 to over 7 million, and its share of national population increase grew proportionately. Its transport system of underground railways and electric tramways had encouraged both suburban growth and technology. Its size and density made heavy demands on technical services – London gradually ceased to be 'a polluted sponge' and became a 'relatively healthy city'.[57] Its industrial base was diversified, highly specialized and skilled, and organized in comparatively small units. London was in fact 'by far the biggest centre of manufactures in the whole country', and the 'second industrial revolution' of the later nineteenth century shifted the industrial balance of the nation further south.[58] London, as a contemporary wrote, could be regarded too much as 'existing on its immense intermediary and financial business', to the neglect of the really important producing industries carried on within its limits; 'industrial London occupies a position of importance ranking it properly almost on a level with any of the branches into which the trade and commerce of London may be subdivided'.[59] Strictly beyond its boundaries were industrial settlements such as Watford with its railway works, the ordnance factories at Enfield, cement works at Grays and Northfleet, dockyards at Tilbury and Chatham, Greenwich and Woolwich with their naval and military complexes, but all these were 'economically closely dependent on London'.[60] And while this quickening and expanding life was drawn more and more to the suburbs, the perimeter, and served by a swarming, travelling army of workmen on foot or with cheap railway tickets, or by the end of the century on bicycles, at the centre lay a remarkable range of institutions for scientific and technical study. These included the great teaching hospitals, University and King's Colleges, the Society of Arts, the Royal Society, the Royal Astronomical Society, the Royal Institution, the Chemical Society, the Royal College of Chemistry, the Royal School of Mines, the Geological Survey, the Museum of Practical Geology. There were also professional associations such as the Institutes of Civil Engineers (1771, and reformulated and granted a Charter 1828) and of Mechanical Engineers (1846), and specialist colleges such as the Royal Military Academy at

Woolwich.[61] Underpinning these was the work of the Department of Science and Art (1856) with its examinations and 'payment by results' for schools, and its College at South Kensington,[62] and the survivals of the Mechanics' Institute movement of an earlier age of technical education. The London Mechanics' Institution from 1823 had given training in 'Every branch of art, science and literature' and in 1874 had over 2700 students. It was already known as 'the Birkbeck' and moving towards its later collegiate and university status.[63] The London Institution, formed in 1805 and housed in a handsome building in Finsbury Circus in 1815, had from the beginning a fine library, especially 'well-furnished' in mathematical sciences. By 1874 there were 62,000 volumes but only proprietors could use them; its lectures, though given sometimes by eminent scientists, were infrequent; and more regular courses were often on dilettante or ornamental subjects.[64]

London in fact had many of the demands, expectations, institutions and skills needed for an onslaught on the problem of technical education. But it also had in spite of its 'grim, livid, fierce and unmerciful' appearance what Henry James described as its 'most general characteristic . . . absence of insistence. . . . The spirit of the great city is not analytic, and, as they come up, subjects rarely receive at its hands a treatment drearily earnest or tastelessly thorough.'[65] What London lacked was sharpness of focus, a sense of urgency, and an energizing and organizing agency. And surprisingly these were supplied by Turtledom itself. Useful as were the general secondary schools provided or administered by the Livery Companies, it was their work for technical education which enabled them to survive the enquiry of 1884 not only by inherent impregnability and a measure of luck, but also by recognition of achievement. Hare said: 'They recognize their duty, they have taken it up in a manner which I consider highly creditable.'[66] How far the City responded from within to this need and what part was played by pressure from without is not easy to determine. In the early 1870s the Royal Society of Arts began an 'unpretentious scheme of examinations for the teaching of Technology, which is the distinguishing mark of Industrial Education'.[67] Already there must have been interest and concern in the City when in 1871 Thomas Hughes, as Chairman of the Crystal Palace Company at Sydenham, wrote to the Lord Mayor suggesting that 'the progress of the cause of Technical Education in the City of London' encouraged him and his fellow directors to appeal to the 'Corporation and the trading companies of the City' for help in organizing an exhibition of arts and manufacturers at the Crystal Palace. The Lord Mayor, Sills John Gibbons, convened a meeting with Hughes and Groves, Secretary of the Company, at the Mansion House in January 1872 'to consider how Technical Education can best be promoted . . .'. Although a committee and subcommittee were set up and reminded that the 'Society for the Encouragement of Fine Arts were making efforts to carry out the objects of this meeting, which if not voluntarily undertaken by the City Companies would probably be arbitrarily forced on them', it cannot be said that much practical progress was made, though various notions of prizes and premiums, public exhibitions, lectures and so forth were aired. When Waterlow became Lord Mayor he pushed the discussion further, 'recommending that Evening Lectures be delivered at the various Companies' Halls, and that a fund be formed for founding a College to develop Technical Education . . .'. A new subcommittee under his chairmanship was formed and some attempt was made to find which Companies were prepared, or had taken steps, to promote such work; lists of sheep and goats and 'don't knows' were drawn up. Two important other agencies were investigated. The first was a report introduced by Henry Cole of the Science and Art Department, of a meeting at Marlborough House (21 July 1873) under the chairmanship of the Prince of Wales, to discuss 'how Technical Instruction might be promoted by the City Companies acting in concert with the International Exhibitions'. This was 'the great question of the present day', and the Companies could use their wealth to no better purpose than 'in this work of allying Science and Art with Productive Industry'. Waterlow, as Lord Mayor, tactfully emphasized that 'the City Companies had already done much to promote the cause of Technical Instruction' through prizes and scholarships and lectures, but admitted that 'much more important results could be obtained by union, and especially by a union promoted by His Royal Highness'. The practical or immediate outcome of this high-powered encounter was a scheme for tickets at 3*d* a time for London School Board pupils and those from middle-class and Company schools to visit the South Kensington exhibtitions.

The second movement examined was the Guild 'for the Promotion of Technical and Higher Education among the Working Classes of the United Kingdom', led by the Reverend Henry Solly, which had its headquarters in the Strand, and powerful patronage from Earl Granville, Lord Lyttelton, men of learning and literature, Christian Socialists, Matthew Arnold, J. A. Froude, Tennyson, Kingsley and Hughes. Waterlow and Lubbock were among its City patrons. Its Council contained working men, some of them former Chartists, trade unionists, and members of the London School Board and of the Working Men's College, and this was what gave the Guild its short-lived significance, especially after it had got rid of the somewhat over-assiduous Solly. This Guild was able to give the City committee a more practical view of the problems of technical education. The decline of apprenticeship, the subdivision of skills, and 'the large Capital now employed' meant that 'able workmen should give instruction to their own shop mates' and that mechanics should be enabled to 'obtain any special knowledge they might require', as they could abroad. For its short history this Guild was able to advocate the interpretation of technical education which working men themselves wanted.

The meeting of the City subcommittee which received this report and deputation was its most substantial session and it was almost its last. In October 1873 its minutes were approved and signed and there for the moment the matter rested.[68] Perhaps it was the end of Waterlow's year of office, perhaps between the Prince of Wales and Mr Solly the City needed time for reflection, or men such as Waterlow more time to build up opinion within the Companies. The function of this committee had been exploratory.

During this same crucial period, influences from without were also at work. Britain was in one of her recurrent periods of anxiety over industrial progress and foreign competition. 'No doubt when we have grumbled sufficiently we should set to work to put it right,' said Bishop Temple down at Exeter. Huxley was not only championing science education, but exploring both the nature of technical education and its provision. London, he considered, came off badly in comparison with northern cities. From about 1870 he began to dine more frequently at the Mansion House and he later claimed considerable influence in unlocking the City's coffers in this cause. In 1879 in *Nature* he reminded the Livery Companies of their enormous wealth 'which had been left to them for the benefit of the trades they represent', and by 1880 he had evidently persuaded himself that he was playing a major part in getting a response; 'The animal is moving and by a judicious combination of carrots in front and kicks from behind, we shall get him into a fine trot presently.'[69] Huxley was perhaps not without arrogance and that tendency of reformers to try to advance their cause by disparaging those whom they consider to be opponents. A great deal had been achieved by 1880 and he was metaphorically referring to men of the calibre of the President of the Royal Society, Selborne, Frederick Bramwell and Waterlow and fellow members of the X Club. Education rarely advances by reformers acting upon inert bodies.

In 1875 in presenting Science and Art prizes at Greenwich Gladstone spoke of the desirability of such instruction to help the British workman to 'hold his position in the world'. Assistance was needed, and 'I confess that I should like to see a great deal of this work done by the London companies. I have not been consulted . . . but if *so* I would have besought and entreated them to consider whether it was not in their power to make themselves that which they certainly are not now, illustrious in the country by endeavouring resolutely and boldly to fulfil the purposes for which they were founded.' Selborne, quoting it in his evidence in 1884, speculated on the influence of this speech 'upon other people's minds' ('I mention it because it had certainly some influence on mine').[70]

Activity mounted in a series of City meetings. In 1876 at the Mansion House the Livery Companies resolved that their energies should be 'directed to the promotion of Education not only in the Metropolis, but throughout the country, and especially to technical education, with the view of educating young artisans and others in scientific and artistic branches of their trades'.[71] In February 1877 a meeting was held at the Drapers' Hall 'in furtherance of a proposal to establish a Central Technical University, with affiliated schools of technical instruction'. Waterlow was acting as chairman of a joint committee of the Drapers' and Clothworkers' Companies, both of which promised £2000 a year and further assistance if necessary.[72] As a start had to be made somewhere, at the suggestion of Dr Wormell classes for artisans were begun in the basement of the Cowper Street Schools, and the Clothworkers sent a deputation abroad to study methods of technical instruction.[73] In June 1877 came the meeting from which the movement is usually dated, held at the Mercers' Hall, 'to initiate a national scheme of technical education'. The Corporation sent three delegates, most of the Companies were represented by such men as Selborne, Bramwell, Waterlow, and men of science such as Armstrong and Huxley attended and also Colonel Donnelly and Captain Galton from the Science and Art Department. All were agreed that the best plan was to establish a Central Institute or Technical University for the training of teachers and advanced students, with 'elementary' schools of science and art in London and other large towns, together with the encouragement of technical studies in other institutions by scholarships and grants. The Mercers, Drapers, Fishmongers, Goldsmiths, Salters, Ironmongers, Clothworkers, Armourers, Cordwainers, Coopers, Plaisterers and Needlemakers agreed to provide about £12,000 per annum for these purposes.[74] In July 1878 Common Council received and printed the report which resulted from this committee on the 'extension and improvement of Technical Education'. While not committing itself to details Common Council expressed 'approval of the general outlines and objects involved in the Report', and identified itself 'with the Livery Companies in endeavouring to give effect thereto'.[75] Thus was the City and Guilds' Institute born, one of the most significant contributors to the formulation and direction of secondary education in these decades.

The usefulness of these few years of preparation and apparently unproductive discussions was demonstrated by the fact that this report of 1878 provided a fairly complete plan for the Institute as it was eventually realized. Assistance had been sought of 'men of high standing and varied pursuits', chosen as 'employers of labour' as well as for their 'knowledge of pure Science, their acquaintance with Scientific Education and with Technical Examination' – among the latter Armstrong, Donnelly, Galton, Huxley. They all agreed that it was not desirable to try to teach workmen their handicraft but to give knowledge of the 'Scientific or Artistic principles upon which the particular manufacture may depend'; that tuition should be designed to produce 'a supply of superior Workmen, Foremen, Managers and Principals of Manufactures'; that first a Central Institution and then later local trade schools would be the best means; that examinations and prizes should be organized; that the scheme would depend on the 'energy and ability' of the professors and teachers at all levels. 'Teaching and not examination is the pressing necessity', though Donnelly advocated a system of payment by results as 'auxiliary'. A broad outline of the content of the course had been drawn up – applied physics, chemistry, mechanics and art. The cost of such a scheme had been estimated – £10,000 p.a. for salaries, £1000 for rent of temporary buildings, £3000 outlay on equipment, library, etc., £10,000 p.a. for scholarships, both at the Central Institution and at King's College and elsewhere, and grants towards trade schools, and about £1500 for administration. The Livery Companies would have to contribute an income of not less than £20,000 for the scheme even to be started, and over £11,000 had already been promised by twelve of them. An appendix drew up a scheme of government for this City and Guilds of London Institute for the Advancement of Technical Education.[76] In October 1878 Common Council accepted the report which provided the basis of the new Institute. In December a motion to appoint governors to the new body had a fairly stiff passage through the Court, and was cautiously amended to prevent any specific financial commitment, but was eventually carried, and the Lord Mayor, six Aldermen, the Recorder and twelve members of Common Council were duly appointed to serve.[77] One of the Aldermen was the elderly Sir Thomas Dakin, who had in his early life been an active promoter of mechanics' institutes and lectured on electricity and chemistry. In November the Institute was inaugurated in a first lecture at the Cowper Street Schools by Professor Ayrton on 'The improvements science can effect in our trades and in the condition of our workmen'.[78]

In 1879 202 candidates took the new examinations at 23 centres and by 1880 examinations were already offered in twenty-four subjects and taken by 816 candidates, of whom 575 passed. Three years later 2397 candidates entered at 154 centres. The Institute had taken over the technological examinations of the Society of Arts.[79] The effects of these examinations were rapid and nation-wide. Mechanics' Institutes and the schools attached to them were given objectives, help, and advice.[80] The secretary of the Institute and schools at Manchester in 1879 described his feeling of despair at their moribund condition. 'I could see no way open; when one day I got the Programme of the City and Guilds' Institute establishing examinations of a distinctly industrial and technical character, and I at once induced the directors to establish classes to meet the demands of these examinations.' He had a vivid recollection of the visit of the City and Guilds' 'Organising Director and Secretary', Mr Philip Magnus, who had been appointed in 1880, and of the 'hope with which you inspired me, when you said that the . . . Institute would grant immediate aid if certain things were done . . .'.[81] Mr George Hooper, a coachbuilder in Victoria Street, a member of the Coachmakers' Company, had built up St Mark's Technical School through which nearly 150 apprentices and workmen had passed. Some had visited the Paris

Exhibition of 1878, and presented a report. The City and Guilds' examinations helped them to think of reasons for what they were doing, and 'above all breaks down old prejudices and hindrances to progress'.[82]

Although the original scheme had given priority to the higher Central College, it was the institution for more practical studies which was first established, partly because the pioneer work of the Cowper Street Schools gave it a location and an educational base. The Schools were used at first for classes, and it was decided to erect a college next to them in Tabernacle Row, 'as an institution intermediate between' these schools and the projected 'Central Institution', at a cost of £20,000. Already a system of technical education, and its place in an educational process, were being worked out. The organization of the Finsbury Technical College was one of the first problems faced by Magnus, who became its acting principal in 1882. Armstrong and Ayrton had established highly successful evening classes for artisans, emphasizing practical laboratory work with supervision by the professors themselves, and the skills needed in local industries – cabinet-making, engineering, chemical, electrical, brewing trades. Evening classes were held in carpentry, joinery, metal-plate work, bricklaying, drawing, painting, modelling and design.[83] Day students, who had to take an entrance examination in elementary mathematics, followed a complete course – practical science, freehand and mechanical drawing, at least three hours a week in the workshop – and they learnt one modern language. This day school was 'new and experimental'.[84] By 1883 the college had a 'splendid apparatus of physical and chemical laboratories', and afforded 'technical instruction to upwards of 1000 students'.

Whilst Armstrong and his colleagues had worked out full theoretical and practical courses in sciences and mathematics, this college kept its aims firmly tied to the needs of students 'actually engaged in the staple industries of the district'. The Artisans' Institute of St Martin's Lane (another of Solly's interests) had been incorporated within it and the City School of Art was installed in the basement.[85] In south London, the Art School in Kennington Park Road, the Lambeth School of Art, had been adapted in the same way, and gave instruction to artisans, some from the nearby Doulton Pottery, where 'art aptitude is indispensable for success'.[86] Grants had been made to provincial technical colleges and the London colleges had also reached out to help other institutions, the British Horological Institute at Clerkenwell, the London School of Woodcarving, for example.[87] An approach had been 'made to the establishment of a relationship' between the Finsbury College and 'the principal middle-class schools of the Metropolis, by the award to selected pupils from these schools' of exhibitions.[88] Eventually the scientific side of the Cowper Street School teaching was absorbed into the College. In 1884 it was suggested that if the relationship between the school and the college 'could be made still closer, and the school could be brought *under* the direct control of the Institute, a technical school might be created in London which would serve as a model for others throughout the kingdom'.[89] At the other end of this emerging process of education connections were being explored. The Clothworkers had given two exhibitions to the London School Board and the hope was expressed that the way would be opened to boys of exceptional merit 'from the primary schools' to the 'highest technical instruction'.[90]

This upper end of the process, the Technological University, was rather more controversial. Magnus himself feared that a 'limited view of the scope of technical instruction' might prevail, yet not only did 'so-called captains of industry' need education, but scientific research was essential, and without good teachers the whole structure would collapse.[91] In 1880 the Commissioners of the 1851 Exhibition offered a site at South Kensington at a peppercorn rent, and the Institute was granted £2000 a year for five years by the City Corporation.[92] At an estimate £76,000 was needed. The Fishmongers, Goldsmiths, Clothworkers and Cordwainers agreed to subscribe another £30,000, and by 1884 most of the Companies had 'associated themselves' and £100,000 had been raised. Waterhouse was employed to produce a design which while 'not of a meagre and improper character for the neighbourhood . . . is by no means ostentatious, and by no means extravagant'. Its location and its apparent opulence however caused criticism. Some sections of City opinion, including Cotton, operating with a narrower definition of technical education, argued that it was unnecessarily extravagant and ambitious; it was far from 'the homes of those for whom it was designed . . . the artisan and labouring classes'; it overlapped the work of its neighbour, the Normal School of Science; it would draw funds away from the Finsbury Technical College. The governors replied that the Metropolitan District Railway, the numerous inexpensive lodgings nearby, the advantages of the neighbouring museums and other colleges, made the site suitable for the students for whom it was intended, future teachers, 'managers of works, engineers, industrial chemists and others who have a desire for superior education and instruction in the branches of their industry'. Without this Central Institute 'the system of technical education' would 'be incomplete'.[93] 'As soon as the correct idea of the object of the Central College had taken shape, the difficulty of the site was overcome . . .', and the building was opened by the Prince of Wales in July 1884.[94]

That was the year in which the reports of the Royal Commission on Technical Instruction (of which Magnus was a member) and that on the Livery Companies were both produced, giving occasion not only for rehearsing the history of the City and Guilds' Institute but also a thorough examination of its work. Before the Livery Companies' Commissioners Spottiswoode, then President of the Royal Society, submitted a full discussion of the philosophy and practice of technical education as it had been formulated in civic action. It was 'lack of understanding of the principles on which his handicraft is (often uncon-

Central Institution of City and Guilds' Institute

sciously) based, and a better acquaintance with the nature and uses of the materials which he employs' which made the British workman inferior to his foreign competitors. 'This knowledge forms part of general science and may be made a part of an educational system.' Taking the commissioners thoroughly through the achievements of the institute, he maintained that its colleges, scholarships, grants, advice and examinations were now providing 'a systematic and progressive course of instruction' and that experts from the Continent were in their turn visiting England in order to enquire into the scheme.[95] The Lord Chancellor, Selborne, discussed the extent to which the advice of Huxley had been followed; the question 'turns mainly on the supply of teachers good enough, but not too good, for the purpose' and the South Kensington college was therefore crucial to success.[96] Bramwell, with his great technical experience, was an especially valuable witness in discussing the relation between the workshop and this kind of education, enabling men to work 'with a knowledge of what they are doing instead of being compelled to undertake it upon a sort of rough practical teaching'. When the question of an adequate base of general education was raised, Bramwell was of the opinion that so far this had not been a problem, though some students 'may have been debarred from coming'.[97]

The Institute therefore felt able to make strong claims. 'The commons of London have thus founded in England a system of technical education, a service to the state which it is difficult to overvalue.'[98] Moreover, this was a continuing process. Selborne maintained that it was his impression that 'whatever funds are needed will be forthcoming'.[99] Bramwell referred to the interest of the Companies, their concern to provide the right governors. The Mercers had sent himself and Mr George Matthey, 'a most scientific metallurgist', and when, because their subscription had been doubled, they became entitled to two more, they had made Dr Siemans a liveryman by special grant. They had 'plenty of well qualified men but they thought they could do better' and he 'would be for the benefit of the institution'.[100]

Behind this success lay unsolved problems which were more fully investigated by the Samuelson Commission.[101] The balance between theory and practice, the economic and educational ability of the workman to take up opportunities, were explored in the evidence of the Professor of Engineering from University College, who criticized evening classes as too fatiguing. A deputation of working men led by Solly argued for a system of day release on three afternoons a week.[102] Experiments had already begun. Spottiswoode himself had a school for between 300 and 400 boys who worked in his firm, the Queen's Printers, and had two hours a day compulsory instruction.[103] At this period however workmen would usually have had to sacrifice wages for such a scheme, making it impracticable as a general solution.[104] Long-term advantages in better wages and security of employment were luxuries few workmen could afford to await, and this was probably why at this period the trade unions 'were by no means active supporters of technical education, its necessity and advantages'.[105] It was not only at this level that there were problems. The partner in an Erith Iron Works, a member of both the Institute of Civil and of Mechanical Engineers, complained savagely of the deficient education of boys from public schools. 'The modern schools such as Owen's College and University College' gave a 'really useful education' but their pupils could not afford his premium. Technical preparation for the managerial level was in 'a very lamentable state'.[106] The part played by technical instruction in elementary schools was also a matter of controversy. In 1886 the London School Board had approached the City and Guilds' for grants to finance evening technical classes in Board school premises and experiments began in Hackney and Southwark in such subjects as art, practical chemistry, magnetism, electricity and manual training.[107] As part of the day curriculum of such schools, manual training, it was argued by men such as Lubbock, should be part of general education, one which would induce parents to keep their boys longer at school, but should not attempt to 'give a boy a trade'.[108] In 1886 Magnus discussed the continuing deficiencies of London endowed schools and of the process of education in the capital in this respect. It was 'intermediate technical schools or middle-grade schools' which were lacking and the scholarships of the London School Board had often to be 'diverted into literary or clerical channels' at for example the City of London or King's College Schools, 'where there is no technical education, whatever'. The United Westminster School gave a fairly good science education, 'but even there the defect of the school is the large amount of time that is spent in teaching Latin grammar'. He wanted schools which could lead up to technical colleges, the Central College of the City and Guilds', and even the universities. Scholarships would provide a 'missing link' with the elementary schools and tap the 'intellectual wealth found in the children of the working classes' who should be educated in these intermediate technical schools alongside pupils paying about £4 a year fees.[109]

Ambiguity of definition and lack of co-ordination had persisted through the years during which the City was creating a system of technical education. The formation of the National Association for the Promotion of Technical Education in 1886, its campaigns culminating in the Technical Instruction Act of 1889, and the formation of county and municipal committees, to some extent masked the same problem. When the Technical Education Committee of the LCC was formed it included three representatives of the City and Guilds' Institute,[110] which felt justified in claiming that it had solved 'the difficult problem of adapting the teaching of science to the wants of artisans and of differentiating practical trade teaching from the teaching of the practice of a trade'.[111] But had it? As a contribution to secondary education this must be seen either in a very long perspective or to some extent as an alternative system. The City and Guilds' Institute in its early days had tried both to provide for the education of the workman, or the future workman, and to construct a whole process of education in conjunction with the emerging institutions of a national system. But although it had provided the ingredients of a system of technical education and the technical components of a system of education, the result for the most part remained a mixture and not a compound, as the experience of the next century showed. In 1911 the Dyke Acland Report referred to the City and Guilds' annual examinations, then taken by 22,443 candidates *in the evenings*, as 'not likely to be taken by more than a very small number of pupils in Secondary Schools'.[112] And at this same period of consolidation the Institute's Central Technical College was moving into the University orbit as part of the Imperial College of Science and Technology.[113] In 1933 Lord Eustace Percy complained that 'until recently our technical education has had little or no connexion with our secondary and elementary education' and the Board of Education's chief technical inspector wrote: 'The advocates of technical education in this country have always been a comparatively small body of interested persons . . .'.[114] Amongst these the City of London had been pre-eminent. The wealth of the City had provided a reservoir of capital which had given life to a whole area of education.

Commercial education

The Guilds of the City of London had made this effective contribution to technical education not only because they understood their obligations or felt the threat of public criticism but because it was a good investment. But the immediate demands which the City made upon such education were more often clerical and commercial than industrial, and it was another City business institution, the London Chamber of Commerce, which at the same period addressed itself to this problem.

London private schools had long attempted to supply this need, with varying success, and a number of proprietary and reformed endowed schools had also prepared for this rapidly expanding labour market. The Taunton Commissioners had noted the requirements of the 'third grade' of school as 'very good reading, very good writing, very good arithmetic', and the philosopher T. H. Green had concluded that the demand for 'a *clerk's education*; namely a thorough knowledge of arithmetic, and the ability to write a good letter' was low, but 'thoroughly sensible'. The steady increase in the volume of government business, the introduction of competitive examinations, and the attempts of the Civil Service Commissioners to distinguish between 'intellectual and mechanical work' all had impact on the schools. Jowett, in calculating that there would be 10,000 candidates a year for the lower grade, recommended that they be examined in dictation, arithmetic, geography, and in either writing a letter or making an abstract, with a *viva* for estimating general intelligence. In Trevelyan's estimate, 'In respect of the lower class, quick and legible handwriting, facility in deciphering, familiarity with all the ordinary arithmetical processes and knowledge of book-keeping should be the principal subjects of examinations.' For many of these clerks work consisted in the drudgery or copying, and of the boys taken on for this at fourteen or fifteen, many were discharged at nineteen or twenty. It was only towards the end of the century that this work was taken over by machines and women.[115] Whilst the reform of the higher Civil Service had an impact on schools of Taunton's first grade throughout the country, it was London and suburban schools which responded most keenly to the demands of the lower grade.

It is impossible to distinguish consistently between official and commercial clerks when estimating the increase in their number during the 1851–1901 period when census officials made constant experiments in classification. Nevertheless the overall picture is clear. 'Commercial clerks' rose around 1000 per cent, from 37,529 to 363,673, in the nation as a whole. In London, which had long ago begun the transition from production to service occupations, the rise was less spectacular than in some Midland cities, but in numbers the capital still kept its lead, clerks growing from 12,310 in 1851 to 103,414 in 1901. Other commercial occupations, merchants, brokers, agents and factors, accountants, commercial travellers, banking and insurance service employees, also showed a remarkable overall rise, slowing down after 1871. After 1861 London lost its lead in the growth of insurance occupations, but had the most spectacular rise in banking employees, as the centralized control of the credit structure was strengthened. Accountants increased only slowly in number, probably because of their highly specialized training. The general pattern of growth was little affected by so-called years of depression.[116]

These cohorts of Cratchits put great pressure on slender educational resources and it has been argued that commercial education was at its lowest ebb in the decade or so after the Great Exhibition, just when apprenticeship for entry to the business world declined, and mercantile houses had not time, because of the growing complexities of business practice, to train boys more informally on the job. Poor education lowered the prestige and value of clerks at a time when increasing scale of business made promotion to responsible positions less likely, and variety of experience less easy to gain. This not only depressed the position and market value of clerks but employers were in difficulties through lack of any external qualifications.[117] The College of Preceptors was the first in this field in 1851 with a brief experiment in examinations in book-keeping and for commercial certificates. The Royal Society of Arts was the first to give systematic examinations in commerce from 1852, and from 1856 a scheme for taking trade and commercial schools 'into union' was launched, to encourage more systematic courses in mathematical, experimental, observational, mechanical and social sciences, in moral and metaphysical studies, the fine arts and literature. Commercial subjects were parcelled out amongst these fine-sounding divisions of the curriculum, but by 1859 were given a clearer identity and shorthand was introduced as an examination subject in 1876. Six months' attendance at a school in union was necessary before a certificate could be gained. These RSA examinations were used by the Civil Service until 1864, when its own competitive entry was organized.[118]

During the 1870s the commercial aspect was subsumed in the mounting discussion and action over technical education, but in reality received little effective attention, in spite of the fact that the National Association for Technical and Secondary Education did address itself to the problem. Evidence was collected from Consular Reports on the effectiveness of foreign competition on overseas trade, and Dr Percival prepared a paper on *Commercial Education and Our Higher Schools*. His argument was a powerful indictment of insularity. Humboldt had given Germany fifty years' start, but Britain had 'ignored new methods of industrial and commercial instruction'. Defects of education had contributed 'in no small degree' to the way 'foreigners are beating us'. The school system needed to be 'modified from top to bottom' to give mastery of one or two foreign languages, and also 'the arithmetic of commerce, commercial and industrial geography, the products of the different parts of the world, and the principles of economics'. Here was a whole structure and philosophy for secondary education.[119] The operation of the Education Act of 1870 may however have had more influence, for effective and thorough instruction in some London Board schools presented a challenge to the private, proprietary and endowed schools whose products faced unwelcome and wholesome competition, later increased by higher grade schools and evening classes in Board schools. From 1890 the elementary Code included book-keeping, in part the result of otherwise ineffectual attempts to ensure that the Technical Instruction Act included commercial education. It was a Sheffield member who raised the question in the House, asking 'if the definition of the Technical Instruction Bill is clearly understood to embrace commercial instruction . . . for the study of foreign languages, commercial correspondence, advanced book-keeping, the principles of banking, exchange, discount, customs, and mercantile law . . .'. A deputation including Mundella, Playfair, Samuelson and Lubbock had waited on the Committee of Council to press the same general point, but while the Act in its definition of technical education included its commercial aspect in parenthesis, in practice very little was done. It was left to the local authorities, subject to the approval of the Science and Art Department, not particularly imaginative or sympathetic to this need.[120]

In the City men such as Lubbock were acutely aware of the problem. He proposed that the Civil Service examinations should be extended to candidates for commercial posts. This was implemented by the City of London College which in 1880 began to conduct examinations on behalf of banking employers.[121] In the autumn of 1881 a meeting was called at the Mansion House to establish a London Chamber of Commerce, which held its first meeting in January 1882,[122] and from the outset one of 'the main objects they had in view was that of improving the commercial education of the people of this country'. 'The national preference for self help, in place of state-aid or state-supervision, being practically unanimous, it falls to the duty of private associations and private initiative . . .'.[123] Its early efforts were directed to helping the technical education movement but whilst arguing that the capital's industrial base was important, the London Chamber was particularly sensitive to its 'immense intermediary commission and financial business',[124] and the lack of 'corresponding improvement of education of those destined to a mercantile career. Nationally speaking, there will be but little use in producing a more highly skilled class of manufacturers and artisans if we do not simultaneously improve the powers and capacities of the merchants, travellers and clerks, whose function is to obtain orders and information for and distribute the produce of the industrial commonwealth . . .'.[125] It had some pungent things to say about the London business community. Leaving 'middle-class education' to the laws of supply and demand had failed. Commercial men were to blame for the poor state of commercial education. They educated their own sons 'more with a social object in view, than with the purpose of launching them on the world carefully trained for a definite career'. Merchants did not want to train their own sons as clerks, they forgot the source of their own success. Like the fifteenth-century merchant dynasties, city firms had a short life, and until recently money had been easily made, 'which favoured a tendency to invest in landed property, and encouraged living on interest rather than by personal effort'. Now money was more difficult to make, real estate depreciating, competition keener. The same competition was pressing on clerks, the market was overstocked, fewer were able to 'migrate from the bench or stool' without a foreign language and shorthand. The London Chamber printed a sample letter from the 'Principal of a leading school in London' saying that boys did not take up a commercial course. Out of a hundred boys less than half a dozen took shorthand, less than a dozen book-keeping, and evening classes in more advanced subjects such as commercial law had been a total failure. His pupils came from the wealthier classes, were intended for public schools, the services or professions, or had no particular career in mind. Merchants 'think it *infra dig* that their sons should learn what they will be able to pay clerks to do'. Moreover pressure of examinations worked against commercial subjects, foreign languages could only be learnt abroad, and his boys did not work hard enough to master such subjects.[126] 'We have grown rich and prosperous upon the system of our forefathers, and are only be-ginning to find, under pressure of competition, that the old system no longer produces an easy competency' declared the London Chamber.[127] Its campaign was strengthened by mounting foreign competition and economic depression. The Royal Commission on the Depression of Trade and Industry of 1888 made the point: 'In the matter of education, we seem to be particularly deficient in comparison with some of our foreign competitors; and this remark applies not only to what is usually called technical education, but to the ordinary commercial education which is required in mercantile houses and especially in foreign languages.'[128] But such requirements were far from ordinary in English schools. The problem was one of complacency. 'An ordinary school routine is considered as giving sufficient groundwork on which . . . a few years' experience in the office, warehouse or factory . . . may be satisfactorily grafted. . . . The whole training of men of business has been left to the vagaries of individual fancy.'[129]

Through study of other aspects of technical education, contacts and investigations abroad, examination of economic reports of consuls throughout the world, the London Chamber prepared its campaign.[130] In July 1886 a Congress of Chambers of Commerce of the British Empire was held at South Kensington, and the London Chamber was responsible for an extended conference 'to consider the best means of educating young men intended for a commercial career, so as to fit them for competition with those of the continent . . .'. Samuelson's paper took the discussion straight into the matter of definition, arguing that vocational training was best done on the job, the British business house giving the best training in the world, but that it was general education which was deficient. A German or Swiss youth came to the counting house well grounded in commercial geography, natural science, 'and more especially with the natural habitations of animals and plants'; he was a 'correct and rapid arithmetician', and above all was correct and fluent in writing and speaking one or more modern languages. Young Englishmen educated at 'Classical and Commercial Academies' could not compete with this, especially as the low fees of European state schools placed them within the reach of classes who wished their sons to rise by industry and were prepared to work hard.[131]

This led the London Chamber during 1887 to investigate, at first casually, the need of the City to employ foreign clerks, and then by systematic enquiry through a questionnaire to members. Replies showed that about 35 per cent of firms could not get English clerks who could use foreign languages, and found that German youths especially were not only better qualified but worked for less pay, considering it part of their training. The general opinion was that the foreigner was not only a better technician, but had a 'wider culture which enables him to adapt his knowledge and training to the varying demands of modern commerce'.[132]

During this enquiry Dr Percival, again enlisted in the cause, was at the instance of Morley compiling a report on *Commercial Education Abroad*, in Europe and the USA, for presentation to the Associated Chambers of Commerce meeting at Exeter in September 1887. This discussed an impressive conception of graded technical schools, leading from elementary to secondary levels, then 'to the highest grades in the country', available not only to the élite but to 'the poorer part of the working classes'.[133] In November the London Chamber convened a meeting of 'business men and representative schoolmasters' at the Cannon Street Hotel.[134] Lubbock analysed the problem in its context of the long struggle to reduce the 'exclusive devotion to classics' and of the 'neglect of science and modern languages', especially for boys who left school at fifteen or sixteen. He himself had instituted an enquiry into the time given to science teaching at 240 principal schools and had found only 20 which gave as much as 'four hours to this important subject'. French and German when taught at all were usually taught as dead languages. Pressure from the universities was partly responsible, though London at least insisted on science and one modern language. The Oxford and Cambridge Schools Examination Board grouped its subjects in such a way that a boy might choose his five subjects without the 'slightest knowledge of history and geography, of English and . . . of any branch of science'. Reform could be demanded here and also in the balance and scale of marks adopted by the Civil Service Commissioners, placing 'French and German on the same footing as Greek and also to admit other modern languages'.

In exploring ways of rendering 'our school system more practical and useful', Lubbock was redefining secondary education rather than pleading for a special vocational preparation, and moreover was insisting on its place in the whole process or system of education. This emphasis was sustained in discussion. Dr Percival argued that in preparing young men vocationally to go into the world, their intellectual tastes and faculties would be best stimulated. The Cowper Street Schools were cited as an example of what could be done. From his experience at the Board of Trade, Mundella enlarged on the need for foreign languages if full benefit was to be derived from commercial treaties. It was from middle-class schools, made cheap and accessible, that such education should come, and London had the financial resources to make it available for 10,000 boys. Other speakers urged reform of endowments along these lines, and Waterlow suggested the United Westminster Schools as a model. The conference drew its debate together in a resolution which not only urged the use of endowments and the reform of the curriculum, but strongly supported the proposal to appoint a Minister of Education.[135]

The immediate result was the setting up of an impressive Commercial Education Committee including the Lord Mayor, Mundella, Lubbock, Samuelson, Roscoe, Waterlow, Huxley, Percival, Quintin Hogg, Dr Wace of King's College, the Reverend J. R. Diggle from the London School Board: amongst those later added were Philip Magnus, Canon Rogers, and one of the staff of the City of London School.[136] From this there emerged a scheme for school examinations. From 1888 to 1895 the Oxford and Cambridge Schools Examinations Board, after 'discussions with the various Chambers of Commerce', experimented with commercial certificates which could be taken at about sixteen, whether the candidates were at school or not. These never attracted more than a few candidates, for the Joint Board was geared to the needs of 'first grade schools'.[137] The London Chamber recognized the need for examinations under its own auspices and a scheme was hammered out between 1888 and 1890 in consultation with the Joint Board and leading schoolmasters and businessmen. Junior and senior examinations were proposed after a progressive course. The first scheme included Latin, but 'many schoolmasters themselves urged' its omission, much to the committee's astonishment.[138] Particular stress was laid on modern foreign languages but the intention to insist on two was dropped 'in the face of the decided opinion of the Oxford and Cambridge representatives, that the Chamber would probably not secure a single candidate . . .'[139] The scheme as it emerged had ten obligatory subjects for the Junior Commercial Certificates: English, including handwriting, orthography, grammar and composition; the Commercial History of the British Isles, Colonies and Dependencies; Geography, the elements of physical geography, and 'ordinary geography' with special reference to commerce and industry; Arithmetic including 'general knowledge of Foreign Weights and Measures, Currencies and Exchanges'; Algebra including quadratic equations; Euclid, Books I to III; the Elementary Mechanics of Solids and Fluids; Book-keeping and Accounts; modern foreign languages, French, German, Spanish, Portuguese, Italian, comprising translation, composition, dictation and conversation; Elementary drawing ('Free-hand *or* Geometrical *or* Designing'). Then the candidate had to choose at least one optional subject from a higher knowledge of mechanics and hydrostatics; shorthand; advanced drawing; theoretical and practical chemistry; 'sound, light and heat'; electricity and magnetism; natural history with a choice of two from the elements of botany, zoology, geology, physiology; and a further foreign language.[140] This was backed up by a prescribed course of instruction covering the years from ten to fifteen or sixteen, giving the number of hours a week to be given to each branch of study. The Chamber made a serious attempt to ensure that the course was not mere cramming for examinations, but was taken as a whole and 'thoroughly and loyally acted up to', to induce proper understanding.[141] The senior course taken between sixteen and eighteen or nineteen included more advanced vocational studies such as banking and insurance, commercial and industrial law, drawing, photography and the sciences in relation to commerce.[142] The London Chamber was promulgating a complete and systematic scheme of secondary education. To induce 'parents and schoolmasters to prepare youths for the test' two hundred City firms agreed to give preference to holders of these Junior Commercial Certificates.[143]

The examinations were entrusted to the administration of the College of Preceptors and in 1890 there were 17 passes out of the 65 London candidates. By 1893 these had risen to 46 out of 76, and a centre at Ipswich also entered a few candidates.[144] Modifications were introduced, arranging subjects into seven obligatory and nine optional groups, and Latin was added as an optional subject.[145] After the fourth year, the London Chamber decided to take over the examinations itself, and the Senior Certificate was elaborated, giving a 'Full Commercial Certificate' for a whole series of obligatory and optional subjects, and a 'Special Senior Commercial Certificate' for subjects selected by the candidates; the latter could be taken especially by 'studious clerks' who had not had the opportunity to take the Junior Certificates.[146]

There was some response from the schools and a number set up courses or 'sides' to prepare for the examinations. Dr Wace had thrown the 'whole weight of his scholastic experience' behind the scheme, and King's College School opened a commercial side which was 'worked with considerable success'.[147] University College School did likewise and later opened what it claimed to be 'the first public commercial school on anything like the lines of Continental commercial education ever instituted in the United Kingdom'.[148] The newly appointed headmaster of the City of London School was 'strongly in favour' and began a commercial side.[149] Owen's School under Easterbrook was the most successful school in the examinations;[150] and candidates were entered by the Central Foundation (Cowper Street), Archbishop Tenison's, and Parmiter's among endowed schools, and the Boys' Public Day School, Clapham, among proprietary schools, and by polytechnic and commercial schools and a number of suburban private schools.[151] Educationalists such as Dr Percival considered that the scheme had been a great stimulus, as 'if education had suffered from one fault more than another, it was not the fault of being too utilitarian, but of . . . being too sluggish . . .'. It had run along 'traditional lines in a sluggish and mechanical fashion'.[152]

But although the number of candidates rose steadily, it remained low in proportion to the needs of London. Some commercial 'sides' fitted uneasily into established schools – that at University College School came to an end when the school moved to Hampstead.[153] The hope that the London example would be the beginning of a 'single scheme of commercial education through the entire kingdom' was disappointed. London refused to operate its own scheme nation-wide and other Chambers were both reluctant to act as centres, or to work out their own examinations. The strong 'individualism of the local business communities' worked against any agreement as to 'what constitutes a satisfactory system of commercial education'.[154]

During the last decade of the century this movement became entangled in the national debate over secondary education. Moreover the rising standard of such education and the rising demands of commerce interacted, while the obstinate insularity of the British acted as a barrier to both. It was the 'business of foreigners to learn our language . . . if they wished to enjoy the privilege of dealing with us . . . as a rule we still expect foreigners to adapt to our custom, to our metrical system, to our language' as a contemporary wrote in 1890.[155] This was in painful contrast to the attitudes which Lord Reay, in his evidence to the Bryce Commission, wished to see developed by modern studies in secondary schools: 'more knowledge and more versatility' were essential as the protectionist policies of other countries and rising competition made the work of for example a commercial traveller more difficult. Thorough knowledge of foreign languages, ability to 'insinuate himself into the society' of a foreign country, to create new outlets by understanding their 'social characteristics' ('which to a race with migratory instincts is of the highest importance') were needed. These might not be easy to teach and emphasis was being increasingly placed on the qualities of character needed in commerce, 'industry, resourcefulness, self-reliance, imagination, and the ability to form swift and accurate judgements of men . . .'.[156] When, in 1899, the Vice President of the London Chamber of Commerce contributed to the series of essays edited by Scott, the headmaster of Parmiter's School, under the title *What is Secondary Education?*, he distinguished between the mechanical and intellectual abilities needed for commercial success. He included qualities of character, such as *longue patience*, humility and a 'determination to take business, even in its dull and early stages, seriously, and not to sub-ordinate it to games and amusements', and a formidable list of skills, 'accuracy and thoroughness' especially in modern languages ('railway chatter is worth very little'), and if mathematical understanding was not often directly used in the counting house, 'rare is the accountant who, without a mathematical training, can keep his head clear through a mass of complex figures'. He was analysing a high quality of general sec-ondary education which had imparted the art of learning, 'thought and originality combined with accuracy', 'the power of making a way where there is none, not the power of running along the road', and 'a broad and deep fund of general knowledge'.[157] Over and over again in the debates of the time this note is sounded. Gorst, who among statesmen was perhaps most alive to the need for commercial eduction, at a Guildhall Conference in 1898 emphasized the need for a *system* of education: 'All education of every kind is indissolubly linked together.... You cannot build a superstructure of art, of science, of commercial, or technical education unless you have a sound and solid base upon which to build.'[158]

From their side many educationalists were prepared to accept the need for vocational preparation. The Incorporated Association of Headmasters, formed by Scott, agreed that 'the aim of secondary schools is to provide more extended courses of study, (a) adapted to higher commercial scientific or professional requirements; (b) varying according as they are planned to terminate normally at 17 or 19'. The Assistant Masters' Association agreed that these schools should provide 'curricula adapted to professional, scientific, mercantile and higher industrial requirements, or those of the public services'.[159] Others were less ready to compromise. Morant in 1898, addressing the International Congress on Commercial Education at Antwerp, declared that 'England wished to maintain her primary and secondary schools for the purpose of general education ... [They] are schools for life, not for livelihood.'[160] A year later, he was writing that the greatest function of our secondary schools was to 'produce this, this magnificent re-quirement of our great imperial destiny as a race – something quite different from the technical education of our industries, or the com-mercial education of our business houses....'.[161]

The Technical Education Board of the LCC could not afford to adopt such an inflated posture, and increasingly by the end of the century the concept of secondary schooling in the capital was being worked out by the interaction of this powerful body with the other agencies of both general and vocational education. The London busi-ness community was heavily committed on both sides of this dialogue. Sidney Webb had been responsible for remodelling the Technical Education Board to conciliate the City Companies and businessmen as well as trade unionists, the London School Board and the teachers. He had appointed Hubert Llewellyn Smith, formerly Secretary of the

National Association for the Promotion of Technical and Secondary Education, to make a masterly survey of London's technical education provision.[162] Llewellyn Smith in 1892 wrote in the *Journal of the London Chamber of Commerce* that commercial education could only be organized through the secondary schools, where curricula could be infused with a commercial spirit, after which definitely commercial subjects could be taken up in evening classes or higher commercial schools.[163] This same point was made by Lubbock to the Special Subcommittee on Commercial Education of the Technical Education Board appointed in 1897: 'his opinion leans to the perfecting of the existing agencies'.[164]

In 1899 the Report of this committee, which included Easterbrook of Owen's and Gull of the Grocers' School, surveyed the whole field on the eve of the establishment of the Board of Education and the Local Education Authorities. While the subject was one of national importance, for reports of British consuls spoke of the 'want of linguistic training, of local knowledge, of insight and adaptability' shown by British firms and their representatives abroad, it concerned 'citizens of London more than any other British subjects' for it was not only the greatest commercial centre of the world, and the heart of the British Empire, it had a greater population of 'clerks' than any city in the world. Not only was good general education the foundation of any superstructure of vocational subjects, but 'commercial education must be regarded as covering a considerable part of the field of what is known as 'general education'. This term had 'for too long been usurped by the supporters of the classical system. . . . We see no reason why it should not be possible to give a good general education by means of different combinations of subjects.' Commercial education of this kind was 'already provided in London to a considerable and increasing extent', at schools such as Parmiter's, the Whitechapel Foundation, Central Foundation, the Mercers', Sir Walter St John's, United Westminster. But the examinations of the London Chamber of Commerce had 'not yet been able to make a very marked impression' and it was clear that the time had come for a more unified system of schools and examinations. The University Locals and London Matriculation might be combined in some way and the London School of Economics was now providing an apex to the structure. The London Chamber had already revised its senior law examinations to bring them into line with its lectures.[165]

This Report makes clear the position of the LCC, decisively rejecting separate commercial schools.[166] The evidence which it collected of the views and needs of a wide range of employers – banker, underwriter, estate agent, broker, actuary, milling engineer, department store directors, shopkeepers, tradesmen of all kinds, manufacturers – revealed the variety and uncertainty of the labour market to be satisfied. Industrial and commercial change were heightening the character of London as a distributive and servicing centre. The rise of the department store, for example, added the demand for Kipps as well as Cratchit, and the army of 'lady typewriters' now taking over some of the office drudgery pushed up demands on male employees at a time when business scale meant fewer promotion prospects. Some London schools earned approval from the range of employers interviewed. The London and East India Docks spoke highly of the City of London School; a manufacturing chemist in Islington preferred to employ girls from Owen's School; Chappell, the music publisher and piano manufacturer, drew his best boys from the Philological School; but in general the greatest defects in clerks were 'want of knowledge of foreign languages, shorthand and book-keeping, and the absence of that energy, push and exactness which were to be found with the American and the foreigner'. A draper of Islington, on the other hand, declared that 'nobody could beat an Englishman' as a clerk. Unfortunately he went on to say that the 'unsatisfactory nature of the present-day clerk was due to too much leisure at school. People do not think now-a-days.' Attitudes to special commercial training varied widely and at best were ambivalent. Some employers were uneasy lest it would make young men dissatisfied with routine tasks and raise their market value. Docility was often implied as desirable. Sir J. B. Maple frankly preferred boys from charity schools: 'Public school boys do not mould well.' Employers looked for high skills but did not want to pay for them and distrusted specialization which might make young employees less adaptable or amenable. On their side the schoolmasters knew that high standards might also raise aspirations. Wormell gave evidence that boys from good schools wanted to go into the professions, and this was of particular significance from the headmaster of a school designed to educate boys for the City.[167] Good general education had dangers for the supply of labour for commerce; and an avid labour market often uncertain of its own demands and perhaps unprepared to pay for a good article, gave an unstable foundation to the effort of the leaders of the London business community to define both content and standards of secondary education.

The polytechnics

It was during the last two decades of the century, when administrative and political controversy over the government of London was both intense and confused, that the City made another important contribution to the interpretation and provision of education including the secondary level. The creation of the London network of polytechnics may usually be considered as part of the higher education sector, but the age of a large number of the early students, the courses provided, the social philosophy which lay behind the movement, have significance for the education of the adolescent, and many polytechnics included a secondary school within their range of activities.

A large proportion of the capital and income which the City contributed to this polytechnic movement came from its parochial charities, archaic and chaotic survivals providing an 'incomparable museum' for the discerning critic. *The Times* defined a charity as 'an institution which labours under a perpetual tendency to fall out of repair'.[168] These parish benefactions related to a social, economic and topographical order which had long since passed away, to a time when 'London had meant the City', when 'south of the Thames were a few steady-going villages and the quaint "Boro"; the East-end instead of teaming with that dull, uncomplaining laborious life of which few of us know much was dotted with picturesque hamlets'.[169] The writer, the Reverend R. H. Hadden, had been curate to Rogers at Bishopsgate and kept in consultation with him after 1888, when he was given the living of St Botolph Aldgate, 'perhaps the richest parish in London', and one where the battle over charities was to be at its most sordid, even violent.[170]

For decades the attack mounted and became part of the general debate on the concept of metropolis. Sir Charles Trevelyan coined the phrase 'phantom parishes' to describe those which had been de-populated or obliterated in a City which had become a gigantic counting and warehouse. 'The Cannon Street station accounted for the major part of All Hallows the Great, the General Post Office for three-quarters of St Anne and St Agnes, while the Bank of England wiped out St Christopher le Stock.'[171] The best-informed and most persevering critic was Hare, the Charity Commissioner. As early as 1857 he con-tributed to the Social Science Congress a paper 'On the Application of Endowed Charities in the Improvement of the Education and Condition of the Poor'. The 'London poor' no longer lived in London as defined by history. All round the City, where formerly had been open fields, 'within stone's throw of the richest establishments of the city, are at this day really "the poor of the city", and entitled to the benefits of the endowments created for their predecessors under a different condition of things'. He cited the experience of Rogers at the Charterhouse, unable to get funds for his 'Costermongria', and the case of Alleyn's Charity. Painful legislation would be needed to solve these topographical and demographic anomalies, and to bring benefactions into line with contemporary needs and theories of social benefit. Not only was there maladministration (too much sherry in the vestry and whitebait at Greenwich) but even trustees anxious to do their duty found it difficult to track down amidst the warehouses and banks 'one poor honest ancient washerwoman', or maidens suitable for dowries, or apprentices in a city where the system had virtually disappeared. 'The money is there, but no-one claims it.' Rarely was a solution sought unless personal initiative found a way round legal difficulties. St Margaret's Lothbury had an apprenticeship fund which reached over £1300 before one of its churchwardens used his connection with the Middle Class Schools' Corporation to assign it to Rogers's useful enterprise.[172] To make matters more unsatisfactory, while between 1851 and 1881 the population of the City shrank from 131,000 to

52,000, between 1865 and 1876 a number of leases were being re-
negotiated and the receipts of the City Charities rose substantially by as
much as 50 per cent to nearly £100,000.[173] Much of the capital consisted of real estate administered by innumerable little trusts, while the
immense problems of the expanding and changing city needed
capitalization, as Sir Charles Trevelyan insisted.[174]

This provided ammunition for the various campaigners for London
government reform, and criticism of *parochial* charities perhaps unjustly
exacerbated hatred of the *City* as a 'fortress of ancient and selfish
privilege'.[175] Hare's series of critical reports, the polemic of men such as
Gilbert,[176] Trevelyan's articles, built up pressure in 1877–8. Liberal
parliamentarians finally prevailed on Disraeli's Home Secretary, Cross,
to appoint a Royal Commission. The majority report of this undistin-
guished body was timid and tepid, but Rogers, Albert Pell and Farrer
Herschell presented a minority report, sweeping aside difficulties of
distinguishing eleemosynary from ecclesiastical benefactions and demanding an administrative body representing the whole metropolis
rather than only City interests.[177] Fortunately Bryce assisted by
Hobhouse took up the cause and introduced legislation which embodied
these more advanced views in the Parochial Charities' Act of 1883,[178]
passed during the furore of Parnell's parliamentary campaign. It was a
drastic attack on the doctrine of *cy pres* and provided a powerful body of
commissioners to execute its proposals. This, even compared with the
Endowed Schools' Act, was the high-water mark of Victorian charity
reform, with immense implications for London education.

London parishes were divided into two categories. Five large and
comparatively populous ones ringing the City, St Andrew Holborn, St
Botolph Bishopsgate, St Botolph Aldgate, St Bride Fleet Street, St
Giles Cripplegate, with a combined population of 31,000, were to be
responsible for their own benefactions; 107 others, including many
'phantom parishes', were to be combined in the City Parochial Foundation. The Bryce Act gave the Charity Commission stronger than usual
powers to frame Schemes, if necessary overriding founders' wishes; they
were to 'proceed on a utilitarian basis', and the 'beneficial area' was to
be not the City but the Metropolis. Two additional commissioners, Sir
Francis Sandon and James Anstie, were appointed to tackle the framing
of 1300 Schemes, classifying each charity as ecclesiastical or general and
adapting it to the new needs of the new city. It was not only the size and
complexity of the task which took nearly ten years, but the violent
opposition of many vestrymen and officials, who resorted to almost every
kind of legal, and even illegal, opposition to changes which they regarded as little short of red revolution. But the City in this respect was
divided against itself. In this reform it was the clerical hierarchy which
was all-important. Some, such as Archdeacon Hale, fought a stubborn
rearguard action against change, but many of the clergy such as Rogers
and Hadden lined themselves behind the Bryce Act, and Temple, as

Bishop of London, stood by to throw cold water over the more hysterical tactics of churchwardens, trustees and vestrymen. By 1887 the endowments had been classified. The five large parishes emerged with £2601 ecclesiastical and £24,015 general income, the rest with £35,459 and £56,567 respectively. Hadden considered that, if anything, Anstie as a Nonconformist had tended to generosity in assigning the ecclesiastical share.[179] From this Trollopian and sometimes sordid struggle there emerged in 1891 the City Parochial Foundation with its experienced and powerful Central Governing Body.[180]

Hadden of St Botolph Aldgate gives the best account of the struggle and is corroborated by other evidence. The parish was large and populous, including the Tower of London and St Katherine's ancient precinct, and was divided into two parts, the 'Freedom' parish lying within the bounds of the City and the 'Lordship' parish in the old County of Middlesex. Hadden arrived after some years' interregnum and found what he described as 'a sort of moral paralysis . . . a parish in which the forces of evil and wrong had got a firm upper hand . . . a reign of terror' comparable with Tammany Hall. Educational endowments amounted to about £8000 a year, 'administered by a mysterious body called "the Inquest of the Ward of Portsoken and the Leet Jury of the Manor of East Smithfield"', a self-perpetuating body of twenty-one trustees, 'impervious to criticism', 'serene in their tenure of the choicest parochial patronage', 'a spectacle', wrote Hadden drily, 'at least worthy of observation'. Every possible subterfuge was used to preserve this patronage and at the same time to limit 'the number of eligible candidates to the school . . .'.[181] This was the foundation of Sir John Cass (1665–1718), Alderman and Member of Parliament for the City, who had endowed a small school already existing in the parish to prepare boys both for the universities and apprenticeships. He had died while actually executing his elaborate will, and a macabre touch was added to the antics of the Victorian trustees by the school badge of a bloodstained quill pen, to them a symbol of its ancient values and traditions.[182] Hare reported on it several times; the Schools' Inquiry Commission 'came and went, and left it alone'; even the City Parochial Charities Act at first ignored it warily. The problem was left to Hadden and his supporters in the parish. To prevent the Vestry, in order to preserve its control, from letting leases at much below their value, he called in the Charity Commissioners and the Attorney General was notified. Hadden's right to preside at the Vestry was challenged, it was invaded and packed and at the Easter meeting of 1890 he sat for four hours in the chair, protected by two stalwarts from an organization formed by a number of reforming parishioners, while 'there was almost a free fight in the body of the room and the police were brought in'. The matter got into the Queen's Bench and into the courts thirteen times in all and the Vicar's right was upheld. The Charity Commissioners did not hesitate to use their full powers and vested the parish charities in a new Aldgate Freedom Foundation (1891) and proposed a radical reform on the educational side. Four more years of hysterical opposition had to be overcome before the trustees, who tried to claim that the parish was a kind of 'no-go' area as far as the Commissioners were concerned, were borne down and the claims of Hackney parish, where some of the more valuable endowments lay, were assuaged.[183] Aldgate was now provided with a whole range of scholastic institutions relevant to its needs. Provision for secondary education was defined in this decade and for this area as provision for scholarships and as technical education built on a basis of good elementary schools. Hadden not only secured the reform of the endowed and voluntary elementary schools but encouraged the building of two good Board schools in the parish. The Aldgate and All-Hallows Barking Exhibition Foundation was formed, incorporating the former Alderman Hickson's Grammar School on Tower Hill with two other relevant bequests, amounting in all to about £1800 a year, and a 'system of scholarships at secondary schools' was established. The interests of girls were recognized and the awards were made through the LCC's Technical Education Board. Residents and workers in the parishes were given preference, and after them children of the City and Tower Hamlets, a suggestion of Hadden himself. 'Four scholarships of £90 a year at Oxford or Cambridge added the top rungs of the educational ladder', which Hadden regarded, with a complacency reflecting much progressive contemporary opinion, as 'complete'.

The technical side was secured by the almost forcible transformation of the Sir John Cass benefaction into a Technical Institute, containing classrooms for a day school, dining-hall, assembly hall, technical library, lecture rooms, laboratories, drawing-rooms, workshops and 'studios for the teaching of certain trade subjects, including artistic crafts', and domestic economy. Recreation rooms including a gymnasium and a swimming bath were considered important, and the whole was planned to be 'a centre of learning and social intercourse to the young people of this crowded industrial neighbourhood', defined as not only the parish but the eastern half of the City and Whitechapel, Spitalfields, St George's in the East, and Horsleydown over the river.[184]

This combination of technical and vocational instruction with social and pastoral concern was the especial characteristic of the City's educational aims at the end of the century and inspired the polytechnic movement just at the time when funds were becoming available through the City Parochial Foundation. The mood was general, lay and secular as well as clerical, for the attitude to the city, to urbanism, was complex, even ambivalent. The last hundred years had seen an aggregation, a scale of expansion and proliferation, which was an achievement, multiplying possibilities, civilizing, but which increasingly was known to be also submerging and corrupting.[185] Earlier in the century the need for training in urban living was recognized but had on the whole been directed to adapting children and young people to make the most of the opportunities of city life and the competition of a market economy, and these were seen as progressive if imperfect. Now, in the later decades, the city was seen as antipathetic to childhood and to youth. Collectivist policies and the movement of secular idealist philosophy as well as doctrinal and liturgical movements in the church emphasized the need to reassert the importance of community and co-operation, and to restore the moral and civic purposes of education at all levels. The behaviour, and the problems, of unorganized urban youth caused much criticism and alarm. At this period the London School Board was grappling with compulsory attendance at elementary level. Young traders, once regarded as enterprising capitalists, were now seen as deviant and undisciplined. This attitude was strengthened by changes in the labour market where young boys were taken on in large numbers as messenger boys, for example, but were turned off at eighteen unless they were skilled enough to be transferred to other work. A further influence, not unconnected with those economic changes, was the lengthening period of adolescence in more prosperous sections of society, demonstrated by the growth of organized games and ceaseless supervision of so-called 'free time' in public schools and in endowed schools of lesser rank. The needs of urban youth and of public school boys reflected in different styles the same attitudes to adolescence. It needed not independence but institutionalized dependence, *esprit de corps*, moral supervision, a chance to enjoy and refine leisure pursuits and sports.[186] The idea of education for leisure had not yet been born, but training for healthy and constructive recreation was being incorporated into the concept of education, and the unique characteristic of English scholastic institutions as moral, social and recreational as well as intellectual and religious communities was taking shape. The newly emerged girls' secondary sector reinforced this development; from the beginning the polytechnic movement was coeducational, and the secondary schools attached to polytechnics were among the earliest coeducational schools above elementary level.

The polytechnic movement therefore was not only a logical extension of the City's already active interest in technical education, but incorporated new and progressive elements. The acceptance of the idea of polytechnic education was in itself some indication of innovatory attitudes in a supposedly conservative, even reactionary, sector. Almost a century had passed since the establishment of the first polytechnic by the National Convention in Paris in 1794. In the 1830s the word began its slow migration towards insular respectability as the title for a centre in Regent Street for industrial exhibitions and lectures. When Quintin Hogg moved his enterprise to help the boys of the slums around Charing Cross into this Polytechnic building in 1880, expending something like £100,000 of his own money on it, the last taint of Jacobinism was purged by philanthropy and rendered ideologically acceptable, although Sidney Webb considered that the name of the polytechnics sprang from a 'local accident of no significance'. By 1888 the concept had been sufficiently detached from its republican and revolutionary origins to emerge in a resolution at a Mansion House meeting on the needs of technical and commercial education.[187] Hogg's devoted work for 'the instruction of artisans and clerks in the principles, and, to some extent, the practice of their breadwinning pursuits', with a strong emphasis on rescue and recreative work for neglected urban boys and youths, linked the idea with new concerns and preoccupations and to some extent provided a pattern.[188] By the 1880s the City was committed to the polytechnic idea.

The Livery Companies were already espousing the cause. The history of Queen Mary College of the University of London illustrates the processes at work. The Beaumont Institute had been founded by a philanthropic artist, author and businessman who wished to improve the quality of life of the people of Mile End, Poplar. The New Philosophic Institute contained lecture rooms and a museum. After his death in 1841 his trust continued the work until 1879 when support failed and new local efforts were needed to re-establish the charity. The site of the old Bancroft School and almshouses was fixed on and the Drapers enlisted. They provided £20,000 on condition that the trustees incorporated a technical school in the scheme. At this point these proposals were combined with those which had grown from the work of Sir Walter Besant and Henry Cunynghame. Besant's *All Sorts and Conditions of Men* (1882), based on his tramps through the East End, was one of the works which helped to fix this area in the consciousness of Londoners as an expiatory symbol, to some extent a sentimental projection of the guilt of the Metropolis for its own agglomeration; the dark side of its own success. Plans for a People's Palace of Delights enlisted royal support and the interest of Quintin Hogg, and raised a substantial sum. In 1886 the Prince of Wales laid the foundation stone for the recreational and cultural centre and the Queen herself laid that of the technical school a year later. The funds of the Beaumont Trustees were however still not adequate, and the Drapers' Company once again came to the rescue with £70,000 as endowment and an annual grant of £7000. Between 1884 and 1917 the Drapers gave a substantial proportion of their educational expenditure from corporate funds, nearly £960,000 overall, to the People's Palace. The City Parochial Foundation contributed £3500 a year from 1892.

The union of a Palace of Delights and a Technical College was always ill-assorted, and the Company had stipulated that education rather than recreation should be emphasized. Soon the People's Palace was on its way to higher things, but although it eventually achieved full university status, its origins illustrate the characteristic blend of technical and recreative, vocational and ameliorative elements which made up the mood of the 1880s.[189]

Royal patronage combined with the interest of the City Companies extended south of the river. In 1887 the Prince of Wales became President of the South London Polytechnic Committee which had under its care the Borough and Battersea Colleges and the Goldsmiths' Company's Technical and Recreative Institute, opened by the Prince in the old Royal Naval School's building at New Cross in 1891. It was maintained by the Company on 'entirely unsectarian and undenominational' lines, for the 'promotion of technical skill, knowledge, health and general well-being among men and women of the industrial, working and artisan classes . . . equal prominence being given to the education and recreative aspects of the work'. Its School of Art quickly achieved a high reputation. During the first year 4000 members, a quarter of them women, enrolled at 'Goldsmiths".[190]

When the Central Governing Body of the City Parochial Foundation was ready to begin its operations, enthusiasm for the polytechnic idea and some solid achievements on the ground ensured that there were few rivals for its funds and expertise. The open space societies, reflecting the same preoccupations with the dangers of unchecked urbanism, secured some share; but other and substantial claims were set aside. The Charity Commissioners favoured the polytechnic idea, not only as an 'educational and cultural panacea' for urban needs, but to attract further funds from the City Companies and civic circles, and it was made clear that grants would be made conditional on local response.[191]

The City Parochial Foundation therefore proposed grants of more than £160,000 from capital to the polytechnics, and in perpetuity an income of £22,500 a year for them with a further £5000 a year for technical institutions not yet specified. This was not without opposition, for the polytechnics were experimental, in fact only three (Regent Street, the People's Palace and Goldsmiths') were in operation, and a very high proportion of the funds available to the Central Governing Body would be committed in this way, especially if its income from capital were so drastically reduced. But apart from the intrinsic merits of the scheme, matters had gone too far, local fund-raising campaigns had been launched in, for example, South London and Chelsea, and the Companies had promised contributions. Parliament approved the Schemes in 1891.[192]

As this was one of the last major sources of capital and income to be released for education from the 'dead hand' of the past, and as this was at the beginning of the decade when the whole nature, development and purpose of secondary education was under national review, critical caution was understandable. It was quickly countered by the success of the polytechnics and the varied contribution they made to ideas and experience of secondary and tertiary education in the capital and its spreading suburbs. By 1896 there were eleven polytechnics with a roll of about 30,000 individual students, representing between 40,000 and 50,000 class entries. The Birkbeck Institute, the City of London College in Moorfields and the Woolwich Polytechnic, which had existed before in rather different forms, had been brought within the scheme, and as well as the three already functioning in 1891, the Borough, Battersea College, Chelsea (South-West), the Northern (Holloway) Polytechnics and the Northampton Institute, Clerkenwell, were all at work. The eleven represented a capital outlay of £500,000 and cost £120,000 a year to maintain.[193] Plans were being made to establish a North-Western Polytechnic in Paddington, and the Sir John Cass Institute was battling its way into existence in Aldgate and was soon taken under the polytechnic wing.[194] The Hackney Institute dated from the beginning of the next century.[195] In 1896 the eleven polytechnics then functioning were described as promoting the 'industrial skill, general knowledge, health and well-being of young men and young women belonging to the poorer classes', through classes in arts and sciences and their practical application, and in 'other branches and subjects of art, science, and literature and general knowledge', as well as public lectures, entertainments, exhibitions, instruction and practice in gymnastics and drill, and reading-rooms, libraries, museums, clubs and societies.[196]

Each institution had a local character and seemed to 'create its own public'. Regent Street and Goldsmiths' emphasized the social and recreational side, members did not have to attend educational classes. At Battersea and Chelsea only students could use the recreational facilities. Battersea was 'immediately surrounded by a population chiefly composed of clerks and artisans, estimated to number at least 150,000 within a radius of one mile', and was well served by rail and tramways. Even since its opening there had been considerable building of small houses and flats suitable for the working classes in its neighbourhood. Large chemical and engineering works were nearby. The Polytechnic had departments of mechanical engineering and building trades, chemistry and physics, art, electrical engineering, women's work, and a teaching staff of seventy. Its courses, in both day and evening classes, covered almost every sector of technology, science, art, music, domestic economy, commercial and general education, and the subjects ranged from elementary to the highest stages. Students came from almost every social class, the sexes met on an equal footing (domestic economy classes were only open to women). Women comprised about one-third of the enrolment. Most of the students were 'casual and temporary' with practical and utilitarian motives for study, but the institution tried to systematize courses and introduce 'subjects of general culture'.[197]

Battersea and Chelsea Polytechnics were only a little over a mile apart, but as well as being divided by the river, they appealed to 'very different constituencies'.[198] Chelsea, which was opened in 1896 and in its first session had 1553 students, quickly adapted itself 'rather to a clerkly population'.[199] The City of London College which with the Birkbeck Institute constituted the City Polytechnic College emphasized commercial subjects. The retirement in 1889 of Prebendary

Whittington from the honorary principalship, and his replacement as principal by Mr S. Humphries, symbolized the transition from the earlier, clerically directed phase of the College's history to the new interpretation encouraged by the polytechnic movement. Humphries had been educated at the Central Foundation School and at Cambridge, where he had been senior optime and then taken the Law Tripos. As well as practising in the Inner Temple he had lectured at the College in higher mathematics and commercial law. The commercial side of this College was further developed by E. H. Spencer in the early years of the next century.[200]

The educational doubts of 1891 must soon have been dispelled, but financial criticisms proved to be better founded. The cost of establishing this ring of polytechnics far exceeded the Central Parochial Fund's expectations or resources. The situation was saved by two factors: the enormous rise in the value of London property (the City Parochial Fund trebled between 1891 and 1950); and the arrival on the scene of the Technical Education Board (TEB) of the LCC in 1893.

It was clear that overlapping of functions and confusion would arise and the Central Governing Body proposed a conference with the Technical Education Board and the City and Guilds' Institute to co-ordinate their work. Under the chairmanship of Lord Reay of the Central Governing Body, with Sidney Webb and Llewellyn Smith representing the TEB, this set up the London Polytechnic Council, representing the three agencies. Later direct representation of the Goldsmiths' Institute and the People's Palace was added. Its functions were to inspect and if necessary examine polytechnics, to disseminate information and reports, and to 'make suggestions for the better co-ordination' of their work.[201] A policy of uniformity was disclaimed. The polytechnics had 'by a natural process of selection, endeavoured to adapt themselves to the requirements of their district . . .'. The only common stipulation was that there must be 'Industrial Classes at a Fee not exceeding 10*s* per annum for theoretical and practical work combined'. Any attempt to destroy variety and receptivity to the diversity of London would 'prove injurious to the educational interests of the county'.[202] From April 1894 the London Polytechnic Council provided supervision and regulation of this highly complex and fluid sector as well as stimulating and guiding expansion and experiment.[203] The governing bodies of individual polytechnics were reorganized to represent this partnership; that of Battersea for example included three representatives of the City Parochial Foundation, two each from the LCC and the London School Board, and three from the Technical Education Board. The financing of the polytechnics was equally complex. In 1895–6 Battersea received £2500 from endowment; £3166 and grants for equipment from the TEB; £1000 special grant from the Central Governing Body; £2254 from students' fees; and £653 and £1024 in grants from the Science and Art Department and the City and Guilds' Institute respectively.[204] The

Technical Education Board provided the highest proportion of the *revenue*, and this was general for all the institutions throughout the London Polytechnic Council's life. Heavy demands on equipment grants were clearly pressure from success, and the same applied to the need for costly building extensions.

Here City sources still played the larger part and the Council sent forward a resolution to the Central Governing Body urging them to seek Charity Commission authorization for £40,000 of this sum.[205] Between 1891 and 1951 the London polytechnics received about £25 million from the City Parochial Foundation.[206]

The foundations of the polytechnic system were therefore the result of a partnership stemming from legislation – the Bryce Act and the Technical Instruction Acts. The part played by the Technical Education Board was crucial and when the LCC was constituted the Local Education Authority in 1903, the London Polytechnic Council was wound up.[207] As is often the case, the inheriting institution has tended to take the whole credit. The claim made by Sidney Webb in 1903 that the LCC had 'laid down the lines of a highly complex system of specialised education, partly in the dozen great polytechnics, partly in its own technical institutes and art schools and culminating in the technical faculties of the reorganized University of London',[208] seems at least ungenerous and obscures almost as much as it discloses about the origins and development of an interesting sector of education.

The part which the polytechnics played in the development of secondary education is difficult to assess. Webb considered that they were entirely extra to the system of both secondary schools and university when neither exhibited 'any signs of growth'. The influence of the Technical Education Board, and of Webb in particular, strengthened their ties with the higher sector. His involvement in the reform of the University of London enabled him to steer polytechnic policy towards university level, and to use LCC grants as a means of persuading the university to take certain polytechnic courses within its system. But it is difficult to distinguish Webb's personal or ideological contribution from that of his colleagues. The London Polytechnic Council arranged an interview with Herschell, then Lord Chancellor and in charge of the Bill for the reconstruction of the University of London, and urged that a 'definite status should be given to the polytechnic classes' and that 'students who can study only in the evenings and regularly attend laboratory instruction should have access to a degree as internal students of the University. This was ... secured in the University Statutes, together with the direct representation of the polytechnic teachers on an academic council.'[209] This had repercussions on the status and salaries of polytechnic teachers.[210] From the beginning, advanced work and research were encouraged and by careful monitoring of examination results the Polytechnic Council recognized with satisfaction that there was a steady increase in the proportion of honours and advanced candidates. By 1899 these had nearly doubled overall, while ordinary level candidates had increased by 17 per cent and elementary ones by 2 per cent. The steady climb of the polytechnics to university status began from their very earliest years.[211]

The continuing experience of the twentieth century however has emphasized that education is rarely a tidy process, that its stages are difficult to distinguish clearly and to define. In the circumstances of the late nineteenth century, a large number of students had had no access to formal and systematic secondary education, and used the polytechnics either to fill gaps or to supply a whole stage of learning. In 1896 the London Polytechnic Council made a survey of classes other than those in sciences, art and technology. It is impossible to distinguish students studying such subjects for general interest from those who were aiming at filling 'secondary' gaps, and attempting qualifications which would usually have rounded off that stage; but it is clear that, for example, some of the 164 in the Latin class at Birkbeck (the largest apart from music with 188) were doing this, while the Matriculation class was 43 strong. At Chelsea classes were held for the Matriculation examination 'on the literary side' in Latin, English language, history and geography.[212] It was not only the students who were aware of the need for general or remedial education of this kind. The lecturers often recognized that progress in vocational and technical subjects was held back by its deficiencies. In 1898 the report of the electricity department at Chelsea deplored the lack of mathematical foundations but 'no amount of persuasion and advice moved the students to attend a mathematical class pure and simple'. The devices of an inclusive fee and of introducing an 'electrical flavour' into mathematical problems, had been successful. A 'working knowledge of the calculus' was needed by advanced students, and those at the elementary stage required 'a thorough knowledge of decimals, mensuration and simple equations'. Students therefore spent one of their three evenings a week on technical subjects, another on mathematical foundations, and the third on the science on which the technical subjects were based.[213] Such experience convinced the London Polytechnic Council that while examination results for London as a whole were good, 'it will be seen that the general education of a large number of students . . . is still very defective, and that they are consequently unable to profit as much as they should do by the special instruction they receive . . .'.[214] Polytechnic courses were not only supplying but revealing the needs of secondary instruction. This was one of the problems which arose on a national scale when the Technical Instruction Act began to be implemented. Some Technical Instruction Boards were obliged to open secondary schools to fill the need. The London Technical Education Board did not do so, but the secondary schools attached to the polytechnics filled the same purpose.

Not all polytechnics had such schools. By 1897 they had been established at Regent Street, Battersea, the Borough, South-West London

(Chelsea) and Woolwich Polytechnics and at the People's Palace. The nearness of Aske's Hatcham Schools, the Roan Schools and the Addey and Stanhope School made it unnecessary to establish one at the Goldsmiths' Institute, but in the Northern Polytechnic 'there is room for a good day school . . . especially since the Islington High School has been closed'. This was set up shortly afterwards. The schools were inspected by the Technical Education Board, and their inspector, C. W. Kimmins, helped in the planning and systematization of courses. Schools were set on their feet by the London Polytechnic Council's providing funds during early difficulties. The Borough Polytechnic Day School opened in 1897 'under the most favourable auspices'. There was a distinct want for it in the district, but at first it ran at a loss. It not only fed the college, but as the evening lecturers were employed there during the day this enabled the governors to pay higher salaries and get better teachers, who then devoted their whole time to the institution and took a keener academic and pastoral interest.[215] The London Polytechnic Council pursued an empirical policy towards the schools as a whole and decided in 1898 to postpone any formulation of conditions of grants until the imminent legislation on secondary education had been passed.[216]

In the meantime this remarkable group of schools illustrated the interaction of the polytechnic idea with other developments at secondary level. In them new and old ideas were consolidated into scholastic institutions which are recognizable as the 'county secondary schools' of the first half of the twentieth century. Yet some of the features of these schools which seem today to be most traditional, were in fact the most experimental and progressive.

The principal of the Battersea Polytechnic considered that these schools were one of the most interesting features of the polytechnics, an 'experiment in the coeducation of boys and girls', and a bridge between elementary and technical education. In Battersea there was no school of this character, and there was a need for better preparation for the college course. In 1894 the school opened with 45 boys who had passed through the elementary standards, and in that autumn became an Organized Science school qualifying therefore for the maximum grants from the Science and Art Department. The next year it was opened for girls. The fees were 10s a half-term including all books and materials. There were three scholarships a year to the Polytechnic and a liberal provision of junior scholarships from the Technical Education Board. By 1896 there were 100 boys and 39 girls; the average age of the senior division was fifteen and of the junior fourteen years three months.

A 'larger view of school life' was deliberately fostered. Thring's work at Uppingham was cited as the philosophic basis of the attitude to discipline and the organization and ethos of the school community. The teaching force came from the polytechnic but was imbued with the pastoral ideas which formed one of the bases of that movement. The school had an assembly for prayers conducted by the principal (a conscience clause operated), forms with form masters, pupils who were trusted and treated as if they had 'given up childish things'. They ran their own library, school magazine, field club for natural history rambles, debating society, and sports, even mixed inter-form hockey teams. All these things had arisen 'as a natural outcome of the carefully trained *esprit-de-corps* and general tone of the school . . .'. This tone had been built up carefully, and one master, 'a man of exceptional powers in this direction', had been recognized as 'out of school master' and acted as 'guide, counsellor and restraining influence'. The coeducational nature of the school had created little difficulty, though 'there is need for constant watchfulness of course'. Apart from coeducation, the chief experiment had been in applying to 'students from a different class', and teachers from a polytechnic, practices and ideas which would have been a matter of course in public or other high-class secondary schools.[217] The whole notion of organized leisure, of games played according to set rules, of the school community as a social, cultural, moral entity, had become part of a national ethos in remarkably few decades. That parents using these schools recognized and valued this is indicated by the application in 1903 of the school attached to the Northern Polytechnic for permission to raise its fees from £5 5s to £6 6s a year to meet the cost of a cricket ground; this increase would not militate against the success of the school in that neighboiurhood.[218]

By the end of the nineteenth century London had been provided with a reformed structure of government which by no means satisfied the more radical reformers, but which enabled 'functionalists' such as Sidney Webb to work out a theory of education recognizable as that of the first part of the twentieth century. Ideas of meritocracy, of education for national efficiency, of collectivism, have sometimes been termed 'social imperialism'.[219] The contribution of the City to this achievement was considerable; sometimes reluctant, sometimes voluntary, often altruistic as well as utilitarian, and usually enlightened when either self-interested or philanthropic purposes were being served, for in the last resort the wants and needs of what the critics were pleased to call turtledom and of the ordinary inhabitants and workers of the now vast metropolis coincided. A cricket ground in Tufnell Park, an 'Economic (summer) reading circle' in the Borough, a 'labour and reception bureau' at Regent Street, a Harriers' and Rambling Club in Battersea,[220] as well as classical and commercial schools, schemes for technical instruction, examinations in commercial education, symbolized for the increasing number of families concerned with secondary education the organic nature of civic society: threatened, distorted, ignored, but never extinguished in nineteenth-century London.

IX

'A directing and supervising intelligence'

London schools in the nineties

By the decade which led to the direct intervention of the State in secondary education, London's extent and 'horrible numerosity' was the wonder of the world. Yet to Henry James it still offered 'on the whole the most possible form of life'.[1] This unique and open city would have been wholly unrecognizable by the men of that thriving little town which had laid the foundation of its first schools. Its vitality and versatility however still placed vast economic and human resources at the disposal of education, and its shifting and confused demands stimulated and pressed upon its ramshackle and experimental provision of schooling. Perhaps by this period Londoners were beginning to get London into perspective. Panic reaction to the 'singularity of the urban achievement', to this 'climax of the Victorian city', was giving way to a more constructive and political response to the operations of the reformed structure of local government with which London was now provided. The population also became largely dependent on natural increase rather than devouring immigrants. In no other European country did urban population come so near to reproducing itself. This contributed to stability, yet this population was itself migratory, continually exporting numbers to its fringes.[2] The London which contributed to the shaping and launching of a national system of secondary schooling was predominantly a suburban London. A contemporary investigating one topographical sector noted that 'the dominant social factor observable is the steady northward movement of the people'.[3] A recent writer has likened this outward movement to 'an unstoppable lava flow; the encrustations that eventually cooled behind it seemed to take on the dull unworkability of pumice'.[4]

But the hardening may be exaggerated. Still it moved. Developments in transport both disclosed and facilitated the directions of the flow and the pattern on the ground. Older expansion had created 'walking suburbs', and only the more affluent and less regimented had travelled to the City by private transport or omnibuses. Railways served suburbs already created, especially south of the river.[5] The complexities of London's railway system were for the most part complete by the last decade of Victoria's reign, and the northern main lines were opening stations along their routes to serve areas already developed.[6] These suburban services north of the river were especially significant for

London's expansion, for example the GNR's low fares to Edgware, Alexandra Palace, Barnet and Enfield, the GER's also as far as Enfield. The workman's ticket took you further on the northern and eastern lines and this had a marked effect on London's social geography. By 1884 8000 people were using the GER's suburban trains daily. By 1900 the GNR provided about 30 million single journeys a year.[7] The era of the 'tubes' was also dawning as methods of deep tunnelling were discovered. The first was built in 1890 and by 1900 the London Bridge–Moorgate –Stockwell underground was constructed and later in the same year reached Clapham Common. Electrification was the key to this expansion. The Metropolitan and District lines were electrified from 1900. Suburban London was being given new arteries.[8] Socially and culturally such suburbs lay somewhere between the eras of Mr Pooter and John Betjeman, for while Metroland is a twentieth-century phenomenon, the old Holloway tied so closely emotionally as well as economically to the City began to have an outdated air.

The City, now largely uninhabited at night except for the very poorest trapped in its interstices, remained the hub of the transport system, and the West End was for most of the century protected from penetration by railways or from plebeian horse-trams when these began operating from the 1870s within the suburbs. The tubes opened up the West End as it was being transformed into a shopping and business centre, providing new kinds of employment.[9]

The suburbs which fed and fed upon the wealth at the centre, each with its own diverse and particular character, were all created partly by the typically English desire for rural surroundings, partly by the passion for social distancing. One-upmanship lay behind the constant movement of population. Education was of course an important element in maintaining these social distinctions and their economic base. Moreover the new suburbs, beyond the older fringe of genteel villas for more established older families and carriage-folk, contained a comparatively high proportion of young families. Even before 1902 Middlesex had a high demand for secondary education and an early-twentieth-century report of its Education Committee remarked of Southgate, 'as a general rule the class of house erected . . . is one from which scholars for Secondary Schools are likely to be obtained'.[10] The Bryce Report discerned that Surrey with its scattered towns varying from 20,000 to 30,000 inhabitants, stretching out and nearly meeting, connected by numerous lines of railway, had a higher proportion of population needing more than elementary education than most countries, making the provision of secondary education very important. The question was complicated by the social distinctions eagerly preserved between the 'villa population' and the local population, whose growth had been stimulated by the services and commodities demanded by the more affluent commuters and their households.[11]

This outward movement of population posed problems for London schools. In the middle decades of the century centrally placed schools were used as day schools by the middle classes. 'By any of the early trains you may meet the sons of those of them who live in the suburbs coming up to the schools . . . Breakfast is early that the boys may be off . . .'. Lingen, who gave this evidence to Taunton, approved of this on moral and social grounds, and thought that the outward movement of King's or University College Schools, Westminster, St Paul's, or Charterhouse would be 'greatly against the interest of the classes who use them to such purpose'.[12] Witnesses before the Clarendon Commission had been less favourable. The high master of St Paul's thought boys were fatigued – travelling two hours a day was too much for a little boy, and it was worse when they used the omnibuses and got wet ('They do not like to be shut up'). Lyttelton, with an equal discernment of the universal reaction of schoolboys to all forms of public transport, also asked whether 'it is apt to over-excite them?'[13] In 1870 a schoolmaster complained of the distances his boys travelled to Merchant Taylors' – only 3 of his 48 in class were from walking distance, others came even from beyond the suburbs, from Gravesend, Erith, Ewell, Sutton, Crawley. They learnt their lessons in the train and were subject to many corrupting influences from forward young women or profane talk by young clerks.[14] The system was somewhat eased by the old style of informal boarding – some houses catered for boys from several schools. One Clarendon witness described his migratory years at Merchant Taylors', boarding in Doctors' Commons, or out at Wimbledon, or for a short time with his mother in Highgate. 'It was very much the practice . . . so that instead of exercise they had travelling in a railway carriage.'[15]

It was the new attitude to adolescence and its emphasis on health and sports which eventually caused the outward migration of these schools. Not only did travel deprive boys of the time for games, but central sites were too cramped to provide for them. Boarding-schools were particularly affected. Charterhouse, under the energetic Dr Haig Brown, moved to Surrey in 1872. He became schoolmaster while the Clarendon Commissioners were still sitting, and seems to have believed in the removal from the time of his appointment. He had to fight hard to gain his point, and the master, Archdeacon Hale, a kind of one-man home of lost causes, was one of his stronger opponents. The matter became political, with Lord Derby and Gladstone ranged on opposite sides, but was eventually resolved by Act of Parliament. After the move to Godalming numbers rose dramatically.[16] King's College School moved to Wimbledon in 1897,[17] University College School to Hampstead early in the next century – the move had first been proposed in 1888 by the great Dr Eve, when already a high proportion of its boys came from the north-western suburbs.[18]

The two greatest transplants, from the point of view of London's life and history, were Christ's Hospital and St Paul's, both part of the very fabric of the City. Christ's Hospital, huddled in a 'colony of tenements, small houses and shops and public walks' between Newgate and St Bartholomew's Hospital, was gradually over the centuries welded into 'a great coherent whole', the last rebuilding beginning in 1795 and continuing well into the era of reform – the 'Grecians' Cloister' dated from 1836.[19] Citizens peered fascinated through the railings at the boys, the 'Blues'. These were part of the sights of London, regarded with real affection, and always hoping, when allowed out on a 'ticket', to meet 'the Bob Gent' who pressed a shilling into the hand, 'in memory of Charles Lamb'.[20] The school and its ceremonies were part of the City's life – 'Public Suppings' in the Lent Term, the St Matthew's Day procession to Christ Church and then the Mansion House for the dole and feast from the Lord Mayor, and so forth. 'Any boy who had sufficient assurance to present himself to the Archdeacon of London could obtain a pass . . . to ascend at least as high as the "Stone Gallery" of the Cathedral.'[21] Relations were not of course always smooth and there were some notable scandals and quarrels about rights of patronage which were to some extent resolved by Act of Parliament in 1782, but in general the City regarded Christ's Hospital with pride.[22]

It could not however escape the attention of the nineteenth-century reformers. The Charity Commisioners reported cautiously on it in 1840; the Taunton Commissioners placed it first on their list of 'Eight of the Largest Endowments'. 'Is it the best possible application of a net income of £40,000 or £50,000 to have a large middle-class boarding-school in the heart of London?' the Report asked. Its recommendations were predictable. Christ's Hospital 'is a thing without parallel in the country, and *sui generis*', but admission was never confined to London and the school could not 'be considered as the exclusive property of the metropolis'. Londoners might 'fairly claim a share', but the London school, and its Hertford branch for girls and little boys, should be transformed into boarding- and day schools filled with scholars entering by competitive examination, and with a modernized governing body appointed by the Lord Mayor and the Crown. A greater share of the endowment should be used for girls – the number of whom, 18, compared poorly with 1192 boys (large and small).[23]

Nothing happened until 1877 when a new Commission made further enquiries and eventually from this stemmed a Scheme for a boys' boarding-school for 700 'to be maintained within a convenient distance from the City of London', and a girls' school for 350 to use and adapt the Hertford buildings. This was approved in 1891, but ten years' battle lay ahead. Controversy arose over the interpretation of 'convenient distance'. Wimbledon was proposed but was said to be too suburban and populous. Then a large Horsham site was found. It was immediately claimed that this would 'destroy the metropolitan character of the foundation . . .' and travelling would be a cruel imposition of expense on working-class parents. The London Brighton and South Coast Railway

Bluecoat boys plead with the Duke of Sussex to be moved to green fields, 1870 responded swiftly with promises of a new station and cheap fares. Financial objections and gloomy prognostications about the water supply were also countered, and an outbreak of scarlet fever which closed the school in 1893 clinched the matter, though the Duke of Cambridge, as President, continued to moan and mutter. Dr Bell, Master of Marlborough and formerly of Christ's Hospital, tried to be educationally reassuring. Under the Scheme and on its new site 'drawing into its class-rooms the pick of the elementary schools of London, and of the Endowed Schools of the Kingdom, its future reputation will be such that Blues will find a better welcome than ever in the public services and in professional and commercial life'.[24] Dr Haig Brown, an 'Old Blue' and governor, who had so successfully moved the Charterhouse to Surrey, was active in promoting the move. Christ's Hospital eventually assembled in its new buildings at Horsham in 1902. The boys of the Mathematical School no longer took a separate place in the school but were provided with special classes and continued to wear a distinguishing badge.[25] The preparatory boys were also transferred, leaving the girls' school at Hertford to develop its own life.[26]

St Paul's moved to Hammersmith in 1884. Throughout the nineteenth century it had preserved its essential character as a City school. Before the mid century its sixteenth-century routine had to some extent increased the number of boarders, but when by 1862 school hours had been brought into line with contemporary practice, a nine-to-four day, boys 'once again tended to be drawn from purely London homes'.[27] The connection between school and City was zealously preserved. But its site was hopelessly constricted and its huge revenues had no scope; from 1860 the idea of removing the school was canvassed. The Mercers' Company contemplated a move to the country, perhaps of buying the site and buildings of the East India Company's school at Haileybury. But this was rejected; the Clarendon Commission recommended another site in London. Although the Mercers were successful in securing the exclusion of St Paul's from the Public Schools' Bill of 1865, this meant that it fell into the jurisdiction of the Endowed Schools and Charity Commissioners and this undoubtedly prolonged negotiations for a new Scheme and the removal.[28] By 1879 it was possible to buy a site on the borders of Hammersmith and Fulham, known as Dead Man's Fields, and here Alfred Waterhouse erected one of his characteristic red and writhing educational structures, with all the classrooms facing away from the sun (the High Master 'inclined to the view that heat was an enemy of an active brain . . .').[29]

This High Master was Frederick Walker who as a boy had been at St Saviour's, Southwark, and had already demonstrated his conception of civic education by his work at Manchester where, as High Master since 1859, he had persuaded its citizens to restore their Grammar School. To some of his sometimes harassed staff he was 'the Man from Manchester'. His technique was one of 'energetic ubiquity'; asked how he achieved his success he replied, 'I walked about.' There may have been rather more to it than this but, by whatever means, he brought St Paul's to a standard and range of scholarship which was unparalleled, and his huge bearded awe-inspiring figure must have galvanized many of the 600 boys to reach heights they had not contemplated unassisted. This was a demonstration of the academic potential of education worthy of a metropolis. Walker was unconcerned about the social origin of his boys. 'Madam', he said to a pretentious woman who was worried about the exclusiveness of the school, 'so long as your son behaves and his school fees are paid we shall ask no embarrassing questions about your social status.'[30] But the tenacity of St Paul's in preserving its academic standing had social consequences. The fees and the curriculum were the problems. From 1893 a new Scheme fixed fees at £15 a year and proposed that one-third of the foundation scholarships should be reserved for boys either from other endowed schools with low fees or for those who had been for three years at a public elementary school within the Metropolitan area. This plan had to be abandoned as it was maintained that it would lower the academic standards of what *The Times* called 'the greatest, the most successful and the most popular of London day schools'. 'Popular' here must be translated in strictly scholastic terms. In 1900 a solution of a kind was reached: one-third of the scholarships were to be weighted to modern subjects and Greek was not to be required.[31]

Not all schools, however, moved to the suburbs. The City of London School and the Central Foundation Schools demonstrated the continuing viability of civic education, St Olave's was erecting its new building near Tower Bridge as late as the 1890s,[32] and Merchant Taylors' moved only into the vacated Charterhouse buildings, getting them as a bargain for £90,000. St Clement Danes did not move till the next century. Westminster, true to its court tradition, remained where it was although the Clarendon Commission had recommended its removal to the country.[33]

That the educational vitality and needs of the urban centre still held for varying social and academic levels was demonstrated by the school which moved into the premises vacated by King's College School. In 1875 Mr William Braginton's classes training for the competitive boy clerks' examination of the second and third grade of the Civil Service were 'taken into connexion' by King's College as evening classes. In 1892 day classes were begun by candidates for 'boy clerkships' and 'boy copyists' in the public offices. These classes had to be housed in premises near Blackfriars Bridge, later in the Waterloo Road, and developed into a 'high grade commercial school'. More than 50 per cent of these appointments, and others of similar grade such as telegraph learners, excise and customs posts, assistant surveyors of taxes, were secured by its pupils. In 1895 125 appointments were offered, 1100 candidates entered, and Mr Braginton's pupils got 88 of them. When

King's College School moved, these day classes were installed in its vacant basement and became known as the Strand School. In 1900 this was recognized by the LCC for holding county scholarships and later for bursaries for intending teachers, and by 1907 it had 804 pupils. It moved to Brixton in 1913 as a highly successful general secondary school, with a former Rugby master, an Oxford mathematician, as its headmaster, and Cambridge scholars on its staff.[34]

This school in origin was partly an Anglican enterprise, and although at this period national attention was much focused on the need to apply state funding to education at all levels, older methods of financing schools remained active in London. Some endowments were still being redeployed and aided both by new-style private benefactions and the new local government structures. The Isleworth Grammar School seems to have been born of a conversation on the train to Waterloo between Mr William Regester, Chairman of the Middlesex Technical Education Committee, and Mr Andrew Pears. From about 1883 the old Blue Coat School had aimed at secondary schooling to about fourteen or fifteen in its Upper Department, and the Borough Road Training College, now in the former International School Buildings,[35] planned to use this as a practising school. Lack of funds frustrated this until wealth from soap made it possible. Pears produced the site, the British and Foreign School Society had financial responsibility, Blue Coat funds supported 20 scholars, and management was shared between society, charity and county council. From 1895, and from 1897 in its new building, the school provided modern secondary and technical education, 'suited to the needs of the locality', and students from the college used it for carefully restricted practice and observation. It was a risky, vague experiment which 'fell wretchedly between the old era of richly endowed grammar schools and the new era of the twentieth-century "county school"'. Three years of difficulty and negotiation ended in its being handed over to the Middlesex County Council in 1906. For ten years it was the only secondary school in West Middlesex, except Hampton Grammar School,[36] and while its scholarship holders came from the parish, fee-paying boys came from far afield – Ashford, Bedfont, Feltham, Staines, Brentford, Ealing, Acton, Chiswick, Clapham Junction. Its complicated and shaky origins did not detract from its educational efficiency and usefulness.[37]

Soap and compost: domestic cleanliness and a reinterpretation of London's environs' long tradition of market gardening: a similar injection of wealth from the new consumer economy enabled the Rutlish School at Merton to make a like contribution to secondary education. A foundation of 1687 for putting poor children to prentice was re-established by a Charity Commission Scheme of 1895, on the initiative of Mr John Innes, as a school for boys from ten to seventeen, to teach science and 'subjects usually taught in middle-class schools'. Plumbing, wood-carving and the use of tools were included. The Surrey

County Council played its part here and its Technical Instruction Board and also Science and Art Department funds enabled Rutlish to be constituted as a 'Science School'. From 1897 the headmaster was Alfred Disney, from Trinity Cambridge, and with a London BSc. He had been headmaster of Islington High School for ten years and brought Rutlish School to a high state of efficiency – by 1905 it held 202 boys and was giving a general secondary education.[38]

Financing by proprietors still played a precarious part in the provision of secondary schooling, especially for girls. The Boys' Public Day School Company, however, was much less successful and in London its Kentish Town School, opened in 1883, had a very short life.[39] The Church Schools' Company continued Anglican provision by this means from 1883, but only their girls' schools had much success nationally. In the metropolis they were unsuccessful for both sexes – their Kensington Park School, founded in 1896, was sold to St Mary's College in 1904 and soon closed, and the girls' Stoke Newington School (1886) did reasonably well until it was killed by the Skinners' Company School. The Tottenham girls' school was sold to the Drapers' Company.[40] Booth was critical of this method of providing schools for London. Inability to adapt to changing needs was a 'fatal flaw . . . to the self-supporting proprietary school as a link in our educational machinery'.[41] London however had profited greatly earlier in the century and did gain one new school by this means in this *fin de siècle* period, one moreover which conveys its exact flavour – King Alfred's School, Hampstead. This was founded by a society incorporated in 1898, whose members were required to subscribe as long as their children were in the school, while for £100 life members could nominate a pupil for half fees at this or the other schools which were planned, though only one was in fact set up. Fees were quite high – £10 10s a term at secondary age – and the schools, as in earlier proprietary schemes, were eventually to be self-supporting. The objects of the school were progressive – 'to give practical expression to the best theories of Education extant . . . such as [those of] Pestalozzi, Froebel, Herbart, Herbert Spencer, Louis Compton Miall, and others working on similar lines'. Co-operation rather than competition, coeducation, absence of punishment and rules, the cultivation of a sense of beauty and 'what is comely and valuable in the world, in art, in literature, in human character', of 'working power', interest, curiosity were stressed, and great emphasis was placed on 'bodily health and vigour'. Vegetarian dinners were provided but no religious teaching – this was considered 'unsuitable as an element in the education of children' – Jaeger underwear and brown bread no doubt were considered more important. The second headmaster was John Russell, formerly assistant at University College School in this secular tradition. Supporters included Sir James Crichton Browne, the doctor who had roused the famous controversy about over-pressure on schoolchildren,[42] Professors Miall and Findlay, representatives from the

British Child Study Association, the Childhood Society, the Royal Sanitary Institute, and Cecil Sharp, whose very name conveys that epoch of the arts and crafts movement, folk art, and *art nouveau*.[43]

King Alfred's School clearly catered for a very particular clientèle, and some private schools also fulfilled this purpose. The function of the majority continued to be the relief of 'pressure on the weak points of the major educational structure' and to provide a 'safety valve'. The debate about the status of private schools was very much an open question.[44] Such schools still swarmed and came and went. In 1891 a well-informed witness guessed that of the 2300 or 2400 schools (elementary as well as secondary) in London and its suburbs, considerably less than one-tenth were public, endowed or proprietary schools.[45] The Private Schools' Association was formed when this sector felt the threat of state intervention, both central and local, and no longer had confidence in the College of Preceptors. This, by its collaboration with the endowed and proprietary schools, its policy over teachers' registration, and its admission of elementary teachers, had failed as a pressure group for the private sector.[46] Any hopes of private enterprise providing an adequate *system* of secondary schooling faded and a largely defensive policy was now adopted, to 'unite the members in a common bond, to protect the interests of the profession, and to hold periodic meetings . . . for the discussion of educational topics, more especially such as relate to the position and status of the private schoolmaster'. The Association seems to have dated from a dinner held in the Holborn Restaurant in 1878, but was not securely in being until 1883, and was slow in building up membership. In 1891 this was only 177, but after that interest quickened. By 1894 there were 600 members, the Association was called to give evidence to the Bryce Commission, it founded its own journal, *Secondary Education*, and had a further spurt of growth before the legislation of 1902 – by the following year membership was 1500, though this was partly the result of admitting assistant teachers.[47]

There was a similar drawing together as an interest group at this same period by the preparatory schools. The ingredients of a system of such schools had long been present in London and its suburbs, but earlier in the century the characteristic school combined preparation for professions, public schools and universities. Often however such schools were used more for younger boys. At Burlington House, Isleworth, attended by R. L. Stevenson for a short time in the early 1860s the 'small fry' greatly outnumbered the 'middling size' and the 'big boys'.[48] As the age of entry to public schools rose, with the standards required, the number of specialist schools grew. Arnold preferred not to take boys before twelve or thirteen. An outstanding example of a successful school of this type was Temple Grove at Sheen, whose headmaster, O. C. Waterfield, a former fellow of King's and master at Eton, was examined by the Taunton Commission. His school had already been established for sixty years, and had 100 boys, almost all being prepared for public schools or the Navy. He would not keep boys after fifteen, they then needed more liberty and would require an unfair share of teaching – morever it was morally 'desirable to enforce a strict separation of ages'. It was to Dr Waterfield that Benson, when headmaster of Wellington, entrusted his eldest son, who won a Winchester scholarship. Another school of similar standards and prestige was the Eagle House at Hammersmith from 1820, in Wimbledon from 1860. From 1833 to 1847 the Reverend E. Wickham was headmaster and he restricted boys to preparatory age – at one time he had seven future public-school headmasters under his charge and he seems to have imbued them with a belief in compulsory games as part of a manly education.[49] Other schools in the London orbit were more modest in reputation. In 1855 Miss Innes opened a school in Highbury Park to prepare boys under twelve for the public schools, such as Islington Proprietary School.[50] In 1879 at the St John's Wood Preparatory School for the Sons of Gentlemen the 'terms correspond to Eton and Harrow'.[51] Hampstead was a favourite district, and as early as 1860 'two or three preparatory schools for boys divided the field'. One opened in 1860 and still prepared for 'professional life' in 1872, but after its removal to Heath Mount in 1876 under Mr Goldsmith, who had been a public schoolmaster, it prepared for public schools alone, teaching classics, mathematics and French.[52] The Harrow neighbourhood also acted as a hothouse for the newer kind of school. In 1872 Harrow-on-the-Hill Preparatory School helped boys to gain a 'good position' at entrance to Harrow and other public schools, and at Pinner Mrs Martin prepared for 'Eton, Harrow, Rugby, and the London Public Schools'.[53] By 1879 there were two more such schools.[54] Some schools opened their own preparatory departments – for example University College School in 1891 at Hampstead in Holly Hill House.[55] Dulwich College Preparatory School (a separate institution) was founded in 1885 with 10 boys. By 1914 it had 400.[56]

From 1892–3 the Preparatory Schools' Association helped to give coherence of aim and policy. By 1900 competition had done its work, 'no eligible spot remained unoccupied', and the supply of boys was said to be running out. Sir Michael Sadler, who took Heddon Court, Rosslyn Hill, as a case study, considered that preparatory-school tuition was of a secondary character. Children from state schools could rarely compete against boys already advanced in academic subjects, especially languages.[57] The private sector of education had responded to threats from the public sector by closing its ranks, providing an enclosed system of its own.

It was not only impending enquiry and legislation on secondary education which was seen as a threat, but the progress and vitality of elementary and technical education. After 1870 the London School Board began its work and in a remarkably short time reached the boundary between elementary and secondary education – a boundary the cause of dispute which reverberates to this day.

Compared with the great centres of the North and Midlands, London was slow off the mark in creating any kind of higher grade schools, and still had none at the time of the Cross Commission.[58] There were several reasons – the sheer volume and intensity of the need for basic elementary education in inner London, the comparatively good supply of secondary schools, the triumph of the 'Economical Party' at the School Board elections. When the number of London children staying on through the 'Standards' grew steadily, when the success of Board schools increased the appetite for education, especially in the upper working and lower middle classes, the issue became prominent. One London sub-inspector told the Cross Commission that he considered that ambitious parents would keep their children at school till fifteen or sixteen – 'if they found they were receiving instruction that would benefit them, they would make a sacrifice . . .'.[59] The emerging Progressive Party on the Board pressed the case. Lyulph Stanley especially became its champion and in 1881 a committee recommended a system of selected schools with higher classes. Political wrangling further delayed action until 1886 when the number of pupils in Standard V or above had increased to 12.9 per cent of the total number and their teaching was posing a serious problem to the schools. By 1887 the London School Board at last committed itself to a policy of providing 'upper standard schools ten years after the idea was first mooted'.[60]

But these 'central' schools, drawing their pupils from assigned 'feeder schools', were not fully effective. Schools were unwilling to send on their best pupils, classes were too small to justify properly paid teachers. They served mainly skilled workers' childen though the LSB did pursue the fairly radical policy of keeping the weekly charge to parents no higher than other elementary schools – Stanley declared that 'none of its schools shall be class schools' – and the higher standard schools were made free when fees were abolished in 1891.[61]

Progress was uneven and slow. By the end of the century better staffing, competitive entry to ensure 'scholars with the capacity and inclination to benefit from advanced instruction and whose parents had expressed their support for an extended schooling', better structuring of the system of schools, even the establishment of some purpose-built higher grade schools 'along provincial lines', had enabled the LSB in this respect to substantiate its reputation for progressive educational practice.[62]

Were they secondary schools in all but name? As early as 1893 the Education Department suspected the legality of such provision.[63] Such was the bitter complaint of the private sector. The organ of the Private Schools' Association quoted an article from the *Finchley Free Press* on 'Secondary Education for Nothing', describing the Long Lane Board School, an 'Organized Science School' whose aim was to give a 'good thorough secondary education', with equal attention given to English and commercial subjects. Parents should give prompt consideration to the opportunity.[64] These 'upper standard' or 'higher grade' schools could only legitimately draw their funds from the local rates if they were classed as giving 'elementary' instruction. The more liberal Codes allowed grants from the Education Department for a wider curriculum of both 'class' and 'specific' subjects and these London schools were thus able to offer a curriculum 'overlapping between Primary and Secondary Education'.[65] Subjects were to be chosen according to the needs of the neighbourhood – boys in Limehouse, for example, took magnetism and electricity because of the proximity of the Silvertown Electrical Engineering Works. For London as a whole, French increased in importance, especially for girls, and so did shorthand, botany and chemistry.[66] But the most important source of revenue was the Science and Art Department, and for London schools, as compared with those in industrial areas, these grants distorted the curriculum away from the more literary and linguistic studies which were needed for commercial employment. In 1899 just when such schools were to be disallowed, the LSB drew up a scheme, supported by the TEB, for higher elementary education more suited to the 'city of clerks'.[67] Claims by the LSB to educate pupils even up to university standards, and its opposition to the TEB's application to become the sole authority for Science and Arts Grants in its area, determined Gorst, at the Committee of Council on Education, to destroy such pretensions. The result was the Elementary School Minute of 1900 which reduced higher grade to higher elementary schools, restricted in curriculum, intake, age-range, and prevented from competing with secondary schools. The challenge of the LSB in evening classes was dealt with through the action of the District Auditor, Cockerton, disallowing expenditure at the Camden School of Art from rates raised solely for elementary education. The judgment was eventually upheld in the Court of Appeal (1901). The very success of the LSB led to the abolition of the school boards in the Education Act of 1902. A London row about elementary schooling had shaped the national system of education at all levels. This whole complex, disreputable and highly controversial episode brings up in acute form the question of the educational status of the higher grade schools.

Co-operation between the London School Board and the Technical Education Board was precarious. Over the previous decade the TEB had been able to bring pressure to bear through its scholarship system,[68] 'the best means yet in existence for enabling the clever boy or girl to climb up from Board School to the University'.[69] These scholarships were awarded from 1893 and from the beginning Board schools regularly won 95 per cent of them, and a high proportion of these successes came from the higher grade schools. 'Upper standard' Schools which had a low success rate were usually demoted by the School Board.[70]

Scholarships could also be held at such higher grade elementary schools as the TEB approved, and this, as much as their curriculum and quality of teaching, was seen as a threat by the endowed secondary schools. These TEB scholarships were giving them a new lease of life[71] and 'it is not surprising that London's grammar schools felt the pressure of the competition'. More dangerous from the LSB's point of view were the growing tensions between it and the TEB and these were eventually to destroy the School Boards – here London reflected and perhaps exacerbated and precipitated a national crisis.[72]

The London School Board of course only covered part of the open and sprawling London of the end of the nineteenth century, and to see more truthfully how higher grade schools operated in the emerging secondary school system it is well to balance the inner city with the suburb. Tottenham provides a useful example. It was typical of suburban growth, developing from a rural retreat for the mercantile gentry to a prosperous middle-class village, and then rapidly, with the coming of cheap railway travel, into a densely populated working-class area, with skilled artisans able to afford to travel to work or use the horse-trams for local journeys, and more impoverished workers increasing in numbers as the new population engendered more casual and low-paid work.[73] Wood Green, its more hilly 'suburb', where cheap terrace housing was inappropriate to the terrain, remained largely free of the less prosperous and more precarious families. In 1870 the ratepayers were still predominantly middle-class, and stoutly resisted the setting up of a School Board for nearly ten years until in 1879 the Education Department, finding the parish short of 2000 school places, ordered the formation of a Board. When elected it largely represented the supporters of the voluntary schools.[74]

Here the chief point of interest is the speed with which demand for higher grade elementary education emerged in this suburb – four months after the Board's formation, the matter is recorded in its minutes.[75] Secondary education was ill-served. Tottenham Grammar School was now provided with a Scheme which made it largely fee-paying.[76] The example of successful higher grade schools in other parts of the country was before the eyes of the local ratepayers. In spite of protests from the private school interest the matter was pressed forward. Wood Green was decided upon as the site and in 1884 two higher grade schools, one for boys in the Trinity Road Wesleyan Chapel Hall, and one for girls in a Presbyterian Sunday School, were opened.[77]

The fortunes of these schools were uneven until in 1896 they were established in new buildings where 900 children could be accommodated. What is significant here is that from the outset these schools set out to provide a higher kind of education for a higher cost – 9d a week – and this in spite of much opposition from the Education Department which wanted a more open kind of school. The local Board managed to get round the problem and justify the use of public money by providing scholarships from what it unashamedly called the 'Ordinary Public Elementary Schools'. In this way was laid on for the lower-middle-class and more prosperous working-class parents of Tottenham and Wood Green a curriculum which included as well as the 'usual Elementary subjects', 'Latin, French, Physiology, Euclid, Algebra, Composition, History,' etc.[78] Soon the school was entering pupils for the Pupil-Teacher examinations, County Council and other scholarships, Oxford and Cambridge Locals, and setting its sights towards London Matriculation. By the end of the century no school in the London orbit was more successful in preparing pupils for London employment – 'for some years [it] presented some of the most efficient and best pupils who ever entered for the London Chamber of Commerce examinations'.[79] The Wood Green Higher Grade School was, throughout its history, firmly in control of the middle classes and this makes explicit what has been implied even for the London higher grade schools, that it is dangerous to claim that these schools were 'citadels of radicalism' or even that they might have extended secondary education 'on an open-ended basis'[80] to any significant extent. In other parts of the country some of the higher elementary schools into which higher grade schools were transposed after the crisis of the Cockerton Judgment were later to become county secondary schools. In Middlesex, short of secondary schools, this happened to the higher grade schools at Finchley and Hornsey. London, however, had a relatively good supply of reformed endowments,[81] and schools attached to the polytechnics.

Another type of school engendered on the borderlines of secondary and elementary education was the pupil-teacher centre. The LSB was from 1874 attending to the 'conditions under which their pupil-teachers were appointed and taught', and by 1882 a scheme for pupil-teacher schools was in operation – improved two years later by reducing over-pressure on instruction out of school hours. In London junior pupil-teachers attended a centre for part of each day and on Saturday mornings, the seniors on two half days and Saturday mornings.[82] Improvement in performance in the Queen's scholarship examination was proof of the advantages of the scheme, and the 'centre system' was considered to have attracted candidates from beyond the elementary school circle, young people of more liberal education, who had attended secondary schools.[83]

The response of the voluntary sector to this developing demand for more than elementary education was hesitant. Faced with the financial difficulties of keeping up with the Board schools, the National Society criticized a 'system of advanced or secondary instruction under cover of rules which profess to provide for elementary education'. Grants for specific subjects such as Latin, French, botany, animal physiology, chemistry, physics, were unsuitable for elementary schools and hindered the need to develop secondary education. Reasonable assistance should be given to promising pupils to 'obtain a superior education', schools should be graded and children should be able to pass from one grade to another with scholarships.[84] In London St Thomas Charterhouse, Latymer's School at Hammersmith, the Boutcher and Raines Foundation Schools, operated as higher grade schools.[85] Endowments helped other voluntary elementary schools to keep pace with higher aspirations. In Bermondsey Bacon's School, founded in 1703, was enlarged and rebuilt in 1891 with a curriculum 'adapted to the changing requirements of education', and in 1899 attracted further endowments.[86] When the higher elementary schools were under discussion in 1901, the National Society took the line that they should not aspire to a secondary curriculum and that too much science was proposed. Staffing and laboratory equipment would be too expensive.[87]

Their long tradition of teacher training equipped the Churches better to meet the need for pupil-teacher centres. St Aloysius Convent School in St Pancras began such classes in 1893.[88] The Islington Convent of Notre Dame de Sion High School began as a pupil-teacher centre.[89] The first Anglican example was proposed by the Church Schools' Union of Lambeth, Newington and Kennington under the chairmanship of Canon Charles Edward Brooke. The Union being hesitant, Canon Brooke took personal action and circulated the managers of the local voluntary schools announcing that 'Central Classes for Girl Pupil-Teachers' were to be held in Longfield Hall, Camberwell, under 'the superintendence of the lady principal, Miss Evers, LLA St Andrews, who has great experience in the training of pupil-teachers', having been a governess in training colleges and senior assistant at another centre. The Centre opened in January 1898 with 30 students. In 1904 it was converted into a Church of England secondary school, then called Kennington School for Girls. Later it adopted its founder's name.[90]

Other agencies which were both sustaining and challenging the older kinds of secondary school in this formative decade were the Technical Education Boards.[91] In inner London the TEB was able to act through existing schools, sometimes sharply redefining their character. In Surrey lack of suitable schools obliged its Technical Instruction Committee to establish schools – Richmond County School was one of these, opened in 1896, with an annual grant of £450 and the services of a modern languages master. It earned good grants from the Science and Art Department, and charged Surrey pupils a £6 fee; £10 for ex-county pupils.[92] Richmond would perhaps scorn to be called a suburb of London. That most suburban of counties, Middlesex, faced the same problem of dearth of schools. Its Technical Education Committee was one of the last to be formed, in 1893. It had strong City representation, which helped to shape its concept of education – its members saw Middlesex as a dormitory for London.[93] Unlike London it was not confronted with a powerful and unified School Board, but with a number of small and weak ones – only Tottenham was strong enough to criticize its policy. But when in 1897 the Science and Art Department Directory enabled TEBs to become the sole recognized authority for the awarding of its grants and Middlesex used this as a way of asserting 'its exclusive powers in the post elementary field', Tottenham's objections were to no avail. Schools which were recognized for such grants under the 'Clause VII' included the Enfield and Tottenham Grammar Schools, the Tottenham High School for Girls (Drapers' School), Tottenham Collegiate School, St Ignatius College, Tottenham, and the practising school of St Katherine's Training College, as well as two schools of art at Chiswick and Hornsey.[94]

The dependence of boys and girls in the Middlesex suburbs on London schools can be seen from the operation of the TEB's scholarship system from 1893–1903.[95]

*Schools attended by Middlesex scholarship-holders
1893–1903*

Boys	Numbers attending
Owen's School Islington	64
United Westminster School	27
Enfield Grammar School	13
Tottenham Grammar School	9
Cowper Street Schools	9
Tiffins School Kingston	6
Isleworth County School	6
Latymer Upper School Hammersmith	4
Stationers' Company School Hornsey	3
Polytechnic School Regent Street	3
City of London School	3
Tottenham Polytechnic Day School	2
John Lyon School Harrow	2
William Ellis School	1
St Marylebone Grammar School	1
Girls	
Skinners' Company School Stamford Hill	9
Tottenham High School (Drapers')	5
Owen's School Islington	3
North London Collegiate School	2
Queen's Park Institute	1
Latymer Upper School Hammersmith	1
Church High School Richmond	1
Brondesbury High School	1
Tottenham Polytechnic Day School	1

This drawing away of able pupils to London schools was considered a 'waste of resources' which did not 'benefit Middlesex schools', and it was only slowly and reluctantly that the TEB created a system of its own schools. Grants to some existing grammar schools rescued them from decay or extinction – for example, Tottenham, Enfield.[96] An interesting case was Hampton Grammar School. Throughout the century its fortunes had fluctuated and it had difficulties in dividing its endowments between elementary and more ambitious education. By 1896 it had dwindled to only 12 boys. Its reluctance to change from a first-grade classical school to one offering technical and science subjects, in an area with low population and a poor train service, had brought it to near ruin. A new Charity Commission Scheme enabled it to qualify for County Council aid, and from 1896 fees were reduced to £6, science and commercial subjects were taught, science and modern languages masters appointed, and a physics laboratory built. By 1902 it was able to apply for status as a 'school of science' under the Board of Education regulations, and by 1906 there were 195 boys.[97] The John Lyon School at Harrow was given science apparatus by the Middlesex TEB and a grant towards a physics laboratory in 1897.[98] The newly opened Isleworth School was also aided.[99] The crucial importance of the TEB in seeing schools through this crisis period can be seen from the demise and rebirth of the Latymer foundation at Edmonton.[100] The table shows the new balance of financial resources of the aided schools.[101]

Income from endowment, school fees, County Council and Science and Art Department grants 1897–1900

	School	Endowment	Fees	County Council	Science & Art Dept
		£ s d	£ s d	£ s d	£ s d
1897	Enfield	158 9 5	941 16 0	200 0 0	41 15 0
	Hampton	239 13 3	105 17 0	—	—
	Isleworth	100 0 0	508 10 0	100 0 0	—
	Tottenham	279 5 0	1002 10 0	200 0 0	111 7 6
1900	Enfield	252 2 9	987 8 0	300 0 0	38 10 0
	Hampton	130 1 5	358 11 8	300 0 0	125 18 6
	Isleworth	75 0 0	641 10 6	300 0 0	52 14 6
	Tottenham	243 13 3	1090 5 0	300 0 0	—

To some extent the existence of such schools excused the Middlesex TEB from vigorous action and from seeing 'the need for secondary education as a solid basis for technical educaton', and it frittered much of its funds away on small grants to evening classes and so forth. But under the energetic and enlightened Benjamin Gott, appointed as organizing secretary and inspector in 1898, a much more progressive policy was gradually adopted. Christ's College at Finchley was purchased as a secondary school for the district in 1901.[102] A day school at Tottenham Polytechnic was opened in 1901, planned for 200 pupils paying fees of £4 10s. It earned large Science and Art Department

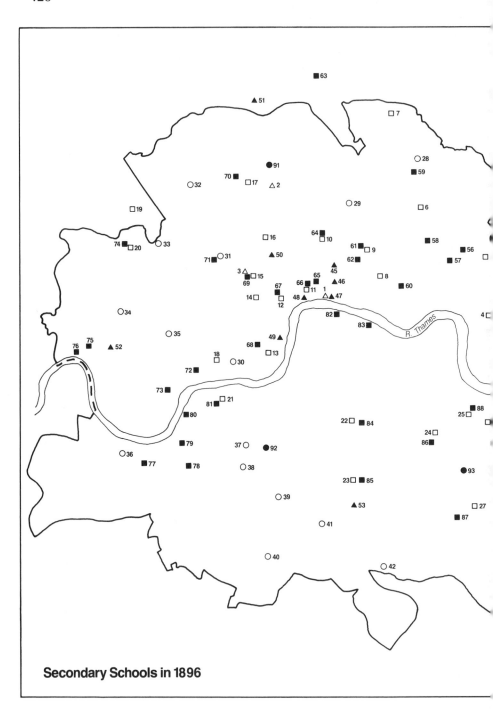

Secondary Schools in 1896

1 City of London School for Girls
2 North London Collegiate School
3 Queen's College
4 George Green's School
5 Coborn School
6 Lady Holles' School
7 Skinners' School
8 Central Foundation School
9 Haberdashers' (Aske's) School, Hoxton
10 Owen's School
11 St Clement Danes School
12 St Martin's High School
13 Grey Coat Hospital
14 Burlington School
15 Regent Street Polytechnic Day School
16 Convent School (RC) Clarendon Sq.
17 Camden School
18 Whitelands College School
19 Kilburn and Brondesbury High School
20 Queen's Park College
21 Battersea Polytechnic Day School
22 Mary Datchelor School
23 James Allen's School
24 Haberdashers' (Aske's) School, Hatcham
25 Addey and Stanhope School
26 Roan School

27 Lewisham Grammar School
28 Clapton Modern School GPDS
29 Highbury High School
30 Church of England High School, Pimlico
31 Church of England High School, Upper Baker Street
32 South Hampstead High School GPDS
33 Maida Vale High School GPDS
34 Notting Hill High School GPDS
35 Kensington High School GPDS
36 East Putney High School GPDS
37 Clapham Modern School GPDS
38 Clapham High School GPDS
39 Streatham and Brixton Hill High School GPDS
40 Streatham High School (Church Schools Co.)
41 Dulwich High School GPDS
42 Sydenham High School GPDS
43 Blackheath High School GPDS
44 Woolwich High School (Church Schools Co.)
45 Merchant Taylors' School
46 Christ's Hospital
47 City of London School
48 King's College School
49 Westminster School
50 University College School
51 Highgate School
52 St Paul's School
53 Dulwich College
54 Blackheath Proprietary School
55 George Green's School
56 Coopers' Company School
57 People's Palace Day Technical School
58 Parmiter's School
59 Grocers' Company School
60 New Commercial School, Whitechapel
61 Haberdashers' (Aske's) School, Hoxton
62 Central Foundation School
63 Stationers' School
64 Owen's School
65 Mercers' School
66 St Clement Danes School
67 Tenison's School
68 United Westminster School
69 Regent Street Polytechnic Day School
70 William Ellis School
71 Philological School
72 South-West London Polytechnic Day School
73 St Mark's College, Upper School
74 Queen's Park College
75 Godolphin School
76 Latymer Upper School
77 Wandsworth Technical Institute Day School
78 Emanuel School
79 Battersea Grammar School
80 Sir Walter St John's School
81 Battersea Polytechnic Day School
82 St Saviour's Grammar School
83 St Olave's School
84 Wilson's Grammar School, Camberwell
85 Alleyn's School
86 Haberdashers' (Aske's) School, Hatcham
87 St Dunstan's College
88 Addey and Stanhope School
89 Colfe's Grammar School
90 Roan School
91 Kentish Town High School BPDS
92 Clapham High School BPDS
93 West Kent Grammar School (Church Schools Co.)
94 Woolwich and Plumstead High School (Church Schools Co.)

■ 90

94 ● ○ 44

○ 43
▲ 54

▲ First Grade Schools, Boys

△ First Grade Schools, Girls

■ Second Grade Schools, Boys

□ Second Grade Schools, Girls

● Proprietary Schools, Boys

○ Proprietary Schools, Girls

grants.[103] Secondary schools were planned in Acton, Uxbridge, Twickenham, Chiswick and Hanwell, and the help of the Duke of Northumberland provided a girls' school from the old 'Green School' at Isleworth.[104] The work of these schools belongs to the history of the twentieth century but they demonstrate the vital part played by the TEB in creating secondary education in Middlesex during its decade of activity.

Nearly all the schools of London and its surrounding villages founded in the sixteenth and seventeenth centuries had survived to serve the new city and its suburbs on the threshhold of the twentieth century. Some had moved, others stood their ground in the centre or had been revitalized by outward movements of population. Other ways of providing schools, by private enterprise or proprietary investment, retained enough vitality to service some sections of the new society or satisfy minority needs. Demands and pressures from the elementary and technical sectors were creating newer kinds of school with secondary pretensions or aspirations. It is not surprising that contemporaries as well as later historians found the scene confusing and perhaps wasteful and ineffective.

A decade of enquiry

London was perhaps only a particularly complex example of the shifting and lively state of secondary education which became a matter of urgent national enquiry at this time. Charles Booth had already cast a searching eye over the educational scene in his massive survey of the *Life and Labour of the People in London* from 1889. 'At present', he concluded, 'secondary schools mean schools in which the children of clerks, tradesmen, managers, manufacturers, and professional men receive their education.' This was not a 'fundamental definition, being merely an accident of the existing distribution of wealth'.[105] His assistant, H. Llewellyn Smith, became Secretary to the LCC's Special Committee on Technical Education, and in 1891 was commissioned to carry out an 'Inquiry into the needs of London with regard to Technical Education . . .' and the result, presented in 1892, provides one of the best contemporary analyses of the whole range of education in the LCC area, for he interpreted his brief liberally.[106] His report on 'Secondary Education in London' begins by quoting the Royal Commission on Technical Instruction: 'The best preparation for technical study is a good modern secondary school.' He therefore included the 'whole field of secondary education' – the first- and second-grade schools, and added consideration of the higher departments of elementary schools. He identified forty-five secondary schools under some kind of public management, but having eliminated proprietary schools, whose element of profit excluded them from benefit under the Technical Instruction Acts, endowments in a state of transition

(Christ's Hospital and Southwark), those owned or managed by City Companies, the City of London School because it was owned by the Corporation, Westminster as a public school under a Scheme resulting from the Public Schools' Commission, King's College School because it lacked a conscience clause, he was left with thirty schools eligible for aid from the TEB. Four he placed in the 'high school class' – Dulwich College, St Paul's, University College School and St Dunstan's – with fees varying from £12 to £25 4s a year. The remaining twenty-six were 'second-grade' schools charging fees averaging £6 a year.[107] Yet Llewellyn Smith calculated that a good education 'giving good teaching in general subjects, including practical science, drawing, and manual work, for boys up to the age of 16 cannot be carried on efficiently at an annual cost of less than £9 to £10 a boy, supposing buildings already found'. For girls the figure would be lower – £7 a head.[108] The schools were unevenly distributed through the School Board Districts.[109]

District	Attendance per 1000 of population
Tower Hamlets	2.7
Hackney	2.7
Marylebone	2.8
Westminster and City	7.4
Chelsea	1.7
Finsbury	3.0
East and West Lambeth	2.1
Greenwich	3.0

He appended a Table showing for 1891 the income from various sources and expenditure of boys' and girls' endowed schools, and the GPDS Company schools.[110] The chief defects of these schools, he considered, were their 'isolation and want of relation to elementary schools', their insufficiency in number, the 'great inequality and general insufficiency of their resources', the absence of the stimulus of any 'central co-ordinating power'. He recommended that the LCC should give aid as capital grants towards equipment and as annual grants 'to enable schools to be efficiently maintained', this being 'mainly intended to enable the schools to provide a good secondary and technical education at a low cost for children of artizans . . .'. The 'Higher divisions of Elementary Schools' should receive capitation grants on condition that these 'ex-standard' pupils were taught separately by 'special and qualified' teachers, and grants should treat the curriculum as a whole, which should include drawing, science and manual instruction.[111] A considerable section of the Report studied the question of scholarships and exhibitions[112] and this had especial force in guiding the policy of 'Wily Webb', and 'William the Builder' when the TEB began its operation in April 1893.[113]

Llewellyn Smith, fresh from his own enquiry, was appointed to the Bryce Commission in 1894. During the thirty years between the Taunton and this Commission, ways and means of providing secondary education had taken on all the complexity and secret selectivity of the jungle, and the London scene was particularly luxuriant and confused. The Bryce enquiry was made necessary primarily by administrative confusion between the Education Department, the Science and Art Department, the Charity Commission, the County and County Borough Technical Education Committees, and the School Boards. But these complexities were matched by local problems.[114] The Report, in paying tribute to the 'rich variety of our educational life, and to the active spirit which pervades it', warned the observer 'to expect the usual results of dispersed and unconnected forces, needless competition between the different agencies, and a frequent overlapping of effort, with much consequent waste of money, time, and of labour'.[115]

The number of London boys and girls concerned in this inquiry – at least the number in the LCC area – can be discovered from the Report.[116]

Bryce 9: Appendix D – Table III
Showing the total number of boys and girls in London
receiving education in Secondary Schools in London

	Under 13		13–16		Over 16		Total of all ages	
	Boys	*Girls*	*Boys*	*Girls*	*Boys*	*Girls*	*Boys*	*Girls*
Receiving education in the 84 public endowed and public proprietary schools	4042	3348	5747	3712	929	1114	10,838*	8234
Receiving education in the 126 private or semi-private schools	2279	2080	1045	1100	142	461	3466	3641
TOTAL	6321	5428	6792	4812	1071	1574	14,304*	11875

GRAND TOTAL 26,179   *including 120 whose ages were not specified

There was no separate treatment of London in this great national enquiry, but there can be discerned a metropolitan dimension. London experience was important as a contribution to that of the nation, and its very diffuseness and contradictions were factors which helped to shape, or perhaps distort, the outcome. The Report's conclusion that 'the ground of Secondary Education is ... already almost covered with buildings so substantial that the loss to be incurred in clearing it for the erection of a new or symmetrical pile cannot be contemplated',[117] was more true of London than of any other part of the country. Above all, clarity of definition of secondary education was less likely in London's 'comprising atmosphere' discerned so shrewdly earlier in the century by an observer operating with the European perspective of the Roman Catholic tradition.[118]

Two notable and particularly clear-headed London head-teachers served on the Bryce Commission – Dr Sophie Bryant of the North London Collegiate School, and Dr Richard Wormell of the Central Foundation School. London provided also important witnesses including the Bishop of London, Mr Brown and Miss Olney of the Private Schools' Association, Dr Eve of University College School, Mr Easterbrook of Owen's School and R. P. Scott of Parmiter's School as representatives of the Headmasters' Association, Mrs Witheil of Notting Hill High School from the Association of Assistant Mistresses, Miss Wood of the Maria Grey College, F. Storr, master of modern subjects at Merchant Taylors' and here representing the Teachers' Guild, E. E. Pinches, Treasurer of the College of Preceptors and from a family of London schoolmasters, and D. R. Fearon, whose unrivalled knowledge of London secondary education in the 1860s had since been increased by his experience with the Charity Commission. Lyulph Stanley represented the London School Board, Sidney Webb and William Garnett the Technical Education Board of the LCC, and Joshua Fitch, with a lifetime of active work in all sectors of education, was then principally connected with the University of London.[119] All these witnesses took a national perspective but their opinions were strongly imbued with their experience of schooling in an expanding city, its social life continually drawn towards its open boundaries, both its central and peripheral economic vitality providing diverse, often ill-defined and precarious opportunities for employment, its educational provision in luxuriant disarray. It is not surprising that the evidence they gave was often contradictory even when it was convinced, divergent even when dogmatic. Take for example their views on the important matter of building a coherent structure for secondary education. Here the question of the status of private schooling was crucial. Eve considered that a 'private school that is well founded in every way should be considered to fill its place in a general scheme';[120] Easterbrook that they should be taken into consideration, and submit to registration and inspection;[121] Storr that the contribution of private schooling to educational advance entitled them to consideration as a valuable part of the system;[122] Pinches emphasized their 'gradual and uninterrupted improvement' and the injustice of competing against them with education 'under cost price'.[123] Fitch was largely in agreement but was prepared to let local authorities, probably less well disposed to the private sector, 'determine whether they should be reckoned as part of the secondary provision of the place'.[124] Stanley considered that it was not possible to distinguish in law between proprietary schools such as those of the invaluable GPDS Company (for which his mother had done so much), and those which worked for profit, and that therefore there should be 'amplest recognition of all existing efficient schools'.[125] But Webb and Garnett were not prepared to send pupils with scholarships from the TEB to private schools and they included proprietary schools in this category. 'In certain districts, notably in north-west London and west London, we have been obliged to send children a very long way to find a satis-factory secondary school. For example, we have had to send a boy from Shepherd's Bush to the Regent Street Polytechnic.' They admitted that this was merely a departmental opinion and had not been tried in the courts.[126] Fearon was emphatic that scholarship holders should not remain at or be sent to private schools, which were necessarily ephemeral, 'here today and gone tomorrow', or worse 'here good today and here bad tomorrow'. Only endowed schools had enough stability and public character to entitle them to profit from imminent state participation in the financing of secondary education. Private schools should have no 'other advantages than those of recognition'.[127] The divergence is broadly speaking between the administrators, concerned with a tidy and manageable structure, and educators active in the field, or perhaps jungle, but on each side there were grades and shades of opinion. The same ambiguities and disagreements were shown over methods of inspection, the powers and nature of the proposed central and local authorities, and the possibilities of uniting secondary and elementary teachers on one register. All these arguments were redeployed at the Cambridge Conference on Secondary Education which followed the Bryce Re-port a year later.[128] These were national questions on which London witnesses could advance contradictory arguments each supported by metropolitan and suburban educational experience. Such ambiguities clouded the debate and relaxed its moral and political tension together with any articulation of secondary education which had resulted from the process of growth and development. At Cambridge this very confusion under the names of 'freedom, variety, elasticity', was exalted as a national advantage – Miss Olney declared that France might have clarity of educational provision and definition, due to its military system:

The very position of continental countries renders uniformity and machine- like precision of more value than originality and independence. But for England with its extensive and varied Empire, the very reverse is needed. Without that individuality, independence, and power for adaptation to circumstances, which Secondary Education has hitherto developed, England's sons would be ill-fitted for the battle of life they have to fight. Character is of far more importance to the nation than any number of facts crammed into the mind according to some specific system.[129]

This was the authentic voice of Hampstead; matters might have seemed different in, say, Birmingham or Sheffield where the 'cold and paralysing hand' of the State upon the 'sacred ark of Secondary Education' was not so much dreaded as sought as a 'directing and supervising intelligence'.[130] Secondary education was in danger of becoming suburban schooling. Suburban life may not have been easier for the hard-pressed middle classes of the late nineteenth century than it was in the northern and Midland regions, but its edges were certainly less clearly defined.

What is secondary education?

The national structure of educational administration was decided by the Board of Education Act of 1899[131] and the Education Act of 1902.[132] For London an Act of 1903 constituted the LCC as the local education authority[133] – this in spite of hopes and intrigues by the London School Board which might have given London a directly elected authority, and some movement to hand education over to the London boroughs.[134] This devolution of provision of secondary schooling to some extent preserved that variety and elasticity so highly prized by some educationalists, but it left its definition unresolved. What had London experience to contribute to this debate? 'So unaware are we Londoners of what London is, that few of us realize that the great city has now a more extensive series of secondary schools, under essentially public management, maintained out of public funds ... than any other city in the world' wrote Sidney Webb on the eve of his taking over responsibility for London education.[135] Evidence suggests that the demands of London, and this diverse and comparatively rich provision of schools, concentrated attention on the fundamental question of its nature and purpose.

Secondary education could be defined as part of a system or process, by function, by clientèle, by content; defined administratively, socially, academically, educationally, culturally.[136] All these definitions were actively operating or being discussed in the London arena and none could be easily isolated or distinguished from the others. Apart from the supremely bureaucratic tautology put forward by the officials of the

Science and Art Department, that it should be defined by its administering agency,[137] the most straightforward and logical definition of secondary education would be as its name implies as part of a process or system. But this was frustrated by the fact that most grammar and high schools had their own preparatory departments and that private schools acted as feeders to them. There were some points of contact between elementary and private schools – Tollington Park College for example took pupils from the VII Standard but found that their lack of subjects such as botany and French was a disadvantage.[138] The London School Board used such schools as the Philological School, the proprietary schools in Islington and Kensington, the Maria Grey Girls' School, the Cowper Street Schools, King's College School and St Mark's College Schools in Chelsea for its scholarship holders.[139] But social attitudes tended to nullify such hopeful points of contact within the system.

There is ample evidence of the importance of such attitudes. The Bishop of London (Temple) was amongst those who considered that 'social motives' were particularly important in London and the south. 'I have not any doubt that especially in London, the social feeling operates very largely indeed.'[140] The three levels of 'middle-class schooling' of the Taunton period had consolidated into two by this time, with leaving ages of perhaps sixteen and eighteen/nineteen.[141] Adolescence was now firmly established as an acknowledged stage of human development which needed some special recognition, at any rate in more prosperous levels of society; standards of education had risen, demands of examinations and employers were more stringent.[142] Llewellyn Smith reported that different classes of school were broadly distinguished by levels of fees.[143] His 'high schools' represented a social polarization within secondary schooling. The 'first-grade schools', or public schools as they were now usually called, were recognized by the emerging state system as part of its provision. In 1905 Garnett writing to Sir William Collins, the first chairman of the Education Committee of the LCC, discussed the removal of University College School to Hampstead as 'simply working out its destiny in connection with the natural evolution of secondary education in London, which must inevitably tend towards the establishment of one first-grade school in each "division" surrounded by second-grade secondary schools, the areas of which constitute smaller districts'. Charterhouse had moved beyond the London orbit, but its site was used by Merchant Taylors', Christ's Hospital had 'gone away . . . and its place in London is unoccupied', the City of London School 'remains very near to its old neighbourhood . . . but is readily accessible to the east and the north-east', St Paul's provided for west London, King's College School at Wimbledon for the south-west, and Dulwich for the south and east. 'It may be left to the future development of the Grocers' School to provide . . . for the north-east . . . I think we should lay stress upon the system of distribution of secondary schools in London, with special reference to the localization of the first-grade schools.'[144] This policy would apply especially to day schools. Other schools in this category, some beyond the LCC area, still included Blackheath[145] and Highgate. This since 1876 had been provided with a governing body in line with public school status, and had an increased number of foundationers and scholarships to help boarders, and its own junior school from 1889.[146] Harrow preserved its pre-eminence and to some extent its isolation – judicious purchases of land kept suburban development at bay and the school was almost exclusively boarding.[147] Chigwell out in its forest region made a slow ascent to public-school status. The difficulties of a double foundation and disagreements among the governors hampered plans for reform, but after an expensive suit in Chancery an interim Scheme was agreed, the lower or English school was removed to a new building, and the grammar school, freed from an 'inconvenient class of boy', was able to adopt a wide and liberal curriculum. Under a new headmaster, from Lancing College, numbers rose from 47 in 1869 to 142 in 1875. The Endowed Schools' Commission eased the path to loans for extending the building, including a chapel, playing fields were acquired, a prefect system stabilized. In 1894 a new Scheme raised the fees to £20, incorporated Greek in the general course and raised the leaving age to nineteen. A Board of Education official described it as a first-grade boarding- and day school meeting a local want, but 'with a very scanty endowment and inadequate premises'. The school was glad to accept help from the new Local Education Authority – in this case the Essex County Council.[148] In a somewhat similar way Whitgift's School out at Croydon struggled slowly towards first-grade status, rising socially by also casting off a less academic lower school. In 1907 its headmaster was elected to the Headmasters' Conference and the school was in an academically flourishing state which attracted new benefactors.[149]

Within the ranks of the first-grade schools there were gradations, and they defined themselves in academic as well as social terms. The long and seemingly unscrupulous struggle of Dr Walker to preserve St Paul's from a scholarship system which he considered would lower its classical standards as well as perhaps its social tone, was a case in point.[150] The second-grade schools also had their variations of fees and levels of academic aspiration. The social definition of secondary education undoubtedly was entangled with its academic definition.

Was such education to be defined by the ability of pupils to profit from it? Was it a standard, rather than a stage of education? The concept of secondary education for all lay in the future. Conscious and active demand from the working classes was growing, but slowly.[151] 'The feeling is at present less noticeable among the labouring classes themselves', wrote a contemporary observer in the East End of London. Even progressive thinkers such as Huxley assumed that:

The great mass of mankind have neither the liking, nor the aptitude, for either literary or scientific or artistic pursuits; nor indeed for excellence of any sort. . . . But a small proportion of the population is born with that most excellent quality, a desire for excellence, or with special aptitude of some sort or another. . . . Now the most important object of all educational schemes is to catch these exceptional people, and turn them to account for the good of society.[152]

This was the philosophy behind the scholarship ladder. But again, this operated socially as well as academically. Llewellyn Smith and Booth for example in surveying the social class of scholarship holders in London grammar schools had found that they were not the children of the poor but of the lower middle class and the upper fringe of the working class, the 'aristocracy, no less socially than intellectually', of the elementary schools from which they were drawn.[153] Even by 1910 the efforts of the LCC to change this had not been effective.[154] The valuable entrance scholarships to some endowed schools of first and second grades could not always be filled.[155]

London amply demonstrated however one revolution in the definition of secondary education by clientèle – this now included girls,[156] though rarely alongside the boys. Perhaps for social reasons, but also because of the rich provision of schools, coeducation was not the London style. Only in ideological provision, such as King Alfred's or the polytechnic secondary schools, was the experiment made.[157] The victory of the struggle for girls' education was even producing a reaction. One notable suburban school was due to this. Charlotte Cowdroy, educated at Stockwell Practising School and then, after being a pupil-teacher, at Stockwell Training College, opened a private school in Crouch End, Hornsey, in 1900 to put into practice her ideas. 'Girls are not boys and they should not be educated as boys.' Her success gave her an almost world-wide reputation. 'The Crouch End High School and College' was considered one of the most remarkable schools in the country and many people moved to the neighbourhood in order to send their daughters to it.[158] Philip Magnus discussed the wider application of this to the debate about the function of schooling in relation to its content: '. . . education should not be aimless, but should have some definite relation to the life interests and occupations of the individual – the training of girls ought to be on very different lines from that of boys'. This he interpreted as partly due to the out-of-date ('medieval') concentration on classics and mathematics in boys' schools, but he also emphasized the current debate about the vocational aspects of the curriculum, inevitably here the need for 'including the domestic arts among the subjects of instruction of girls' schools of every grade'.[159] But this limited and limiting practical outcome does not invalidate the significance of the argument for defining secondary education. One of the most valuable contributions which the girls' schools made at this period was to concentrate attention on the curriculum. The concept of secondary education was being formed by this debate on the relation of its content to its function – surely more fundamental than its social purposes or temporary distribution.

Contemporary curriculum debate tended to concentrate on the place of technical and scientific education in relation to general or liberal education.[160] Practice was distorted by the operations of the Science and Art Department grants, for to earn these many grammar schools, for boys and for girls, and higher grade and higher elementary schools, gave heavy emphasis to technical or science subjects. The Technical Education Boards of the County Councils reinforced this tendency.[161] The Bryce Commission paid direct attention to this problem and warned against early specialization, whether in classics or science. Technical education was part of secondary education, and a good general education was the best preparation for vocational studies.[162] Webb in discussing London secondary schools felt obliged to take a less cloudy view. London was a 'city of offices'[163] and a good general education to be a practical preparation for commercial work, required some differentiation.

> We want, in fact, at least three kinds of secondary schools – one aiming at university scholarships; another giving a carefully devised, predominantly scientific training, with languages and literature taking a second place; and yet a third, in which languages, literature, and history of at least two modern countries beside our own will be made the basis of the intellectual training, with economics, geography and physical science holding a subordinate position.[164]

When in 1897 the government set out to investigate the supply of schools over the whole nation, it was obliged to describe them as 'Secondary and Other Schools'.[165] Thus the nineteenth century ended with the definition of secondary education still unresolved. 'Neither aim nor curriculum necessarily corresponds to any definite conception: in consequence the education given at a Secondary School in England and the conditions under which it is given are alike indeterminate ....'.[166]

This despondent judgement by a leading London schoolmaster, R. P. Scott, came at the end of a decade of provision, experiment and enquiry. But such uncertainties had served to stir professional activity – both theoretical and practical. Girls' education, perhaps on account of the very need for definitions in an emerging and experimental sector, had led the way in the professional training and organization of secondary teachers.[167] Now the Headmasters' Association was formed in 1890 as a result of professional concern and to act as an interest group. It aimed to define secondary as opposed to, or in connection with, higher elementary schooling, and to initiate a uniform and nation-wide scholarship examination for pupils from elementary schools with School

Board finance, and attract county scholars whose fees would be paid by the Technical Education Boards. The Association was defensive – it wished to combat the School Boards' 'intrusions into secondary education' – and it was also positive – it aimed to raise standards at endowed schools by more purposeful courses and teaching and by attracting finance.[168] Its secretary was R. P. Scott, headmaster of Parmiter's School and formerly of the George Green Schools, and from the staff of the Cowper Street Schools. His evidence before Bryce described the way the scholarship system operated. In London the TEB had close relations with the examining board, Garnett even making suggestions for modifying the papers, and the Board allocated scholarships from the pass list, but by districts, to secure a fairer distribution, and operated a parental means test for its own scholarships. The London School Board was considering using the same scheme. Through this scholarship system the age of transfer from elementary and secondary schools was more firmly fixed at eleven/twelve, which enabled such pupils to catch up in subjects not before studied and to pursue a full five-year course.[169]

In 1898 the Headmasters' Association secured a concordat with the headmasters of higher grade schools on the whole question of the relations 'of primary and secondary schools to each other in a national system of education'.[170] In these national negotiations the northern schools played a large part. No London higher grade schools were represented but Scott and the headmaster of Chigwell School were at the conference and signed the Joint Memorandum. This agreed that elementary and secondary schools were differentiated by age of leaving, determined by family circumstances, that a 'Secondary School . . . aims at the development of a broad and well-trained mind, rather than the development of aptitude in some specific direction, and which can only be imparted under conditions of teaching staff and general efficiency consistent with liberal culture'. While School Boards had done great service in extending the age of elementary education, pupils with scholarships should be passed on at an early enough age to profit from secondary schooling and the schools should adopt such classifications and curricula 'that scholars from the top standards of the Elementary School may be able, with reasonable diligence, in a short time to take up the ordinary work of a Secondary School'.[171]

These were empirical and pragmatic solutions to conceptual problems. The associations of secondary teachers appointed a committee to examine such experiments and reflect on such experience. It included staff from Owen's School, Blackheath High School (GPDSC), Chigwell School, Merchant Taylors', Parmiter's. In 1899 it published its deliberations in *What is Secondary Education? . . . a Handbook for Public Men and for Parents*. Scott was its editor and his experience of small endowments working under intense urban pressure[172] and 'in danger of sinking in the educational plane' was reflected in his introductory rationale, and his emphasis on the need for proper finance. 'We are a practical, not an intellectually imaginative people. . . . At bottom we feel that character, not intellect, governs this world and inherits the next.' But the recent concordat with the higher grade schools would only work if secondary education was more systematically defined.[173] Miss Page, of the Skinners' Company School at Stamford Hill, also explored this relationship 'between Secondary and Elementary Education' in a nation where 'the so-called High School is not an organic part of a national system . . . but has to adapt itself to the circumstances of the locality in which it is placed . . .'. Difficulties of transferring girls from one school to another had to be worked through subject by subject, pupil by pupil, in both social and academic terms.[174] Secondary education as a process was coming into conflict with secondary education as a social alternative.

London contributions on the content of secondary education also disclosed tensions which experience was beginning to resolve. The Vice-President of the London Chamber of Commerce was forthright on the question of vocational preparation: 'Unless a broad and deep foundation of general knowledge is laid, a mere superficial acquirement of commercial technique is worse than useless.'[175] Canon Barnett of St Jude's Whitechapel and founder of Toynbee Hall, pleaded for education for citizenship. His East End experience emphasized the need for collectivist action, and the reformed structure of London government was creaking into action. 'The Vestry, the Board, or the Council has to a large extent in its hands the making or marring of the lives of the citizens whose votes will decide the destinies of the Nation and the Empire. On its knowledge and activity depend in a great measure the health and prosperity of the community . . .'. Only a good and thorough secondary education could produce citizens who could grasp the distant as well as the near, the foreign as well as the native, 'to imagine a future with which to fit the present, or to introduce into England . . . methods approved on the Continent . . .'.[176] Whitechapel and the City both demanded a truly liberal education, a schooling which made sense of immediate complexities, widened the horizons, and brought moral action to bear on the personal and public challenges and duties perceived by an enlightened intellect.

It would be unwise as well as unhistorical to criticize the late nineteenth century for failure to define secondary education. All that can be asked of any age is that it should provide schools which attempt to meet its intellectual, cultural, social, economic, political needs, as these are discerned at the time, and to be aware of their deficiencies. It is a matter of national history that secondary *schools* were at last defined by the crudest category, the financial/administrative. By the famous Board of Education Minute of 1904, while no definition of such education was offered, only schools which complied with its conditions received grants under the Secondary School Regulations. But these required *general* and *complete* courses for children up to the age of sixteen, and the exact content and balance of curriculum was laid down.[177]

It is usual to attribute the Minute of 1904 to the influence of the public schools on the reformed endowed schools,[178] and even to assume that, therefore, Morant deliberately intended to preserve secondary schools for the middle classes. A closer examination of the schools on the ground and their development over the centuries suggests that response to local needs had brought into being many kinds of school which had helped to reshape and give new content to changing concepts of secondary education and that the so-called public schools of the late nineteenth century were also part of this process. These in turns influenced Morant and the framers of the Minute. As an example: the coeducational secondary school attached to Battersea Polytechnic may have acknowledged the influence of Thring of Uppingham but itself represented a movement which contributed to the formation of newer content for education at all grades. University College School had its commercial course,[179] Dulwich College after the appointment of F. W. Sanderson in 1885 had its workshops as well as its laboratories.[180] London schools in fact gave as good as they got. The curriculum of the 1904 Regulations, which restored the balance between literary, scientific, practical subjects, and insisted on Latin unless special circumstances justified its exclusion, seems to have accorded with national consensus. It complied for example with the needs of the 'City of Offices'[181] and the scientific lobby acknowledged that it established science as an integral part of general education instead of a matter for separate, and distorting, grants. The inclusion of Latin was not only culturally accepted, it enhanced chances of social mobility, especially important in a constantly aspiring suburban environment.[182]

The way the London schools responded to these Regulations belongs to twentieth-century history though its agents operated with nineteenth-century experience. R. P. Scott, for example, became Staff Inspector for Secondary Schools in 1904, Assistant Secretary of the Secondary Branch of the Board of Education in 1911, and from 1920 to 1926 was a member of its Consultative Committee.[183] Centuries of tradition and experiment in secondary education bequeathed to the present century a wealth, variety, complexity, even ambiguity of experience, particularly important to a nation which proceeds pragmatically and empirically rather than systematically and theoretically.[184] London's educational history embodied such experience. Even from the Dark Ages, through the medieval centuries, Renaissance, Reformation, Ages of Observation and Enlightenment, Commercial, Industrial, Consumer Revolutions, a constantly changing and expanding city had provided and adapted schools to prepare boys, and later girls, for the public world. This preparation responded, however imperfectly, to changing civic and national needs and appetites and to ever more complex and diverse realms of meaning, to greater demands of powers of criticism and reflection. The content of such schooling expanded to include the skills and knowledge necessary to use and explain new experience and meet new challenges. It is only to be expected that London should have played a key part in the development of secondary education, for there is in London, as one of its greatest citizens said, 'all that life affords', and ultimately learning has to keep pace with living, education has to try to make sense out of life and to increase our powers of action.

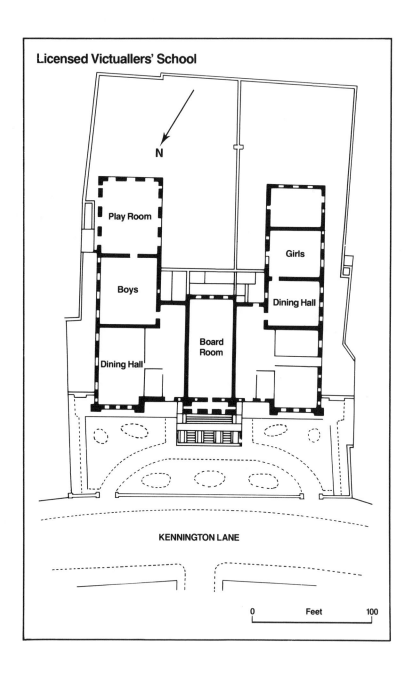

Licensed Victuallers' School

N

Play Room

Girls

Boys

Dining Hall

Board
Room

Dining Hall

KENNINGTON LANE

0   Feet   100

Notes

I The early grammar schools

1 G. A. Williams, *Medieval London, from Commune to Capital* (1963), pp. 307–8, 313–14; R. W. Southern, 'Master Vacarius and the Beginning of an English Academic Tradition', in J. J. G. Alexander and M. T. Gibson (eds), *Medieval Learning and Literature: Essays presented to Richard William Hunt* (1976), p. 266.
2 E. M. Veale, 'Craftsmen and the Economy of London in the 14th century', in A. E. J. Hollaender and W. Kellaway (eds), *Studies in London History* (1969), pp. 136–9; S. Thrupp, *The Merchant Community of Medieval London 1300–1500* (1962), pp. 2–3, 27–9, 51–2; C. Morris, *The Discovery of the Individual 1050–1200* (1972), pp. 124–5; R. L. Storey, 'Gentlemen Bureaucrats', in C. H. Clough (ed.), *Profession, Vocation & Culture in Later Medieval England* (1982), pp. 90ff.
3 H. Pirenne, *Medieval Cities, Their Origins and the Revival of Trade* (1925; 1952 edn), Chap. V *passim* and p. 123.
4 C. N. L. Brooke, assisted by C. Keir, *London 800–1216: The shaping of a city* (1975), p.77.
5 Pirenne, p. 117; Thrupp, p. xvii.
6 J. Huizinga, *The Waning of the Middle Ages* (1924; 1965 edn), pp. 147ff.
7 Thrupp, p. 318; Morris, *passim*, and esp. pp. 120–2; Pirenne, p. 125.
8 M. T. Clanchy, *From Memory to Written Record, England 1066–1307* (1979), Chap. 7, pp. 175ff.
9 G. R. Potter, 'Education in the 14th and 15th Centuries', in *Cambridge Medieval History*, Vol. VIII (1936), p. 689.
10 J. W. Adamson, 'The Extent of Literacy in England in the 15th and 16th centuries; Notes and Conjectures', *The Library*, Transactions of the Bibliographical Society Second Series, Vol. X (1929–30), pp. 163–93; J. N.T. Miner, 'Schools and Literacy in Later Medieval England', *British Journal of Educational Studies*, XI, 1962; Margaret Aston, 'Lollardry and Literacy', *History*, Vol. 62, No. 206, October 1977; J. Simon, *Education and Society in Tudor England* (1966), p. 15; Thrupp, p. 158.
11 Potter, p. 689; Thrupp, pp. 159–60; F. W. Steer, *A History of the Worshipful Company of Scriveners of London* (1973), Vol. I, pp. 10–11; Simon, p. 15.
12 N. Orme, *English Schools in the Middle Ages* (1973), pp. 143–5.
13 A. F. Leach, 'St Paul's School before Colet', *Archaeologia*, lxii, pt 1 (1910), pp. 191ff; Leach, *The Schools of Medieval England* (1915), esp. pp. 141–2. St Paul's also had an almonry school for the choristers and if they required to learn Latin the grammar master was paid to teach them. Ibid., p. 214.
14 William Fitzstephen's *Description of London*, trans. H. E. Butler, in F. M.

445

Stenton, *Norman London* (Historical Association Leaflets Nos 93, 94 (1934).

15 A. F. Leach, 'The Ancient Schools in the City of London', in W. Besant, *London in the Nineteenth Century* (1910), p. 393; Marjorie Honeybourne, 'London, History', *Chamber's Encyclopaedia*, Vol. 8 (1950), pp. 659–60; D. W. Robertson Junior, *Chaucer's London* (1968), pp. 196–8; A. G. B. Atkinson, *St Botolph's Aldgate, the story of a City parish* (1898), pp. 10–12; Thrupp, p. 158ff; Brooke, *Shaping of a City*, p. 323.

16 Orme, p. 212; Leach, 'Ancient Schools . . . ,' pp. 407–26; *Victoria County History of London* (1909), Vol. I, pp. 581ff, 555–65 (hereafter *VCH*); T. L. Humberstone, 'Education in London', British Association for the Advancement of Science, *London and the Advancement of Science* (1931), pp. 134ff; *DNB*, John Carpenter (Bishop of Worcester), Thomas More.

17 Leach, *Schools of Medieval England*, pp. 266.

18 Orme, p. 212.

19 V. H. Galbraith, 'John Seward and his Circle', *Medieval and Renaissance Studies*, I (1941), pp. 85–104; Leach, *Schools of Medieval England*, pp. 143, 260–67; Orme, 'Schoolmasters 1307–1509' in Clough, *Profession, Vocation & Culture*, pp. 223–4.

20 Orme, loc. cit., p. 190, f.n.2, quot. Cal. of Plea and Memoranda Rolls of London 1381–1412, A. H. Thomas (ed.) (1932), p. 182.

21 W. K. Jordan, *Charities of London 1480–1660* (1960), p. 212.

22 M. McDonnell, *Annals of St Paul's School* (1959), p. 28.

23 Orme, *Schools*, p. 212.

24 Thrupp, p. 160; Simon, p. 14.

25 H. S. Bennett, *Chaucer in the 15th Century* (1948), p. 31; *DNB*, Chaucer.

26 *DNB*, Colet.

27 Galbraith, loc. cit., pp. 98, 86.

28 Thrupp, p. 156; Simon, pp. 22–6; Leach, 'Ancient Schools . . .', pp. 406–7; *VCH, London*, I, pp. 555–65; Humberstone, loc. cit.

29 Simon, p. 25; L. F. Morris, *A History of St Dunstan's College* (1970).

30 *DNB*, Lichfield; Leach, 'Ancient Schools . . .', p. 427; Simon, p. 25.

31 Simon, p. 27.

32 Clanchy, *passim*, esp. Chaps 7 and 10; Pirenne, pp. 231–4; Thrupp, p. 162.

33 Brooke, p. 80; *DNB*, Lichfield, John Carpenter 1370?–1441? (not to be confused with Bishop of Worcester; see note 16); W. A. Pantin, 'Instructions for a Devout and Literate Layman', in Alexander and Gibson, *Medieval Learning . . .* , pp. 398ff; Simon, p. 9.

34 Orme, *Schools*, p. 194; H. A. Miskimin, 'The Legacies of London, 1259–1330', in H. A. Miskimin, D. Herlihy and A. L. Uldovitch (eds), *The Medieval City* (1977), pp. 209–27; J. A. F. Thomson, 'Piety and Charity in Late Medieval London', *Journal of Ecclesiastical History*, XVI (1965), pp. 178ff.

35 Thrupp, pp, 312–13.

36 Simon, pp. 31, 94; Orme, *Schools*, p. 194.

37 Simon, p. 25; Thrupp, p. 156; Jordan, *London*, p. 210; Orme, *Schools*, pp. 3–7, 213; Galbraith, f.n. 3, p. 89.

38 Thrupp, p. 163; Orme, *Schools*, pp. 203–5; Thomson, 'Piety and Charity . . .', pp. 194–5.

39 Orme, *Schools*, pp. 221, 151–3.
40 F. Seebohm, *The Oxford Reformers* (1914 edn), Chap. I.
41 McDonnell, p. 4; C. Picciotto, *St Paul's School* (1939); Leach, 'St Paul's before Colet', pp. 202ff; K. Charlton, *Education in Renaissance England* (1965), pp. 31ff.
42 C. L. Kingsford (ed.), J. Stow, *A Survey of London reprinted from the text of 1603* (1908), pp. 74–5; McDonnell, p. 24.
43 Jordan, *London*, p. 17.
44 Brooke, p. 70; Dorothy George, *London Life in the 18th Century* (1966 edn), pp. 78–80; Jordan, *London* p. 18.
45 Jordan, *London*, p. 19; C. Hill, *Intellectual Origins of the English Revolution* (1965), p. 97; C. W. K. Jordan, *Philanthropy in England 1480–1660* (1959), pp. 280, 156.
46 *VCH, Essex*, II (1907), pp. 527ff.
47 Sometimes called St Dunstan's in the East. *VCH, Middlesex*, I (1969), p. 291.
48 J. Watney, *An Account of the Mistery of Mercers in the City of London* (1914), pp. 78–85.
49 E. H. Pearce, *Annals of Christ's Hospital* (1901), p. 24.
50 B. Garside, *The history of Hampton School from 1556 to 1700 with a brief account of the years between 1700 and the present day* (1931); *VCH, Middlesex*, I, p. 298.
51 Above, p. 9; *VCH, Middlesex*, I, p. 294; L. B. Marshall, *A Brief History of Enfield Grammar School* (1958).
52 F. W. M. Draper, *Four Centuries of Merchant Taylors' School* (1962); L. Tanner, *Westminster School, A History* (1934); J. D. Carleton, *Westminster School, A History* (1965).
53 R. C. Carrington, *Two Schools: a history of the St Olave's and St Saviour's Grammar School Foundation* (1971).
54 *VCH, Middlesex*, I, p. 302.
55 Ibid., p. 299.
56 F. H. G. Percy, *History of Whitgift School* (1976).
57 *VCH, Middlesex* I, p. 310; R. A. Dare, *A History of Owen's School* (n.d.).
58 G. S. Davies, *The Charterhouse in London* (1921).
59 *VCH, Surrey*, II (1905), pp. 198–210 (Dulwich), 210–17 (Wilson's).
60 W. Wheatley, *The History of Edward Latymer and his Foundations* (1936); *VCH, Middlesex*, I, p. 305.
61 G. S. Stott, *A History of Chigwell School* (1960).
62 K. S. Binnie, *The Story of the Roan Schools 1643–1956* (1957).
63 L. L. Duncan, *The History of Colfe's Grammar School 1652–1952* (1952); *VCH, Kent*, II (1926), pp. 210–17.
64 J. P. Anglin, 'Frustrated Ideals; the case of Elizabethan grammar school foundations', *History of Education*, Vol. II, No. 4, 1982, pp. 267ff; Jordan, *London*, p. 219.
65 Orme, *Schools*, p. 7.
66 Simon, pp. 182–7; Tanner, *passim*; Charlton, p. 92.
67 Simon, p. 240.
68 S. T. Bindoff, *Tudor England* (1950), pp. 139–40.
69 McDonnell, p. 112; Leach, 'Ancient Schools . . .', pp. 419–26.
70 *VCH, Essex*, II, pp. 527ff.

71 A. H. Johnson, *A History of the Worshipful Company of Drapers* (1915), II, pp. 94–101; Simon, p. 239.
72 Simon, p. 189.
73 Watney, esp. pp. 79–80; Simon, p. 187; Jordan, *London*, p. 212.
74 Pearce, *Annals, passim*; Jordan, *London*,, pp. 212–14; Ivy Pinchbeck and Margaret Hewitt, *Children in English Society*, Vol. I (1969), pp. 127–33.
75 Simon, p. 302; McDonnell, pp. 77, 80, 87.
76 Draper, pp. 5ff; Simon, pp. 306–7; Jordan, *London*, pp. 215, 251–2.
77 Carrington, esp. pp. 21, 23, 29–30; Jordan, *London*, pp. 215–16.
78 Carrington, pp. 33–5, 38.
79 Jordan, *London*, pp. 47, 67–8.
80 Jordan, p. 211; *VCH, Middlesex*, I, p. 291.
81 *VCH, Middlesex*, I. p. 294.
82 *DNB*, Owen; Dare, esp. pp. 13–14; Jordan, *London*, pp. 150, 235, 360.
83 Jordan, *Philanthropy*, p. 283
84 *DNB*, Sutton; Davies, *Charterhouse*, Chaps XVIII and XIX; Jordan, *London*, pp. 151–3.
85 Simon, p. 373, quot. Mulcaster's *Positions*.
86 Jordan, *London*, pp. 58–61.
87 Thrupp, pp. 279–87, 311–12.
88 Garside, *passim*; *VCH, Middlesex*, I, p. 298.
89 *VCH, Middlesex*, I, p. 299; Jordan, *London*, pp. 229–30; Simon, p. 372.
90 Jordan, *London*, p. 61; Simon, pp. 372–3.
91 Jordan, *London*, pp. 55–6, 82–4.
92 *VCH, Middlesex* I, p. 302; Jordan, *London*, p. 217.
93 Wheatley, Chap. IV.
94 Jordan, *London*, p. 83.
95 Jordan, *London*, p. 155; Carrington, p. 25; W. H. Blanch, *Ye Parish of Camberwell* (1877), pp. 420ff; W. Young, *History of Dulwich College* (1899), Vol. I, esp. pp. 77–8; Sheila Hodges, *God's Gift – A living history of Dulwich College* (1981), Chap. I.
96 Jordan, *London*, pp. 61–3.
97 *VCH, Essex*, II, pp. 544ff. The governors included the incumbents of Chigwell and Loughton, and the Bishop of London was Visitor.
98 Simon, p. 180; Charlton, p. 162.
99 D. H. Allport, *Camberwell Grammar School: a short history of the foundation under Royal Charter, of Edward Wilson* . . . (1964), esp. pp. 27–8, 35–7.
100 L. L. Duncan, *History of the Borough of Lewisham* (1908), p. 40.
101 Duncan, *Colfe's*, esp. pp. 20–2, 29, 30–9, 52.
102 Simon, p. 291.
103 Ibid., pp. 91–2.
104 Below, pp. 31–2.
105 Simon, Chap. XIII.
106 Carrington, pp. 17–18; *DNB*, Alexander Nowell; Simon, p. 307.
107 Carrington, pp. 48–9, 74.
108 Ibid., p. 29.
109 J. Hurstfield, *Liberty and Authority under Elizabeth I*, an Inaugural Lecture delivered at University College, London (1960), *passim*. esp. p. 8.
110 Subscription Books for Diocese of London, Guildhall MS 9539 A, Vol. I 1627–44; Vol. 2 1631–48 and 1660–69; Vol 3 1663–75; MS 9539 B,

1662; MS 9539 C, 1662–64; MS 9540, Vol. I 1662–83/4; MS 10144, 1662–83: Consistory Court Books, 1520–1685, Greater London Record Office, DL/C/330/45.

111   S. W. Wide and J. A. Morris, 'The Episcopal Licensing of Schoolmasters in the Diocese of London, 1627–1685', *Guildhall Miscellany*, Vol 2, 1967.

112   43 Eliz. C. 4; W. H. G. Armytage, *Four Hundred Years of English Education* (1964), p. 7; W. Beveridge, *Voluntary Action* (1948), p. 187ff.

113   Anglin, 'Frustrated ideals . . .', p. 268.

114   Anglin, p. 274; McDonnell, p. 42; Picciotto, p. 7.

115   Duncan, *Colfe's*, pp. 46–7.

116   Dare, pp. 37–8.

117   *VCH, Middlesex*, I, p. 291.

118   Duncan, *Colfe's*, pp. 33, 56.

119   Picciotto, pp. 16–17.

120   Draper, pp. 12–14.

121   Duncan, *Colfe's*, p. 50.

122   Dare, p. 36.

123   Above, p. 28; Dare, p. 40.

124   Dare, pp. 39–41.

125   Carrington, pp. 41, 69, 85–7.

126   Allport, pp. 34–5, 56, 65.

127   Simon, p. 291; above, p. 28.

128   Anglin, 'Frustrated ideals . . .', p. 279.

129   Above, p. 10.

130   E. Ives, 'Queen Elizabeth and the People of England', *The Historian*, No. 1, Autumn 1983, p. 5.

131   Carrington, pp. 26–7, 39.

132   Duncan, *Colfe's*, p. 34; Allport, p. 33.

133   Carrington, pp. 27, 39.

134   Picciotto, p. 11; Duncan, *Colfe's*, pp. 34–5.

135   Carrington, pp. 26–7.

136   D. Hay, *The Italian Renaissance in its Historical Background* (1966 edn), p. 200.

137   Charlton, p. 117.

138   Duncan, *Colfe's*, p. 34.

139   Allport, p. 29; VCH, Essex, II, p. 544; Charlton, p. 117; above, p. 26.

140   Simon, pp. 363–4.

141   Ibid.

142   Ibid., pp. 353–4; Charlton, pp. 119ff.

143   Simon, pp. 363–4.

144   Pearce, *Annals*, pp. 26, 146–53.

145   Carrington, pp. 38–9.

146   *VCH, Middlesex*, I, pp. 294, 302; Dare, p. 20.

147   *VCH, Essex*, II, p. 544; Duncan, *Colfe's*, pp.36, 47, 34; Allport, p. 33 f.n.

148   *VCH, Middlesex*, I, p. 291.

149   Picciotto, p. 10.

150   Carrington, p. 26; Allport, pp. 32–3, 48.

151   Carrington, pp. 80–4.

152   Above, p. 25.

153   *VCH, Middlesex*, I, p. 293.

154 Ibid., p. 296.
155 *VCH, Surrey*, II, pp. 218–19.
156 *Reports of the Commissioners... concerning Charities... Kent* 1819–37 99/21.
157 *VCH, Essex*, II, pp. 547–8.
158 Canon G. V. Bennett, 'Archbishop Tenison and the Reshaping of the Church of England', *Friends of Lambeth Palace Library, Annual Report*, 1981, pp. 10ff.
159 R. S. Tompson, *Classics or Charity? The dilemma of the eighteenth-century grammar school* (1971), p. 54.
160 Wide and Morris, 'Episcopal Licensing...', p. 405.
161 *VCH, Middlesex*, I, p. 314.
162 Garside, p. 120.
163 Picciotto, pp. 7, 10; above, p. 10.
164 Draper, pp. 5ff; McDonnell, pp. 39–40; Simon, p. 297.
165 Davies, p. 248.
166 Order Book 7, quot. Tompson, p. 79.
167 Allport, p. 32.
168 Duncan, *Colfe's*, pp. 33, 43.
169 Picciotto, p. 10; A. M. Stowe, *The English Grammar Schools in the Reign of Queen Elizabeth* (1908; reprinted 1973), p. 132.
170 Carrington, p. 26.
171 Allport, p. 33.
172 Simon, p. 95; Pepys's *Diary*, ed. H. B. Wheatley, Vol. I (1928), Introduction, p. xxii.
173 McDonnell, p. 38; Simon, p. 95.
174 Carrington, pp. 26, 39.
175 Allport, p. 32.
176 Duncan, *Colfe's*, p. 33.
177 *VCH, Middlesex*, I, p. 299.
178 Tompson, pp. 88ff.
179 *VCH, Middlesex*, I, p. 295.
180 Above, p. 19; Carrington, pp. 39, 85.
181 Jordan, *London*, pp. 251–2.
182 Carrington, pp. 60–1, 85–6.
183 Duncan, *Colfe's*, pp. 36, 51–2, 54, 59–60.
184 Ibid., p. 58.
185 McDonnell, p. 42.

II The Court and the City

1 H. S. Bennett, *English Books and Readers, 1475–1557* (2nd edn 1969), pp. 16, 20–1, 180–1, 186; Simon, *Education and Society in Tudor England*, pp. 383–92; D. Hay, *Annalists and Historians, Western Historiography from the VIIIth to the XVIIIth Century* (1977), pp. 85–6, 118.
2 Charlton, *Education in Renaissance England, passim*.
3 M. Reeves, 'The European University from Medieval Times', in W. R. Niblett (ed.), *Higher Education, Demand and Response* (1970), pp. 71–5;

E.W. Ives, 'The Common Lawyers', in Clough, *Profession, Vocation & Culture...*', Chap. 7, pp. 181ff; Simon, pp. 8ff.

4 Orme, *Schools of Medieval England*, pp. 217ff; Simon, pp. 9ff; J. J. Scarisbrick, *Henry VIII* (1968), p. 15.

5 E. G. R. Taylor, *The Mathematical Practitioners of Tudor and Stuart England* (1970), pp. 16–17, Works No. 15. p. 314.

6 Ibid., Biog. 14, p. 169.

7 Ibid., Biog. 9, p. 168.

8 Simon, p. 98; Scarisbrick, pp. 14–15. Croke was also useful later in negotiations over Henry's divorce.

9 J. Hexter, *Reappraisals in History* (1961), pp. 45–70, and *The History Primer* (1971), pp. 263–71.

10 Charlton, pp. 72–5; Simon, p. 160.

11 Simon, pp. 99, 155–6; J. Hurstfield, *The Queen's Wards* (1958), Chap. III.

12 G. R. Batho, 'The Education of a Stuart Nobleman', *British Journal of Educational Studies*, Vol. V, No. 2, May 1957, pp. 131–43.

13 Simon, pp. 8–13, 99–100, 117–21, 353ff; Charlton, Chap. VI; R. Tittler, 'Education and the Gentleman in Tudor England: the case of Sir Nicholas Bacon', *History of Education*, Vol. 5, No. 1, Feb 1976, pp. 3–10; T. K. Rabb, 'Population, economy and society in Milton's England', in C. A. Patrides and R. B. Waddington (eds.), *The Age of Milton – Background to seventeenth century literature* (1980), p. 95.

14 Hurstfield, pp. 25ff; Hill, *Intellectual Origins*, p. 138; Charlton, pp. 156–7; Simon, pp. 341–4; J. Conway Davies, 'Elizabethan Plans and Proposals for Education', *Durham Research Review*, No. 5, Sept. 1954, pp. 1–8; Sir John E. Sandys, 'Education', in W. Raleigh (ed.), *Shakespeare's England* (1916), Vol. I, pp. 246–9.

15 E. K. Chambers, 'The Court', in Raleigh (ed.), *Shakespeare's England*, Vol. I, pp. 110ff; Hill, pp. 213–19; Taylor, *Practitioners*, p. 49, Biog. 53, pp. 181–2, and Biog. 37.

16 E. M. Portal, 'The Academ Roiall of King Jas I', *Proceedings of the British Academy* (1915–16), pp. 192ff; Hill, p. 216; Charlton, pp. 217–18; Foster Watson, *Beginnings of the Teaching of Modern Subjects in England* (1909), pp. xxxiii, 220–1.

17 L. Aiken, *Memoirs of the Court of Charles I* (1833), Vol. ii, p. 31; W. E. Houghton, 'The English Virtuoso in the 17th Century', *Journal of the History of Ideas*, Vol. III, 1942, pp. 51–73.

18 G. G. Turnbull, *Hartlib, Drury and Comenius* (1947), pp. 17, 57.

19 Aiken, p. 31; D. Lysons, *Collectanea*, I, p. 24; *DNB*, Gerbier; J. Harris, S. Orgel, R. Strong, *The King's Arcadia: Inigo Jones and the Stuart Court* (Arts Council, 1973), pp. 188, 201; P. W. Thomas, 'Two Cultures? Court and Country under Charles I', in C. Russell (ed.), *The Origins of the English Civil War* (1973), *passim*; Pepys's *Diary* (ed. Wheatley), III, p. 147 and fn., 28 May 1663.

20 C. L. Kingsford, *Early Days of Piccadilly, Leicester Square and Soho* (1925), p. 128; J. Evelyn, *Diary*, E. S. de Beer (ed.), IV, pp. 257 n. 5, 290, 400; Hist. MSS Commission, *Ormonde* V, pp. 165, 300–1, 345, 375, 385; VI, pp. 76, 128; *Hastings* II, pp. 250–1, 255, 260; *Cal. Treas. Bks*, 1679–80, pp. 132, 140.

21 Rabb, 'Population, economy and society...' in Patrides (ed.), p. 93;

L. Stone, 'The Residential Development of the West End of London in the 17th Century', in B. C. Malament (ed.), *After the Reformation, essays in honor of J. H. Hexter* (1980), pp. 167–212.

22   Foster Watson, *Modern Subjects*, pp. xxi-iii; Rabb, loc. cit., p. 94, Table VI.

23   L. B. Wright, *Middle Class Culture in Elizabethan England* (1935), pp. 43–4.

24   Hill, *Intellectual Origins, passim.*

25   R. Williams, *The Long Revolution* (1961, 1965 edn), pp. 277, 237–43; Hill, p. 130; Victoria and Albert Museum, *The Orange and the Rose, Holland and Britain in the Age of Observation* (1964), p. 10.

26   Reeves, 'The European University . . .', in Niblett (ed.), pp. 71–5.

27   Hill, p. 15.

28   Quoted Wright, pp. 30–1.

29   *The Orange and the Rose*, p. 13.

30   P. M. Rattansi, 'The Scientific Background', in Patrides (ed.), pp. 209, 223.

31   Above, p. 3.

32   A. Heal, *The English Writing Masters and their Copy Books 1570–1800, a biographical dictionary* (1931), pp. 9–11.

33   Charlton, p. 268; Heal, p. 9; Sir Edward Thompson, 'Handwriting', in Raleigh (ed.), Vol. I, Chap. X, pp. 284ff.

34   Hill, p. 133 and f.n. 4.

35   Charlton, pp. 229–30; Foster Watson, pp. 412–14; Kathleen Lambley, *The Teaching and Cultivation of the French Language in England during Tudor and Stuart Times* (1920), *passim.*

36   Charlton, p. 230; Foster Watson, pp. 425ff.

37   Charlton, p. 233; Foster Watson, pp. 427–31.

38   Foster Watson, p. 266.

39   Taylor, *Mathematical Practicioners* pp. 27ff.

40   Hill, pp. 16–17; Wright, Chap. XV.

41   Foster Watson, pp. 260, 300; Charlton, p. 164; Taylor, Biog. 5, p. 167.

42   Foster Watson, p. 321; Simon, p. 386.

43   Foster Watson, pp. 262–6.

44   Taylor, Biog. 19, p. 171; Francis R. Johnson, 'Thomas Hood's Inaugural Address as Mathematical Lecturer of the City of London, 1588', *Journal of the History of Ideas*, Vol. III, 1942, p. 94 f.n.

45   Taylor, p. 26, Biog. 17, pp. 170–1.

46   Taylor, p. 32, and Biog. 20, pp. 171, 33–4, and Biog. 38, p. 176.

47   Taylor, pp. 40–1, Biog. 48, p. 179; Johnson, 'Hood's Inaugural Address . . .'; Charlton, p. 281; Hill, pp. 33–4.

48   Taylor, Biog. 58, p. 184.

49   Ibid., p. 47, Biog. 53, pp. 181–2; Charlton, p. 283.

50   Taylor, Biog. 91, p. 191.

51   Hill, pp. 35–61.

52   Taylor, Biog. 114, p. 199; Biog. 138, pp. 205–6; Biog. 106, p. 196.

53   Ibid., Biog. 95, p. 193.

54   Ibid., Biog. 98, p. 194.

55   Ibid., Biog. 128, George Gilden *fl.* 1614–31, p. 203.

56   Foster Watson, pp. 279, 145.

57   Wright, *Middle Class Culture*, pp. 62–3; Simon, pp. 386, 395 f.n. 3.

58 Hill, *Intellectual Origins*, p. 69, quot. J. Jones, *The Jurors: Judges of Law and Fact* (1650) and p. 61.
59 Ibid., p. 95.
60 Thomas, 'Two Cultures, Court and Country . . .' in Russell (ed.), *Origins of the . . . Civil War, passim*.
61 Thomas, loc. cit., p. 176; C. V. Wedgwood, *Truth and Opinion, Historical Essays* (1960), 'The Last Masque', pp. 139–56; O. Millar, *The Age of Charles I* (Tate Gallery, 1972), Introduction and esp. pp. 37–45; J. Harris *et al.*, *The King's Arcadia, passim*; V. Pearle, *London and the Outbreak of the Puritan Revolution, City Government and National Politics* (1961), esp. p. 27.
62 Hill, pp. 100–9; H. M. Knox, 'William Petty's Advice to Samuel Hartlib', *British Journal of Educational Studies*, Vol. I, No. 2, May 1953; Turnbull, *Hartlib, Drury and Comenius, passim*.
63 Rabb, 'Population, economy and society . . .' in Patrides (ed.), p. 90.
64 M. Hunter, *Science and Society in Restoration England* (1981), esp. pp. 77–8.
65 See for example C. Webster, 'Science and the Challenge to the Scholastic Curriculum', in History of Education Society, *The Changing Curriculum* (1971), pp. 21–35.
66 Hunter, pp. 62–3.
67 Heal, *Writing Masters*, pp. 33–6, xi–xii.
68 Ibid., p. 106.
69 Ibid., p. 73.
70 Ibid., pp. 81–2.
71 Ibid., pp. 7–8.
72 Ibid., p. 72.
73 Ibid., p. 112; N. Hans, *New Trends in Education in the Eighteenth Century* (1951), p. 22.
74 Heal, pp. 67–8.
75 K. Charlton, 'The Educational Background', in Patrides (ed.), pp. 105–6.
76 Simon, p. 363.
77 *DNB*, T. Farnaby 1575?–1674; Sir John Bramston, *Autobiography* (Camden Society No. 32, 1845), pp. 101–2; Foster Watson, pp. 103, 3; M. L. Clarke, *Classical Education in Britain 1500–1900* (1959), p. 37.
78 Foster Watson, pp. 21–3; J. P. Tuck, 'The Beginnings of English Studies in the Sixteenth Century', *Durham Research Review*, No. 7, Sept. 1956, pp. 65–73.
79 Above, p. 53; Taylor, Biog. 103, p. 195.
80 Above, pp. 27, 59; Duncan, *Colfe's*, p. 18.
81 Foster Watson, 'Notes and Materials on Religious Refugees in their Relation to Education in England', *Proceedings of the Huguenot Society of London*, IX, 1911, pp. 80–1; Lambley, *French Language*, pp. 301ff.
82 W. J. Pinks, *History of Clerkenwell* (1856), p. 101.
83 *DNB*, Edward Wolley d. 1684; *Cal. State Papers Domestic*, 1655–6, p. 76.
84 A. à Wood, *Athenae Oxoniensis* (1817), Vol. III, p. 887.
85 Ibid., p. 882; D. Lysons, *Environs of London* (1792–6),iii, p. 139.
86 Lysons, Vol. iii, p. 184; J. Norris Brewer, *London and Middlesex* (1816), Vol. iv of the ref. work by Edward Wedlake Brayley, p. 240.
87 *DNB*, Fuller; Pepys's *Diary*, ed. Wheatley, I, p. 20.

88 Foster Watson, *Modern Subjects*, p. 330.

89 A. Browning (ed.), *Memoirs of Sir John Reresby* (1936), p. 2.

90 Mark Lewis, *Model for a School for the better education of youth* (1675?) and *Plan and Short Rules for pointing periods (1675?)*; Lambley, pp. 396ff.

91 F. P. and M. M. Verney, *Memoirs of the Verney Family in the Seventeenth Century* (1907), iii, p. 356.

92 J. Simon, 'The History of Education in Past and Present', *Oxford Review of Education*, Vol. 3, No. 1, 1977, p. 80.

93 *DNB*, Willis; Lysons, *Environs*, iii, p. 585; Foster Watson, *Modern Subjects*, p. 21.

94 *DNB*, Wyatt.

95 A. à Wood, *Athenae Oxoniensis*, Vol. III, pp. 1260–1; J. Nelson, *History, Topography and Antiquities of the Parish of St Mary, Islington* (1811, 1823 edn), p. 356.

96 Mark Pattison, *Milton* (English Men of Letters) (1879), pp. 43–9.

97 *DNB*, Woodward; Irene Parker, *Dissenting Academies in England* (1914), pp. 23, 37; Foster Watson, *Modern Subjects*, pp. xxiii, 18–19, 146–7, 195, 281.

98 Turnbull, *Hartlib . . .*, pp. 33, 90–1, 350, 372.

99 Foster Watson, *Modern Subjects*, p. 327.

100 J. Foster, *Sir John Eliot* (1865), Vol. 2, pp. 602–3 (reference kindly given by Mrs Joan Simon).

101 Chambers, Mary C. E., *The Life of Mary Ward, 1585–1645*, H. J. Coleridge, (ed.), (2 vols, 1882), i, pp. 107, 196, 215ff, 267–8, 273–4, 285–321, 327, 366, 423–8, ii, 22, 43ff, 53–4, 324–6, 452–74, 511–18, 235, 525; A. C. F. Beales, *Education under Penalty* (1963), pp. 98, 103, 203–5, 226–7, 254, 258; Mary D. R. Leys, *Catholics in England 1559–1829* (1961), p. 166; Lysons, *Environs*, ii, pp. 420–1; *The Laity's Directory* (1835–6); *Catholic Directory* (1854 and 1865). This school was later placed under the Benedictine Convent of the Immaculate Conception and moved to Teignmouth, Devon.

102 J. O. Halliwell (ed.), *The Autobiography and Correspondence of Sir Simonds D'Ewes Bart during the reigns of James I and Charles I* (1845), I, p. 157 (reference kindly given by Mrs Joan Simon).

103 D. Gardiner, *English Girlhood at School* (1929), p. 211; Pepys's *Diary*, ed. Wheatley, VI, p. 264.

104 *Cal. State Papers Domestic* 1635–6, p. 523; 1637, p. 422; Gardiner, pp. 211, 214, 224–6.

105 Gardiner, p. 211 and f.n.; Elizabeth, M. D. Morris, 'The Education of Girls in England from 1660–1800', (unpublished MA thesis, University of London, 1926), p. 142, Appendix VI, pp. xvii-xviii; Lysons, *Environs*, ii, p. 494; W. Robinson, *History of Hackney* (1842), i, p. 212; John Batchiler, *The Virgin's Pattern* (1661).

106 Gardiner, p. 211; Morris, p. xvi; Bramston, *Autobiography*, pp. 108, 111; *Diary of the Revd Ralph Josselin* (Camden Society Third Series, xv, 1908), p. 167; J. Aubrey, *Brief Lives*, A. Clark (ed.), (1898), ii, p. 153; *DNB*, Katherine Philips (1631–64); Lambley, *French Language*, p. 323; Doris Stenton, *The Englishwoman in History* (1957), p. 167; Lysons, *Environs*, ii, p. 510.

107 *DNB*, Wolley; Stenton, pp. 188–91.

108 Aubrey, *Miscellanies* (1857 edn), p. 219; W. Wycherley, *The Gentleman Dancing Master* (1671–2).
109 Turnbull, *Hartlib . . .*, pp. 117–21.
110 *DNB*; Bathsua Makin, *Essay to revive the Antient Education of Gentlewomen in Religion, Manners, Arts and Tongues* (1673); Gardiner, pp. 224–5, 244–5; Morris, p. 144, Appen. II, p. iii.
111 *DNB*, John Tutchin 1661–1707.
112 *DNB*; Mary Astell, *Essay in Defence of the Female Sex* (1696) and *Serious Proposal for Ladies* (1694 and 1697); Stenton, pp. 184–8, 220–4; Lysons, *Environs*, ii, pp. 137–8; L. Stone, *The Family, Sex and Marriage in England 1500–1800* (1970), p. 240, quot. Astell, *Reflections on Marriage* (1706, 1730 edn).
113 Lysons, *Environs*, iii, p. 157; Gardiner, p. 214.
114 Stone, Chap. 6, pp. 267–9.
115 A. Beaver, *Memorials of Old Chelsea* (1892), p. 150; Gardiner, pp. 215–16; Morris, p. 251, Appen. VII pp. xix–xxi; Purcell, *Dido and Aeneas*, (*c.* 1689); *Memoirs of the Verney Family*, ii, p. 366, iv, p. 221.
116 T. D'Urfey, *Love for Money or the Boarding School* (1691), *Beauties Triumph* (1676).
117 Stone, pp. 10, 652.
118 Ibid., pp. 203–4.
119 K. Charlton, '"Tak the to thi distaff . . .": the education of girls and women in early modern England', [1] *Westminster Studies in Education*, Vol. 4, 1981, pp. 3–18.
120 One notable private schoolmaster was also an insurance pioneer: see P. J. Wallis, 'Thomas Watts, Academy Master, Freemason, Insurance Pioneer, MP', *History of Education Society Bulletin.*, No. 32 Autumn 1983 pp. 51–3.

III From observation to Enlightenment

1 Lucy S. Sutherland, *A London Merchant, 1695–1774* (1933, 1962 edn), *passim.*
2 George, *London Life in the 18th Century*, pp. 16ff.
3 Ibid.; D. Jarrett, *England in the Age of Hogarth* (1974), pp. 12, 36–7.
4 George, pp. 15–16; R. Porter, *English Society in the Eighteenth Century* (1982), esp. pp. 235ff.
5 A. R. Humphreys, 'The Social Setting', in B. Ford (ed.), *From Dryden to Johnson* (Vol. 4, The Pelican Guide to English Literature, (1968 edn), pp. 15–48.
6 E. A. Wrigley, 'A Simple Model of London's Importance in Changing English Society and Economy, 1650–1750', *Past and Present*, No. 37, 1967, pp. 44ff.
7 George, Chap. I; G. Rudé, *Hanoverian London* (1971), Chap. 4.
8 George, p. 23, quot. Price, *Observations on . . . Population* (1779).
9 J. Boswell, *Life of Johnson*, G. B. Hill and L. F. Powell (eds), (1934), iii, p. 85.
10 P. Gay, *The Enlightenment: An Interpretation* (1967), Chap. I.
11 Clarke, *Classical Education*, p. 46.

12 H. Honour, 'Neo-Classicism', in Arts Council, *The Age of Neo-Classicism* (1972), p. xxiii.
13 E. Gombrich, *Ideals and Idols* (1979), p. 127.
14 N. Annan, *Leslie Stephen* (1951), p. 18.
15 Clarke, p. 75; R. M. Ogilvie, *Latin and Greek* (1964), esp. pp. 74ff.
16 W. Haig Brown, *Charterhouse Past and Present* (1879), p. 144.
17 W. A. L. Vincent, *The Grammar Schools . . . 1660–1714* (1969), pp. 125–6.
18 *VCH, Middlesex*, I, p. 303.
19 Vincent, pp. 125–6.
20 Ibid.
21 A. M. d'I Oakeshott, 'English Grammar Schools 1660–1714' (unpublished PhD thesis, University of London, 1969), pp. 38–40.
22 Picciotto, *St Paul's*, pp. 22–5; McDonnell, *St Paul's*, p. 339.
23 Oakeshott, pp. 38–40; Vincent, p. 129; F. Sargeaunt, *Annals of Westminster School* (1898), pp. 81ff.
24 Oakeshott, pp. 55–6, 61, 87; Draper, *Merchant Taylors'*, Chap. VIII; Dare, *Owen's*, pp. 36–8.
25 Oakeshott, pp. 32–8, 86–9.
26 Tompson, *Classics or Charity*, pp. 56ff.
27 Stott, *A History of Chigwell School*, Chaps. 3 and 4.
28 Tompson, *passim*.
29 Above, p. 48.
30 Oakeshott, p. 48.
31 *VCH, Middlesex*, I, p. 298.
32 Ibid., p. 314.
33 Ibid., p. 298.
34 Ibid., p. 310; Dare, pp. 45–6.
35 Carrington, *Two Schools*, Chap. 3.
36 Ibid., p. 90.
37 Draper, p. 107.
38 Ibid., pp. 95–6.
39 Tompson, pp. 95–9, esp. Tables 10 and 11.
40 Picciotto, p. 28.
41 McDonnell, pp. 329, 333, 357, 364; Picciotto, pp. 29–35.
42 Pearce, *Annals*, pp. 93–4.
43 Above, pp. 43–4; McDonnell, p. 332.
44 Sargeaunt, p. 103.
45 Ibid., pp. 105–6.
46 M. V. Wallbank, 'Eighteenth-Century Public Schools and the Education of a governing Elite', *History of Education*, Vol. 8, No. 1, March 1979, pp. 1–19.
47 Charles Lamb, *Essays of Elia* (1823, 1901 edn), 'Christ's Hospital five-&-thirty years ago', esp. pp. 25–32. Lamb's description of the Grecians of his time is a good record of the public work for which they were prepared. For a comparable description of Thackeray's experiences at the Charterhouse, see Davies, *Charterhouse*, pp. 263, 282.
48 Tompson, pp. 90–1, quot. Lambeth Palace Library, V, 1392; *VCH, Middlesex*, I, pp. 299–300; Trevor May, 'The Other Harrovians, Local Boys at Harrow School in the Nineteenth Century', in P. Searby, (ed.)

Educating the Victorian Middle Classes (History of Education Society, 1982), pp. 88–92.

49 Warren Derry, *Dr Parr: A portrait of the Whig Dr Johnson* (1966), *passim*; *DNB*, Parr; T. Maurice, *Memoirs of the Author of Indian Antiquities* (1819–1822), 3 vols., *passim*; Hist. Mss Com., *Du Cane*, pp. 228–32; *Dartmouth, 15th Rep. App.1*, III, pp. 194–6.

50 *VCH, Middlesex*, I, p. 300; E. Halévy, *A History of the English People in 1815* (1924, 1938 edn), Book III, pp. 162–5.

51 Wallbank, loc. cit., p. 11.

52 McDonnell, p. 336: Tompson, p. 66 and for a discussion of the Leeds case, pp. 116–24.

53 A. W. Trollope, *History of the Royal Foundation of Christ's Hospital* (1834), p. 137; M. Elwin, *The First Romantics* (1947), pp. 76–7.

54 Draper, p. 127; below, p. 368.

55 Draper, pp. 86–7; *DNB*, Edmund Calamy 1671–1732.

56 Pearle, *London and the Outbreak of the Puritan Revolution*, pp. 167–8.

57 G. N. Clark, *The Later Stuarts* (1940), pp. 20–2.

58 Parker, *Dissenting Academies*, p. 138; N. G. Brett-James, *Mill Hill* (1938), pp. 11–16.

59 H. McLachlan, *English Education under the Test Acts* (1931), p. 12.

60 Parker, pp. 57, 138; McLachlan, pp. 2, 10; J. W. Ashley Smith, *The Birth of Modern Education* (1954), pp. 2–3.

61 A. D. Morris, *Hoxton Square and the Hoxton Academies* (1957, printed for the author, Dr Williams's Library).

62 Nelson, *Islington*, p. 116 f.n.; S. Lewis, *The History and Topography of the Parish of St Mary Islington* (1842), pp. 267–70, f.n., 314–15, 319; Parker, pp. 57, 138; McLachlan, p. 10.

63 *DNB*, Morton 1627–1698; Parker, pp. 51, 58–63, 138; McLachlan, pp. 11, 24, 76–80; Ashley Smith, pp. 10, 56–61.

64 *DNB*, Dolittle 1630–1707, Edmund Calamy 1671–1732, Matthew Henry 1662–1714, Thomas Vincent 1634–1678; Parker, pp. 62, 138; McLachlan, pp. 11, 49–52; Ashley Smith, pp. 24–5, 87–90.

65 *DNB*, Gale 1628–1718, Thomas Rowe 1657–1705; Parker, pp. 62, 138; McLachlan, pp. 11, 49–52; Ashley Smith, pp. 41ff, 87–90.

66 *DNB*, Brand 1635–91; McLachlan, pp. 6, 85–6.

67 Parker, p. 138; Ashley Smith, pp. 72–4; McLachlan, p. 86.

68 Parker, pp. 59, 139; McLachlan, p. 14.

69 *DNB*, Oldfield 1656–1729, Tonge 1662–1726/7; Parker, p. 141; McLachlan, p. 9; Ashley Smith, pp. 70–1, 121–6; J. Oldfield, *Essay towards the Improvement of Reason* (1707); Morris, *Hoxton Square, passim*.

70 McLachlan, pp. 2–3, 9, 85–90; HMC National Register of Archives, *List of Archives of New College London* (1968).

71 McLachlan, p. 11; *DNB*, Pike 1772–1773.

72 Morris, *Hoxton Square*; Parker, p. 142; Ashley Smith, pp. 71, 95–6, 180–7; McLachlan, pp. 9, 18, 23–4, 117–25; *DNB*, Isaac Chauncey 1632–1712, Thomas Ridgeley 1667?–1734, John Eames d. 1744, David Jennings 1691–1762, Samuel Morton Savage 1721–1791, Abraham Rees 1743–1825, Andrew Kippis 1725–1795.

73 McLachlan, pp. 9, 236–9; Ashley Smith, pp. 227–8; Lewis, *Islington*, pp. 191–2; *DNB*, Stephen Addington 1729–96.

74   Parker, p. 141; Ashley Smith, pp. 192–7; McLachlan, pp. 9, 175–88;
     A. Cave, *Story of the Founding of Hackney College*, Hampstead Public Library
     Loc. Collec., MSS Notes on New College; *Hampstead Annual, 1905–6*,
     G. E. Matheson and S. C. Mayle (eds), pp. 118–27; *DNB*, Thomas Gibbons
     1720–85, John Conder 1714–81, John Pye Smith 1774–1851, Henry Mayo
     1733–93; Lysons, *Supplement to Environs* (1811), pp. 169–70; G. F. Nuttall,
     New College, London and its Library (Dr Williams's Trust, 1977).
75   Parker, p. 96; Ashley Smith, p. 152; Nuttall, op. cit.
76   *DNB*, J. Eyre 1754–1803; Cave, *Hackney College*, pp. 13–18, 42–51;
     Robinson, *Hackney*, ii, pp. 295–302.
77   *DNB*, R. Aspland 1782–1845; McLachlan, p. 9.
78   Lysons, *Environs*, ii, p. 480, iii, p. 633; *Supp.* p. 169; Robinson, *Hackney*, ii,
     pp. 290–4; Millicent Rose, *East End of London* (1951), p. 117; (eds) A.
     Aspinall and E. A. Smith, *English Historical Documents*, XI, pp. 701–2;
     McLachlan, pp. 9, 23, 38, 246–55; Ashley Smith, pp. 152–9, 171–8;
     Gentleman's Magazine, 1790 lx (2), p. 793; 1791 lxi (1), pp. 509–10; 1791
     lxi (2), pp. 621–2, 755, 984, 1022, 1025, 1026; 1793 lxiii (1), pp. 334, 409,
     412; 1796 lxvi (1), pp. 458–9; lxvi (2), p. 555; *DNB*, Thomas Belsham
     1750–1829, William Hazlitt 1778–1830, Richard Price 1723–91, Joseph
     Priestley 1733–1804, Abraham Rees 1743–1825, Hugh Worthington
     1752–1813.
79   Below, pp. 213ff.
80   B. Willey, *The Eighteenth-Century Background* (1940), Chap. X.
81   F. D. Klingender, *Art and the Industrial Revolution* (A. Elton (ed.), 1968), pp.
     34–5; (ed.) P. Rogers, *The Context of English Literature, the Eighteenth Century*
     (1978), pp. 168–9.
82   See G. E. Davie, *The Democratic Intellect, Scotland and her Universities in the
     Nineteenth Century* (1961).
83   Ibid., p. xii.
84   V. H. H. Green, *The Universities* (1969), p. 91.
85   H. Perkin, *The Origins of Modern English Society, 1780–1880* (1969), *passim*.
86   D. Davie, *A Gathered Church: The Literature of the English Dissenting Interest,
     1700–1930* (1978), pp. 26–7.
87   Ibid., p. 14.
88   A. Richardson, *History, Sacred and Profane* (1964), p. 85.
89   J. W. Ashley Smith, 'Modern History as Subject Matter for Higher
     Education; the Contribution of Francis Tallents, *Pedagogica Historica*, XVI
     (1975), pp. 5–15.
90   Nuttall, p. 52; McLachlan, p. 36.
91   McLachlan, pp. 122ff, 291; Ashley Smith, *Modern Education*, pp. 154ff,
     quot, Priestley, 'Lectures on History', *Works*, XXIV.
92   McLachlan, p. 27.
93   Ibid., pp. 118–19, quot. Wilson, *Dissenting Churches*, II, p. 75.
94   Parker, p. 55.
95   Ashley Smith, *Modern Education*, p. 157, quot. Priestley, *Works*, XXV, p. 368.
96   McLachlan, pp. 180ff.
97   Nuttall, pp. 21, 27–8; McLachlan, p. 123; Ashley Smith, *Modern Education*,
     pp. 196–7, 262–4.
98   Ashley Smith, p. 158, quot. 'Preface to Experiments . . . on . . . Air', *Works*,
     XXV, p. 375.

99 Ashley Smith, p. 175, quot. *Sermon*, 25.4.1787, pp. 41–2.
100 McLachlan, p. 27, quot. J. H. Colligan, *Eighteenth Century Nonconformity*, p. 73; A. W. Ward and A. R. Waller (eds), *Cambridge History of English Literature, X, The Age of Johnson* (1913), W. A. Shaw, 'The Literature of Dissent, 1660–1760', p. 382.
101 *DNB*, Joseph Gerrald.
102 Nuttall, p. 22.
103 Above, Chap. II; E. G. R. Taylor, *The Mathematical Practitioners of Hanoverian England. 1714–1840* (1966), p. 3.
104 Ibid., p. 14.
105 Ibid., p. 33, Biog. 385, p. 213, and 548, p. 249.
106 Taylor, p. 32, Biog. 526, p. 244; Z. Williams, *An Account of an Attempt to Ascertain the Longitude at Sea, by an Exact Theory of the Variations of the Magnetic Needle . . .* (1755), in fact written by Samuel Johnson, whose compassion helped Williams and then Williams's blind daughter Anna, to whom Johnson gave a home. See *Samuel Johnson. 1709–1984: A Bicentenary Exhibition* (Arts Council, 1984), No. 48, p. 85.
107 Taylor, pp. 43, 58.
108 Ben Ross Schneider Junior, *Wordsworth's Cambridge Education* (1957), p. 11.
109 Taylor, pp. 617, Biog. 49, p. 121; 117, p. 143; 35, p. 116.
110 Ibid., p. 7, Biog. 132, pp. 146–8; G. S. Rousseau, 'Science' in Rogers (ed.), *Context of Literature, the Eighteenth Century*, p. 162.
111 Taylor, Biog. 248, p. 174.
112 Ibid., Biog. 507, pp. 238–9.
113 Ibid., Biog. 68, pp. 129–30.
114 Ibid., Biog. 300, p. 189.
115 Ibid., Biog. 249, p. 174.
116 Ibid., p. 14, Biog. 136, pp. 149–50.
117 Ibid., Biog. 95, p. 136.
118 Ibid., Biog. 61, pp. 127–8; Hans, *New Trends*, p. 106; *DNB*, Haselden.
119 Hans, pp. 106, 67.
120 *DNB*, Walkingame; *Notes and Queries*, cci, pp. 256–61; J. Shield, *Preceptor's Assistant* (1780), preface.
121 Taylor, Biog. 348, pp. 204–5, Biog. 685, p. 280; Hans, pp. 106, 67; *DNB*, Samuel Dunn d. 1799; T. Faulkner, *An historical and topographical description of Chelsea . . . (1810)*, ii, pp. 210–11; Chelsea Public Library Loc. Collec; J. Bettesworth, *The New Universal ready reckoner* (1780); J. Bettesworth and H. Fox, *Observations on Education in general but particularly on Naval Education with a Plan for a Naval Academy* (1782).
122 Taylor, Biog. 77, p. 131; *DNB*.
123 *DNB*, Canton; *Biog. Brit.* (2nd edn), ii, pp. 215–22; LCC, *Survey of London*, xxvii, p. 57; Taylor, Biog. 239, p. 172.
124 Above, p. 65–6; Hans, p. 82ff; Taylor, Biog. 131, p. 146; 218, pp. 166–7; 142, p. 151; 124, pp. 144–5; 204, p. 164; 18, p. 113.
125 Taylor, p. 26, Biog. 93, p. 135.
126 Ibid., Biog. 318, pp. 194–5; 412, p. 218.
127 Letter 24 July 1783, quot. E. J. Holmyard, 'Science, Mathematics and Astronomy' in A. S. Turberville (ed.), *Johnson's England* (1933), Vol. II, Chap. XXIII, p. 243.

128 Davie, *Gathered Church*, p. 39.
129 Taylor, Biog. 688, pp. 280–1; *DNB*, Bonnycastle; Hans, p. 112; *Gent. Mag.*, 1821, xci (1), pp. 472, 482.
130 A. C. T. White, *The Story of Army Education* (1963), pp. 20–1.
131 B. H. Becker, *Scientific London* (1874, reprinted 1968), p. 89.
132 Taylor, p. 4.

IV The contribution of private adventure schools

1 Lysons, *Environs*, ii, p. 477, *Supplement*, p. 168; Robinson, *Hackney*, p. 140; R. Parkinson (ed.), *Autobiography of Henry Newcombe, MA* (Chetham Society, XXVI 1852), *passim*; N. Hans, *New Trends*, pp. 69, 70–4; *DNB*; *Gent. Mag.*, 1851, NS. xxxvi (2) pp. 88–9, NS. xxxv (1), pp. 198–200, NS. xvii (1), pp. 667–8; J. Gore (ed.), *The Creevey Papers* (1963), p. 12, and Appendix II, 'Creevey's School at Hackney', pp. 266–70; Elwin, *The First Romantics*, p. 74.

2 G. Clinch, *Marylebone and St Pancras* (1890), pp. 7, 98; Hans, pp. 127–8; W. H. Manchée, 'Marylebone and its Huguenot Associations', *Proc. Huguenot Soc. of London*, xi, pp. 58–128; *Gent. Mag.*, 1814, 1xxiv (2), p. 122, 1828, xcviii (2), p. 86; Marylebone Public Library Loc. Collec., Ashbridge, p. 315; *DNB*, G. Colman 1762–1836, William Cox 1747–1828, Charles Grey 1764–1845, Archibald Rowan 1751–1834.

3 M. Weekley, *Thomas Bewick* (1953), pp. 133, 152; F. S. de Carteret Bisson, *Our Schools and Colleges* (1872), p. 270, *Our Endowed and Private Schools* (1879), i, p. 710; Esther Greenberg, 'The Contribution to Education of Private Schools in the First Half of the Nineteenth Century', (unpublished MA thesis, University of London, 1953), p. 26; J. T. Smith, *A Book for a Rainy Day* (1905), p. 41.

4 Above, p. 45; J. Thorne, *Handbook to the Environs of London arranged alphabetically* (1876), p. 175; Lysons, *Environs*, ii, p. 285; *DNB*, Robert Uvedale 1642–1722; W. Robinson, *History of Enfield* (1843), i, pp. 48–9, 74, 115, 120, ii, p. 42; W. Hodson and E. Ford, *History of Enfield* (1873), pp. 28, 224; C. W. Whitaker, *Illustrated historical and statistical and topographical account of ... Enfield* (1911), pp. 185–92; G. W. Sturges, *Schools of Edmonton Hundred* (privately printed 1949), p. 87; Bisson, *Endowed Schools*, i, p. 613.

5 C. Warburton James, *Chief Justice Coke, his family and descendants*, extracts in Hounslow Public Library Loc. Collec.; Hans, p. 230.

6 G. Redford and T. H. Riches, *The History of the Ancient Town of Uxbridge* (1885), p. 177; Lysons, *Collectanea*, i, p. 22; Hans, p. 115; *Autobiography of William Jerdan* (1852), i, pp. 22–3.

7 *DNB*, John Ryland 1723–92, Charles Cowden Clarke 1787–1877, John Keats 1788–1821, Edward Holmes 1797–1859; Charles and Mary Cowden Clarke, *Recollections of Writers* (1878, reprint 1969), pp. 1–4, 9–10, 120–4; Hans, p. 61; Sturges, pp. 87–8; Hodson and Ford, p. 224; Whitaker, pp. 174–6; M. R. Watts, *The Dissenters* (1978), p. 459.

8 Robinson, *Enfield*, ii, p. 82; John Hope, *Occasional Attempt at Sentimental Poetry by a man in Business* (1769), p. 54; *DNB*, John Hope 1739–85.

9 Lewis, *Islington*, p. 320; Nelson, *Islington*, p. 49; W. Robinson, *History and*

Antiquities of Stoke Newington (1820), p. 91; Hans, p. 60; *Edinburgh Review*, Vol. 104, July 1856, p. 76.

10 Lewis, p. 152.

11 Greenberg, 'Private Schools', pp. 28, 77; *The Times*, 17 July 1821; *DNB*, Elhanan Bicknell 1788–1861.

12 Above, p. 112, *DNB*, Eliezer Cogan 1762–1855, Samuel Solly 1805–1871.

13 W. Draper, *Chiswick* (1923), p. 134.

14 Islington Public Library Loc. Collec., YA. 160.

15 Chelsea Public Library Loc. Collec.

16 Hans, pp. 67, 92–3; Nelson, *Islington*, p. 195; Lewis, pp. 351–2 and f.n.

17 G. O. Trevelyan, *The Early History of Charles James Fox* (1880, 1923 edn), pp. 44–5.

18 Lord Herbert (ed.), *The Pembroke Papers, 1734–80* (1942), pp. 18–22.

19 Lysons, *Environs*, ii, p. 193; T. Faulkner, *History and Antiquities of Brentford, Ealing and Chiswick* (1845), pp. 329, 368; P. W. Phillimore and W. H. Whitear (eds), *Historical Collections relating to Chiswick* (1897), pp. 25, 268; J. L. and Barbara Hammond, *Shaftesbury* (1925; Penguin edn 1969), p. 12; Hans, pp. 129–30.

20 Above, p. 127.

21 Faulkner, *Brentford, Ealing...*, p. 236; Edith Jackson, *Annals of Ealing* (1898), p. 98; Greenberg, p. 27; *DNB*, Samuel Goodenough 1743–1827; J. Nichols, *Illustrations of the Literary History of the Eighteenth Century* (1817–58), vi, pp. 245–56.

22 *DNB*, Weedon Butler 1742–1823; *Gent. Mag.*, 1823, xciii (2), pp. 182, 1832, ci (2), p. 186; J. Nichols, *Literary Anecdotes of the Eighteenth Century* (1812–15), ix, p. 223; R. Blunt, *An Illustrated Historical Handbook to the Parish of Chelsea* (1900), p. 113; N. Annan, 'The Intellectual Aristocracy', in J. H. Plumb (ed.), *Studies in Social History: A Tribute to G. M. Trevelyan* (1955).

23 *DNB*, Samuel Rose 1767–1804; Boswell, *Johnson*, Hill and Powell (eds), i, p. 46 f.n.; Faulkner, *Brentford, Ealing...*, pp. 348–54; *Gent. Mag.*, 1804, lxxiv (2), p. 1249; Nichols, *Lit. Anec.*, iii, pp. 386–7; Phillimore and Whitear, pp. 178, 247; Draper, *Chiswick*, p. 120; Hans, p. 130.

24 Hans, p. 130; *DNB*, Charles Burney 1757–1817; C. Buxton (ed.), *Memoirs of Sir Thomas Fowell Buxton* (1848), and *DNB*; *DNB*, Henry Milman 1791–1868; C. Lloyd, *Fanny Burney* (1937), p. 267.

25 Hans, pp. 77–8; *DNB*, James Elphinston 1721–1809; Boswell, *Johnson*, Hill and Powell (eds), ii, pp. 171, 226, 494, iii, p. 379; Nichols, *Lit. Anec.*, iii, p. 30; T. Faulkner, *History and Antiquities of Kensington* (1820), pp. 393–4; *Notes and Queries* Fifth Series, viii, p. 20; James Elphinston, *Plan of Education at Kensington Academy* (1764); *Principles of English Grammar Digested* (2 vols, 1765); *Education, a Poem in Four Books* (1763).

26 Hans, pp. 66–9, 87–91, 114–15; *DNB*, William Barrow 1754–1836, James Boswell the younger 1778–1822, Joseph Holman 1764–1817, Thomas Morton 1764–1838, Thomas Rowlandson 1765–1827, John Horne Tooke 1736–1812, Joseph Turner 1775–1851; Tompson, *Classics or Charity*, p. 43; M. Clare, *Youth's Introduction to Trade and Business* (1720); M. Clare and the Revd C. Barwis, *Rules and Orders for the Government of Soho Academy, London* (1744?–1751?); Dr W. Barrow, *An Essay...* (1802).

27 Hans, op. cit., *passim*; J. Simon, 'Private classical schools in eighteenth-

century England: a critique of Hans; *History of Education*, Vol. 8, No. 3, Sept. 1979, pp. 179ff.

28 D. P. Leinster-Mackay, 'The English Private School 1830–1914, with special reference to the private preparatory school' (unpublished PhD thesis, University of Durham, 1971/2), Chap. 4, f.n. 24.

29 John Locke, *Some Thoughts Concerning Education* (1693); *An Essay Concerning Human Understanding* (1690); M. V. C. Jeffreys, *John Locke, Prophet of Common Sense* (1967); James Barclay, *Treatise on Education* (1743).

30 *DNB*, R. Ainsworth; R. Ainsworth, *A Most Natural and Easy Way . . .* (1698); Nichols, *Lit. Anecs.*, v, pp. 248–54; *Notes and Queries*, Sixth Series, vii, pp. 65–6; *Gent. Mag.*, 1736, vi, p. 491; Lysons, *Environs*, ii, p. 32, iii, p. 463.

31 Lysons, *Collectanea*, i, p. 20; *Morning Post*, 4 Oct 1788.

32 W. A. C. Stewart and W. P. McCann, *The Educational Innovators 1750–1880* (1967), esp. pp. 23, 34–5.

33 Ibid., pp. 35ff; David Williams, *Lectures on Education* (1774); J. J. Rousseau, *Emile*, Bk V.

34 W. Johnstone, *Result of Experience in the Practice of Instruction, or Hints for the improvement of the Art of Tuition as regards the Middling and Higher Classes of Society* (1818); Greenberg, pp. 53, 79–80, 144, 147, 160–4.

35 M. Miall, *Practical Remarks on Education* (1822); Greenberg, pp. 77–85, 147, 164–71; Nelson, *Islington*, p. 354; *DNB*, Miall.

36 *DNB*, John Evans; John Evans, *Essay on the Education of Youth* (1799); *The Times*, 17 Jan. 1810, 6 Jan. 1821; Greenberg, pp. 29, 83–4 and f.n., 137, 146, 149; Lewis, *Islington*, p. 349; Nelson, *Islington*, p. 52; Islington Public Library Loc. Collec., YA. 160.

37 Katharine M. Rogers, *Feminism in Eighteenth-Century England* (1982), Chap. 1. See Stone, *The Family, Sex and Marriage . . .* for the most elaborate theory of the 'Closed Domestic Nuclear Family' and its emphasis on 'Affective Individualism' binding a closed group of kindred together by emotion and sentiment as well as by social and economic interdependence.

38 Lysons, *Environs*, iii, pp. 138, 299; Nelson, pp. 167, 239, 258; Robinson, *Stoke Newington*, p. 82.

39 Norris Brewer, *London and Middlesex . . .*, iv, p. 216 f.n.; Pigot's *Directory, Middlesex*, 1832/4, 'Edmonton'.

40 *Spectator*, I, No. 18, p. 345; Gardiner, *English Girlhood*, p. 401.

41 Stenton, *Englishwoman*, p. 252.

42 Morris, *Education of Girls*, p. 147 f.n.; Clinch, *Marylebone*, p. 8; Manchée, 'Marylebone and Huguenot Associations', pp. 89–90; Lysons, *Environs*, ii, p. 245; Gardiner, p. 339; Cobden Sanderson (ed.), *Memoirs of the late Mrs Robinson Written by herself* (1801, 1930 edn), pp. 23–5.

43 Greenberg, p. 181; *The Times*, 13 July 1828; T. Crofton Croker, *A Walk from London to Fulham* (1860, 1836 edn), p. 206; T. Faulkner, *History and Antiquities of Fulham* (1813), p. 329; C. J. Ferét, *Fulham Old and New . . .* (1890), ii, pp. 192, 265; P. Barfoot and J. Wilkes, *The Universal British Directory . . .* (1791–7), v, pp. 222–4; W. M. Thackeray, *Vanity Fair* (1848).

44 J. H. Plumb, 'The Walpoles, Father and Son', in (ed.) Plumb, *Studies in Social History*, p. 203.

45 Katherine E. Farrer (ed.), *Correspondence of Josiah Wedgwood 1781–1794* (1906), ii, pp. 190–1, 322–3.

46 Above, p. 77; Obituary of Mrs Pemberton, *Gent. Mag.*, 1815, ii, p. 571;

M. E. Grimshaw *Pre Victorian medals* (1985), pp 5–6; Lysons, *Environs*, ii, p. 90; Beaver, *Chelsea*, pp. 92, 150, 189, 246, 319, 343; R. Davies, *Chelsea Old Church* (1904), p. 210; Faulkner, *Chelsea*, pp. 350, 366; A. G. K. L'Estrange, *Village of Palaces* (1880), I, p. 180 f.n.; G. Bryan, *Chelsea* (1869), p. 176; Morris, 'Education of Girls', pp. 147, 251, Appendix 7, pp. xix-xxi; Gardiner, *English Girlhood*, pp. 215–16, 220ff; John Jenkins, *Female Education and Christian Fortitude under Affliction* (1772).

47 *London Gazette*, No. 1625, 13–16 June 1682, No. 1839, 2–5 July 1683; Gardiner, p. 216; Lysons, iii, p. 180; Norris Brewer, *London and Middlesex*, iv, p. 147; Florence M. Gladstone, *Aubrey House, Kensington*, pp. 7, 32, 28, 38–9, in Kensington Public Library Loc. Collec., 36556.

48 Croker, *Walk from London*, pp. 40–1; *DNB*, Letitia Landon 1802–38; *Life of Mrs Sherwood*, ed. by her daughter Sophia Kelly (1854), pp. 87, 91, 108, 118, 125, 159; Frances Kemble, *Record of a Girlhood* (1878), pp. 73, 99, 109

49 Lysons, *Collectanea*, i, p. 15; Chelsea Public Library Loc. Collec., Scrapbook 9.

50 Croker, *Walk*, pp. 137–9; *Memoirs of the late Mrs Robinson*, pp. 16–20.

51 Gardiner, pp. 339, 340.

52 Mona Wilson, *Jane Austen and Some Contemporaries* (1938), p. 10.

53 H. Chorley (ed.), *Letters of M. R. Mitford* (1872), i, p. 6; Revd A. G. L'Estrange (ed.), *Life of Mary Russell Mitford* (1970 edn), i, pp. 11–14; A. C. Percival, *The English Miss* (1939), p. 86; Morris, p. 156; James Rice, *Plan for Female Education* (1791); M. E. Grimshaw, *Silver Medals, Badges and Trophies from Schools in the British Isles 1550–1850* (n.d.), pp. 20–1; Lewis, *Islington*, p. 321; C. Tomalin, *The Life and Death of Mary Wollstonecraft* (1974).

54 G. B. Whittaker, *The Boarding School and London Masters' Directory, or the Addresses of the First Teachers in Every Department of Education and of the Principal Finishing and Preparatory Seminaries of Young Ladies and Gentlemen in and near the Metropolis* (1828).

55 Perkin, *Origins of Modern English Society*, p. 62 and *passim*.

56 See F. K. Brown, *Fathers of the Victorians* (1961).

57 P. Collins, 'Dickens and London' in H. J. Dyos and M. Wolff (eds), *The Victorian City* (2 vols, 1973), Chap. 23, pp. 537ff; F. Schwarzbach, *Dickens and the City* (1979).

58 Perkin, p. 117.

59 E. E. Lampard, 'The Urbanizing World' in Dyos and Wolff, I, pp. 4, 10ff.

60 J. T. Coppock, 'A General View of London and its Environs' in J. T. Coppock and H. C. Prince (eds), *Greater London* (1964), pp. 28–9.

61 Rudé, *Hanoverian London*, p. 3.

62 H. C. Prince, 'North West London, 1814–1863', in Coppock and Prince (eds), Chap. 4, esp. p. 81.

63 P. Hall, 'The Development of Communications', in Coppock and Prince (eds), esp. pp. 52–9.

64 Prince, 'North West London, 1814–1863', op. cit., p. 107; G. Weightman and S. Humphries, *The Making of Modern London 1815–1914* (1983), Chap. 4.

65   T. C. Barker and M. Robbins, *A History of London Transport*, Vol. I, *The Nineteenth Century* (1963), pp. 3–6, 320 f.n., xxvi; J. R. Kellett, *The Impact of Railways on Victorian Cities* (1969), pp. 365ff.

66   Kellett, esp. p. 367; Hall, 'Development of Communications' in Coppock and Prince (eds), *passim*; J. Simmons, 'The Power of the Railway', in Dyos and Wolff (eds), pp. 285ff.

67   Faulkner, *Brentford, Ealing...*, p. 236; Jackson, *Annals*, p. 98; Greenberg, p. 27; *DNB*, Samuel Goodenough; Nichols, *Illustrations of Literary History*, vi, pp. 245–56.

68   Thorne, *Environs*, p. 160; Faulkner, *Brentford, Ealing...*, *p. 249*; C. Jones, *Ealing from Village to Corporate Town* (n.d.), pp. 87, 148; Jackson, p. 160; Maurice, *Memoirs of the Author of Indian Antiquities*, i, pp. 31–2; Bisson, *Schools and Colleges*, p. 297; *DNB*, Thomas Maurice 1754–1824, George Selwyn 1809–1878; J. Jackson, 'John Henry Newman, the origins and application of his educational ideas' (unpublished PhD thesis, University of Leicester, 1968).

69   Above, p. 128; Bisson, *Endowed Schools*, i, p. 613.

70   *The Times*, 6 Jan. 1835; Greenberg, pp. 27, 136; Islington Public Library Loc. Collec., YA. 160 ISL, V. p. 59, X, p. 210 FLO, pp. 228–9; Hans, *New Trends*, p. 79; *Gent. Mag.*, 1786, lvi (2), pp. 269–70; Nelson, *Islington*, pp. 116–17; Lewis, *Islington*, pp. 162 and f.ns, 176; *DNB*, John Nichols 1745–1826, William Tooke 1744–1820.

71   Hans, p. 111; *DNB*, Thomas Stamford Raffles 1781–1826.

72   *DNB*, Thackeray; L. S. Stevenson, *Showman of Vanity Fair, The Life of William Makepeace Thackeray* (1947), pp. 8ff; G. N. Ray, *Thackeray, the Uses of Adversity* (1955), pp. 71–2, 76.

73   M. Robbins, *Middlesex* (1953), p. 133; *Middlesex Chronicle*, 7 Jan. 1939; *Isleworth Citizen*, Sept. 1925; *DNB*, Shelley; Shelley, Dedicatory Epistle of 'Laon and Cythna'.

74   Chelsea Public Library Loc. Collec.; Faulkner, *Chelsea*, ii, p. 214; Bryan, *Chelsea*, p. 186; J. B. Ellenor, *Rambling Recollections of Chelsea* (1901), pp. 19–23.

75   Whittaker, *Directory ...* (1828), p. 37.

76   *The Times*, 13 Jan. 1821; Greenberg, p. 126.

77   Whittaker, *Directory* (1828), p. 27; *The Times*, 27 Jan. 1814; Greenberg, pp. 39, 44, 83, 92, 122–4; D. Dowling, op. cit. in text.

78   Greenberg, p. 114, ref. *The Times*, 19 March 1821.

79   Ibid., p. 113, ref. *The Times*, 24 Dec. 1822.

80   Ibid., p. 113, ref. *The Times*, 4 Jan. 1840.

81   Ibid., pp. 39, 56, 71 and f.n., ref. *The Times*, 6 Jan. 1835, 20 Jan. 1838; G. J. Aungier, *History and Antiquities of Syon Monastery ...* (1840), p. 212; BM Catalogue lists 26 publications of Alexander Jameson, AM, LLD, between 1814–46.

82   Greenberg, p. 91, ref. *The Times*, 22 Oct. 1835; *VCH, Middlesex*, III, pp. 231, 236.

83   Greenberg, p. 93; *British Educational Magazine*, ii, 1835, p. 256; Islington Public Library Loc. Collec., YA16 COL.

84   Greenberg, pp. 61, 90, ref. *The Times*, 16 Sept. 1835.

85   Ibid., p. 142, ref. *The Times*, 3 July 1821.

86   Ibid., p. 138, ref. *The Times*, 15 Aug. 1835.

87 Ibid., p. 44, ref. *The Times*, 8 Jan. 1840.
88 Ibid., pp. 44, 150; Islington Public Library Loc. Collec., YA166 MAN, cuttings from *The Times*, 23 June 1835, 1 Jan. 1840, *Morning Herald*, 1 Jan. 1831, *Morning Chronicle*, 18 July 1836.
89 Greenberg, pp. 139, 145, 151, ref. *The Times*, 14 March 1835; Islington Public Library Loc. Collec., YA160 COL, cuttings from *Morning Herald*, 15 July 1826, *Morning Chronicle*, 1825 and 1835.
90 Greenberg, p. 140, ref. *The Times*, 9 July 1840.
91 Ibid., ref. *The Times*, 8 July 1835.
92 Ibid., ref. *The Times*, 8 Jan. 1835; Grimshaw, *Silver Medals*, pp. 18–30.
93 D. Newsome, *Godliness and Good Learning* (1961), pp. 38ff; E. C. Mack, *Public Schools and British Opinion* (1938), I, pp. 151ff, 218.
94 Sturges, *Schools of Edmonton Hundred*, pp. 77–9.
95 Ibid., pp. 80–1.
96 Below, pp. 175ff; H. Hayman, *Can We Adapt the Public School System to the Middle Classes?* (1858), quot. T. W. Bamford, *The Rise of the Public Schools* (1967), p. 49.
97 BPP *Commissioners appointed by Her Majesty to inquire into the education given in schools in England, not comprised within Her Majesty's two recent commissions on popular education and on public schools* 1867–8 [C.3966] comprising Vol. XXXVIII of Sessional Papers (hereafter Schools Inquiry (*SIC*) or Taunton Commission) Vol. IV, Minutes of Evidence Q.3144–3502, Q.3850–3986
98 *SIC*, V, p. 885, Q.17417, and Appendix, pp. 894–7.
99 *Crockford's Scholastic Directory for 1861, Being an Annual Work of Reference for Facts relating to Educators, Education and Educational Establishments (Public and Private) in the United Kingdom* (1861).
100 Bisson, op. cit.
101 Below, p. 253; BPP *Report of the Select Committee to inquire into the education of the lower orders in the Metropolis . . .* HC 1816–1818, 1816 [498] IV 1, 1817 [479] III 81, 1818 [136] IV 1; *Education Enquiry Abstract of Answers and Returns* 1833 Vol. 1; 1835 Vol. II, xli–xlii.
102 G. Baron, 'The Secondary Schoolmaster, 1895–1914' (unpublished PhD thesis, University of London, 1952), pp. 1–2; Laadan Fletcher, *The Teachers' Press in Britain 1802–1888* (1978), p. 41; *Scholastic Journal* (1839–40), New Series (1856–7).
103 *Fifty Years of Progress in Education*, a Review of the Work of the College of Preceptors from its Foundation in 1846 to its Jubilee in 1896 (pub. by the College, 1896), pp. 3–6
104 Evidence of the Secretary, J. Robson, *SIC*, IV, p. 4; *Fifty Years*, pp. 6–8; *Transactions of the National Association of Social Science* (hereafter *TNASS*) (1862), pp. 235ff, paper of Dr G. A. Jacob, Master of Christ's Hospital and Dean of the College.
105 *Fifty Years*, pp. 4, 6–15; *SIC*, IV, pp. 1, 7ff; Baron, pp. 433–4.
106 *TNASS* (1862), pp. 245–9, 334–6; this grew from the Benthamite Law Reform Society.
107 *Fifty Years*, pp. 22–6, 33–4; *DNB*, Joseph Payne 1808–1876; BPP *Special Report from the Select Committee on Teachers' Registration and Organization Bill* 4 July 1891 (C. 335) XVII, pp. 42, 47.
108 *Fifty Years*, pp. 15–16; *SIC*, IV, pp. 31ff.

109 *Fifty Years, passim.*
110 G. B. Robinson, 'A Study of the Private Schools' Association (latterly Independent Schools') in relation to changing policies in the administration of education by national and local government agencies, 1880–1944' (unpublished MA thesis, University of London, 1966), p. 38; Baron, 'Secondary Schoolmaster', p. 100; below, p. 419.
111 *Scholastic World*, 1 July 1879; Bisson, *Schools and Colleges*, p. 289; BPP . . . *Report from Select Committee on Teachers' Registration . . .* 1891, pp. 116–42; BPP *Special Reports on Educational Subjects* II 1898 (C. 8943) HC, p. 269, XXIV; Baron, pp. 65, 79, 88, 418ff.
112 *Scholastic Gazette* (No. 83 NS. No. 7), 1 Jan. 1882.
113 BPP *Report of the Royal Commission on Secondary Education* 1894–5 (C.7862 i) (hereafter called the *Bryce Report*), I, pp. 51–2, III, pp. 279–82.
114 C. Booth, *Life and Labour of the People in London* (1889–1903), First Series, *Poverty*, iii, pp. 248–50, 263.
115 'Difficulties of a Middle–Class Schoolmaster', *The Academia*, 14 March 1868, p. 257.
116 Bisson, *Endowed Schools*, i, pp. 885, xlv.
117 *Crockford's Scholastic Directory*, p. xx.
118 A. A. Milne, *It's Too Late Now* (1939), pp. 2–8, 21–22, 81; Bisson, *Endowed Schools*, i, p. 722.
119 *Report . . . Sel. Com. . . . Teachers' Registration* 1891, p. 42; Department of Education School File 6388.
120 *Crockford's Directory*, p. viii; Sturges, pp. 83ff, quot. E. Clarke, *The Story of My Life*; personal reminiscences of Mrs Lacy, daughter of C. F. H. White, headmaster.
121 For a discussion in sociological theoretical terms see K. Hoskin, 'Examinations and the Schooling of Science', in R. MacLeod (ed.), *Days of Judgement* (1982), pp. 213ff.
122 Bisson, *Schools and Colleges*, p. 269; Bisson, *Endowed Schools*, i, p. 709; Islington Public Library Loc. Collec., YA 166 SHA.
123 Quot. Sturges, pp. 84ff.
124 Milne, pp. 47–8; J. Van Gogh-Bonger (ed.), *Letters of Vincent van Gogh to his brother, 1872–1886* (1927–29), 1, pp. 62, 71–84, 89.
125 *Report Sel. Com. Teachers' Registration* 1891, pp. 142–3; Baron, 'Secondary Schoolmaster', pp. 142ff; *Report of a Conference on Secondary Education convened by the Vice-Chancellor of the University of Cambridge* (1896) (hereafter *Cambridge Conference 1896*), pp. 65–6.
126 *TNASS*, 1857, Inaugural Address of W. Cowper, pp. 59–62.
127 G. O. Trevelyan, *Life and Letters of Lord Macaulay* (1901 edn), p. 240. Letter to sister Hannah, 14 Oct. 1833.
128 Bisson, *Endowed Schools*, i, p. 712.
129 Ibid., p. 754.
130 Ibid., p. 760.
131 Ibid., p. 719.
132 Bisson, *Schools and Colleges*, p. 474.
133 *SIC*, VII, pp. 233ff.
134 G. Kitson Clark, *The Making of Victorian England* (1962), Chap. VIII, esp. pp. 255ff.
135 *SIC*, I, p. 15.

136 A. Trollope, *Autobiography* (1883, 1953 edn), pp. 4, 30–1.

137 See J. Roach, *Public Examinations in England 1850–1900* (1971), and Roach, 'Middle Class Education and Examinations: Some Early Victorian Problems', *British Journal of Educational Studies*, X, May 1962.

138 *SIC*, IV, pp. 82ff.

139 *SIC*, IV, pp. 492ff, below, pp. 188–9.

140 *SIC*, V, pp. 22ff, and Appendix to evidence, p. 42.

141 Bisson, *Schools and Colleges*, p. 271.

142 Bisson, *Endowed Schools*, i, p. 710; *Crockford's . . . Directory*, p.x.

143 Bisson, *Endowed Schools*, i, pp. 718–19; the Board of Trade examinations for the Masters and Mates of Merchantmen began in 1850.

144 See J. Hearl, 'Military Examinations and the Teaching of Science, 1857–1879', in MacLeod (ed.), *Days of Judgement*, pp. 109–49.

145 *SIC*, VII, pp. 354ff.

146 *SIC*, IV, pp. 187ff and 195.

147 Bisson, *Schools and Colleges*, p. 275.

148 Ibid, p. 297; Bisson, *Endowed Schools*, i, pp. 754, lxxxviii, 755, lxxvi.

149 Bisson, *Endowed Schools*, p. 871.

150 'Training for the Army and Navy, A Successful Tutorial System', *St James Budget*, 11 Jan. 1895, Kensington Public Library Loc. Collec., Box H. 1005; W. S. Churchill, *My Early Life* (1944 edn), p. 36.

151 Bisson, *Endowed Schools*, i, p. 759.

152 Greenberg, 'Private Schools', pp. 71, 152–4, *The Times*, 4 July 1835, 23 July, 10 Dec. 1840; see Gladstone Pottery Museum, Stoke-on-Trent, ceramic tile collection.

153 Greenberg, p. 70, *The Times*, 14 Dec. 1840.

154 BPP *Royal Commission on Technical Instruction* 1884 (C.3981) (hereafter called the Samuelson Commission), Vol. 1, pp. 417–18; *Journal of the London Chamber of Commerce*, 5 Oct. 1885, p. 267.

155 *Hampton's Scholastic Directory and Hotel Guide* (1893–4), p. 8.

156 Sturges, pp. 118–19.

157 Greenberg, pp. 711, 404.

158 Bisson, *Endowed Schools*, i, pp. 404, 401.

159 *Bryce Report*, I, pp. 1–2.

160 See D. L. Leinster-Mackay, 'Private or Public Schools: the Educational Debate in Laissez-faire England', *Journal of Educational Administration and History*, Vol. XV, No. 2, July 1983, pp. 1ff.

161 *Bryce Report*, II, p. 453.

V The middle-class education question

1 J. H. Higginson, 'The Evolution of Secondary Education', *British Journal of Educational Studies*, XX, No. 2, June 1972, pp. 165ff.

2 *English Journal of Education*, Vol. VI, 1852, pp. 202–3.

3 *The Times*, 1 July 1861; B. Heeney, *Mission to the Middle Classes, The Woodard Schools 1848–1891* (1969), p. 12.

4 Higginson, loc. cit., quot. Arnold's letter on 'The Education of the Middle Classes', *Sheffield Courant*, April 1832.

5 See M. Arnold, *Culture and Anarchy* (1869, ed. J. Dover Wilson, 1966).

6   Lord Norton, 'Middle Class Education', *The Nineteenth Century*, Vol. XIII, Feb. 1883, pp. 233ff; *DNB*, Norton (Charles Bowyer Adderley), Conservative MP for N Staffs 1841–78, Vice-President of Committee of Council for Education 1858–9, Charity Commissioner 1856–7.

7   Lord Fortescue, *Public Schools for the Middle Classes* (1864), pp. 1–12.

8   Dyos and Wolff (eds), *The Victorian City*, Vol. II, Chap. 38, editors' summary.

9   Ibid., Chap. 37, S. Pierson, 'The Way Out', p. 875; F. Schwarzbach, *Dickens and the City*, *passim*.

10   B. Simon, *Studies in the History of Education 1780–1870* (1960), pp. 78, 119–20; F. H. W. Sheppard, *London 1808–1870: The infernal wen* (1971), p. 217.

11   W. H. Burston, *James Mill on Philosophy and Education* (1973), pp. 69–72.

12   Hans, *New Trends*, p. 61; *DNB*, Thomas Wright Hill 1763–1851; above, p. 107.

13   These counters used the decimal system and their usage was so elaborate that 'one wonders how there could have been time for any teaching . . .' A number of schools copied the system. See The British Association of Numismatic Societies, R. N. P. Hawkins, *Four Studies of British Metallic Tickets and Commercial Checks of the 19th–20th Centuries*, Doris Stockwell Memorial Papers, No. 2, 1975, pp. 4, 8–9, 16–18, plate III.

14   A. T. Milne, *Catalogue of the MSS of Jeremy Bentham in the Library of University College London* (1937), Box XVIII, 178–182, 183–7; Folder 22 (Box X); *Public Education: Plan for the Government and Liberal Instruction of Boys in large numbers* (anon., 1822, 1825); *Edinburgh Review*, Vol. XLI, No. 82, Jan. 1825, pp. 315ff; *Quarterly Journal of Education*, Vol. VI, July/October 1833, pp. 115ff; *SIC*, V, pp. 838ff, Examination of Birkbeck Hill; *Scholastic Journal*, NS. XV, 30 Nov. 1856, p. 90; *Scholastic World*, 1 Sept. 1878; *Gent. Mag.*, 1851, NS. XXVI (2), p. 326; National Register of Archives, *Tottenham Exhibition Catalogue* (1956), pp. 24–6; W.Robinson, *The History and Antiquities of the parish of Tottenham in the county of Middlesex* (1840), pp. 219ff; Thorne, *Environs*, pp. 618–19; Sturges, *Schools of Edmonton Hundred*, p. 71; Greenberg, 'Private Schools', pp. 19, 87; Bisson, *Schools and Colleges*, p. 272, *Endowed Schools*, i, p. 885; R. L. Archer, *Secondary Education in the 19th Century* (1921, reprinted 1966), pp. 90–6; Mack, *Public Schools and British Opinion*, I, pp. 147, 168–70; J. L. Dobson, 'The Hill Family and Educational Change', *Durham Research Review*, Vol. III, No. 10, Sept. 1959, No. 11, Sept. 1960, No. 12, Sept. 1961.

15   H. J. K. Usher, C. D. Black Hawkins, C. J. Carrick, *et al.*, *An Angel without Wings: The History of UCS 1830–1980* (UCS, 1981); *SIC*, IV, pp. 313ff; *Bryce Commission*, II, pp. 218ff; Bisson, *Schools and Colleges*, p. 310, *Endowed Schools*, i, p. 763, ii, p. 193; Mack, *Public Schools*, I, p. 159; H. C. Barnard, 'A Great Headmaster: John Lewis Paton, 1863–1946', *British Journal of Educational Studies*, XI (1), Nov. 1962.

16   Thorne, p. 561; *VCH, Middlesex*, III, p. 137; *English Journal of Education*, 1863, pp. 298–9; *Illustrated London News*, 7 Sept. 1867; Bisson, *Schools and Colleges*, p. 303, *Endowed Schools*, i, p. 863; M. Hewlett, 'The Gods in the Schoolhouse', *The English Review*, XIII, pp. 43ff, Hounslow Public Library Loc. Collec.; C. Bibby, 'A Victorian Experiment in International Education', *British Journal of Educational Studies*, V, Nov. 1956, pp. 23–36.

17   V. G. Toms, 'Secular Education in England 1800–1870' (unpublished PhD thesis, University of London, 1972), pp. 144–7.

18   Ibid., pp. 382–3.

19 *SIC*, IX, p. 245.

20 'The Employment of Machinery', *Westminster Review*, Vol. 5, pp. 101–30.

21 See F. W. Robinson, 'William Ellis and his work for education' (unpublished MA thesis, University of London, 1919); Toms, 'Secular Education', esp. Chaps 1, 6, 7 and 9; E. K. Blyth, *Life of William Ellis* (1889); BPP *Report of the Commission on Popular Education* 1861 [C.2794] HC (hereafter called the Newcastle Commission), V, pp. 179–82, 406–10, 593ff; *SIC*, VII, pp. 351, 533ff; BPP *Report of the Royal Commission on Scientific Instruction and the Advancement of Science* 1872 (C.536) (hereafter called the Devonshire Report), 1st, 2nd and 3rd Reports, p. 594, Examination of William Ellis, p. 99, letter from Ellis; *TNASS*, 1857, W. Mathieu Williams, 'On the Teaching of Social Economy', pp. 509–17; G. Combe 'On Teaching Physiology . . . in Common Schools', pp. 208–19; 1862, E. K. Blyth, 'On the more Systematic Teaching of Rules of Conduct in Harmony with the Truths of Economic Science', pp. 309–19, 352; *Lectures in Connection with the Educational Exhibition of the Royal Society of Arts, 1854*, pp. 269ff, W. A. Shields, 'On the Inspector and the Schoolmaster', pp. 115ff, W. Ellis, 'On Economic Science'; Florence F. Miller, 'William Ellis and his Work as an Educationist', *Fraser's Magazine*, Feb. 1882, pp. 233–52; ed. R. H. Hadden, *Reminiscences of the Revd William Rogers* (1888), p. 87; Bisson, *Endowed Schools*, ii, p. 533; T. D. Wickenden, *William Ellis School, 1862–1962* (n.d.), esp. Chaps II–IV.

22 S. T. Coleridge, *The Constitution of Church and State* (1829); B. M. G. Reardon, *From Coleridge to Gore; A century of religious thought in Britain* (1971), esp. pp. 84–9.

23 G. Kitson Clark, *Churchmen and the Condition of England, 1832–1885* (1973), *passim*; A. R. Vidler, *The Church in an Age of Revolution* (Pelican History of the Church, Vol. 5) (1961), Chap. 4; D. Newsome, *The Parting of Friends* (1966), Chap. 5, Sec. 1, pp. 211ff.

24 P. J. Welch, 'Bishop Blomfield' (unpublished PhD thesis, University of London, 1952); *DNB*, C. J. Blomfield 1786–1857.

25 Welch, p. 45; J. Avery, *Bishopsgate Schools 1702–1889* (1932), pp. 1–10; BPP *Endowed Charities London* 1900, LXI, 15, pp. 646–72.

26 See G. F. A. Best, *Temporal Pillars, Queen Anne's Bounty, the Ecclesiastical Commissioners and the Church of England* (1964).

27 Welch, p. 338.

28 Sheppard, *The Infernal Wen*, pp. 210–11, 213–14; Lewis, *Islington*, pp. 118–22.

29 Kitson Clark, *Churchmen . . .*, p. 47; Charlotte Brontë', *Shirley* (1849), Chap. I.

30 *Quarterly Review*, VIII, Feb. 1837, pp. 237ff; Sheppard, pp. 214–15.

31 Welch, pp. 280, 286; *DNB*, Blomfield.

32 Welch, pp. 472–3.

33 *DNB*, Charles Richard Sumner 1790–1874; Newsome, *Parting of Friends*, *passim*.

34 Welch, Chap. VIII; Letter 1 Dec. 1856 to Archdeacon Sinclair, *The Times* 13 Dec. 1856, quot. Welch, p. 690.

35 Best, *Temporal Pillars*, pp. 154ff.

36 BPP *Return of Endowed Charities London* 1896 (144, 306) LXIII Pt 1, 555;

SIC, X, p. 106; *Crockford's Directory*, p. 232; Kitson Clark, *Churchmen . . .*, p. 72; *DNB*, W. Champneys; C. N. Lee, *St Pancras Church and Parish* (1955), Chap. X.

37 H. Prince, 'NW London', in Coppock and Prince (eds), *Greater London*, p. 123; Sheppard, p. 228.

38 Lee, *St Pancras*, Chap. IX; Palmer, *St Pancras*, pp. 159–62; Welch, pp. 604–7, 661; D. J. Palmer, *The Rise of English Studies* (1965), pp. 18–25; F. Boase, *Modern English Biography* (1892–1921), I p. 802, II, p. 278.

39 Palmer, p. 142; F. Miller, *St Pancras Past and Present* (1874), pp. 239ff; *Crockford's Directory*, p. xiii; Boase, *Biography*, VI, W. C. Williams; *SIC*, IV, pp. 488ff; *Scholastic World*, No. 2, Vol. 11, 1 Aug. 1878.

40 A. T. Milne (ed.), *Centenary Book of Christ's College 1857–1957* (1957); Bisson, *Schools and Colleges*, pp. 269, 463, *Endowed Schools*, i, p. 707; below, p. 427.

41 Welch, pp. 355–6, quot. Church Commissioners' File 15450.

42 Hadden, *Reminiscences . . .*, p. 48; National Society School File, St Mary's Charterhouse, letter 29 Dec. 1875.

43 *Newcastle Commission* IV, pp. 313ff.

44 Hadden, *Reminiscences*, esp. pp. 87–8; Bisson, *Schools and Colleges*, p. 261; National Society School File, St Thomas Charterhouse.

45 Kitson Clark, *Churchmen . . .*, p. 87.

46 *Quarterly Review*, CIII (1858), 'Church Extension', p. 143.

47 For example, Sheppard, *Infernal Wen*, Chap. 6, 'Church, School and State'.

48 *Quarterly Review*, loc. cit., pp. 169–70.

49 National Society, 28th Report, 1839, p. 84, Appendix VI, General Committee Minutes, No. 4, Jan. 1838–July 1847, pp. 18, 53; C. K. F. Brown, *The Church's Part in Education 1833–1941* (1942), pp. 110–12.

50 Newsome, *Parting of Friends*, pp. 219–22; National Society, 28th Report, 1839, pp. 8–10, 29th Report, 1840, pp. 2–7, 14; *SIC*, V, Minute of Evidence 13099; Heeney, *Mission to the Middle Classes*, pp. 14ff; R. Hussey, *A Letter to Thos Dyke Acland . . . on the System of Education to be Established in the Diocesan Schools for the Middle Classes* (1839); J. Roach, *Public Examinations in England* (1971), pp. 46ff; H. J. Burgess, *Enterprise in Education* (1958), pp. 68ff.; *Monthly Paper* of National Society, 29 Feb. 1848, p. 11, Prospectus of Middle or Commercial School attached to St Mark's College, Chelsea, 30 Sept. 1843, pp. 26, 40.

51 Below, p. 199; National Society, *Report of London Diocesan Board of Education* (1840–42), pp. 22–3, *First Report of the Metropolitan Institution for the Establishment and Improvement of Commercial Schools in the Metropolis and its Suburbs, in connexion with the National Church* (1840); G. Chandler, *An Address Delivered at the Opening of the Church of England Metropolitan Commercial School, Rose Street, Soho Square, Jan. 28, 1839* (1839).

52 National Society, *Metropolitan Institution Report* (1840), *passim*; National Society, *2nd Report of the London Diocesan Board of Education* (1841), Appendix IV, General Report of Central Commercial School.

53 *First Report of Metropolitan Institution*, pp. 9–10, 12.

54 Ibid., pp. 11–14, 22–3; *2nd Report of London Diocesan Board of Education*, p. 32; King's College *Calendar*, 1848/9, 1850/1; below, p. 200; Greenberg, pp. 21ff; Brown, *Church's Part*, pp. 110ff; Lewis, *Islington*,

p. 330; Richard Burgess, *Address delivered at the opening of the East Islington Commercial School* (1841).

55   *2nd Report of London Diocesan Board* . . ., pp. 13–16.
56   *3rd Report of London Diocesan Board* . . . 1842, p. 5, *4th Report* (1843), p. 9, *5th Report* (1844), p. 14, *6th Report* (1845), p. 9.
57   *Saturday Review*, 16 July 1864.
58   Woodard, letter to Bishop Fraser, 13 June 1871, quot. Bamford, *Rise of Public Schools*, p. 30.
59   National Society *Report* (1866), pp. xi–xii, (1867), pp. 11–12.
60   National Society Records, Vol. (a), *Battersea Sub-Committee*, 1847–9, end of volume, esp. pp. 47, 58.
61   National Society *Report*, (1869), pp. 17, 29–33, *First Report of the Middle Class Schools' Committee*.
62   National Society *Report* (1873), p. 14.
63   Ibid. (1870–6).
64   A. Highmore, *Pietas Londinensis* (1808), pp. 872–6; *Report of the Philological School or School of General Instruction* (1834); *SIC*, VII, pp. 347–8; Marylebone Public Library Loc. Hist. Collec., *The Builder*, 17 Oct. 1857; *Crockford's Directory*, p. 218; P. Wayne, *The Philological School, or St Marylebone Grammar School Past and Present* (1953), *passim; VCH, Middlesex*, I, pp. 306–7; R. Pound and A. G. Harmsworth, *Northcliffe* (1959), p. 64; D. Batten, *Clapham with its Common and Environs* (1841), p. 93; King's College *Calendar*, 1848/9.
65   *SIC*, X, pp. 138–9; D. Dymond, *The Forge* (1955), pp. 1–2 and f.n. A girls' school, St Margaret's, was founded in 1840, Bisson, *Endowed Schools* . . ., ii, p. 455.
66   *DNB*, George D'Oyley, William Otter, John Lonsdale; J. Tanswell, *The History and Antiquities of Lambeth* (1858), pp. 116–30; J. F. C. Hearnshaw, *The Centenary History of King's College, London, 1828–1928* (1929), pp. 16, 36–7.
67   Hearnshaw, p. 79.
68   Ibid., pp. 80, 66, 101–3, 154, 192; Bisson, *Schools and Colleges*, p. 307.
69   Hearnshaw, pp. 81–2; Hackney Public Library Loc. Collec., 'Some Records of Clapton Past and Present', compiled by F. Bagust, Vol. 7, pp. 42–8, and File, Schools A–K, Hackney Collegiate School; Guildhall Library, S. Curtis, *Strictures on the Hackney Grammar School, by a Proprietor* (1831) and S. Roper, *A few more words in defence of Hackney Grammar School* (1831); Robinson, *Hackney*, II, pp. 222–30.
70   Kensington Public Library Loc. Collec., Cutting 2415, 1835; *Quarterly Journal of Education*, IV, July/Oct. 1832, pp. 183–4; Crofton Croker, *Walk* . . ., p. 83.
71   *Quarterly Journal of Education*, I, 1831, pp. 199–203.
72   King's College *Calendars*, 1848/9–1871/2; Hearnshaw, pp. 82, 103–4; *SIC*, IV, p. 162, Evidence of Dean Plumptre; Enid and Cecil Samuel, 'The Villas of Regent's Park and their Residents', *St Marylebone Society Publication* No. 1, 1959, pp. 10–11.
73   Greenberg, p. 21.
74   King's College *Calendar*, 1846/7, p. 118, 1863/4, p. 458; Hearnshaw, pp. 51–2, 104.
75   N. G. L. Hammond, *Centenary Essays on Clifton College* (1962), pp. 2–3.

76   *SIC*, VII, pp. 340ff; Brown, *Church's Part...*, p. 116.
77   Islington Public Library Loc. Collec., YA160 ISL, Notice of 1830, Yp 160 Cr163498, Rules and Regulations (1832) and Two Annual Reports, 1st Report of the Directors; Lewis, *Islington*, p. 270; *SIC*, VII, pp. 239, 343ff.
78   Newsome, *Parting of Friends*, p. 171 f.n. quot. letter of 1836, Oratory Misc. Letters 1829–36, No. 99.
79   Islington . . . Loc. Collec., YpA160 Cr163497, Revd John Owen Parr MA, *An Address delivered at the opening of the Islington Proprietary School before . . . the Bishop of London, President, Vice-Presidents, Directors and Proprietors of that Institution; and printed at their request* (1830).
80   Islington . . . Loc. Collec., YA160 ISL, Printed papers relating to the dismissal of the Second Master, the Revd Mark Cooper, by the Directors; *DNB*, John Jackson 1811–1885.
81   Lewis, *Islington*, p. 367.
82   See J. W. Kirby, *The History of the Blackheath Proprietary School* (1933); H. W. Ord, *The Adventures of a Schoolmaster* (1936), p. 34.
83   *SIC*, VII, p. 342.
84   King's College *Calendar*, 1863/4, p. 471; 1871/2, p. 472.
85   King's College *Calendar*, 1850/1, p. 263.
86   Kirby, p. 15; Ord, p. 40.
87   *SIC*, VII, p. 343; Hearnshaw, pp. 191–3, 261–5, 324–7; Bisson, *Schools and Colleges*, p. 307; *Devonshire Commission*, 1872, *1st, 2nd and 3rd Reports*, p. 451. The holder of the Chair of Natural Philosophy described the boys from the modern side of the school as 'very well prepared', but most left early and went into business.
88   Kirby, p. 57.
89   Kensington Public Library Loc. Collec., F722, *Kensington News*, May 1910, 36556 pl. 154 *Prospectus*; King's College *Calendar*, 1840–9, p. 216; Major-General Sir G. Marshall, 'Kensington Proprietary School', in H. E. Haig Brown (ed.), *William Haig Brown* (1908), Chap. 3.
90   King's College *Calendar*, 1871/2, p. 474.
91   *SIC*, VII, p. 343; Islington . . . Loc. Collec., YA160 ISL, cutting *Standard* 21 Dec. 1857, Report of Bishop of London's Visitation; YA160 1SL, Report of Examiners, June 1848.
92   *SIC*, VII, p. 342.
93   G. G. Bradley, 'My Schooldays 1830 to 1840', *The Nineteenth Century*, Vol. XV, 1 March 1884, pp. 455–74; *DNB*; Bradley became Headmaster of Marlborough and Dean of Westminster.
94   *DNB*, Charles Pritchard; Leinster-MacKay, 'English Private School', pp. 116–18, and 'Pioneers in Progressive Education . . .', *History of Education*, Vol. 9, No. 3, Sept. 1980, pp. 213–14.
95   Kirby, pp. 103, 55.
96   E.g. Kempthorne, Sur-master of St Paul's, succeeded Selwyn at Blackheath and was followed by a man from Christ's Hospital. Blackheath staff moved to St Edmund's Canterbury, Eastbourne College, Haileybury, St Paul's, Sherborne, Malvern, Uppingham. Kensington supplied Marlborough with its first headmaster, Wilkinson, and then W. Haig Brown to Charterhouse.
97   Kensington . . . Loc. Collec., Box C, 310–33, *Kensington News*, May 1910, F722, Box N.
98   *DNB*, J. L. Brereton 1822–1901.

99 Kirby, p. 90.
100 Alicia Percival, *Very Superior Men* (1973), p. 145.
101 Above, p. 203.
102 Leinster-Mackay, 'English Private School', pp. 165–71.
103 Bisson, *Endowed Schools*, i, p. xxi.
104 *SIC*, VII, p. 343–4.
105 Kensington . . . Loc. Collec., 36556/154.
106 Kirby, pp. 73, 136, 113.
107 Hearnshaw, pp. 207, 354–5, 373–4, 376; below, p. 412.
108 London School Board, *Schedule of Secondary Schools* (1891); BPP *Charities of the County of London, Parish of Kensington* 1900 LXXII, pp. 59–63.
109 King's College *Calendar* 1891/2, pp. 663, 677.
110 Kirby, pp. 157–62.
111 Below, p. 412.
112 King's College *Calendar* 1890/1, p. 661.
113 Above, p. 112.
114 N. G. Brett-James, *Mill Hill School 1807–1907* (1924), pp. 14–15, 17–18; N. G. Brett-James, *Mill Hill* (1938), p. 10.
115 Brett-James, *Mill Hill School*, p. 20.
116 Ibid., pp. 15–16, 19, 34, 41; Brett-James, *Mill Hill*, p. 21; *VCH, Middlesex* I, p. 308.
117 Brett-James, *Mill Hill School*, pp. 36–7, and *Mill Hill*, p. 29; in B. Simon and I. Bradley (eds), *The Victorian Public School* (1974), M. Seaborne, 'The Architecture of the Victorian Public School', p. 180.
118 Brett-James, *Mill Hill*, pp. 38–41, 44; *Mill Hill School*, pp. 211ff.
119 Bisson, *Endowed Schools*, i, p. 723; Brett-James, *Mill Hill*, pp. 48–9, 52, Chap. IX, *passim; VCH, Middlesex*, I, p. 308.
120 B. Gardner, *The Public Schools* (1973), p. 148; *SIC*, Vol. XVIII, pp. 320, 329.
121 Gardner, p. 150.
122 Ibid., p. 163; above, p. 197; Constance E. Curryer and U. K. Moore, *The Story of Walthamstow Hall* (1973), Chaps. I and II.
123 Kitson Clark, *Making of Victorian England*, pp. 270–3.
124 F. C. Pritchard, *Methodist Secondary Education* (1949), p. 220.
125 Ibid., p. 130; W. R. Ward, *Religion and Society in England 1790–1850* (1972), esp. Chap. 6.
126 Pritchard, pp. 139ff, 166ff, 224.
127 G. F. A. Best, *Mid-Victorian Britain, 1851–75* (1971), p. 181.
128 Pritchard, p. 132.
129 Ibid., pp. 193, 218ff, 224, 260ff.
130 Ibid., pp. 152, 174; H. F. Mathews, *Methodism and the Education of the People 1791–1851* (1949), *passim*.
131 Minutes of Committee of Council on Education, 1858/9, pp. 148–50, 1855/6, pp. 472–6.
132 Ibid., 1853/4, M. Arnold's report on the Wesleyan Training College, Horseferry Road, pp. 312ff; *Newcastle Commission*, VI, pp. 256–7, Q.2055.
133 *The Watchman*, VI, p. 175, quot. Pritchard, p. 217.
134 *Newcastle Commission*, VI, p. 250, Q.1981–6.

135 Pritchard, p. 187.
136 See W. A. Campbell Stewart, *Quakers and Education* (1953).
137 R. S. Mortimer, 'Quaker Education' (review article), *Journal of the Friends' Historical Society*, Vol. XXXIX, 1947, pp. 66–70; Campbell Stewart, pp. 62–3, 134 f.n.5.
138 N. Penney (ed.), 'Pen Pictures of the London Yearly Meeting, 1789–1833', *Friends' Historical Society* Supplements 16, 17, *London Yearly Meeting during 250 years* (1919), p. 55; Campbell Stewart, p. 63.
139 Campbell Stewart, pp. 91, 79, 94.
140 *DNB*, William Allen.
141 S. W. Brown, *Leighton Park* (1952), pp. 7–8.
142 *DNB*, Richard Claridge; Sturges, *Schools of Edmonton Hundred*, pp. 71–3; HMC NRA *Tottenham Exhibition Catalogue*, pp. 2, 20; T. Compton, *Recollections of Tottenham Friends and the Forster Family* (1893). Josiah Forster II came to London in 1710 to teach in the Clerkenwell Workhouse School, and moved to Tottenham in 1752.
143 Brown, *Leighton Park*, pp. 8, 15–16.
144 Brown, p. 8; *SIC*, V, Minute of Evidence 11896; *DNB*, W. E. Forster 1818–1886.
145 Brown, pp. 20–1, 23; Bisson, *Endowed Schools*, i, pp. 885, xlv; Sturges, pp. 74ff; NRA *Exhibition Catalogue*, pp. 3, 23–6; Robinson, *Tottenham*, I, pp. 102ff, 117ff.
146 Brown, p. 35; Campbell Stewart, pp. 81–2; Gardner, p. 45. Continuity with the Tottenham school was maintained by personal and financial connections, and the invested capital of the former school eventually provided a boarding-house at Leighton Park.
147 Beales, *Education under Penalty*, pp. 207ff, 250–3, 254; T. G. Holt, 'Some Early London Catholic Schools', *London Recusant*, Vol. 5, No. 1, 1975, pp. 45–53.
148 *DNB*, James Usher 1720–72; J. Gillow, *Literary and Biographical Dictionary of English Catholics* (1885), Vol. V, p. 569.
149 *DNB*, Richard Challoner, 1691–1781, worked from 1730 in London Mission and from 1740 as coadjutor to Dr Benjamin Petre, and then his successor (1758); Gillow, *Biographical Dictionary*, I, pp. 447–57; W. J. Battersby, 'Middle Class Education', *Month*, Vol. CLXXXVI, No. 973, Sept. 1948; Gardner, *Public Schools*, p. 142.
150 Battersby, loc. cit., pp. 82–3; for pressure from the parallel demand for popular education see A. C. F. Beales, 'The Beginnings of Elementary Education in England in the Second Spring', *Dublin Review*, Vol. 205, Nos 410 and 411, 1939.
151 H. O. Evenett, *The Catholic Schools of England and Wales* (1944), pp. 64–72; Gardner, pp. 142–5.
152 In G. A. Beck (ed.), *The English Catholics 1850–1950* (1950), P. Hughes, 'The English Catholics in 1850', *passim*.
153 *Catholic Directory* (1841), p. 97; M. A. Murphy, 'The Origin, Growth and Development of Schools for Roman Catholic Poor Children in the Archdiocese of Westminster' (unpublished MPhil thesis, University of London, 1979), p. 194ff.
154 Cardinal Manning in *Dublin Review*, Oct. 1867, pp. 381ff, quot. V. A. McClelland, *English Roman Catholics and Higher Education 1830–1903* (1972).

155 *DNB*, T. W. Allies, 1813–1903; D. E. Selby, 'Henry Edward Manning and the Catholic Middle Class', *Paedagogica Historica*, X, No. 1 1970, pp. 149–70.

156 *Catholic Middle School Log Book, 1848–51*, St Edmund's Papers, Archbishop's House, Westminster, 19.1.17.

157 Denis Gwynn, 'The Irish Immigration', in Beck (ed.), *English Catholics*, pp. 265ff.

158 Gordon Wheeler, 'The Archdiocese of Westminster', in Beck (ed.), op. cit., pp. 154ff.

159 Battersby, 'Middle Class Education', loc. cit, p. 85.

160 Evenett, p. 49.

161 W. J. Battersby, *The De La Salle Brothers in Great Britain* (1954), pp. 6–7, 15, 16–21, 38; Battersby, 'Secondary Education for Boys', in Beck (ed.), op. cit., p. 322–36.

162 Above, pp. 207, 210.

163 Battersby, *Brother Potamian, Educator and Scientist* (1953), esp. pp. 68, 28–9, 76, 73, Chap. VI, *passim*.

164 Battersby, 'Secondary Education . . .', in Beck (ed.), pp. 329, 331; Evenett, p. 51.

165 Selby, ' . . . Manning and the Catholic Middle Class', loc. cit.; Evenett, p. 46–7.

166 Selby, loc. cit., quot. *Report of a Meeting on Higher Middle Class Education of Catholics of London*, held at Archbishop's House, 5 Oct. 1880 (Manning Papers); McClelland, 'The 1880 Central School Scheme', *Tablet*, Vol. 219, No. 6532, 1965, p. 853.

167 McClelland, . . . *Higher Education*, p. 233.

168 P. Hughes, loc. cit., in Beck (ed.), p. 68.

169 See J. D. Holmes, 'Newman and the Kensington Scheme', *Month*, Jan. 1965, Vol. 3, No. 1, pp. 12–23; McClelland's reply, March 1965, pp. 173–82.

170 Manning in *Dublin Review*, Jan. 1874, Vol. 22, pp. 187–204 and Oct. 1874, Vol. 23, pp. 441–75.

171 Selby, loc. cit., quot. Ripon MSS. BM Add MSS. 43 545 ff32.

172 Bisson, *Endowed Schools*, i, p. 931.

173 McClelland, . . . *Higher Education*, pp. 118, 331–2.

174 Wheeler, 'Archdiocese of Westminster', in Beck (ed.), pp. 330–1.

175 McClelland, op. cit., pp. 325–7; Gardner, p. 181.

176 McClelland, *Cardinal Manning* (1962), pp. 54–5.

177 Battersby, *Potamian*, pp. 53, 46–9; McClelland, *Manning*, p. 55.

178 See McClelland, 'The 1880 Central School Scheme', *Tablet* Nos 6532/3/4, 1965; Selby, ' . . . Manning and the Catholic Middle Class', p. 161; McClelland, *Manning*; Battersby, *Potamian*; W. R. Conolly and W. A. Dalton, *Prospectus for Establishing in London a Great Catholic Central Middle-Class School for Boys, on the Great Commercial Principles of the Age, Cooperation and Limited Liability* (June 1880).

179 McClelland, 'Central School Scheme', *Tablet* No. 6534, 1965, pp. 902–3; and *Manning*, p. 57; Battersby, *Potamian*, pp. 56, 59, 61.

180 Battersby, 'Secondary Education . . .', in Beck (ed.), p. 331; Evenett, pp. 50, 52.

181 Evenett, p. 47; Sturges, *Schools of Edmonton Hundred*, p. 112.

182 Battersby, *Potamian*, pp. 66, 114, Chap. VII, *passim*; *De La Salle*, p. 70; *St Joseph's College, Beulah Hill, 1855–1955* (1955).

183 P. L. S. Quinn, 'Jewish Schooling Systems of London 1656–1965' (unpublished PhD thesis, University of London, 1950), I, p. 73; V. D. Lipman, *Social History of the Jews in England* (1954), p. 1.

184 Lipman, pp. 6–8.

185 Quinn, I, pp. 181–3.

186 Ibid., I, pp. 195–6.

187 Ibid., I, p. 195; Lipman, p. 8.

188 Quinn, I, pp. 316ff; Lipman, pp. 76–7.

189 (United Synagogue, London, n.d.), V. D. Lipman, 'The Development of London Jewry', p. 47 in S. S. Levin (ed.), *A Century of Anglo-Jewish Life, 1870–1970*; Lipman, *Social History*, pp. 16–17.

190 E. Jamilly, 'Synagogue Art and Architecture', in Levin (ed.), *passim*; A. N. Newman, 'The United Synagogue, Growth and Change', *passim*; Lipman, 'London Jewry', pp. 48–50 in Levin (ed.), op. cit.; Quinn, I, pp. 579ff.

191 Quinn, I, p. 183.

192 Newman, 'Setting the Scene, Anglo-Jewry in 1870', in Levin (ed.) p. 11, Rabbi R. Apple, 'United Synagogue, Religious Founders and Leaders', p. 17 in Levin (ed.), op. cit..

193 Quinn, I, pp. 183, 321–5, 367–8, II, pp. 563, 604; S. S. Levin, 'The Origins of the Jews' Free School', *Transactions of the Jewish Historical Society of England*, XIX (1960); S. S. Levin, 'The Changing Pattern of Jewish Education', in Levin (ed.), op. cit., pp. 58–61; Bisson, *Endowed Schools*, i, p. 695; *Endowed Charities (County of London) Return . . . of Parish of Christ Church Spitalfields*, 1895 (425–I), pp. 22–38; *Times Educational Supplement*, 30 April 1965.

194 Levin, 'Changing Pattern . . .', p. 58.

195 A. Barnett, 'Sussex Hall – the First Anglo-Jewish Venture in Popular Education', *Transactions of the Jewish Historical Society of England*, XIX, 1955–9, pp. 65–79; Quinn, I, pp. 339ff; for the Anglican venture see *TNASS*, 1862, E. G. Clarke, 'The City of London College', pp. 297ff.

196 For example H. N. Solomon's school at Enfield (Sturges, *Schools of Edmonton . . .*, p. 82) and that in Highgate of Hyman Hurwitz which had its own synagogue (Brayley/Norris Brewer, *Middlesex* (1816), p. 216); Levin, 'Changing Pattern . . .' in Levin (ed.) op. cit., p. 59; Quinn, I, p. 180.

197 C. E. Cassell, 'The West Metropolitan Jewish School', *Transactions of the Jewish Historical Society of England*, XIX, 1960, pp. 115–28; *Jewish Chronicle*, No. 270, p. 138; Quinn, II, App. VIII, pp. 1v–1viii; Lipman, *Social History*, pp. 45–9.

198 Newman, 'Setting the Scene . . .', p. 11, Apple, 'United Synagogue . . .', p. 14 in Levin (ed.), op. cit.; Quinn, I, pp. 383, 398; A. M. Hyamson, *Jews' College* (1955), p. 14.

199 Apple, op. cit., p. 14.

200 Hyamson, *passim*; Quinn, I, pp. 397, 445; *Jews' College Jubilee Volume* (1906); *SIC*, V, pp. 22ff; Bisson, *Endowed Schools*, i, pp. 695, 705.

201 Quinn, I, p. 278, II, pp. 1i–1ii.

202 Above, p. 231, and below, p. 268; Quinn, I, pp. 279–80.

203 Ibid., I, pp. 430–1, 436, 438.

204 Below, p. 243; Quinn, I, p. 436.

205   Ibid., I, p. 460.
206   Ibid., II, pp. 671, 824ff; Gardner, p. 221; *The Times*, 2 Oct. 1975, Letter
      J. Rosen, Carmel College.
207   Obituary of Canon William Rogers, *Daily Chronicle*, 20 Jan, 1896, cutting
      in Bishopsgate Institute.
208   Above, p. 189f.
209   See Hadden, *Reminiscences of . . . Rogers, passim*.
210   Avery, *Bishopsgate Schools*, pp. 12–23.
211   Obituaries, *Westminster Gazette* and *Daily Telegraph*, 20 Jan. 1896,
      cuttings in Bishopsgate Institute.
212   Below, p. 272.
213   *SIC*, V, pp. 472ff, Evidence of Revd William Rogers; Hadden, *Reminis-
      cences*, pp. 157–72.
214   Hadden, p. 159; *Minute Book of Middle Class Schools' Corporation*, I
      (hereafter *MCSC*), printed circular in front cover.
215   *MCSC*, I, pp. 1–3, 14.
216   Ibid., pp. 6, 10–12.
217   Ibid., p. 10, Meeting of Subcommittee, 30 Nov. 1865.
218   Ibid., pp. 62ff, 100, 44–5; *Minutes of the Proceedings of the Court of Common
      Council*, 21 Feb. 1866, p. 41.
219   *Middle Class Schools' Corporation*, IV, List of Governors and Subscribers.
220   *MCSC*, I, pp. 126, 148, 150; *MCSC, Minutes of Council*, II, 6 Dec. 1871;
      MCSC Minutes of Governors' Meetings, III, 18 March 1867; see below, pp.
      396ff..
221   *MCSC*, I, pp. 62, 64; III, p. 1, 23 July 1866, first meeting of Governors.
222   *MCSC*, I, pp. 86–127.
223   *MCSC*, I, pp. 78–92; III, 18 March 1867; *SIC*, V, p. 472.
224   *SIC*, V, p. 475.
225   *The Times*, Obituary, 20 Jan. 1896.
226   *MCSC*, IV and I, pp. 117, 124, 187ff.
227   Heeney, *Mission to the Middle Classes*, pp. 96–8, 166–7.
228   *MCSC*, I, pp. 58, 63, 113–14, II, p. 4.
229   Above, p. 203; *MCSC*, III, 12 March 1869; *The Times*, 13 March 1869,
      Jackson's reply to Address of Lord Mayor at AGM of *MCSC*.
230   Hadden, *Reminiscences*, p. 170; above, p. 238; Quinn, 'Jewish Schooling
      Systems', I, pp. 413, 437; *Jewish Chronicle*, 10 Jan. 1868, 'A Middle Class
      Man'.
231   *MCSC*, I, pp. 75–9; III, 18 March 1867; *SIC*, V, p. 475.
232   *MCSC*, I, pp. 131–2; *The Times*, 16 Dec. 1868.
233   *Scholastic World*, 1 July 1878, April 1879; *Academia*, 7 March 1868;
      Hadden, p. 171; Bisson, *Schools and Colleges*, p. 265, *Endowed Schools*, i,
      p. 704.
234   *The Times*, 16 Dec. 1868.
235   *MCSC*, III, 11 March 1870.
236   *Special Report . . . on the Teachers' Training and Organization Bill*, p. 25,
      Minutes of Evidence 481–6.
237   *MCSC*, I, p. 71.
238   *The Times*, 16 Dec. 1868.
239   *MCSC*, I, pp. 84, 160–1, 181, III, 17 March 1875.
240   *MCSC*, III, 11 March 1870, 7 March 1873.

241   *MCSC*, I, pp. 73, 75, 94, 118, 159, III, 11 March 1870.
242   *MCSC*, III, 11 March 1870; Hearl, 'Military Examinations...', in MacLeod (ed.), *Days of Judgement*, pp. 133ff.
243   Hadden, *Reminiscences...*, p. 171.
244   Bisson, *Endowed Schools*, i. p. 704.
245   *MCSC*, III, 25 Feb. 1885, Headmaster's Report on the Condition of the School.
246   Hadden, p. 170.
247   Ibid.
248   *MCSC*, III, 7 March 1873; below, pp. 336–7.
249   *MCSC*, II, 17 July 1874, 7 March 1877.
250   *The Times*, 16 Dec. 1868.
251   P. Smith and G. Summerfield (eds), *Matthew Arnold and the Education of the New Order* (1969), p. 67.

VI   'It's past praying for'

1   D. Owen, *English Philanthropy, 1660–1960* (1964), Chap. VI; M. D. W. Jones, 'Brighton College v. Marriott', *History of Education*, Vol. 12, No. 2, June 1983, pp. 121ff.
2   M. L. Simmons, *Register of the Clergy Orphan School for Boys, 1751–1896*, St Augustine's College Canterbury (1897), pp. vii–x.
3   *SIC*, X, pp. 211–18; Bisson, *Schools and Colleges*, p. 260; *Public and Preparatory Schools' Year Book* (1979); *VCH, Surrey*, II, p. 221.
4   Sturges, *Schools of Edmonton Hundred*, p. 75. For the girls' school see R. M. Handfield Jones, *The History of the Royal Masonic Institution for Girls, 1788–1974* (1974).
5   *Rules and Bye-Laws of the Society of Licensed Victuallers* (1911 edn); LCC, *Survey of London: St Mary Lambeth*, Pt 11, Vol. XXVI (1956), p. 43.
6   *DNB*, G. Moore; M. Arnold, *Culture and Anarchy*, ed. Wilson, p. 118.
7   *DNB*, ibid.; *SIC*, IV, pp. 567ff, Evidence of W. F. Richards; Bisson, *Endowed Schools*, i, p. 814, ii, p. 581.
8   Arnold, op. cit., pp. 118–19.
9   *SIC*, IV, p. 567.
10   *Quarterly Review*, CIX, 1861, pp. 447–8.
11   BPP *Endowed Charities (County of London) Return ... for Parish of Poplar, All Saints* 1895 (425–IV), pp. 21–31; below, pp. 292ff.
12   Owen, *Philanthropy*, p. 247.
13   Daniel Robert Fearon, b.1835, son of a Suffolk clergyman. Educ. Winchester and Balliol, 1860 Assistant Inspector of Schools, only layman to inspect Anglican schools before 1870. 1864, HMI. After Taunton Inquiry called to Bar, became Assistant Charity Commissioner, 1886 Secretary to Charity Commission. See J. E. Dunford, 'Biographical Details of Her Majesty's Inspectors of Schools appointed before 1870', *History of Education Society Bulletin*, No. 28, Autumn 1981, p. 13.
14   *SIC*, VII, pp. 271ff.
15   W. L. Burn, *The Age of Equipoise* (1968 edn), p. 226.
16   Owen, pp. 183–4; BPP *Report of the Select Committee ... into the education of the lower orders in the Metropolis* 1816 HC [498] IV 1.

17 Owen, pp. 187–8.
18 BPP *Select Committee on Public Charities* 1835 [C.449] *VII*, Q115 . . . Evidence of W. Grant.
19 BPP *Digest of Reports of . . . Inquiry into Charities* 1843 XVI 1, *City of London*, pp. 672–775; *City of Westminster*, pp. 776–83; *Middlesex*, pp. 784–825; *Kent*, pp. 456–515; *Surrey*, pp. 420–55.
20 Owen, p. 192.
21 *Charitable Trusts' Act* 16 and 17 Vict. c. 137.
22 *Westminster Review*, Vol. III, July 1824, pp. 149ff.
23 Owen, p. 169.
24 J. A. Morris, *A History of the Latymer School at Edmonton* (1975), pp. 92–5, 100, 112, 128; *VCH, Middlesex*, I, p. 305; *SIC*, VII, p. 308.
25 *VCH, Middlesex*, I, p. 303.
26 *Reports of the Commissioners . . . Charities . . . Kent* 1819–37, p. 99; BPP *Endowed Charities (County of London) Return . . . Parishes of St Nicholas and St Paul, Deptford* 1897 (222–1) LXVI Pt 1. pp. 7–17
27 Allport, *Camberwell Grammar School*, pp. 74–80; *SIC*, VII, pp. 469–73.
28 *VCH, Middlesex*, I, p. 292; *SIC*, X, p. 73; BPP *Return of Charity Commissioners, Parish of Stepney* 1895 (425–VI), esp. pp. 1–10.
29 Owen, pp. 194–5.
30 Percy, *Whitgift School*, pp. 68–9, 70, 77, 130–1; this Charity was outside the powers of the Brougham inquiry until 1831 because it was under a special Visitor. See Owen, pp. 186, 188.
31 Owen, p. 195.
32 Carrington, *Two Schools*, p. 143.
33 *VCH, Middlesex*, I, p. 295.
34 R. J. B. Pooley, 'The History of St Clement Danes Holborn Estate Grammar School, 1552–1952' (unpublished MA thesis, University of London, 1955), Conclusion, pp. 174ff; *SIC*, VII, pp. 248, 409, 454; BPP *Endowed Charities Report (County of London)* (combined form) Vol. V, 1903 (181) xlix 1, pp. 33–62.
35 *SIC*, VII, pp. 271–4, 276.
36 Percy, *Whitgift*, pp. 134–5; *VCH, Surrey*, II, pp. 195–6.
37 *VCH, Middlesex*, I, pp. 303–4; See forthcoming article, Dr Joan Schwitzer, 'A Schoolmaster caught in the Crossfire: Letters from Highgate School, 1818–1832'.
38 *VCH, Middlesex*, I, p. 314; *SIC*, VII, pp. 306–7.
39 *VCH, Surrey*, II, p. 218; F. T. Smallwood, *Sir Walter St John's School* (two typewritten essays, 1967, Guildhall Library).
40 Dare, *Owen's*, pp. 49–55, Chap. XI; Lewis, *Islington*, pp. 420–2; *VCH, Middlesex*, I, pp. 310–11.
41 J. Maskell, *Collections in illustration of the Parochial History and Antiquities of the Ancient Parish of All Hallows Barking . . .* (1864); *SIC*, X, pp. 7ff; BPP *Return of Parish of St Botolph without Aldgate . . . Charity Commissioners* 1897 (86) LXVI Pt 1; below, p. 400.
42 Allport, pp. 84–7, 90–1; King's College *Calendar*, 1846, p. 118, 1848/9, p. 212, 1864/5, p. 476; above, p. 200.
43 3 and 4 Vict. c.77, the Eardley Wilmot Act designed to give governing bodies a freer hand in applying endowments, but circumscribed and lacking precision. See Owen, p. 249.

44 Allport, pp. 91–6; *VCH, Surrey*, II, p. 216.
45 *VCH, Middlesex*, I, p. 295; above, p. 256.
46 Davies, *Charterhouse*, pp. 264–5; Carrington, *Two Schools*, pp. 146–66, 170–1, 185ff; *SIC*, VII, pp. 331–3.
47 Owen, pp. 205, 207–8.
48 Below, p. 359.
49 A. E. Douglas-Smith, *The City of London School* (1965 edn), p. 32; above, p. 9.
50 Ibid., pp. 30–5, 38 quot. X *Report of Charity Commission* 1823. The will did not come to light until 1961 with the publication of the *Calendar of Plea and Memoranda Rolls 1458–1482* (ed. Dr Jones of the Guildhall Record Office). See Douglas-Smith, pp. 22ff.
51 Douglas-Smith, pp. 39–40.
52 Ibid., pp. 41–5.
53 Ibid., pp. 45–9.
54 Ibid., pp. 53ff.
55 4 and 5 Wm. IV c.35; Douglas-Smith, Appendix VI, pp. 515ff.
56 Ibid., pp. 58, 63, 150–2; *Middle Class Schools' Corporation, Minute Book I*, 7 Nov. 1865.
57 Douglas-Smith, p. 66.
58 Ibid., pp. 61–2, 97–9, 128; *DNB*, Sir William Tite 1798–1873.
59 Douglas-Smith, p. 68.
60 Ibid., p. 80; above, pp. 200, 259.
61 Douglas-Smith, p. 86; Kensington Public Library Loc. Collec., 2415; above, p. 199.
62 Above, pp. 196–7.
63 BPP, *Her Majesty's Commissioners to inquire into the revenues and management of certain colleges and schools . . .* 1864 [C.3288] I, p. 37 (hereafter Clarendon Commission).
64 R. Jenkins, *Asquith* (1967 edn), pp. 14–15; Douglas-Smith, Introduction, xvi.
65 Above, pp. 237–8.
66 Jenkins, p. 14; Cf. Benjamin Jowett who went to St Paul's in 1829 aged twelve and lodged by himself somewhere in the City Road. He was exiled from home even in holiday time. See G. Faber, *Jowett: A portrait with background* (1957).
67 Douglas-Smith, p. xvi.
68 *SIC*, VII, pp. 277ff.
69 Above, p. 149.
70 Carrington, *Two Schools*, p. 139; *SIC*, VII, p. 333.
71 Carrington, pp. 144–6, 224–5; *VCH, Surrey*, II, pp. 180–1; *SIC*, X, pp. 119–27.
72 Morris, *St Dunstan's*, pp. 14, 17, 18–21; BPP *Select Committee on the Endowed Schools' Act* 1873 (C.254) VIII Q.4366, Evidence of E. Shearman.
73 Ibid., Q.4376, 511, 4340–4541.
74 Morris, *St Dunstan's*, pp. 26ff.
75 *VCH, Surrey*, II, p. 201; Young, *Dulwich*, II, pp. 496ff; *SIC*, I, pp. 495–502.
76 20 and 21 Vict. c. 84.
77 Allport, *Camberwell Grammar School*, pp. 96, 104–5.

78 *Minutes of the Vestry of St Botolph's Bishopsgate*, Guildhall MS 4526/7, f16–18, 175–7, 191, 209, 389.
79 *VCH, Surrey*, II, pp. 207–8.
80 For the setting up of the Taunton Commission see Owen, pp. 250ff; P. Gordon, *Selection for Secondary Education* (1980), pp. 8–10. The deputation from the National Association for Social Science which urged it upon the Prime Minister, Palmerston, included Brougham, Lord Lyttelton, the Bishop of London. The Members of the Commission were Henry Labouchère, Lord Taunton (Chairman), Thomas Dyke Acland, Frederick Temple, Lord Lyttelton, W. E. Forster, E. Baines, Lord Northcote. Its terms were the examination of all types of school other than elementary. Assistant Commissioners included Fearon, T. H. Green, James Bryce, Joshua Fitch, Matthew Arnold, James Frazer, H. J. Roby.
81 Burn, *Equipoise*, p. 226.
82 'Educational Endowments', *Fraser's Magazine*, Vol. 79, Jan. 1869.
83 *Fortnightly Review*, April 1869.
84 *DNB* (2nd Supplement), Arthur Hobhouse 1819–1904, Charity Commissioner 1866, Endowed Schools' Commissioner 1869; quoted by Beveridge, *Voluntary Action*, pp. 195–6.
85 D. Roberts, *Victorian Origins of the British Welfare State* (1960), pp. 88–9; see also G. Kitson Clark, *An Expanding Society* (1967), Chap. 8.
86 H. J. Roby in E. G. Sandford (ed.), *Memoirs of Archbishop Temple* (1906), I, p. 128, and Chaps IV and V.
87 P. Magnus, *Gladstone* (1963 edn), pp. 154–5.
88 *The Times*, 10 Nov. 1865, Editorial.
89 *SIC*, I, p. 6.
90 *SIC*, X, p. 1.
91 Owen, pp. 250–1; below, pp. 413ff..
92 *SIC*, I, pp. 338–43.
93 *SIC*, VII, pp. 352–3, 340ff.
94 Ibid., pp. 240ff.
95 Ibid., pp. 243ff, 304ff; below, p. 412.
96 *SIC*, VII, pp. 236–7.
97 *SIC*, I, p. 15.
98 *SIC*, VII, Appendix iii, p. 454.
99 Ibid., pp. 277–86; above, p. 267.
100 *SIC*, VII, p. 288; below, p. 413.
101 *SIC*, X, pp. 7–10, 40–1, VII, pp. 288ff.
102 *SIC*, I, p. 340.
103 *SIC*, VII, p. 289.
104 *SIC*, X, pp. 70–2, 106–7, 73–9, 119–27.
105 Ibid., pp. 131–7.
106 Ibid., pp. 62–9, VII, pp. 241–2, 304.
107 *SIC*, VII, pp. 303ff.
108 Ibid., pp. 303–4.
109 Ibid., pp. 304–6, 307–8.
110 Ibid., pp. 335–9.
111 Ibid., pp. 289ff, 297, 302.
112 Ibid., pp. 292–5, 310, 320.

113 Ibid., pp. 314–19.

114 Ibid., pp. 312–14.

115 Ibid., pp. 321–5.

116 *SIC*, Vol. I; Sandford, *Temple*, I, Chap. V; Owen, p. 252; *Select Committee on Endowed Schools' Act* 1873, Evidence of Lyttelton.

117 32 and 33 Vict. c.56 Sec. 9.

118 Owen, pp. 253–6.

119 Boase, *Modern English Biography*, III (1887); Owen, p. 255.

120 Carrington, *Two Schools*, pp. 197–217.

121 Ibid., pp. 219–26, 231; *VCH, Surrey*, II, pp. 174–87; S. Fletcher, *Feminists and Bureaucrats* (1980), p. 217.

122 BPP *Select Committee Endowed Schools' Acts* 1886 (191) IX 1 Q. 1091ff; *VCH, Middlesex* I, pp. 296–7; BPP *Endowed Charities (County of London) Return . . . of the Parish of St Leonard, Shoreditch* 1897 (222–II) LXVI Pt 1, pp. 74–96, 79–80; PRO Ed. 27/2971, 1870 Memo. by Haberdashers' Company to Charity Commissioners (reference supplied by Mr Raymond Thatcher). In 1890 a new girls' school was built at Hatcham. In 1898 the boys' Hoxton school was moved to West Hampstead and the girls' to Acton.

123 BPP *Report of the Endowed Schools' Commissioners to the Committee of Council on Education* 1872 (C.524) XXIV, p. 37.

124 Owen, pp. 258, 259–62.

125 *Report of Endowed Schools' Commissioners . . .* 1872, pp. 7, 27.

126 C. W. Scott-Giles, *The History of Emanuel School 1594–1964* (1966), pp. 47, 56–9, 71–2.

127 Ibid., pp. 75–7.

128 Owen, pp. 257–9; Scott-Giles, pp. 76–9; *The Times*, 17 and 25 April 1871.

129 Scott-Giles, pp. 79–80.

130 Westminster Public Library Loc. Collec., PB20, R. E. H. Goffin, *A Brief Account of the Foundation and History of the United Westminster Schools* (1894).

131 *Select Committee on Endowed Schools' Act* 1873, pp. iii and xiv.

132 *The Times*, 14 May 1873; Scott-Giles, p. 81; below, Chap. IX.

133 This was planned for parents of moderate means; *Select Committee on Endowed Schools' Act* 1873, Q.840, Evidence of Roby.

134 Scott-Giles, pp. 102, 117, and Chap. IX, *passim*; Goffin, *A Brief Account . . . passim*.

135 *Select Committee . . .* 1873, Q.181.

136 Wheatley, *Latymer*, p. 94.

137 *VCH, Middlesex*, I, p. 306.

138 Wheatley, pp. 104–6.

139 Below, p. 415f.

140 *VCH, Middlesex*, I, p. 306; in 1927 the St Clement Danes School moved to Shepherd's Bush (Pooley, Conclusion).

141 Above, p. 187.

142 *VCH, Middlesex*, I, pp. 293–4.

143 Above, p. 251; BPP *Return of Charity Commissioners . . . County of London, Poplar, Parish of All Saints* 1895 (425–IV,) pp. 21–31. See H. C. Wilks, *George Green's School 1828–1978* (1979).

144 Above, pp. 200, 210, 255; *VCH, Middlesex*, I, pp. 290, 293; BPP *Return of Charity Commissioners . . . Parish of Stepney* 1895 (425–VI). pp. 1–59.

145 BPP 1883 (91–III) LIII–275, 1884 LXI (21–1) 351; BPP *37th Report of Charity Commissioners* 1890 (C.5986) XXVI 24.
146 *VCH, Middlesex*, I, pp. 312–14.
147 Above, p. 246, and below, pp. 336–7.
148 Schools' Committee of the Council of Citizens of East London, Fourth Bulletin, *Our East London: The story of our schools* (Winter 1950).
149 Owen, p. 252; *SIC*, I, pp. 26–7; Hadden, *Reminiscences of . . . Rogers*, p. 171; *Report of Endowed Schools' Commissioners* (1872), pp. 19–20.
150 Extract from Gilkes's diary kindly supplied by Sheila Hodges (Mrs S. Bush). See her *God's Gift*, pp. 53ff; *VCH, Surrey*, II, pp. 207–8.
151 Loc. cit; *The Edward Alleyn Magazine*, Dec. 1912, July 1918.
152 Below, p. 339.
153 BPP *Endowed Charities (London)* (Combined form) III 1900 (252) LXI 1, pp. 656ff; Guildhall MS 4526/9 *Vestry Minutes of St Botolph's . . .* 1889, f 53–7; below, p. 336f.
154 *VCH, Surrey*, II, pp. 207–8.
155 Bridget Cherry and N. Pevsner (eds), *London, 2, South* (The Buildings of England, 1983), pp. 199ff; Percy, *Whitgift, passim*; *VCH, Surrey*, II, pp. 195–6; *Endowed Schools' Enquiry* 1873, Q.885–900; below, p. 437.
156 *VCH, Surrey*, II, pp. 218–19; Cherry and Pevsner, p. 671.
157 *Report of the Endowed Schools' Commissioners* 1872, pp. 29–32; *Endowed Schools' Enquiry* 1873, Q.168, 174, 1280.
158 *SIC*, X, p. 2.
159 BPP *30th Report of the Charity Commissioners* 1883 (C.3537) XXI 337, p. 16.
160 *Vestry Minutes of St Botolph's; Endowed Charities (London)* (Combined form) III 1900, pp. 657–65.
161 Above, p. 291; BPP 1886 IX, pp. 1682–96; A. Tropp, *The School Teachers* (1957), pp. 121–2; BPP . . . *Select Committee on Mr Goffin's Certificate . . .* 1878/9 (334) X; Goffin, *Brief Account . . .*, pp. 45–51; but for Philip Magnus's criticism of this school for wasting time on Latin, see BPP 1886 IX, Q.3278.
162 BPP *Endowed Charities (County of London) Return . . . for the Parish of Greenwich* 1895 (425–II), pp. 4ff and 66ff.
163 *Return for Parishes of . . . Deptford* 1897 (222–I), pp. 32–9.
164 Dare, *Owen's . . .*, pp. 65–80.
165 Above, p. 269f.
166 Morris, *St Dunstans . . .*, pp. 35–65; W. H. Brock, *H. E. Armstrong and the Teaching of Science* (1973).
167 Allport, *Camberwell Grammar School*, pp. 105, 109, 118–32.
168 *SIC*, VII, pp. 248, 409; Pooley, 'History of St Clement Danes', Conclusion *passim*, and pp. 102–5, 115; above, p. 256.
169 *VCH, Middlesex*, I, pp. 295–6; below, p. 426.
170 *VCH, Middlesex*, I, p. 314; below, p. 426.
171 Morris, *Edmonton*, pp. 144–209; above, p. 254; below, p. 426.
172 See for example P. Gordon, 'The Endowed Schools and the Education of the Poor', *Durham Research Review*, V, No. 17, Sept. 1966, pp. 47–58.
173 H. Perkin, 'Middle Class Education and Employment in the 19th Century; A Critical Note', *Economic History Review*, XIV, 1961, pp. 122ff.
174 *Beehive*, 26.3.1870 quot. C. Griggs, 'The Trades' Union Congress and

the Question of Educational Endowments, 1868–1925', *History of Education Society Bulletin*, No. 28, Autumn 1981, p. 45. See also his *The Trades' Union Congress and the Struggle for Education, 1868–1925* (1983).

175 *Select Committee to Inquire into the . . . Endowed Schools' Act* 1873, Q.1278, 352, 265, 490, 828, 823, 825–6, 595–6, 488, 491; P. Searby, 'The Schooling of Kipps; the Education of Lower Middle Class Boys in England, 1860–1918', in History of Education Society, *Educating the Victorian Middle Class* (1982), pp. 113ff.

176 *Select Committee . . .* 1872, Q.320–3, 317, 822, 1261, 1040.

177 Griggs, 'The TUC and . . . Endowments', p. 45.

178 BPP *30th Report of Charity Commissioners* 1883 (C.3537) XXI 337, p. 15; *31st Report* 1884 (C.3936) X, pp. 18–20.

179 House of Lords' Sessions Papers, 1884 Vol. 1, Paper No. 29 (Shelf Mark BS9/1).

180 BPP *Select Committee on the Endowed Schools' Acts* 1886 IX; *Select Com. on Endowed Schools' Acts*, Further Report 1887 (120) IX 235, Q. 7709–24, Evidence of Jesse Collings; Owen, *Philanthropy*, pp. 265ff.

181 *SC* 1886, Q.1682–1696.

182 Ibid., Q.1101–5, 1107, 1109–12; below, p. 416.

183 BPP *40th Annual Report of Charity Commissioners* 1893/4 (C.6960) XXV 15.

184 Owen, p. 269; below, pp. 425ff.

185 *SC Enquiry . . . Endowed Schools* 1873, Q.3857.

186 BPP *38th Annual Report of Charity Commissioners* 1891/2 (C.6301) XXVI 15.

187 *40th Annual Report . . .*, pp. 32–4.

188 *SIC*, VII, p. 271.

VII   'The most important event in the history of the country'

1 Sir Walter Besant, *Survey of London: London in the Nineteenth Century* (1909), p. 36.

2 Above, p. 21; Thrupp, *Merchant Community of Medieval London*, pp. 169–74.

3 G. M. Young, 'Portrait of an Age', *Early Victorian England* (1934), Vol. 2, pp. 445ff, f.n.1.

4 Quot. Vera Brittain, *The Women at Oxford* (1960), p. 48.

5 Ibid., p. 45.

6 Margaret Bryant, *The Unexpected Revolution* (1979), esp. pp. 103–6.

7 Above, pp. 143ff.

8 Above, p. 188.

9 Elaine Kaye, *A History of Queen's College* (1972), pp. 11–13.

10 Rosalie G. Grylls, *Queen's College, 1848–1948* (1948), pp. 2ff; Shirley C. Gordon, 'Demands for the Education of Girls, 1790–1865' (unpublished MA thesis, University of London, 1950), pp. 210ff, quoting GBI Reports, 1844, 1845, 1848; H. M. Stanley of Alderley, 'Personal Recollections of Women's Education', *The Nineteenth Century*, VI, August 1879, pp. 308ff; *DNB*, F. D. Maurice.

11 Gordon, pp. 60–1; Stanley, loc. cit.

12 Gordon, pp. 396–9, 221–3, 218ff; Stanley, loc. cit.

13 *Quarterly Review*, LXXXVI, Dec. 1849, pp. 369ff; Grylls, pp. 8, 16; Stanley, loc. cit; J. Killham, *Tennyson and 'The Princess'* (1958), pp. 130–2.

14 Gordon, pp. 391–412, 422ff and Appendix A, pp. 515–43 for courses and organization of studies; Grylls, pp. 71–8; Bessie Rayner Parkes, *Essays on Women's Work* (1865), pp. 203–4.

15 Gordon, pp. 418–21.

16 Margaret J. Tuke, *The History of Bedford College for Women 1849–1937* (1939), pp. 23–5; Boase, *Modern English Biography*, III, p. 986.

17 Tuke, pp. 73ff, 97, 99–103, 110–12, 119–30; *SIC*, V, pp. 697ff, Examination of Miss E. E. Smith, and VII, pp. 581–7, 602.

18 See Sara A. Burstall, *Frances Mary Buss* (1938); M. Scrimgeour (ed.), *The North London Collegiate School* (1950); *SIC*, V, pp. 252ff, Examination of Miss Buss; Josephine Kamm, *How Different from Us: A biography of Miss Buss and Miss Beale* (1958), Chap. V; Bryant, pp. 93–6.

19 PMY, 'Woman and her Social Position', *Westminster Review*, XXXV, Jan. 1841, pp. 24–52.

20 Bryant, Chap. 3; Ray Strachey, *The Cause: A short history of the women's movement in Great Britain* (1928), p. 64; Patricia Hollis (ed.), *Pressure from Without* (1974), pp. vii-viii; H. Burton, *Barbara Bodichon* (1949), pp. 59–73; B. Rayner Parkes, *Women's Work*, p. 67; Barbara Stephen, *Emily Davies and Girton College* (1927), pp. 51ff.

21 *English Woman's Journal*, X, Jan. 1863, pp. 312–15; Gordon, pp. 118–19, 448, 450, 458–60; *Women of the Day* (1884), p. 21; *Newcastle Commission*, V, p. 105; W. T. Hill, *Octavia Hill* (1956), p. 56.

22 M. C. Bradbrook, *'That Infidel Place': A short history of Girton College 1869–1969* (1969), pp. 6, 8–10; Bryant, pp. 61ff, 82ff; Stephen, pp. 29, 109, 118–19.

23 Bryant, pp. 96–7; Stephen, pp. 82–105.

24 Bryant, p. 98; Stephen, Chap. VIII; *SIC* II, p. 272; *DNB*, H. J. Roby 1830–1915.

25 *SIC*, I, pp. 548–9.

26 *SIC*, VII, p. 238.

27 *SIC*, X, pp. 93–5.

28 *SIC*, X, pp. 286–7, VII, p. 410.

29 *SIC*, X, p. 299, VII, p. 410.

30 *SIC*, VII, pp. 386, 581.

31 *SIC*, VII, pp. 384ff, 635, 653.

32 *SIC*, VII, pp. 412–13.

33 *SIC*, V, pp. 252ff, Evidence of Miss Buss.

34 Menella B. Smedley, 'The English Girl's Education', *Contemporary Review*, XIV, April/July 1870, pp. 37ff, discussion of Cambridge Higher Local.

35 *SIC*, V, pp. 697ff.

36 *SIC*, V, pp. 676ff.

37 Bryant, pp. 86–8.

38 Ibid., Chap. 1, 'The Task'.

39 Emily Davies Papers, Girton College, Box IX, Reports and Minute Books, LAS.

40 BPP *Endowed Charities London* (Combined form) III 1900 (252) LXI 1, pp. 769–88.

41 Janet Sondheimer and Prunella Bodington (eds), *The Girls' Public Day School Trust 1872–1972. A Centenary Review* (1972), p. 6.

42 Josephine Kamm, *Indicative Past: A hundred years of the Girls' Public Day School Trust* (1971), pp. 32–5, 24–5.

43 Ibid., p. 38; *The Times*, 28 March 1871.

44 Mary Gurney, *Are We to Have Education for Our Middle-Class Girls? Or the history of the Camden Collegiate Schools* (1872).

45 Kamm, *Indicative Past*, pp. 38–42. The National Union was wound up in 1882, see Fletcher, *Feminists and Bureaucrats*, p. 180; its objects are set out in Sondheimer and Bodington, pp. 11–12.

46 Kamm, pp. 45–7; Sondheimer and Bodington, p. 36.

47 Kamm, pp. 43ff.

48 Ibid., p. 48 and Chap. 4; Sondheimer and Bodington, pp. 10, 52; *Bryce Commission Report*, VII, pp. 4–5, 21–2.

49 Kamm, pp. 42–3, 62; Sondheimer and Bodington, p. 42; Bisson, *Endowed Schools*, ii, pp. 428–30.

50 Sondheimer and Bodington, p. 29; *Bryce Commission Report*, II, pp. 168ff and 240ff, Evidence of W. H. Stone, Chairman of Council of GPDSCo., and Miss Gurney; Stanley, 'Personal Recollections', pp. 316–17.

51 Sondheimer and Bodington, p. 101.

52 Ibid., p. 29; Kamm, p. 96.

53 Sondheimer and Bodington, p. 14; Bisson, *Endowed Schools*, ii, p. 428.

54 Kamm, pp. 50, 67.

55 Above, p. 330; E. Gadesden, *The Education of Girls and the Development of Girls' High Schools* (1900), quot. in Jan Milburn, 'The Secondary Schoolmistress: A study of her professional views and their significance in the educational developments of the period 1895–1914' (unpublished PhD thesis, University of London, 1969), p. 84.

56 Kamm, pp. 67, 72ff.

57 *SIC*, V, Q15040–7, pp. 625–32.

58 Nonita Glenday and Mary Price, *Reluctant Revolutionaries: a century of headmistresses, 1874–1974* (for Association of Headmistresses, 1974), p. 3; Kamm, p. 8.

59 Kamm, p. 60.

60 *Bryce Commission Report*, II, p. 544, Statistics of University Careers of GPDSCo. Pupils, Dec. 1893 (claimed as an underestimate as some particulars not registered).

61 See E. Moberly Bell, *Francis Holland Schools* (1938) and *A History of the Church Schools' Company 1883–1958* (1958); Bisson, *Endowed Schools*, ii, p. 439; Alice Zimmern, *The Renaissance of Girl's Education* (1898), p. 59.

62 *Bryce Commission Report*, II, pp. 240–1.

63 *Select Committee Endowed Schools' Act* 1873, Q.4179, Evidence of Mrs Maria Grey; Smedley, 'The English Girl's Education'.

64 Zimmern, Chap. V, 'Endowments for girls', pp. 84ff.

65 Fletcher, *Feminists and Bureaucrats*, pp. 178–82.

66 Ibid., pp. 53–9; BPP *Endowed Charities London* (Combined form) III 1900, pp. 769–88; S. M. Fletcher, 'The Part Played by Civil Servants in Promoting Girls' Secondary Education, 1869–1902: Some aspects of the administration of the Endowed Schools' Acts' (unpublished PhD

thesis, University of London, 1976), pp. 112ff; Doris Burchell, *Miss Buss' Second School* (1971), Chaps. 3 and 4.

67 These were: before 1874, Palmer's 1871, Bow (Prisca Coborn) 1873, Greenwich (Roan) 1873, Hoxton (Aske's) 1873, West Ham (Bonnell's) 1873, Westminster (Greycoat and St Martin's) 1873: Schemes submitted and later approved, Camberwell (Central Foundation) 1874, Datchelor's 1874, St Paul's 1874 (opened 1904), Lady Eleanor Holles's 1874, North London Collegiate 1874, Westminster (St Clement Danes) 1874: after 1874, Burlington School 1875, Dame Alice Owen 1878, James Allen's 1882, George Green's 1883, Skinners' 1886, Lewisham (Prendergast) 1887, Christ's Hospital 1890, Central Foundation 1891, Addey and Stanhope (mixed) 1893, St Saviour's and St Olave's 1899, Godolphin and Latymer 1903. Fletcher, *Feminists and Bureaucrats*, Appendix I, pp. 192ff.

68 BPP *SC Endowed Schools' Acts* 1886 IX, Q.624, 848–9, 1594, 5906–10.

69 Central Foundation School Archives, I *Minute Book*, 1 June 1870, p. 173; 23 June, p. 183; III Minutes of Governors' Meetings, 24 March, 5 July 1871; II, Minutes of Council, 6 Dec. 1871, 24 Jan., 20 March 1872.

70 Anne Caroline Creed, 'The Life and Educational Work of Anne Clough, 1820–1892' (unpublished MA dissertation, University of London, 1972), p. 81, quot. correspondence at Balliol, Typescript 179, 181, 190, Letter of Jowett to F. Nightingale, 17 Oct. 1869; Blanche A. Clough, *A Memoir of Anne Jemima Clough* (1903), pp. 145–61; Rita McWilliams-Tullberg, *Women at Cambridge: A men's university – though of a mixed type* (1975), pp. 57–8.

71 Central Foundation School Archives, *Log Book of Bishopsgate School for Girls*.

72 Below, pp. 350ff.

73 BPP *Endowed Charities (London)* (Combined form) III 1900, pp. 658ff; Central Foundation School Archives, in *Bicentenary Magazine*, 1926, Mary Hanbridge, History of School.

74 See R. N. Pearse (ed.), *The Story of the Mary Datchelor School* (1957), collected papers; *VCH, Surrey*, II, pp. 219–20.

75 Above, p. 287; BPP *Endowed Charities Return* 1897 (222-II) LXVI Pt I, pp. 89ff.

76 Ibid., pp. 93ff.

77 Above, p. 323; Bisson, BPP *Endowed Schools*, ii, p. 534; BPP *Endowed Charities London* (Combined form) III 1900, p. 673; Fletcher, *Feminists and Bureaucrats*, p. 201.

78 *VCH, Essex*, II, pp. 546–7.

79 BPP *Select Committee . . . Endowed Schools' Acts* 1887, Q.7230–1.

80 Above, p. 296; M. A. Wren and P. Hackett, *James Allen, a portrait enlarged* (1968), esp. pp. 57–9, 78–82; Fletcher, *Feminists and Bureaucrats*, pp. 106–7; BPP *Charities of the County of London, Parish of Camberwell* 1900 LXXII, pp. 54–61; Bryant, pp. 100–1.

81 Dora H. Thomas, *A Short History of St Martin's High School for Girls* (1929); BPP *Charities of the County of London, Parish of St Martin's-in-the-Fields* 1900 LXII, 390–III Sess. 2 32–V, p. 617.

82 Zimmern, p. 102.

83 Below, p. 373; J. F. Wadmore, *Some Account of the Worshipful Company of*

Skinners of London (1902), pp. 250ff; see Miss H. Page (headmistress), detailed account of the school in R. P. Scott (ed.), '*What is Secondary Education?*' (1899), pp. 213–21.

84   BPP *Endowed Charities London* (Combined form) III 1900, pp. 139–45, 160–70; above, p. 287.

85   BPP 1899 (112) LXXVI Part VI, pp. 13ff.

86   BPP *Charities of the County of London, Parish of Hammersmith* 1900 LXXII 390–I Sess. 2, pp. 315, 25.

87   Above, p. 292; *VCH, Middlesex*, I, p. 306.

88   Morris, *St Dunstan's*, pp. 29–30.

89   *Select Committee . . . Endowed Schools' Acts* 1887, Q.7230–6; Q.539–40.

90   Minutes of Methodist Conference XVII, p. 593, quot. Pritchard, *Methodist Secondary Education*, pp. 276–81, 289, 283.

91   Glenday and Price, *Reluctant Revolutionaries*, pp. 13–14; Curryer and Moore, *Walthamstow Hall*, Chapter II.

92   See M. Williams, *Sainte Madeleine Sophie, her life and letters* (1965) and *The Society of the Sacred Heart* (1978).

93   Hounslow Public Library Loc. Collec., *Middlesex Chronicle*, 27 June 1891, 14 and 21 March 1958; Bisson *Endowed Schools*, ii, pp. 625, 624, 623; Department of Education School File, 5750.

94   *Catholic Directory* (1900), pp. 450–9.

95   *Bryce Commission Report*, III, p. 298; Bisson, *Endowed Schools . . .*, ii, p. 430; below, p. 433.

96   Bisson, *Endowed Schools . . .*, ii, p. 435.

97   Ibid., pp. 556, 560, 568, 537.

98   Below, pp. 407ff, 420ff, 424f; above, p. 249ff.

99   BPP *Endowed Charities . . . Parish of Stepney* 1895 (425–VI) LXXIV Pt 1, pp. 59ff.

100   J. A. Banks, 'The Contagion of Numbers', in Dyos and Wolff (eds), *Victorian City*, I, p. 116.

101   Fabian Tract 157, *The Working Life of Women* (1911).

102   'M. A.', Fabian Tract 175, *The Economic Foundations of the Women's Movement* (1914).

103   S. Alexander, 'Women's Work in Nineteenth-Century London: A study of the years 1820–1850', in J. Mitchell and A. Oakley (eds), *The Rights and Wrongs of Women* (1976); J. B. Mayor, 'The Cry of the Women', *Contemporary Review*, XI, May/Aug. 1869, pp. 196–215.

104   Above, p. 320; *TNASS*, 1859, Bessie Rayner Parkes, 'The Market for Educated Female Labour', 'A Year's Experience . . .'; J. B. Kinnear, 'The Social Position of Women in the Present Age', in Josephine Butler (ed.), *Women's Work and Women's Culture* (1869), pp. 344ff.

105   D. R. Fearon, 'Girls' Grammar Schools', *Contemporary Review*, II, May/Aug. 1869, pp. 333–54.

106   *SIC*, V, Q.15999–16065, pp. 718–22.

107   *TNASS*, 1862, Louisa Gann, 'Schools of Art', pp. 304–8; S. Macdonald, *The History and Philosophy of Art Education* (1970), p. 146; BPP *Royal Commission on the Livery Companies* 1884 (c. 4073), (hereafter called the Livery Companies' Commission), I, Minute of Evidence 1676.

108   Below, pp. 407f, 425f.

109   Zimmern, p. 246.

110 Review article, 'Employment of Women in the Public Service', *Quarterly Review*, Vol. 151, Jan. 1881, pp. 181ff; Margaret E. Harkness, 'Women as Civil Servants', *The Nineteenth Century*, Vol. 10, Sept. 1881, pp. 369ff; S. Gwynn, 'Bachelor Women', *Contemporary Review*, LXXIII, June 1898, pp. 866ff; W. Besant, 'The Endowment of the Daughter', *Longman's Magazine*, Vol. 11, 1888, p. 604.
111 Above, pp. 299f.
112 J. A. and O. Banks, *Feminism and Family Planning* (1964), Chap. 6.
113 *Bryce Commission Report*, VII, p. 29.
114 Bisson, *Endowed Schools...*, ii, pp. 530, 568.
115 *Paddington and Maida Vale High School Magazine*, Dec. 1894, pp. 17–18, July 1898, p. 1, March 1907, pp. 30–31; *Report of Headmistress*, 1908, p. 17.
116 Milburn, 'Secondary Schoolmistress', pp. 248–50.
117 W. Jacob, 'The London Secondary Technical Schools for Girls', *Journal of Education*, Vol. 86, No. 1, 21 August 1954, pp. 365–6.
118 See Glenday and Price, *Reluctant Revolutionaries*.
119 Milburn, p. 82.
120 A. M. A. Archives, *Special Conferences 1890–1894*, Miss Buss's Minute Book, press–cutting 16 June 1887, quot. Milburn, p. 7.
121 Above, pp. 158ff.
122 *National Society Report* (1844), p. 115; *Minutes of Committee of Council* (1874), pp. 397–400; E. Moberly Bell, *The History of Lady Margaret School 1851–1951* (1951).
123 *SIC*, V, p. 259.
124 *The Times*, 14 April 1975, letter from Dr Donald Clarke, Headmaster, Princess Helena College.
125 *Report of the Adult Orphan Asylum*, 1823, pp. 1–8, 10–11, 1826, pp. 5–6; MSS notes, 1822–3.
126 *Reports*, 1823, pp. 10–11, 1833, pp. 10–12.
127 *Report*, 1823, MSS notes 1822.
128 *Report*, 1833, p. 6.
129 *Reports*, 1832, pp. 7, 10, 1823, p. 33; *Prospectus*, p. 3.
130 *Report*, 1832, pp. 18–19.
131 *SIC*, X, pp. 301–3.
132 *SIC*, V, pp. 255ff; VII, p. 589, Appendix XIII.
133 Above, p. 313ff.
134 *SIC*, V, p. 265.
135 See M. Vivian Hughes, *A London Girl in the 1880s* (1946 edn), Chap. 2, 'Under Law'.
136 Irene M. Lilley, *Maria Grey College 1878–1976* (1981), Chap. 2.
137 *Special Report from the Select Committee on Teachers' Registration and Organization Bill* 1891, Evidence of Miss A. J. Ward, Principal of the College, Minute of Evidence 2016.
138 Kamm, *Indicative Past*, p. 87.
139 Central Foundation School Archives, *Log Book of Bishopsgate School for Girls*, 1873–1891, pp. 295–301, 399, 426.
140 Lilley, pp. 20, 10–11.
141 *Select Committee... on Teachers' Registration... Bill* 1891, Minute of Evidence 2017; Kamm, p. 87.

142 Lilley, p. 24; Hounslow Public Library Loc. History Collec., *Middlesex Chronicle*, 3, 10, 17 Jan. 1958, articles W. Bennett.

143 *Bryce Commission Report*, IV, pp. 1–21, Evidence of Miss Alice Woods; *Log Book of Bishopsgate School*, p. 439.

144 Ferét, *Fulham Old and New*, II, p. 279.

145 Lilley, p. 41.

146 *Bryce Commission Report*, I, p. 71; *Paddington and Maida Vale High School Magazine*, June 1900, pp. 9–10, 1901, p. 23.

147 Kamm, *Indicative Past*, p. 147; Laurie Magnus, *The Jubilee Book of the Girls' Public Day School Trust* (1923), pp. 75–9.

148 Kamm, p. 88.

149 *Provisional Scheme for Training Graduate Teachers*, Dec. 1902 and April 1904, GPDST Archives, quot. Milburn, pp. 181–2 and Appendix A.

150 *VCH, Surrey*, II, pp. 219–20; C. S. Bremner, *Education of Girls and Women in Great Britain* (1897), pp. 170–77.

151 Tuke, *Bedford College*, p. 136; M. Vivian Hughes, *A London Home in the 1890s*, Chaps. II and VII give a delightful account of this course and its genesis.

152 Hughes, op. cit.; University of London Institute of Education *Handbook* (1964/5), p. 35. The College was closed in 1969.

153 *Report of Adult Orphan Institution*, 1876, pp. 13–14, 36–41, *Prospectus*, p. 3.

154 Lilley, p. 31.

155 Bisson, *Endowed Schools . . .*, ii, p. 433.

156 *Report of Adult Orphan Institution*, 1881, pp. 9–10.

157 *Report*, 1882, pp. 9–12.

158 *Reports*, 1886, p. 12; 1888, p. 22; 1892, p. 10; 1889, p. 10; 1890, p. 10.

159 *Reports*, 1888, p. 11; 1890, p. 10; 1891, p. 11; 1892, p. 11; Bisson, *Endowed Schools . . .*, ii, pp. 433–4.

160 Baron, 'Secondary Schoolmaster', pp. 142ff; *Select Committee . . . on Teachers' Registration . . . Bill* 1891, pp. 142–3; *Report of a Conference on Secondary Education convened by the Vice-Chancellor of the University of Cambridge* (1896), pp. 65–6.

161 Above, p. 339; Fletcher, *Feminists and Bureaucrats*, pp. 106ff.

162 Kamm, pp. 144–6; C. Dyhouse, 'Social Darwinistic ideas and the development of women's education', *History of Education* Feb. 1976, Vol. 5, No. 1, pp. 41–5; Milburn, pp. 234–47, 289–91.

163 *SIC*, V, p. 265; Milburn, pp. 263–4; London Association of Schoolmistresses, *Minute Book*, I, 19 March 1866; Kamm, *How Different from Us*, p. 171; Joan N. Burstyn, *Victorian Education and the Ideal of Womanhood* (1980), Chap. 5; P. Atkinson, 'Fitness, Feminism and Schooling', in S. Delamont and L. Duffin (eds), *The Nineteenth-Century Woman: Her Cultural and Physical World* (1978), pp. 92ff; P. McIntosh, *Physical Education in England since 1800* (1968), Chap. 8, pp. 140ff, and Appendix A, J. May, 'The Bergman-Österberg Physical Training College'.

164 Alice R. James, *Girls' Physical Training, being a series of healthy and artistic movements to music* (1898); Bryant, p. 110.

165 Presidential Address to AHM, 1908, and *Journal of Education*, August 1908, quot. Milburn, pp. 120, 124.

166 Presidential Address to AHM, 1904, quot. Milburn, p. 149.
167 Above, pp. 327–8.
168 Bisson, *Endowed Schools . . .*, ii, p. 528.
169 A former resident on 'The Educational Opportunities of Old Hampstead', *Hampstead Annual* (1906–7), p. 75.
170 Hearnshaw, *King's College*, pp. 313–18, 376–8; Appendix A, Hilda D. Oakeley, 'King's College for Women', pp. 489–509; Mrs Stepney Rawson, 'Where London Girls May Study', Kensington Public Library Loc. Collec., J1437; Carol Dyhouse, *Girls Growing up in Late Victorian and Edwardian England* (1981), pp. 167–9.
171 Below, p. 401.
172 Presidential Address of Miss Drummond of the North London Collegiate School, AHM, 1914, quot. Milburn, p. 107.

VIII 'Reorganizing the metropolis of a nation'

1 K. Young and Patricia Garside, *Metropolitan London: Politics and Urban Change 1837–1981* (1982), p. 1.
2 See *The Corporation of London, its Origin, Constitution, Powers and Duties* (1950).
3 BPP *Report of the Commissioners to inquire into the existing state of the Corporation of the City of London* 1854 (8) 1772, Vol. XXVI, p. x (under chairmanship of Henry Labouchère, later Lord Taunton).
4 F. W. Maitland, 1885, quot. in BPP *Royal Commission on the Government of London* 1894 (C.7493) XVII, XVIII, Paper 5, Memorandum on County of London and the County of the City of London, p. 2.
5 Toms, 'Secular Education', p. 24; E. J. T. Brennan, *Education for National Efficiency* (1975), p. 19. The significance of the interaction of debates over local government and education reform is discussed in R. Aldrich, '1870, a Local Government Perspective', *Journal of Educational Administration and History*, Vol. XV, No. 1, Jan. 1983, pp. 22ff.
6 Young and Garside, pp. 14–15. In 1851 the boundaries adopted for London defined the metropolis as a full census division.
7 Op. cit., pp. xiii-xiv.
8 Young and Garside, p. 17, quot. Rosa Lynn Pinkus, 'The Conceptual Development of Metropolitan London 1800–1855' (unpublished PhD thesis, State University of New York at Buffalo, 1975).
9 G. Gibbon and R. W. Bell, *History of the London County Council 1889–1939* (1939), p. 65.
10 *Westminster Review*, XXXIX, No. 11, 1843, art. X, pp. 497–587; above, pp. 262ff.
11 A. Bassett Hopkins, *The Boroughs of the Metropolis* (1900), pp. 8–11; Young and Garside, p. 19.
12 W. Newall, 'The Municipality of London', *Contemporary Review* Vol. XXV, Feb. 1875, p. 437; A. Hobhouse, 'Local Self-government in London', *Contemporary Review*, Vol. LIII, June 1888, pp. 773–86; *Royal Commission on Government of London* 1893/4, pp. 22–3; K. Young, 'The Conservative Strategy for London, 1855–1975', *The London Journal*, Vol. 1, No. 1, May 1975, pp. 57–102; Young and Garside, pp. 34ff.

13 *RC London Government* 1894, LCC Papers, C, Synopsis of the observations and recommendations of Royal Commissions and Special Committees as to the government of the Metropolis, and a short account of Bills introduced for the Reform of London, 18 May 1893, pp. 17–22; Bassett Hopkins, p. 12; Gibbon and Bell, Chapter 3; Brennan, p. 20; Young and Garside, p. 38.

14 W. Eric Jackson, *Achievement: A short history of the LCC* (1965), pp. 5, 23.

15 Young, 'Conservative Strategy . . .', pp. 61–5; Young and Garside, pp. 62, 70ff.

16 52 and 53 Vict. c.76.

17 P. R. Sharp, '"Whiskey Money" and the Development of Technical and Secondary Education in the 1890s', *Journal of Educational Administration and History*, Vol. IV, No. 1, Dec. 1971, pp. 33ff.

18 Gibbon and Bell, p. 246; Brennan, p. 23; P. Gosden, 'Technical instruction committees', History of Education Society, *Studies in the government and control of education since 1860* (1970), pp. 27ff.

19 *RC London Government* 1893/4 I, p. 274.

20 TUC *Annual Report* (1885), p. 19, quot. C. Griggs, 'The Trades' Union Congress and the Question of Educational Endowments, 1868–1925', *History of Education Society Bulletin*, No. 28, Autumn 1981, pp. 45–6.

21 Owen, *Philanthropy*, pp. 284ff; BPP *Royal Commission on the Livery Companies* 1884 (C.4073) XXXIX (hereafter Livery Companies' Commission).

22 *Livery Companies' Commission*, I, pp. 31–9; Owen, pp. 284–90.

23 Owen, p. 288; *Who Was Who*, 1897–1916; *Livery Companies' Commission*, I, pp. 76–88, 71–75.

24 Owen, pp. 284–5, 288–9.

25 *Livery Companies' Commission*, I, pp. 49ff, 89ff.

26 BPP *Report of the Committee on the Law and Practice Relating to Charitable Trusts* 1952 (C.8710), Q.5189, quot. Owen, pp. 289–90.

27 Owen, p. 288.

28 Above, p. 242.

29 *Who Was Who*, 1897–1916.

30 *DNB*, Samuel Morley 1809–1886; J. B. Paton, 'Mr Samuel Morley – In Memoriam', *Contemporary Review*, Vol. L, Oct 1886, pp. 549–53; E. Hodder, *Life and Letters of Samuel Morley* (1889).

31 *DNB*, William Spottiswoode 1825–1883; D. Layton, 'The educational work of the Parliamentary Committee of the British Association for the Advancement of Science', *History of Education*, Vol. 5, No. 1, Feb. 1976, p. 36.

32 *DNB*, John Lubbock 1803–1865, John Lubbock 1834–1913; J. Lubbock, 'On the Present System of Public School Education' (1876), pp. 44–69, in *Addresses: Political and Educational* (1879); 'Manual Instruction', *Fortnightly Review*, CCXXXV N.S., Oct. 1886.

33 *DNB*, Frederick Bramwell 1822–1906, George Bramwell 1808–1892; above, p. 150.

34 *DNB*, Roundell Palmer 1812–1895.

35 *DNB*, Sydney Waterlow 1822–1906; Scott-Giles, *Emanuel*, p. 102.

36 P. Thompson, *Socialists, Liberals and Labour: The struggle for London 1885–1914* (1967), p. 7.

37 Draper, *Merchant Taylors'*, pp. 116, 139, 146; H. T. Wilkins, *Great English Schools* (1925), pp. 241, 244, 272; H. Dunn, *Eight Years a Blue Coat Boy*, quot. in E. Blunden, *The Christ's Hospital Book*, (1953), p. 228; Douglas-Smith, *City of London School*, pp. 131–2.

38 A forester and Labour Party organizer quoted in R. Blythe, *Akenfield* (1969 edn), p. 106.

39 *Clarendon Commission*, I, pp. 50–2; Draper, p. 159.

40 *The Times*, 15 June 1869.

41 *Clarendon Commission*, I, pp. 83, 202ff.

42 Watney, *Mercers . . .*, pp. 80–1, 85; *Livery Companies' Commission*, I, pp. 110–12; C. Welch, *Modern History of the City of London* (1896), p. 436; BPP *The Endowed Charities of the City of London, reprinted at large from the 17 Reports of the Commissioners for inquiry concerning Charities* 1829, pp. 42–3.

43 Cyprian Blagden, *The Stationers' Company . . . 1403–1959* (1960), pp. 256–7; *SIC*, VII, p. 465, V, Minutes of Evidence 9160–5; *Livery Companies' Commission*, V, pp. 278ff; Appendix, pp. 283–5.

44 *SIC*, V, Minutes of Evidence 9145–9303.

45 *Livery Companies' Commission*, I, Minutes of Evidence 1533–7.

46 Blagden, p. 257.

47 *Livery Companies' Commission*, I, p. 287.

48 G. Alderman, *The History of Hackney Downs School, formerly the Grocers' Company's School* (1972), pp. 1–27; *Livery Companies' Commission*, I, Minutes of Evidence 418, 450, 454; see Guildhall MS. 11, 633, Minutes of Governing Body of Grocers' Company School, 1873–1906.

49 J. F. Wadmore, *The Worshipful Company of Skinners*, pp. 244, 247–50; above, p. 340.

50 Johnson, *Drapers . . .*, III, pp. 449–50; *Livery Companies' Commission*, II, p. 202, IV, p. 154; Sturges, *Schools of Edmonton Hundred*. It was closed in 1885 and three years later opened as a High School for Girls.

51 *Livery Companies' Commission*, IV, p. 154; *SIC*, X, pp. 80–2.

52 *Livery Companies' Commission*, II, pp. 122–5, 173–5, 178–85, 202; I, p. 113, Minutes of Evidence 446–7; Johnson, III, pp. 477–8.

53 *Livery Companies' Commission*, IV, pp. 125–32; Johnson, III, pp. 479–81; Greenwich Royal Hospital School, *Old Boys' Association Gazettes*; BPP *Report of Commissioners appointed to inquire into the affairs of the Greenwich Hospital* 1860 [C.2670] XXX 1.

54 'What is true technical education?', *The Economist*, 25 Jan. 1868, pp. 87–8, quot. P. W. Musgrave, 'The Definition of Technical Education, 1860–1910', *Vocational Aspects of Secondary and Further Education*, Vol. XVI, No. 34, Summer 1964, pp. 105–11.

55 Tabled in Session 1867, *Report relative to Technical Education* [C.3898], XXVI, pp. 3–30.

56 *Bryce Commission Report*, I, p. 28, III, Samuelson's evidence, Q.6243–8.

57 Thompson, *Socialists, Liberals and Labour . . .*, p. 9.

58 A. E. Musson, 'The British Industrial Revolution', *History*, Vol. 67, No. 220, June 1982, pp. 257–8.

59 London Chamber of Commerce, *Commercial Education*, Guildhall Pamphlet 6841, pp. 1–2.

60 Thompson, loc. cit.

61 B. H. Becker, *Scientific London* (1874 and 1968), *passim*; W. H. G. Armytage, *The Rise of the Technocrats* (1965), Chap. 7; Humberstone, 'Education in London', *London and the Advancement of Science*, pp. 159–76.

62 H. Butterworth, 'The Science and Art Department Examinations: Origins and Achievements', in MacLeod (ed.), *Days of Judgement*, pp. 27–44.

63 Becker, pp. 201–14.

64 Ibid., pp. 196–7.

65 Henry James, *English Hours* (ed. A. C. Lowe, 1962), pp. 7, 97–8.

66 *Livery Companies' Commission*, I, Minute of Evidence 131.

67 Philip Magnus, 'Industrial Education', in R. D. Roberts (ed.), *Education in the Nineteenth Century* (1901), pp. 164–5; F. Foden, 'The Technology Examinations of the City and Guilds', in MacLeod (ed.), *Days of Judgement*, pp. 69ff.

68 City Record Office, Committee for the Promotion of Technical Education, *Minute Book*, Jan. 1872–Oct. 1873; Butterworth, 'Science and Art Department Examinations . . .', pp. 28ff; *DNB*, Henry Cole 1808–1882; W. P. McCann, 'The Trade Guilds of Learning', *Vocational Aspects of Secondary and Further Education*, Vol. XIX, Spring 1967, pp. 34–40.

69 Sandford, *Memoirs of Temple*, I, pp. 325–6; C. Bibby, *T. H. Huxley and Education* (1971), pp. 45–6.

70 *Livery Companies' Commission*, I, Minute of Evidence 1675.

71 M. Argles, *South Kensington to Robbins* (1964), pp. 22–3.

72 Welch, *Modern History of the City . . .* , p. 305.

73 Magnus, in Roberts (ed.), pp. 164–6.

74 *Livery Companies' Commission*, I, pp. 66–9.

75 City Record Office, Minutes of Court of Common Council, 18 July 1878, p. 183, and *Report* No. 24.

76 *Report* No. 24, pp. 1–15.

77 Minutes of Court of Common Council, October 1878, pp. 222, 283, 297–9.

78 Welch, pp. 404, 328–9.

79 *Samuelson Commission*, I, pp. 402–3; *Livery Companies' Commission*, I, Minute of Evidence 1675.

80 *Livery Companies' Commission*, I, pp. 67–8.

81 P. Magnus, *Educational Aims and Efforts 1880–1910* (1910), p. 84, and Magnus in Roberts, p. 154.

82 *Samuelson Commission*, III, pp. 217–26, esp. Q.2189.

83 *Livery Companies' Commission*, I, pp. 67–8 and Minute of Evidence 1695.

84 *Samuelson Commission*, I, pp. 405–9; Magnus, *Educational Aims . . .*, p. 88.

85 *Livery Companies' Commission*, I, p. 68, Appendix A for detailed syllabuses, staffing, timetabling, etc.; Minute of Evidence 1695.

86 *Samuelson Commission*, I, pp. 403ff, 528; III, pp. 96–111.

87 *Livery Companies' Commission*, I, pp. 67–8.

88 *Samuelson Commission*, I, p. 403.

89 *Livery Companies' Commission*, I, Minute of Evidence 1731.

90 *Samuelson Commission*, I, pp. 408–9.

91 Magnus, *Educational Aims . . .*, p. 86.

92 Welch, *Modern History . . .* , p. 332.

93 *Livery Companies' Commission*, I, pp. 67–8, Minutes of Evidence 1676, 1753, 1756, 1772.
94 Magnus, *Educational Aims . . .*, pp. 98–9.
95 *Livery Companies' Commission*, I, pp. 198–201.
96 Ibid., I, pp. 185ff.
97 Ibid., I, Minutes of Evidence 1709, 1721.
98 Ibid., I, p. 69.
99 Ibid., I, Minute of Evidence 1704.
100 Ibid., I, Minute of Evidence 1707.
101 See M. Argles, 'The Royal Commission on Technical Instruction; Its Inception and Composition', *Vocational Aspects . . .*, Vol. XI, Autumn 1959, pp. 97ff.
102 *Samuelson Commission*, III, Minutes of Evidence 2016, 2114–17.
103 *SIC*, V, Minutes of Evidence 9254–5.
104 *Samuelson Commission*, III, Minutes of Evidence 2132–7.
105 Magnus, *Educational Aims . . .*, pp. 111–12.
106 *Samuelson Commission*, III, p. 169, Minute of Evidence 1752.
107 PRO Ed. 14, London and General Files, File E25/29, List and Index Society, Vol. 21, DES Class List Pt 1, p. 226.
108 Lubbock, 'Manual Instruction', *Fortnightly Review*, Vol. CCXXXV N.S., Nov. 1886.
109 BPP *Select Committee Report . . . on Endowed Schools' Acts* 1886 IX 188, Q.3133–9, 3152–9, 3161–72, 3278.
110 Gosden, 'Technical instruction committees . . .', pp. 31–2; the London Technical Education Board was of the 'hybrid' type, containing 15 co-opted members and 20 Councillors.
111 Magnus, in Roberts, pp. 167–8.
112 BPP *Report of Consultative Committee on Examinations in Secondary Schools* 1911 (C.6004) XVI-159, p. 290; for a full discussion of these examinations see Foden, ' . . . Examinations of the City and Guilds', in MacLeod (ed.), pp. 74–82.
113 Magnus, *Educational Aims . . .*, pp. 76–80; D. S. L. Cardwell, *The Organization of Science in England* (1957), p. 197.
114 A. Abbott, *Education for Commerce and Industry* (1933), pp. vii, 3–4.
115 O. G. Pickard, 'Office Work and Eduction, 1848–1948', *Vocational Aspects . . .*, Vol. 1, Nov. 1949, pp. 222–8.
116 M. A. Dalvi, 'Commercial Education in England during 1851–1902: An institutional study' (unpublished PhD thesis, University of London 1957), pp. 99, 114–17.
117 Ibid., pp. 286, 303–12; Abbott, pp. 122–4.
118 Dalvi, pp. 321–4, 327.
119 Ibid., pp. 370–1.
120 Ibid., pp. 454, 378.
121 *Journal of London Chamber of Commerce*, Vol. VI, No. 70, 5 Dec. 1887; Pickard, loc. cit., p. 443; above, p. 235.
122 Welch, *Modern History . . .*, pp. 344, 351.
123 Leader in *Journal of London Chamber of Commerce* Vol. VI, No. 70, 5 Dec. 1887; Vol. VI, No. 66, 5 Aug. 1887.
124 London Chamber of Commerce, *Pamphlet 6841*, p. 1.
125 *Journal of London Chamber of Commerce*, Vol. VI, No. 70, 5 Dec. 1887.

126 Ibid., Vol. VI, No. 66, 5 Aug. 1887.
127 Ibid., Vol. V, No. 55, 6 Sept. 1886.
128 Final Report, p. XXIV, quot. Dalvi, 'Commercial Education', p. 175.
129 *Journal of London Chamber of Commerce*, Vol. V, No. 55, 6 Sept. 1886.
130 Ibid., Vol. V, 5 April, 5 June, 6 Dec. 1886.
131 Ibid., Supplement, 5 Aug. 1886.
132 Ibid., Vol. VI, No. 66, 5 Aug. 1887; *Pamphlet* 6841, p. 2.
133 *London Chamber of Commerce* Supplement, 5 Oct. 1887.
134 *Pamphlet* 6841, p. 3.
135 *Journal of London Chamber of Commerce*, Vol. VI, 5 Dec. 1887.
136 *Pamphlet* 6841, p. 4.
137 G. M. D. Howat, *The Oxford and Cambridge Schools' Examinations Council, 1873–1973* (1973), pp. 5–6.
138 *Pamphlet* 6841, §14, p. 5.
139 Ibid,. §15, pp. 5–6.
140 *Journal of London Chamber of Commerce*, Vol. IX, 5 Feb. 1890.
141 Ibid., 5 March 1890, pp. 55–7, Professor Bodington of Leeds speaking at Mansion House Conference; Dalvi, pp. 504–5.
142 Dalvi, p. 506.
143 *Pamphlet* 6841, §19, p. 6.
144 Ibid., §21–3, pp. 6–7.
145 *Journal of London Chamber of Commerce*, Vol. X, 6 Oct. 1890.
146 *Pamphlet* 6841 §31–33, pp. 9–10.
147 *Journal of London Chamber of Commerce*, Vol. X, 5 March 1890; Dalvi, p. 493.
148 Dalvi, pp. 624–5.
149 Ibid., p. 493; *Journal of London Chamber of Commerce*, Vol. X, 5 March 1890.
150 Ibid., Vol. XI, 10 Nov. 1891; above, p. 301.
151 *Pamphlet* 6841 §35, p. 10; Dalvi, p. 539.
152 Report of Conference at Mansion House, *Journal of London Chamber of Commerce*, Vol. X, 5 March 1890.
153 Usher *et al.*, *Angel without Wings*, p. 55.
154 *Journal of London Chamber of Commerce*, Vol. X, 5 March 1890; Dalvi, pp. 642–3, quot. enquiry instituted by the Bradford Chamber of Commerce, 1901.
155 Dalvi, p. 450.
156 *Bryce Commission Report*, IV, pp. 279–80.
157 D. Howard, 'The Relations of Commercial to Secondary Education', in Scott (ed.), *'What is Secondary Education?'* pp. 240–44; Abbott, pp. 122–4; below, p. 439.
158 Dalvi, p. 586.
159 F. C. Campbell, 'The Changing Environment of the London Grammar School', (unpublished PhD thesis, University of London, 1953), pp. 344–5.
160 Dalvi, pp. 590, 592, quot. *Technical Education Gazette*, May 1898, p. 65.
161 Ibid., *Educational Review*, Aug. 1899, p. 500.
162 Brennan, *Education for National Efficiency*, pp. 26–7; below, p. 430f.
163 Dalvi, pp. 541–2, quot. *Journal of London Chamber of Commerce*, Dec. 1892.

164 LCC Technical Education Board, *Report of Special Committee on Commercial Education* (1899) (TEB 80/4), p. 27.

165 Ibid., pp. ii-ix, 70–1, 12.

166 Ibid., *passim*; Campbell, 'London Grammar School', p. 345.

167 TEB *Report of Special Committee . . .*, Appendix II, pp. 25–36, 14.

168 *The Times*, 3 Sept. 1880, quot. Owen, *Philanthropy*, pp. 276–84; BPP 1843, XVI, pp. 722–775.

169 Revd R. H. Hadden, 'City Parochial Charities', *The Nineteenth Century*, Vol. IX, Feb. 1881, pp. 324–37.

170 Hadden, 'The Last Ten Years', in Atkinson, *St Botolph's Aldgate . . .*, pp. 208–10.

171 Owen, p. 277; BPP *Report of the Royal Commission on the London Parochial Charities* 1880 (C.2522) XX 1, Q.1406, 267, 6176.

172 *TNASS*, 1857, pp. 232–41; Hadden, 'City . . . Charities', pp. 328–9.

173 Owen, p. 277.

174 Hadden, 'City . . . Charities', p. 336.

175 Owen, p. 281.

176 Eg. *Contrasts* (1873), *The City* (1877), *The City: An enquiry into the Corporation, its Livery Companies and the Administration of their Charities and Endowments* (1877).

177 Owen, pp. 280ff; Hadden, 'City . . . Charities', pp. 333–7.

178 46 and 47 Vict. c. 36.

179 Owen, pp. 290–8; *DNB*, Francis Richard Sandford 1824–1893; Hadden, 'The Last Ten Years', p. 221.

180 *A History of the City Parochial Foundation, 1891–1951* (published by the Foundation); Ernald R. Warre, *Report of CPF* (1927).

181 Hadden, 'The Last Ten Years', *passim*; Owen, p. 294: BPP *Endowed Charities (County of London), Return for Parish of St Botolph without Aldgate* 1897 (86) LXVI Pt I, 1, pp. 34–5.

182 Oakeshott, 'Grammar Schools', p. 112; Atkinson, pp. 171–82.

183 Hadden, 'The Last Ten Years', *passim*.

184 *Return . . . Parish of St Botolph without Aldgate*, 1897 (86) LXVI Pt I, 1, pp. 57, 69–84; Hadden, loc. cit.

185 See A. Briggs, 'The Human Aggregate', and J. A. Banks, 'The Contagion of Numbers' in Dyos and Wolff (eds), *'The Victorian City*, I.

186 D. Reeder, 'Predicaments of City Children: late-Victorian and Edwardian Perspectives on Education and Urban Society', in Reeder (ed.) for the History of Education Society, *Urban Education in the Nineteenth Century* (Proceedings of Annual Conference, 1976), pp. 75ff.

187 *Oxford English Dictionary*, 'Polytechnic'; S. Webb, 'The London Polytechnic Institutes', BPP *Special Reports on Educational Subjects* II 1898 (C.8943), p. 59.

188 Ibid., pp. 60–1.

189 Owen, pp. 292ff; T. Kelly, *A History of Adult Education in Great Britain* (1962), pp. 192–3; *VCH, Middlesex*, I, pp. 353–5.

190 BPP *Special Reports on Educational Subjects* I 1896–7 (C.8447), S. H. Wells, 'The Secondary Day School attached to the Battersea (London) Polytechnic', p. 19; Dymond, *The Forge*, pp. 2–4; BPP *36th Report of Charity Commissioners* 1889 (C.5685) XXVIII.

191 Owen, p. 290; Webb, loc. cit., p. 62.

192 Owen, pp. 294–6, quot. BPP *Return of Certain Objections to the Central Scheme* LV 33 1890 (142).
193 Guildhall MSS 8971, City Parochial Council, London Polytechnic Council, *Minute Books*, 1894–1904 (hereafter LPC); BPP *37th Report of Charity Commissioners* 1890 (C.5986) XXVI, pp. 27–55 for discussion of beginning of system of Polytechnics in relation to needs of Metropolis; Webb, loc. cit., p. 63.
194 Above, pp. 399–400; *LPC*, Vol. I, 1 July 1898, Minute 2.
195 Ibid, Vol. II, 30 April 1903, Minute 9.
196 Wells, ' . . . Battersea Polytechnic', pp. 196ff.
197 Ibid.; Webb, loc. cit., p. 74.
198 *LPC*, Vol. II, 25 Nov. 1903, Minute 34.
199 See H. Silver, *Chelsea College, A History* (1977); S. J. Teague, 'Thoughts Towards the Early History of Chelsea College of Science and Technology', *British Journal of Educational Studies*, XVII, Oct. 1969.
200 Above, p. 235; *LPC*, Vol. I, 8 Dec. 1899, Minute 8; 12 Dec. 1902, Appen. Report of TEB, p. 4; E. H. Spencer, *An Inspector's Testament* (1938), pp. 225–39.
201 *LPC*, Vol. I, 27 Nov. 1893, p. 5.
202 *LPC*, Vol. II, 25 Nov. 1903, Minute 34.
203 *LPC*, Vol. II, 29 April 1904, Final Report on handing over to LCC 1904.
204 Wells, pp. 197ff.
205 *LPC*, Vol. I, 8 Dec. 1899, Appendix A; 14 Dec. 1900, Appendix A and Appendix C; Vol. II, 28 Feb. 1902, Minute 4, p. 11.
206 Owen, p. 297.
207 *LPC*, Vol. II, 2 April 1904, Minute 8.
208 *The Nineteenth Century*, XX, Oct. 1903, pp. 561ff.
209 Brennan, pp. 24, 34; *LPC*, Vol. II, 29 April 1904, Final Report to LCC §6, p. 8.
210 *LPC*, Vol. II, 6 Dec. 1901, Appendix D.
211 *LPC*, Vol. I, 8 Dec. 1899, Appendix B, p. 17.
212 *LPC*, Vol, I, 1 May 1896, Appendix, 'Work of the Polytechnics'.
213 *LPC*, Vol. I, 25 Nov. 1898, Appendix A, pp. 2–3.
214 *LPC*, Vol. II, 6 Dec. 1901, Appendix B, p. 1.
215 *LPC*, Vol. I, 19 Nov. 1897, Minute 5 and Appendix Report from TEB, p. 15, Kimmins's report on day school attached to Woolwich Polytechnic, the scheme of work overcomplicated and requires more staff than is necessary.
216 *LPC*, Vol. I, 5 April 1898, Minute 5.
217 Wells pp. 202ff.
218 *LPC*, Vol. II, 2 July 1903, Minute 15.
219 Brennan, pp. 9–10.
220 *LPC*, Vol. I, 1 May 1896, Appendix, 'The Work of the Polytechnics', pp. 1–4.

IX 'A directing and supervising intelligence'

1 *Notebooks of Henry James*, F. O. Mattheissen and K. B. Murdock (eds) (1961), quot. A. Briggs, 'The Human Aggregate', in Dyos and Wolff (eds), *The Victorian City*, I, p. 93.

2 E. E. Lampard, 'The Urbanizing World', Dyos and Wolff (eds), I, pp. 10ff.
3 Campbell, ' . . . the London Grammar School', quot. Booth, *Life and Labour . . . Religious Influences: London North of the Thames*, Vol. 1, 1904.
4 H. J. Dyos and D. A. Reeder, 'Slums and Suburbs', Dyos and Wolff (eds), I, p. 376.
5 Above, pp. 148–9; Weightman and Humphries, *The Making of Modern London*, Chapter Four.
6 Ibid., p. 109.
7 Royston Toon, 'The Work of the Middlesex Technical Education Committee' (unpublished MA dissertation, University of London, 1979), p. 9.
8 G. A. Sekon, *Locomotion in Victorian London* (1938), pp. 193–200; J. Simmons, 'The Power of the Railway', in Dyos and Wolff (eds), op. cit., I, pp. 284–5.
9 Above, p. 346; Weightman and Humphries, Chap. 2, 'The West End, from Season to Shopping Centre'.
10 M. Rees, 'The Economic and Social Development of Extra-Metropolitan Middlesex during the nineteenth century' (unpublished MSc (Econ) thesis, University of London, 1955), p. 442; below, pp. 423ff.
11 *Bryce Report*, VII, pp. 4–5; Dyos and Reeder, loc. cit., pp. 370ff.
12 *SIC*, V, pp. 423ff, Q.13082–3.
13 *Clarendon Commission*, IV, pp. 591–3.
14 Alfred Church, 'Day Schools, their Advantages and Disadvantages', *Contemporary Review*, XV, Aug./Nov. 1870.
15 *Clarendon Commission*, IV, pp. 968ff.
16 Davies, *Charterhouse*, pp. 276ff; Bamford, *Rise of the Public Schools*, pp. 10–16; R. W. Macan, 'The Removal of Charterhouse School', in H. E. Haig Brown (ed.), *William Haig Brown of Charterhouse*. Chap. III, pp. 42ff.
17 Above, p. 211.
18 Senate House Library, University of London Collection, ULC/PC/33/22/1–3; Usher *et al*, *Angel without Wings*, pp. 40–2, 52ff.
19 G. A. T. Allan, *Christ's Hospital* (1937), pp. 27–8.
20 Ibid., p. 88.
21 Ibid., pp. 47–9.
22 22 Geo. III c. 77; Allan, pp. 10–11.
23 *SIC*, Fearon's Report VII, p. 474–89, Digest, X, pp. 11–19; Evidence, IV, pp. 748–859; Recommendations, I, pp. 474–91.
24 Allan, pp. 80–2; R. J. N. Neville, 'Early Days', in Haig Brown (ed.), Chap. I, pp. 18–26.
25 Allan, Chap. VII; N. M. Plumley, 'The Royal Mathematical School, Christ's Hospital', *History Today*, Vol. XXIII, No. 8, August 1973, pp. 581ff.
26 See W. Lemprière, *History of the Girls' School of Christ's Hospital* (1924).
27 Picciotto, *St Paul's*, pp. 45–6.
28 Ibid., pp. 53–5: G. Cannell, 'Resistance to the Charity Commissioners: the case of St Paul's Schools', 1860–1904', *History of Education*, Vol. 10, No 4, Dec 1981.
29 Picciotto, *St Paul's*, pp. 57–8.
30 Ibid., p. 66.
31 Ibid., pp. 82–5.
32 Above, pp. 286–7.
33 Davies, *Charterhouse*, p. 278; Draper, *Merchant Taylors'*, p. 164; above, pp. 367–8.

34 Hearnshaw, *King's College*, pp. 309, 371, 422; typescript history of the school provided by the headmaster; Kirby, *Blackheath School*, pp. 112–13.
35 Above, pp. 179–80.
36 Below, p. 427.
37 Hounslow Public Library Loc. Collec., *Middlesex Chronicle*, 24 and 31 Jan. 1958, *Richmond and Twickenham Times*, 7 Aug. 1937; R. H. Hyam, *History of Isleworth Grammar School* (1968).
38 Information from C. Williams, Student at West London Institute of Higher Education.
39 London School Board *Schedule of Secondary Schools, 1891*; *Special Report from Select Committee on Teachers' Registration and Organization Bill* 1891, Minute of Evidence 4280ff.
40 *Bryce Report*, I, pp. 49–51; E. Moberly Bell, *History of the Church Schools' Company 1883–1958*, pp. 39, 84–5.
41 Booth, *Life and Labour* (1890), Third Series, *Poverty*, p. 247.
42 BPP 1884 Paper 293 HC LXI 259.
43 Hampstead Public Library Loc. Collec., H370 6 Prospectus, etc.; J. Russell, 'On some of the aims and methods of the King Alfred School Society', *Journal of the Royal Sanitary Institute*, Vol. XXXII, No. 2 (1911), pp. 161–3; Alice Woods, *Educational Experiments in England* (1920), p. 25; W. A. C. Stewart, *Progressives in English Education 1750–1970* (1972), pp. 173ff.
44 Robinson, 'Private Schools', pp. 20–2; D. P. Leinster-Mackay, 'Private or Public Schools: the Educational Debate in laissez-faire England', *Journal of Educational Administration and History*, XV, No. 2, July 1983, pp. 1ff.
45 *Special Report on Teachers' Registration... Bill*, Minute of Evidence 148, Evidence of Hodgson, Secretary of College of Preceptors.
46 Above, p. 161; Robinson, 'Private Schools', p. 38.
47 Baron, 'Secondary Schoolmaster', pp. 100ff; *Secondary Education*, Vol. I, No. 1, 1 Oct. 1896, p. 5, and Supplement, No. 5, 1 Feb. 1897.
48 Hounslow Public Library Loc. Collec., J. Cooper 'Literary Associations of Heston and Isleworth'.
49 Newsome, *Godliness and Good Learning*, pp. 161ff, 222; Leinster-Mackay, 'English Private School', II, pp. 24–6; *SIC*, V, pp. 761–72.
50 *Crockford's Directory*, p. x; Bisson, *Schools and Colleges*, p. 269.
51 Bisson, *Endowed Schools*, i, pp. 726, 724.
52 Bisson, *Schools and Colleges*, p. 298; Hampstead Public Library Loc. Collec., *Hampstead Annual* (1906–7) 'The Educational Opportunities of Old Hampstead', p. 69.
53 Bisson, *Schools and Colleges*, pp. 230, 339.
54 Bisson, *Endowed Schools*, i, pp. 641, 814.
55 Usher *et al.*, *An Angel without Wings*, pp. 43–4.
56 Leinster-Mackay, 'English Private Schools', II, p. 98.
57 BPP *Special Reports on Educational Subjects* 1900 (C.418) HC XXII (2).
58 A. Mann, 'The Achievement of the London Higher Grade Schools, 1887–1904' (unpublished MA dissertation, University of London, 1979), p. 22.
59 Ibid., p. 23; Evidence of William Martin, Sub-inspector for Marylebone, BPP *Cross Commission Third Report* 1887 (C.5158), pp. 496–7, Minutes of Evidence 55, 483ff.
60 Mann, p. 28.

61 Ibid., pp. 31–5.
62 Ibid., p. 62.
63 R. C. Lilley, 'Attempts to Implement the Bryce Commission's Recommendations – and the consequences', *History of Education*, Vol. II, No. 2, June 1982, pp. 99ff.
64 *Secondary Education*, 1 Dec. 1897, Vol. 11, No. 15, p. 163.
65 Report of Revd T. W. Sharpe, HMI, quot. Mann, p. 77.
66 Ibid., pp. 78–9.
67 Ibid, pp. 93, 97; S. Webb, *London Education (1904)*, p. 107.
68 Above, pp. 308–9; below, pp. 425ff.
69 H. B. Philpott, *London at School: The Story of the London School Board*, p. 170, quot. Mann, p. 86.
70 Mann, pp. 86–7.
71 Above, p. 303; Mann, p. 89.
72 Ibid., p. 89; For the Cockerton Judgement see E. J. R. Eaglesham, *The Foundations of 20th-Century Education in England* (1967), pp. 32–5; Maclure, *One Hundred Years . . .*, pp. 73–6; J. Lawson and H. Silver, *A Social History of Education in England* (1973), pp. 368–72.
73 P. J. Prior, 'The Higher Grade Schools in Tottenham and Wood Green, 1884–1914' (unpublished MA dissertation, University of London, 1981), Chap. 1.
74 Ibid., pp. 9–13.
75 Ibid., p. 17.
76 Ibid., pp. 16ff; above, p. 303.
77 Prior, p. 18.
78 Ibid., pp. 21–2.
79 Ibid., pp. 46, 92; above, pp. 391ff.
80 Maclure, *One Hundred Years . . .*, p. 50.
81 Middlesex Education Committee, *Secondary Schools and Technical Institutes in the Administrative County of Middlesex* (1915); *Report of the Consultative Committee of the Board of Education on Secondary Schools* (the 'Spens Report', 1938), p. 65.
82 In 1886 such centres were at William Street, Chelsea, Victoria Place, Clyde Street, New Road, Tottenham Road, Priory Grove, Sumner Road, Surrey Lane, 'The Brecknock', Marylebone, Nelson Street, Trafalgar Square: *Cross Report, Final Report* 1888 (C.5485), pp. 88–90.
83 *Cross Report, 2nd Report* 1887 (C.5056), Evidence of Revd J. R. Diggle, Q.30, 373–7, 29, 950, Appendix D, Paper VIII, Return Showing Number of Pupil Teachers, at present attending Pupil Teacher Schools, who have previously attended Secondary Schools, p. 1036.
84 *71st Annual Report of National Society* (1882), pp. 19–20; *72nd . . .* (1883), pp. 16–17.
85 LSB, *Schedule of Secondary Schools to which scholarship holders may be sent*, 1891; TEB, Report of Llewellyn Smith, p. 67.
86 G. T. Gray, *The Parish Church of Saint Mary Magdalen Bermondsey* (1958), p. 52.
87 *90th Annual Report of National Society (1890)*, pp. 26ff.
88 Department of Education School File 5754.
89 DES School File 5734; LCC *School List* 1959, Division 3, p. 10.
90 The Charles Edward Brooke School, *Memories of a School 1898–1973* (published by the School, 1973).

91 Above, p. 385.
92 Gosden, 'Technical Education Committees . . .' in History of Education Society, *Studies in the Government . . . of Education . . .*', p. 37.
93 Toon, '. . . Middlesex Technical Education Committee', pp. 40–1, 106–7.
94 Ibid., pp. 47–8.
95 Ibid., Table 15, p. 79.
96 Ibid., pp. 56–7; above, p. 303.
97 Toon, pp. 58–9; Garside, *Hampton School*, pp. 194–206.
98 Toon, pp. 58–9.
99 Ibid., p. 59; above, p. 417.
100 Toon, p. 60; above, p. 303f.
101 Toon, Table 8, p. 61.
102 Ibid., p. 65; above, p. 189.
103 Toon, p. 64.
104 Ibid., p. 65.
105 Booth, First Series, *Poverty*, iii, pp. 248–50.
106 LCC, *Report to the Special Committee on Technical Education* (1892).
107 *Report . . . on Technical Education*, pp. 62–3.
108 Ibid., pp. 66, 69.
109 Ibid., p. 63.
110 Ibid., Appendix K, pp. 173–4.
111 Ibid., pp. 69ff.
112 Ibid., XVII, pp. 78–82.
113 Above, pp. 385, 394.
114 J. S. Maclure, *Educational Documents, England and Wales, 1816–1967* (1968 edn), pp. 140–1.
115 *Bryce*, I, pp. 18–19.
116 Ibid., IX, Appendix D, Table III.
117 Ibid., I, pp. 1–2.
118 Above, p. 228.
119 *Bryce*, II, pp. 236ff, 264ff, 513ff, III, pp. 1ff, 130ff, 270ff, 435ff, IV, pp. 1ff, 42ff, 474ff.
120 Ibid., II, p. 236.
121 Ibid., III, p. 9.
122 Ibid., III, p. 147.
123 Ibid., II, pp. 513–15.
124 Ibid., III, pp. 270–1.
125 Ibid., IV, p. 474.
126 Ibid., II, p. 264.
127 Ibid., III, pp. 435ff.
128 *Cambridge Conference* (1896) *passim*.
129 Ibid., pp. 64–5, 24–5.
130 College of Preceptors, *Fifty Years of Progress . . .* (1896), pp. 35, 39; G. Baron, 'The Teachers' Registration Movement', *British Journal of Educational Studies*, II, May 1954, pp. 133–7; Tropp, *School Teachers*, pp. 53–4, 99–100.
131 62 and 63 Vict. c. 33.
132 2 Edw. VII c. 42.
133 3 Edw. VII c. 24.

134 Maclure, *One Hundred Years . . .*, pp. 75–6.
135 Webb, *London Education*, pp. 110–11.
136 *Bryce*, I, pp. 130–5.
137 Ibid., and pp. 98–101.
138 *Report of Select Committee on Teachers' Registration . . . Bill* 1891, pp. 44, 48.
139 LSB, *Schedule of Secondary Schools . . .* (1891).
140 *Bryce*, II, p. 360.
141 Ibid., I, pp. 132–3; Campbell, 'London Grammar School', pp. 270–1.
142 Above, pp. 301, 401.
143 Above, p. 431.
144 Letter 25 Oct. 1905, ULC/PC33/22/1–3; I am indebted to Mr G. Cannell of Kingsway-Princeton College for drawing my attention to this letter.
145 Above, p. 212; Webb, pp. 111–12.
146 Above, p. 284; *VCH, Middlesex*, I, p. 304.
147 Ibid., p. 301.
148 Stott, *Chigwell*, pp. 96, 111–13, 136.
149 Percy, *Whitgift's*, pp. 306–7, 251–4, 256–8.
150 Above, pp. 415–6.
151 Scott, '*What is Secondary Education?*', p. 6.
152 Quoted in P. Chalmers Mitchell, *Thomas Henry Huxley* (1913), pp. 195–6.
153 Booth, First Series, *Poverty*, iii, p. 277.
154 Campbell, 'London Grammar School', p. 227.
155 Webb, p. 111.
156 Above, Chap. VII.
157 Above, pp. 418, 407f; see Woods, *Educational Experiments*.
158 See C. Cowdroy, *Wasted Womanhood*, together with *A Biography of the Author* by M. Bennell (1933).
159 Magnus, *Educational Aims and Efforts*, pp. 41–6.
160 Above, Chaps VI and VIII.
161 Above, pp. 425f; E. W. Jenkins, *From Armstrong to Nuffield* (1979), Chap. 1.
162 *Bryce*, I, pp. 134–6.
163 Webb, p. 99.
164 Ibid., p. 115.
165 BPP *Return of the Pupils in Public and Private Secondary and other Schools (not being Public Elementary or Technical Schools) in England on July 1, 1897* June 1898 (C.8634); H. Bendall, 'Secondary and other Schools', in Scott (ed.), p. 45; Higginson, 'The Evolution of Secondary Education', pp. 172ff.
166 Scott, p. 15.
167 Above, pp. 347ff.
168 Baron, 'Secondary Schoolmaster', *passim*; Gordon, 'Endowed Schools and the Education of the Poor', pp. 70–1.
169 *Bryce*, IV, pp. 156ff.
170 BPP, No. 381, Aug. 1898; Scott, pp. 222–30.
171 Scott, pp. 225, 226–8, 229.
172 H. C. Wilks, *George Green's School 1828–1978* (1979), pp. 121–2.
173 Scott, '*What is Secondary Education?*', pp. 1–18, 58–66.

174　Ibid., pp. 213–21.
175　Ibid., p. 243; above, p. 393.
176　Scott, pp. 67, 69.
177　Board of Education, *Regulations for Secondary Schools*, 1904 (C.2128) lxxv 533; Higginson, loc. cit.; Maclure, *Documents*, pp. 156–9; Roy Lowe, 'Robert Morant and the Secondary School Regulations of 1904', *Journal of Educational Administration and History*, XVI, No. 1, Jan. 1984, pp. 37ff.
178　See for example N. Whitbread, 'The early twentieth century secondary curriculum debate in England', *History of Education*, Vol. 13, No. 3, Sept. 1984, pp. 221ff.
179　Above, p. 392.
180　R. Palmer, 'The Influence of F. W. Sanderson on the development of science and engineering at Dulwich College, 1885–1892', *History of Education*, Vol. 6, No. 2, June 1977, pp. 121–30.
181　Above, p. 422.
182　Jenkins, *From Armstrong to Nuffield*, pp. 6–7; Maclure, *One Hundred Years . . .*, pp. 87, 89.
183　Wilks, *George Green's School*, pp. 121–2.
184　C. Cookson (ed.), *Essays on Secondary Education by various contributors* (1898).

Bibliography

(A)   Primary sources
(B)   Contemporary periodicals and newspapers
(C)   Works of Reference
(D)   Books and Pamphlets
(E)   Articles
(F)   Theses

(A)   Primary sources

Adult Orphan Asylum (Institution) (at Princess Helena College)
   Annual Reports, 1823–98
Bishopsgate Institute
   Papers relating to the Revd William Rogers
Calendar of State Papers Domestic
   1635–6, 1637, 1655–6.
Calendar of Treasury Books, 1679–80
Central Foundation School Archives
   I   *Minute Book* 1865–73 with Committee Minutes from 1866
   II   Minutes of Council 1866–89
   III   Minutes of Governors' Meetings 1866–89
   IV   List of Governors and Subscribers
   Log Book of the Bishopsgate School for Girls
      Bicentenary Magazine of School 1926
City of London Record Office
   Minute Book of the Committee for the Promotion of Technical Education,
      Jan. 1872–Oct. 1873
   Minutes of the Court of Common Council, 1866, 1878, and Report No. 24
Fabian Tracts
   157   *The Working Life of Women* (1911)
   175   *The Economic Foundations of the Women's Movement* (1914)
Girton College
   Emily Davies Papers, *Reports* and *Minute Books* of the London Association of
      Schoolmistresses, Box IX.
Greater London Record Office
   Consistory Court Books, Diocese of London, 1520–1685
Guildhall Library
   City Parochial Council, *Minute Books* of the London Polytechnic Council,
      2 vols, 1894–1904 (Guildhall MS 8971)
   Diocese of London, *Subscription Books*, 1627–83 (Guildhall MS 9539 A,
      9539 B, 9539 C, 9540, 10144)

Vestry of St Botolph's Bishopsgate, Minutes (Guildhall MS 4526/7)
Historical Manuscripts Commission
  Du Cane
  Dartmouth (*15th Report, Appendix 1*)
  Hastings II
  Ormonde V, VI
HMC National Register of Archives
  List of Archives of New College London (1968)
  Tottenham Exhibition Catalogue (1956)
King's College London
  Calendars, 1846–90/1
Local Collections:
  Chelsea Central Library
  Enfield Central Library
  Hackney Central Library
  Hampstead Central Library
  Hounslow and District Central Library
  Islington Central Library
  Kensington Central Library
  Marylebone Central Library
  Tottenham, Bruce Castle Museum
  Uxbridge Central Library
  Westminster Public Library
London Chamber of Commerce
  Journal and *Commercial Education* (Guildhall Pamphlet 6841)
London County Council, County Record Office
  Annual Reports, 1893/4–1903/4
  Report of Special Subcommittee on Commercial Education, and 1 vol. MSS loose
    papers TEB 20
    Technical Education Board TEB 80/52, 53, 54, 55
    TEB 80/39 Reports of Inspectors
London School Board
  Schedule of Secondary Schools to which scholarship holders may be sent (1891)
Middlesex Education Committee
  Secondary Schools and Technical Institutes in the Administrative County of
    Middlesex (1915)
Miscellaneous School Papers
  Charles Edward Brooke School, *Memories of a School 1898–1973* (1973)
  Edward Alleyn School, *Magazine*, 1912–18
  Greenwich Royal Hospital School. *Old Boys' Association Gazettes*
  Paddington and Maida Vale High School, *Headmistress's Report* 1908, and
    School Magazine 1894–1907
  Society of Licensed Victuallers, *Rules and Bye-Laws* (1911 edn).
  Strand School, typescript history
National Society
  Annual Reports
  *First Report of the Metropolitan Institution for the Establishment and Improvement
    of Commercial Schools in the Metropolis and its Suburbs in connexion with the
    National Church* (1840)
  First Report of the Middle Class Schools' Committee (Ann. Rep. LX 1869)

General Committee Minutes
Records Vol. (a) *Battersea Subcommittee, 1847–9*
Reports of London Diocesan Board of Education
School Files
New College, Hampstead
  A. Cave, *The Story of the Founding of Hackney College* (MSS notes, Hampstead
    Central Library Loc. Collec.)
Official publications
  Department of Education School Files
  Minutes of Committee of Council on Education, 1853–4, 1855–6, 1858–9
Parliamentary Papers
(i) BPP *Report of the Select Committee to inquire into the education of the lower
     orders in the Metropolis and to consider what may be done with children of
     paupers found begging in the streets in and near the Metropolis*
     1816 [498] IV 1
     1817 [479] III 81
     1818 [136] IV 1
     1818 [356] IV 3
     1818 [426] IV 55
     1818 [427] IV 223
     1818 [428] IV 367
   BPP *Education Enquiry Abstract of Answers and Returns* 1833 Vol. I; 1835
     Vol. II, xli–xlii
   BPP *Report of the Commission on Popular Education* 1861 [C.2794] xx1, Pt
     11 (Newcastle Commission)
   BPP *Her Majesty's Commissioners to inquire into the revenues and management
     of certain colleges and schools and the studies pursued and instruction given
     therein* 1864 [C.3288] (Clarendon Commission)
   BPP *Commissioners appointed by Her Majesty to inquire into the education given
     in schools in England, not comprised within Her Majesty's two recent commis-
     sions on popular education and on public schools* 1867–8 [C.3966] 21 vols
     comprising Vol. XXXVIII of Sessional Papers (Taunton or Schools'
     Inquiry Commission)
   BPP *Report relative to Technical Education* tabled in Session 1867, XXVI
   BPP *Report of the Endowed Schools' Commissioners to the Committee of Council
     on Education* 1872 (C.524) XXIV
   BPP *Select Committee on the Endowed Schools' Act* 1873 (C.254) VIII
   BPP *Reports of Select Committee: Endowed Schools' Acts* 1886 (191 Sess. 1)
     IX 1
   Further Report with Proceedings, Evidence and Appendix 1887 (120) IX 235
   BPP *Select Committee on Scientific Instruction* 1867–8 [C.432] XV
     (Samuelson Committee)
   BPP *Royal Commission on Scientific Instruction and the Advancement of Science*
     1872 (C.536) XXV 1 (Devonshire Commission)
   BPP *Royal Commission on Technical Instruction Second Report* 1884 (C.3981)
     XXIX, XXX, XXXI, XXXII (Samuelson Commission)
   House of Lords Sessions Papers, 1884 Vol. 1 No. 29 (Shelf mark B59/1)
     (the Fortescue Returns)
   BPP *Report from the Select Committee on Mr Goffin's Certificate* 1878/9 (334)
     X

BPP 1884 Paper 293 HCLXI 259 (Dr Crichton-Brown's report on over-pressure on schoolchildren)

BPP *Report of the Royal Commission appointed to inquire into the working of the Elementary Education Acts, England and Wales*

First Report 1886 (C.4863) XXVI

Second Report 1887 (C.5056) XXIX 1

Third Report 1887 (C.5158) XXX 1

Final Report 1888 (C.5485)

Appendices 1888 (C.5485 II to IV) XXXVI 1 (Cross Commission)

BPP *Special Report from the Select Committee on the Teachers' Registration and Organization Bill* 4 July 1891 (C.335) XVII

BPP *Royal Commission on Secondary Education* 1894–5 (C.7862 i) (Bryce Commission)

BPP *Return of the Pupils in Public and Private Secondary and other Schools (not being Public Elementary or Technical Schools) in England on 1 July 1897* June 1898 (C.8634)

BPP *Special Reports on Educational Subjects*

I 1896 (C.8447)

II 1898 (C.8943)

VI 1900 (C.418)

BPP *Board of Education Regulations for Secondary Schools* 1904 (C.2128) LXXV 533

BPP *Report of the Consultative Committee on Examinations in Secondary Schools* 1911 (C.6004) XVI 159 (Dyke-Acland Report)

(ii) BPP *Report from the Select Committee to examine and consider the Evidence in the several Reports presented to The House from the Commissioners of Charities in England and Wales* 1835 [C.449] VII 631

BPP *Analytical Digest of the Reports of the Commissioners of Inquiry into Charities* 1843 [433, 434] XVI 1, XVII 1

The Endowed Charities of the City of London, reprinted at large from the 17 Reports of the Commissioners for inquiry concerning Charities (1829)

Reports of the Commissioners to inquire concerning Charities . . . relating to the County of Kent 1819–37 (compiled from relevant Parliamentary Papers each with Command no.)

BPP *Report of the Commissioners appointed to inquire into Greenwich Hospital* 1860 [C.2670] XXX 1

BPP *Scheme for the Management of the Foundation of Thomas Parmiter*
1883 (91–III) LIII–275
1884 (21–1) LXI–351

BPP *Annual Reports of the Charity Commissioners*

30th 1883 (C.3537) XXI 337

31st 1884 (C.3936) X

36th 1889 (C.5685) XXVIII

37th 1890 (C.5986) XXVI

38th 1891/2 (C.6301) XXVI § 15

40th 1893/4 (C.6960) XXV 15

BPP *Returns . . . made to the Charity Commissioners. In the result of an Inquiry held in every parish in each county in England and Wales*

London 1894 (261, 231) LXIII 13

1895 (35, 235, 304, 392, 425, 465) LXXIV 195

1896 (144, 306) LXIII Pt 1 555
1897 (86, 128, 222, 393) LXVI Pt 1 1
1898 (44, 112, 222, 389) LXVI Pt 11 1
1899 (200, 101, 256, 161) LXX 1
1900 LXXII

BPP *Returns . . . to the Charity Commissioners . . . and a Digest showing, in the case of each parish . . . , what such Endowments are recorded in the books of the Charity Commission in the parish*

London (Combined form)
Vol. I 1897 (394) LXVI Pt II 1
Vol. II 1899 (93) LXIX 1
Vol. III 1900 (252) LXI 1
Vol. V 1903 (181) xlix 1
Vols VI–VII 1904 (79, 333, 334) lxxi, lxxii, lxxiii 1

(iii) BPP *Report of the Commissioners to inquire into the existing state of the Corporation of London* 1854 (8) XXVI 1772

BPP *Report of the Royal Commission appointed to inquire into the Condition and Administration of the Parochial Charities in the City of London* 1880 (C.2522) XX 1

BPP *Royal Commission appointed to inquire into the Livery Companies of the City of London*

Vol. I Reports, memoranda and the oral inquiry 1884 (C.4073–I) XXXIX Pt I 1
Vol. II Returns of the Great Companies 1884 (C.4073–I) XXXIX Pt II 1
Vol. III Returns of the Minor Companies 1884 (C.4073–II) XXXIX Pt III 1
Vol. IV Mr Hare's Reports . . . twelve Great Companies 1884 (C.4073) XXXIX Pt IV 1
Vol. V Reports as to the Charities of the Minor Companies 1884 (C.4073–IV) XXXIX Pt V 1

BPP *Royal Commission on the Government of London* 1893–4 (C.7493) XVII, XVIII

BPP *Report of the Royal Commissioners appointed to consider the proper conditions under which the Amalgamation of the City and County of London can be effected . . .* 1894 (C.7493) XVII, XVIII

Senate House Library
University of London Collection ULC/PC/33/22/1–3
St Edmund's Papers, Archbishop's House, Westminster
Catholic Middle School Log Book, 1848–51 (19.1.17)

(B) Contemporary periodicals and newspapers

The Academia
Contemporary Review
Dublin Review
Edinburgh Review
English Journal of Education
The Englishwoman's Journal
Fraser's Magazine

Gentleman's Magazine
Illustrated London News
Journal of the London Chamber of Commerce
Longman's Magazine
The Nineteenth Century
Quarterly Journal of Education
Saturday Review
The Scholastic Gazette
Scholastic Journal
Scholastic World
The Times
Westminster Review

(C) Works of reference

à Wood, Anthony, *Athenae Oxoniensis* (1691–2; ed. P. Bliss, 1813–20)
Barfoot, P. and Wilkes, J., *The Universal British Directory of Trade, Commerce and Manufactures* (5 vols, 1791–7)
Biographia Britannica, or the lives of the most eminent persons who have flourished in Great Britain and Ireland from the earliest age down to the present time (7 vols, 1747–66)
Bisson, F. S. de Carteret, *Our Schools and Colleges* (1872)
    Our Endowed and Private Schools, Vol. i, For Boys (1879), Vol. ii, For Girls (1884)
Boase, F., *Modern English Biography* (6 vols, 1892–1921)
Brayley, Edward Wedlake, *London and Middlesex or an Historical Commercial and Descriptive Survey of the Metropolis of Great Britain, including sketches of its Environs, etc.*:
Vols I and II (1810)
Vol. III by J. Nightingale (1815)
Vol. IV by Norris Brewer (1816)
Catholic Directory and Annual Register.
Crockford's *Scholastic Directory for 1861. Being an Annual Work of Reference for Facts relating to Educators, Education and Educational Establishments (Public and Private) in the United Kingdom* (1861)
Dictionary of National Biography (1885–1900) and *Supplements*
Foster, J., *Alumni Oxonienses* (1887–92)
Gillow, J., *A literary and biographical history or bibliographical dictionary of English Catholics from the Breach with Rome in 1534 to the present time* (1885–95)
Hampton's *Scholastic Directory and Hotel Guide* (1893–4)
Heal, A., *The English Writing Masters and their Copy Books 1570–1800*, a biographical dictionary (1931)
Laity's Directory
London County Council, *Survey of London* (1900–)
Lysons, the Revd Daniel, *Environs of London* (4 vols, 1792–6), *Supplement, An Historical Account of those parishes in the Conty of Middlesex which are not described in the Environs of London* (1808).
    Collectanea (2 vols BM)
Pigot's *Directories*

Post Office *Directories*
Public and Preparatory Schools' Year Book
Thorne, J., *Handbook to the Environs of London*, alphabetically arranged in two parts (1876)
Whittaker, G. B., *The Boarding School and London Masters' Directory, or the Addresses of the First Teachers in Every Department of Education and of the Principal Finishing and Preparatory Seminaries of Young Ladies and Gentlemen in and near the Metropolis* (1828).
Who was Who (1897–1916)
Women of the Day (1884)

(D) Books and pamphlets

Abbott, A., *Education for Commerce and Industry* (1933)
Aiken, Lucy, *Memoirs of the Court of Charles I* (1833)
Ainsworth, R., *Compendious Dictionary of the Latin Tongue* and *Thesaurus* (1736) and *A Most Natural and Easy Way of Institution containing Proposals for making a Domestic Education less Chargeable to Parents and More Easy and Beneficial to Children* (1698)
Alderman, G., *The History of Hackney Downs School, formerly the Grocers' Company's School* (1972)
Alexander, J. J. G. and Gibson, M. T., *Medieval Learning and Literature: Essays presented to Richard William Hunt* (1976)
Allan, G. A. T., *Christ's Hospital* (1937)
Allport, D. H., *Camberwell Grammar School: a short history of the foundation under Royal Charter of Edward Wilson . . .* (published by the Governors of the School, 1964)
Annan, N., *Leslie Stephen* (1951)
Archer, R. L., *Secondary Education in the 19th Century* (1921, reprinted 1966)
Argles, M., *South Kensington to Robbins* (1964)
Armytage, W. H. G., *Four Hundred Years of English Education* (1964)
    The Rise of the Technocrats (1965)
Arnold, M., *Culture and Anarchy* (1869; ed. J. Dover Wilson, 1966)
Arts Council, *The Age of Neo-Classicism* (1972).
Ashley Smith, J. W., *The Birth of Modern Education: the Contribution of the Dissenting Academies 1660–1800* (1954)
Astell, Mary, *Essay in Defence of the Female Sex* (1696)
    Serious Proposal for Ladies (1694 and 1697)
    Reflections on Marriage (1706, 1730 edn)
Atkinson, A. G. B., *St Botolph's Aldgate, the Story of a City Parish* (1898)
Aubrey, J., *Brief Lives* (ed. A. Clark, 1898) and *Miscellanies* (1857 edn)
Aungier, G. J., *History and Antiquities of Syon Monastery, the Parish of Isleworth and the Chapelry of Hounslow* (1840)
Avery, J., *Bishopsgate Schools, 1702–1889* (1932)
Bamford, T. W., *The Rise of the Public Schools* (1967)
Banks, J. A. and O., *Feminism and Family Planning* (1964)
Barclay, J., *Treatise on Education* (1743)
Barker, T. C. and Robbins, M., *A History of London Transport, Vol. I, The Nineteenth Century* (1963)

Bassett Hopkins, A., *The Boroughs of the Metropolis* (1900)

Batchiler, J., *The Virgin's Pattern* (1661)

Batten, D., *Clapham with its Common and Environs* (1841)

Battersby, W. J., *Brother Potamian, Educator and Scientist* (1953)
   The De la Salle Brothers in Great Britain: the story of a century of effort and achievement in the domain of English education (1954)
   St Joseph's College, Beulah Hill, 1855–1955 (1955)

Beales, A. C. F., *Education under Penalty: English Catholic Education from the Reformation to the fall of James II 1547–1689* (1963)

Beaver, A., *Memorials of Old Chelsea* (1892)

Beck, G. A. (ed.), *The English Catholics 1850–1950* (1950)

Becker, B. H., *Scientific London* (1874, reprinted 1968)

de Beer, E. S. (ed.), *Diary of John Evelyn* (6 vols, 1955)

Bennett, H. S., *Chaucer in the 15th Century* (1948)
   English Books and Readers 1474–1557, being a study in the history of the Book trade from Caxton to the incorporation of the Stationers' Company (1969)

Besant, W., *Survey of London* (8 vols, 1903–10), *London in the Nineteenth Century* (1909)

Best, G. F. A., *Mid-Victorian Britain 1851–75* (1971).
   Temporal Pillars, Queen Anne's Bounty, the Ecclesiastical Commissioners and the Church of England (1964)

Bettesworth, J., *The New Universal ready reckoner* (1780)

Bettesworth, J. and Fox, H., *Observations on Education in general but particularly on Naval Education with a Plan for a Naval Academy* (1782)

Beveridge, W., *Voluntary Action* (1948)

Bibby, C., *T. H. Huxley and Education* (1971)

Bindoff, S. T., *Tudor England* (1950)

Binnie, K. S., *The Story of the Roan Schools, 1643–1956* (1957)

Blagden, Cyprian, *The Stationers' Company . . . 1403–1959* (1960)

Blanch, W. H., *Ye Parish of Camberwell* (1877)

Blunden, E., *The Christ's Hospital Book 1553–1953* (1953)

Blunt, R., *An Illustrated Historical Handbook to the Parish of Chelsea* (1900)

Blyth, E. K., *Life of William Ellis* (1889)

Booth, C., *Life and Labour of the People in London* (1889–1903, 1903 edn)

Boswell, J., *Life of Johnson* (G. B. Hill and L. F. Powell (eds) 1934)

Bradbrook, M. C., *'That Infidel Place', A Short History of Girton College 1869–1969* (1969)

Bremner, C. S., *Education of girls and women in Great Britain* (1897)

Brennan, E. J. T., *Education for National Efficiency: the Contribution of Sidney and Beatrice Webb* (1975)

Brett-James, N. G., *Mill Hill School 1807–1907* (1924)
   The Growth of Stuart London (1935)
   Mill Hill (1938)

British Association for the Advancement of Science, *London the Advancement of Science* by various Authors (issued on occasion of . . . centenary meeting in London, 1931).

Brittain, Vera, *The Women at Oxford* (1960)

Brock, W. H., *H. E. Armstrong and the Teaching of Science* (1973)

Brooke, C. N. L., assisted by Keir, C., *London 800–1216: The shaping of a city* (1975)

Brown, C. K. F., *The Church's Part in Education 1833–1941* (1942)

Brown, F. K., *Fathers of the Victorians* (1961)

Brown, S. W., *Leighton Park* (1952)

Browning, A. (ed.), *Memoirs of Sir John Reresby* (1936)

Bryan, G., *Chelsea in the Olden and Present Times* (published by the author, 1869)

Bryant, Margaret, *The Unexpected Revolution* (1979)

Burchell, Doris, *Miss Buss' Second School* (1971)

Burgess, H. J., *Enterprise in Education: the story of the work of the Established Church in the education of the people prior to 1870* (1958)

Burgess, R., *Address delivered at the opening of the East Islington Commercial School* (1841)

Burn, W. L., *The Age of Equipoise* (1964, 1968 edn)

Burstall, Sara A., *Frances Mary Buss* (1938)

Burston, W. H., *James Mill on Philosophy and Education* (1973)

Burstyn, Joan N., *Victorian Education and the Ideal of Womanhood* (1980)

Burton, H., *Barbara Bodichon* (1949)

Butler, Josephine (ed.), *Women's Work and Women's Culture* (1869)

Buxton, C., *Memoirs of Sir Thomas Fowell Buxton* (1848)

Camden Society, *Autobiography of Sir John Bramston* (No. 32, 1845)
   Diary of the Revd Ralph Josselin (3rd Series, XV, 1908)

Campbell Stewart, W. A., *Quakers and Education* (1953)

Cardwell, D. S. L., *The Organization of Science in England* (1957)

Carleton, J. D., *Westminster School, A History* (1965)

Carrington, R. C., *Two schools: a history of the St Olave's and St Saviour's Grammar School Foundation* (published for the Governors, 1971)

Chambers, Mary C., *The Life of Mary Ward, 1585–1645*, H. J. Coleridge (ed.), (1882)

Chandler, G., *An Address Delivered at the opening of the Church of England Metropolitan Commercial School, Rose Street, Soho Square, Jan. 28, 1839* (1839)

Charlton, K., *Education in Renaissance England* (1965)

Cherry, Bridget and Pevsner, N. (eds), *London, 2, South* (The Buildings of England) (1983)

Chetham Society, *Autobiography of Henry Newcombe MA*, R. Parkinson (ed.) (Vol. XXVI, 1852)

Chorley, H. (ed.), *Letters of M. R. Mitford* (1872)

Churchill, W. S., *My Early Life* (1944 edn)

Clanchy, M. T., *From Memory to Written Record, England 1066–1307* (1979)

Clark, G. N., *The Later Stuarts* (1940)

Clarke, C. Cowden and Mary Victoria, *Recollections of Writers* (1878, reprinted 1969)

Clarke, M. L., *Classical Education in Britain, 1500–1900* (1959)

Clinch, G., *Marylebone and St Pancras* (1890)

Clough, Blanche A., *A Memoir of Anne Jemima Clough* (1903)

Clough, C. H., *Profession, Vocation and Culture in Later Medieval England*, Essays dedicated to the memory of A. R. Myers (1982)

Coleridge, S. T., *The Constitution of Church and State* (1829)

College of Preceptors, *Fifty Years of Progress in Education*, a Review of the Work of the College of Preceptors from its Foundation in 1846 to its Jubilee in 1896 (1896)

Compton, T., *Recollections of Tottenham Friends and the Forster Family* (1893)

Conolly, W. R. and Dalton, W. A., *Prospectus for Establishing in London a Great Catholic Central Middle-Class School for Boys, on the Great Commercial Principles of the Age, Cooperation and Limited Liability* (1880)

Cookson, C. (ed.), *Essays on Secondary Education by various authors* (1898)

Coppock, J. T. and Prince H. C. (eds), *Greater London* (1964)

Cowdroy, Charlotte, *Wasted Womanhood* together with *A Biography of the Author* by M. Bennett (1933)

Crofton Croker, T., *A Walk from London to Fulham* (1860, enlarged, etc, B. E. Horne, 1896)

Curryer, Constance E. and Moore, U. K. (Katharine), *The Story of Walthamstow Hall* (1973)

Curtis, S., *Strictures on the Hackney Grammar School, by a Proprietor* (1831)

Dare, R. A., *A History of Owen's School* (n.d.)

Davie, D., *A Gathered Church: The Literature of the English Dissenting Interest, 1700–1930* (Clark Lecture 1976, pub. 1978)

Davie, G. E., *The Democratic Intellect, Scotland and her Universities in the Nineteenth Century* (1961)

Davies, G. S., *The Charterhouse in London* (1921)

Davies, R., *Chelsea Old Church* (1904)

Delamont, S. and Duffin, L. (eds.), *The Nineteenth-Century Woman: Her cultural and physical world* (1978)

Derry, Warren, *Dr Parr: A portrait of the Whig Dr Johnson* (1966)

Dolittle, I. G., *The City of London and its Livery Companies* (1982)

Douglas-Smith, A. E., *The City of London School* (2nd edn 1965)

Dowling, D., *An Improved System of Arithmetic for the Use of Schools and the Counting House* (1818)
 A New and Improved System of Calculation (1829)
 Key to Hutton's Course of Mathemetics (1818)

Draper, F. W. M., *Four Centuries of Merchant Taylors' School* (1962)

Draper, W., *Chiswick* (1923)

Duncan, L. L., *History of the Borough of Lewisham* (1908)
 The History of Colfe's Grammar School 1652–1952 (1910, 1952 edn).

D'Urfey, T. *Love for Money, or the Boarding School* (1691)
 Beauties Triumph (1676)

Dyhouse, Carol, *Girls Growing Up in Late Victorian and Edwardian England* (1981)

Dymond, Dorothy, *The Forge* (1955)

Dyos, H. J. and Wolff, M., *The Victorian City* (2 vols, 1973)

Eaglesham, E. J. R., *The Foundations of 20th century Education in England* (1967)

Ellenor, J. B., *Rambling Recollections of Chelsea and the surrounding District* (1901)

Elphinston, J., *Plan of Education at Kensington Academy* (1764)
 Principles of English Grammar Digested (2 vols, 1765)
 Education, a Poem in Four Books (1763)

Elwin, M., *The First Romantics* (1947)

Evenett, H. O., *The Catholic Schools of England and Wales* (1944)

Faber, G., *Jowett: A portrait with background* (1957)

Farrer, Katherine E. (ed.), *Correspondence of Josiah Wedgwood 1781–1794* (1906)

Faulkner, T., *An historical and topographical description of Chelsea and its environs etc.* (1810)
 History and Antiquities of Fulham including Hammersmith (1813)

History and Antiquities of Kensington (1820)

History and Antiquities of Brentford, Ealing and Chiswick (1845)

Ferét, C. J., *Fulham Old and New, being an Exhaustive History of the Ancient Parish of Fulham, London* (3 vols, 1890)

Fletcher, Laadan, *The Teachers' Press in Britain 1802–1888*, Educational Administration and History Monograph No. 7 (Museum of the History of Education, University of Leeds, 1978)

Fletcher, S., *Feminists and Bureacrats: A study in the development of girls' education in the nineteenth century* (1980)

Ford, B. (ed.), *From Dryden to Johnson* (Vol. 4, Pelican Guide to English Literature) (1968 edn)

Fortescue, Lord, *Public Schools for the Middle Classes* (1864)

Foster, J., *Sir John Eliot* (1865)

Foster, Watson, *Beginnings of the Teaching of Modern Subjects in England* (1909)

Gardiner, Dorothy, *English Girlhood at School: a study of women's education through twelve centuries* (1929)

Gardner, B., *The Public Schools* (1973)

Garside, B., *The history of Hampton School from 1556 to 1700 with a brief account of the years between 1700 and the present day* (1931)

Gay, P., *The Enlightenment: An interpretation* (1967)

George, M. Dorothy, *London Life in the Eighteenth Century* (1925, 1966 edn)

Gibbon, G. and Bell, R. W., *History of the London County Council, 1889–1939* (1939)

Gilbert, W., *The City. An Enquiry into the Corporation, its Livery Companies, and the Administration of their Charities and Endowments* (1877)

Gladstone, Florence M., *Aubrey House, Kensington, 1698–1920* (Kensington Public Library Loc. Collec. 36556)

Glenday, Nonita and Price, Mary, *Reluctant Revolutionaries: a century of headmistresses* (for Association of Headmistresses, 1974)

Goffin, R. E. H., *A Brief Account of the Foundation and History of the United Westminster Schools* (1894)

van Gogh-Bonger, J. (ed.), *Letters of Vincent van Gogh to his brother, 1872–1886* (3 vols, 1927–29)

Gombrich, E., *Ideals and Idols* (1979)

Gordon, P., *Selection for Secondary Education* (1980)

Gore, J. (ed.), *The Creevey Papers* (1963)

Gott, B. and Maples, E., *Higher Education in the Administrative County of Middlesex 1907* (1907)

Gray, G. T., *The Parish Church of Saint Mary Magdalen, Bermondsey* (1958)

Green, V. H. H., *The Universities* (1969)

Grimshaw, M. E., *Silver Medals, Badges and Trophies from Schools in the British Isles 1550–1850* (n.d., privately printed Cambridge)

Pre-Victorian Silver School Medals (1985)

Grylls, Rosalie G., *Queen's College, 1848–1948* (1948)

Gurney, Mary, *Are We to Have Education for Our Middle-Class Girls? Or the History of the Camden Collegiate Schools* (1872)

Hadden, R. H. (Compiler), *Reminiscences of the Reverend William Rogers, Rector of St Botolph Bishopsgate* (1888)

Haig Brown, H. E. (ed.), *William Haig Brown of Charterhouse: A short biographical memoir, written by some of his pupils* (1908)

Haig Brown, W., *Charterhouse Past and Present* (1879)

Halévy, E., *A History of the English People in 1815*, Book III, Religion and Culture (1924, 1938 edn)

Halliwell, J. O. (ed.), *The Autobiography and Correspondence of Sir Simonds D'Ewes Bart during the reigns of James I and Charles I* (1845)

Hammond, J. L. and Barbara, *Shaftesbury* (1925; Penguin edn 1969)

Hammond, N. G. L., *Centenary Essays on Clifton College* (Clifton College, 1962)

Handfield Jones, R. M., *The History of the Royal Masonic Institution for Girls, 1788–1974* (The Institution, 5th edn 1974)

Hans, N., *New Trends in Education in the Eighteenth Century* (1951)

Harris, J., Orgel, S., Strong, R., *The King's Arcadia: Inigo Jones and the Stuart Court* (Arts Council, 1973)

Hay, D., *Annalists and Historians: Western historiography from the VIIIth to the XVIIIth century* (1977)

    The Italian Renaissance in its Historical Background (1966 edn)

Hearnshaw, J. F. C., *The Centenary History of King's College, London, 1828–1928* (1929)

Heeney, B., *Mission to the Middle Classes; The Woodard Schools 1848–91* (1969)

Herbert, Lord, *The Pembroke Papers (1734–1780): Letters and Diaries of Henry, Tenth Earl of Pembroke and his Circle* (1939, 1942 edn)

Hexter, J., *Reappraisals in History* (1961)

    The History Primer (1971)

Highmore, A., *Pietas Londinensis* (1808 and 1810)

Hill Brothers (anon in BM catalogue), *Public Education, Plans for the Government and Liberal Instruction of Boys in large numbers* (1822 and 1825)

Hill, C., *Intellectual Origins of the English Revolution* (1965)

Hill, W. T., *Octavia Hill* (1956)

History of Education Society, *Studies in the Government and Control of Education since 1860* (1970)

    The Changing Curriculum (1971)

    Reeder, D. (ed.), *Urban Education in the Nineteenth Century* (1976)

    Searby, P. (ed.), *Educating the Victorian Middle Class* (1982)

Hodder, E., *Life and Letters of Samuel Morley* (1889)

Hodges, Sheila, *God's Gift: A living history of Dulwich College* (1981)

Hodson, W. and Ford, E., *History of Enfield* (1873)

Hollaender, A. E. J. and Kellaway, W. (eds), *Studies in London History* (1969)

Hollis, Patricia (ed.), *Pressure from Without* (1974)

Howat, G. M. D., *The Oxford and Cambridge Schools' Examinations Council, 1873–1973* (The Board, 1973)

Hughes, M. Vivian, *A London Family 1870–1900* (1946 edn); 3 vols, *A London Girl in the 1880s* being the 2nd, and *A London Home in the 1890s* the 3rd.

Huizinga, J., *The Waning of the Middle Ages* (1924, 1965 edn)

Hunter, M., *Science and Society in Restoration England* (1981)

Hurstfield, J., *The Queen's Wards* (1958)

    Liberty and Authority under Elizabeth I, an Inaugural Lecture delivered at University College, London (1960)

Hussey, R., *A Letter to Thos Dyke Acland . . . on the System of Education to be Established in the Diocesan Schools for the Middle Classes* (1839)

Hyam, R. H., *History of Isleworth Grammar School* (1968)

Hyamson, A. M., *Jews' College* (1955)

Jackson, Edith, *Annals of Ealing* (1898)

Jackson, W. Eric, *Achievement: a short history of the LCC* (1965)

James, Alice R., *Girls' Physical Training, being a series of healthy and artistic movements to music* (1898)

James, H., *English Hours* (1962 edn)

Jarrett, D., *England in the Age of Hogarth* (1974)

Jeffreys, M. V. C., *John Locke, Prophet of Common Sense* (1967)

Jenkins, E. W., *From Armstrong to Nuffield* (1979)

Jenkins, J. (Revd), *Female Education and Christian Fortitude under Affliction* (1772)

Jenkins, R., *Asquith* (1967 edn)

Jerdan, W., *Autobiography of William Jerdan* (1852)

Jews' College Jubilee Volume (1906)

Johnson, A. H., *A History of the Worshipful Company of Drapers* (4 vols, 1914–22).

Johnson, S., *Lives of the Poets* (1779–81)

Jones, C., *Ealing, from Village to Corporate Town or Forty Years of Municipal Life* (n.d. Ealing)

Jordan, W. K., *Philanthropy in England 1480–1660* (1959)
    The Charities of London 1480–1660 (1960)

Kamm, Josephine, *How Different from Us: A biography of Miss Buss and Miss Beale* (1958)
    Indicative Past: A hundred years of the Girls' Public Day School Trust (1971)

Kaye, Elaine, *A History of Queen's College* (1972)

Kellett, J. R., *The Impact of Railways on Victorian Cities* (1969)

Kelly, Sophia (ed.), *Life of Mrs Sherwood, chiefly autobiographical* (1854)

Kelly, T., *A History of Adult Education in Great Britain* (1962)

Kemble, Frances, *Record of a Girlhood* (3 vols, 1878)

Killham, J., *Tennyson and 'The Princess'* (1958)

Kingsford, C. L. (ed.), John Stow, *A Survey of London reprinted from the text of 1603* (1908 edn)

Kingsford, C. L., *Early Days of Piccadilly, Leicester Square and Soho* (London Topographical Society Pub. No. 55, 1925)

Kirby, J. W., *The History of The Blackheath Proprietary School* (Blackheath, 1933)

Kitson Clark, G., *The Making of Victorian England* (1962)
    An Expanding Society: Britain 1830–1900 (1967)
    Churchmen and the Condition of England 1832–1885 (1973)

Klingender, F. D., *Art and the Industrial Revolution* (ed. A. Elton, 1968)

Lamb, Charles, *Essays of Elia* (1823, 1901 edn)

Lambley, Kathleen, *The Teaching and Cultivation of the French Language in England during Tudor and Stuart Times* (1920)

Lawson, J. and Silver, H., *A Social History of Education in England* (1973)

Leach, A. F., *The Schools of Medieval England* (1915)

Lee, C. N., *St Pancras Church and Parish* (1955)

Lemprière, W., *History of the Girls' School of Christ's Hospital* (1924)

L'Estrange, A. G. K., *Village of Palaces, or Chronicles of Chelsea* (1880)
    Life of Mary Russell Mitford (1970 edn)

Levin, S. S. (ed.), *A Century of Anglo-Jewish Life, 1870–1970* (United Synagogue, London, n.d.)

Lewis, Mark, *Model for a School for the better education of youth* (1675?)
    Plan and Short Rules for pointing periods (1675?)

Lewis, S. (Junior), *The History and Topography of the Parish of St Mary, Islington* (1842)

Leys, Mary D. R., *Catholics in England 1559–1829: A social history* (1961)

Lilley, Irene M., *Maria Grey College 1878–1976* (1981)

Lipman, V. D., *Social History of the Jews in England* (1954)

Lloyd, C., *Fanny Burney* (1937)

Locke, J., *Some Thoughts Concerning Education* (1693)
    An Essay Concerning Human Understanding (1690)

Low, Sampson, *Charities of London* (1850, 2nd edn 1861)

Lubbock, John, *Addresses: Political and educational* (1879)

McClelland, V. A., *Cardinal Manning: his public life and influence* (1962)
    English Roman Catholics and Higher Education, 1830–1903 (1972)

Macdonald, S., *The History and Philosophy of Art Education* (1970)

McDonnell, M., *Annals of St Paul's School* (1959)

McIntosh, P., *Physical Education in England since 1800* (1968)

Mack, E. C., *Public Schools and British Opinion 1780–1860* (1938)

McLachlan, H., *English Education under the Test Acts* (1931)

MacLeod, R. (ed.), *Days of Judgement, Science, Examinations and the Organization of Knowledge* (1982)

Maclure, J. Stuart (ed.), *Educational Documents, England and Wales, 1816–1967* (1968 edn)

Maclure, J. Stuart, *One Hundred Years of London Education 1870–1970* (1970)

McWilliams-Tullberg, Rita, *Women at Cambridge: A men's university – though of a mixed type* (1975)

Magnus, Laurie, *The Jubilee Book of the Girls' Public Day School Trust 1873–1923* (1923)

Magnus, P., *Educational Aims and Efforts 1880–1910* (1910)

Magnus, P., *Gladstone* (1954, 1963 edn)

Makin, Bathsua, *Essay to revive the Antient Education of Gentlewomen in Religion, Manners, Arts and Tongues* (1673)

Malament, Barbara C., *After the Reformation: Essays in honor of J. H. Hexter* (1980)

Marshall, L. B., *A Brief History of Enfield Grammar School* (1958)

Maskell, J., *Collections in illustration of the Parochial History and Antiquities of the Ancient Parish of All Hallows Barking . . .* (1864)

Matheson, G. E. and Mayle, S. C. (eds), *Hampstead Annual*, 1905–6.

Mathews, H. F., *Methodism and the Education of the People 1791–1851* (1949)

Maurice, T., *Memoirs of the Author of Indian Antiquities* (1819–22)

Millar, O., *The Age of Charles I* (Tate Gallery, 1972)

Miller, F., *St Pancras Past and Present* (1874)

Milne, A. A., *It's Too Late Now: The autobiography of an author* (1939)

Milne, A. T. (ed.), *Centenary Book of Christ's College, Finchley, 1857–1957* (1957)

Milne, A. T., *Catalogue of the MSS of Jeremy Bentham in the Library of University College London* (1937)

Miskimin, H. A., Herlihy, D., Uldovitch, A. L,. *The Medieval City* (1977)

Mitchell, J. and Oakley, A. (eds), *The Rights and Wrongs of Women* (1976)

Mitchell, P. Chalmers, *Thomas Henry Huxley: A sketch of his life and work* (1913)

Moberly Bell, E., *The History of Lady Margaret School 1851–1951* (?1951)
    Francis Holland Schools (1938)
    A History of the Church Schools' Company, 1883–1958 (1958)

Morris, A. D., *Hoxton Square and the Hoxton Academies* (printed for the author, Dr Williams's Library, 1957)

Morris, C., *The Discovery of the Individual 1050–1200* (Church History Outlines 5, ed. V. H. H. Green, 1972)

Morris, J. A., *A History of the Latymer School at Edmonton* (printed for the Foundation, 1975)

Morris, L. F., *A History of St Dunstan's College* (for the Old Dunstan's Association, 1970)

Nelson, J., *History, Topography and Antiquities of the Parish of St Mary, Islington* (1811; 1823 edn).

Newsome, D., *Godliness and Good Learning* (1961)
   The Parting of Friends (1966)

Niblett, W. R. (ed.), *Higher Education, Demand and Response* (1970)

Nichols, J., *Literary Anecdotes of the Eighteenth Century* (9 vols, 1812–15)

Nichols, J. and Bowyer, J., *Illustrations of the Literary History of the Eighteenth Century* (1817–58)

Nuttall, G. F., *New College, London and its Library* (Dr Williams's Trust, 1977)

Ogilvie, R. M., *Latin and Greek* (1964)

Oldfield, Joshua, *Essay towards the Improvement of Reason* (1707)

Ord, H. W., *The Adventures of a Schoolmaster* (1936)

Orme, N., *English Schools in the Middle Ages* (1973)

Owen, D., *English Philanthropy, 1660–1960* (1964)

Palmer, D. J., *The Rise of English Studies* (1965)

Palmer, S., *St Pancras* (1870)

Parker, Irene, *Dissenting Academies in England* (1914)

Parr, John Owen, *An Address delivered at the opening of the Islington Proprietary School before... the Bishop of London, President, Vice-Presidents, Directors and Proprietors of that Institution, and printed at their request* (1830)

Patrides, C. A. and Waddington, R. B. (eds), *The Age of Milton* (1980)

Pattison, Mark, *Milton (English Men of Letters)* (1879)

Pearce, E. H., *Annals of Christ's Hospital* (1901)

Pearle, V., *London and the Outbreak of the Puritan Revolution, City Government and National Politics* (1961)

Pearse, R. N. (ed.), *The Story of the Mary Datchelor School, 1877–1957* (1957)

Percival, Alicia C., *The English Miss Today and Yesterday* (1939)
   Very Superior Men (1973)

Percy, F. H. G., *History of Whitgift School* (1976)

Perkin, H., *The Origins of Modern English Society 1780–1880* (1969)

Phillimore, P. W. and Whitear, W. H., *Historical Collections relating to Chiswick* (1897)

Picciotto, C., *St Paul's School* (1939)

Pinchbeck, Ivy and Hewitt, Margaret, *Children in English Society*, Vol. I (1969)

Pinks, W. J., *History of Clerkenwell* (1865)

Pirenne, H., *Medieval Cities: Their origins and the revival of trade* (1925, 1952 edn)

Plumb, J. H. (ed), *Studies in Social History: A tribute to G. M. Trevelyan* (1955)

Porter, R., *English Society in the Eighteenth Century* (1982)

Pound, R. and Harmsworth, A. G., *Northcliffe*, (1959)

Preceptors, College of, see College.

Pritchard, F. C., *Methodist Secondary Education*, a history of the contribution of Methodism to secondary education in the United Kingdom (1949)

Raleigh, W. (ed), *Shakespeare's England*, Vols. I and II (1916)

Ray, G. N., *Thackeray, the Uses of Adversity* (1955)

Rayner Parkes, Bessie, *Essays on Women's Work* (1865)

Redford, G. and Riches, T. H., *The History of the Ancient Town of Uxbridge* (1885)

Rees, A., *Cyclopaedia, or a Universal Dictionary of Arts, Sciences and Literature* (39 vols, 1802–19)

Rice, J., *Plan for Female Education* (1791)

Richardson, A., *History, Sacred and Profane* (1964)

Roach, J., *Public Examinations in England 1850–1900* (1971)

Robbins, M., *Middlesex* (New Survey of England) (1953)

Roberts, D., *Victorian Origins of the British Welfare State* (1960)

Roberts, R. D. (ed.), *Education in the Nineteenth Century* (1901)

Robertson, D. W., Junior, *Chaucer's London: New dimensions in history, historic cities* (1968)

Robinson, Mary, *Memoirs of the late Mrs Robinson Written by herself* (1801; R. Cobden Sanderson, 1930 edn)

Robinson, W., *History and Antiquities of Stoke Newington* (1820)
> *History and Antiquities of the parish of Tottenham in the county of Middlesex* (1840)
> *History of Hackney* (1842)
> *History of Enfield* (1843)

Rogers, Katharine M., *Feminism in Eighteenth-Century England* (1982)

Rogers, P. (ed.), *The Context of English Literature, the Eighteenth Century* (1978)

Roper, S., *A few more words in defence of Hackney Grammar School* (1831)

Rose, Millicent, *The East End of London* (1951)

Rudé, G., *Hanoverian London* (1971)

Russell, C. (ed.), *The Origins of the English Civil War* (1973)

Sandford, E. G. (ed.), *Memoirs of Archbishop Temple* (2 vols, 1906)

Sargeaunt, F., *Annals of Westminster School* (1898)

Scarisbrick, J. J., *Henry VIII* (1968)

Schneider, Ben Ross, *Wordsworth's Cambridge Education* (1957)

Schwarzbach, F,. *Dickens and the City* (1979)

Scott, R. P. (ed.), '*What is Secondary Education?' and other short essays: A handbook for public men and parents on the national organization of Education in England* (1899)

Scott-Giles, C. W., *The History of Emanuel School 1594–1964* (1966)

Scrimgeour, M., *The North London Collegiate School* (1950)

Seebohm, F., *The Oxford Reformers* (1914 edn)

Sekon, G. A., *Locomotion in Victorian London* (1938)

Sheppard, F. H. W., *London 1808–1870, The Infernal Wen* (1971)

Shield, J., *The Preceptor's Assistant* (1780)

Silver, H., *Chelsea College: A history* (pub. by the College, 1977)

Simmons, M. L., *Register of the Clergy Orphan School for Boys, 1751–1896* (St Augustine's College Canterbury, 1897)

Simon, B., *Studies in the History of Education 1780–1870* (1960)

Simon, B. and Bradley, I. (eds.), *The Victorian Public School* (1974)

Simon, Joan, *Education and Society in Tudor England* (1966)

Smith, J. T., *A Book for a Rainy Day* (ed. W. Whitten, 1905)

Smith, J. W. Ashley, see Ashley

Smith, P. and Summerfield, J. (eds), *Matthew Arnold and the Education of the New Order: A selection of Arnold's writings on education* (1969)

Sondheimer, Janet, and Bodington, Prunella (eds.), *The Girls' Public Day School Trust 1872–1972. A Centenary Review* (1972)

Spencer, E. H., *An Inspector's Testament* (1938)

Steer, F. W., *A History of the Worshipful Company of Scriveners of London* (1973)

Stenton, Doris, *The Englishwoman in History* (1957)

Stenton, F. M., *Norman London* with William Fitzstephen's *Description of London* (Historical Association Leaflets Nos 93 and 94, 1934)

Stephen, Barbara, *Emily Davies and Girton College* (1927)

Stevenson, L. S., *Showman of Vanity Fair, the Life of William Makepeace Thackeray* (1947)

Stewart, W. A. C., *Progressives in English Education 1750–1970* (1972)

Stewart, W. A. C. and McCann, W. P., *The Educational Innovators 1750–1880* (1967)

Stone, L., *The Family, Sex and Marriage in England 1500–1800* (1970)

Stott, G. S., *A History of Chigwell School* (1960)

Stowe, A. M., *The English Grammar Schools in the Reign of Queen Elizabeth* (1908, reprinted 1973)

Strachey, Ray, *The Cause, A Short History of the Women's Movement in Great Britain* (1928)

Sturges, G. W., *Schools of Edmonton Hundred* (privately printed 1949)

Sutherland, Lucy S., *A London Merchant 1695–1774* (1933; 1962 edn)

Tanner, L., *Westminster School: a history* (1934)

Tanswell, J., *The History and Antiquities of Lambeth* (1858)

Taylor, E. G. R., *The Mathematical Practitioners of Hanoverian England 1714–1840* (1966)
  The Mathematical Practitioners of Tudor and Stuart England (1970)

Thomas, Dora H., *A Short History of St Martins-in-the-Fields High School for Girls* (1929)

Thompson, P., *Socialists, Liberals and Labour: The struggle for London 1885–1914* (1967)

Thrupp, Sylvia, *The Merchant Community of Medieval London, 1300–1500* (1962)

Tomalin, C., *The Life and Death of Mary Wollstonecraft* (1974)

Tompson, R. S., *Classics or Charity? The dilemma of the eighteenth century grammar schools* (1971)

Trevelyan, G. O., *The Early History of Charles James Fox* (1880, 1923 edn)
  Life and Letters of Lord Macaulay (1901 edn).

Trollope, A., *Autobiography* (1883, World's Classics edn 1953)

Trollope, A. W., *History of the Royal Foundation of Christ's Hospital* (1834)

Tropp, A., *The School Teachers* (1957)

Tuke, Margaret J., *The History of Bedford College for Women 1849–1937* (1939)

Tuberville, A. S. (ed.), *Johnson's England* (2 vols, 1933)

Turnbull, G. G., *Hartlib, Drury and Comenius* (1947)

Usher, H. J. K., Black Hawkins, C. D., Carrick, C. J. *et al.*, *An Angel without Wings: The history of University College School 1830–1980* (UCS, 1981)

Verney, F. P. and M. M., *Memoirs of the Verney Family in the Seventeenth Century* (1907)

Victoria and Albert Museum, *The Orange and the Rose: Holland and Britain in the Age of Observation* (1964)

Victoria County History, *London*, I (1909), *Middlesex*, I (1969), *Essex*, II (1907), *Kent*, II (1926), *Surrey*, II (1905)

Vidler, A. R., *The Church in an Age of Revolution* (Pelican History of the Church, Vol. 5) (1961)

Vincent, W. A. L., *The Grammar Schools, Their Continuing Tradition . . . 1660–1714* (1969)

Wadmore, J. F., *Some Account of the Worshipful Company of Skinners of London* (1902)

Ward, A. W. and Waller, A. R. (eds), *The Cambridge History of English Literature*, Vol. X, *The Age of Johnson* (1913)

Ward, W. R., *Religion and Society in England 1790–1850* (1972)

Watney, Sir J., *An Account of the Mistery of Mercers in the City of London* (1914)

Watts, M. R., *The Dissenters* (1978)

Wayne, P., *The Philological School, or St Marylebone Grammar School Past and Present* : An Address by the Headmaster . . . to The St Marylebone Society (22 April 1953)

Webb, S., *London Education* (1904)

Wedgwood, C. V., *Truth and Opinion*, Historical Essays (1960)

Weekley, M., *Thomas Bewick* (1953)

Weightman, G. and Humphries, S., *The Making of Modern London 1815–1914* (1983)

Welch, C., *Modern History of the City of London* (1896)

Wheatley, W., *The History of Edward Latymer and his Foundations* (1936)

Wheatley, W. H. (ed.), *Pepys's Diary* (1928)

Whitaker, C. W., *Illustrated historical and statistical and topographical account of . . . Enfield* (1911)

White, A. C. T., *The Story of Army Education* (1963)

Wickenden, T. D., *William Ellis School 1862–1962* (n.d.)

Wilkins, H. T., *Great English Schools* (1925)

Wilks, H. C., *George Green's School 1828–1978* (1979)

Willey, B., *The Eighteenth-Century Background* (1940)

Williams, G. A., *Medieval London: From commune to capital* (1963)

Williams, Margaret, *Sainte Madeleine Sophie, her Life and Letters* (1965)
    The Society of the Sacred Heart (1978)

Williams, R., *The Long Revolution* (1961; 1965 edn)

Wilson, Mona, *Jane Austen and Some Contemporaries* (1938)

Woods, Alice, *Educational Experiments in England* (1920)

Wren, M. A. and Hackett, P., *James Allen, a Portrait Enlarged* (1968)

Wright, L. B., *Middle Class Culture in Elizabethan England* (1935)

Wycherley, W., *The Gentleman Dancing Master* (1671–2)

Young, G. M., *Portrait of an Age* (1936) and *Early Victorian England* (2 vols, 1934; 1951 edn)

Young, K. and Garside, Patricia, *Metropolitan London: Politics and Urban Change 1837–1981* (1982)

Young, W., *The History of Dulwich College* (1889)

Zimmern, Alice, *The Renaissance of Girls' Education* (1898)

(E) Articles

Adamson, J. W., 'The extent of literacy in England in the 15th and 16th centuries', *The Library*, Transactions of the Bibliographical Society Second Series, X (1929–30)

Aldrich, R., '1870: A local government perspective', *Journal of Educational Administration and History*, XV, No. 1, Jan. 1983

Anglin, J. P., 'Frustrated ideals; the case of Elizabethan grammar school foundations', *History of Education*, Vol. 11, No. 4, Dec. 1982

Argles M., 'The Royal Commission on Technical Instruction; Its inception and composition', *Vocational Aspects of Secondary and Further Education*, XI, Autumn 1959

Ashley Smith, J. W., 'Modern History as subject matter for Higher Education: The contribution of Francis Tallents', *Pedagogica Historica*, XVI, 1975.

Aston, Margaret, 'Lollardry and literacy', *History*, Vol. 62, No. 206, Oct. 1977.

Barnard, H. C., 'A great headmaster: John Lewis Paton, 1863–1946', *British Journal of Educational Studies*, XI (1), Nov. 1962.

Barnett, A., 'Sussex Hall – the first Anglo-Jewish venture in popular education', *Transactions of the Jewish Historical Society of England*, XIX, 1955/9.

Baron, G., 'The Teachers' registration movement', *British Journal of Educational Studies*, II, May 1954.

Batho, G. R., 'The Education of a Stuart Nobleman', *British Journal of Educational Studies*, V (2), May 1967.

Battersby, W. J., 'Middle-class education', *Month*, CLXXXVI, No. 973, Sept. 1948.

Beales, A. C. F., 'The beginning of elementary education in England in the second spring', *Dublin Review*, Vol. 205, Nos 410 and 411, 1939.

Bennett, G. V., 'Archbishop Tenison and the reshaping of the Church of England', *Friends of Lambeth Palace Library*, Annual Report 1981.

Besant, W., 'The endowment of the Daughter', *Longman's Magazine*, Vol. 11, 1888.

Bibby, C., 'A Victorian experiment in international education', *British Journal of Educational Studies*, V, Nov. 1956.

Bradley, G. G., 'My schooldays from 1830 to 1840', *The Nineteenth Century*, XV, 1 March 1884.

Campbell Stewart, W. A., 'The staffing of Friends' schools in England during the nineteenth century' and 'Punishment in Friends' schools 1779–1900', *Journal of the Friends' Historical Society* XLI and XLII, 1949–50.

Cannell, G., 'Resistance to the Charity Commissioners: The case of St Paul's Schools, 1860–1904', *History of Education*, Vol. 10, No. 4, Dec. 1981.

Cassell, C. E., 'The West Metropolitan Jewish School', *Transactions of the Jewish Historical Society of England*, XIX, 1960.

Charlton, K., "Tak the to thi distaff . . .": The education of girls and women in early modern England', *Westminster Studies in Education*, Vol. 4, 1981.

Church, A., 'Day schools, their advantages and disadvantages', *Contemporary Review*, XV, Aug./Nov. 1870.

Conway Davies, J., 'Elizabethan plans and proposals for education', *Durham Research Review*, No. 5, Sept. 1954.

Dobson, J. L., 'The Hill family and educational change', *Durham Research Review*, III, No. 10, Sept. 1959, No. 11, Sept. 1960, No. 12, Sept. 1961.

Dunford, J. E., 'Biographical details of Her Majesty's Inspectors of Schools appointed before 1870', *History of Education Society Bulletin*, No. 28, Autumn 1981.

Dyhouse, C., 'Social Darwinistic ideas and the development of women's education', *History of Education* (1976), Vol. 5, No. 1.

Fearon, D. R., 'Girls' grammar schools', *Contemporary Review*, II, May/Aug. 1869.

Fitch, J., 'Educational endowments', *Fraser's Magazine*, Vol. 79, Jan. 1869.

Foster, Watson, 'Notes and materials on religious refugees in their relation to education in England', *Proceedings of the Huguenot Society of London*, IX, 1911.

Galbraith, V. H. 'John Seward and his Circle', *Mediaeval and Renaissance Studies*, I, 1941.

Gordon, P., 'The Endowed Schools and the education of the poor', *Durham Research Review*, V, No. 17, Sept. 1966.

Griggs, C., 'The Trades' Union Congress and the question of educational endowments, 1868–1925', *History of Education Society Bulletin*, No. 28, Autumn 1981.

Gwynn, S., 'Bachelor women', *Contemporary Review*, LXXIII, June 1898.

Hadden, R. H., 'City parochial charities', *The Nineteenth Century*, IX, Feb. 1881.

Harkness, Margaret E., 'Women as Civil Servants', *The Nineteenth Century*, X. Sept. 1881.

Hawkins, R. N. P., 'Four studies of British metallic tickets and commercial checks of the 19th–20th Centuries', *British Association of Numismatic Societies*, Doris Stockwell Memorial Papers, No. 2, 1975.

Higginson, J. H., 'The evolution of secondary education', *British Journal of Educational Studies*, XX, No. 2, June 1972.

Hobhouse, A., 'Local self-government in London', *Contemporary Review*, LIII, June 1888.

Holmes, D. J., 'Manning and the Kensington Scheme', *Month*, Vol. 3, No. 1, Jan. 1965.

Holt, T. G., 'Some early London Catholic schools', *London Recusant*, Vol. 5, No. 1, 1975.

Honeybourne, Marjorie, 'London, History', *Chambers's Encyclopaedia*, Vol. 8 (1950 edn).

Houghton, W. E., 'The English virtuoso in the 17th century', *Journal of the History of Ideas*, III, 1942.

Ives, E., 'Queen Elizabeth and the people of England', *The Historian*, No. 1, Autumn 1983.

Jacob, W., 'The London secondary technical schools for girls', *Journal of Education* Vol. 86, No. 1, Aug. 1954.

Johnson, Francis R., 'Thomas Hood's inaugural address as mathematical lecturer of the City of London, 1588', *Journal of the History of Ideas*, III, 1942.

Jones, M. D. W., 'Brighton College v. Marriott', *History of Education*, Vol. 12, No. 2, June 1983.

Knox, H. M., 'William Petty's Advice to Samuel Hartlib', *British Journal of Educational Studies*, Vol. I, No. 2, May 1953.

Layton, D., 'The educational work of the Parliamentary Committee of the British Association for the Advancement of Science', *History of Education*, Vol. 5, No. 1, Feb. 1976.

Leach, A. F., 'St Paul's School before Colet', *Archaeologia*, lxii, pt 1, 1910.

Leinster-Mackay, D. P., 'Pioneers in progressive education . . .', *History of Education*, Vol. 9, No. 3, Sept. 1980.

'Private or Public Schools: The educational debate in laissez-faire England', *Journal of Educational Administration and History*, XV, No. 2, July 1983.

'The evolution of t'other schools: an examination of the 19th century development of the private preparatory school', *History of Education*, Vol. 5, No. 3, Oct. 1976.

Levin, S. S., 'The origins of the Jews' Free School', *Transactions of the Jewish Historical Society of England*, XIX, 1960.

Lilley, R. C., 'Attempts to implement the Bryce Commission's recommendations – and the consequences', *History of Education*, Vol. 11, No. 2, June 1982.

Lowe, R., 'Robert Morant and the Secondary School Regulations of 1904', *Journal of Educational Administration and History*, XVI, No. 1, Jan. 1984.

Lubbock, J., 'Manual instruction', *Fortnightly Review*, CCXXXV N.S., Oct. 1886.

McCann, W. P., 'The Trade Guilds of Learning', *Vocational Aspects of Secondary and Further Education*, XIX, Spring 1967.

McClelland, V. A., 'The 1880 Central School scheme', *The Tablet*, Vol. 219, No. 6532, No. 6533, No. 6534, 1965.

Reply to Holmes, *Month*, March 1965.

Magnus, P., 'Manual training', *Contemporary Review*, L, Nov. 1886.

Manchée, W. H., 'Marylebone and its Huguenot associations', *Proc. of Huguenot Society of London*, XI, 1915–17.

Manning, H. E. and Ward, W. G., 'Catholic higher studies in England', 'The infidelity of the day: The new scheme of Catholic higher education', *Dublin Review*, Vol. 22, Jan. 1874, Vol. 23, Oct. 1874.

Manning, H. E., 'The Works and wants of the Church in England', *Dublin Review*, 3rd Series, Vol. 1, Jan. 1879.

Mayor, J. B., 'The cry of the women', *Contemporary Review*, XI, May/Aug. 1869.

Miller, Florence F., 'William Ellis and his work as an educationist', *Fraser's Magazine*, Vol. 105 O.S., 25 N.S. Feb. 1882.

Miner, J. N. T., 'Schools and literacy in later medieval England', *British Journal of Educational Studies*, XI, 1962.

Mortimer, Russell S., 'Quaker Education' (review article), *Journal of the Friends' Historical Society*, Vol. XXXIX, 1947.

Musgrave, P. W., 'The definition of technical education, 1860–1910', *Vocational Aspects*, XVI, No. 34, Summer 1964.

Musson, A. E., 'The British Industrial Revolution', *History*, Vol. 67, No. 220, June 1982.

Newall, W., 'The municipality of London', *Contemporary Review*, XXV, Feb. 1875.

Norton, Lord (Charles Bowyer Adderley), 'Middle class education', *Nineteenth Century*, XIII, Feb. 1883.

Palmer, R. J., 'The influence of F. W. Sanderson on the development of science and engineering at Dulwich College, 1885–1892', *History of Education*, Vol. 6, No. 2, June 1977.

Paton, J. B., 'Mr Samuel Morley – In Memoriam', *Contemporary Review*, L, Oct. 1886.

Penney N. (ed.), 'Pen pictures of the London Yearly Meeting, 1789–1833', *Friends' Historical Society*, Supplements 16, 17.

Perkin, H., 'Middle class education and employment in the 19th century: A critical note', *Economic History Review*, XIV, 1961.

Pickard, O. G., 'Office work and education, 1848–1948', *Vocational Aspects . . .*, Vol. 1, Nov. 1949.

Plumley, N. M., 'The Royal Mathematical School, Christ's Hospital', *History Today*, XXIII, No. 8, Aug. 1973.

Portal, E. M., 'The Academ Roiall of King Jas I', *Proceedings of the British Academy*, 1915–16.

Potter, G. R., 'Education in the 14th and 15th centuries', *Cambridge Medieval History*, Vol. VIII (1936).

Review Article, 'Employment of women in the public service', *Quarterly Review*, Vol. 151, Jan. 1881.

Roach, J., 'Middle class education and examinations: Some early Victorian problems', *British Journal of Educational Studies*, X, May 1962.

Russell, John, 'On some of the aims and methods of the King Alfred School Society', *Journal of the Royal Sanitary Institute*, XXXII, No. 2, 1911.

Samuel, Enid and Cecil, 'The villas of Regent's Park and their residents', *St Marylebone Society Publication*, No. 1, 1959.

Schools' Committee of the Council of Citizens of East London, Fourth Bulletin, 'Our East London: The story of our schools', Winter 1950.

Selby, D. E., 'Henry Edward Manning and the Catholic middle class', *Paedagogica Historica* X, No. 1, 1970.

Sharp, P. R., 'Whiskey Money' and the development of technical and secondary education in the 1890s', *Journal of Educational Administration and History*, IV, No. 1, Dec. 1971.

Simon, J., 'The history of education in *Past and Present*', *Oxford Review of Education*, Vol. 3, No. 1, 1977.
 'Private classical schools in eighteenth century England', *History of Education*, Vol. 8, No. 3, Sept. 1979.

Smedley, Menella B., 'The English girl's education', *Contemporary Review*, XIV, April/July 1870.

Lady Stanley of Alderley (H. M.), 'Personal recollections of women's education', *The Nineteenth Century*, VI, Aug. 1879.

Teague, S. J., 'Thoughts towards the early history of Chelsea College of Science and Technology', *British Journal of Educational Studies*, XVII, Oct. 1969.

Thomson, J. A. F., 'Piety and charity in late medieval London', *Journal of Ecclesiastical History*, XVI, 1965.

Tittler, R., 'Education and the gentleman in Tudor England: The case of Sir Nicholas Bacon', *History of Education*, Vol. 5, No. 1, Feb. 1976.

Tuck, J. P., 'The beginnings of English Studies in the sixteenth century', *Durham Research Review*, No. 7, Sept. 1956.

Wallbank, M. V., 'Eighteenth-century Public Schools and the education of a governing élite', *History of Education*, Vol. 8, No. 1, March 1979.

Wallis, P. J., 'Thomas Watts, Academy Master, Freemason, Insurance Pioneer, M. P.', *History of Education Society Bulletin*, No. 32, Autumn 1983.

Webb, S., 'London education', *The Nineteenth Century*, XX, Oct. 1903.

Wide, S. W. and Morris, J. A., 'The episcopal licensing of schoolmasters in the Diocese of London, 1627–1685', *Guildhall Miscellany*, Vol. 2, 1967.

Wrigley, E. A., 'A simple model of London's importance in changing English society and economy, 1650–1750', *Past and Present*, No. 37, 1967.

Young, K., 'The Conservative strategy for London, 1855–1975', *The London Journal*, Vol. 1, No. 1, May 1975.

(F) Theses (unpublished)

Baron, G., 'The Secondary Schoolmaster, 1895–1914' (PhD, University of London, 1952)

Campbell, F. C., 'The Changing Environment of the London Grammar School 1900–1950' (PhD, University of London, 1953)

Creed, Anne Caroline, 'The Life and Educational Work of Anne Clough, 1820–1892' (MA dissertation, University of London, 1972)

Dalvi, M. A., Commercial Education in England during 1851–1902: An institutional study' (PhD, University of London, 1957)

Fletcher, Sheila M. 'The Part Played by Civil Servants in Promoting Girls' Secondary Education 1869–1902: Some aspects of the administration of the Endowed Schools' Acts' (PhD, University of London, 1976).

Gordon, Shirley C., 'Demands for the Education of Girls, 1790–1865' (MA, University of London, 1950)

Greenberg, Esther, 'The Contribution to Education of Private Schools in the First Half of the Nineteenth Century' (MA, University of London, 1953)

Jackson, J., 'John Henry Newman, the origin and application of his educational ideas' (PhD, University of Leicester, 1968)

Leinster-Mackay, D. P., 'The English Private School 1830–1914, with special reference to the private preparatory school' (PhD University of Durham, 1971/2)

Mann, A., 'The Achievement of the London Higher Grade Schools, 1887–1904' (MA dissertation, University of London, 1979)

Milburn, Jan, 'The Secondary Schoolmistress: A study of her professional views and their significance in the educational developments of the period 1895–1914' (PhD, University of London, 1969)

Morris, Elizabeth M. D., 'The Education of Girls in England from 1660 to 1800' (MA, University of London, 1926)

Murphy, M. A., 'The Origin, Growth and Development of Schools for Roman Catholic Poor Children in the Archdiocese of Westminster from 1760 to 1861' (MPhil, University of London, 1979)

Oakeshott, A. M. d'I, 'English Grammar Schools 1660–1714' (PhD, University of London, 1969)

Pooley, R. J. B., 'The History of St Clement Danes Holborn Estate Grammar School, 1552–1952' (MA, University of London, 1955)

Prior, P. J., 'The Higher Grade Schools in Tottenham and Wood Green, 1884–1914' (MA dissertation, University of London, 1981)

Quinn, P. L. S., 'Jewish Schooling Systems of London 1656–1965' (PhD, University of London, 1950)

Rees, Merlyn, 'The Economic and Social Development of Extra-Metropolitan Middlesex during the nineteenth century (1800–1914)' (MSc (Econ), University of London, 1955)

Robinson, F. W., 'William Ellis and his work for education' (MA, University of London, 1919)

Robinson, G. B., 'A Study of the Private Schools' Association (latterly Independent Schools') in relation to changing policies in the administration of education by national and local government agencies, 1880–1944' (MA, University of London, 1966)

Toms, V. G., 'Secular Education in England 1800–1870' (PhD, University of London, 1972)

Toon, Royston, 'The Work of the Middlesex Technical Education Committee' (MA dissertation, University of London, 1979)

Welch, P. J., 'Bishop Blomfield' (PhD, University of London, 1952)

Index